BEN JONSON
AND THE CAVALIER POETS

AUTHORITATIVE TEXTS
CRITICISM

NORTON CRITICAL EDITIONS

BEN JONSON
AND THE CAVALIER POETS

AUTHORITATIVE TEXTS
CRITICISM

⇶ ⋘

Selected and Edited by

HUGH MACLEAN

STATE UNIVERSITY OF NEW YORK AT ALBANY

⇶ ⋘

W · W · NORTON & COMPANY · INC · *New York*

W. W. NORTON & COMPANY, INC.
also publishes

THE NORTON ANTHOLOGY OF ENGLISH LITERATURE
edited by M. H. Abrams et al.

THE NORTON ANTHOLOGY OF POETRY
edited by Arthur M. Eastman et al.

WORLD MASTERPIECES
edited by Maynard Mack et al.

THE NORTON FACSIMILE OF

THE FIRST FOLIO OF SHAKESPEARE
prepared by Charlton Hinman

and the NORTON CRITICAL EDITIONS

FIRST EDITION

Library of Congress Cataloging in Publication Data

Maclean, Hugh, 1919–   comp.
  Ben Jonson and the cavalier poets.
  (A Norton critical edition)
  Bibliography: p.
  1. English poetry—Early modern, 1500–1700
I. Title.
PR1205.M37   821'.008   74–2109
ISBN 0–393–04387–8
ISBN 0–393–09308–5 (pbk.)

Published simultaneously in Canada
by George J. McLeod Limited, Toronto

PRINTED IN THE UNITED STATES OF AMERICA

1 2 3 4 5 6 7 8 9 0

Contents

Preface

The primary aim of this Critical Edition is to make available to modern readers full and appropriately varied selections from a body of seventeenth-century poetry that has not received its critical due. Ben Jonson (to quote Douglas Bush) "gave poetry a new charter through his dynamic assimilation of the main tradition of the past"; if the charm of Cavalier poetry goes without saying, its special quality resides rather in an eminently Jonsonian combination of strength and wit, one that finds its most felicitous expression in celebrating "the mysteries of manners, arms, and arts." Over the years, however, the tides of literary taste have taken their toll. Jonson considered that Donne's poetry "for not being understood would perish"; he directed his own nondramatic verse chiefly to those who cared to understand it, and for those readers alone he reserved his trust. By a curious irony, it was Jonson's poetry that fell gradually into disrepute and relative obscurity. His reputation as a dramatist remained high, but the poems (save for a few isolated pieces) have been savagely neglected until quite recent times. By consequence, as Joseph Summers remarks, modern readers "are likely to miss a good deal of Jonson's range and strength and art." The poetry of Jonson's heirs and followers has also been seriously underrated: generations of readers, dazzled by Donne's fireworks and the curiously wrought fancies of metaphysical poetry, have scarcely noticed the witty variety of Cavalier verse, not to mention its moving reflection of a once confident society grown desperate under the pressures of time and change. The poems collected in this volume comprise an especially copious and representative sampling of Jonson's nondramatic verse and that of the Cavalier poets; they enable modern readers once again distinctly to perceive the vital character of Jonson's contribution in this kind, and to relish the challenging wit and art of Cavalier verse.

The strength and scope of Jonson's poetry are fully represented here. A wide selection from the *Epigrams* includes satiric and commendatory poems, together with the mock epic, "On the Famous Voyage." *The Forest* is here complete; its fifteen diversified poems provide an intriguing microcosm of Jonson's larger achievement. From *Underwood*, such well-known pieces as "A Celebration of Charis" and the Cary-Morison ode are included among the selections; I have drawn attention to less familiar but equally significant aspects of Jonson's verse by the inclusion of "An Execration Upon Vulcan" and, in particular, the "Epithalamion" on the Weston-Stuart nuptials, a poem that repays comparison with Spenser's marriage ode and with Herrick's "A Nuptial Song," also given in this volume. The earliest of Jonson's three odes to himself is here, as well as that which marks the poet's furious reaction to the failure of *The New Inn* in 1629; a group of the more delightful songs from the plays and masques makes up the tally. These selections will permit judicious readers to recognize that, if the wit of Jonson's poetry may well be described (by F. J. Warnke) as "the ability to give terse and memorable expression to generally acknowledged truths," it is conditioned (even, perhaps, defined) by Jonson's consistent attention to the criterion of a larger decorum.

Almost everyone can agree that Suckling, Lovelace, and (probably) Carew may appropriately be termed "Cavalier poets"; but that rubric need not be too exclusively delimited. It is evidently of some importance to be aware that "Cavalier wit" is touched and in some degree transmuted by the influence of metaphysical poetry, notably that of Donne. Carew's verse is a case in point; but the images and rhythms of verses by several poets included here more than once recall those of the metaphysical manner. In any event, my selection has been guided in the first instance by Douglas Bush's discussion of these figures in *English Literature in the Earlier Seventeenth Century 1600–1660*, 2nd ed. (New York, 1962), an account that would support the inclusion, as "Jonsonian cavalier poets," of some eleven authors represented in this Critical Edition. By another reckoning, the group includes members of the "Tribe of Ben," courtly gentlemen who took the king's part during the civil war, and such figures as Waller, Denham, and Cowley, whose classical affinities enabled them to compose verses recalling the manner and (from time to time) the substance of Jonson's poetry, even as their own "sweetness and strength" prepared the way for Dryden and the Augustans. In this regard, I have included a number of poems in which the authors address themselves to Jonson or to each other: the poems to Jonson's memory, drawn from *Jonsonus Virbius*, are no less instructive than Carew's candid response to his mentor's "Ode to Himself," while Herrick's verses to Fane and Denham, and the poetical exchanges among Shirley, Stanley, and Habington, illuminate the social fabric within which these men pursued their several interests and careers. Finally, the socially oriented wit of all these men echoes their mutual concern for those values that Earl Miner identifies as the salient marks of Cavalier poetry: a consistent urge to define and explore the features of "the good life," an eager desire to cope with and neutralize the threat of time, a fascinated attention "to idealized as well as re-

alistic versions of the psychology of love," a profound (and Jonsonian) faith in the power of friendship.

The spelling and (in some degree) the punctuation of poems
in this Critical Edition have been brought into accord with modern
practice. The principles governing these and other alterations of
the early editions are discussed in the Textual Notes. Footnotes
serve primarily to gloss unfamiliar terms, to clarify the syntax of
especially complex or gnomic constructions, and to explain allusions to mythological figures or episodes, and to historical personages
and events. Now and again, footnotes draw attention to formally
or thematically comparable passages in other poems included in
this edition. Since readers may very probably not undertake to
proceed steadily through this volume, from Jonson's first epigram
to Stanley's "Expectation," I have exercised some discretion in
explaining those mythological and classical names which appear
with some frequency (e.g., Apollo, Anacreon, Orpheus, etc.). In
general, for Jonson's poetry and that of Corbett, Herrick, and
Carew, footnotes to often-repeated allusions refer the reader to the
first such footnoted allusion in the volume; thereafter, as a rule,
footnotes are omitted in these cases, or, where the allusion bears
a rather distinct emphasis, footnotes briefly explain such allusions
in terms that draw attention to that emphasis.

The selection of appropriate critical materials for this volume
has presented some problems. Until quite recent times, informed
and detailed criticism of Jonson's nondramatic verse can scarcely
be said to have flourished; typically, those critics who discuss
Jonson's art lavish attention on the plays, but slight or altogether
ignore the poems. As for the other figures represented here (Dr.
Johnson's *Lives* excepted), "criticism" before the modern era consists chiefly in scattered, almost random asides. Nevertheless, it has
seemed reasonable to arrange these materials chronologically, if
only to indicate the great gap of time that yawns between the
perception of Jonson's own critical pronouncements and the renewed interest in his nondramatic verse and that of the Cavaliers
which in our own day springs up on every hand. Among the modern
essays collected here, Patrick Cruttwell's provides the larger context
within which the Jonsonian tradition develops. Joseph Summers
considers Jonson's verse in relation to the contrasting manner of
Donne, while Earl Miner shows how Johnson's poetry reflects a
significant Cavalier ideal. Five other scholars discuss particular
aspects of Jonson's art. It has not been possible to include critical
essays that deal directly with each one of the Cavaliers whose work
is represented here, but the six remaining essays raise issues which
are by no means relevant only to the poet with whom each critic

deals. The Textual Notes provide lists of chiefly substantive variants. In this regard, I gratefully acknowledge my indebtedness to the full critical apparatus provided by C. H. Herford and Percy and Evelyn Simpson in their definitive edition of Jonson's works (11 vols., Oxford, 1925–1952), and by the modern editors of the poetry of other authors represented in this edition; these scholars are individually identified in the Textual Notes. A Selected Bibliography includes those books and articles that the present editor has found especially useful.

For various kinds of assistance in the preparation of this volume, I am deeply grateful to a number of persons and institutions. Chief among these are the librarian and the staff of the Cambridge University Library, and of Christ's College, Trinity College, and Emmanuel College in Cambridge University, for making available to me the early editions on which the texts of a majority of the poems in this Critical Edition are based. I wish also to thank the librarians of the Newberry Library and of the University of Illinois Library for providing me with microfilm copies of early editions of poems by Corbett, Fane, Vaughan, and Stanley. I must further acknowledge the willing and co-operative assistance over a long period rendered by the librarian and the staff of the Library of the State University of New York at Albany. Among my colleagues at this university, Townsend Rich and Walter Knotts have been steadfast in their support; I am particularly grateful for the cheerful aid and comfort provided by Edward Le Comte, Frank Sypher, and Donald Prakken. Let me not forget, at last, two generous scholar-teachers from whom I have learned much, and whose characters exemplify the virtues of the period they have made their own: Norman Endicott and Arthur Barker.

HUGH MACLEAN

The Texts of
the Poems

Ben Jonson

1572 (or 1573)	Born in London, a month or so after the death of his father, a minister. Attends Westminster School, perhaps through the good offices of William Camden (then second master), until 1589.
1589	Apprenticed to the bricklayer's trade, that of his stepfather.
1591–1592	Serves with the army in the Low Countries.
1594	Marriage to Anne Lewis.
1597	Playwright and actor in London. Imprisoned in consequence of his connection with the (lost) play, *The Isle of Dogs*, held by the Privy Council to be "lewd . . . seditious and slanderous."
1598	*The Case Is Altered* acted by the boys' company, the Children of the Chapel Royal; *Every Man In His Humour* acted by the Lord Chamberlain's Men (Shakespeare took one of the roles). Kills a fellow actor, Gabriel Spencer, in a duel, escaping the gallows only by pleading benefit of clergy. Converted to Roman Catholicism while awaiting trial; remains a Catholic until about 1610. Included in Francis Meres's list, in *Palladis Tamia*, of those who are "our best for tragedy."
1599	*Every Man Out Of His Humour* acted by the Lord Chamberlain's Men.
1600	*Cynthia's Revels* acted by the Children of the Chapel Royal, who perform *Poetaster* in 1601.
1602–1607	Living in the house of his patron, Esmé Stewart, Lord of Aubigny.
1603	Death of Queen Elizabeth, March 24. Commissioned to write *An Entertainment at Althorpe* in connection with James I's journey from Edinburgh to London for his coronation; thereafter a regular contributor of masques (twenty-four in all) for entertainments at the royal court, often in uneasy collaboration with the designer, Inigo Jones. *Sejanus* acted by the Lord Chamberlain's Men. Death of Jonson's first son.
1604–1605	Imprisoned, with Marston and Chapman, for supposedly anti-Scottish elements in the play *Eastward*

3

	Ho! acted at this time by the boys' company, now termed the Children of the Queen's Revels.
1606	*Volpone* performed by the King's Men (formerly the Lord Chamberlain's Men).
1609–1610	*Epicoene* and *The Alchemist* acted by, respectively, the Children of the Queen's Revels and the King's Men.
1611	*Catiline* acted by the King's Men.
1612–1613	In France, serving as tutor and companion to Sir Walter Raleigh's son. From 1613 (perhaps), Jonson makes one of a group of poets, intellectuals, and "wits" meeting regularly at the Mermaid Tavern in London.
1614	*Bartholomew Fair* acted by Lady Elizabeth's Men.
1616	Publication of Jonson's *Works*. Awarded a royal pension.
1618–1619	Walking tour to Scotland; well received by persons of standing in Edinburgh, and honored by the town council of that city. Resides for two or three weeks with William Drummond of Hawthornden. Awarded an honorary M.A. by Oxford University.
1620	Residing in Gresham College, London; perhaps lecturing in rhetoric at that institution. Until at least 1625, the central figure of a congenial group ("the Tribe of Ben") meeting in the "Apollo Room" of the Devil Tavern in London.
1623	Jonson's books and manuscripts destroyed by fire.
1625	Death of James I; Jonson's influence at court declines steadily from this time.
1626	*The Staple of News* acted by the King's Men.
1628	Suffers a paralytic stroke. Appointed historiographer of the City of London (a sinecure).
1629	*The New Inn* acted by the King's Men; a resounding failure.
1630	Jonson's pension increased to £100 annually, together with a tierce of Canary wine.
1631–1635	Years of declining health and influence. A *Tale of a Tub* acted by Queen Henrietta's Men in 1633; Jonson's last masque, *Love's Welcome at Bolsover*, presented in 1634. Death of Jonson's second son, 1635.
1637	Death, August 6. Buried three days later in Westminster Abbey.
1640–1641	Publication of Jonson's *Works*, in two volumes, seen through the press by Sir Kenelm Digby.

From THE WORKS OF
BENJAMIN JONSON (1616)

From Epigrams[1]

I: To the Reader

Pray thee, take care, that tak'st my book in hand,
To read it well: that is, to understand.[2]

II: To My Book

It will be looked for, book, when some but see
    Thy title, Epigrams, and named of me,
Thou should'st be bold, licentious, full of gall,
    Wormwood and sulphur,[3] sharp, and toothed withal;
Become a petulant[4] thing, hurl ink and wit   5
    As madmen stones, not caring whom they hit.
Deceive their malice, who could wish it so.
    And by thy wiser temper, let men know
Thou are not covetous of least self-fame
    Made from the hazard of another's shame;   10
Much less, with lewd, profane, and beastly praise,
    To catch the world's loose laughter, or vain gaze.
He that departs with[5] his own honesty
    For vulgar praise, doth it too dearly buy.

IV: To King James[6]

How, best of kings, dost thou a scepter bear!
    How, best of poets, dost thou laurel wear!
But two things, rare, the Fates had in their store,
    And gave thee both, to show they could no more.

---

1. Jonson dedicated his Epigrams to William Herbert, third Earl of Pembroke (1580–1630), son of that Countess of Pembroke who was Sir Philip Sidney's sister; in the dedicatory epistle, Jonson calls these poems "the ripest of [his] studies." In form and spirit, they reflect primarily the work of the Roman epigrammatist Martial (c. 40–c. 104); for a useful account of Jonson's conception of the epigram, cf. Ben Jonson, ed. C. H. Herford, P. and E. M. Simpson, 11 vols. (Oxford, 1925–1952), II, pp. 342–360. This edition is cited hereafter as H & S.
2. Cf. The Alchemist, To the Reader: "If thou beest more, thou art an understander, and then I trust thee."
3. I.e., full of bitterness derived from several aspects of being; with that rancor supposed to have its seat in the gall bladder are conjoined the bitter-tasting plant Artemisia absinthium and the pungently odorous mineral sulphur, respectively associated in Jonson's day with whatever is bitter and grievous to the soul, and with Satan's abode in hell. The expression is ultimately scriptural: cf. Deuteronomy 29:18.
4. Peevishly aggressive.
5. I.e., gives up.
6. James I (James VI of Scotland) had published His Majesties Poeticall Exercises in 1591, and Essayes of a Prentise in the Divine Art of Poesie in 1584, at the age of eighteen.

For such a poet, while thy days were green,   5
    Thou wert, as chief of them are said t'have been.
And such a prince thou art, we daily see,
    As chief of those still promise they will be.
Whom should my Muse then fly to, but the best
    Of kings for grace; of poets for my test?   10

IX: *To All, To Whom I Write*

May none, whose scattered names honor my book,
    For strict degrees of rank or title look;
'Tis 'gainst the manners of an epigram;
    And I a poet here, no herald am.

XI: *On Something That Walks Somewhere*

At court I met it, in clothes brave[7] enough
    To be a courtier, and looks grave enough
To seem a statesman; as I near it came,
    It made me a great face; I asked the name.
"A lord," it cried, "buried in flesh and blood,   5
    And such from whom let no man hope least good,
For I will do none: and as little ill,
    For I will dare none." Good lord, walk dead still.

XIV: *To William Camden*[8]

Camden, most reverend head, to whom I owe
    All that I am in arts, all that I know
(How nothing's that?); to whom my country owes
    The great renown and name wherewith she goes.[9]
Than thee the age sees not that thing more grave,   5
    More high, more holy, that she more would crave.
What name, what skill, what faith hast thou in things![1]
    What sight in searching the most antique springs!
What weight and what authority in thy speech!
    Man scarce can make that doubt, but thou canst teach.   10
Pardon free truth, and let thy modesty,
    Which conquers all, be once overcome by thee.
Many of thine this better could than I,
    But for their powers, accept my piety.

---

7. Fine.
8. William Camden (1551–1623), antiquarian and historian, was Jonson's teacher at Westminster School. Jonson dedicated *Every Man In His Humour* to him.

9. Jonson here alludes to the international reputation of Camden's *Britannia* (1586), and probably also to the equally admired *Remaines of a Greater Worke concerning Britaine* (1605).
1. Facts, events.

XVIII: To My Mere[2] English Censurer

To thee, my way in epigrams seems new,
    When both it is the old way, and the true.
Thou say'st, that cannot be; for thou hast seen
    Davies, and Weever,[3] and the best have been,
And mine come nothing like. I hope so. Yet,   5
    As theirs did with thee, mine might credit get,
If thou'dst but use thy faith, as thou didst then,
    When thou wert wont t'admire, not censure men.
Prithee believe still, and not judge so fast;
    Thy faith is all the knowledge that thou hast.   10

XXII: On My First Daughter

Here lies, to each her parents' ruth,[4]
Mary, the daughter of their youth;
Yet all heaven's gifts being heaven's due,
It makes the father less to rue.
At six months' end,[5] she parted hence   5
With safety of her innocence;
Whose soul heaven's queen, whose name she bears,
In comfort of her mother's tears,
Hath placed amongst her virgin-train:
Where, while that severed doth remain,[6]   10
This grave partakes the fleshly birth;
Which cover lightly, gentle earth!

XXIII: To John Donne

Donne, the delight of Phoebus, and each Muse,
    Who, to thy one, all other brains refuse;[7]
Whose every work, of thy most early wit,
    Came forth example, and remains so yet;
Longer a-knowing than most wits do live,   5
    And which no affection praise enough can give!
To it,[8] thy language, letters, arts, best life,
    Which might with half mankind maintain a strife.

2. Absolute.
3. The epigrams of Sir John Davies (1569–1626) had appeared c. 1590; John Weever (1576–1632) published *Epigrammes in the oldest cut, and newest fashion* in 1599.
4. Grief.
5. The dates of Mary's life are not known.
6. I.e., while the soul remains separate from the body (until souls and bodies are reunited at the Resurrection).
7. I.e., Phoebus Apollo (the god of poetry and music) and the nine Muses, who reject all other brains matched with yours. According to William Drummond of Hawthornden, Jonson considered Donne to be "the first poet in the world in some things"; cf. p. 418 of this edition.
8. I.e., add to it.

All which I meant to praise, and yet I would,
   But leave, because I cannot as I should!   10

XLV: *On My First Son*

Farewell, thou child of my right hand, and joy;[9]
   My sin was too much hope of thee, loved boy.
Seven years thou wert lent to me, and I thee pay,
   Exacted by thy fate, on the just day.
O, could I lose all father now![1] For why   5
   Will man lament the state he should envy?
To have so soon 'scaped world's and flesh's rage,
   And, if no other misery, yet age?
Rest in soft peace, and asked, say, "Here doth lie
   Ben Jonson his best piece of poetry,   10
For whose sake, henceforth, all his vows be such
   As what he loves may never like too much."[2]

LV: *To Francis Beaumont*[3]

How I do love thee, Beaumont, and thy Muse,
   That unto me dost such religion[4] use!
How I do fear myself, that am not worth
   The least indulgent thought thy pen drops forth!
At once thou mak'st me happy, and unmak'st;   5
   And giving largely to me, more thou tak'st.
What fate is mine, that so itself bereaves?
   What art is thine, that so thy friend deceives?
When even there, where most thou praisest me,
   For writing better, I must envy thee.   10

9. Jonson's son Benjamin (the name, literally "child of the right hand" in Hebrew, implies the meaning "dexterous" or "fortunate"), born in 1596, died of the plague in 1603, while Jonson was absent from London. Drummond observes that the poet, "being in the country at Sir Robert Cotton's house with old Camden . . . saw in a vision his eldest son, then a child and at London, appear unto him with the mark of a bloody cross on his forehead as if it had been cutted with a sword; at which amazed, he prayed unto God, and in the morning he came to Mr. Camden's chamber to tell him, who persuaded him it was but an apprehension of his fantasy, at which he should not be dejected. In the meantime comes there letters from his wife of the death of that boy in the plague. He appeared to him, he said, of a manly shape, and of that growth that he thinks he shall be at the Resurrection" (*H & S*, I, pp. 139–140).
1. I.e., relinquish every thought of fatherhood.
2. These lines (with their echo of line 2) appear to reflect the classical belief that excessive good fortune is likely to excite the jealousy of the gods. Cf. Martial, *Epigrams*, VI. xxix. 8: *Quidquid amas, cupias non placuisse nimis* ("Whatever you love, may you wish not to have been overly pleased by [it]"). Cf. also the comments of L. A. Beaurline on the poem, on p. 517 of this edition.
3. Francis Beaumont (c. 1584–1616) collaborated with John Fletcher (1597–1625) chiefly in the genre of romantic tragicomedy, over a period of some ten years early in the seventeenth century. For his verse "Letter to Ben Jonson," cf. p. 421 of this edition.
4. Faithfulness.

LIX: On Spies[5]

Spies, you are lights in state, but of base stuff,
Who, when you've burnt yourselves down to the snuff,[6]
Stink, and are thrown away. End fair enough.

LXIX: To Pertinax Cob[7]

Cob, thou nor soldier, thief, nor fencer art,
Yet by thy weapon liv'st! Th'hast one good part.

LXXVI: On Lucy, Countess of Bedford[8]

This morning, timely rapt with holy fire,
    I thought to form unto my zealous Muse
What kind of creature I could most desire
    To honor, serve, and love; as poets use.
I meant to make her fair, and free, and wise,   5
    Of greatest blood, and yet more good than great;
I meant the day-star should not brighter rise,
    Nor lend like influence from his lucent seat.
I meant she should be courteous, facile,[9] sweet,
    Hating that solemn vice of greatness, pride;   10
I meant each softest virtue there should meet,
    Fit in that softer bosom to reside.
Only a learned and a manly soul
    I purposed her; that should, with even powers,
The rock, the spindle, and the shears[1] control   15
    Of destiny, and spin her own free hours.
Such when I meant to feign, and wished to see,
    My Muse bade, "Bedford write," and that was she.

5. Drummond reports that "in the time of [Jonson's] close imprisonment under Queen Elizabeth [i.e., in 1598], his judges could get nothing of him to all their demands but aye and no; they placed two damned villains to catch advantage of him, with him, but he was advertised [i.e., warned] by his keeper. Of the spies he hath an epigram" (*H & S*, I, p. 139). Cf. also Epigram CI, p. 13, n. 7.

6. Candle end.

7. Latin *pertinax* means "stubborn, obstinate" (also "stiff"); "cob" has the double sense of "something big or stout" and "something forming a rounded lump." In northern English rustic dialect, "cob" came to mean "testicle."

8. Daugher (1581–1627) of Sir John Harington, the Countess of Bedford was friend and patron to Jonson, Donne, Daniel, and other literary figures; she took part in several of Jonson's masques. Cf. also Epigram XCIV, p. 11.

9. Affable, unconstrained.

1. Distaff ("rock"), spindle, and shears are the emblems of the three Fates—Clotho spins the thread of life; Lachesis determines its length; Atropos cuts it with her shears. Cf. Hesiod, *Theogony*, 217–223, 904–906; and Plato, *Republic*, X. 617–621.

LXXIX: To Elizabeth, Countess of Rutland[2]

That poets are far rarer births than kings
    Your noblest father proved; like whom, before,
Or then, or since, about our Muses' springs,
    Came not that soul exhausted so their store.
Hence was it that the destinies decreed   5
    (Save that most masculine issue of his brain)[3]
No male unto him, who could so exceed
    Nature, they thought, in all that he would feign.
At which she, happily[4] displeased, made you;
    On whom if he were living now to look,   10
He should those rare and absolute numbers[5] view,
    As he would burn, or better far his book.

LXXXIII: To a Friend

To put out the word, *whore*, thou dost me woo,
Throughout my book. 'Troth, put out *woman* too.

XCI: To Sir Horace Vere[6]

Which of thy names I take, not only bears
    A Roman sound, but Roman virtue wears,
Illustrous Vere, or Horace; fit to be
    Sung by a Horace, or a Muse as free,
Which thou art to thyself: whose fame was won   5
    In th'eye of Europe, where thy deeds were done,
When on thy trumpet she did sound a blast,
    Whose relish[7] to eternity shall last.
I leave thy acts, which should I prosecute[8]
    Throughout, might flatt'ry seem; and to be mute   10
To any one were envy, which would live
    Against my grave, and time could not forgive.
I speak thy other graces, not less shown,
    Nor less in practice, but less marked, less known:

2. The daughter (1584–1612) of Sir Philip Sidney; according to Drummond, Jonson thought her "nothing inferior to her father . . . in poesie" (*H & S*, I, p. 138).
3. I.e., Sidney's prose romance *Arcadia*.
4. By good fortune.
5. I.e., perfectly harmonious proportions.
6. A distinguished English soldier (1565–1635), Vere campaigned with considerable success against the forces of Spain in the Netherlands. Thomas Fuller notices his "excellent temper, it being true of him what is said of the Caspian Sea,

that it doth never ebb nor flow; observing a constant tenor, neither elated nor depressed with success." Comparing him to his brother, Sir Francis Vere, Fuller observes, "Sir Francis was more feared, Sir Horace more loved, by the soldiery" (*The Worthies of England*, ed. J. Freeman [London, 1952], p. 180). The *Odes* and *Satires* of Horace (65–8 B.C.) were admired and imitated by Jonson, who translated the Roman poet's *Ars Poetica*. Latin *vere* means "truly."
7. Lingering and agreeable trace or echo.
8. Pursue in detail.

Humanity and piety, which are   15
    As noble in great chiefs as they are rare;
And best become the valiant man to wear,
    Who more should seek men's reverence, than fear.

XCIV: *To Lucy, Countess of Bedford,*
with Mr. Donne's Satires[9]

Lucy,[1] you brightness of our sphere, who are
    Life of the Muses' day, their morning-star!
If works, not th'author's, their own grace should look,[2]
    Whose poems would not wish to be your book?
But these, desired by you, the maker's ends   5
    Crown with their own. Rare poems ask rare friends.
Yet satires, since the most of mankind be
    Their unavoided subject, fewest see;
For none e'er took that pleasure in sin's sense,
    But, when they heard it taxed, took more offence.   10
They, then, that living where the matter is bred,[3]
    Dare for these poems, yet, both ask, and read,
And like them too, must needfully, though few,
    Be of the best; and 'mongst those, best are you,
Lucy, you brightness of our sphere, who are   15
    The Muses' evening, as their morning-star.

XCVI: *To John Donne*

Who shall doubt, Donne, where[4] I a poet be,
    When I dare send my epigrams to thee?
That so alone canst judge, so alone dost make;
    And, in thy censures, evenly, dost take
As free simplicity to disavow,   5
    As thou hast best authority t'allow.
Read all I send; and if I find but one
    Marked by thy hand, and with the better stone,[5]
My title's sealed. Those that for claps do write,
    Let puisnees',[6] porters', players' praise delight,   10
And, till they burst, their backs, like asses load;[7]
    A man should seek great glory, and not broad.

9. Donne's *Satires,* perhaps composed c. 1593–1595, were circulating in manuscript before their publication in 1633.
1. "Lucy" derives from Latin *lux,* "light, brightness."
2. Seek.
3. I.e., in the society being satirized.
4. Whether.
5. The ancient Romans marked joyful or successful days on their calendars with white stones (thought to be auspicious); cf. Pliny, *Natural History,* VII. 40; and *Letters,* VI. 11.
6. Inferiors, underlings.
7. I.e. (as foolish men overload beasts of burden), accept ever greater loads (of vulgar praise) until their backs break.

CI: Inviting a Friend to Supper[8]

Tonight, grave sir, both my poor house and I
    Do equally desire your company;
Not that we think us worthy such a guest,
    But that your worth will dignify our feast
With those that come, whose grace may make that seem   5
    Something, which else could hope for no esteem.
It is the fair acceptance, sir, creates
    The entertainment perfect; not the cates.[9]
Yet shall you have, to rectify your palate,
    An olive, capers, or some better salad   10
Ushering the mutton; with a short-legged hen,
    If we can get her, full of eggs, and then
Lemons and wine for sauce; to these, a coney[1]
    Is not to be despaired of, for our money;
And though fowl, now, be scarce, yet there are clerks,   15
    The sky not falling, think we may have larks.
I'll tell you of more, and lie, so you will come:
    Of partridge, pheasant, woodcock, of which some
May yet be there; and godwit, if we can,
    Knat, rail, and ruff too.[2] Howsoe'er, my man   20
Shall read a piece of Vergil, Tacitus,
    Livy, or of some better book[3] to us,
Of which we'll speak our minds, amidst our meat;
    And I'll profess no verses to repeat;
To this, if ought appear which I know not of,   25
    That will the pastry, not my paper, show of.
Digestive cheese, and fruit there sure will be;
    But that which most doth take my Muse, and me
Is a pure cup of rich Canary wine,
    Which is the Mermaid's[4] now, but shall be mine;   30
Of which had Horace or Anacreon tasted,
    Their lives, as do their lines, till now had lasted.

8. The versified invitation to share a frugal or lavish repast is a popular variety of the classical and Renaissance verse epistle. Jonson took several hints from Martial's poems in this kind, e.g., *Epigrams*, V. lxxviii; XI. lii. Cf. also Habington, "To a Friend, Inviting Him to a Meeting upon Promise," p. 225.
9. Dainties, delicacies.
1. Rabbit.
2. Edible birds of English marshlands and waterways; in modern usage, curlew, sandpiper, corn crake, pigeon.
3. With Vergil (70–19 B.C.), author of the *Aeneid*, Jonson conjoins the Roman historian Livy (59 B.C.–A.D. 17) and Tacitus (c. A.D. 60–c. 120), whom he especially admired; cf. *H & S*, I, p. 136. By "some better book" is meant, perhaps, the Bible.
4. The Mermaid Tavern in London was frequented by Jonson and his fellows; cf. Francis Beaumont, "A Letter to Ben Jonson," p. 422, ll. 44–58. For Horace, cf. Epigram XCI, p. 10, and note; the lyric poet Anacreon of Teos (born c. 550 B.C.) gave his name to a genre of amatory verse much favored by Jonson's predecessors.

Tobacco, nectar, or the Thespian spring[5]
    Are all but Luther's beer[6] to this I sing.
Of this we will sup free, but moderately,   35
    And we will have no Pooly, or Parrot by;[7]
Nor shall our cups make any guilty men,
    But at our parting we will be as when
We innocently met. No simple word
    That shall be uttered at our mirthful board   40
Shall make us sad next morning, or affright
    The liberty that we'll enjoy tonight.

CXX: *Epitaph on S. P., a Child of Q. El. Chapel*[8]

Weep with me, all you that read
    This little story;
And know, for whom a tear you shed
    Death's self is sorry.
'Twas a child that so did thrive   5
    In grace and feature,
As Heaven and Nature seemed to strive
    Which owned the creature.
Years he numbered scarce thirteen
    When Fates turned cruel,   10
Yet three filled zodiacs[9] had he been
    The stage's jewel;
And did act (what now we moan)
    Old men so duly,
As, sooth, the Parcae[1] thought him one,   15
    He played so truly.
So, by error, to his fate
    They all consented;
But viewing him since (alas, too late),
    They have repented,   20
And have sought, to give new birth,
    In baths to steep him;
But, being so much too good for earth,
    Heaven vows to keep him.

---

5. Thespiae lies at the foot of Mount Helicon, in Greece; the "Thespian spring" was associated with the Muses. Tobacco appears in this context, perhaps, because it was often said to be drunk; cf. *Every Man In His Humour*, III. v. 137; "The most divine tobacco that ever I drunk."

6. I.e., German beer.

7. Robert Pooly and (probably) Henry Parrot were government spies; Pooly was present when Christopher Marlowe was killed in a tavern brawl. Cf. Mark Eccles, "Jonson and the Spies," *RES*, XIII (1937), 385–397; and Epigram LIX, p. 9. Jonson punningly suggests the loose chatter associated with ("polly") parrots.

8. Salomon Pavy, a boy actor with the Children of Queen Elizabeth's Chapel, took part in two of Jonson's plays: *Cynthia's Revels*, in 1600, and *Poetaster*, in 1601. He died in 1602. On his name and career, cf. G. E. Bentley, "A Good Name Lost," *TLS* (May 30, 1942).

9. I.e., he had acted for three years.

1. The Fates. Cf. Epigram LXXVI, p. 9, n. 1.

CXXIV: *Epitaph on Elizabeth, L.H.*[2]

Wouldst thou hear what man can say
    In a little? Reader, stay.
Underneath this stone doth lie
    As much beauty as could die;
Which in life did harbor give   5
    To more virtue than doth live.
If, at all, she had a fault,
    Leave it buried in this vault.
One name was Elizabeth;
    Th'other, let it sleep with death: 10
Fitter, where it died, to tell,
    Than that it lived at all.   Farewell!

CXXVIII: *To William Roe*[3]

Roe (and my joy to name), th'art now to go
    Countries, and climes, manners, and men to know,
T'extract, and choose the best of all these known,
    And those to turn to blood, and make thine own:
May winds as soft as breath of kissing friends   5
    Attend thee hence; and there, may all thy ends,
As the beginnings here, prove purely sweet,
    And perfect in a circle always meet.
So, when we, blessed with thy return, shall see
    Thy self, with thy first thoughts, brought home by thee,   10
We each to other may this voice inspire:
    "This is that good Aeneas, passed through fire,
Through seas, storms, tempests; and, embarked for hell,
    Came back untouched. This man hath travailed[4] well."

CXXXIII: *On the Famous Voyage*

No more let Greece her bolder fables tell
    Of Hercules, or Theseus going to hell,
Orpheus, Ulysses; or the Latin Muse,
    With tales of Troy's just knight,[5] our faiths abuse;

2. The identity of the lady has not been positively established. On the poem's structure and style, cf. H. S. Babb, "The 'Epitaph on Elizabeth, L. H.' and Ben Jonson's Style," *JEGP*, LXII (1963), 738–744; and the response by G. N. Murphy and W. C. Slattery, "Meaning and Structure in Jonson's 'Epitaph on Elizabeth, L. H.,' " *Re: Arts and Letters*, II (1969), 1–3.
3. William Roe (1585–1667) was the brother of Sir John Roe, Jonson's close friend; cf. *H & S*, I, pp. 136–137. Jonson appeared as a witness in William Roe's behalf in a lawsuit, in 1610.
4. I.e., worked (travailed) and traveled to good purpose.
5. Aeneas, the virtuous hero of the *Aeneid*, composed by Vergil ("the Latin Muse"). In the course of his mock-epic, Jonson makes play with the apparatus of classical epic (invocation, heroic quest, descent to the underworld, etc.). Students of the poem may wish to consult Edmund Wilson's essay, "Morose Ben Jonson," in *The Triple Thinkers: Twelve Essays on Literary Subjects* (New York, 1940), pp. 213–232.

We have a Shelton[6] and a Heyden got,　　　　　　　　5
　　Had power to act, what they to feign had not.
All that they boast of Styx, of Acheron,
　　Cocytus, Phlegethon,[7] ours have proved in one;[8]
The filth, stench, noise: save only what was there
　　Subtly distinguished, was confuséd here.　　　　　10
Their wherry[9] had no sail, too; ours had none;
　　And in it, two more horrid knaves than Charon.[1]
Arses were heard to croak instead of frogs;[2]
　　And for one Cerberus,[3] the whole coast was dogs.
Furies there wanted not; each scold was ten.　　　　15
　　And, for the cries of ghosts, women and men,
Laden with plague-sores, and their sins, were heard,
　　Lashed by their consciences, to die affeard.
Then let the former age with this content her,
　　She brought the poets forth, but ours th' adventer.[4]　20

THE VOYAGE ITSELF

I sing the brave adventure of two wights,
And pity 'tis, I cannot call 'em knights:
One was; and he, for brawn and brain, right able
To have been styléd of King Arthur's table.
The other was a squire of fair degree,　　　　　　　25
But in the action greater man than he
Who gave, to take at his return from Hell,
His three for one.[5] Now, lordings, listen well.

　　It was the day, what time the powerful moon
Makes the poor Bankside creature wet its shoon　　30
In its own hall,[6] when these (in worthy scorn
Of those that put out moneys on return
From Venice, Paris, or some inland passage
Of six times to and fro without embassage,[7]
Or him that backward went to Berwick,[8] or which　　35

6. Sir Ralph Shelton was knighted in 1607; Heyden's identity is unknown.
7. I.e., the four rivers of Hades; cf. Homer, *Odyssey*, X. 513–515.
8. I.e., ours have experienced in the Fleet Ditch, a thoroughly polluted stream running south into the Thames. "The Fleet . . . had become a shallow, silt-choked, rubbish-filled abomination 'very stinking and noisome' . . . little better, indeed, than a sewer. As early as 1390 the White Friars had complained that the stench arising from it, impossible to deaden with the strongest incense, had been responsible for the death of several of their brethren" (Christopher Hibbert, *London: The Biography of a City* [New York, 1969],p. 74).
9. I.e., the vessel(s) in which the figures named in lines 2–4 were embarked.
1. The boatman who ferried the souls of the dead across the river of Hades is a familiar figure in classical literature; cf. Vergil, *Aeneid*, VI. 298–315.
2. The allusion refers to Aristophanes' comedy, *The Frogs*.
3. The monstrous watchdog of Hades; cf. Hesiod, *Theogony*, 311.
4. Adventure.
5. I.e., his large profit.
6. I.e., at high tide. The Bankside, or southern bank of the Thames, was a notoriously raffish district.
7. I.e., without acting as official ambassadors.
8. William Rowley, in *A Search for Money* (London, 1609), discussing the contemporary passion for eccentrically conceived travels, alludes to "the fellows going backward to Berwick, another hopping from York to London" (A 4).

Did dance the famous morris unto Norwich)[9]
At Bread Street's Mermaid, having dined, and merry,
Proposed to go to Holborn[1] in a wherry:
A harder task than either his to Bristo',
Or his to Antwerp.[2] Therefore, once more, list ho.   40
    A dock[3] there is that calléd is Avernus,
Of some Bridewell, and may, in time, concern us
All, that are readers; but methinks 'tis odd
That all this while I have forgot some god
Or goddess to invoke, to stuff my verse;   45
And with both bombard-style and phrase rehearse
The many perils of this port, and how,
Sans help of Sibyl, or a golden bough,[4]
Or magic sacrifice, they passed along!
Alcides,[5] be thou succoring to my song.   50
Thou hast seen Hell, some say, and know'st all nooks there,
Canst tell me best how every Fury looks there,
And art a god, if fame thee not abuses,
Always at hand to aid the merry Muses.
Great club-fist,[6] though thy back and bones be sore   55
Still with thy former labors; yet once more
Act a brave work, call it thy last adventry;[7]
But hold my torch, while I describe the entry
To this dire passage. Say, thou, stop thy nose:
'Tis but light pains; indeed this dock's no rose.   60
    In the first jaws appeared that ugly monster
Yclepéd[8] Mud, which, when their oars did once stir,
Belched forth an air as hot as at the muster
Of all your night-tubs, when the carts do cluster,
Who shall discharge first his merde-urinous[9] load;   65
Thorough her womb they make their famous road
Between two walls; where, on one side, to scare men,
Were seen your ugly Centaurs, ye call carmen,[1]
Gorgonian scolds, and Harpies; on the other
Hung stench, diseases, and old Filth, their mother,   70

9. Rowley also mentions Will Kemp's "wild morris to Norwich"; Kemp's exploit took place in 1599. In 1600 he published *Kemps nine daies wonder. Performed in a daunce from London to Norwich.*
1. In Jonson's day, Holborn was a residential area lying to the northwest of the city walls.
2. These feats of rowing are noticed by Samuel Rowlands in verses prefixed to John Taylor, *The Sculler, Rowing from Tiber to Thames* (London, 1612), A 4.
3. Bridewell Dock was situated at the junction of the Fleet Ditch and the Thames. The pun on "dock" (the place where prisoners stand in a court of law) would have reminded Jonson's readers that Bridewell Prison stood nearby.

4. Aeneas was so aided; cf. *Aeneid,* VI, 1 ff.
5. I.e., Hercules, who rescued Alcestis from Hades; cf. Euripides, *Alcestis.*
6. Hercules, usually represented as carrying a club cut from a wild olive tree, accidentâlly killed Eurynomus with a blow of his fist; cf. Diodorus Siculus, *Bibliotheca Historica,* IV. 36.
7. Adventure.
8. Called.
9. I.e., composed of excrement and urine.
1. I.e., men who drive carts carrying dung. Centaurs, Gorgons, and Harpies, monstrous beings from the realm of classical mythology, variously combine the characteristics of beasts and men.

With famine, wants, and sorrows many a dozen,
The least of which was to the plague a cousin.
But they unfrighted pass, though many a privy
Spake to 'em louder than the ox in Livy,[2]
And many a sink[3] poured out her rage anenst[4] 'em.   75
But still their valor and their virtue fenced[5] 'em,
And on they went, like Castor brave and Pollux,[6]
Plowing the main. When, see, the worst of all lucks,
They met the second prodigy, would fear a
Man that had never heard of a Chimaera.[7]   80
One said it was bold Briareus,[8] or the beadle[9]
Who hath the hundred hands when he doth meddle;
The other thought it Hydra,[1] or the rock
Made of the trull that cut her father's lock;[2]
But coming near, they found it but a lighter,   85
So huge, it seemed, they could by no means quite[3] her.
"Back," cried their brace of Charons; they cried, "No,
No going back; on still, you rogues, and row.
How hight[4] the place?" A voice was heard, "Cocytus."[5]
"Row close then, slaves." "Alas, they will beshite us."   90
"No matter, stinkards, row. What croaking sound
Is this we hear? of frogs?" "No, guts windbound,
Over your heads." "Well, row." At this loud
Crack did report itself, as if a cloud
Had burst with storm, and down fell, *ab excelsis*,[6]   95
Poor Mercury, crying out on Paracelsus[7]
And all his followers, that had so abused him;
And, in so shitten sort, so long had used him,
For (where he[8] was the god of eloquence,
And subtlety of metals) they dispense   100
His spirits, now, in pills, and eke in potions,

2. Cf. Livy's history of Rome, XXXV. 21.
3. Sewage drain.
4. Against.
5. Protected.
6. In classical mythology, Castor and Pollux, the Dioscuri, were the sons of Zeus; by a variant account, Pollux alone was Zeus' offspring and, therefore, immortal, while Castor, the son of Tyndareus, was mortal. Cf. *Odyssey*, XI. 300 ff.; Pindar, *Nemean Odes*, X. 80.
7. A fire-breathing monster combining the head of a lion, the body of a goat, and a dragon's tail.
8. A huge monster with a hundred hands and fifty heads, Briareus was the son of Uranus (Heaven) and Gaea (Earth); cf. Hesiod, *Theogony*, 149–150.
9. Parish official.
1. Hydra, a sea monster wtih nine heads, was slain by Hercules; cf. Ovid, *Metamorphoses*, IX. 67–74.
2. Jonson confuses the sea monster Scylla, guardian of a dangerous rock in the Straits of Messina (Ovid, *Metamorphoses*, XIII. 897–968; XIV. 1–74), with Scylla the daughter of King Nisus, who, to win the love of Minos, cut off a lock of her father's hair, on which his life depended (*Metamorphoses*, VIII. 1–151).
3. Avoid.
4. I.e., what is the name of.
5. The river of lamentation, in Hades.
6. I.e., from the heavens.
7. Mercurial compounds were employed as purgatives; the followers of Paracelsus (Theophrastus Bombastus von Hohenheim, 1493–1541), physician and alchemist, assigned special importance to the role of mercury in medical and alchemical processes. Jonson's view of the alchemist's art is dramatically set out in his comedy, *The Alchemist*.
8. I.e., whereas Mercury. Mercury was also the divinity of commerce and gain.

Suppositories, cataplasms,[9] and lotions.
"But many moons there shall not wane," quoth he,
"(In the meantime, let 'em imprison me)
But I will speak, and know I shall be heard,   105
Touching this cause, where they will be afeared
To answer me." And sure, it was the intent
Of the grave fart, late let in parliament,[1]
Had it been seconded, and not in fume
Vanished away; as you must all presume   110
Their Mercury did now. By this, the stem
Of the hulk touched, and, as by Polypheme
The sly Ulysses stole in a sheepskin,[2]
The well-greased wherry now had got between,
And bade her farewell sough unto the lurden;[3]   115
Never did bottom more betray her burden;
The meat-boat of bears' college, Paris Garden,[4]
Stunk not so ill; nor, when she kissed, Kate Arden.[5]
Yet, one day in the year, for sweet 'tis voiced,
And that is when it is the Lord Mayor's foist.[6]   120
   By this time had they reached the Stygian pool
By which the Masters swear, when, on the stool
Of worship,[7] they their nodding chins do hit
Against their breasts. Here several ghosts did flit
About the shore, of farts but late departed,   125
White, black, blue, green, and in more forms outstarted
Than all those atomi ridiculous,
Whereof old Democrite and Hill Nicholas,[8]
One said, the other swore, the world consists.
These be the cause of those thick frequent mists   130
Arising in that place, through which who goes
Must try the unused valor of a nose,
And that ours did. For yet no nare[9] was tainted,
Nor thumb nor finger to the stop acquainted,
But open and unarmed encountered all,   135
Whether it languishing stuck upon the wall
Or were precipitated down the jakes,[1]
And, after, swum abroad in ample flakes,
Or that it lay, heaped like an usurer's mass,

9. Poultices.
1. This alludes to "a discussion [in 1607] in the House of Commons on the peculiar manner in which Henry Ludlow said 'no' to a message brought . . . from the Lords" (*H & S*, X, p. 74).
2. Cf. *Odyssey*, IX. 431–434.
3. I.e., gave a parting sigh to the clumsy slowness (of the lighter).
4. Offal from the meat markets in London was transported across the Thames to Paris Garden, in Southwark, where bears and bulls were "baited" by mastiffs.
5. A celebrated prostitute; cf. "An Exe-

cration Upon Vulcan," p. 71, ll. 148–149.
6. I.e., used as the Lord Mayor's barge. "Foist" means also "stink."
7. I.e., on the toilet.
8. Democritus (born c. 460 B.C.) is generally regarded as the founder of the atomic theory of matter; Nicholas Hill (c. 1570–1610) in 1601 published a philosophical text touching on Democritus and other ancient thinkers.
9. Nostril.
1. Privy.

All was to them the same, they were to pass;   140
And so they did, from Styx to Acheron,
The ever-boiling flood, whose banks upon
Your Fleet Lane Furies[2] and hot cooks do dwell
That, with still-scalding steams, make the place hell.
The sinks ran grease and hair of measled[3] hogs,   145
The heads, houghs,[4] entrails, and the hides of dogs;
For to say truth, what scullion is so nasty
To put the skins and offal in a pasty?
Cats there lay divers had been flayed and roasted,
And, after moldy grown, again were toasted;   150
Then, selling not, a dish was ta'en to mince 'em,
But still it seemed the rankness did convince[5] 'em.
For here they were thrown in with the melted pewter,
Yet drowned they not. They had five lives in future.
    But 'mongst these tiberts,[6] who do you think there
       was?   155
Old Banks the juggler,[7] our Pythagoras,
Grave tutor to the learned horse. Both which,
Being beyond sea, burned for one witch,
Their spirits transmigrated to a cat;
And now above the pool a face right fat,   160
With great gray eyes, is lifted up, and mewed;
Thrice did it spit; thrice dived. At last it viewed
Our brave heroes with a milder glare,
And in a piteous tune began. "How dare
Your dainty nostrils (in so hot a season,   165
When every clerk eats artichokes and peason,[8]
Laxative lettuce, and such windy meat[9])
Tempt such a passage, when each privy's seat
Is filled with buttock, and the walls do sweat
Urine and plasters;[1] when the noise doth beat   170
Upon your ears of discords so unsweet,
And outcries of the damnéd in the Fleet?[2]
Cannot the plague-bill[3] keep you back; nor bells
Of loud Sepulchre's[4] with their hourly knells,
But you will visit grisly Pluto's hall?   175
Behold where Cerberus, reared on the wall
Of Holborn (three sergeants'[5] heads), looks o'er,
And stays but till you come unto the door!

2. I.e., the cooks of Fleet Lane.
3. Leprous.
4. Hocks.
5. Convict.
6. Cats.
7. Entertainer. Banks trained and exhibited the famous performing horse, Morocco, over a period of years toward the close of the sixteenth century. Notwithstanding the allusion to Pythagoras (540–510 B.C.), who believed in the transmigration of souls, Banks was still

living in 1625.
8. Peas.
9. Food.
1. I.e., excrement.
2. I.e., the Fleet Prison.
3. I.e., the weekly list of those dead of the plague.
4. Saint Sepulchre's Church stood just to the west of the city proper.
5. Lawyers'; but here alluding to the three judges named in lines 187–190.

Tempt not his fury, Pluto is away;
And Madame Caesar, great Proserpina,[6]   180
Is now from home. You lose your labors quite,
Were you Jove's sons, or had Alcides' might."
They cried out, "Puss!" He told them he was Banks,
That had so often showed 'em merry pranks.
They laughed at his laugh-worthy fate, and passed   185
The triple head without a sop.[7] At last,
Calling for Rhadamanthus,[8] that dwelt by,
A soap-boiler; and Aeacus him nigh
Who kept an alehouse; with my little Minos,
An ancient purblind fletcher,[9] with a high nose;   190
They took 'em all to witness of their action;
And so went bravely back, without protraction.[1]

    In memory of which most liquid deed,
The city since hath raised a pyramid.
And I could wish for their eternized sakes,   195
My Muse had plowed with his that sung A-jax.[2]

The Forest[3]

I: Why I Write Not Of Love

Some act of Love's bound to rehearse,[4]
I thought to bind him in my verse;
Which when he felt, "Away," quoth he,
"Can poets hope to fetter me?
It is enough they once did get   5
Mars and my mother in their net;[5]

6. I.e., the queen of Hades.
7. I.e., a bribe of food. Cerberus was propitiated in this way; cf. *Aeneid*, VI. 415–425.
8. Rhadamanthus, Aeacus, and Minos were the three judges of Hades; cf. Plato, *Apology*, 41a.
9. I.e., blind or partly blind makers of arrows.
1. Delay.
2. I.e., with that of Sir John Harington (c. 1561–1612), who wrote the Rabelaisian *The Metamorphosis of Ajax* (with a pun on "a jakes," i.e., a privy).
3. It seems likely that Jonson regarded the fifteen poems that comprise *The Forest* with special affection; he appears to have thought them superior to those "lesser poems, of later growth," that make up *Underwood* (as he remarks in his prefatory note to that collection), and also to have regarded them as in some ways more serious and exploratory even than the *Epigrams,* from which *The Forest* diverges in range, tone, and variety of verse form. The clipped brevity of the epigrammatic mode yield here, thought the verse is as delicately chiseled as before,
to the ampler design of the verse epistle and the ode, and to lyric poetry in various kinds; the dominantly critical stance of the *Epigrams* is less in evidence than are forthright expressions of allegiance to the highest standards of moral conduct, often exemplified by aristocratic figures whom Jonson especially admired. Then, too, while the couplet is not abandoned, other verse forms and structural patterns come into view; and these anticipate the haunting measures of such poems as "The Hourglass" or "The Dream" as well as the complexities of the "Epithalamion" for the Weston-Stuart nuptials. It may be, finally, that the arrangement of these fifteen poems is deliberate; certainly it is of interest that the first poem bids a sad farewell to Cupid while the last affirms the poet's love of God.
4. I.e., bound to relate some act performed by Cupid, the god of love.
5. Discovering his consort Venus in the embraces of her lover Mars, Vulcan threw a net over the guilty pair and invited the other gods to witness the scene; cf. Ovid, *Metamorphoses*, IV. 171–189.

I wear not these my wings in vain."
With which he fled me; and again
Into my rhymes could ne'er be got
By any art. Then wonder not   10
That since, my numbers[6] are so cold,
When Love is fled, and I grow old.

II: To Penshurst[7]

Thou are not, Penshurst, built to envious show
    Of touch,[8] or marble; nor canst boast a row
Of polished pillars, or a roof of gold;
    Thou hast no lantern,[9] whereof tales are told,
Or stair, or courts; but stand'st an ancient pile,   5
    And, these grudged at, art reverenced the while.[1]
Thou joy'st in better marks, of soil, of air,
    Of wood, of water: therein thou art fair.
Thou hast thy walks for health, as well as sport;
    Thy Mount,[2] to which the dryads[3] do resort,   10
Where Pan and Bacchus their high feasts have made
    Beneath the broad beech and the chestnut shade;
That taller tree, which of a nut was set,
    At his[4] great birth, where all the Muses met.
There in the writhéd bark are cut the names   15
    Of many a sylvan, taken with his flames.[5]
And thence the ruddy satyrs oft provoke
    The lighter fauns to reach thy Lady's oak.[6]
Thy copse, too, named of Gamage,[7] thou hast there,
    That never fails to serve thee seasoned deer   20
When thou wouldst feast, or exercise thy friends.
    The lower land, that to the river bends,

---

6. Verses.
7. Penshurst Place, in Kent, was, and remains, the home of the Sidney family. The poem, perhaps the first successful example of the "topographical" or "country house" poem in English, was much admired and imitated by Jonson's contemporaries; cf. Carew's "To Saxham," and Waller's two poems "At Penshurst" (on pp. 164, 235, and 236 respectively). Marvell's "Upon Appleton House" is also relevant. A useful study, which attends to the poem in its classical and English contexts, is G. R. Hibbard, "The Country House Poem of the Seventeenth Century," *JWCI*, XIX (1956), 159 ff.
8. Touchstone; here, fine black marble or basalt.
9. I.e., a glassed-in cupola or small room on the top of a house. To what other storied "lantern" the line may refer is unknown.
1. I.e., while other buildings are envied, you are admired.
2. Some high ground on the estate.
3. Wood nymphs.
4. I.e., Sir Philip Sidney's (on November 30, 1554, when an oak was planted to commemorate the occasion).
5. I.e., of many woodsmen, or country-folk, stirred by Sidney's love poetry.
6. According to tradition, Lady Leicester's labor pains began under an oak on the estate, afterward called "My Lady's Oak."
7. Sir Robert Sidney (1563–1626), brother of the poet and owner of Penshurst when Jonson wrote this poem, had married Barbara Gamage in 1584. A grove near the entrance of the park bore her name.

Thy sheep, thy bullocks, kine, and calves do feed;
   The middle grounds thy mares and horses breed.
Each bank doth yield thee coneys;[8] and the tops   25
   Fertile of wood, Ashore and Sidney's copse,[9]
To crown thy open table, doth provide
   The purpled pheasant with the speckled side;
The painted partridge lies in every field,
   And, for thy mess, is willing to be killed.   30
And if the high-swol'n Medway[1] fail thy dish,
   Thou hast thy ponds, that pay thee tribute fish,
Fat, aged carps, that run into thy net,
   And pikes, now weary their own kind to eat,
As loath the second draught or cast to stay,[2]   35
   Officiously[3] at first themselves betray;
Bright eels that emulate them, and leap on land
   Before the fisher, or into his hand.
Then hath thy orchard fruit, thy garden flowers,
   Fresh as the air, and new as are the hours.   40
The early cherry, with the later plum,
   Fig, grape, and quince, each in his time doth come;
The blushing apricot and woolly peach
   Hang on thy walls[4] that every child may reach.
And though thy walls be of the country stone,   45
   They're reared with no man's ruin, no man's groan;
There's none that dwell about them wish them down;
   But all come in, the farmer, and the clown,[5]
And no one empty-handed to salute
   Thy lord and lady, though they have no suit.[6]   50
Some bring a capon, some a rural cake,
   Some nuts, some apples; some that think they make
The better cheeses bring 'em, or else send
   By their ripe daughters whom they would commend
This way to husbands, and whose baskets bear   55
   An emblem of themselves, in plum or pear.
But what can this (more than express their love)
   Add to thy free provisions, far above
The need of such whose liberal board doth flow
   With all that hospitality doth know!   60
Where comes no guest but is allowed to eat
   Without his fear, and of thy lord's own meat;
Where the same beer and bread and self-same wine
   That is his lordship's shall be also mine.

8. Rabbits.
9. These two small groves still survive.
1. The river Medway borders the estate
2. I.e., as if they were reluctant to wait
for the second cast and drawing-in of the
net.
3. Dutifully.
4. I.e., on the espaliered walls.
5. I.e., the rustic.
6. Request or special petition.

And I not fain to sit, as some, this day,   65
  At great men's tables, and yet dine away.[7]
Here no man tells[8] my cups; nor, standing by,
  A waiter doth my gluttony envy,
But gives me what I call and lets me eat,
  He knows, below, he shall find plenty of meat.   70
Thy tables hoard not up for the next day,
  Nor when I take my lodging need I pray
For fire, or lights, or livery;[9] all is there
  As if thou, then, wert mine, or I reigned here:
There's nothing I can wish, for which I stay.   75
  That found King James, when hunting late this way
With his brave son, the Prince,[1] they saw thy fires
  Shine bright on every hearth as the desires
Of thy Penates[2] had been set on flame
  To entertain them; or the country came,   80
With all their zeal, to warm their welcome here.
  What (great, I will not say, but) sudden cheer
Didst thou then make them! and what praise was heaped
  On thy good lady then! who therein reaped
The just reward of her high huswifery;   85
  To have her linen, plate, and all things nigh,
When she was far; and not a room but dressed,
  As if it had expected such a guest!   ·
These, Penshurst, are thy praise, and yet not all.
  Thy lady's noble, fruitful, chaste withal.   90
His children thy great lord may call his own,
  A fortune in this age but rarely known.
They are and have been taught religion; thence
  Their gentler spirits have sucked innocence.
Each morn and even they are taught to pray   95
  With the whole household, and may, every day,
Read, in their virtuous parents' noble parts,
  The mysteries[3] of manners, arms and arts.
Now, Penshurst, they that will proportion[4] thee
  With other edifices, when they see   100
Those proud, ambitious heaps, and nothing else,
  May say, their lords have built, but thy lord dwells.

---

7. I.e., to be given less satisfying or choice fare than that reserved for the host (and so be forced to go elsewhere for a full meal). Drummond reports that Jonson complained of such treatment by the Earl of Salisbury; cf. *H & S*, I, p. 141.
8. Counts.
9. Food, provisions.

1. I.e., Prince Henry, who died in November, 1612.
2. The Roman household gods.
3. Crafts, arts; but there is also the sense of "high mysteries," implying a set of cultural attainments into which one must be initiated.
4. Compare.

III: *To Sir Robert Wroth*[5]

How blest are thou, canst love the country, Wroth,
    Whether by choice, or fate, or both;
And, though so near the city and the court,
    Art ta'en with neither's vice nor sport;
That, at great times, are no ambitious guest   5
    Of sheriff's dinner or mayor's feast,
Nor com'st to view the better cloth of state,
    The richer hangings, or crown-plate,
Nor throng'st, when masquing is, to have a sight
    Of the short bravery[6] of the night,   10
To view the jewels, stuffs, the pains, the wit
    There wasted, some not paid for yet;
But canst at home in thy securer[7] rest
    Live, with un-bought provision blessed,
Free from proud porches, or their gilded roofs,   15
    'Mongst lowing herds and solid hoofs,
Alongst the curléd woods and painted meads
    Through which a serpent river leads
To some cool, courteous shade, which he calls his,
    And makes sleep softer than it is!   20
Or, if thou list the night in watch to break,
    Abed canst hear the loud stag speak
In spring, oft rouséd for thy master's[8] sport,
    Who, for it, makes thy house his court;
Or with thy friends, the heart of all the year,[9]   25
    Divid'st upon the lesser deer;
In autumn at the partridge makes a flight,
    And giv'st thy gladder guests the sight;
And in the winter hunt'st the flying hare
    More for thy exercise than fare,   30
While all that follow their glad ears apply
    To the full greatness of the cry;[1]
Or hawking at the river, or the bush,
    Or shooting at the greedy thrush,

---

5. Sir Robert Wroth (1576–1614) married Lady Mary Sidney, the daughter of Sir Robert Sidney, in 1604; his country estate at Durrants, northeast of London, is the setting for Jonson's tribute. While the poem has something in common with "To Penshurst," its informing idea is rather that of "the happy life" which is good "because it possesses, or may possess, enjoyments and a fullness of comfort," and which reflects the Stoic ideal of Cicero's *De Senectute*: "How blessed it is for the soul, after having, as it were, finished its campaigns of lust and ambition, of strife and enmity and of all the passions, to return within itself, and, as the saying is, 'to live apart!' " (XIV. 49; cf. Earl Miner, *The Cavalier Mode from Jonson to Cotton* [Princeton, 1971], pp. 76, 95). The theme often recurs in the work of Jonson's followers: cf. Herrick's "The Country Life," Fane's "To Retiredness," and Randolph's "An Ode to . . . Stafford . . ." (on pp. 137, 206, and 212 respectively). For a discussion of Jonson's art in this poem, cf. the essay by Stephen Orgel on p. 525.
6. I.e., ephemeral and showy appearance.
7. More free from care.
8. I.e., the king's.
9. I.e., in summer.
1. I.e., the baying of hounds.

Thou dost with some delight the day out-wear,   35
    Although the coldest of the year!
The whilst the several seasons thou hast seen
    Of flow'ry fields, of copses green,
The mowéd meadows with the fleecéd sheep,
    And feasts that either shearers keep,   40
The ripened ears, yet humble in their height,
    And furrows laden with their weight,
The apple-harvest, that doth longer last,
    The hogs returned home fat from mast,[2]
The trees cut out in log; and those boughs made   45
    A fire now, that lent a shade!
Thus Pan and Sylvan having had their rites,
    Comus[3] puts in for new delights,
And fills thy open hall with mirth and cheer
    As if in Saturn's reign[4] it were;   50
Apollo's harp and Hermes' lyre resound,
    Nor are the Muses strangers found;
The rout of rural folk come thronging in
    (Their rudeness[5] then is thought no sin),
Thy noblest spouse affords them welcome grace,   55
    And the great heroes of her race
Sit mixed with loss of state or reverence:
    Freedom doth with degree dispense.
The jolly wassail walks the often round,[6]
    And in their cups their cares are downed;   60
They think not, then, which side the cause shall leese,[7]
    Nor how to get the lawyer fees.
Such, and no other, was that age of old
    Which boasts t'have had the head of gold;
And such, since thou canst make thine own content,   65
    Strive, Wroth, to live long innocent.
Let others watch in guilty arms, and stand
    The fury of a rash command,
Go enter breaches, meet the cannon's rage,
    That they may sleep with scars in age,   70
And show their feathers shot, and colors torn,
    And brag that they were therefore born.
Let this man sweat and wrangle at the bar
    For every price, in every jar,
And change possessions oftener with his breath   75
    Than either money, war, or death;
Let him than hardest sires more disinherit,[8]
    And each where boast it as his merit

2. Nuts, mashed to serve as food for hogs.
3. In later antiquity, Comus was the god of festive mirth and jollification.
4. I.e., in the Golden Age; cf. ll. 63–64.
5. Rustic, unsophisticated manner.
6. I.e., the drinking cups are regularly refilled.
7. Lose; i.e., they forget everyday cares.
8. I.e., let him disinherit more children than the most severe fathers do.

To blow up orphans, widows, and their states,[9]
    And think his power doth equal Fate's.   80
Let that go heap a mass of wretched wealth,
    Purchased by rapine, worse than stealth,
And brooding o'er it sit with broadest[1] eyes,
    Not doing good, scarce when he dies.
Let thousands more go flatter vice, and win   85
    By being organs[2] to great sin;
Get place, and honor, and be glad to keep
    The secrets that shall break their sleep,
And, so they ride in purple, eat in plate,[3]
    Though poison, think it a great fate.   90
But thou, my Wroth, if I can truth apply,
    Shalt neither that nor this envy;
Thy peace is made; and when man's state is well,
    'Tis better if he there can dwell.
God wisheth none should wreck on a strange shelf;[4]   95
    To Him, man's dearer than t'himself.
And howsoever we may think things sweet,
    He always gives what He knows meet,
Which who can use is happy: such be thou.
    Thy morning's and thy evening's vow   100
Be thanks to Him, and earnest prayer to find
    A body sound, with sounder mind;
To do thy country service, thyself right,
    That neither want do thee affright
Nor death; but when thy latest sand is spent,   105
    Thou may'st think life a thing but lent.[5]

IV: To the World:
A Farewell for a Gentlewoman,[6] Virtuous and Noble

False world, good-night; since thou hast brought
    That hour upon any morn of age,
Henceforth I quit thee from my thought,
    My part is ended on thy stage.
Do not once hope that thou canst tempt   5
    A spirit so resolved to tread
Upon thy throat, and live exempt
    From all the nets that thou canst spread.

9. I.e., deprive orphans and widows of their property and possessions.
1. Wide open, staring.
2. Instruments.
3. I.e., dine off gold or silver platters.
4. Shoal.
5. The view that man's life is lent to him by God, and that God takes account of the fashion in which man uses it, often recurs in Jonson's poetry; cf. Epigrams XXII and XLV, pp. 7 and 8 respec-tively.
6. The unidentified gentlewoman is the speaker of the poem, which advocates an austerely Stoic self-sufficiency, derived primarily from Horace, and involving "self-knowledge and wisdom, living a life relying on oneself, and refusing to be distracted by the baubles of the world" (Miner, *op. cit.*, p. 90). Lines 25–32 may be compared with Horace, *Satires,* II. vii. 68–71.

I know thy forms are studied arts,
    Thy subtle ways be narrow straits,   10
Thy courtesy but sudden starts,
    And what thou call'st thy gifts are baits.
I know, too, though thou strut and paint,
    Yet art thou both shrunk up and old,
That only fools make thee a saint,   15
    And all thy good is to be sold.
I know thou whole[7] art but a shop
    Of toys and trifles, traps and snares,
To take the weak, or make them stop;
    Yet art thou falser than thy wares.   20
And, knowing this, should I yet stay,
    Like such as blow away their lives,
And never will redeem a day,
    Enamored of their golden gyves?[8]
Or, having 'scaped, shall I return   25
    And thrust my neck into the noose
From whence, so lately, I did burn
    With all my powers myself to loose?
What bird or beast is known so dull,
    That fled his cage or broke his chain,   30
And, tasting air and freedom, wull
    Render[9] his head in there again?
If these, who have but sense,[1] can shun
    The engines that have them annoyed,[2]
Little for me had reason done   35
    If I could not thy gins[3] avoid.
Yes, threaten, do. Alas, I fear
    As little as I hope from thee;
I know thou canst nor show nor bear
    More hatred than thou hast to me.   40
My tender, first, and simple years
    Thou didst abuse, and then betray;
Since, stirr'dst up jealousies and fears,
    When all the causes were away.
Then in a soil[4] hast planted me   45
    Where breathe the basest of thy fools,
Where envious arts professéd be,
    And pride and ignorance the schools
Where nothing is examined, weighed,
    But as 'tis rumored, so believed;   50
Where every freedom is betrayed,
    And every goodness taxed or grieved.

---

7. Wholly.
8. Fetters.
9. I.e., will put back.
1. I.e., who lack reasoning power.

2. I.e., the devices that have troubled them.
3. Snares.
4. I.e., at court.

But what we're born for, we must bear;
    Our frail condition it is such
That, what to all may happen here,   55
    If't chance to me, I must not grutch.[5]
Else, I my state should much mistake,
    To harbor a divided thought
From all my kind, that for my sake
    There should a miracle be wrought.   60
No, I do know that I was born
    To age, misfortune, sickness, grief;
But I will bear these with that scorn
    As shall not need thy false relief.
Nor for my peace will I go far,   65
    As wand'rers do, that still do roam,
But make my strengths, such as they are,
    Here in my bosom, and at home.

V: *Song: To Celia*[6]

Come, my Celia, let us prove,[7]
While we may, the sports of love;
Time will not be ours forever;
He at length our good will sever.
Spend not then his gifts in vain.   5
Suns that set may rise again;
But if once we lose this light,
'Tis with us perpetual night.
Why should we defer our joys?
Fame[8] and rumor are but toys.   10
Cannot we delude the eyes
Of a few poor household spies?
Or his[9] easier ears beguile,
So removéd by our wile?
'Tis no sin love's fruit to steal;   15
But the sweet theft to reveal,
To be taken, to be seen,
These have crimes accounted been.

VI: *To the Same*[1]

Kiss me, sweet; the wary lover
Can your favors keep, and cover,

5. Complain.
6. These lines appear in Jonson's *Volpone,* III. vii. 166–183; Volpone employs the song as part of his campaign to seduce the virtuous Celia, wife to Corvino. The lines are based on Catullus, *Odes,* iv. 3–6. The poem was set to music by Alphonso Ferrabosco (d. 1628) and published in that composer's *Ayres* (1609); Jonson addressed two epigrams to Ferrabosco (CXXX and CXXXI).
7. Experience.
8. Reputation.
9. I.e., Corvino's.
1. The poem is based on Catullus, *Odes,* v. 7–13, and vii. Lines 19–22 appear in *Volpone,* III. vii. 236–239.

When the common courting jay
All your bounties will betray.
Kiss again; no creature comes.   5
Kiss, and score up wealthy sums
On my lips, thus hardly sundered
While you breathe. First give a hundred,
Then a thousand, then another
Hundred, then unto the t'other   10
Add a thousand, and so more;
Till you equal with the store
All the grass that Romney² yields,
Or the sands in Chelsea fields,
Or the drops in silver Thames,   15
Or the stars that gild his streams
In the silent summer nights
When youths ply their stol'n delights;
That the curious may not know
How to tell 'em³ as they flow,   20
And the envious, when they find
What their number is, be pined.⁴

VII: *Song: That Women Are But Men's Shadows*⁵

Follow a shadow, it still flies you;
  Seem to fly it, it will pursue;
So court a mistress, she denies you;
  Let her alone, she will court you.
Say, are not women truly, then,   5
  Styled but the shadows of us men?
At morn, and even, shades are longest;
  At noon, they are or short or none;
So men at weakest, they are strongest,
  But grant us perfect, they're not known.   10
Say, are not women truly, then,
  Styled but the shadows of us men?

VIII: *To Sickness*

Why, Disease, dost thou molest
Ladies, and of them the best?
Do not men enough of rites

2. Romney Marsh is in Kent; Chelsea, in Jonson's time "but a group of isolated houses amidst six hundred acres of arable fields and pasture, orchards, gardens, and riverside meadows" (Hibbert, *London*, p. 93), derives its name from "chesil" (gravel).
3. I.e., count them.
4. I.e., be pained or dismayed.
5. The lines are based on a Latin poem by Barthelemi Aneau; cf. the note by O. Wallace, *N & Q*, III/8 (1865), 187. Drummond describes the occasion of the poem's composition: "Pembroke and his Lady discoursing, the Earl said [that] women were men's shadows, and she maintained them; both appealing to Jonson, he affirmed it true, for which my Lady gave a penance to prove it in verse; hence his epigram" (*H & S*, I, p. 142).

To thy altars, by their nights
Spent in surfeits, and their days,   5
And nights too, in worser ways?
   Take heed, Sickness, what you do;
   I shall fear you'll surfeit too.
Live not we, as all thy stalls,
Spitals,[6] pest-house, hospitals   10
Scarce will take our present store?
   And this age will build no more;
Pray thee, feed contented, then,
Sickness, only on us men;
   Or if needs thy lust will taste   15
   Womankind, devour the waste
   Livers round about the town.
But forgive me; with thy crown[7]
They maintain the truest trade,
And have more diseases made.   20
   What should yet thy palate please?
   Daintiness, and softer ease,
   Sleekéd limbs, and finest blood?
If thy leanness love such food,
There are those that for thy sake   25
Do enough, and who would take
Any pains, yea, think it price,[8]
To become thy sacrifice:
That distill their husbands' land
In decoctions,[9] and are manned   30
With ten emp'ricks, in their chamber,
Lying for the spirit of amber;
That for th'oil of talk dare spend
More than citizens dare lend
Them, and all their officers;   35
That to make all pleasure theirs,
Will by coach and water go,
Every stew in town to know;
Dare entail[1] their loves on any,
Bald, or blind, or ne'er so many,   40
   And for thee, at common game,
   Play away health, wealth, and fame.
These, Disease, will thee deserve;
And will, long ere thou should'st starve[2]

---

6. Hospitals for poor folk.
7. I.e., allied to you, or following your leadership (perhaps also with a play on "crown" as a piece of money).
8. Choice, highly desirable.
9. I.e., by their luxurious habits, ruin their husbands financially. Lines 29–33 employ alchemical expressions: *decoction* means "reduction by boiling down"; an *empiric* is an experimenter (here in a sexual sense); *spirit of amber* is an acid formed by dry distillation of amber; *oil of talk* (i.e., talc) a cosmetic (here, figuratively, courtly compliment and gossip).
1. In law, to entail is to settle lands inalienably on a person and his descendants; the term is employed here in a sexual sense.
2. Die.

On their beds, most prostitute,   45
Move it as their humblest suit
In thy justice to molest
None but them, and leave the rest.

IX: Song: To Celia[3]

Drink to me only with thine eyes,
   And I will pledge with mine;
Or leave a kiss but in the cup,
   And I'll not look for wine.
The thirst that from the soul doth rise   5
   Doth ask a drink divine:
But might I of Jove's nectar sup,
   I would not change for thine.
I sent thee, late, a rosy wreath,
   Not so much honoring thee,   10
As giving it a hope that there
   It could not withered be.
But thou thereon did'st only breathe,
   And sent'st it back to me;
Since when it grows, and smells, I swear,   15
   Not of itself, but thee.

X[4]

And must I sing? What subject shall I choose?
Or whose great name in poets' heaven use
For the more countenance to[5] my active Muse?

Hercules? Alas, his bones are yet sore
With his old earthly labors.[6] T' exact more   5
Of his dull godhead were sin. I'll implore

Phoebus. No: tend thy cart[7] still. Envious day
Shall not give out[8] that I have made thee stay,
And foundered thy hot team, to tune my lay.

---

3. Jonson's poem is based on five separate passages in the *Epistles* of the Greek rhetorician Philostratus (c. A.D. 170–c. 245). For a variant MS. version, cf. Textual Notes, p. 370. Cf. also, for comment on Jonson's art in selectively arranging his materials, the article by L. A. Beaurline, p. 516.
4. This poem (together with "Epode" and two other poems by Jonson) first appeared in 1601, in an appendix to Robert Chester's poem, "Love's Martyr"; the appendix also includes Shakespeare's "The Phoenix and the Turtle" and other verses on that theme by Marston and Chapman, allegorically figuring the phoenix and turtledove as idealized types of female and male virtue. An earlier version of this poem, preserved in MS., appears in *H & S*, VIII, p. 108.
5. I.e., for the higher repute of.
6. The twelve labors of Hercules were performed for Eurystheus, at the behest of Juno; cf. Apollodorus, *The Library*, II. iv–v; also Ovid, *Metamorphoses*, IX. 182–198.
7. Chariot (of the sun, pulled by Phoebus Apollo's team of horses; cf. Ovid, *Metamorphoses*, II. 47–48).
8. I.e., report.

Nor will I beg of thee, lord of the vine,[9]   10
To raise my spirits with thy conjuring wine,
In the green circle of thy ivy twine.

Pallas, nor thee I call on, mankind[1] maid,
That at thy birth mad'st the poor smith afraid,
Who, with his axe, thy father's midwife played.[2]   15

Go, cramp dull Mars, light Venus, when he snorts,[3]
Or with thy tribade trine[4] invent new sports,
Thou nor thy looseness with my making sorts.[5]

Let the old boy, your son,[6] ply his old task,
Turn the stale prologue to some painted mask,   20
His absence in my verse is all I ask.

Hermes, the cheater,[7] shall not mix with us,
Though he would steal his sisters' Pegasus[8]
And riffle him; or pawn his petasus.[9]

Nor all the ladies of the Thespian lake[1]   25
Though they were crushed into one form could make
A beauty of that merit that should take

My Muse up by commission;[2] no, I bring
My own true fire. Now my thought takes wing,
And now an *Epode*[3] to deep[4] ears I sing.   30

XI: *Epode*

Not to know vice at all, and keep true state,
    Is virtue, and not fate;[5]
Next to that virtue is to know vice well,
    And her black spite expel.

---

9. I.e., Bacchus, ordinarily represented as wearing an ivy garland.
1. Masculine.
2. Pallas Athene, goddess of wisdom, was born from the head of Zeus when Hephaestus (Vulcan) struck it with an axe; cf. Apollodorus, *The Library*, I. iii.
3. I.e., Go, wanton Venus, pinch dull Mars (to awaken him) when he snores. Cf. "Why I Write Not Of Love," p. 20, n. 5.
4. I.e., the three Graces, who attended Venus after Vulcan had revealed her infidelity; cf. *Odyssey*, VIII. 364–365. A *tribade* is "a woman who practices unnatural vice with other women" (*OED*). Jonson's is the first recorded use of the term in English.
5. I.e., is suitable for my poetry.
6. Cupid was traditionally the eldest of the gods; cf. Plato, *Symposium*, 178b–c.

7. Hermes (Mercury) was the god of merchants and thieves.
8. The winged horse Pegasus created the Hippocrene spring for the Muses by striking the ground with his hoof; cf. Ovid, *Metamorphoses*, V. 257–258.
9. I.e., and gamble him away; or pawn his own winged hat.
1. I.e., the Muses; cf. Epigram CI, p. 13, n. 5.
2. I.e., by command.
3. The Greek poet Archilochus (c. 714– c. 676 B.C.) invented the epode, a lyric poem in lines alternately long and short, on a serious subject.
4. Wise, profound.
5. I.e., the virtue that is altogether untouched by vice achieves that condition by exercise of the will (not by the force of an external influence).

Which to effect, since no breast is so sure   5
    Or safe but she'll procure[6]
Some way of entrance, we must plant a guard
    Of thoughts to watch and ward
At th'eye and ear, the ports[7] unto the mind,
    That no strange or unkind[8]   10
Object arrive there, but the heart, our spy,
    Give knowledge instantly
To wakeful reason, our affections' king;
    Who, in th' examining,
Will quickly taste[9] the treason, and commit   15
    Close, the close cause of it.[1]
'Tis the securest policy we have
    To make our sense our slave.
But this true course is not embraced by many;
    By many? scarce by any.   20
For either our affections do rebel,
    Or else the sentinel
That should ring 'larum to the heart doth sleep,
    Or some great[2] thought doth keep
Back the intelligence, and falsely swears   25
    They're base and idle fears
Whereof the loyal conscience so complains.
    Thus, by these subtle trains,[3]
Do several passions invade the mind,
    And strike our reason blind.   30
Of which usurping rank some have thought love
    The first, as prone to move
Most frequent tumults, horrors, and unrests
    In our enflaméd breasts;
But this doth from the cloud of error grow,   35
    Which thus we overblow.[4]
The thing they here call love is blind desire,[5]
    Armed with bow, shafts, and fire;
Inconstant, like the sea of whence 'tis born,
    Rough, swelling, like a storm;   40

6. I.e., vice will obtain (as a pimp practices his trade).
7. Gates. Lines 9–30 are based on Renaissance "faculty psychology": reason ought properly to restrain and control the senses and the emotions, but in fact most men and women, for a variety of causes, are ruled by their emotions or passions.
8. Unnatural.
9. Apprehend, identify.
1. I.e., and bring its immediate cause under strict control.
2. Dominant.
3. Stratagems, deceitful tricks.
4. Overcome.
5. Lines 37–48 are based on a passage from *In Praise of Demosthenes*, a work

of the fourth century A.D. attributed to an imitator of the Greek satirist Lucian (died c. A.D. 185): "You could wax philosophical in your discourse about the two impulses of love that come upon men, the one that of a love like the sea, frenzied, savage, and raging like stormy waves in the soul, a veritable sea of earthy Aphrodite surging with the fevered passions of youth, the other the pull of a heavenly cord of gold that does not bring with fiery shafts affecting wounds hard to cure, but impels man to the pure and unsullied Form of absolute beauty . . ." (*Lucian*, ed. and trans. M. D. MacLeod, 8 vols. [Cambridge, Mass., 1921–1967], VIII, p. 253).

With whom who sails, rides on a surge of fear,
    And boils, as if he were
In a continual tempest. Now, true love
    No such effects doth prove;[6]
That is an essence far more gentle, fine,   45
    Pure, perfect, nay divine;
It is a golden chain let down from heaven,[7]
    Whose links are bright and even;
That falls like sleep on lovers, and combines
    The soft and sweetest minds   50
In equal knots; this bears no brands, nor darts
    To murder different hearts,
But, in a calm and godlike unity,
    Preserves community.
O, who is he that, in this peace, enjoys   55
    Th' elixir[8] of all joys?
A form more fresh than are the Eden bowers,
    And lasting[9] as her flowers;
Richer than time, and as time's virtue[1] rare.
    Sober as saddest[2] care,   60
A fixéd thought, an eye untaught to glance;
    Who, blessed with such high chance,
Would, at suggestion of a steep[3] desire,
    Cast himself from the spire
Of all his happiness?[4] But soft: I hear   65
    Some vicious fool draw near,
That cries, we dream, and swears there's no such thing
    As this chaste love we sing.
Peace, Luxury,[5] thou art like one of those
    Who, being at sea, suppose,   70
Because they move, the continent doth so;
    No, Vice, we let thee know,
Though thy wild thoughts with sparrow's[6] wings do fly,
    Turtles can chastely die;[7]

---

6. I.e., produce.
7. Homer's is the earliest reference to the "golden rope" of Zeus, suspended from heaven, to which gods, men, and the entire universe are attached; cf. *Iliad*, VIII. 18–27. The figure was variously interpreted by later writers; in a note to line 320 of his masque *Hymenaei*, Jonson indicates his sympathy with the view of the Roman grammarian Macrobius (fl. c. A.D. 400), who emphasizes the divine origin of *mens* (mind), which "forms and suffuses all below with life. . . . from the Supreme God even to the bottommost dregs of the universe there is one tie, binding at every link and never broken. This is the golden chain of Homer" (*Commentary on the Dream of Scipio*, ed. and trans. W. H. Stahl [New York, 1952], p. 145).
8. Quintessence.
9. I.e., eternal.
1. I.e., Truth, the daughter of Time. Cf. Aulus Gellius, *Noctes Atticae*, XII. xi.
2. Most firmly fixed.
3. Headlong.
4. Jonson alludes to Satan's temptation of Christ, in Luke 4:9: "And he brought him to Jerusalem, and set him on a pinnacle of the temple, and said unto him, If thou be the Son of God, cast thyself down from hence." Cf. also Matthew 4: 5–6.
5. Lust.
6. The sparrow was a symbol of lechery.
7. I.e., turtledoves can achieve sexual consummation and yet remain chaste.

And yet (in this t'express ourselves more clear)   75
    We do not number here
Such spirits as are only continent
    Because lust's means are spent,
Or those who doubt the common mouth of fame,[8]
    And for their place and name   80
Cannot so safely sin. Their chastity
    Is mere necessity.
Nor mean we those whom vows and conscience
    Have filled with abstinence;
Though we acknowledge, who can so abstain   85
    Makes a most blessèd gain.
He that for love of goodness hateth ill
    Is more crown-worthy still
Then he which for sin's penalty forbears;
    His heart sins, though he fears.   90
But we propose a person like our dove,[9]
    Graced with a phoenix[1] love;
A beauty of that clear and sparkling light
    Would make a day of night,
And turn the blackest sorrows to bright joys;   95
    Whose odorous breath destroys
All taste of bitterness, and makes the air
    As sweet as she is fair;
A body so harmoniously composed,
    As if nature disclosed   100
All her best symmetry in that one feature!
    O, so divine a creature
Who could be false to; chiefly, when he knows
    How only she bestows
The wealthy treasure of her love on him,   105
    Making his fortunes swim
In the full flood of her admired perfection?
    What savage, brute affection
Would not be fearful to offend a dame
    Of this excelling frame?   110
Much more a noble and right generous mind,
    To virtuous moods inclined,
That knows the weight of guilt; he will refrain
    From thoughts of such a strain,
And to his sense object this sentence ever:[2]   115
    Man may securely[3] sin, but safely never.

---

8. I.e., who fear scandal.
9. I.e., the turtledove, symbol of man's faith.
1. The phoenix, traditionally an emblem of immortality, here represents primarily a Platonic ideal of womanly perfection.
2. I.e., and always present to his senses this (controlling) maxim.
3. Carelessly, confidently.

XII: *Epistle to Elizabeth, Countess of Rutland*[4]

Madame:
Whilst that for which all virtue now is sold,
    And almost every vice, almighty gold,
That which, to boot[5] with hell, is thought worth heaven,
    And for it, life, conscience, yea, souls are given,
Toils, by grave custom, up and down the court   5
    To every squire or groom that will report
Well or ill only, all the following year,
    Just to the weight their this day's presents bear;[6]
While it makes ushers[7] serviceable men,
    And some one apteth[8] to be trusted, then,   10
Though never after; while it gains the voice
    Of some grand peer, whose air[9] doth make rejoice
The fool that gave it, who will want and weep
    When his proud patron's favors are asleep;
While thus it buys great grace and hunts poor fame,   15
    Runs between man and man, 'tween dame and dame,
Solders cracked friendship, makes love last a day,
    Or perhaps less; whilst gold bears all this sway,
I, that have none to send you, send you verse.
    A present which (if elder writs rehearse   20
The truth of times) was once of more esteem
    Than this our gilt nor golden[1] age can deem;
When gold was made no weapon to cut throats,
    Or put to flight Astraea;[2] when her ingots
Were yet unfound, and better placed in earth   25
    Than, here, to give pride fame, and peasants birth.[3]
But let this dross carry what price it will
    With noble ignorants, and let them still
Turn upon scorned verse their quarter-face;[4]
      With you, I know, my off'ring will find grace.   30
For what a sin 'gainst your great father's[5] spirit
    Were it to think that you should not inherit

---

4. Cf. Epigram LXXIX, p. 10. Elizabeth Sidney had married the fifth Earl of Rutland in 1599; this poem was a gift for New Year's Day, 1600. Jonson evidently considered the genre of the verse epistle well suited to his personality, his moral convictions, and what he conceived to be his social role. For a full discussion of the epistolary tradition, cf. W. Trimpi, *Ben Jonson's Poems: A Study of the Plain Style* (Stanford, Calif., 1962), pp. 60–75; for detailed commentary on individual verse epistles, cf. Miner, *op. cit.,* pp. 144–146, 170–174, 271–275; and also the essay by Hugh Maclean on p. 496 of this edition.
5. I.e., to be of avail.
6. I.e., precisely in proportion to the gifts bestowed today.

7. Servants, attendants.
8. Most fit.
9. Manner.
1. I.e., neither gilded nor golden. The text of 1616 has "our guilt, nor golden age."
2. Astraea, the goddess of justice, lived among men during the Golden Age; but when their wickedness increased, she returned to heaven and was stellified as the constellation Virgo; cf. Ovid, *Metamorphoses,* I. 127–150.
3. I.e., to give high reputation and place to the proud and to those of low character.
4. I.e., all but turn away, contemptuously, from poetry.
5. I.e., Sir Philip Sidney's.

His love unto the Muses, when his skill
　　Almost you have, or may have when you will;
Wherein wise nature you a dowry gave　　　　　　　35
　　Worth an estate treble to that you have.
Beauty, I know, is good, and blood is more;
　　Riches thought most. But, madame, think what store
The world hath seen, which all these had in trust,
　　And now lie lost in their forgotten dust.　　　　　　40
It is the Muse alone can raise to heaven,
　　And, at her strong arms' end, hold up, and even,
The souls she loves. Those other glorious[6] notes
　　Inscribed in touch or marble, or the coats[7]
Painted or carved upon our great mens' tombs,　　　45
　　Or in their windows, do but prove the wombs
That bred them, graves; when they were born, they died,
　　That had no Muse to make their fame abide.
How many, equal with the Argive queen,[8]
　　Have beauty known, yet none so famous seen?　　　50
Archilles was not first that valiant was,
　　Or, in an army's head, that locked in brass[9]
Gave killing strokes. There were brave men before
　　Ajax or Idomen,[1] or all the store
That Homer brought to Troy; yet none so live,　　　55
　　Because they lacked the sacred pen could give
Like life unto them. Who heaved Hercules[2]
　　Unto the stars? or the Tyndarides?
Who placéd Jason's Argo in the sky,
　　Or set bright Ariadne's crown so high?　　　　　　60
Who made a lamp of Berenice's hair,
　　Or lifted Cassiopeia in her chair,
But only poets, rapt with rage divine?[3]
　　And such, or my hopes fail, shall make you shine.
You and that other star, that purest light　　　　　　65
　　Of all Lucina's[4] train, Lucy the bright,[5]

---

6. Pompous, boastful; cf. "To Pens-hurst," p. 21, ll. 1–2.
7. Coats of arms.
8. I.e., Helen of Troy; "Argive" by metonymy for "Grecian."
9. I.e., in armor, leading an army.
1. Ajax, the son of Telamon, and Ido-meneus of Crete commanded subdivisions of the Greek host; cf. *Iliad, passim.*
2. For Hercules, in this regard, cf. Ovid, *Metamorphoses,* IX. 241–273. The Tyn-darides are Castor and Pollux (sons of Leda, whose consort was Tyndareus), placed in the constellation Gemini; cf. Apollodorus, *Library,* III. xi. 2. Accord-ing to Hyginus, *Fables,* xiv, Minerva (Pallas Athene) placed the Argonauts' vessel in the heavens. Ariadne, deserted by Theseus on the isle of Naxos, became the consort of Dionysus, who placed her marriage crown among the stars; cf. Ovid, *Metamorphoses,* VIII. 177–179. Berenice (c. 273–221 B.C.) married Ptol-emy III of Egypt, who named a star "the lock of Berenice" in her honor; in *The Masque of Queens,* 546–560, Jonson gives Catullus (*Odes,* lxvi) as his source. For the story of Cassiopeia, culminating in her elevation to the heavens ("Cas-siopeia's chair"), cf. Ovid, *Metamor-phoses,* IV. 663–803.
3. I.e., ravished by divine inspiration.
4. I.e., Queen Elizabeth's. "Lucina" de-rives from *lux,* "light, brightness."
5. I.e., Lucy Harington, Countess of Bedford.

Than which a nobler, heaven itself knows not,
    Who, though she have a better verser[6] got
(Or poet, in the court account) than I,
    And who doth me, though I not him, envy,   70
Yet, for the timely favors she hath done
    To my less sanguine Muse, wherein she'hath won
My grateful soul, the subject of her powers,
    I have already used some happy hours
To her remembrance; which, when time shall bring   75
    To curious light, to notes[7] I then shall sing
Will prove old Orpheus' act[8] no tale to be,
    For I shall move stocks, stones no less than he.
Then all that have but done my Muse least grace
    Shall thronging come, and boast the happy place   80
They hold in my strange poems, which as yet
    Had not their form touched by an English wit.[9]
There, like a rich and golden pyramid
    Borne up by statues, shall I rear your head
Above your under-carvéd ornaments,   85
    And show how, to the life, my soul presents
Your form impressed there; not with tickling rhymes
    Or commonplaces filched, that take these times,
But high and noble matter, such as flies
    From brains entranced and filled with ecstasies;   90
Moods which the godlike Sidney oft did prove,[1]
    And your brave friend[2] and mine so well did love.
Who, wheresoe'er he be . . . .

                    The rest is lost.[3]

XIII: *Epistle to Katharine, Lady Aubigny*[4]

'Tis grown almost a danger to speak true
    Of any good mind, now: there are so few.
The bad by number are so fortified
    As what they've lost t'expect, they dare deride.

6. Jonson may allude to Samuel Daniel, whom he thought "no poet," according to Drummond (*H & S*, I, p. 132); or to Michael Drayton, as R. W. Short suggests in "Ben Jonson in Drayton's Poems," *RES*, XV (1939), 149–158.
7. In *The Masque of Queens*, 666–669, Jonson refers to plans for a poem celebrating British ladies.
8. According to legend, stones and trees moved in response to the power of Orpheus' musical art; cf. Ovid, *Metamorphoses*, XI. 1–2.
9. I.e., my poems, unfamiliar in mode, which exemplify an art not attained by other English poets.
1. Experience.
2. I.e., the Earl of Rutland.
3. Cf. Textual Notes, p. 371, for the concluding lines, dropped from the poem in the *Works* of 1616 since by that time it had become known that the Earl was impotent. Cf. *H & S*, I, pp. 139, 163.
4. Jonson lived in the house of his patron, Esme Lord Aubigny (1574–1624), from 1602 to 1607; the poet acknowledged these favors in Epigram CXXVII, and dedicated his tragedy *Sejanus* to Lord Aubigny, who married Katharine Clifton in 1609. Three of Lady Aubigny's four sons, who fought on the royalist side in the Civil Wars, were killed in battle. Her daughter Frances was married to Jerome Weston, son of Richard Lord Weston, Lord High Treasurer (from 1628); Jonson celebrated the nuptials in his "Epithalamion" (cf. p. 80 of this volume).

So both the praised and praisers suffer. Yet   5
   For others' ill, ought none their good forget.
I, therefore, who profess my self in love
   With every virtue, wheresoe'er it move
And howsoever; as I am at feud
   With sin and vice, though with a throne endued,   10
And, in this name, am given out[5] dangerous
   By arts and practice of the vicious,
Such as suspect themselves, and think it fit
   For their own capital crimes t'indict my wit;
I, that have suffered this, and, though forsook   15
   Of fortune, have not altered yet my look
Or so my self abandoned, as because
   Men are not just, or keep no holy laws
Of nature and society, I should faint,
   Or leave to draw true lines 'cause others paint;   20
I, madame, am become your praiser. Where,
   If it may stand with your soft blush to hear
Your self but told unto yourself, and see
   In my character[6] what your features be,
You will not from the paper slightly[7] pass;   25
   No lady but at some time loves her glass.[8]
And this shall be no false one, but as much
   Removed as you from need to have it such.
Look, then, and see your self. I will not say
   "Your beauty," for you see that every day,   30
And so do many more; all which[9] can call
   It perfect, proper, pure, and natural,
Not taken up o' th'doctors,[1] but as well
   As I can say and see it doth excel.
That asks but to be censured by the eyes,   35
   And in those outward forms all fools are wise.
Nor that your beauty wanted not a dower[2]
   Do I reflect. Some alderman has power,
Or coz'ning farmer of the customs[3] so,
   T'advance his doubtful issue, and o'erflow   40
A prince's fortune; these are gifts of chance,
   And raise not virtue; they may vice enhance.
My mirror is more subtle, clear, refined,
   And takes and gives the beauties of the mind,
Though it reject not those of fortune: such   45
   As blood, and match.[4] Wherein, how more than much

5. I.e., reputed to be.
6. I.e., in my detailed description of your qualities. The "character" was an ancient literary genre revived and polished in the seventeenth century by, for example, Sir Thomas Overbury and John Earle.
7. Indifferently, uncaringly.
8. Mirror.
9. Of whom.
1. I.e., not dependent on artificial or medical aids.
2. I.e., a natural gift.
3. I.e., a deceitful exciseman who holds his post by virtue of having paid a fee for the right to collect customs duties.
4. Marriage.

Are you engagéd to your happy fate
    For such a lot![5] that mixed you with a state
Of so great title, birth, but virtue most,
    Without which all the rest were sounds, or lost.   50
'Tis only that can time and chance defeat,
    For he that once is good is ever great.
Wherewith then, madame, can you better pay
    This blessing of your stars than by that way
Of virtue which you tread? What if alone,   55
    Without companions? 'Tis safe to have none.
In single paths, dangers with ease are watched;
    Contagion in the press[6] is soonest catched.
This makes that wisely you decline[7] your life
    Far from the maze of custom, error, strife,   60
And keep an even and unaltered gait,
    Not looking by,[8] or back (like those that wait
Times and occasions, to start forth, and seem);
    Which though the turning world may disesteem,
Because that studies spectacles and shows,   65
    And after varied as fresh objects goes,
Giddy with change, and therefore cannot see
    Right, the right way; yet must your comfort be
Your conscience, and not wonder if none asks
    For truth's complexion, where they all wear masks.   70
Let who will follow fashions and attires,
    Maintain their liedgers forth, for foreign wires,[9]
Melt down their husbands' land to pour away
    On the close-groom[1] and page, on New Year's Day,
And almost all days after, while they live   75
    (They find it both so wittty and safe to give).
Let 'em on powders, oils, and paintings[2] spend
    Till that no usurer nor his bawds[3] dare lend
Them, or their officers;[4] and no man know
    Whether it be a face they wear or no.   80
Let 'em waste body and state; and after all,
    When their own parasites laugh at their fall,
May they have nothing left whereof they can
    Boast but how oft they have gone wrong to man,[5]
And call it their brave[6] sin. For such there be   85
    That do sin only for the infamy,
And never think how vice doth every hour
    Eat on her clients, and some one devour.
You, madame, young have learned to shun these shelves[7]
    Whereon the most of mankind wreck themselves,   90

And, keeping a just course, have early put
    Into your harbor, and all passage shut
'Gainst storms, or pirates, that might charge[8] your peace;
    For which you worthy are the glad increase
Of your blessed womb, made fruitful from above,   95
    To pay your lord the pledges of chaste love,
And raise a noble stem to give the fame
    To Clifton's blood, that is denied their name.[9]
Grow, grow, fair tree, and as thy branches shoot,
    Hear what the Muses sing about thy root   100
By me, their priest (if they can ought divine):
    Before the moons have filled their triple trine[1]
To crown the burden which you go withal,
    It shall a ripe and timely issue fall
T'expect the honors of great Aubigny;   105
    And greater rites, yet writ in mystery,
But which the Fates forbid me to reveal.
    Only thus much, out of a ravished[2] zeal
Unto your name, and goodness of your life,
    They speak; since you are truly that rare wife   110
Other great wives may blush at, when they see
    What your tried manners are, what theirs should be;
How you love one, and him you should; how still
    You are depending on his word and will;
Not fashioned for the court, or strangers' eyes,   115
    But to please him, who is the dearer prize
Unto himself by being so dear to you.
    This makes that your affections still be new,
And that your souls conspire,[3] as they were gone
    Each into other, and had now made one.   120
Live that one, still; and as long years do pass,
    Madame, be bold to use this truest glass,
Wherein your form you still the same shall find,
    Because nor it can change, nor such a mind.

XIV: *Ode to Sir William Sydney,*[4] *on His Birthday*

Now that the hearth is crowned with smiling fire,
    And some do drink, and some do dance,
        Some ring,
        Some sing,
    And all do strive t'advance   5

8. Threaten.
9. Lady Aubigny's father, Sir Gervase Clifton, had no sons.
1. I.e., have completed nine months.
2. I.e., an enraptured.
3. Harmonize (literally, "breathe together").
4. Sir William Sidney (1590–1612), the son of Sir Robert Sidney, was knighted in January, 1611. As W. B. Hunter, Jr., observes, this "early attempt to introduce the complex form of the classical ode into English" anticipates Jonson's later and more ambitious efforts in the genre (*Complete Poetry of Ben Jonson* [New York, 1968], p. 75). For a discussion of Jonson's contributions in tihs kind, cf. Carol Maddison, *Apollo and the Nine: A History of the Ode* (Baltimore, Md., 1960), pp. 296–304.

The gladness higher;
    Wherefore should I
    Stand silent by,
      Who not the least
      Both love the cause, and authors of the feast?   10
Give me my cup, but from the Thespian well,[5]
  That I may tell to Sydney, what
      This day
      Doth say,
And he may think on that   15
Which I do tell,
    When all the noise
    Of these forced joys
      Are fled and gone,
      And he with his best Genius[6] left alone.   20
This day says, then, the number of glad years
  Are justly summed, that make you man;
      Your vow
      Must now
Strive all right ways it can   25
T'outstrip your peers;
    Since he doth lack
    Of going back
      Little, whose will
      Doth urge him to run wrong, or to stand still.   30
Nor can a little of the common store
  Of nobles' virtue show in you;
      Your blood,
      So good
And great, must seek for new,   35
And study more;
    Not weary, rest
    On what's deceased.
      For they that swell
      With dust of ancestors in graves but dwell.   40
'Twill be exacted of your name, whose son,
  Whose nephew, whose grand-child you are;[7]
      And men
      Will, then,
Say you have followed far,   45
When well begun;
      Which must be now;
      They teach you how.

5. Cf. Epigram 1, p. 13, l. 33, and note.
6. I.e., protecting spirit. "According to the opinion of the Romans, every human being at his birth obtained a genius, whom he worshipped as [the holiest of gods], especially on his birthday, with libations of wine, incense, and garlands of flowers" (*A Smaller Classical Dictionary*, ed. E. H. Blakeney *et al.* [London, 1949], p. 225.
7. Sir William was the nephew of Sir Philip Sidney and the grandchild of Sir Henry Sidney, who was named Queen Elizabeth's Lord Deputy in Ireland three times.

And he that stays
  To live until tomorrow hath lost two days.   50
So may you live in honor, as in name,
  If with this truth you be inspired;
      So may
      This day
Be more and long desired;   55
And with the flame
  Of love be bright,
  As with the light
    Of bonfires. Then
    The birthday shines, when logs not burn, but men.

                                                       60

XV: *To Heaven*[8]

Good and great God, can I not think of Thee,
  But it must, straight, my melancholy be?
Is it interpreted in me disease,
  That, laden with my sins, I seek for ease?
O, be Thou witness, that the reins[9] dost know,   5
  And hearts of all, if I be sad for show,
And judge me after: if I dare pretend
  To ought but grace, or aim at other end.
As Thou art all, so be Thou all to me,
  First, midst, and last, converted[1] one, and three; 10
My faith, my hope, my love; and in this state,
  My judge, my witness, and my advocate.
Where have I been this while exiled from Thee?
  And whither raped,[2] now Thou but stoop'st to me?
Dwell, dwell here still: O, being everywhere,   15
  How can I doubt to find Thee ever here?
I know my state, both full of shame and scorn,
  Conceived in sin, and unto labor born,
Standing with fear, and must with horror fall,
  And destined unto judgment after all.   20
I feel my griefs too, and there scarce is ground
  Upon my flesh t'inflict another wound.
Yet dare I not complain, or wish for death
  With holy Paul,[3] lest it be thought the breath
Of discontent; or that these prayers be   25
  For weariness of life, not love of Thee.

8. On Jonson's religious poems, cf. P. Cubeta, "Ben Jonson's Religious Lyrics," *JEGP*, LXII (1963), 96–110.
9. Physiologically, the reins (or kidneys) were considered to be the seat of the affections or feelings; but Jonson has an eye to Psalms 7:9: "for the righteous God trieth the hearts and reins."
1. Appearing as (the eternal Godhead who sits, as Milton puts it in "On the Morning of Christ's Nativity," "the midst of Trinal Unity").
2. Ravished (in the sense of "enraptured").
3. Cf. Romans 7:24: "O wretched man that I am: who shall deliver me from the body of this death?"

From *THE WORKS OF BENJAMIN JONSON* (1640–1641)

From *Underwood*[4]

A *Hymn to God the Father*

Hear me, O God!
   A broken heart
   Is my best part;
Use still Thy rod,
   That I may prove[5]   5
   Therein, Thy Love.

If Thou hadst not
   Been stern to me,
   But left me free,
I had forgot   10
   My self and Thee.

For sin's so sweet
   As minds ill bent
   Rarely repent,
Until they meet   15
   Their punishment.

Who more can crave
   Than Thou hast done,
   That gav'st a Son
To free a slave?   20
   First made of nought,
   With all since bought.[6]

---

4. Sir Kenelm Digby (1603–1665), scientist, diplomat, and friend to Jonson, took charge of the poet's manuscripts after Jonson's death in 1637, and included the eighty-nine poems and translations comprising *Underwood* in the *Works* of 1640–1641. The order in which the earlier poems appear seems to reflect Jonson's own concern with establishing their connection to *The Forest* (as the poet's prefatory note to *Underwood* suggests); thus, three doctrinal poems are followed by a group of metrically various love poems, and these in turn by an epitaph and three verse epistles. Thereafter, to speak generally, the collection follows the poems' order of composition, although the five translations from Horace, Petronius, and Martial with which *Underwood* concludes were probably composed between 1612 and 1622. The twenty-three poems included in the present edition may be thought to provide a sufficiently representative sampling of Jonson's extraordinary range in *Underwood*: here are lyrics, epigrams and epitaphs, elegies, Pindaric and Horatian odes, even a sonnet; poems in Jonson's most classically lapidary style are companioned by others that strikingly recall the manner of Donne.

5. Experience.

6. I.e., redeemed by Christ.

Sin, Death, and Hell,
His glorious Name
Quite overcame, 25
Yet I rebel
And slight the same.

But I'll come in
Before my loss,
Me farther toss, 30
As sure to win
Under His Cross.

A Hymn on the Nativity of My Saviour

I sing the birth was born tonight,
The Author both of life and light,
The angels so did sound it;
And like[7] the ravished shepherds said,
Who saw the light, and were afraid, 5
Yet searched, and true they found it.[8]

The Son of God, th'eternal King,
That did us all salvation bring,
And freed the soul from danger;
He whom the whole world could not take,[9] 10
The Word which heaven and earth did make,[1]
Was now laid in a manger.

The Father's wisdom willed it so,
The Son's obedience knew no No,
Both wills were in one stature;[2] 15
And as that wisdom had decreed,
The Word was now made flesh indeed,[3]
And took on Him our nature.

What comfort by Him do we win,
Who made Himself the price of sin,[4] 20
To make us heirs of glory!
To see this Babe, all innocence,
A Martyr born in our defence,
Can man forget this story?

---

7. I.e., similar things.
8. Cf. Luke 2:8–16.
9. I.e., contain.
1. Cf. John 1:3.
2. I.e., the wills of the First and Second Persons of the Trinity were perfectly at one.
3. Cf. John 1:14.
4. Cf. I. Corinthians 6:20.

A Celebration of Charis in Ten Lyric Pieces[5]

1. HIS EXCUSE FOR LOVING

Let it not your wonder move,
Less your laughter, that I love.
Though I now write fifty years,
I have had, and have, my peers;
Poets, though divine, are men,   5
Some have loved as old again.[6]
And it is not always face,
Clothes, or fortune gives the grace,
Or the feature,[7] or the youth;
But the language and the truth,   10
With the ardor and the passion,
Gives the lover weight and fashion.
If you then will read the story,
First, prepare you to be sorry
That you never knew till now   15
Either whom to love or how;
But be glad, as soon with me,
When you know that this is she
Of whose beauty it was sung,
She shall make the old man young,   20
Keep the middle age at stay,
And let nothing high decay;
Till she be the reason why
All the world for love may die.

2. HOW HE SAW HER

I beheld her on a day,
When her look out-flourished May;
And her dressing did out-brave[8]
All the pride the fields then have;
Far I was from being stupid,   5
For I ran and called on Cupid,
"Love, if thou wilt ever see
Mark of glory, come with me;
Where's thy quiver? Bend thy bow;
Here's a shaft, thou art too slow!"   10
And, withal, I did untie

5. Although Jonson may have arranged these lyrics as they stand, they were not composed as a unit: lines 11–30 of "Her Triumph" appear in *The Divell Is An Ass* (1616), at II. vi. 94–113; and "His Excuse for Loving" was presumably written in 1623. The identity of Charis (from Latin *caritas*, "love") is unknown. On the structure of the poem as a whole, cf. P. Cubeta, " 'A Celebration of Charis': An Evaluation of Jonson's Poetic Strategy," *ELH*, XXV (1958), 163–180; and also W. Trimpi, *Ben Jonson's Poems*, pp. 209–227.
6. I.e., at the age of one hundred.
7. Beauty.
8. Surpass.

Every cloud about his eye;[9]
But he had not gained his sight
Sooner than he lost his might
Or his courage; for away   15
Straight he ran and durst not stay,
Letting bow and arrow fall,
Nor for any threat or call
Could be brought once back to look.
I, foolhardy, there up took   20
Both the arrow he had quit
And the bow; with thought to hit
This my object. But she threw
Such a lightning, as I drew,
At my face, that took my sight   25
And my motion from me quite;
So that there I stood a stone,
Mocked of all; and called of one
(Which with grief and wrath I heard)
Cupid's statue with a beard,   30
Or else one that played his ape,
In a Hercules-his shape.

3. WHAT HE SUFFERED

After many scorns like these,
Which the prouder beauties please.
She content was to restore
Eyes and limbs to hurt me more,
And would on conditions be   5
Reconciled to Love,[1] and me.
First, that I must kneeling yield
Both the bow and shaft I held
Unto her; which Love might take
At her hand, with oath to make   10
Me the scope of his next draught.[2]
Arméd with that self-same shaft
He no sooner heard the law,
But the arrow home did draw,
And, to gain her by his art,   15
Left it sticking in my heart;
Which when she beheld to bleed,
She repented of the deed,
And would fain have changed the fate,
But the pity comes too late.   20
Loser-like, now, all my wreak[3]

9. Cupid was traditionally represented as blind; cf. E. Panofsky, "Blind Cupid," in *Studies in Iconology* (New York, 1962), pp. 95–128.

1. I.e., Cupid.
2. I.e., the object at which he next aimed.
3. Revenge.

Is that I have leave to speak,
And in either prose or song
To revenge me with my tongue,
Which how dexterously I do,   25
Hear and make examples too.

4. HER TRIUMPH

See the chariot at hand here of Love
   Wherein my lady rideth!
Each that draws is a swan or a dove,[4]
   And well the car Love guideth.
As she goes, all hearts do duty   5
      Unto her beauty;
And enamored, do wish so they might
      But enjoy such a sight,
That they still[5] were to run by her side,
Through swords, through seas, whither she would ride.   10

Do but look on her eyes, they do light
   All that Love's world compriseth!
Do but look on her hair, it is bright
   As Love's star[6] when it riseth!
Do but mark, her forehead's smoother   15
      Than words that soothe her!
And from her arched brows, such a grace
      Sheds itself through the face,
As alone there triumphs to the life
All the gain, all the good, of the elements' strife.[7]   20

Have you seen but a bright lily grow
   Before rude hands have touched it?
Ha' you marked but the fall o' the snow
   Before the soil hath smutched it?
Ha' you felt the wool of beaver?   25
      Or swan's down ever?
Or have smelt o' the bud o' the brier?
      Or the nard[8] in the fire?
Or have tasted the bag of the bee?
O so white! O so soft! O so sweet is she![9]   30

---

4. Venus' chariot was drawn by swans or doves; cf. Ovid, *Metamorphoses*, X. 718.
5. Continually.
6. I.e., Venus.
7. It was thought that from the original clash and conflict of the four elements emerged, by divine arrangement, the harmonious order of the universe. Cf. Ovid, *Metamorphoses*, I. 1–31.
8. An aromatic herb.
9. With this stanza cf. Shirley's "Would you know what's soft?" and Suckling's "A Song to a Lute," on pp. 190 and 271 respectively.

5. HIS DISCOURSE WITH CUPID

Noblest Charis, you that are
Both my fortune and my star!
And do govern more my blood
Than the various[1] moon the flood!
Hear what late discourse of you   5
Love and I have had; and true.
'Mongst my Muses finding me,
Where he chanced your name to see
Set, and to this softer strain;
"Sure," said he, "if I have brain,   10
This here sung can be no other
By description than my mother![2]
So hath Homer praised her hair;
So Anacreon drawn the air[3]
Of her face, and made to rise,   15
Just about[4] her sparkling eyes,
Both her brows, bent like my bow.
By her looks I do her know,
Which you call my shafts. And see!
Such my mother's blushes be,   20
As the bath your verse discloses
In her cheeks, of milk and roses;
Such as oft I wanton in.
And, above her even chin,
Have you placed the bank of kisses,   25
Where, you say, men gather blisses,
Ripened with a breath more sweet
Than when flowers and west winds meet;
Nay, her white and polished neck
With the lace that doth it deck   30
Is my mother's! Hearts of slain
Lovers, made into a chain!
And between each rising breast
Lies the valley, called my nest,
Where I sit and proyne[5] my wings   35
To my shafts! Her very name
With my mother's is the same."[6]
"I confess all," I replied,
After flight; and put new stings
"And the glass hangs by her side,   40
And the girdle 'bout her waist,
All is Venus; save unchaste.

---

1. Changing.
2. I.e., Venus, whose hair Homer calls "lovely as the Graces' "; cf. *Iliad*, XVII. 51. For Anacreon, cf. Epigram CI, p. 12, l. 30 and note.
3. Expression.
4. I.e., above.
5. Preen.
6. In the *Odyssey* (VIII. 364) the name of Vulcan's consort is Venus; in the *Iliad* (XVIII. 382) she is named Charis.

But alas, thou seest the least
Of her good, who is the best
Of her sex; but could'st thou, Love,   45
Call to mind the forms that strove
For the apple,[7] and those three
Make in one, the same were she.
For this beauty yet doth hide
Something more than thou hast spied.   50
Outward grace weak love beguiles;
She is Venus, when she smiles,
But she's Juno, when she walks,
And Minerva, when she talks."

6. CLAIMING A SECOND KISS BY DESERT

Charis, guess, and do not miss,
Since I drew a morning kiss
From your lips, and sucked an air
Thence, as sweet as you are fair,
    What my Muse and I have done;   5
Whether we have lost or won,
If by us the odds were laid,
That the bride, allowed a maid,
Looked not half so fresh and fair,
With th'advantage of her hair   10
And her jewels, to the view
Of th'assembly, as did you!
    Or that did you sit or walk,
You were more the eye and talk
Of the court, today, than all   15
Else that glistered in Whitehall;[8]
So as those that had your sight[9]
Wished the bride were changed tonight,
And did think such rites were due
To no other Grace[1] but you!   20
    Or if you did move tonight,
In the dances, with what spite
Of your peers you were beheld,
That at every motion swelled
So to see a lady tread   25
As might all the Graces lead,
And was worthy, being so seen,

7. Eris, angered at not having been invited to the marriage of Thetis and Peleus, threw among the invited goddesses a golden apple inscribed, "Let it be given to the fairest." The subsequent contest between Juno, Minerva, and Venus, decided by Paris in favor of Venus (who had promised him Helen), led to the Trojan War. Cf. Ovid, *Heroides*, xvi; Hyginus, *Fables*, xcii.
8. The king's palace at Westminster.
9. I.e., saw you.
1. The Graces (Euphrosyne, Aglaia, and Thalia) personified grace and beauty to the ancients; cf. Hesiod, *Theogony*, 907–911, for an initial reference.

To be envied of the queen.
Or if you would yet have stayed,
Whether any would upbraid   30
To himself his loss of time;
Or have charged his sight of crime,
To have left all sight for you.
     Guess of these, which is the true;
And if such a verse as this   35
May not claim another kiss.

7. BEGGING ANOTHER, ON COLOR[2] OF MENDING THE FORMER

For love's sake, kiss me once again;
I long, and should not beg in vain,
  Here's none to spy or see;
    Why do you doubt, or stay?
I'll taste as lightly as the bee,   5
That doth but touch his flower and flies away.
  Once more, and, faith, I will be gone:
  Can he that loves ask less than one?
    Nay, you may err in this,
      And all your bounty wrong;   10
  This could be called but half a kiss.
What we're but once to do, we should do long;
  I will but mend the last, and tell
  Where, how it would have relished well;
    Join lip to lip, and try;   15
      Each suck other's breath.
And whilst our tongues perplexéd lie,
Let who will think us dead, or wish our death.

8. URGING HER OF A PROMISE

Charis one day in discourse
Had of Love, and of his force,
Lightly promised she would tell
What[3] a man she could love well;
And that promise set on fire   5
All that heard her, with desire.
With the rest, I long expected[4]
When the work would be effected;
But we find that cold delay
And excuse spun every day,   10
As, until she tell her one,
We all fear she loveth none.
Therefore, Charis, you must do't,

2. Pretence.
3. What kind of.
4. I.e., eagerly awaited.

For I will so urge you to't
You shall neither eat nor sleep,   15
No, nor forth your window peep
With your emissary[5] eye,
To fetch in the forms go by;[6]
And pronounce which band or lace
Better fits him than his face;   20
Nay, I will not let you sit
'Fore your idol glass a whit,
To say over every purl[7]
There, or to reform a curl;
Or with secretary Sis[8]   25
To consult, if fucus[9] this
Be as good as was the last.
All your sweet of life is past,
Make account unless you can,
And that quickly, speak[1] your man.   30

9. HER MAN DESCRIBED BY HER OWN DICTAMEN[2]

Of your trouble, Ben, to ease me,
I will tell what man would please me.
I would have him, if I could,
Noble, or of greater blood;
Titles, I confess, do take me,   5
And a woman God did make me;
French to boot, at least in fashion,
And his manners of that nation.
    Young I'd have him too, and fair,
Yet a man; with crispéd[3] hair   10
Cast in thousand snares and rings
For Love's fingers, and his wings;
Chestnut color, or more slack[4]
Gold, upon a ground of black.
Venus' and Minerva's eyes,[5]   15
For he must look wanton-wise.
    Eyebrows bent like Cupid's bow;
Front,[6] an ample field of snow;
Even nose and cheek withal
Smooth as is the billiard ball;   20
Chin, as woolly as the peach;
And his lip should kissing teach,

---

5. Spying.
6. I.e., to consider the men who pass by.
7. Loop of lace.
8. I.e., with a confidential maid named Sis (or Cis, the name originally assigned to the chambermaid Prudence in Jonson's play, *The New Inn*).

9. Cosmetic.
1. Describe.
2. Pronouncement.
3. Curled.
4. I.e., duller.
5. I.e., bright blue.
6. Forehead.

Till he cherished too much beard,
And make Love or me afeard.
    He would have a hand as soft   25
As the down, and show it oft;
Skin as smooth as any rush,
And so thin to see a blush
Rising through it ere it came;
All his blood should be a flame   30
Quickly fired, as in beginners
In love's school, and yet no sinners.
    'Twere too long to speak of all;
What we harmony do call
In a body should be there.   35
Well he should his clothes to wear;
Yet[7] no tailor help to make him;
Dressed, you still for man should take him;
And not think h' had eat a stake,
Or were set up in a brake.[8]   40
    Valiant he should be as fire,
Showing danger[9] more than ire;
Bounteous as the clouds to earth
And as honest as his birth.
All his actions to be such,   45
As to do nothing too much.
Nor o'er-praise, nor yet condemn;
Nor outvalue, nor contemn;
Nor do wrongs, nor wrongs receive;
Nor tie knots, nor knots unweave;   50
And from baseness to be free,
As he durst love truth and me.
    Such a man, with every part,
I could give my very heart;
But of one, if short he came,   55
I can rest me where I am.

10. ANOTHER LADY'S EXCEPTION PRESENT AT THE HEARING

For his mind, I do not care,
That's a toy that I could spare;
Let his title be but great,
His clothes rich, and band[1] sit neat,
Himself young, and face be good,   5
All I wish is understood.
What you please, you parts may call,
'Tis one good part I'd lie withal.

---

7. I.e., yet even if.
8. I.e., in a stiff framework.

9. Courage.
1. Collar (or ruff).

The Musical Strife, in a Pastoral Dialogue[2]

SHE

Come, with our voices let us war,
    And challenge all the spheres,[3]
Till each of us be made a star
    And all the world turn ears.

HE

At such a call, what beast or fowl   5
    Of reason empty is?
What tree or stone doth want[4] a soul?
    What man but must lose his?

SHE

Mix then your notes, that we may prove[5]
    To stay the running floods,   10
To make the mountain quarries move,
    And call the walking woods.[6]

HE

What need of me? Do you but sing,
    Sleep and the grave will wake;
No tunes are sweet, nor words have sting,   15
    But what those lips do make.

SHE

They say the angels mark each deed
    And exercise[7] below,
And out of inward pleasure feed
    On what they viewing know.   20

HE

O sing not you, then, lest the best
    Of angels should be driven
To fall again; at such a feast,
    Mistaking earth for heaven.

2. According to Drummond, Jonson was especially fond of quoting this poem (*H & S*, I, p. 134). Cf. John Hollander, *The Untuning of the Sky: Ideas of Music in English Poetry 1500–1700* (New York, 1970), pp. 338–342, 408–409.
3. I.e., match our voices with the music of the spheres.
4. Lack.
5. Attempt.
6. Cf. *The Forest*, XII, p. 38, l. 77–78 and note.
7. Action.

SHE

Nay, rather both our souls be strained   25
   To meet their high desire;
So they in state of grace retained
   May wish us of their choir.

In the Person of Womankind:
A Song Apologetic

Men, if you love us, play no more
   The fools or tyrants with your friends,
To make us still sing o'er and o'er
   Our own false praises, for your ends;
     We have both wits and fancies too,   5
     And if we must, let's sing of you.

Nor do we doubt but that we can,
   If we would search with care and pain,
Find some one good, in some one man;
   So going thorough all your strain,[8]   10
     We shall, at last, of parcels[9] make
     One good enough for a song's sake.

And as a cunning painter takes
   In any curious[1] piece you see
More pleasure while the thing he makes   15
   Than when 'tis made, why, so will we.
     And having pleased our art, we'll try
     To make a new, and hang that by.[2]

Another, in Defence of Their Inconstancy:
A Song

Hang up those dull and envious fools
   That talk abroad of woman's change;
We were not bred to sit on stools,
   Our proper virtue is to range;[3]
     Take that away, you take our lives: 5
     We are no women then, but wives.

Such as in valor would excel
   Do change,[4] though man, and often fight;

---

8. I.e., race, stock (of men).
9. I.e., of separate parts of individual men.
1. Intricate.
2. I.e., put the first one aside.

3. I.e., the virtue peculiarly appropriate to women is to rove at will (by implication, to embody changefulness).
4. I.e., vary their styles of combat.

Which we, in love, must do as well
   If ever we will love aright.   10
      The frequent varying of the deed
      Is that which doth perfection breed.

Nor is't inconstancy to change
   For what is better, or to make
(By searching) what before was strange,   15
   Familiar, for the use's sake;
      The good from bad is not descried
      But as 'tis often vexed[5] and tried.

And this profession of a store[6]
   In love doth not alone help forth[7]   20
Our pleasure; but preserves us more
   From being forsaken than doth worth;
      For were the worthiest woman cursed
      To love one man, he'd leave her first.

A Nymph's Passion[8]

I love, and he loves me again,
   Yet dare I not tell who;
For if the nymphs[9] should know my swain,
   I fear they'd love him too;
      Yet, if it be not known,   5
      The pleasure is as good as none,
For that's a narrow joy is but[1] our own.

I'll tell, that if they be not glad,
   They yet may envy me;
But then if I grow jealous mad,   10
   And of them pitied be,
      It were a plague 'bove scorn,
      And yet it cannot be forborne,[2]
Unless my heart would as my thought be torn.

He is, if they can find him, fair   15
   And fresh and fragrant too,
As summer's sky, or purgéd[3] air;
   And looks as lilies do

5. I.e., searchingly examined.
6. I.e., an abundance.
7. I.e., contribute to.
8. S. T. Coleridge thought enough of this poem to revise it and publish the revision (in *Sibylline Leaves*, 1817), describing it merely as "a song modernized, with some additions, from one of our elder poets." Cf. the comments on Jonson's poem by A. C. Swinburne, on p. 445.
9. I.e., the other nymphs, or young girls.
1. Merely.
2. Avoided.
3. Purified.

That are this morning blown;[4]
Yet, yet I doubt he is not known,   20
And fear much more that more of him be shown.

But he hath eyes so round and bright
    As make away my doubt,
Where Love may all his torches light,
    Though hate had put them out;   25
        But then, t'increase my fears,
        What nymph soe'er his voice but hears
Will be my rival, though she have but ears.

I'll tell no more; and yet I love,
    And he loves me; yet no,   30
One unbecoming thought doth move
    From either heart, I know;
        But so exempt from blame
        As it would be to each a fame,
If love, or fear, would let me tell his name.   35

The Hourglass[5]

Do but consider this small[6] dust,
    Here running in the glass,
        By atoms moved;
    Could you believe that this
        The body was   5
            Of one that loved?
And in his mistress' flame, playing like a fly,
    Turned to cinders by her eye?
    Yes; and in death, as life, unblessed,
        To have't expressed,   10
    Even ashes of lovers find no rest.

My Picture Left in Scotland[7]

I now think Love is rather deaf than blind,
    For else it could not be
        That she,
Whom I adore so much, should so slight me
    And cast my love behind;   5
I'm sure my language to her was as sweet,
    And every close[8] did meet
    In sentence[9] of as subtle feet,

---

4. I.e., fully open.
5. Drummond gives a slightly different version of this "madrigal"; cf. *H & S*, I, p. 150. Cf. also Herrick's "The Hourglass," p. 110.
6. Fine.

7. Jonson sent a version of this poem to Drummond on January 19, 1619 (*H & S*, I, p. 151).
8. I.e., concluding phrase (as in music).
9. The term combines the sense of pithy meaning with that of a period in music.

As hath the youngest he
That sits in shadow of Apollo's[1] tree.   10

Oh, but my conscious fears,
    That fly my thoughts between,
    Tell me that she hath seen
My hundreds of gray hairs,
    Told seven and forty years;   15
Read so much waste,[2] as she cannot embrace
My mountain belly, and my rocky face;
And all these through her eyes have stopped her ears.

The Dream

Or scorn or pity on me take,
I must the true relation make:
    I am undone tonight.
    Love, in a subtle dream disguised,
    Hath both my heart and me surprised,   5
Whom never yet he durst attempt t'awake;
Nor will he tell me for whose sake
    He did me the delight,
        Or spite,
    But leaves me to inquire,   10
    In all my wild desire
    Of sleep again, who was his aide;
    And sleep so guilty and afraid,
As[3] since he dares not come within my sight.

An Epitaph on Master Vincent Corbett[4]

I have my piety too, which could
It vent itself but as it would,
    Would say as much as both have done
    Before me here, the friend and son;[5]
For I both lost a friend and father   5
Of[6] him whose bones this grave doth gather:
    Dear Vincent Corbett, who so long
    Had wrestled with diseases strong
That, though they did possess each limb,
Yet he broke them, ere they could him,   10
    With the just canon[7] of his life,
    A life that knew nor noise nor strife;

1. Apollo was the god of poetry and song.
2. Jonson puns on "waist."
3. That.
4. Vincent Corbett, who died in 1619, was the father of Bishop Richard Corbett; cf. the latter's "An Elegy Upon the Death of His Own Father," p. 97.
5. The expression may refer to two separate persons, or simply to Richard Corbett, Jonson's friend.
6. In.
7. Rule.

But was by sweet'ning so his will,
All order, and disposure[8] still.
    His mind as pure and neatly kept   15
    As were his nurseries,[9] and swept
So of uncleanness or offence
That never came ill odor thence;
    And add his actions unto these,
    They were as specious[1] as his trees.   20
'Tis true, he could not reprehend;
His very manners taught[2] t'amend,
    They were so even, grave, and holy;
    No stubbornness so stiff, nor folly
To license ever was so light[3]   25
As twice to trespass in his sight,
    His looks would so correct it, when
    It chid the vice, yet not the men.
Much from him I profess I won,
And more, and more, I should have done   30
    But that I understood him scant;
    Now I conceive him by my want,
And pray who shall my sorrows read
That they for me their tears will shed;
    For truly, since he left to be,   35
    I feel, I'm rather dead than he![4]

An Epistle to Master John Selden[5]

I know to whom I write. Here, I am sure,
Though I am short,[6] I cannot be obscure;
Less shall I for the art or dressing care:
Truth and the Graces best when naked are.
Your book, my Selden, I have read, and much   5
Was trusted that you thought my judgment such
To ask it; though in most of works it be
A penance, where a man may not be free,
Rather than office, when it doth or may
Chance that the friend's affection proves allay   10
Unto the censure.[7] Yours all need doth fly

---

8. Arrangement.
9. I.e., horticultural nurseries; Corbett was a gardener.
1. I.e., outwardly pleasing.
2. I.e., taught others.
3. Careless.
4. See Textual Notes, p. 373.
5. A famous legal authority and antiquarian (1584–1654), Selden is best known to students of literature for *Table Talk* (1689), his secretary's record of Selden's observations on men and manners. According to Drummond, Jonson called Selden "the law book of the judges of England, the bravest man in all languages" (*H & S*, I, p. 149). This poem is prefixed to Selden's *Titles of Honor* (1614), a study of the history of regal and honorific titles.
6. Brief.
7. I.e., he who is asked for an opinion of another's work often feels constrained not to speak with candor; but if a friend requests that "office," the bonds of friendship will permit perfect frankness.

Of this so vicious humanity,[8]
Than which there is not unto study a more
Pernicious enemy. We see before
A many[9] of books, even good judgments wound   15
Themselves through favoring what is there not found;
But I on yours far otherwise shall do,
Not fly the crime, but the suspicion too,
Though I confess (as every Muse hath erred,
And mine not least) I have too oft preferred   20
Men past their terms,[1] and praised some names too much;
But 'twas with purpose to have made them such.
Since, being deceived, I turn a sharper eye
Upon myself, and ask to whom, and why,
And what I write; and vex[2] it many days   25
Before men get a verse, much less a praise;
So that my reader is assured I now
Mean what I speak, and still will keep that vow.
Stand forth, my object, then: you that have been
Ever at home, yet have all countries seen,   30
And, like a compass keeping one foot still
Upon your center,[3] do your circle fill
Of general knowledge; watched men, manners too,
Heard what times past have said, seen what ours do.
Which grace shall I make love to first? Your skill,   35
Or faith in things?[4] Or is't your wealth and will
T'instruct and teach? Or your unwearied pain
Of gathering? Bounty in pouring out again?
What fables have you vexed! What truth redeemed!
Antiquities searched! Opinions dis-esteemed!   40
Impostures branded! And authorities urged!
What blots and errors have you watched and purged
Records and authors of! How rectified
Times, manners, customs! Innovations spied!
Sought out the fountains, sources, creeks, paths, ways,   45
And noted the beginnings and decays!
Where is that nominal mark, or real rite,
Form, act, or ensign[5] that hath 'scaped your sight?
How are traditions there examined; how
Conjectures retrieved![6] And a story now   50
And then of times (besides the bare conduct
Of what it tells us) weaved in to instruct.

---

8. I.e., the need, rooted in imperfect human nature, to silence, or somehow account for, the free expression of perfect truth.
9. I.e., a number.
1. Limits; i.e., extravagantly.
2. I.e., examine stringently.
3. Drummond observes that Jonson's "Impresa [device] was a compass with one foot in center, the other broken; the word [motto] *Deest quod duceret orbem* [There is lacking that which would lead the world]" (*H & S*, I, p. 148).
4. I.e., facts, events.
5. Jonson alludes in these lines to Selden's ability (as demonstrated in *Titles of Honor*) to distinguish among confusing aspects of ceremonial procedures.
6. I.e., recovered from historical obscurity.

I wondered at the richness, but am lost
To see the workmanship so'xceed the cost;
To mark the excellent seas'ning of your style,   55
And manly elocution, not one while
With horror rough, then rioting with wit,
But to the subject still the colors fit[7]
In sharpness of all search, wisdom of choice,
Newness of sense, antiquity of voice!   60
    I yield, I yield: the matter of your praise
Flows in upon me, and I cannot raise
A bank against it. Nothing but the round
Large clasp of nature[8] such a wit can bound.
Monarch in Letters! 'Mongst thy titles shown   65
Of other honors, thus enjoy thine own.
I first salute thee so; and gratulate[9]
With that thy style, thy keeping of thy state,
In offering this thy work to no great name,[1]
That would, perhaps, have praised, and thanked the same,   70
But nought beyond. He thou hast given it to,
Thy learned chamber-fellow, knows to do
It true respects. He will not only love,
Embrace, and cherish; but he can approve[2]
And estimate thy pains, as having wrought   75
In the same mines of knowledge; and thence brought
Humanity enough to be a friend,
And strength to be a champion, and defend
Thy gift 'gainst envy. O, how I do count
Among my comings-in,[3] and see it mount,   80
The gain of your two friendships! Hayward and
Selden! Two names that so much understand!
On whom I could take up[4] and ne'er abuse
The credit what would furnish a tenth Muse!
But here's no time, nor place, my wealth to tell;   85
You both are modest. So am I. Farewell.

A *Little Shrub Growing By*

Ask not to know this man. If fame should speak
    His name in any metal, it would break.
Two letters[5] were enough the plague to tear
    Out of his grave, and poison every ear.
A parcel of court-dirt, a heap and mass   5
    Of all vice hurled together, there he was,

7. I.e., continually employ suitable rhetorical figures of speech.
8. I.e., the entire creation.
9. Hail.
1. *Titles of Honor* was dedicated to Edward Hayward (d. 1658), who, like Selden, had studied law at the Inner Temple; cf. l. 72.
2. Confirm.
3. Income; i.e., the fruitful aspects of my life.
4. I.e., get.
5. The person alluded to is unknown.

Proud, false, and treacherous, vindictive, all
 That thought can add, unthankful, the lay-stall[6]
Of putrid flesh alive! Of blood the sink![7]
 And so I leave to stir him, lest he stink.   10

An Elegy[8]

Though beauty be the mark of praise,
 And yours of whom I sing be such
 As not the world can praise too much,
Yet is't your virtue now I raise.

A virtue, like allay,[9] so gone   5
 Throughout your form as, though that[1] move,
 And draw, and conquer all men's love,
This[2] subjects you to love of one.

Wherein you triumph yet; because
 'Tis of yourself, and that you use   10
 The noblest freedom, not to choose
Against or faith, or honor's laws.

But who should less expect from you,
 In whom alone Love lives again,
 By whom he is restored to men,   15
And kept, and bred, and brought up true?

His falling temples you have reared,
 The withered garlands ta'en away;
 His altars kept from the decay
That envy wished, and nature feared;   20

And on them burn so chaste a flame,
 With so much loyalties' expense,
 As Love, t'acquit[3] such excellence,
Is gone himself into your name.[4]

And you are he: the deity   25
 To whom all lovers are designed
 That would their better objects find;
Among which faithful troop am I.

---

6. Dung heap.
7. Sewer, cesspool.
8. Cf. the comments on this poem in Miner, *op. cit.*, pp. 11–12.
9. Alloy.
1. I.e., your beauty.

2. I.e., your virtue.
3. I.e., to reward.
4. I.e., the letters of the word "love" make part of your name (on this hint, scholars have suggested Lady Covell as the person addressed).

Who, as an off-spring[5] at your shrine,
    Have sung this hymn, and here entreat   30
    One spark of your diviner heat
To light upon a love of mine.

Which if it kindle not, but scant
    Appear, and that to shortest view,
    Yet give me leave t'adore in you   35
What I in her am grieved to want.

An Ode to Himself[6]

Where dost thou careless lie
    Buried in ease and sloth?
Knowledge that sleeps doth die;
And this security,
    It is the common moth   5
That eats on wits and arts, and destroys[7] them both.

Are all the Aonian[8] springs
    Dried up? Lies Thespia waste?
Doth Clarius' harp want strings,
    That not a nymph now sings?   10
    Or droop they as disgraced,
To see their seats and bowers by chatt'ring pies[9] defaced?

If hence thy silence be,
    As 'tis too just a cause,
Let this thought quicken thee: 15
Minds that are great and free
    Should not on fortune pause;
'Tis crown enough to virtue still, her own applause.

What though the greedy fry
    Be taken with false baits   20
Of worded balladry,[1]
And think it poesy?
    They die with their conceits,
And only piteous scorn upon their folly waits.

---

5. Cf. Textual Notes, p. 373.
6. Cf. the later "Ode to Himself," composed in 1629, on the failure of Jonson's play, *The New Inn.*
7. Cf. Textual Notes, p. 373. The figure of lines 5–6 recalls Matthew 6:19–21.
8. Mount Helicon and the Aganippean well, sacred to the Muses, were situated in Aonia; for Thespia, cf. Epigram CI, p.

13, 1. 33 and note. *Clarius* is a term for Apollo, from his temple at Claros, on the Ionian coast.
9. Magpies.
1. Jonson regularly distinguished between poets and poetasters; cf. his contemptuous remark to Drummond, "a poet should detest a ballad-maker" (*H & S, I, p.* 145).

Then take in hand thy lyre,   25
   Strike in thy proper strain,
With Japhet's line,[2] aspire
Sol's chariot for new fire
   To give the world again;
Who aided him will thee, the issue of Jove's brain.[3]   30

And since our dainty age
   Cannot endure reproof,
Make not thyself a page
To that strumpet, the stage,
   But sing high and aloof,   35
Safe from the wolf's black jaw, and the dull ass's hoof.

An Ode

High-spirited friend,[4]
I send nor balms nor corr'sives[5] to your wound;
   Your fate hath found
A gentler and more agile hand to tend
The cure of that which is but corporal,   5
And doubtful days, which were named critical,
   Have made their fairest flight,
   And now are out of sight.
Yet doth some wholesome physic[6] for the mind
   Wrapped in this paper lie,   10
Which in the taking if you mis-apply,
     You are unkind.[7]

   Your covetous hand,
Happy in that fair honor it hath gained,
   Must now be reined.   15
True valor doth her own renown command
In one full action, nor have you now more
To do than be a husband of that store.
   Think but how dear you bought
   This same[8] which you have caught;   20
Such thoughts will make you more in love with truth:
   'Tis wisdom, and that high,
For men to use their fortune reverently,
     Even in youth.

2. Prometheus, who stole fire from heaven, was the son of Iapetus; cf. Ovid, *Metamorphoses*, I. 82.
3. I.e., Minerva (Pallas Athene); cf. *The Forest*, X, p. 32, l. 15 and note.
4. The identity of the friend is unknown.
5. I.e., harsh medicines.
6. Medicine.
7. I.e., wanting in kindness; also, unnatural.
8. Cf. Textual Notes, p. 373.

A Sonnet to the Noble Lady, the Lady Mary Wroth[9]

I that have been a lover, and could show it,
   Though not in these,[1] in rithmes not wholly dumb,
   Since I exscribe[2] your sonnets, am become
A better lover, and much better poet.
Nor is my Muse or I ashamed to owe it   5
   To those true numerous graces, whereof some
   But charm the senses, others overcome
   Both brains and hearts; and mine now best do know it:
For in your verse all Cupid's armory,
   His flames, his shafts, his quiver, and his bow,   10
   His very eyes are yours to overthrow.
But then his mother's sweets you so apply,
   Her joys, her smiles, her loves, as readers take
   For Venus' ceston[3] every line you make.

A Fit of Rhyme Against Rhyme[4]

Rhyme, the rack of finest wits,
That expresseth but by fits
     True conceit,
Spoiling senses of their treasure,
Cozening judgment with a measure,[5]   5
     But false weight;
Wresting words from their true calling,
Propping verse for fear of falling
     To the ground;
Jointing[6] syllabes, drowning letters,   10
Fast'ning vowels, as with fetters
     They were bound!
Soon as lazy thou wert known,
All good poetry hence was flown,
     And art banished.[7]   15

9. Mary Lady Wroth was the daughter of Sir Robert Sidney; she had married Sir Robert Wroth in 1604. Jonson dedicated *The Alchemist* to her. Other sonnets by Jonson include Epigram LVI; "An Epigram to the Household" (on p. 75 of this edition); and the verses prefixed to Nicholas Breton's *Melancholike Humours* (1600) and to the second edition of Thomas Wright's exposition of psychological theory, *The Passions of the Minde in Generall* (1604).
1. I.e., not in the rhyme scheme and metrical arrangement of the sonnet.
2. Copy out.
3. Girdle (from Latin *cestus*).
4. "Fit" in the title signifies primarily "canto"; in line 2, "by fits" has the sense rather of "fitfully," and also "paroxysms of lunacy." Jonson told Drummond that "cross rhymes and stanzas . . . were all forced" (*H & S*, I, p. 132). Cf. also his remarks on "tuning and rhyming" in *Timber*, on p. 405 of this edition. Given these views (and Jonson's preference for the couplet), this poem is something of a *jeu d'esprit*.
5. I.e., deceiving the judgment by the use of rhythmical verse.
6. I.e., disjointing, pulling apart.
7. Greek and Latin poetry did not deliberately employ rhyme, which apparently originated with the sacred poetry of the early Christian church, in the time of Tertullian (c. 160–c. 230); by the fourth century, a tradition of rhymed sacred poetry was established. In Jonson's view, "rhyme's wrongs" (l. 35) defaced the purity of Latin verse.

For a thousand years together
All Parnassus'[8] green did wither,
    And wit vanished.
Pegasus did fly away,
At the wells no Muse did stay,   20
    But bewailed
So to see the fountain dry,
And Apollo's music die,
    All light failed!
Starveling rhymes did fill the stage;   25
Not a poet in an age
    Worth crowning;
Not a work deserving bays,[9]
Nor a line deserving praise,
    Pallas frowning.   30
Greek was free from rhyme's infection,
Happy Greek by this protection
    Was not spoiled.
Whilst the Latin, queen of tongues,
Is not yet free from rhyme's wrongs,   35
    But rests foiled.
Scarce the hill[1] again doth flourish,
Scarce the world a wit doth nourish
    To restore
Phoebus to his crown again,   40
And the Muses to their brain
    As before.
Vulgar[2] languages that want
Words, and sweetness, and be scant
    Of true measure,[3]   45
Tyrant rhyme hath so abuséd
That they long since have refuséd
    Other ceasure.[4]
He that first invented thee,
May his joints tormented be,   50
    Cramped forever;
Still may syllabes jar with time,
Still may reason war with rhyme,
    Resting never.
May his sense, when it would meet   55
The cold tumor in his feet,
    Grow unsounder;
And his title be long fool,[5]

---

8. Mount Parnassus was sacred to Apollo and the Muses. For Pegasus and the (Hippocrene) well, cf. *The Forest*, X, p. 32, l. 23 and note.
9. I.e., the laurel garland traditionally awarded to poets of distinction.
1. I.e., Parnassus.
2. Vernacular.

3. I.e., quantitative verse (the scansion of English verse is accentual).
4. Caesura.
5. Concluding a succession of puns (in ll. 48, 56, 57), Jonson puns on the expression *ars longa, vita brevis* ("art is long, life is short").

That in rearing such a school
    Was the founder.   60

An Execration Upon Vulcan

And why to me this, thou lame lord of fire,[6]
    What had I done that might call on thine ire?
Or urge thy greedy flame, thus to devour
    So many my years' labors in an hour?
I ne'er attempted, Vulcan, 'gainst thy life,   5
    Nor made least line of love to thy loose wife,[7]
Or, in remembrance of thy affront and scorn,
    With clowns and tradesmen kept thee closed in horn.[8]
'Twas Jupiter that hurled thee headlong down,
    And Mars that gave thee a lanthorn for a crown;   10
Was it because thou wert of old denied
    By Jove to have Minerva for thy bride,[9]
That since thou takst all envious care and pain
    To ruin any issue of the brain?
Had I wrote treason there, or heresy,   15
    Imposture, witchcraft, charms, or blasphemy,
I had deserved then thy consuming looks,
    Perhaps to have been burnéd with my books.
But, on thy malice, tell me, didst thou spy
    Any least loose or scurrile paper lie   20
Concealed or kept there that was fit to be,
    By thy own vote, a sacrifice to thee?
Did I there wound the honors of the crown?
    Or tax the glories of the church and gown?[1]
Itch to defame the state? or brand the times?   25
    And myself most, in some self-boasting rhymes?
If none of these, then why this fire? Or find
    A cause before, or leave me one behind.
Had I compiled from *Amadis de Gaul*,[2]
    Th'Esplandians, Arthurs, Palmerins, and all   30
The learned library of Don Quixote,
    And so some goodlier monster had begot,

6. Jonson's house was consumed by fire in November, 1623; his books, manuscripts, and works in progress were utterly destroyed. Vulcan, god of fire, was lamed when Jupiter threw him down from heaven to the Aegean isle of Lemnos; cf. Homer, *Iliad,* I. 590–594.
7. I.e., Venus; cf. *The Forest,* X, p. 32, l. 16 and note.
8. Vulcan was scorned (as a cuckold) by the other gods; Jonson alludes also to the casing of horn that enclosed the flame in a horn lantern. These are combined in "lanthorn" (l. 10).
9. Cf. Hyginus, *Fables,* clxvi.
1. I.e., of the legal profession.
2. This well-known Spanish romance by García Ordóñez de Montalvo, published in 1510, was translated (c. 1590) by Anthony Munday, who also translated the romances *Palmerin d'Oliva* and *Palmerin of England.* Esplandian was the son of Amadis. For Don Quixote's library, cf. the novel by Cervantes, I. vi.

Or spun out riddles, and weaved fifty tomes
  Of logogriphs[3] and curious palindromes,[4]
Or pumped[5] for those hard trifles, anagrams   35
  Or eteostichs,[6] or those finer flams[7]
Of eggs and halberds, cradles and a hearse,
  A pair of scissors and a comb in verse,[8]
Acrostichs[9] and telestichs, on jump[1] names,
  Thou then hadst some color[2] for thy flames,   40
On such my serious follies. But thou'lt say
  There were some pieces of as base allay[3]
And as false stamp there; parcels of a play,
  Fitter to see the firelight than the day;
Adulterate[4] moneys, such as might not go;   45
  Thou should'st have stayed[5] till public fame said so.
She is the judge, thou executioner.
  Or, if thou needs would'st trench[6] upon her power,
Thou might'st have yet enjoyed thy cruelty
  With some more thrift and more variety;   50
Thou might'st have had me perish, piece by piece,
  To light tobacco, or save roasted geese,
Singe capons, or poor pigs, dropping their eyes;[7]
  Condemned me to the ovens with the pies;
And so have kept me dying a whole age,   55
  Not ravished all hence in a minute's rage.
But that's a mark whereof thy rites do boast,
  To make consumption, ever, where thou go'st;
Had I foreknown of this thy least desire
  T'have held a triumph, or a feast of fire,   60
Especially in paper; that, that steam
  Had tickled your large nostril; many a ream
To redeem mine, I had sent in. "Enough!"
  Thou should'st have cried, and all been proper stuff.
The Talmud[8] and the Alcoran had come,   65
  With pieces of the *Legend*; the whole sum

3. Word puzzles.
4. I.e., words or sentences that read the same backward or forward (e.g., the palindrome epitomizing General Goethals: "A man, a plan, a canal, Panama").
5. Worked.
6. Chronograms (riddles involving numerals).
7. Flames; i.e., conceits, fancies.
8. Lines 37–38 allude to poems visually shaped so as to represent their subjects; cf. for example, Herrick's "The Pillar of Fame," on p. 147 of this edition. George Puttenham, *The Arte of English Poesie* (1589), devotes a chapter (II. xi) to these matters.
9. I.e., acrostics; verses of which the initial letters in each line spell a name; telestichs employ the final letters in each line to the same end.
1. I.e., exactly corresponding.
2. Excuse.
3. Alloy.
4. I.e., counterfeit.
5. Waited.
6. Encroach.
7. I.e., whose eyes fell out as they were roasted on a spit.
8. I.e., the body of Jewish civil and ceremonial law. The "Alcoran" is the Koran; Jacobus de Voragine's thirteenth century *Legenda Aurea*, a collection of saints' lives, was translated by Caxton in the fifteenth century.

Of errant[9] knighthood, with the dames and dwarfs,
   The charméd boats, and the enchanted wharfs;
The Tristrams, Lancelots, Turpins, and the Peers,
   All the mad Rolands and sweet Olivers;[1]   70
To Merlin's marvels and his cabal's loss,[2]
   With the chimaera of the Rosy-Cross,[3]
Their seals, their characters, hermetic rings,
   Their gem of riches, and bright stone that brings
Invisibility, and strength, and tongues;   75
   The art of kindling the true coal, by lungs;[4]
With Nicholas Pasquil's *Meddle with your match*,[5]
   And the strong lines that so the times do catch;[6]
Or Captain Pamphlet's horse and foot, that sally
   Upon the Exchange, still, out of Pope's Head Alley.[7]   80
The weekly corants, with Paul's seal,[8] and all
   Th'admired discourses of the Prophet Ball.[9]
These, hadst thou pleased either to dine or sup,
   Had made a meal for Vulcan to lick up.
But in my desk, what was there to excite   85
   So ravenous and vast an appetite?
I dare not say a body, but some parts
   There were of search and mast'ry in the arts.
All the old Venusine in poetry,
   And lighted by the Stagirite, could spy   90

9. Wandering; cf. Spenser's allusion to Una, in *The Faerie Queene*, II. i. 19, as "the errant damozell." The vessel "withouten ore [oar]" in which Phaedria overtakes Guyon's craft (*FQ*, II. xii. 15–16) is one instance of the "charméd boats" Jonson has in mind.

1. Tristram and Lancelot appear in Arthurian story. The others are associated with the Charlemagne cycle of romances: Turpin, Archbishop of Rheims, died in battle at Roncesvalles, together with the Twelve Peers (Charlemagne's elite bodyguard); Roland, hero of the *Chanson de Roland* (with his thoughtful companion Oliver), is celebrated also by Ariosto, in *Orlando Furioso* (1532).

2. Merlin, the magician of Arthurian legend, was overcome at last by Nimue, the Lady of the Lake; cf. Malory's *Le Morte d'Arthur*, IV. i.

3. The Rosicrucians, a society concerned with esoteric lore and occult knowledge, had existed since the fifteenth century; in 1614, the publication of *Fama Fraternitatis*, by Johann Andrea (known as Christian Rosenkreuz), gave new impetus to their activities. Although Jonson's friend Sir Kenelm Digby interested himself in Rosicrucianism, Jonson remained skeptical (as the line indicates).

4. Lines 73–76 reflect the association of Rosicrucianism with the alchemists of Jonson's day, who sought (or pretended to seek) the "philosopher's stone," which would give man supranatural powers. The assistant who attended an alchemist's furnace was often known as "Lungs"; cf. Jonson's *The Alchemist*.

5. Nicholas Breton (c. 1555–c. 1626) published several pamphlets under the pseudonym "Pasquil"; *Meddle with your match* probably refers to one such pamphlet, now lost.

6. "Strong lines" alludes to the metaphysical manner in poetry. Cf. Carew's "Elegy" on Donne, ll. 38–39, 49–53 (on p. 174 of this edition).

7. Thomas Gainsford, a soldier turned pamphleteer, made his headquarters in Pope's Head Alley, near the Royal Exchange in Cornhill.

8. Early precursors of the modern newspaper were published from Saint Paul's churchyard.

9. Jonson alludes to one of two Puritan preachers, either John Ball (1585–1640) or Thomas Ball (1590–1659).

Was there made English;[1] with the grammar too,
  To teach some that their nurses could not do,
The purity of language; and among
  The rest, my journey into Scotland sung,
With all the adventures;[2] three books not afraid   95
  To speak the fate of the Sicilian maid
To our own ladies,[3] and in story there
  Of our fifth Henry, eight of his nine year;
Wherein was oil, beside the succor spent,
  Which noble Carew, Cotton, Selden lent;[4]   100
And twice-twelve-years' stored up humanity,[5]
  With humble gleanings in divinity,
After the Fathers,[6] and those wiser guides
  Whom faction had not drawn to study sides.
How in these ruins, Vulcan, thou dost lurk,   105
  All soot and embers! odious as thy work!
I now begin to doubt if ever Grace
  Or goddess could be patient of thy face.
Thou woo Minerva! or to wit aspire!
  'Cause thou canst halt with us in arts[7] and fire!   110
Son of the wind! for so thy mother gone
  With lust conceived thee; father thou hadst none;[8]
When thou wert born, and that thou look'st at best,
  She durst not kiss, but flung thee from her breast.
And so did Jove, who ne'er meant thee his cup;[9]   115
  No marvel the clowns of Lemnos took thee up,
For none but smiths would have made thee a god.
  Some alchemist there may be yet, or odd
Squire of the squibs against the pageant day,[1]
  May to thy name a Vulcanale[2] say;   120
And for it lose his eyes with gunpowder,
  As th'other may his brains with quicksilver.
Well fare the wise men yet, on the Bankside,[3]
  My friends the watermen! They could provide

---

1. I.e., a translation of *Ars Poetica*, by Horace (born in Venusia, modern Venossa), with a commentary based on the *Poetics* of Aristotle (born in Stagira, in Macedonia). Another version was published in Jonson's *Works* (1640–1641), together with his *English Grammar*.

2. Jonson's walking trip to Scotland was undertaken in 1618–1619; cf. Drummond's notes on his conversations with the poet at that time (*H & S*, pp. 128–151).

3. At the request of James I, Jonson had undertaken to translate *Argents*, a Latin romance by the Scottish John Barclay (1588–1621).

4. Richard Carew (1555–1620) and Sir Robert Cotton (1571–1631) were distinguished antiquaries of Jonson's acquaintance. For Selden, cf. Jonson's Epistle to him, p. 59 and the first note.

5. I.e., probably, a commonplace book similar to *Timber*.

6. I.e., the early Christian writers.

7. I.e., in the art of metalwork.

8. Jonson follows Apollodorus, *Library*, I. iii. 5; cf. also notes to ll. 1–12.

9. Cf. *Iliad*, I. 584–600, where Vulcan, acting as cupbearer to the gods, arouses their derision.

1. John Squire was the author of an entertainment, *The Triumphs of Peace*, composed. for the Lord Mayor's Show (and display of fireworks) in October, 1620.

2. I.e., a hymn to Vulcan.

3. Cf. Epigram CXXXIII, p. 000, l. 30 and note. "Watermen" are the boatmen who ferried passengers across the Thames.

Against thy fury, when to serve their needs   125
     They made a Vulcan of a sheaf of reeds,[4]
Whom they durst handle in their holiday coats,
     And safely trust to dress, not burn their boats.
But O those reeds! thy mere disdain of them
     Made thee beget that cruel stratagem,   130
Which some are pleased to style but thy mad prank,
     Against the Globe,[5] the glory of the Bank,
Which, though it were the fort of the whole parish,
     Flanked with a ditch and forced out of a marish,[6]
I saw with two poor chambers[7] taken in   135
     And razed; ere thought could urge, "This might have
         been!"
See the world's ruins! Nothing but the piles
     Left; and wit since to cover it with tiles.[8]
The brethren,[9] they straight noised it out for news;
     'Twas verily some relic of the stews,[1]   140
And this a sparkle of that fire let loose
     That was locked up in the Winchestrian goose[2]
Bred on the bank, in time of popery,
     When Venus there maintained the mystery.[3]
But others fell with that conceit by the ears,   145
     And cried[4] it was a threat'ning to the bears,
And that accurséd ground, the Paris Garden.[5]
     "Nay," sighed a sister, " 'twas the nun,[6] Kate Arden,
Kindled the fire!" But then did one return,
     "No fool would his own harvest spoil, or burn!   150
If that were so, thou rather would'st advance
     The place that was thy wife's inheritance."
"O no," cried all, "Fortune, for being a whore,
     'Scaped not his justice any jot the more;[7]
He burnt that idol of the revels too;   155
     Nay, let Whitehall[8] with revels have to do,
Though but in dances, it shall know his power;
     There was a judgment shown too in an hour.
He is true Vulcan still! He did not spare
     Troy, though it were so much his Venus' care."[9]   160

4. I.e., a torch.
5. The Globe Theater, destroyed by fire on June 29, 1613, was rebuilt in the following year.
6. Marsh.
7. Cannon (used for sound effects); burning wadding from them set fire to the thatched roof of the Globe.
8. The rebuilt theater was provided with a tile roof.
9. Jonson alludes either to pamphleteers who issued ballads and news reports about the fire, or (more probably) to Puritans, who considered the destruction of the Globe a sign of divine displeasure.
1. Brothels.
2. I.e., venereal disease. The brothels of Southwark were located in an area belonging to the Bishop of Winchester.
3. Trade.
4. I.e., cried that.
5. Cf. Epigram CXXXIII, p. 14, ll. 117–118 and notes.
6. I.e., whore; for "nunnery" in the sense of "brothel," cf. *Hamlet*, III. i. 143–157.
7. The Fortune, another theater, was burned in 1621.
8. The royal banqueting house at Whitehall burned in 1618.
9. Venus, who favored the Trojans, protected Aeneas, who eventually founded Rome.

Fool, wilt thou let that in example come?
    Did not she save from thence, to build a Rome?
And what hast thou done in these petty spites,
    More than advanced the houses and their rites?[1]
I will not argue thee, from those of guilt,   165
    For they were burnt but to be better built.
'Tis true that in thy wish they were destroyed,
    Which thou hast only vented,[2] not enjoyed.
So wouldst th'have run upon the Rolls by stealth,
    And didst invade part of the commonwealth   170
In those records, which, were all chroniclers gone,
    Will be remembered by Six Clerks, to one.[3]
But say, all six good men, what answer ye?
    Lies there no writ out of the Chancery
Against this Vulcan? No injunction?   175
    No order? No decree? Though we be gone[4]
At common law, methinks in his despite
    A court of equity should do us right,
But to confine him to the brew-houses,
    The glass-house, dye-vats, and their furnaces;   180
To live in sea-coal,[5] and go forth in smoke;
    Or, lest that vapor might the city choke,
Condemn him to the brick-kilns, or some hill-
    foot (out in Sussex) to an iron mill;
Or in small fagots have him blaze about   185
    Vile taverns, and the drunkards piss him out;
Or in the bellman's[6] lanthorn, like a spy,
    Burn to a snuff, and then stink out and die:
I could invent a sentence yet were worse;
    But I'll conclude all in a civil curse.   190
Pox on your flameship, Vulcan; if it be
    To all as fatal as't hath been to me
And to Paul's steeple,[7] which was unto us
    'Bove all your fireworks had at Ephesus
Or Alexandria;[8] and, though a divine   195
    Loss, remains yet as unrepaired as mine.
Would you had kept your forge at Etna still,
    And there made swords, bills, glaives,[9] and arms your
        fill,

---

1. I.e., your spiteful pleasure in these destructive fires is futile, since the theaters and their activities flourish more than ever.
2. Expressed.
3. The "Six Clerks'" (Rolls) Office in Chancery Lane was destroyed by fire in 1621; but, since the clerks remembered all that the lost records had contained, Vulcan could be said to have been defeated of his purpose.
4. I.e., although our case is lost.

5. I.e., in relatively smoky sea-coal, not charcoal.
6. Night watchman's.
7. The spire of Saint Paul's steeple was struck by lightning on June 4, 1561; the resulting fire destroyed steeple and roof.
8. Herostratus burned the temple of Diana at Ephesus in 356 B.C.; the famous library at Alexandria was burnt in A.D. 640.
9. Broadswords.

Maintained the trade at Bilbo[1] or elsewhere,
    Struck in at Milan with the cutlers there;   200
Or stayed but where the friar[2] and you first met,
    Who from the devil's arse did guns beget;
Or fixed in the Low Countries,[3] where you might
    On both sides do your mischiefs with delight;
Blow up and ruin, mine and countermine,   205
    Make your petards and granats,[4] all your fine
Engines of murder, and receive the praise
    Of massacring mankind so many ways.
We ask your absence here; we all love peace,
    And pray the fruits thereof and the increase;   210
So doth the king, and most of the king's men
    That have good places; therefore, once again,
Pox on thee, Vulcan, thy Pandora's pox,[5]
    And all the evils that flew out of her box
Light on thee; or if those plagues will not do,   215
    Thy wife's pox on thee, and B. B.'s[6] too.

An Epistle Answering to One that Asked to be Sealed of the Tribe of Ben[7]

Men that are safe and sure in all they do
    Care not what trials they are put unto;
They meet the fire, the test, as martyrs would,
    And, though opinion stamp them not, are gold.
I could say more of such, but that I fly[8]   5
    To speak myself out too ambitiously,
And showing so weak an act to vulgar eyes,
    Put conscience and my right to compromise.[9]
Let those that merely talk and never think,
    That live in the wild anarchy of drink,   10
Subject to quarrel only; or else such
    As make it their proficiency how much
They've glutted in and lechered out that week,
    That never yet did friend or friendship seek

1. The finest swords in Europe were made at Bilbao and Milan.
2. The allusions probably refer to Roger Bacon (c. 1214–1294), considered by some of Jonson's contemporaries to have invented guns.
3. Throughout the late sixteenth and early seventeenth centuries, the armies of Spain were opposed by Protestant forces in the Netherlands. Jonson was proud of his own service in these wars; cf. *H & S*, I, p. 139.
4. A petard is an explosive charge used to blast open the gates of besieged cities; "granats" are grenades.
5. I.e., Pandora's curse or Pandora's disease (syphilis). The gods gave to Pandora a box, created by Vulcan, that contained every kind of evil; when she opened the box, these flew out to plague mankind (cf. Hesiod, *Works and Days*, 60–104).
6. I.e., Bess Broughton's; a notorious whore, she is described by John Aubrey as "a most exquisite beauty, as finely shaped as nature could frame, and had a delicate wit. . . . her price was very dear. . . . At last she grew common, and infamous, and had the pox, of which she died" (John Aubrey, *Brief Lives*, ed. A. Powell [London, 1949], p. 373).
7. Cf. Revelation 7:8: "Of the tribe of Benjamin were sealed twelve thousand." *Sealed* here means "assured, accepted."
8. I.e., prefer not.
9. I.e., compromise myself (by boasting).

But for a sealing: let these men protest.   15
    Or th'other on their borders,[1] that will jest
On all souls that are absent, even the dead,
    Like flies or worms which man's corrupt parts fed;
That to speak well, think it above all sin,
    Of any company but that they are in,   20
Call every night to supper in these fits,
    And are receivéd for the covey[2] of wits;
That censure all the town, and all th'affairs,
    And know whose ignorance is more than theirs:
Let these men have their ways, and take their times   25
    To vent their libels, and to issue rhymes;
I have no portion in them, nor their deal
    Of news they get to strew out the long meal;
I study other friendships, and more one[3]
    Than these can ever be, or else with none.   30
What is't to me whether the French design
    Be, or be not, to get the Valteline?[4]
Or the States'[5] ships sent forth belike to meet
    Some hopes of Spain in their West Indian fleet?
Whether the dispensation[6] yet be sent,   35
    Or that the match from Spain was ever meant?
I wish all well, and pray high heaven conspire
    My prince's safety and my king's desire;
But if, for honor, we must draw the sword,
    And force back that which will not be restored,[7]   40
I have a body yet that spirit draws
    To live, or fall a carcass, in the cause.
So far without inquiry what the States,
    Brunsfield and Mansfield[8] do this year, my fates
Shall carry me at call; and I'll be well,   45
    Though I do neither hear these news, nor tell
Of Spain or France, or were not pricked down[9] one
    Of the late mystery of reception,[1]
Although my fame, to his, not under-hears,[2]
    That guides the motions and directs the bears.[3]   50

1. I.e., or others like them.
2. I.e., and are considered to be the fashionable group.
3. I.e., friendships which more truly embody that ideal; or (perhaps) friendships which more completely exemplify a unity of character.
4. A valley near Lake Como, of some strategical importance, the Valteline was seized from Spanish control by the French in 1624.
5. I.e., Dutch.
6. Permission from Rome was necessary to make possible the projected marriage of Prince Charles to the Spanish Infanta.
7. I.e., any aggressively ambitious power, but in particular, the forces of Catholic Spain.
8. Ernest, Count of Mansfield, commanded the army of the Palatinate and Bohemia; the identity of "Brunsfield" is uncertain, although W. B. Hunter, Jr., suggests Christian of Brunswick (*Complete Poetry of Ben Jonson*, ed. cit., p. 202).
9. I.e., singled out.
1. I.e., the committee (including the designer and architect Inigo Jones, whom Jonson bitterly resented) that, in 1623, arranged for the reception of the Spanish Infanta at Southampton.
2. I.e., is not inferior.
3. Jonson contemptuously likens Inigo Jones to a cheap showman, whose undertakings are no better than puppet shows ("motions") and bear baitings.

But that's a blow by which in time I may
    Lose all my credit with my Christmas clay
And animated porcelain of the court;
    Aye, and for this neglect, the coarser sort
Of earthen jars there may molest me too.[4]   55
    Well, with mine own frail pitcher, what to do
I have decreed: keep it from waves, and press,[5]
    Lest it be jostled, cracked, made nought or less;
Live to that point I will for which I am man,
    And dwell as in my center as I can,   60
Still looking to and ever loving heaven,
    With reverence using all the gifts thence given;
'Mongst which, if I have any friendships sent,
    Such as are square, well-tagged,[6] and permanent,
Not built with canvas, paper, and false lights[7]   65
    As are the glorious scenes at the great sights,
And that there be no fev'ry heats nor colds,
    Oily expansions,[8] or shrunk dirty folds,
But all so clear, and led by reason's flame,
    As but to stumble in her sight were shame;   70
These I will honor, love, embrace, and serve,
    And free it[9] from all question to preserve.
So short you read my character, and theirs
    I would call mine, to which not many stairs
Are asked to climb. First give me faith, who know   75
    Myself a little; I will take you so
As you have writ yourself. Now stand; and then,
    Sir, you are sealéd of the Tribe of Ben.

An Epigram to the Household[1]

What can the cause be, when the king hath given
    His poet sack,[2] the household will not pay?
Are they so scanted[3] in their store, or driven
    For want of knowing the poet, to say him nay?
Well, they should know him, would the king but grant   5
    His poet leave to sing his household true;
He'd frame such ditties of their store, and want,
    Would make the very green cloth[4] to look blue,
And rather wish, in their expense of sack,
    So the allowance from the king to use   10

4. In lines 51–55, Jonson acknowledges the uncertainty of his own position at court, notably the likelihood (given Jones's influence) that he may no longer be commissioned to compose masques for the festivities of Christmas.
5. Crowds.
6. Well knit.
7. I.e., not depending on insubstantial devices (like those favored by Inigo Jones).

8. I.e., the stretching of painted canvas.
9. I.e., friendship.
1. I.e., the household of King Charles I.
2. By a royal patent of March 26, 1630, Jonson was to receive £100 and "one tierce [42 gallons] of Canary Spanish wine" (*H & S*, I, pp. 245–247).
3. Diminished.
4. The Board of Green Cloth controlled domestic expenses of the royal household.

As the old bard should no Canary lack.
'Twere better spare a butt than spill[5] his Muse,
For in the genius of a poet's verse
The king's fame lives. Go now, deny his tierce!

To the Immortal Memory and Friendship
of that Noble Pair, Sir Lucius Cary and Sir H. Morison[6]

THE TURN[7]

Brave infant of Saguntum,[8] clear
Thy coming forth in that great year,
When the prodigious[9] Hannibal did crown
His rage, with razing your immortal town.
Thou, looking then about,   5
Ere thou wert half got out,
Wise child, didst hastily return,
And mad'st thy mother's womb thine urn.
How summed a circle didst thou leave mankind
Of deepest lore, could we the center find!   10

THE COUNTER-TURN

Did wiser Nature draw thee back
From out the horror of that sack?
Where shame, faith, honor, and regard of right
Lay trampled on; the deeds of death and night
Urged, hurried forth, and hurled   15
Upon th'affrighted world;
Sword, fire, and famine with fell fury met,
And all on utmost ruin set;
As, could they but life's miseries foresee,
No doubt all infants would return like thee.   20

5. I.e., spare a large cask than spoil (but Jonson's taste for punning adds point to the line).

6. Sir Lucius Cary, second Viscount Falkland (c. 1610–1643), in the view of Douglas Bush "the example *par excellence* of the noble and philosophical cavalier" (*English Literature in the Earlier Seventeenth Century 1600–1660*, 2nd ed., rev. [New York, 1962], p. 343), was the guiding spirit of an intellectual group that met in the 1630s at Cary's estate, Great Tew, in Oxfordshire. Cary contributed an elegy to *Jonsonus Virbius*, the collection of memorial poems published in 1638. Although he was not in sympathy with the views of Archbishop Laud and the Earl of Strafford, Cary allied himself with the royalist forces when the Civil War began; he was killed at the battle of Newbury in September, 1643. Sir Henry Morison (c. 1608–1629) was knighted in 1627; Cary married his sister in 1630.

7. The odes of Pindar (c. 522–442 B.C.), on which this poem is modeled, are typically arranged in groups of three stanzas: strophe, antistrophe, and a formally distinct epode. Jonson's "turn," "counter-turn," and "stand" correspond to these terms and divisions. The complex metrical structure and the elevated tone of Pindar's odes evidently excited the particular admiration of Jonson, who refers more than once to the "fire" of Pindar's genius (cf. "Ode to Himself," on p. 88 of this edition).

8. According to Pliny (*Natural History*, VII. iii.), when Hannibal destroyed the Spanish city of Saguntum (modern Murviedro), in 217 B.C. (and so began the Second Punic War), a newly born child, witnessing the sack of the city, returned to its mother's womb.

9. Like a prodigy; i.e., extraordinary, ominous.

THE STAND

For what is life, if measured by the space,[1]
Not by the act?
Or maskéd man, if valued by his face
Above his fact?[2]
Here's one outlived his peers,   25
And told forth fourscore years;
He vexéd time, and busied the whole state,
Troubled both foes and friends,
But ever to no ends;
What did this stirrer, but die late?   30
How well at twenty had he fall'n or stood!
For three of his fourscore he did no good.

THE TURN

He entered well, by virtuous parts,
Got up, and thrived with honest arts;
He purchased friends, and fame, and honors then,   35
And had his noble name advanced with men;
But weary of that flight,
He stooped in all men's sight
To sordid flatteries, acts of strife,
And sunk in that dead sea of life   40
So deep, as he did then death's waters sup,
But that the cork of title buoyed him up.

THE COUNTER-TURN

Alas, but Morison fell young!
He never fell; thou fall'st, my tongue.
He stood, a soldier to the last right end,   45
A perfect patriot, and a noble friend,
But most, a virtuous son.
All offices were done
By him, so ample, full, and round,
In weight, in measure, number, sound,   50
As, though his age imperfect might appear,
His life was of humanity the sphere.[3]

THE STAND

Go now, and tell out days summed up with fears,
And make them years;
Produce thy mass of miseries on the stage,   55

---

1. I.e., by the length in time.   3. I.e., the perfect model.
2. Deed.

To swell thine age;
Repeat of things a throng,
To show thou hast been long,
Not lived; for life doth her great actions spell[4]
By what was done and wrought   60
In season, and so brought
To light; her measures are, how well
Each syllabe answered, and was formed, how fair;
These make the lines of life, and that's her air.[5]

THE TURN

It is not growing like a tree   65
In bulk, doth make man better be;
Or standing long an oak, three hundred year,
To fall a log at last, dry, bald, and sere;
A lily of a day
Is fairer far in May,   70
Although it fall and die that night;
It was the plant and flower of light.
In small proportions, we just beauties see;
And in short measures, life may perfect be.

THE COUNTER-TURN

Call, noble Lucius, then for wine,   75
And let thy looks with gladness shine;
Accept this garland, plant it on thy head,
And think, nay know, thy Morison's not dead.
He leaped the present age,
Possessed with hóly rage   80
To see that bright eternal day
Of which we priests and poets say
Such truths, as we expect for happy men;
And there he lives with memory, and Ben

THE STAND

Jonson, who sung this of him, ere he went   85
Himself to rest,
Or taste a part of that full joy he meant
To have expressed
In this bright asterism,[6]
Where it were friendship's schism,   90
Were not his Lucius long with us to tarry,
To separate these twi-

---

4. Signify.
5. I.e., her element (or, perhaps, "manner").
6. Constellation.

Lights, the Dioscuri,[7]
And keep the one half from his Harry.
But fate doth so alternate the design,   95
Whilst that in heav'n, this light on earth must shine.

THE TURN

And shine as you exalted are;
Two names of friendship, but one star:
Of hearts the union. And those not by chance
Made, or indentured, or leased out t'advance   100
The profits for a time;
No pleasures vain did chime
Of rhymes, or riots at your feasts,
Orgies of drink, or feigned protests;
But simple love of greatness, and of good;   105
That knits brave minds, and manners, more than blood.

THE COUNTER-TURN

This made you first to know the why
You liked, then after to apply
That liking; and approach so one the t'other,
Till either grew a portion of the other;   110
Each styléd by his end,[8]
The copy of his friend.
You lived to be the great surnames
And titles, by which all made claims
Unto the virtue; nothing perfect done   115
But as a Cary or a Morison.

THE STAND

And such a force the fair example had,
As they that saw
The good, and durst not practise it, were glad
That such a law   120
Was left yet to mankind,
Where they might read, and find
Friendship in deed was written, not in words;
And with the heart, not pen,
Of two so early[9] men,   125
Whose lines her rolls were, and records,
Who, ere the first down blooméd on the chin,
Had sowed these fruits, and got the harvest in.

7. Castor and Pollux; cf. *The Forest*, XII, p. 37, l. 58 and note.
8. Aim, intention.
9. Young.

Epithalamion, or a Song Celebrating the Nuptials of that Noble
Gentleman, Mr. Jerome Weston, Son and Heir of the
Lord Weston, Lord High Treasurer of England, with the
Lady Frances Stuart, Daughter of Esme Duke of Lenox, Deceased,
and Sister of the Surviving Duke of the Same Name[1]

Though thou hast passed thy summer standing,[2] stay
  Awhile with us, bright sun, and help our light;
Thou canst not meet more glory, on the way
    Between thy tropics,[3] to arrest thy sight
      Than thou shalt see today.   5
        We woo thee, stay,
      And see what can be seen,
The bounty of a King, and beauty of his Queen!

See, the procession! What a holy day,
  Bearing the promise of some better fate,   10
Hath filléd, with caroches,[4] all the way
  From Greenwich hither to Roehampton gate!
    When looked the year, at best,
      So like a feast;
      Or were affairs in tune,   15
By all the spheres' consent, so in the heart of June?

What bevy of beauties and bright youths, at charge[5]
  Of summer's liveries and gladding[6] green,
Do boast their loves and brav'ries[7] so at large
    As they came all to see, and to be seen!   20
    When looked the earth so fine,
      Or so did shine
      In all her bloom and flower,
To welcome home a pair, and deck the nuptial bower?

It is the kindly season of the time,   25
  The month of youth, which calls all creatures forth
To do their offices in nature's chime,

---

1. An epithalamion is a nuptial song in honor of the bride and groom; the term, literally "on the bed chamber," derives from Latin and Greek. Edmund Spenser's is the first use of the term in English; the structure and stanzaic form of Jonson's poem generally recall the *Epithalamion* of his Elizabethan predecessor, although the particular emphases of Jonson's marriage ode differ from those of Spenser's poem. Richard Lord Weston (1577–1635) extended patronage to Jonson in the poet's later years; several poems in *Underwood* (not included here) compliment Lord Weston or request his aid. His son Jerome (1605–1663) conducted diplomatic negotiations in France and Italy during 1632–1633, just prior to his marriage, which took place at Roehampton on June 25, 1632. Frances Stuart was the daughter of that Lady Aubigny to whom Jonson addressed *The Forest*, XIII. The marriage, according to Clarendon (*History of the Rebellion* . . . , 7 vols. [Oxford, 1849], I, p. 75), was arranged by King Charles I.

2. I.e., the solstice.

3. I.e., the Tropics of Cancer and Capricorn.

4. Carriages.

5. I.e., who have the expense.

6. Pleasing.

7. Finery (of clothing).

And celebrate (perfection at the worth)
   Marriage, the end[8] of life,
      That holy strife,   30
   And the allowéd war,
Through which not only we but all our species are.

Hark, how the bells upon the waters play
   Their sister-tunes, from Thames his either side,
As they had learned new changes[9] for the day,   35
   And all did ring th'approaches of the bride,
      The Lady Frances, dressed
        Above the rest
      Of all the maidens fair,
In graceful ornament of garland, gems, and hair.   40

See how she paceth forth in virgin white,
   Like what she is, the daughter of a Duke,
And sister; darting forth a dazzling light
   On all that come her simplesse[1] to rebuke.
      Her tresses trim her back   45
        As she did lack
      Nought of a maiden queen,
With modesty so crowned and adoration seen.

Stay, thou wilt see what rites the virgins do,
   The choicest virgin-troop of all the land,   50
Porting the ensigns of united two,[2]
   Both crowns and kingdoms in their either hand,
      Whose majesties appear,
        To make more clear[3]
      This feast than can the day,   55
Although that thou, O sun, at our entreaty stay.

See, how with roses and with lilies shine
   (Lilies and roses, flowers of either sex)[4]
The bright bride's paths, embellished more than thine
   With light of love, this pair doth intertexe![5]   60
      Stay, see the virgins sow,
        Where she shall go,
      The emblems of their way.
O now thou smil'st, fair sun, and shin'st as thou wouldst stay!

---

8. Purpose, object.
9. Sequences (in the "change ringing" of church bells, an ancient English pursuit demanding concentration and stamina).
1. I.e., her simple and pure dress.
2. I.e., carrying the banners of England and France, symbolizing the union of Charles I and his French consort Henrietta Maria.
3. Bright.
4. The English rose is matched by the French fleur-de-lis.
5. Interweave.

With what full hands, and in how plenteous showers   65
    Have they bedewed the earth where she doth tread,
As if her airy steps did spring the flowers,
    And all the ground were garden, where she led!
      See, at another door,
        On the same floor,   70
      The bridegroom meets the bride
With all the pomp of youth, and all our Court beside.

Our Court and all the grandees;[6] now, sun, look,
    And looking with thy best inquiry tell,
In all thy age of journals[7] thou hast took,   75
    Saw'st thou that pair became these rites so well
      Save the preceding two?
        Who, in all they do,
      Search, sun, and thou wilt find
They are th'exampled pair[8] and mirror of their kind.   80

Force from the phoenix,[9] then, no rarity
    Of sex, to rob the creature; but from man,
The king of creatures, take his parity
    With angels, Muse, to speak these; nothing can
      Illustrate these but they   85
        Themselves today,
      Who the whole act express;
All else we see beside are shadows, and go less.[1]

It is their grace and favor that makes seen
    And wondered at the bounties of this day;   90
All is a story of the King and Queen,
    And what of dignity and honor may
      Be duly done to those
        Whom they have chose,
      And set the mark upon   95
To give a greater name and title to: their own.

Weston, their treasure, as their Treasurer,
    That mine of wisdom and of counsels deep,
Great say-master[2] of state, who cannot err,
    But doth his carract[3] and just standard keep   100

---

6. Nobility, great ones.
7. Daily rounds (from Latin *diurnalis*).
8. I.e., the pair held up as an example.
9. According to legend, the phoenix, after an existence of 500 years, was consumed in its own flames, after which it miraculously emerged youthfully alive to renew its cycle of existence. Jonson, however, refers to the phoenix here primarily as an (ultimately Platonic) ideal of human perfection (cf. *The Forest*, XI, p. 35, l. 92 and note), which is inappropriate, because insufficient, as a figure to describe this occasion.
1. I.e., are worth less.
2. Assay master (in his capacity as Lord High Treasurer of the realm).
3. Carat; i.e., worth. Jonson perhaps employs the term to allow also the sense, "character."

In all the proved assays
   And legal ways
   Of trials to work down[4]
Men's loves unto the laws, and laws to love the Crown.

And this well moved the judgment of the King   105
   To pay with honors, to his noble son,
Today, the father's service; who could bring
   Him up to do the same himself had done.
     That far-all-seeing eye
      Could soon espy   110
     What kind of waking man
He had so highly set, and in what barbican.[5]

Stand there; for when a noble nature's raised,
   It brings friends joy, foes grief, posterity fame;
In him the times, no less than Prince, are praised,   115
   And by his rise, in active men his name
     Doth emulation stir;
      To the dull, a spur
     It is; to th'envious meant,[6]
A mere upbraiding grief and torturing punishment.   120

See, now the chapel opens, where the King
   And Bishop[7] stay to consummate the rites;
The holy prelate prays, then takes the ring,
   Asks first, "Who gives her? I, Charles."[8] Then he plights
     One in the other's hand,   125
      Whilst they both stand
     Hearing their charge, and then
The solemn choir cries, "Joy!" and they return, "Amen."

O happy bands! And thou more happy place
   Which to this use were built and consecrate!   130
To have thy God to bless, thy King to grace,
   And this their chosen Bishop celebrate
     And knit the nuptial knot,
      Which time shall not,
     Or cankered jealousy   135
With all corroding arts, be able to untie!

The chapel empties; and thou may'st begone
   Now, sun, and post away the rest of day;

---

4. I.e., bring into proper relationship.
5. Watchtower.
6. I.e., interpreted by the envious as.
7. The presiding bishop on this occasion was William Laud, at this date Bishop of London, who became Archbishop of Canterbury.
8. Charles I gave the bride away since her father was deceased.

These two, now holy church hath made them one,
  Do long to make themselves so, another way;   140
    There is a feast behind[9]
     To them of kind,
    Which their glad parents taught
One to the other, long ere these to light were brought.

Haste, haste, officious sun, and send them night   145
  Some hours before it should, that these may know
All that their fathers and their mothers might
  Of nuptial sweets, at such a season, owe,
    To propagate their names,
     And keep their fames   150
    Alive, which else would die,
For fame keeps virtue up, and it posterity.

Th'ignoble never lived; they were a while,
  Like swine or other cattle, here on earth;
Their names are not recorded on the file   155
  Of life, that fall[1] so. Christians know their birth
    Alone; and such a race
     We pray may grace
    Your fruitful spreading vine,
But dare not ask our wish in language fescennine.[2]   160

Yet as we may, we will,[3] with chaste desires
  (The holy perfumes of the marriage-bed)
Be kept alive those sweet and sacred fires
  Of love between you and your lovelihead,
    That, when you both are old,   165
     You find no cold
    There, but, renewéd, say,
After the last child born, "This is our wedding day."

Till you behold a race to fill your hall,
  A Richard[4] and a Jerome, by their names   170
Upon a Thomas or a Francis call;
  A Kate, a Frank to honor their grand-dames,
    And 'tween their grandsire's thighs,
     Like pretty spies,
    Peep forth a gem,[5] to see   175
How each one plays his part of the large pedigree.

---

9. I.e., still to come.
1. Perish.
2. Obscene, licentious. Marriage ceremonies in ancient Rome included bawdy songs, which were thought to avert evil (cf. Catullus, *Odes*, lxi).

3. I.e., we desire that.
4. The names given here include those of the bride and groom, and several of their relatives. Jerome and Frances had one son, whom they named Charles.
5. I.e. (probably), each like a gem.

And never may there want one of the stem[6]
    To be a watchful servant for this state,
But, like an arm of eminence 'mongst them,
    Extend a reaching virtue, early and late,   180
        Whilst the main tree still found
          Upright and sound,
      By this sun's noon stead's[7] made
So great: his body now alone projects the shade.

They both are slipped to bed. Shut fast the door   185
    And let him freely gather love's first-fruits;
He's master of the office, yet no more
    Exacts than she is pleased to pay; no suits,
        Strifes, murmurs or delay
          Will last till day;   190
      Night, and the sheets, will show
The longing couple all that elder lovers know.[8]

From MR. WILLIAM SHAKESPEARE'S COMEDIES, HISTORIES, AND TRAGEDIES (1623)

To the Memory of My Beloved, The Author,
Mr. William Shakespeare, and What He Hath Left Us[9]

To draw no envy (Shakespeare) on thy name,
    Am I thus ample[1] to thy book, and fame;
While I confess thy writings to be such,
    As neither man nor Muse can praise too much.
'Tis true, and all men's suffrage.[2] But these ways   5
    Were not the paths I meant unto thy praise:
For seeliest[3] ignorance on these may light,
    Which, when it sounds at best, but echoes right;
Or blind affection, which doth ne'er advance
    The truth, but gropes, and urgeth all by chance;   10

---

6. I.e., the family stock or line.
7. I.e., place is.
8. By art or hap the last phrase echoes Marlowe, "Hero and Leander," ll. 69.
9. While there is little reason to doubt that this famous tribute to Shakespeare's genius and art, published in the "First Folio" edition of Shakespeare's plays, represents (in language appropriate to the occasion) Jonson's honest opinion of his fellow dramatist's achievement, the lines should be read in conjunction with those comments on Shakespeare that appear elsewhere in Jonson's work; cf. *Timber*, 647–668 (on p. 404 of this edition), and also the brusque remark, recorded by Drummond, that "Shakespeare wanted art" (on p. 418 of this edition).
1. Copious (i.e., in this relatively lengthy poem).
2. I.e., all men acknowledge it.
3. Simplest.

Or crafty malice might pretend this praise,
    And think to ruin where it seemed to raise.
These are as[4] some infamous bawd or whore
    Should praise a matron. What could hurt her more?
But thou art proof against them, and indeed   15
    Above th'ill fortune of them, or the need.
I, therefore, will begin. Soul of the age!
    The applause, delight, the wonder of our stage!
My Shakespeare, rise; I will not lodge thee by
    Chaucer, or Spenser, or bid Beaumont[5] lie   20
A little further, to make thee a room:
    Thou art a monument without a tomb,
And art alive still, while thy book doth live,
    And we have wits to read, and praise to give.
That I not mix thee so, my brain excuses;   25
    I mean with great, but disproportioned[6] muses:
For if I thought my judgment were of years,[7]
    I should commit thee surely with thy peers,
And tell how far thou didst our Lyly outshine,
    Or sporting Kyd, or Marlowe's mighty line.[8]   30
And though thou hadst small Latin and less Greek,[9]
    From thence to honor thee, I would not seek
For names, but call forth thund'ring Aeschylus,
    Euripides, and Sophocles to us,
Pacuvius, Accius, him of Cordova dead,[1]   35
    To life again, to hear thy buskin[2] tread
And shake a stage; or, when thy socks were on,
    Leave thee alone for the comparison

4. I.e., as if.
5. These three poets are buried in Westminster Abbey; Shakespeare's remains lie in Holy Trinity Church, Stratford-on-Avon. The fancy rejected by Jonson (i.e., that the other three should make room for Shakespeare) is that with which William Basse (d. 1653) began his "Elegy on Shakespeare," printed in the 1633 edition of the poems of John Donne.
6. I.e., not comparable.
7. I.e., a judgment in the context of extended periods of time (whereas in fact Shakespeare "was not of an age, but for all time," l. 43).
8. John Lyly (c. 1554–1606), author of the prose romance *Euphues*, was the prime exponent of Elizabethan "high comedy" (e.g., *Endymion*); Thomas Kyd (c. 1557–c. 1595) wrote *The Spanish Tragedy*. Christopher Marlowe (1564–1593) was universally admired for the quality of his dramatic blank verse, in *Tamburlaine* and later works.

9. This observation should be read in the context of Jonson's own considerable attainments in classical languages and literatures; Shakespeare's learning was by no means inconsiderable. Cf. V. Whitaker, *Shakespeare's Use of Learning: An Inquiry into the Growth of His Mind and Art* (San Marino, Calif., 1953), esp. pp. 14–44.
1. Aeschylus (525–456 B.C.), Sophocles (495–406 B.C.), and Euripides (480–406 B.C.), the masters of Greek tragedy, are grouped with three Roman tragic authors, Pacuvius (c. 220–130 B.C.), Accius (170–c. 90 B.C.), and Lucius Annaeus Seneca, born in Córdoba, Spain (c. 3 B.C.–A.D. 65).
2. The buskin was the high shoe traditionally worn by actors in Greek tragedy; "socks" (l. 37) refers to its counterpart in comedy. The terms in this context represent Shakespeare's tragedies and comedies.

Of all that insolent Greece or haughty Rome
    Sent forth, or since did from their ashes come.   40
Triumph, my Britain, thou hast one to show
    To whom all scenes of Europe homage owe.
He was not of an age, but for all time!
    And all the Muses still were in their prime
When like Apollo he came forth to warm   45
    Our ears, or like a Mercury to charm!
Nature herself was proud of his designs,
    And joyed to wear the dressing of his lines,
Which were so richly spun and woven so fit,
    As, since, she will vouchsafe no other wit;   50
The merry Greek, tart Aristophanes,
    Neat Terence, witty Plautus,[3] now not please,
But antiquated and deserted lie,
    As they were not of nature's family.
Yet must I not give nature all; thy art,   55
    My gentle Shakespeare, must enjoy a part;
For though the poet's matter nature be,
    His art doth give the fashion. And that he[4]
Who casts[5] to write a living line, must sweat
    (Such as thine are), and strike the second heat   60
Upon the Muses' anvil, turn the same
    (And himself with it) that he thinks to frame;
Or for the laurel he may gain a scorn,
    For a good poet's made, as well as born.
And such wert thou. Look how the father's face   65
    Lives in his issue; even so, the race
Of Shakespeare's mind and manners brightly shines
    In his well-turnéd and true-filéd lines,
In each of which he seems to shake a lance,[6]
    As brandished at the eyes of ignorance.   70
Sweet swan of Avon! what a sight it were
    To see thee in our waters yet appear,
And make those flights upon the banks of Thames,
    That so did take Eliza and our James!
But stay, I see thee in the hemisphere   75
    Advanced, and made a constellation[7] there!
Shine forth, thou star of poets, and with rage
    Or influence, chide or cheer the drooping stage;

3. Aristophanes (c. 444–c. 380 B.C.), Publius Terentius Afer, called Terence (195–159 B.C.), and Titus Maccius Plautus (c. 254–184 B.C.) were the most renowned comic writers of classical times.
4. I.e., that man.
5. Undertakes.
6. The pun on Shakespeare's name looks back to another in line 37. Robert Greene, in *Greene's Groatsworth of Wit Bought With A Million of Repentance* (1592), had maliciously attacked Shakespeare for counting himself, "in his own conceit, the only Shake-scene in a county."
7. I.e., Cygnus, the swan.

Which, since thy flight from hence, hath mourned like
    night,
And despairs day, but for thy volume's light.   80

From *BEN JONSON'S EXECRATION AGAINST VULCAN* (1640)

Ode to Himself[8]

Come leave the loathéd stage,
   And the more loathsome age,
Where pride and impudence in faction knit
    Usurp the chair of wit,
Indicting and arraigning, every day,   5
    Something they call a play.
  Let their fastidious, vain
  Commission of the brain
Run on, and rage, sweat, censure, and condemn:
They were not made for thee, less thou for them.   10

   Say that thou pour'st 'em wheat,
   And they would acorns eat;
'Twere simple[9] fury, still thyself to waste
    On such as have no taste;
To offer them a surfeit of pure bread,   15
    Whose appetites are dead;
  No, give them grains[1] their fill,
  Husks, draff[2] to drink, and swill;
If they love lees, and leave the lusty wine,
Envy them not, their palate's with the swine.   20

   No doubt a moldy tale,
   Like *Pericles*,[3] and stale
As the shrive's crusts,[4] and nasty as his fish,
    Scraps out of every dish
Thrown forth, and raked into the common tub,[5]   25
    May keep up the Play Club.[6]

---

8. Outraged by the failure of *The New Inn,* in 1629, Jonson appended this poem, as an epilogue, to the published version of that play (1631). Cf. Carew's response, on p. 172 of this edition.
9. Foolish.
1. I.e., refuse malt left after brewing (commonly thrown to hogs).
2. Dregs.

3. Acts III, IV, and V of the romance *Pericles* were substantially Shakespeare's work; but the play's verse and movement are notably uneven.
4. I.e., the stale bread served in prisons (under a sheriff's authority).
5. I.e., leavings collected for the poor.
6. Jonson apparently alludes to a group of critics and "wits" whom he scorned.

Broome's[7] sweepings do as well
    There as his master's meal;
For who the relish of these guests will fit
Needs set them but the alms-basket of wit.   30

    And much good do't ye then,
        Brave plush and velvet men
Can feed on orts,[8] and safe in your scene clothes,[9]
        Dare quit upon your oaths
The stagers, and the stage-wrights too (your peers)   35
        Of stuffing your large ears
    With rage of comic socks,[1]
    Wrought upon twenty blocks;[2]
Which, if they're torn, and foul, and patched enough,
The gamesters share your guilt,[3] and you their stuff.   40

    Leave things so prostitute,
        And take th'Alcaic lute;[4]
Or thine own Horace, or Anacreon's lyre;
        Warm thee by Pindar's fire;
And though thy nerves[5] be shrunk, and blood be cold,   45
        Ere years have made thee old,
    Strike that disdainful heat
    Throughout, to their defeat;
As curious fools, and envious of thy strain,
May, blushing, swear no palsy's in thy brain.[6]   50

    But when they hear thee sing
        The glories of thy King,
His zeal to God, and his just awe of[7] men,
        They may be blood-shaken, then
Feel such a flesh-quake to possess their powers,   55
        That no tuned harp like ours,
    In sound of peace or wars,
    Shall truly hit the stars
When they shall read the acts of Charles his reign,
And see his chariot triumph 'bove his wain.[8]   60

---

7. Richard Brome (died c. 1652), formerly Jonson's servant, attained some modest success as a playwright, notably with the comedy *The Joviall Crew* (1641).
8. Table scraps.
9. I.e., probably, clothes worn to attend plays.
1. Cf. "To Shakespeare," p. 86, ll. 36–37 and note.
2. I.e., blockheads (with a pun on "molds").
3. I.e. (punningly), your "gilt" (gold) as well as guilt.
4. Alcaeus (fl. c. 611 B.C.) was a Greek lyric poet whose meter was imitated by Horace (65–8 B.C.); for Anacreon, cf. Epigram CI, p. 12, l. 30 and note; for Pindar, cf. the second note to Jonson's poem "To the Immortal Memory . . . of Cary and . . . Morison," p. 76.
5. Sinews (from Latin *nervus*).
6. Jonson had suffered a paralytic stroke in 1628.
7. I.e., over.
8. Wagon; i.e., above the constellation Charles's Wain (with a pun on "wane"). Cf. Textual Notes, p. 375.

SONGS FROM THE PLAYS AND MASQUES

From *The Works* (1616)

"Slow, slow, fresh fount"[9]

Slow, slow, fresh fount, keep time with my salt tears;
Yet slower, yet, O faintly, gentle springs!
List to the heavy part the music bears,
    Woe weeps out her division,[1] when she sings.
        Droop herbs and flowers;   5
        Fall grief in showers;
        Our beauties are not ours;
          O, I could still,
Like melting snow upon some craggy hill,
    Drop, drop, drop, drop,   10
Since nature's pride is, now, a withered daffodil.

"Queen and huntress, chaste and fair"[2]

Queen and huntress, chaste and fair,
Now the sun is laid to sleep,
Seated in thy silver chair,
State in wonted manner keep;
    Hesperus entreats thy light,   5
    Goddess, excellently bright.

Earth, let not thy envious shade
Dare itself to interpose;
Cynthia's shining orb was made
Heaven to clear, when day did close;   10
    Bless us then with wishéd sight,
    Goddess, excellently bright.

Lay thy bow of pearl apart,
And thy crystal-shining quiver;
Give unto the flying hart   15
Space to breathe, how short soever;
    Thou that mak'st a day of night,
    Goddess, excellently bright.

9. This song appears in *Cynthia's Revels* (1600), I. ii, where it is sung by Echo. For a metrical analysis, cf. *The Critical Reader*, eds. R. Lamson *et al.*, 2nd ed. (New York, 1962), pp. 754–756.
1. I.e., divides a succession of long (slow) notes into several short (quick) ones.
2. In *Cynthia's Revels*, V. vi, Hesperus (the evening star) sings this song to Cynthia (i.e., Diana), goddess of chastity and the moon. Since Queen Elizabeth was regularly identified with Cynthia by the poets of her day, the lyric delicately contributes to Jonson's larger dramatic purpose of "invoking [the queen's] immaculate virtue against the serried follies of her court" (*H & S*, I, p. 405).

"If I freely may discover"[3]

If I freely may discover[4]
What would please me in my lover:
  I would have her fair, and witty,
  Savoring more of court than city;
  A little proud, but full of pity;   5
  Light and humorous in her toying,
  Oft building hopes, and soon destroying;
  Long, but sweet, in the enjoying;
Neither too easy nor too hard,
All extremes I would have barred.   10

She should be allowed her passions,
So they were but used as fashions;
  Sometimes froward, and then frowning,
  Sometimes sickish, and then swowning,
  Every fit with change still crowning.   15
  Purely jealous I would have her;
  Then only constant when I crave her,
  'Tis a virtue should not save her.
Thus, nor her delicates[5] would cloy me,
Neither her peevishness annoy me.   20

"Swell me a bowl with lusty wine"[6]

Swell me a bowl with lusty wine,
Till I may see the plump Lyaeus[7] swim
  Above the brim;
I drink as I would write,
In flowing measure, filled with flame and sprite.   5

"Still to be neat, still to be dressed"[8]

Still to be neat, still to be dressed,
As you were going to a feast;
Still to be powdered, still perfumed;
Lady, it is to be presumed,
  Though art's hid causes are not found,   5
All is not sweet, all is not sound.

---

3. The first stanza of this song (from *The Poetaster* [1601], II. ii, is assigned to Crispinus; the second to Hermogenes.
4. Reveal.
5. I.e., her sensuously pleasing parts.
6. This lyric is sung by Horace, Jonson's spokesman in *Poetaster*, III. i.
7. I.e., Bacchus; the term means "deliverer from care."

8. Sung by Clerimont's page in *Epicoene, or The Silent Woman* (1609) I. i, the lyric derives from an anonymous Latin poem in the *Anthologia Latina* (sixteenth century A.D.). For a contrasting treatment of the central motif, cf. Herrick's "Delight in Disorder," on p. 109 of this edition.

Give me a look, give me a face,
That makes simplicity a grace;
Robes loosely flowing, hair as free;
Such sweet neglect more taketh me   10
        Than all th'adulteries of art.
They strike mine eyes, but not my heart.

From *The New Inn* (1631)

"It was a beauty that I saw"[9]

It was a beauty that I saw,
So pure, so perfect, as the frame
Of all the universe was lame
To that one figure, could I draw,
Or give least line of it a law.   5

A skein of silk without a knot;
A fair march made without a halt;
A curious[1] form without a fault;
A printed book without a blot:
All beauty, and without a spot!   10

From *The Works* (1640–1641)

"The faery beam upon you"[2]

The faery beam upon you,
The stars to glister on you;
   A moon of light
   In the noon of night,
Till the fire-drake hath o'ergone you![3]   5

The wheel of fortune guide you,
The boy with the bow beside you;
   Run aye[4] in the way
   Till the bird of day,
And the luckier lot betide you!   10

9. This lyric is assigned to Lovel, "a soldier and a scholar," in IV. iv.
1. I.e., intricately wrought.
2. Jonson's masque, *The Gypsies Metamorphosed,* includes many lyrics in various meters; this is perhaps the most delicately conceived.
3. I.e., until the fire-breathing dragon has passed you by.
4. Ever.

"Here she was wont to go,[5] *and here! and here!"*

Here she was wont to go, and here! and here!
Just where those daisies, pinks, and violets grow;
The world may find the spring by following her,
For other print her airy steps ne'er left;
Her treading would not bend a blade of grass,   5
Or shake the downy blow-ball from his stalk!
But like the soft west wind she shot along,
And where she went the flowers took thickest root,
As she had sowed 'em with her odorous foot.

"Though I am young, and cannot tell"[6]

Though I am young, and cannot tell
   Either what Death or Love is well,
Yet I have heard they both bear darts,
   And both do aim at human hearts;
And then again, I have been told   5
   Love wounds with heat, as Death with cold;
So that I fear they do but bring
   Extremes to touch, and mean one thing.

As in a ruin, we it call
   One thing to be blown up, or fall;   10
Or to our end, like way may have
   By a flash of lightning, or a wave;
So Love's inflaméd shaft, or hand;
   May kill as soon as Death's cold hand;
Except Love's fires the virtue have   15
   To fright the frost out of the grave.

5. These lines open *The Sad Shepherd, or A Tale of Robin Hood,* a dramatic fragment found among Jonson's papers after his death, and presumably the work of his last years; the speaker is Aeglamour, the "sad shepherd" of the title, in whom (according to the Prologue) there is "as much of sadness shown as passion can." It is perhaps not altogether fanciful to associate the aging Jonson with this figure, "dark and discontent," who yearns for youth and joy once his, now lost.
6. This lyric makes part of *The Sad Shepherd,* I. v.

Richard Corbett

1582	Born in Ewell, Surrey. Educated at Westminster School in London.
1598	Enters Broadgates Hall, in Oxford University.
1599	Transfers to Christ Church, Oxford.
1605	Proceeds M.A. At this time, according to Anthony á Wood, the historian of academic Oxford, "esteemed one of the most celebrated wits in the University."
1609	First English poems of substance.
1613	Preaching the Passion sermon at Christ Church, aligns himself with the Arminian (anti-Puritan) party at Oxford, led by William Laud, later Archbishop of Canterbury. From this year, associated with the circle of scholars, lawyers, and poets (including Ben Jonson) that gathered regularly at the Mermaid Tavern in London.
1616	Recommended, by virtue of his Arminian sympathies, for membership in King James I's projected college of theological controversy at Chelsea.
1619	Ben Jonson, following his return from Scotland, resides for a time with Corbett in Oxford, "writing and composing plays."
1619–1620	Undertakes a journey through the Midlands, in company with Leonard Hutten, Canon of Christ Church, and two other clerics; subsequently records the expepedition in his poem, *Iter Boreale*.
1620	Appointed Dean of Christ Church, through the influence of the royal favorite George Villiers, Earl of Buckingham.
1623–1624	Marries Alice Hutten, daughter of his companion on the Midlands journey. A daughter, Alice, was born in 1625; a son, Vincent in 1627.
1628	Installed as Bishop of Oxford.
1632	Appointed Bishop of Norwich.
1635	Death, July 28. Buried in Norwich Cathedral.
1647	Publication of *Certain Elegant Poems*, edited by John Donne, son of the poet.
1648	Publication of *Poetica Stromata*.

From CERTAIN ELEGANT POEMS (1647)

*A Proper New Ballad, Intituled the Fairies' Farewell, or
God-a-Mercy Will: to be sung or whistled, to the tune of*
The Meadow Brow *by the learned, by the unlearned to
the tune of* Fortune.[1]

Farewell, rewards and fairies,
    Good housewives now may say,
For now foul sluts in dairies
    Do fare as well as they;
And though they sweep their hearths no less   5
    Than maids were wont to do,
Yet who of late for cleanliness
    Finds sixpence in her shoe?

Lament, lament, old abbeys,[2]
    The fairies lost command;   10
They did but change priests' babies,
    But some have changed your land;
And all your children sprung from thence
    Are now grown Puritans,
Who live as changelings ever since,   15
    For love of your demesnes.[3]

At morning and at evening both
    You merry were and glad,
So little care of sleep or sloth
    These pretty ladies had;   20
When Tom came home from labor,
    Or Ciss to milking rose,
Then merrily went their tabor,[4]
    And nimbly went their toes.

1. In his own time, Corbett's best-known poem was *Iter Boreale* ("A Northern Journey"), some 500 lines in pentameter couplets, describing a journey through the English Midlands which Corbett and three Oxford companions undertook in the long vacation of (probably) 1619. But it is "The Fairies' Farewell" for which Corbett is chiefly remembered today; not inappropriately, given Aubrey's portrait of this convivial churchman. For comments on "The Meadow Brow" and "Fortune," cf. *The Poems of Richard Corbett*, eds. J. A. W. Bennett and H. R. Trevor-Roper (Oxford, 1955), p. 129. The tune of "The Meadow Brow" may be found in W. E. Chappell, *The Ballad Literature and Popular Music of the Olden Time*, 2 vols. (New York, 1965), I, p. 182.
2. Thomas Hobbes, toward the end of *Leviathan*, remarks on the association of the fairy world and the Roman Catholic Church, but in a tone sharply contrasting with that of Corbett's poem: an extended list of parallels is capped by the observation that "as the fairies have no existence, but in the fancies of ignorant people, rising from the traditions of old wives, or old poets; so the spiritual power of the Pope, without the bounds of his own civil dominion, consisteth only in the fear that seduced people stand in, of their excommunications, upon hearing of false miracles, false traditions, and false interpretations of the Scripture" (*Leviathan*, ed. M. Oakeshott [New York, 1962], pp. 501–502.
3. Domains, estates.
4. Small drum.

Witness those rings and roundelays[5]   25
     Of theirs, which yet remain,
Were footed in Queen Mary's days[6]
     On many a grassy plain;
But since of late Elizabeth,
     And later James, came in,   30
They never danced on any heath
     As when the time hath been.

By which we note the fairies
     Were of the old profession;
Their songs were Ave Maries,   35
     Their dances were procession;
But now, alas, they all are dead,
     Or gone beyond the seas,
Or further from religion fled,
     Or else they take their ease.   40

A tell-tale in their company
     They never could endure,
And whoso kept not secretly
     Their mirth was punished sure;
It was a just and Christian deed   45
     To pinch such black and blue;
O, how the commonwealth doth need
     Such justices as you!

Now they have left our quarters,
     A register[7] they have,   50
Who can preserve their charters,
     A man both wise and grave;
A hundred of their merry pranks
     By one that I could name
Are kept in store; con[8] twenty thanks   55
     To William[9] for the same.

I marvel who his cloak would turn
     When Puck had led him round,
Or where those walking fires[1] would burn
     Where Cureton[2] would be found;   60

---

5. I.e., fairy circles or rings, for dancing.
6. I.e., in the reign of Mary Tudor (1553–1558), when the established religion was that of Rome.
7. Recorder.
8. Offer.
9. Wililam Chourne was the servant of Dr. Leonard Hutten (Corbett's future father-in-law), one of the party that made the journey described in *Iter Boreale*.

When the group lost its way in Charnwood Forest, "William found/A means for our deliverance: 'Turn your cloaks,'/Quoth he, 'for Puck is busy in these oaks' " (*Iter Boreale*, ll. 306–308).
1. I.e., will-o'-the-wisps.
2. Cureton and Broker, presumably, were "Staffordshire worthies whose spirits Chourne could conjure up" (*Poems of Richard Corbett, ed. cit.,* p. 130).

How Broker would appear to be,
    For whom this age doth mourn;
But that their spirits live in thee,
    In thee, old William Chourne.

To William Chourne of Staffordshire   65
    Give laud and praises due,
Who every meal can mend your cheer
    With tales both old and true;
To William all give audience,
    And pray ye for his noddle,   70
For all the fairies' evidence
    Were lost, if that were addle.[3]

An Elegy Upon the Death of His Own Father[4]

Vincent Corbett, farther known
By Poynter's name than by his own,
Here lies engagéd till the day
Of raising bones and quickening clay.
Nor wonder, reader, that he hath   5
Two surnames in his epitaph,
For this one did comprehend[5]
All that two families could lend;
And if to know more arts than any
Could multiply one into many,   10
Here a colony lies, then,
Both of qualities and men.
Years he lived well-nigh fourscore,
But count his virtues, he lived more;
And number him by doing good,   15
He lived the age before the flood.
Should we undertake his story,
Truth would seem feigned, and plainness glory.
Beside, this tablet were too small:
Add too the pillars and the wall.   20
Yet of this volume much is found
Written in many a fertile ground,
Where the printer thee affords
Earth for paper, trees for words.
He was nature's factor[6] here,   25
And liedger lay[7] for every shire,
To supply the ingenious[8] wants
Of soon-sprung fruits and foreign plants.

3. I.e., if his head were addled or confused.
4. Cf. Jonson's "An Epitaph on Master
Vincent Corbett," on p. 58 of this edition. Why Vincent Corbett assumed the
surname "Poynter" is not known.
5. I.e., for this one man encompassed.
6. Agent.
7. I.e., acted as an agent.
8. Sensible.

Simple he was, and wise withal;
His purse nor base nor prodigal;   30
Poorer in substance than in friends,
Future and public were his ends;
His conscience, like his diet, such
As neither took nor left too much,
So that made laws were useless grown   35
To him; he needed but his own.
Did he his neighbors bid, like those
That feast them only to enclose,[9]
Or with their roast meat rack[1] their rents,
And cozen[2] them with their consents?   40
No; the free meetings at his board
Did but one literal sense afford;
No close or acre understood,[3]
But only love and neighborhood.
His alms were such as Paul defines,[4]   45
Not causes to be saved, but signs;
Which alms, by faith, hope, love laid down,
Laid up, what now he wears, a crown.
Besides his fame, his goods, his life,
He left a grieved son and a wife;   50
Strange sorrow, not to be believed,
When the son and heir is grieved.
   Read then, and mourn, whate'er thou art
   That dost hope to have a part
   In honest epitaphs, lest, being dead,   55
   Thy life be written, and not read.

To His Son, Vincent Corbett[5]

What I shall leave thee none can tell,
But all shall say I wish thee well:
I wish thee, Vin, before all wealth,
Both bodily and ghostly[6] health;
Nor too much wealth, nor wit, come to thee,   5
Too much of either may undo thee.
I wish thee learning, not for show,
But truly to instruct and know;
Not such as gentlemen require
To prate at table or at fire.   10

---

9. I.e., to fence in or "enclose" their
neighbors' arable land for the pasturage
of sheep.
1. Raise unreasonably.
2. Cheat.
3. Cf. n. 9 above.
4. Cf. I Corinthians 13:3: "And though
I bestow all my goods to feed the poor,
and though I give my body to be burned,
and have not charity, it profiteth me
nothing."
5. Born in 1627, Corbett's son (by Aubrey's account) grew to be "a very
handsome youth; but he is run out of
all, and goes begging up and down to
gentlemen" (*Brief Lives, ed. cit.*, p. 288).
6. Spiritual.

I wish thee all thy mother's graces,
Thy father's fortunes, and his places.
I wish thee friends, and one at court,
Not to build up but to support,
To keep thee, not in doing many   15
Oppressions, but from suffering any.
I wish thee peace in all thy ways,
Nor lazy nor contentious days;
And, when thy soul and body part,
As innocent as now thou art.   20

From *POETICA STROMATA* (1648)

Upon Fairford Windows[7]

Tell me, you anti-saints,[8] why glass
With you is longer lived than brass?
And why the saints have 'scaped their falls
Better from windows than from walls?
Is it because the brethren's fires   5
Maintain a glass-house at Blackfriars,[9]
Next which the church stands north and south,
And east and west the preachers mouth?
Or is't because such painted ware
Resembles something what you are,   10
So pied,[1] so seeming, so unsound
In manners, and in doctrine, found,
That, out of emblematic wit,
You spare yourselves in sparing it?
If it be so, then, Fairford, boast   15
Thy church hath kept what all have lost,
And is preservéd from the bane
Of either war[2] or Puritan,
Whose life is colored in thy paint:
The inside dross, the outside saint.   20

---

7. The church of Saint Mary the Virgin in Fairford, Gloucestershire, contains twenty-eight stained glass windows, depicting Biblical scenes, which were created between 1495 and 1505. Saint Mary's is the only English parish church to have retained its complete set of such medieval windows; other churches suffered in at least some degree from the excesses of Puritan zeal in the civil war. Since Corbett died in 1635, however, he is perhaps speaking of civil disorders in a sense not narrowly limited to sectarian intransigence.

8. The expression reflects Corbett's opinion of those Puritan zealots who described themselves as "saints," i.e., among the elect. Elaborately designed memorial tablets of brass, set in the floors or walls of churches, were regularly defaced by the Puritans.

9. Jonson also alludes to the glass factory near Blackfriars Church, a center of Puritan activity; cf. "An Execration Upon Vulcan," p. 72, l. 180.

1. I.e., diversely colored.

2. I.e. (perhaps), any violent civil unrest.

The Distracted Puritan

Am I mad, oh noble Festus,[3]
When zeal and godly knowledge
Have put me in hope
To deal with the Pope,
As well as the best in the College?[4]   5
    Boldly I preach, hate a cross, hate a surplice,
        Miters, copes, and rochets;[5]
    Come, hear me pray nine times a day,
        And fill your heads with crotchets.

In the house of pure Emmanuel   10
I had my education,
Where my friends surmise
I dazzled mine eyes
With the light of revelation.
    Boldly I preach, &c.

They bound me like a bedlam,[6]   15
They lashed my four poor quarters;
Whilst this I endure,
Faith makes me sure
To be one of Foxe's martyrs.[7]
    Boldly I preach, &c.

These injuries I suffer   20
Through Anti-Christ's invasions;
Take off this chain,
Neither Rome nor Spain
Can resist my strong persuasions.
    Boldly I preach, &c.

Of the beast's ten horns[8] (God bless us)   25
I have knocked off three already.
If they let me alone,
I'll leave him none;

---

3. Cf. Acts 26:25–26: "Festus said . . . Paul, thou art beside thyself; much learning doth make thee mad. But he said, I am not mad, most noble Festus; but speak forth the words of truth and soberness."
4. I.e., Emmanuel College, known in Corbett's day as the most puritanically inclined of the colleges in Cambridge University.
5. Vestments (worn by Anglican bishops).
6. Lunatic (so called from the name of the London hospital for the insane, Saint Mary of Bethlehem).
7. John Foxe (1516–1587) was the author of *Actes and Monuments of these latter perilous times touching matters of the Church*, popularly known as "the Book of Martyrs"; first published (in Latin) at Strasbourg in 1559, the volume was printed in English in 1563. Foxe places special emphasis on the sufferings of Protestant martyrs during the reign of Mary Tudor.
8. Cf. Revelation 13:1: "And I . . . saw a beast rise up out of the sea, having seven heads and ten horns, and upon his horns ten crowns, and upon his heads the name of blasphemy." Puritan preachers commonly associated this beast with the Church of Rome, and with the Catholic nations of Europe.

But they say I am too heady.
    Boldly I preach, &c.

When I sacked the seven-hilled city,   30
I met the great red dragon;[9]
I kept him aloof
With the armor of proof,
Though here I have never a rag on.
    Boldly I preach, &c.

With a fiery sword and target,   35
There fought I with this monster;
But the sons of pride
My zeal deride,
And all my deeds misconster.
    Boldly I preach, &c.

I unhorsed the whore of Babel   40
With a lance of inspirations;
I made her stink,
And spill her drink
In the cup of abominations.[1]
    Boldly I preach, &c.

I have seen two in a vision,   45
With a flying book between them;[2]
I have been in despair
Five times a year,
And cured by reading Greenham.[3]
    Boldly I preach, &c.

I observed in Perkins' tables[4]   50
The black lines of damnation;
Those crooked veins
So stuck in my brains
That I feared my reprobation.
    Boldly I preach, &c.

In the holy tongue of Canaan[5]   55
I placed my chiefest pleasure;
Till I pricked my foot

9. Cf. Revelation 12:3: "And there appeared . . . a great red dragon, having seven heads and ten horns, and seven crowns upon his heads"; also Ephesians 6:11: "Put on the whole armour of God, that ye may be able to stand against the wiles of the devil."
1. Cf. Revelation 17:3–5.
2. Cf. Zechariah 5:1: "Then I turned, and lifted up mine eyes, and looked, and behold a flying roll."
3. The *Works* of Richard Greenham (c.

1535–c. 1574), Puritan divine and Fellow of Pembroke College, Cambridge, first published in 1599, had appeared in five editions by 1612.
4. William Perkins (1558–1602), Fellow of Christ's College, Cambridge, was the most highly regarded teacher and theologian among the Puritan divines of his day. "The black lines of damnation" refer to Perkins's chart of the causes of damnation in *A Golden Chain* (1600).
5. I.e., in Hebrew.

With an Hebrew root,
That I bled beyond all measure.
   Boldly I preach, &c.

I appeared before the Archbishop   60
And all the High Commission;[6]
I gave him no grace,
But told him to's face
That he favored superstition.
   Boldly I preach, hate a cross, hate a surplice,   65
      Miters, copes, and rochets;
  Come, hear me pray nine times a day,
    And fill your heads with crotchets.

From *POEMS, BY J[OHN] D[ONNE]* (1633)

An Epitaph on Doctor Donne, Dean of Paul's[7]

He that would write an epitaph for thee,
And do it well, must first begin to be
Such as thou wert; for none can truly know
Thy worth, thy life, but he that hath lived so.
He must have wit to spare, and to hurl down;   5
Enough to keep the gallants of the town.
He must have learning plenty; both the laws,
Civil and common, to judge any cause;
Divinity, great store above the rest,
Not of the last[8] edition, but the best.   10
He must have language, travel, all the arts,
Judgment to use, or else he wants thy parts.
He must have friends the highest, able to do,
Such as Maecenas,[9] and Augustus too.
He must have such a sickness, such a death,   15
Or else his vain descriptions come beneath.
Who then shall write an epitaph for thee,
He must be dead first! Let it alone, for me.

---

6. The Court of High Commission was an ecclesiastical tribunal with broad powers, often exercised somewhat arbitrarily.
7. A number of Corbett's Oxford contemporaries belonged to a group of "wits" (including Donne and, on occasion, Jonson) who gathered monthly, during 1612, at the Mermaid Tavern in London; Corbett may have come to know Donne in this connection. Cf. I. Shapiro, "The 'Mermaid Club,'" *MLR*, XLV (1950), 6 ff. Donne died on March 31, 1631; Corbett's poem was written during his tenure as Bishop of Oxford, i.e., before April, 1632.
8. Latest; i.e. (probably), Puritan departures from Anglican doctrine and ceremony.
9. Maecenas, who died in 8 B.C., was the patron of Vergil and Horace; the Roman emperor Augustus (63 B.C.–A.D. 14) commissioned Vergil's *Aeneid*.

Robert Herrick

1591	Born in London, the fourth son of Nicholas Herrick, a well-to-do London goldsmith.
1592	Nicholas Herrick dies, after a fall from the fourth floor of his house in Goldsmith's Row; although suicide is suspected, his estate goes to his wife Julian and her children, in accordance with the terms of the will. Details of Robert Herrick's early education are unknown.
1607	Apprenticed, for the customary term of ten years, to his uncle, the eminently successful goldsmith Sir William Herrick, who had been knighted in 1605.
1613	Enters Saint John's College, Cambridge, as a fellow commoner (i.e., a relatively affluent student).
1615–1616	Transfers to Trinity Hall; graduates B.A. in 1617.
1620	Takes the degree of M.A. Consorting, in the early 1620's, with Ben Jonson and the group meeting regularly at the Devil Tavern in London.
1623	Ordained deacon, April 24; and (exceptionally) ordained priest on the day following, by the Bishop of Peterborough. Presumably residing in London, perhaps employed as a nobleman's chaplain, for some three or four years.
1625	Richard James, in a poem, "The Muses' Dirge," on the death of James I, links Herrick's name to those of (the established poets) Jonson and Drayton.
1627	As chaplain to the Duke of Buckingham, takes part in the unsuccessful military expedition led by that lord against the Île de Ré.
1629	Appointed Vicar of Dean Prior in Devonshire; installed on October 29, 1630.
1633–1634	First published poems: "Upon His Kinswoman Mistress Elizabeth Herrick," in John Stow's *Survey of London* (1633) and an early version of "Oberon's Feast," in A *Description of the King and Queene of Fayries* . . . (1634).
1640	Probably in London; an entry in the Stationers' Register alludes to a forthcoming volume of "Poems written by Master Robert Herrick" (not known to have been published).

1647	Expelled, as a royalist sympathizer, from his vicarage at Dean Prior; returns to London.
1648	Publication of *Hesperides*. Apparently resident in and about Westminster, until the Restoration.
1660	Returns to his Devonshire parish.
1674	Death; buried on October 15, presumably in the churchyard at Dean Prior (no stone marks his grave).

From *HESPERIDES*[1] (1648)

The Argument[2] *of His Book*

I sing of brooks, of blossoms, birds, and bowers;
Of April, May, of June, and July flowers.
I sing of Maypoles, hock-carts,[3] wassails,[4] wakes,
Of bridegrooms, brides, and of their bridal cakes.
I write of youth, of love, and have access   5
By these to sing of cleanly wantonness.
I sing of dews, of rains, and piece by piece
Of balm, of oil, of spice, and ambergris.[5]
I sing of times trans-shifting,[6] and I write
How roses first came red, and lilies white.[7]   10
I write of groves, of twilights, and I sing
The court of Mab, and of the fairy king.[8]

1. The Hesperides, daughters of Night (or, by another tradition, of Atlas and Hesperis), guarded an orchard in the west, "across the fabulous stream of the Ocean," in which was planted a tree with golden apples, originally presented by Earth to Hera (Juno) at her marriage to Zeus: cf. Hesiod, *Theogony*, 215–216; Diodorus Siculus, IV. xxvii. 2. Herrick's title indicates that his poems also are golden apples from a western garden, i.e., Devonshire, where many of these verses were made.
2. Theme, subject matter. Herrick's art was, for the most part, undervalued or dismissed until the early years of the nineteenth century; Edward Phillips, for instance, observed in 1675, "That which is chiefly pleasant in these poems is now and then a pretty flowery and pastoral gale of fancy, a vernal prospect of some hill, cave, rock, or fountain; which but for the interruption of other trivial passages might have made up none of the worst poetic landscapes" ("The Modern Poets," in *Theatrum Poetarum*, p. 162). In fact, as this first poem indicates, Herrick is concerned not merely with the charm and (often rude) vitality of nature, or with the sensuous thrust of human desire, but (and more deeply) with the causes and origins of things, the reality behind appearances: cf. the essay by Ronald Berman on p. 529 of this edition. The forms and modes of classical verse are evidently congenial to Herrick, in some ways the closest to Jonson of all the "Sons of Ben"; as a churchman, he regularly draws into his verse the ceremonies of the Christian year; at the same time, he is fascinated by the timeless realm of myth and legend reflected in the folklore of the English countryside. The arrangement of the 1,100-odd poems in *Hesperides*, finally, appears in some degree to reflect Herrick's conscious design: cf. J. L. Kimmey, "Order and Form in Herrick's *Hesperides*," *JEGP*, LXX (1971), 255–268.
3. I.e., wagons bringing in the last load of the harvest. Cf. "The Hock-Cart," p. 123.
4. I.e., the drinking of healths on festive occasions.
5. A waxy substance used in perfumes.
6. I.e., (1) the transience of history; (2) the interrelated aspects and attributes of time.
7. Cf. the poems on pp. 115 and 125 of this edition.
8. Oberon and Mab are king and queen of the fairies.

I write of hell; I sing (and ever shall)
Of heaven, and hope to have it after all.

When He Would Have His Verses Read

In sober mornings, do not thou rehearse[9]
The holy incantation of a verse;
But when that men have both well drunk and fed,
Let my enchantments then be sung, or read.
When laurel spirts i' th' fire, and when the hearth   5
Smiles to itself, and gilds the roof with mirth;
When up the thyrse[1] is raised, and when the sound
Of sacred orgies[2] flies—a round, a round![3]
When the rose reigns,[4] and locks with ointments shine,
Let rigid Cato[5] read these lines of mine.   10

To Perilla

Ah my Perilla! dost thou grieve to see
Me, day by day, to steal away from thee?
Age calls me hence, and my gray hairs bid come,
And haste away to mine eternal home;
'Twill not be long, Perilla, after this,   5
That I must give thee the supremest kiss;
Dead when I am, first cast in salt, and bring
Part of the cream from that religious spring,[6]
With which, Perilla, wash my hands and feet;
That done, then wind me in that very sheet   10
Which wrapped thy smooth limbs, when thou didst implore
The gods' protection but the night before.
Follow me weeping to my turf, and there
Let fall a primrose, and with it a tear;
Then lastly, let some weekly strewings[7] be   15
Devoted to the memory of me;
Then shall my ghost not walk about, but keep
Still in the cool and silent shades of sleep.

9. Repeat, recite.
1. "A javelin twined with ivy" (Herrick's note); i.e., a symbol of Bacchus, god of revelry and wine.
2. "Songs to Bacchus" (Herrick's note).
3. Rounds are songs for three or more singers, in which the voices enter in succession with the same music and words, sing through the entire song, and return to the first phrase.
4. On Herrick's employment of flower imagery in the context of pagan ceremonies, cf. K. Wentersdorf, "Herrick's Floral Imagery," *SN*, XXXVI (1964), 69–81.
5. Cato the Censor (234–149 B.C.) was an especially severe Roman administrator.
6. I.e., your eyes, from which salt tears flow. The sprinkling of salt is, ultimately, an echo of Roman ritual; in his poetry, Herrick regularly draws together elements from classical and Christian ceremony: cf. R. H. Deming, "Robert Herrick's Classical Ceremony," *ELH*, XXXIV (1967), 327–348.
7. I.e., strewings of flowers on my grave.

The Wounded Heart[8]

Come bring your sampler,[9] and with art
    Draw in't a wounded heart,
      And dropping[1] here and there;
Not that I think that any dart
    Can make yours bleed a tear,   5
      Or pierce it anywhere;
Yet do it to this end: that I
          May by
      This secret see,
        Though you can make   10
That heart to bleed, yours ne'er will ache
          For me.

No Loathsomeness in Love[2]

What I fancy, I approve,
No dislike there is in love:
Be my mistress short or tall,
And distorted therewithal;
Be she likewise one of those   5
That an acre hath of nose;
Be her forehead and her eyes
Full of incongruities;
Be her cheeks so shallow, too
As to show her tongue wag through;   10
Be her lips ill hung, or set,
And her grinders[3] black as jet;
Has she thin hair, hath she none,
She's to me a paragon.

Upon the Loss of His Mistresses[4]

I have lost, and lately, these
Many dainty mistresses:
Stately Julia, prime of all;
Sappho next, a principal;
Smooth Anthea, for a skin   5
White, and heaven-like crystalline;
Sweet Electra, and the choice

---

8. The poem is "shaped" to represent its title and informing idea.
9. I.e., a piece of cloth used for embroidery.
1. I.e., dripping (blood).
2. The poem in ironic praise of an ugly woman is something of a convention in the period; "The Deformed Mistress," by Sir John Suckling, and "Upon A Very Deformed Gentlewoman," by Thomas Randolph, illustrate the genre, which Donne's "The Autumnal" may be said to transcend.
3. Teeth.
4. It is generally accepted that Herrick's Julia, Anthea, Electra, Dianeme, etc. are imaginative creations (which is not to deny the poet's intensely experienced responsiveness to the various charms of women).

Myrrha, for the lute, and voice;
Next, Corinna, for her wit,
And the graceful use of it;   10
With Perilla: all are gone;
Only Herrick's left alone,
For to number sorrow by
Their departures hence, and die.

The Vine

I dreamed this mortal part of mine
Was metamorphosed to a vine,
Which crawling one and every way
Enthralled my dainty Lucia.
Methought her long small legs and thighs   5
I with my tendrils did surprise;
Her belly, buttocks, and her waist
By my soft nervelets[5] were embraced;
About her head I writhing hung,
And with rich clusters, hid among   10
The leaves, her temples I behung,
So that my Lucia seemed to me
Young Bacchus ravished by his tree.[6]
My curls about her neck did crawl,
And arms and hands they did enthrall,   15
So that she could not freely stir,
All parts there made one prisoner.
But when I crept with leaves to hide
Those parts which maids keep unespied,
Such fleeting pleasures there I took   20
That with the fancy I awoke,
And found (ah me!) this flesh of mine
More like a stock[7] than like a vine.

Discontents in Devon

More discontents I never had
    Since I was born, than here;
Where I have been, and still am sad,
    In this dull Devonshire;
Yet justly too I must confess,   5
    I ne'er invented such
Ennobled numbers[8] for the press
    Than where I loathed so much.

5. Tendrils.
6. I.e., by the grapevine.
7. "Hardened stalk or stem of a plant" (*OED*).
8. Verses. *His Noble Numbers,* Herrick's collected religious verse, was published in 1648 (together with *Hesperides*), the year following the poet's expulsion from his vicarage in Dean Prior, Devonshire.

Cherry-Ripe

"Cherry-ripe, ripe, ripe," I cry,
"Full and fair ones; come and buy."[9]
If so be you ask me where
They do grow, I answer, "There,
Where my Julia's lips do smile;   5
There's the land, or cherry-isle,
Whose plantations fully show
All the year where cherries grow."

His Request to Julia

Julia, if I chance to die
Ere I print my poetry,
I most humbly thee desire
To commit it to the fire;
Better 'twere my book were dead   5
Than to live not perfected.

Dreams

Here we are all, by day; by night, we're hurled
By dreams, each one, into a sev'ral[1] world.

To the King,
Upon His Coming with His Army into the West[2]

Welcome, most welcome to our vows and us,
Most great and universal Genius![3]
The drooping west, which hitherto has stood
As one in long-lamented widowhood,
Looks like a bride now, or a bed of flowers,   5
Newly refreshed both by the sun and showers.
War, which before was horrid,[4] now appears
Lovely in you, brave prince of cavaliers!
A deal[5] of courage in each bosom springs
By your access, O you the best of kings!   10
Ride on with all white[6] omens, so that where
Your standard's up, we fix a conquest there.

---

9. The street vendors of London cried their wares in such terms as these.
1. I.e., separate and distinctly individual. Plutarch reports the view of Heraclitus that "men while awake are in one common world; but asleep, each man has a world to himself" (*De Superstitione*, iii).
2. Charles I came to Exeter in the summer of 1644, before marching on into Cornwall.
3. Cf. Jonson, *The Forest*, XIV, p. 42, l. 20 and note. Herrick identifies Charles I as the guardian spirit of all England.
4. I.e., hideous to behold.
5. I.e., a great amount.
6. I.e., auspicious. Cf. Jonson, Epigram XCVI, p. 11, l. 8 and note.

Delight in Disorder[7]

A sweet disorder in the dress
Kindles in clothes a wantonness:[8]
A lawn[9] about the shoulders thrown
Into a fine distraction;[1]
An erring lace, which here and there   5
Enthralls the crimson stomacher;[2]
A cuff neglectful, and thereby
Ribbons to flow confusedly;
A winning wave (deserving note)
In the tempestuous petticoat;   10
A careless shoestring, in whose tie
I see a wild civility:
Do more bewitch me than when art
Is too precise in every part.

Dean-bourn, a Rude River in Devon, By Which Sometimes He Lived

Dean-bourn, farewell; I never look to see
Dean, or thy warty incivility.
Thy rocky bottom, that doth tear thy streams,
And makes them frantic, ev'n to all extremes,
To my content I never should behold,   5
Were thy streams silver, or thy rocks all gold.
Rocky thou art, and rocky we discover
Thy men, and rocky are thy walls all over.
O men, O manners;[3] now and ever known
To be a rocky generation![4]   10
A people currish, churlish as the seas,
And rude, almost, as rudest savages,
With whom I did, and may re-sojourn, when
Rocks turn to rivers, rivers turn to men.

---

7. Cf. Jonson's "Still to be neat," on p. 91 of this edition; also Herrick's "Art Above Nature: To Julia," on p. 135. In his description of the setting for *The Masque of Blackness,* Jonson observes that the effects imitated "that disorderly order, which is common in nature" (*H & S,* VII, p. 170). "E.K." also, in the Dedicatory Epistle prefixed to Spenser's *Shepheardes Calender,* notes that the combination of delicate and "rude" effects in painting causes the viewer to "take pleasure in that disorderly order." The terms employed by Herrick, however, indicate that he may be concerned as much with sensory excitement as with aesthetic pleasure.
8. I.e., an unfettered gaiety (with the secondary sense of "unruliness").
9. I.e., a scarf of fine linen.
1. Confusion.
2. I.e., an ornamental item of dress worn under the lacings of the bodice.
3. The expression echoes Cicero's phrase, *O tempora, O mores,* in the *First Oration Against Catiline.*
4. Cf. Jeremiah 5:31: "they have made their faces harder than a rock"; also Robert Burton's description of "those ordinary boors and peasants" as "a rude, brutish, uncivil, wild, a currish generation" (*Anatomy of Melancholy,* ed. H. Jackson, 3 vols. [London, 1964], II, p. 343). Echoes of Burton's work (published in 1621) often sound in *Hesperides.*

The Definition of Beauty

Beauty no other thing is than a beam
Flashed out between the middle and extreme.

To Anthea Lying in Bed[5]

So looks Anthea, when in bed she lies
O'ercome or half betrayed by tiffanies,[6]
Like to a twilight, or that simp'ring dawn
That roses show when misted o'er with lawn.[7]
Twilight is yet, till that her lawns give way;   5
Which done, that dawn turns then to perfect day.

Upon Scobble. Epigram[8]

Scobble for whoredom whips his wife, and cries
He'll slit her nose. But, blubb'ring, she replies,
"Good sir, make no more cuts i'th'outward skin;
One slit's enough to let adult'ry in."

The Hourglass[9]

That hourglass which there ye see
With water filled (sirs, credit me),
The humor[1] was, as I have read,
But lovers' tears encrystalléd,
Which, as they drop by drop do pass   5
From th'upper to the under-glass,
Do in a trickling manner tell,
By many a wat'ry syllable,
That lovers' tears in lifetime shed
Do restless run when they are dead.   10

His Farewell to Sack

Farewell thou thing, time-past so known, so dear
To me, as blood to life and spirit;[2] near,

---

5. Cf. "Upon Electra," on p. 132 of this edition, for a contrasting view of the relative power of beauty clothed and unclothed. "Delight In Disorder," "Julia's Petticoat," "Upon Julia's Clothes," and, more at large, "The Lily in a Crystal" also bear on this theme.
6. I.e., by fine silks or muslins.
7. I.e., with fine linen.
8. The harsh realism of these lines (not to mention their compressed precision) recalls Jonson's Epigram LXXXIII (p. 10). Herrick seems deliberately to have interspersed such coarse epigrammatic reflections on individual members of his country parish with the delicately charming fancies more often singled out as typical of his art.
9. Cf. Jonson, "The Hourglass," on p. 57 of this edition.
1. Moisture.
2. I.e., as blood is to "vital spirit" (a substance, thought to be formed in the heart, which brings natural heat to every part of the body) and to "animal spirit" (a more refined substance, formed in the brain, which flows through the nerves).

Nay, thou more near than kindred, friend, man, wife,
Male to the female, soul to body, life
To quick action, or the warm soft side   5
Of the resigning, yet resisting bride.
The kiss of virgins, first-fruits of the bed,
Soft speech, smooth touch, the lips, the maidenhead:
These, and a thousand sweets, could never be
So near, or dear, as thou wast once to me.   10
O thou the drink of gods, and angels! Wine
That scatter'st spirit and lust,[3] whose purest shine
More radiant than the summer's sunbeams shows;
Each way illustrious, brave;[4] and like to those
Comets we see by night, whose shagged[5] portents   15
Foretell the coming of some dire events;
Or some full flame, which with a pride aspires,[6]
Throwing about his wild and active fires.
'Tis thou, above nectar, O divinest soul!
Eternal in thyself, that canst control   20
That which subverts whole nature, grief and care,
Vexation of the mind, and damned despair.
'Tis thou alone who, with thy mystic fan,[7]
Work'st more than wisdom, art, or nature can
To rouse the sacred madness, and awake   25
The frost-bound blood and spirits; and to make
Them frantic with thy raptures, flashing through
The soul like lightning, and as active too.
'Tis not Apollo can, or those thrice three
Castalian sisters,[8] sing, if wanting thee.   30
Horace, Anacreon,[9] both had lost their fame,
Hadst thou not filled them with thy fire and flame.
Phoebean splendor! and thou Thespian spring![1]
Of which sweet swans[2] must drink before they sing
Their true-paced numbers and their holy lays,   35
Which makes them worthy cedar,[3] and the bays.
But why, why longer do I gaze upon
Thee with the eye of admiration?
Since I must leave thee, and enforced, must say
To all thy witching beauties, "Go, away."   40
But if thy whimp'ring looks do ask me why,
Then know that nature bids thee go, not I.
'Tis her erroneous self has made a brain
Uncapable of such a sovereign

3. I.e., that distributes animal spirit and vital spirit throughout the body.
4. Magnificent.
5. Hairy (-tailed).
6. I.e., which rises in splendor.
7. I.e., the thyrsus of Bacchus (figured here as a winnowing fan for grain).
8. I.e., the Muses, who frequented the Castalian spring, sacred to Phoebus Apollo, god of poetry and song.
9. Cf. Jonson, Epigrams XCI, CI, pp. 10 and 12 and notes.
1. Cf. Jonson, Epigram CI, p. 13, 1. 33 and note.
2. I.e., poets.
3. Oil of cedar was used to preserve ancient manuscripts.

As is thy powerful self. Prithee not smile;   45
Or smile more inly, lest thy looks beguile
My vows denounced[4] in zeal, which thus much show thee,
That I have sworn but by thy looks to know thee.
Let others drink thee freely, and desire
Thee and their lips espoused; while I admire   50
And love thee, but not taste thee. Let my Muse
Fail of thy former helps, and only use
Her inadult'rate[5] strength: what's done by me
Hereafter shall smell of the lamp, not thee.

To Dianeme

Sweet, be not proud of those two eyes
Which, star-like, sparkle in their skies;
Nor be you proud that you can see
All hearts your captives, yours yet free;
Be you not proud of that rich hair   5
Which wantons with the love-sick air;
Whenas that ruby which you wear,
Sunk from the tip of your soft ear,
Will last to be a precious stone,
When all your world of beauty's gone.   10

To a Gentlewoman, Objecting to Him His Gray Hairs

Am I despised because you say,
And I dare swear, that I am gray?
Know, lady, you have but your day,
And time will come when you shall wear
Such frost and snow upon your hair;   5
And when, though long it comes to pass,
You question with your looking-glass,
And in that sincere crystal seek
But find no rosebud in your cheek,
Nor any bed to give the shew   10
Where such a rare carnation grew.
Ah! then too late, close in your chamber keeping,
      It will be told
      That you are old
By those true tears y'are weeping.   15

Julia's Petticoat

Thy azure robe I did behold,
As airy as the leaves of gold,[6]

---

4. Proclaimed.
5. Pure, not debased.

6. I.e. (probably), the decorative golden leaves on Julia's blue gown.

Which erring here, and wand'ring there,
Pleased with transgression ev'rywhere.
Sometimes 'twould pant, and sigh, and heave,   5
As if to stir it scarce had leave;
But having got it, thereupon
'Twould make a brave expansion,
And pounced[7] with stars, it showed to me
Like a celestial canopy.   10
Sometimes 'twould blaze, and then abate,
Like to a flame grown moderate;
Sometimes away 'twould wildly fling,
Then to thy thighs so closely cling
That some conceit[8] did melt me down,   15
As lovers fall into a swoon,
And all confused I there did lie
Drowned in delights, but could not die.
That leading cloud[9] I followed still,
Hoping t'have seen of it my fill,   20
But ah! I could not; should it move
To life eternal, I could love.

Corinna's Going A-Maying[1]

Get up, get up for shame; the blooming morn
Upon her wings presents the god unshorn.[2]
　　See how Aurora[3] throws her fair
　　Fresh-quilted colors through the air:
　　Get up, sweet slug-a-bed, and see   5
　　The dew bespangling herb and tree.
Each flower has wept, and bowed toward the east,
Above an hour since; yet you not dressed,
　　Nay! not so much as out of bed?
　　When all the birds have matins said,   10
　　And sung their thankful hymns, 'tis sin,
　　Nay, profanation to keep in,
Whenas a thousand virgins on this day
Spring, sooner than the lark, to fetch in May.[4]

Rise, and put on your foliage, and be seen   15
To come forth, like the springtime, fresh and green,
　　And sweet as Flora.[5] Take no care

---

7. Powdered.
8. Fancy.
9. Cf. Exodus 13:21: "And the Lord went before them by day in a pillar of a cloud to lead them the way."
1. A useful analysis of this famous poem on the *carpe diem* theme is that by Cleanth Brooks, " 'Corinna's Going A-Maying'," in *The Well-Wrought Urn* (New York, 1947), ch. IV.

2. I.e., Phoebus Apollo, god of the sun (whose long hair conventionally figures the sun's rays, as well as youthful vitality).
3. Goddess of the dawn.
4. I.e., to gather the white hawthorn flowers (and so to celebrate the coming of full spring).
5. Roman goddess of flowers and spring.

For jewels for your gown or hair:
Fear not; the leaves will strew
Gems in abundance upon you;   20
Besides, the childhood of the day has kept,
Against[6] you come, some orient[7] pearls unwept;
    Come, and receive them while the light
    Hangs on the dew-locks of the night,
    And Titan[8] on the eastern hill   25
    Retires himself, or else stands still
Till you come forth. Wash, dress, be brief in praying:
Few beads[9] are best when once we go a-Maying.

Come, my Corinna, come; and coming, mark
How each field turns a street, each street a park   30
    Made green, and trimmed with trees; see how
    Devotion gives each house a bough
    Or branch; each porch, each door, ere this,
    An ark, a tabernacle is,[1]
Made up of white-thorn neatly interwove,   35
As if here were those cooler shades of love.
    Can such delights be in the street
    And open fields, and we not see't?
    Come, we'll abroad; and let's obey
    The proclamation made for May,[2]   40
And sin no more, as we have done, by staying;
But my Corinna, come, let's go a-Maying.

There's not a budding boy or girl this day
But is got up, and gone to bring in May.
    A deal[3] of youth, ere this, is come   45
    Back, and with white-thorn laden home.
    Some have dispatched their cakes and cream,
    Before that we have left to dream;
And some have wept, and wooed, and plighted troth,
And chose their priest, ere we can cast off sloth.   50
    Many a green-gown[4] has been given;
    Many a kiss, both odd and even;
    Many a glance too has been sent
    From out the eye, love's firmament;
Many a jest told of the keys betraying   55
This night, and locks picked, yet we're not a-Maying.

---

6. Until.
7. Lustrous (also, "eastern").
8. I.e., the sun.
9. I.e., prayers (with an allusion to the beads of a rosary).
1. I.e., each porch and door is thus transformed and made holy. For the Hebraic "Ark of the Covenant" and "Tabernacle," cf. Exodus 37, 40. Herrick combines the religious ceremonies of Holy Scripture with those of a religion of nature.
2. I.e., a proclamation authorizing May-day festivities.
3. I.e., a great number.
4. I.e., a dress stained with green, from rolling in the grass.

Come, let us go, while we are in our prime,
And take the harmless folly of the time.
    We shall grow old apace, and die
    Before we know our liberty.   60
    Our life is short; and our days run
    As fast away as does the sun;
And as a vapor, or a drop of rain
Once lost, can ne'er be found again,
    So when or you or I are made   65
    A fable, song, or fleeting shade,
    All love, all liking, all delight
    Lies drowned with us in endless night.
Then while time serves, and we are but decaying,
Come, my Corinna, come, let's go a-Maying.[5]   70

How Lilies Came White

    White though ye be, yet, lilies, know
    From the first ye were not so;
        But I'll tell ye
        What befell ye:
    Cupid and his mother lay   5
    In a cloud, while both did play;
    He with his pretty finger pressed
    The ruby niplet of her breast,
    Out of the which, the cream of light,
        Like to a dew,   10
        Fell down on you,
        And made ye white.

The Lily in a Crystal

You have beheld a smiling rose
    When virgins' hands have drawn
    O'er it a cobweb-lawn;
And here, you see, this lily shows,
    Tombed in a crystal stone,   5
More fair in this transparent case
    Than when it grew alone,
    And had but single grace.

You see how cream but naked is,
    Nor dances in the eye   10
    Without a strawberry,

5. Classical expressions of the theme informing Herrick's poem include Catullus, *Odes*, v, and Ovid, *Fasti*, VI, 771. In Holy Scripture, it is the ungodly who cling to the thought of *carpe diem*: cf. Proverbs 7:18, and (in the Apocrypha) the Wisdom of Solomon, 2:1–8.

Or some fine tincture, like to this,
    Which draws the sight thereto,
More by that wantoning with it
    Than when the paler hue   15
    No mixture did admit.

You see how amber through the streams
    More gently strokes the sight
    With some concealed delight
Than when he darts his radiant beams   20
    Into the boundless air,
Where either too much light his worth
    Doth all at once impair,
    Or set it little forth.

Put purple grapes or cherries in-   25
    To glass, and they will send
    More beauty to commend
Them, from that clean and subtle skin,
    Than if they naked stood,
And had no other pride at all   30
    But their own flesh and blood,
    And tinctures natural.

Thus lily, rose, grape, cherry, cream
    And strawberry do stir
    More love, when they transfer   35
A weak, a soft, a broken beam,
    Than if they should discover[6]
At full their proper excellence,
    Without some scene[7] cast over
    To juggle with the sense.   40

Thus let this crystalled lily be
    A rule, how far to teach
    Your nakedness must reach;
And that no farther than we see
    Those glaring colors laid   45
By art's wise hand, but to this end
    They should obey a shade,
    Lest they too far extend.

So though y'are white as swan, or snow,
    And have the power to move   50
    A world of men to love;
Yet, when your lawns and silks shall flow,
    And that white cloud divide

6. Reveal.   7. Veil.

Into a doubtful twilight, then,
Then will your hidden pride[8]   55
Raise greater fires in men.

Upon Some Women

Thou who wilt not love, do this:
Learn of me what woman is.
Something made of thread and thrum,[9]
A mere botch of all and some.
Pieces, patches, ropes of hair;   5
Inlaid garbage ev'rywhere.
Outside silk and outside lawn;
Scenes[1] to cheat us, neatly drawn.
False in legs, and false in thighs,
False in breast, teeth, hair, and eyes,   10
False in head, and false enough;
Only true in shreds and stuff.

The Welcome to Sack

So soft streams meet, so springs with gladder smiles
Meet after long divorcement by the isles,
When love, the child of likeness, urgeth on
Their crystal natures to an union;
So meet stol'n kisses, when the moony nights   5
Call forth fierce lovers to their wished delights;
So kings and queens meet, when desire convinces[2]
All thoughts but such as aim at getting princes:
As I meet thee. Soul of my life and fame!
Eternal lamp of love! whose radiant flame   10
Outglares the heav'n's Osiris,[3] and thy gleams
Outshine the splendor of his mid-day beams.
Welcome, O welcome, my illustrious spouse;
Welcome as are the ends unto my vows;
Aye! far more welcome than the happy soil   15
The sea-scourged merchant,[4] after all his toil,
Salutes with tears of joy, when fires betray
The smoky chimneys of his Ithaca.
Where hast thou been so long from my embraces,
Poor pitied exile? Tell me, did thy graces   20
Fly discontented hence, and for a time
Did rather choose to bless another clime?
Or went'st thou to this end, the more to move me,
By thy short absence, to desire and love thee?

---

8. I.e., your hidden splendor.
9. I.e., bits and pieces of yarn.
1. Veils.
2. Conquers.

3. "The Sun" (Herrick's note). Cf.
Spenser, *The Faerie Queene*, V. vii. 4:
"Like as Osyris signifies the Sun."
4. I.e., Odysseus.

Why frowns my sweet? Why won't my saint confer   25
Favors on me, her fierce idolater?
Why are those looks, those looks the which have been
Time-past so fragrant, sickly now drawn in
Like a dull twilight? Tell me, and the fault
I'll expiate with[5] sulphur, hair, and salt;   30
And with the crystal humor of the spring[6]
Purge hence the guilt, and kill this quarreling.
Wo't thou not smile, or tell me what's amiss?
Have I been cold to hug thee, too remiss,
Too temp'rate in embracing? Tell me, has desire   35
To thee-ward died i'th'embers, and no fire
Left in this raked-up ash-heap, as a mark
To testify the glowing of a spark?
Have I divorced thee only to combine
In hot adult'ry with another wine?   40
True, I confess I left thee,[7] and appeal
'Twas done by me more to confirm my zeal
And double my affection on thee, as do those
Whose love grows more inflamed by being foes.
But to forsake thee ever, could there be   45
A thought of such like possibility?
When thou thyself dar'st say, thy isles shall lack
Grapes, before Herrick leaves Canary sack.
Thou mak'st me airy, active to be borne,
Like Iphiclus,[8] upon the tops of corn.   50
Thou mak'st me nimble, as the wingéd hours,[9]
To dance and caper on the heads of flowers,
And ride the sunbeams. Can there be a thing
Under the heavenly Isis[1] that can bring
More love unto my life, or can present   55
My genius with a fuller blandishment?
Illustrious idol! could th'Egyptians seek
Help from the garlic, onion, and the leek,[2]
And pay no vows to thee, who wast their best
God, and far more transcendent than the rest?   60
Had Cassius,[3] that weak water-drinker, known
Thee in thy vine, or had but tasted one
Small chalice of thy frantic liquor, he
As the wise Cato[4] had approved of thee.

5. I.e., with offerings of (echoing classical ceremonies).
6. I.e., with water.
7. Cf. "His Farewell to Sack," p. 110.
8. A celebrated runner, Iphiclus won the longer of two foot-races at the funeral games of Pelias; cf. Hyginus, *Fables*, cclxxviii.
9. I.e., the goddesses of the seasons; cf. Ovid, *Metamorphoses*, II. 26–30.
1. "The Moon" (Herrick's note).

2. Cf. Numbers 11:5: "We remember the fish, which we did eat in Egypt freely; the cucumbers, and the melons, and the leeks, and the onions, and the garlick."
3. Cassius, who conspired with Brutus to assassinate Caesar, drank only water.
4. Cato the Censor (cf. "When He Would Have His Verses Read," p. 105, n. 5) found time to write *De Agri Cultura*, which includes information on vineyards and wine making.

Had not Jove's son,[5] that brave Tyrinthian swain,   65
Invited to the Thespian banquet, ta'en
Full goblets of thy gen'rous blood, his sprite
Ne'er had kept heat for fifty maids that night.
Come, come and kiss me; love and lust commends
Thee and thy beauties; kiss, we will be friends   70
Too strong for fate to break us; look upon
Me with that full pride of complexion
As queens meet queens; or come thou unto me
As Cleopatra came to Antony,
When her high carriage did at once present   75
To the triumvir, love and wonderment.
Swell up my nerves with spirit; let my blood
Run through my veins like to a hasty flood.
Fill each part full of fire, active to do
What thy commanding soul shall put it to.   80
And till I turn apostate to thy love,
Which here I vow to serve, do not remove
Thy fires from me, but Apollo's curse
Blast these-like actions; or a thing that's worse,
When these circumstants[6] shall but live to see   85
The time that I prevaricate from thee,
Call me the son of beer, and then confine
Me to the tap, the toast, the turf;[7] let wine
Ne'er shine upon me; may my numbers all
Run to a sudden death and funeral.   90
And last, when thee, dear spouse, I disavow,
Ne'er may prophetic Daphne[8] crown my brow.

To Live Merrily, and to Trust to Good Verses[9]

Now is the time for mirth,
    Nor cheek or tongue be dumb;
For with the flow'ry earth
    The golden pomp is come.

The golden pomp is come;   5
    For now each tree does wear,
Made of her pap[1] and gum,
    Rich beads of amber here.

---

5. "Hercules" (Herrick's note) was brought up in Tiryns (in Argolis); he enjoyed the favors of King Thespius' fifty daughters in return for ridding that monarch's land of a ravaging lion. Cf. Apollodorus, *Library*, II. iv. 10.

6. Bystanders.

7. I.e., to beer, to beer-soaked bread, and to earth (as distinct from the "airy" element with which wine is associated in line 49).

8. Daphne, pursued by Apollo, was changed into a laurel tree, which Apollo adopted as his sacred tree. Cf. Ovid, *Metamorphoses*, I. 548–567. Poets' achievements were rewarded by laurel garlands.

9. Herrick's poem at several points (notably ll. 5, 10, 41–44) echoes the language of Ovid's *Amores* and *Heroides*; cf. *The Poetical Works of Robert Herrick*, ed. L. C. Martin (Oxford, 1956), p. 517.

1. Pulp.

Now reigns the rose,[2] and now
    Th'Arabian dew besmears   10
My uncontrolléd brow
    And my retorted[3] hairs.

Homer, this health to thee,
    In sack of such a kind
That it would make thee see   15
    Though thou wert ne'er so blind.

Next, Vergil I'll call forth,
    To pledge this second health
In wine, whose each cup's worth
    An Indian commonwealth.   20

A goblet next I'll drink
    To Ovid, and suppose,
Made he the pledge, he'd think
    The world had all one nose.[4]

Then this immensive cup   25
    Of aromatic wine,
Catullus, I quaff up
    To that terse Muse of thine.

Wild I am now with heat;
    O Bacchus! cool thy rays!   30
Or frantic I shall eat
    Thy thyrse,[5] and bite the bays.

Round, round the roof does run;
    And being ravished thus,
Come, I will drink a tun[6]   35
    To my Propertius.[7]

Now, to Tibullus, next,
    This flood I drink to thee;
But stay, I see a text[8]
    That this presents to me.   40

Behold, Tibullus lies
    Here burnt, whose small return
Of ashes scarce suffice
    To fill a little urn.

---

2. Cf. "When He Would Have His Verses Read," p. 105, n. 4.
3. I.e., bent backward.
4. Herrick puns on Ovid's full name, Publius Ovidius Naso ("nose").
5. Cf. "When He Would Have His Verses Read," p. 105, n. 1.

6. Large cask.
7. Propertius (born c. 51 B.C.) and Tibullus (c. 54–18 B.C.) were, with Catullus (87–c. 47 B.C.), the most celebrated of the Roman elegiac poets.
8. I.e., Ovid, *Amores*, III. ix. 39–40. translated in the next stanza.

Trust to good verses, then;   45
   They only will aspire,
   When pyramids, as men,
   Are lost i'th'funeral fire.

And when all bodies meet
   In Lethe to be drowned,   50
Then only numbers sweet
   With endless life are crowned.

To the Virgins, to Make Much of Time[9]

Gather ye rosebuds while ye may,
   Old time is still a-flying;
And this same flower that smiles today,
   Tomorrow will be dying.

The glorious lamp of heaven, the sun,   5
   The higher he's a-getting,
The sooner will his race be run,
   And nearer he's to setting.

That age is best which is the first,
   When youth and blood are warmer,   10
But being spent, the worse, and worst
   Times still succeed the former.

Then be not coy, but use your time,
   And while ye may, go marry;
For having lost but once your prime,   15
   You may for ever tarry.

His Poetry His Pillar

Only a little more
   I have to write,
   Then I'll give o'er,
And bid the world good-night.

'Tis but a flying minute   5
   That I must stay,
   Or linger in it;
And then I must away.

O Time that cut'st down all!
   And scarce leav'st here   10

9. Cf. "Corinna's Going A-Maying," p. 115, ll. 57–70 and note: also, for further examples of the *carpe diem* motif in clas- sical poetry, *The Complete Poetry of Robert Herrick*, ed. J. Max Patrick (New York, 1968), p. 118.

Memorial
Of any men that were.

How many lie forgot
  In vaults beneath,
    And piecemeal rot   15
Without a fame in death?

Behold this living stone
  I rear for me,
    Ne'er to be thrown
Down, envious Time, by thee.   20

Pillars let some set up,
  If so they please;
    Here is my hope
And my pyramides.

Lyric for Legacies

Gold I've none, for use or show,
Neither silver to bestow[1]
At my death; but thus much know,
That each lyric here shall be
Of my love a legacy,   5
Left to all posterity.
Gentle friends, then do but please
To accept such coins as these,
As my last remembrances.

To Music, to Becalm His Fever

Charm me asleep, and melt me so
  With thy delicious numbers,
That being ravished, hence I go
  Away in easy slumbers.
    Ease my sick head,   5
    And make my bed,
Thou power that canst sever
    From me this ill,
    And quickly still,
    Though thou not kill,   10
    My fever.

Thou sweetly canst convert the same
  From a consuming fire
Into a gentle-licking flame,
  And make it thus expire.   15

---

1. Cf. Acts 3:6: "Silver and gold have I none; but such as I have give I thee."

Then make me weep
My pains asleep,
And give me such reposes
That I, poor I,
May think thereby   20
I live and die
   'Mongst roses.

Fall on me like a silent dew,
  Or like those maiden showers
Which, by the peep of day, do strew   25
  A baptime[2] o'er the flowers.
   Melt, melt my pains
   With thy soft strains,
That having ease me given,
   With full delight   30
   I leave this light,
   And take my flight
    For heaven.

To the Rose. Song[3]

Go, happy rose, and interwove
With other flowers, bind my love.
  Tell her, too, she must not be
  Longer flowing, longer free,
  That so oft has fettered me.   5

Say (if she's fretful) I have bands
Of pearl and gold to bind her hands;
  Tell her, if she struggle still,
  I have myrtle rods at will,
  For to tame, though not to kill.   10

Take thou my blessing, thus, and go,
And tell her this; but do not so,
  Lest a handsome anger fly
  Like a lightning from her eye,
  And burn thee up, as well as I.   15

The Hock-Cart, or Harvest Home:
To the Right Honorable Mildmay, Earl of Westmorland[4]

Come, sons of summer, by whose toil
We are the lords of wine and oil;

---

2. Baptism.
3. The opening lines of this poem echo Martial, *Epigrams,* VII. lxxxix. Cf. also Waller's lyric, "Go, lovely rose!," on p. 246 of this edition.
4. The celebration of "harvest home" began with the return from the fields of the hock cart, bringing the last load of the harvest. Herrick's poem, based generally on Tibullus, *Odes,* II. i, bears some slight resemblance to Jonson's "To Penshurst" and "To Sir Robert Wroth," but scarcely reflects their generous spirit, as lines 1–2 indicate.

By whose tough labors and rough hands
We rip up first, then reap our lands;
Crowned with the ears of corn, now come,   5
And, to the pipe, sing harvest home.
Come forth, my lord, and see the cart
Dressed up with all the country art.
See here a maukin,[5] there a sheet,
As spotless pure as it is sweet;   10
The horses, mares, and frisking fillies,
Clad all in linen, white as lilies;
The harvest swains and wenches bound
For joy to see the hock-cart crowned.
About the cart, hear how the rout   15
Of rural younglings raise the shout;
Pressing before, some coming after,
Those with a shout, and these with laughter.
Some bless the cart; some kiss the sheaves;
Some prank them up with oaken leaves;   20
Some cross the fill-horse;[6] some with great
Devotion stroke the home-borne wheat;
While other rustics, less attent[7]
To prayers than to merriment,
Run after with their breeches rent.   25
Well, on, brave boys, to your lord's hearth,
Glitt'ring with fire; where, for your mirth,
Ye shall see first the large and chief
Foundation of your feast, fat beef,
With upper stories, mutton, veal,   30
And bacon, which makes full the meal;
With sev'ral dishes standing by,
As here a custard, there a pie,
And here all-tempting frumenty.[8]
And for to make the merry cheer,   35
If smirking wine be wanting here,
There's that which drowns all care, stout beer,
Which freely drink to your lord's health;
Then to the plow, the commonwealth,
Next to your flails, your fans, your fats;[9]
Then to the maids with wheaten hats;
To the rough sickle, and crook'd scythe,
Drink, frolic boys, till all be blithe.
Feed, and grow fat; and as ye eat,
Be mindful that the laboring neat,[1]   45
As you, may have their fill of meat.

---

5. I.e., a pole bound with cloth, used as a scarecrow.
6. I.e., some bless the horse that draws the cart.
7. Attentive.

8. I.e., pudding made of wheat, milk, and spices.
9. I.e., your winnowing fans, your vats (for storing grain).
1. Cattle.

And know, besides, ye must revoke[2]
The patient ox unto the yoke,
And all go back unto the plow
And harrow, though they're hanged up now.   50
And, you must know, your lord's word's true,
Feed him ye must, whose food fills you,
And that this pleasure is like rain,
Not sent ye for to drown your pain,
But for to make it spring again.   55

How Roses Came Red

Roses at first were white,
    Till they could not agree
Whether my Sappho's breast
    Or they more white should be.

But being vanquished quite,   5
    A blush their cheeks bespred;
Since which, believe the rest,
    The roses first came red.

How Violets Came Blue

Love on a day, wise poets tell,
    Some time in wrangling spent,
Whether the violets should excel,
    Or she, in sweetest scent.

But Venus having lost the day,   5
    Poor girls, she fell on you,
And beat ye so, as some dare say,
    Her blows did make ye blue.

A *Nuptial Song, or Epithalamie, on Sir Clipsby Crew and His Lady*[3]

What's that we see from far? the spring of day
Bloomed from the east, or fair enjewelled May
    Blown out of April, or some new
    Star filled with glory to our view,
        Reaching at heaven,   5
To add a nobler planet to the seven?
    Say, or do we not descry
Some goddess in a cloud of tiffany[4]
        To move, or rather the
    Emergent Venus from the sea?[5]   10

2. Call back (next year).
3. Sir Clipsby Crewe (1599–1649) married Jane Pulteney on July 7, 1625.
4. I.e., of fine silk or muslin.

5. Venus was said to have sprung from the sea foam; cf. Ovid, *Metamorphoses*, IV. 537.

'Tis she! 'Tis she! or else some more divine
Enlightened substance; mark how from the shrine
    Of holy saints she paces on,
    Treading upon vermilion
                And amber; spice-   15
ing the chafed[6] air with fumes of Paradise.
    Then come on, come on, and yield
A savor like unto a blesséd field,[7]
          When the bedabbled morn
    Washes the golden ears of corn.   20

See where she comes, and smell how all the street
Breathes vineyards and pomegranates: O how sweet!
    As a fired altar is each stone,
    Perspiring pounded cinnamon.
          The phoenix' nest,   25
Built up of odors, burneth in her breast.
    Who therein would not consume
His soul to ash-heaps in that rich perfume,
        Bestroking fate the while
    He burns to embers on the pile?   30

Hymen, O Hymen! Tread the sacred ground;[8]
Show thy white feet, and head with marjoram crowned;
    Mount up thy flames, and let thy torch[9]
    Display the bridegroom in the porch,
        In his desires   35
More tow'ring, more disparkling[1] than thy fires;
    Show her how his eyes do turn
And roll about, and in their motions burn
        Their balls to cinders; haste,
    Or else to ashes he will waste.   40

Glide by the banks of virgins, then, and pass
The showers of roses, lucky four-leaved grass,[2]
    The while the cloud of younglings sing,
    And drown ye with a flow'ry spring;
        While some repeat   45
Your praise, and bless you, sprinkling you with wheat;
    While that others do divine,[3]
Blest is the bride on whom the sun doth shine;
        And thousands gladly wish
    You multiply, as doth a fish.[4]   50

6. Warmed.
7. Cf. Genesis 27:27: "the smell of a field which the Lord hath blessed."
8. The practice of going barefoot on sacred ground, common in classical ceremonies, is also enjoined by Holy Scripture; cf. Exodus 3:5 and Acts 7:33.
9. Hymen, god of marriage, is typically represented as a youth bearing a torch.
1. I.e., higher and more widespread.
2. I.e., four-leaf clovers.
3. Prophesy.
4. Cf. Luke 9:13–17.

And beauteous bride, we do confess y'are wise
In dealing forth these bashful jealousies;
    In love's name do so, and a price
    Set on youself, by being nice;[5]
             But yet take heed,   55
What now you seem, be not the same indeed,
    And turn apostate; love will
Part of the way be met, or sit stone-still.
           On then, and though you slow-
ly go, yet, howsoever, go.   60

And now y'are entered; see, the coddled[6] cook
Runs from his torrid zone to pry and look,
    And bless his dainty mistress; see,
    The aged point out, "This is she
            Who now must sway   65
The house (love shield her) with her yea and nay":
    And the smirk[7] butler thinks it
Sin, in's napery, not to express his wit;
          Each striving to devise
Some gin[8] wherewith to catch your eyes.   70

To bed, to bed, kind turtles[9] now, and write
This the short'st day, and this the longest night,
    But yet too short for you; 'tis we
    Who count this night as long as three,
            Lying alone,   75
Telling the clock strike ten, eleven, twelve, one.
    Quickly, quickly then, prepare,
And let the young men and the bride-maids share
         Your garters, and their joints
Encircle with the bridegroom's points.[1]   80

By the bride's eyes, and by the teeming life
Of her green hopes, we charge ye that no strife,
    Farther than gentleness tends, gets place
    Among ye, striving for her lace;
           O do not fall   85
Foul in these noble pastimes, lest ye call
    Discord in, and so divide
The youthful bridegroom and the fragrant bride,
          Which love forfend; but spoken,
Be't to your praise, no peace was broken.   90

Strip her of springtime, tender-whimp'ring maids;
Now autumn's come, when all those flow'ry aids

---

5. I.e., modestly reserved.
6. Parboiled.
7. Spruce.
8. Snare.

9. I.e., turtledoves.
1. Tagged laces called "points" were used to fasten items of clothing.

Of her delays must end; dispose
That lady-smock, that pansy, and that rose
      Neatly apart;   95
But for prick-madam, and for gentle-heart,
  And soft maiden's-blush,[2] the bride
Makes holy these, all others lay aside;
      Then strip her, or unto her
  Let him come who dares undo her.   100

And to enchant ye more, see everywhere
About the roof a Siren[3] in a sphere,
    As we think, singing to the din[4]
  Of many a warbling Cherubim;
      O mark ye how   105
The soul of nature melts in numbers![5] Now
    See, a thouand Cupids fly
To light their tapers at the bride's bright eye.
      To bed, or her they'll tire,
  Were she an element of fire.   110

And to your more bewitching, see, the proud
Plump bed bear up, and, swelling like a cloud,
    Tempting the two too modest; can
  Ye see it brusle[6] like a swan,
      And you be cold   115
To meet it, when it woos and seems to fold
    The arms to hug it? Throw, throw
Yourselves into the mighty overflow
      Of that white pride, and drown
  The night with you in floods of down.   120

The bed is ready, and the maze of love
Looks for the treaders; everywhere is wove
    Wit and new mystery;[7] read,[8] and
  Put in practice, to understand
      And know each wile,   125

---

2. "Maiden's-blush" is a country name for a rose of a delicate pink shade; "lady-smock," "prick-madam," and "gentle-heart" are rustic names for various flowers and herbs of the English countryside.
3. I.e., an angelic being who sings sweetly. Cf. Plato, *Republic*, X. 617; and Milton's allusion to that passage in *Prolusion 2*: "Plato . . . has told us that certain sirens have their respective seats on every one of the heavenly spheres and hold both gods and men fast bound by the wonder of their utterly harmonious song" (John Milton, *Complete Poems and Major Prose*, ed. M. Y. Hughes [New York, 1957], p. 603). Cf. also Milton's poem "At a Solemn Music," 1–8.
4. I.e., the loud, resonant sound.
5. I.e., in harmonious measures.
6. Ruffle up (as feathers).
7. I.e. (primarily), craft or skill.
8. I.e., look with discernment.

Each hieroglyphic[9] of a kiss or smile,
    And do it to the full; reach
High in your own conceit,[1] and some way teach
        Nature and art one more
    Play than they ever knew before.   130

If needs we must for ceremony's sake
Bless a sack-posset,[2] luck go with it; take
    The night-charm quickly; you have spells
    And magics for to end, and hells
        To pass, but such   135
And of such torture as no one would grutch[3]
    To live therein forever; fry
And consume, and grow again to die
        And live, and in that case
    Love the confusion of the place.   140

But since it must be done, despatch, and sew
Up in a sheet your bride; and what if so
    It be with rock, or walls of brass
    Ye tower her up,[4] as Danae was,
        Think you that this   145
Or hell itself a powerful bulwark is?
    I tell ye no; but like a
Bold bolt of thunder he will make his way,
        And rend the cloud, and throw
    The sheet about like flakes of snow.   150

All now is hushed in silence; midwife-moon,
With all her owl-eyed issue, begs a boon
    Which you must grant, that's entrance; with
    Which extract all we can call pith
        And quintessence   155
Of planetary bodies. So commence,
    All fair constellations
Looking upon ye, that two nations[5]
        Springing from two such fires
    May blaze the virtue of their sires.   160

---

9. Sign (of meaning conveyed by kisses and smiles).
1. Fancy.
2. I.e., a mixture of spiced hot milk curdled by sack, traditionally offered to the bridegroom on his wedding night.
3. Resent.
4. I.e., confine in a fortified building. Danae's father thought to keep his daughter safe from the attentions of Zeus by so confining her; but the god visited Danae in a shower of gold. Cf. Apollodorus, *Library*, II. iv. 1.
5. Cf. Genesis 25:23: "The Lord said unto Rebekah, Two nations are in thy womb." The implicit promise of this scriptural allusion caps and confirms the poet's desire that the stars shed propitious influence on the wedded pair.

Oberon's Feast[6]

Shapcot,[7] *to thee the fairy state*
I with discretion dedicate,
Because thou prizest things that are
Curious and unfamiliar.
Take first the feast; these dishes gone,   5
We'll see the fairy court anon.

A little mushroom table spread,
After short prayers, they set on bread;
A moon-parched grain of purest wheat,
With some small glitt'ring grit,[8] to eat   10
His choice bits with; then in a trice
They make a feast less great than nice.
But all this while his eye is served,
We must not think his ear was starved,
But that there was in place to stir   15
His spleen,[9] the chirring grasshopper,
The merry cricket, puling[1] fly
The piping gnat, for minstrelsy.
And now we must imagine first,
The elves present to quench his thirst   20
A pure seed-pearl of infant dew,
Brought and besweetened in a blue
And pregnant[2] violet; which done,
His kitling[3] eyes begin to run
Quite through the table, where he spies   25
The horns of papery butterflies,
Of which he eats, and tastes a little
Of that we call the cuckoo's spittle.[4]
A little fuzz-ball[5] pudding stands
By, yet not blesséd by his hands;   30
That was too coarse; but then forthwith
He ventures boldly on the pith
Of sugared rush, and eats the sag
And well-bestrutted[6] bee's sweet bag,
Gladding his palate with some store   35
Of emmets'[7] eggs; what would he more?
But beards of mice, a newts' stewed thigh,
A bloated earwig, and a fly,

6. A briefer version was published in
1635; cf. *Poetical Works of Robert Herrick,* ed. Martin, p. 454. D. H. Woodward discusses Herrick's art in this poem
and two related pieces in "Herrick's
Oberon Poems," *JEGP,* LXIV (1965),
270–284.
7. Herrick elsewhere describes Thomas
Shapcot (c. 1586–c. 1669) as a "peculiar"
[i.e., particular] friend; "Oberon's Palace," to which Herrick alludes in line
6, is also addressed to Shapcot.

8. Unground oats.
9. I.e., to keep him amused (since cheerful as well as gloomy emotions were
thought to originate in the spleen).
1. Buzzing.
2. Full-blown.
3. Diminutive.
4. I.e., insects' cocoons.
5. Puffball (a species of edible fungus).
6. Swollen.
7. Ants'.

With the red-capped worm that's shut
Within the concave of a nut,   40
Brown as his tooth. A little moth,
Late fattened in a piece of cloth;
With withered cherries, mandrakes' ears,
Moles' eyes; to these, the slain stag's tears,
The unctuous dewlaps of a snail;   45
The broke-heart of a nightingale
O'ercome in music; with a wine
Ne'er ravished from the flattering vine,
But gently pressed from the soft side
Of the most sweet and dainty bride,[8]   50
Brought in a dainty daisy, which
He fully quaffs up to bewitch
His blood to height; this done, commended
Grace by his priest; the feast is ended.

Upon a Child That Died

Here she lies, a pretty bud,
Lately made of flesh and blood;
Who as soon fell fast asleep
As her little eyes did peep.
Give her strewings; but not stir   5
The earth that lightly covers her.

To Daffodils

Fair daffodils, we weep to see
    You haste away so soon;
As yet the early-rising sun
    Has not attained his noon.
          Stay, stay,   5
    Until the hasting day
          Has run
    But to the even-song;
And, having prayed together, we
          Will go with you along.   10

We have short time to stay, as you;
    We have as short a spring;
As quick a growth to meet decay,
    As you, or any thing.
          We die,   15
    As your hours do, and dry
          Away,

8. I.e., probably, meadowsweet or mea-dowwort, used for flavoring wine. Cf. Spenser, *The Faerie Queene,* II. viii. 20, which describes Merlin's creation of the magic sword, Morddure: "The metall first he mixt with medaewart,/That no enchauntment from his dint might save."

Like to the summer's rain;
Or as the pearls of morning's dew,
  Ne'er to be found again.   20

Upon Master Ben Jonson: Epigram

After the rare arch-poet Jonson died,
The sock[9] grew loathsome, and the buskin's pride,
Together with the stage's glory, stood
Each like a poor and pitied widowhood.
The cirque[1] profaned was, and all postures racked,   5
For men did strut, and stride, and stare, not act.
Then temper flew from words, and men did squeak,
Look red, and blow and bluster, but not speak;
No holy rage or frantic fires did stir
Or flash about the spacious theater.   10
No clap of hands, or shout, or praise's proof
Did crack the playhouse sides, or cleave her roof.
Artless the scene was, and that monstrous sin
Of deep and arrant ignorance came in;
Such ignorance as theirs was, who once hissed   15
At thy unequalled play, *The Alchemist.*
Oh, fie upon 'em! Lastly too, all wit
In utter darkness did, and still will sit
Sleeping the luckless age out, till that she
Her resurrection has again with thee.   20

Upon Electra

When out of bed my love doth spring,
  'Tis but as day a-kindling;
But when she's up and fully dressed,
  'Tis then broad day throughout the east.

Upon Parson Beanes

Old Parson Beanes hunts six days of the week,
And on the seventh, he has his notes to seek.
Six days he hollows[2] so much breath away
That on the seventh he can nor preach or pray.

To Daisies, Not To Shut So Soon

Shut not so soon; the dull-eyed night
  Has not as yet begun
To make a seizure on the light,
  Or to seal up the sun.

9. Sock (the high shoe worn by actors of comedy in ancient times) and buskin (the high boot worn by actors of tragedy) in this context symbolize English comic and tragic drama.
1. Circus (i.e., theater).
2. I.e., shouts, "Halloo!" (as the huntsmen pursue the fox).

No marigolds yet closéd are,   5
    No shadows great appear;
Nor doth the early shepherd's star
    Shine like a spangle here.

Stay but till my Julia close
    Her life-begetting eye,   10
And let the whole world then dispose
    Itself to live or die.

To the Right Honorable Mildmay, Earl of Westmorland[3]

You are a lord, an earl, nay more, a man,
Who writes sweet numbers well as any can;
If so, why then are not these verses hurled,
Like sibyls' leaves, throughout the ample world?[4]
What is a jewel if it be not set   5
Forth by a ring, or some rich carcanet?[5]
But being so, then the beholders cry,
"See, see a gem as rare as Belus' eye!"[6]
Then public praise does run upon the stone
For a most rich, a rare, a precious one.   10
Expose your jewels then unto the view,
That we may praise them, or themselves prize you.
Virtue concealed (with Horace you'll confess)
Differs not much from drowsy slothfulness.[7]

To Blossoms

Fair pledges of a fruitful tree,
    Why do ye fall so fast?
    Your date is not so past
But you may stay yet here a while,
    To blush and gently smile,   5
        And go at last.

What, were ye born to be
    An hour or half's delight,
    And so to bid good-night?
'Twas pity nature brought ye forth   10
    Merely to show your worth,
        And lose you quite.

3. It is arguable that this poem contributed to Mildmay Fane's decision to publish *Otia Sacra* in 1648.
4. Of the various prophetesses or sibyls to whom ancient authors allude, the most celebrated was the Sibyl of Cumae, in Campania; her prophecies were written on palm leaves and placed at the entrance to her cave, whence the wind often carried them away. Cf. Vergil, *Aeneid*, VI.

73–76.
5. Necklace, ornamental chain.
6. The Assyrians, who worshiped Baal (Bel, Belus), dedicated to their god a certain white stone with a glittering black center; cf. Pliny, *Natural History*, XXXVII, 55.
7. Lines 13–14 translate Horace, *Carmina*, IV. ix. 29–30.

But you are lovely leaves, where we
  May read how soon things have
    Their end, though ne'er so brave;[8]   15
And after they have shown their pride,
  Like you a while, they glide
    Into the grave.

To the Water Nymphs, Drinking at the Fountain[9]

Reach, with your whiter[1] hands, to me,
  Some crystal of the spring,
And I about the cup shall see
  Fresh lilies flourishing.

Or else, sweet nymphs, do you but this: 5
  To th' glass your lips incline,
And I shall see, by that one kiss,
  The water turned to wine.

Kissing and Bussing

Kissing and bussing differ both in this:
We buss our wantons, but our wives we kiss.

Upon Mistress Susanna Southwell[2] Her Cheeks

Rare are thy cheeks, Susanna, which do show
Ripe cherries smiling, while that others blow.

Upon Her Eyes

    Clear are her eyes,
    Like purest skies,
Discovering from thence
    A baby there
    That turns each sphere,   5
Like an intelligence.[3]

Upon Her Feet

    Her pretty feet
    Like snails did creep
A little out, and then,
    As if they playéd at bo-peep,
    Did soon draw in again.[4]   5

8. Beautiful.
9. Cf. Jonson, *The Forest*, IX, p. 31.
1. I.e., perfectly white.
2. Susanna Southwell was, probably, related to Sir Thomas Southwell (1598–c. 1641), for whose first marriage, in 1618, Herrick wrote an epithalamion.

3. I.e., like the angelic spirits which were thought to control the motion of each "sphere" in the universe, according to Ptolemaic theory.
4. Cf. Sir John Suckling's "A Ballad Upon a Wedding," ll. 43–45 (on p. 267 of this edition).

Art Above Nature: To Julia

When I behold a forest spread
With silken trees upon thy head,
And when I see that other dress
Of flowers set in comeliness;
When I behold another grace   5
In the ascent of curious lace,
Which like a pinnacle doth shew
The top, and the top-gallant[5] too;
Then, when I see thy tresses bound
Into an oval, square, or round,   10
And knit in knots far more than I
Can tell by tongue, or true-love tie;
Next, when those lawny films I see
Play with a wild civility,
And all those airy silks to flow,   15
Alluring me, and tempting so:
I must confess, mine eye and heart
Dotes less on nature, than on art.

Life Is the Body's Light

Life is the body's light, which once declining,
Those crimson clouds i'th'cheeks and lips leave shining.
Those counter-changéd tabbies[6] in the air,
The sun once set, all of one color are.
So, when death comes, fresh tinctures lose their place,   5
And dismal darkness then doth smutch the face.

His Prayer to Ben Jonson

When I a verse shall make,
Know I have prayed thee,
For old religion's[7] sake,
Saint Ben, to aid me.

Make the way smooth for me,   5
When I, thy Herrick,
Honoring thee, on my knee
Offer my lyric.

Candles I'll give to thee,
And a new altar;   10
And thou, Saint Ben, shalt be
Writ in my psalter.

---

5. I.e., the platforms at the heads of the mainmast and mizzenmast.
6. I.e., those varicolored silk taffetas.
7. I.e. (primarily), for the sake of our old friendship, implicitly a sacred bond; but the expression glances also, very aptly, at a classical ideal of duty as well as at the faith and ceremonies of Roman times.

The Bad Season Makes the Poet Sad

Dull to myself, and almost dead to these
My many fresh and fragrant mistresses,
Lost to all music now, since every thing
Puts on the semblance here of sorrowing;
Sick is the land to th'heart, and doth endure   5
More dangerous faintings by her desp'rate cure.
But if that golden age would come again,
And Charles here rule, as he before did reign;
If smooth and unperplexed the seasons were
As when the sweet Maria[8] livéd here;   10
I should delight to have my curls half drowned
In Tyrian dews, and head with roses crowned,
And once more yet, ere I am laid out dead,
Knock at a star with my exalted head.[9]

The Night-Piece, To Julia[1]

Her eyes the glow-worm lend thee;
The shooting stars attend thee;
    And the elves also,
    Whose little eyes glow
Like the sparks of fire, befriend thee.   5

No will-o'-the-wisp mis-light thee;
Nor snake or slow-worm[2] bite thee:
    But on, on thy way,
    Not making a stay,
Since ghost there's none to affright thee.   10

Let not the dark thee cumber;
What though the moon does slumber?
    The stars of the night
    Will lend thee their light,
Like tapers clear without number.   15

Then, Julia, let me woo thee,
Thus, thus to come unto me;
    And when I shall meet
    Thy silv'ry feet,
My soul I'll pour into thee.   20

The Hag

The hag[3] is astride,
This night for to ride,

---

8. I.e., Henrietta Maria, wife of Charles I.
9. Cf. Horace, *Carmina*, I. i. 36.
1. Cf. Jonson's song, "The faery beam upon you," p. 92.
2. Adder (or possibly the blindworm, a small lizard).
3. Witch.

The devil and she together;
    Through thick and through thin,
    Now out and then in,   5
Though ne'er so foul be the weather.

    A thorn or a burr
    She takes for a spur;
With a lash of a bramble she rides now,
    Through brakes and through briers,   10
    O'er ditches and mires,
She follows the spirit that guides now.

    No beast for his food
    Dares now range the wood,
But hushed in his lair he lies lurking;   15
    While mischiefs by these,
    On land and on seas,
At noon of night[4] are a-working.

    The storm will arise
    And trouble the skies   20
This night, and more for the wonder,
    The ghost from the tomb
    Affrighted shall come,
Called out by the clap of the thunder.

The Country Life, To the Honored Mr. Endymion Porter,[5] Groom of the Bedchamber to His Majesty

Sweet country life, to such unknown,
Whose lives are others', not their own!
But, serving courts and cities, be
Less happy, less enjoying thee.
Thou never plow'st the ocean's foam   5
To seek and bring rough pepper home;
Nor to the Eastern Ind dost rove
To bring from thence the scorchéd clove;
Nor, with the loss of thy loved rest,
Bring'st home the ingot from the West.   10
No, thy ambition's masterpiece
Flies no thought higher than a fleece;
Or how to pay thy hinds,[6] and clear
All scores, and so to end the year;
But walk'st about thine own dear bounds,   15
Not envying others' larger grounds,
For well thou know'st, 'tis not th'extent

4. I.e., at midnight.
5. Endymion Porter (1587–1649), an influential courtier during the reigns of James I and, especially, Charles I, extended support to Sir William Davenant and Thomas Randolph; to Herrick he appears to have been friend as well as patron.
6. Farm laborers.

Of land makes life, but sweet content.
When now the cock, the plowman's horn,
Calls forth the lily-wristed morn,   20
Then to thy corn-fields thou dost go,
Which, though well soiled,[7] yet thou dost know
That the best compost for the lands
Is the wise master's feet and hands.
There at the plow thou find'st thy team,   25
With a hind whistling there to them,
And cheer'st them up by singing how
The kingdom's portion is the plow.
This done, then to th'enameled meads
Thou go'st, and as thy foot there treads,   30
Thou seest a present godlike power
Imprinted in each herb and flower,
And smell'st the breath of great-eyed kine,
Sweet as the blossoms of the vine.
Here thou behold'st thy large sleek neat   35
Unto the dewlaps up in meat;
And as thou look'st, the wanton steer,
The heifer, cow, and ox draw near
To make a pleasing pastime there.
These seen, thou go'st to view thy flocks   40
Of sheep, safe from the wolf and fox,
And find'st their bellies there as full
Of short, sweet grass as backs with wool,
And leav'st them, as they feed and fill,
A shepherd piping on a hill.   45
For sports, for pageantry, and plays,
Thou hast thy eves, and holy-days,
On which the young men and maids meet
To exercise their dancing feet,
Tripping the comely country round,   50
With daffodils and daisies crowned.
Thy wakes, thy quintals,[8] here thou hast,
Thy May-poles, too, with garlands graced;
Thy morris-dance, thy Whitsun-ale,
Thy shearing-feast, which never fail;   55
Thy harvest home, thy wassail bowl,
That's tossed up after fox-i'-th'hole,[9]
Thy mummeries,[1] thy Twelfth-tide kings
And queens, thy Christmas revelings,
Thy nut-brown mirth, thy russet[2] wit,   60
And no man pays too dear for it.
To these, thou hast thy times to go
And trace the hare i'th'treacherous snow;

---

7. Manured.
8. Posts used as targets in rustic tilting-matches.
9. I.e., an ancient game similar to hop-scotch.
1. I.e., ceremonies performed by masked actors.
2. Homespun.

Thy witty wiles to draw, and get
The lark into the trammel net;[3]   65
Thou hast thy cockrood[4] and thy glade,
To take the precious pheasant made;
Thy lime-twigs,[5] snares, and pitfalls then,
To catch the pilf'ring birds, not men.
O happy life! if that their good   70
The husbandmen but understood,
Who all the day themselves do please,
And younglings, with such sports as these;
And, lying down, have naught t'affright
Sweet sleep, that makes more short the night.   75

Caetera desunt[6]—

To Master Denham, On His Prospective Poem[7]

Or[8] looked I back unto the times hence flown,
To praise those Muses, and dislike our own,
Or did I walk those pean[9] gardens through
To kick the flow'rs, and scorn their odors too?
I might, and justly, be reputed here   5
One nicely[1] mad, or peevishly severe.
But by Apollo! as I worship wit,
Where I have cause to burn perfumes to it,
So, I confess, 'tis somewhat to do well
In our high art, although we can't excel   10
Like thee, or dare the buskins to unloose
Of thy brave, bold, and sweet Maronian Muse.[2]
But since I'm called, rare Denham, to be gone,
Take from thy Herrick, this conclusion:
'Tis dignity in others, if they be   15
Crowned poets, yet live princes under thee,
The while their wreaths and purple robes do shine,
Less by their own gems, than those beams of thine.

The Maypole

The Maypole is up,
Now give me the cup,
I'll drink to the garlands around it;

3. I.e., a net combining coarse and fine mesh.
4. Nets were stretched across a "cockrood," or open space in a wood, to catch woodcocks.
5. Branches were smeared with sticky substances made from holly bark to catch birds (cf. Wyatt's lyric, "Tangled I was in love's snare").
6. I.e., the rest is wanting.
7. An early version of Sir John Denham's "Cooper's Hill," which describes the view (or "prospect") from that place, was published in 1642.
8. Either.
9. Since the term in heraldry signifies "gold spots on a black field," Herrick probably refers to the visual effect of bright yellow flowers set in black soil.
1. Fastidiously.
2. I.e., Vergilian Muse (Vergil's full name was Publius Vergilius Maro).

But first unto those
    Whose hands did compose   5
The glory of flowers that crowned it.

A health to my girls,
    Whose husbands may earls
Or lords be (granting my wishes);
    And when that ye wed   10
    To the bridal bed,
Then multiply all, like to fishes.[3]

His Return to London[4]

From the dull confines of the drooping west,
To see the day spring from the pregnant east,
Ravished in spirit, I come, nay more, I fly
To thee, blest place of my nativity!
Thus, thus with hallowed foot I touch the ground,   5
With thousand blessings by thy fortune crowned.
O fruitful Genius! that bestowest here
An everlasting plenty, year by year.
O Place! O People! Manners![5] framed to please
All nations, customs, kindreds, languages!   10
I am a free-born Roman; suffer then
That I amongst you live a citizen.
London my home is, though by hard fate sent
Into a long and irksome banishment;
Yet since called back; henceforward let me be,   15
O native country, repossessed by thee!
For, rather than I'll to the west return,
I'll beg of thee first here to have mine urn.
Weak I am grown, and must in short time fall;
Give thou my sacred relics burial.   20

Not Every Day Fit for Verse

'Tis not ev'ry day that I
    Fitted am to prophesy;
No, but when the spirit fills
    The fantastic pannicles[6]
Full of fire, then I write   5
    As the godhead doth indite.[7]
Thus enraged, my lines are hurled,
    Like the Sibyl's, through the world.[8]

3. Cf. "A Nuptial Song," p. 126, l. 50 and note.
4. Herrick presumably returned from Devonshire to London in 1647, the year in which he was expelled from his living at Dean Prior.
5. Cf. "Dean-bourn," p. 109, l. 9 and note.
6. I.e., the brain cells, which were thought to be the seat of imagination.
7. Dictate.
8. Cf. "To the Right Honorable Mildmay, Earl of Westmorland," p. 133, l. 4 and note.

Look how next the holy fire
Either slakes, or doth retire;   10
So the fancy cools, till when
That brave spirit comes again.

His Grange,[9] or Private Wealth

Though clock
To tell how night draws hence, I've none,
    A cock
I have, to sing how day draws on.
    I have   5
A maid, my Prue, by good luck sent
    To save
That little, Fates me gave or lent.
    A hen
I keep, which creaking[1] day by day,   10
    Tells when
She goes her long white egg to lay.
    A goose
I have, which with a jealous ear
    Lets loose   15
Her tongue, to tell what danger's near.
    A lamb
I keep, tame, with my morsels fed,
    Whose dam
An orphan left him, lately dead.   20
    A cat
I keep, that plays about my house,
    Grown fat
With eating many a miching[2] mouse.
    To these   25
A Tracy[3] I do keep, whereby
    I please
The more my rural privacy;
    Which are
But toys to give my heart some ease: 30
    Where care
None is, slight things do lightly please.

Up Tails All[4]

Begin with a kiss,
Go on too with this,
And thus, thus, thus let us smother

---

9. I.e., his country dwelling (the vicarage of Dean Prior).
1. Clucking.
2. Thieving.
3. "His Spaniel" (Herrick's note). Cf.

"Upon His Spaniel Tracy," p. 147.
4. The title is that of a song popular in Herrick's time; cf. Chappell, *Ballad Literature*, I, p. 196.

Our lips for a while,
But let's not beguile   5
Our hope of one for the other.

This play, be assured,
Long enough has endured,
Since more and more is exacted;
For love he doth call   10
For his up tails all,
And that's the part to be acted.

A *Ternary*[5] *of Littles,*
Upon a Pipkin[6] *of Jelly Sent to a Lady*

A little saint best fits a little shrine,
A little prop best fits a little vine,
As my small cruse[7] best fits my little wine.

A little seed best fits a little soil,
A little trade best fits a little toil,   5
As my small jar best fits my little oil.

A little bin best fits a little bread,
A little garland fits a little head,
As my small stuff best fits my little shed.

A little hearth best fits a little fire,   10
A little chapel fits a little choir,
As my small bell best fits my little spire.

A little stream best fits a little boat,
A little lead best fits a little float,
As my small pipe best fits my little note.   15

A little meat best fits a little belly,
As sweetly, lady, give me leave to tell ye,
This little pipkin fits this little jelly.

Upon Julia's Clothes[8]

Whenas in silks my Julia goes,
Then, then, methinks, how sweetly flows
That liquefaction of her clothes.

---

5. I.e., a set of threes.
6. I.e., a small earthenware pot.
7. Cup.
8. Two interesting analyses of this poem are those by C. S. Lewis, "The Personal Heresy in Criticism," *Essays and Studies by Members of the English Association,* XIX (1934), 9–11, and E. M. W. Tillyard, "The Personal Heresy of Criticism: A Rejoinder," *ibid.,* XX (1935), 17–19. Cf. also R. J. Ross, "Herrick's Julia In Silks," *EIC,* XV (1965), 171–180, esp. n. 2.

Next, when I cast mine eyes and see
That brave vibration each way free;   5
O, how that glittering taketh me!

Upon Prue, His Maid[9]

In this little urn is laid
Prudence Baldwin, once my maid,
From whose happy spark here let
Spring the purple violet.

Ceremonies for Christmas

Come, bring with a noise,[1]
My merry, merry boys,
The Christmas log to the firing;
While my good dame, she
Bids ye all be free,   5
And drink to your hearts' desiring.

With the last year's brand
Light the new block, and
For good success in his spending,[2]
On your psalt'ries[3] play,   10
That sweet luck may
Come while the log is a-teending.[4]

Drink now the strong beer,
Cut the white loaf here,
The while the meat is a-shredding;   15
For the rare mince-pie
And the plums stand by
To fill the paste that's a-kneading.

Poetry Perpetuates the Poet

Here I myself might likewise die,
And utterly forgotten lie,
But that eternal poetry
Repullulation[5] gives me here
Unto the thirtieth thousand year,[6]   5
When all now dead shall reappear.

9. The Parish Register at Dean Prior indicates that Prudence Baldwin was in fact buried on January 6, 1678; Herrick had died almost four years earlier.
1. I.e., a joyful noise.
2. I.e., consuming (by the fire).
3. The psaltery was a string instrument akin to the zither.

4. Kindling.
5. Regeneration.
6. I.e., the period of time required, according to some ancient authorities, for the heavenly bodies to return to their original positions; sometimes referred to as a "great Year." Cf. Plato, *Republic*, VIII. 546.

Kisses

Give me the food that satisfies a guest;
Kisses are but dry banquets to a feast.

The Amber Bead

I saw a fly within a bead
Of amber cleanly buriéd;
The urn was little, but the room
More rich than Cleopatra's tomb.

Upon Love

Love brought me to a silent grove,
　And showed me there a tree
Where some had hanged themselves for love,
　And gave a twist to me.

The halter was of silk and gold   5
　That he reached forth to me,
No otherwise than if he would
　By dainty things undo me.

He bade me then that necklace use,
　And told me, too, he maketh   10
A glorious end by such a noose,
　His death for love that taketh.

'Twas but a dream; but had I been
　There, really alone,
My desperate fears in love had seen   15
　Mine execution.

Charms⁷

Bring the holy crust of bread,
Lay it underneath the head;
'Tis a certain charm to keep
Hags away while children sleep.

Another

Let the superstitious wife
Near the child's heart lay a knife,
Point be up, and haft be down,

7. This poem and the three that follow
reflect the continuing strength in Herrick's time, especially in country parishes
such as Dean Prior, of pre-Christian
folklore and ritual designed to ward off
evil spirits. Cf. "The Hag," p. 136.

While she gossips in the town;
This, 'mongst other mystic charms,   5
Keeps the sleeping child from harms.

Another to Bring In the Witch

To house[8] the hag, you must do this:
Commix with meal a little piss
Of him bewitched; then forthwith make
A little wafer or a cake;
And this, rawly baked, will bring   5
The old hag in. No surer thing.

Another Charm for Stables

Hang up hooks and shears to scare
Hence the hag that rides the mare,
Till they be all over wet
With the mire and the sweat;
This observed, the manes shall be   5
Of your horses all knot-free.

Ceremonies for Candlemas Eve[9]

Down with the rosemary and bays,
    Down with the mistletoe;
Instead of holly, now upraise
    The greener box, for show.

The holly hitherto did sway;   5
    Let box now domineer
Until the dancing Easter Day,[1]
    Or Easter's Eve appear.

Then youthful box which now hath grace
    Your houses to renew,   10
Grown old, surrender must his place
    Unto the crispéd[2] yew.

When yew is out, then birch comes in,
    And many flowers beside,
Both of a fresh and fragrant kin   15
    To honor Whitsuntide.

8. I.e., to attract into the house (where the witch might be destroyed).
9. Candlemas, which falls on February 2, commemorates the Purification of the Virgin Mary; candles, especially for the altar, are blessed on this day. It seems probable, however, that Herrick also has in view the pre-Christian symbolic associations of the various flowers and trees mentioned in the course of the poem.
1. It was popularly believed that the sun dances on Easter Day: cf. Sir Thomas Browne, *Pseudodoxia Epidemica*, V. xxii. 16.
2. Curled.

Green rushes then, and sweetest bents,[3]
    With cooler oaken boughs,
Come in for comely ornaments,
    To re-adorn the house.   20
Thus times do shift; each thing his turn does hold;
New things succeed, as former things grow old.

Upon Ben Jonson

Here lies Jonson with the rest
Of the poets; but the best.
Reader, would'st thou more have known?
Ask his story, not this stone.
That will speak what this can't tell   5
Of his glory. So farewell.

An Ode For Him

      Ah, Ben!
    Say how or when
    Shall we, thy guests,
Meet at those lyric feasts
    Made at the Sun,   5
The Dog, the Triple Tun,[4]
    Where we such clusters[5] had
As made us nobly wild, not mad;
    And yet each verse of thine
Outdid the meat, outdid the frolic wine.   10

      My Ben!
    Or come again,
    Or send to us
Thy wit's great overplus;
    But teach us yet   15
Wisely to husband it,
    Lest we that talent spend;
And having once brought to an end
    That precious stock, the store
Of such a wit the world should have no more.   20

To the King, Upon His Welcome to Hampton Court[6]

Welcome, great Caesar, welcome now you are
As dearest peace after destructive war;
Welcome as slumbers, or as beds of ease

---

3. Bent grass.
4. The Sun, The Dog, and The Triple
Tun were taverns in London.
5. Bunches (of grapes)—i.e., wine.

6. On August 24, 1647, by Parliamentary
order, Charles I was sent with a military
escort to Hampton Court.

After our long and peevish sicknesses.
O pomp of glory! Welcome now, and come   5
To re-possess once more your longed-for home.
A thousand altars smoke; a thousand thighs
Of beeves here ready stand for sacrifice.
Enter and prosper, while our eyes do wait
For an ascendant throughly auspicate,[7]   10
Under which sign we may the former stone
Lay of our safety's new foundation.[8]
That done, O Caesar, live, and be to us
Our Fate, our Fortune, and our Genius,
To whose free knees we may our temples tie   15
As to a still protecting deity.
That should you stir, we and our altars too
May, great Augustus,[9] go along with you.
Long live the King! and to accomplish this,
We'll from our own add far more years to his.   20

On Himself

Lost to the world; lost to myself; alone
Here now I rest under this marble stone:
In depth of silence, heard and seen of none.

Upon His Spaniel Tracy

Now thou art dead, no eye shall ever see,
For shape and service, spaniel like to thee.
This shall my love do, give thy sad death one
Tear, that deserves of me a million.

The Pillar of Fame[1]

Fame's pillar here at last we set,
Out-during[2] marble, brass or jet;
Charmed and enchanted so
As to withstand the blow
Of o v e r t h r o w ;   5
Nor shall the seas,
O r   o u t r a g e s
Of storms, o'erbear
What   we   uprear;
Tho' kingdoms fall,   10

7. I.e., for an altogether auspicious aspect of the heavens.
8. Herrick alludes to the ancients' practice of noting the aspect of the stars under which a city was founded, in order to ascertain the most propitious occasions for later actions affecting the city's well-being.
9. Caesar Augustus (63 B.C.–A.D. 14) was considered to have been the most successful of his line.
1. The poem is "shaped" to resemble a column.
2. Outlasting.

This pillar never shall
Decline or waste at all;
But stand for ever by his own
Firm and well-fixed foundation.

To his book's end this last line he'd have placed:
Jocund his Muse was; but his life was chaste.

From *HIS NOBLE NUMBERS*[3] (1647; with *HESPERIDES*, 1648)

His Prayer for Absolution

For those my unbaptizéd rhymes,
Writ in my wild unhallowed times;
For every sentence, clause, and word,
That's not inlaid with Thee, my Lord,
Forgive me, God, and blot each line   5
Out of my book that is not Thine.
But if, 'mongst all, Thou find'st here one
Worthy Thy benediction,
That one of all the rest shall be
The glory of my work and me.   10

To Find God[4]

Weigh me the fire; or canst thou find
A way to measure out the wind?
Distinguish all those floods that are
Mixed in that wat'ry theater,[5]
And taste thou them as saltless there,   5
As in their channel first they were.
Tell[6] me the people that do keep

---

3. The title page of *His Noble Numbers*, comprising 272 "pious pieces" in which Herrick "sings the birth of his Christ, and sighs for his Saviour's sufferings on the cross," bears an epigraph in Greek, drawn from the *Theogony* of Hesiod: "We know how to say many false things that seem like true sayings, but we know also how to speak the truth when we wish to" (*Hesiod*, trans. R. Lattimore [Ann Arbor, 1970], p. 124). The variety and the devotional character of these poems are discussed by Miriam K. Starkman, "*Noble Numbers* and The Poetry of Devotion," in *Reason and the Imagination: Studies in the History of Ideas 1600–1800*, ed. J. A. Mazzeo (New York, 1962), pp. 1–28.

4. Cf. Donne's lyric, "Go and catch a falling star," which also (in quite another context) confronts the reader initially with a series of impossible demands, the better to enforce the poet's concluding emphasis. Herrick's poem, however, looks in the first instance specifically to II Esdras, in the Apocrypha: "Weigh me the weight of fire, or measure me a measure of wind, or call back for me the day that is past. . . . How many dwellings are there in the heart of the sea, or how many streams at the source of the deep, or how many ways above the firmament . . ." (4:5–7).

5. I.e., the oceans.

6. Count.

Within the kingdoms of the deep;
Or fetch me back that cloud again,
Beshivered into seeds of rain.   10
Tell me the motes, dust, sands, and spears
Of corn, when summer shakes his ears;
Show me that world of stars, and whence
They noiseless spill their influence.
This if thou canst;[7] then show me Him   15
That rides the glorious cherubim.[8]

What God Is

God is above the sphere of our esteem,
And is the best known, not defining Him.

God's Mercy

God's boundless mercy is, to sinful man,
Like to the ever-wealthy ocean,
Which, though it sends forth thousand streams, 'tis ne'er
Known, or else seen to be the emptier;
And though it takes all in, 'tis yet no more   5
Full, and filled-full, than when full-filled before.

Calling, and Correcting

God is not only merciful, to call
Men to repent, but when He strikes withal.[9]

Upon Time[1]

Time was upon
The wing, to fly away,
And I called on
Him but a while to stay;
But he'd be gone,   5
For ought that I could say.

He held out then
A writing, as he went,
And asked me when

7. Lines 10–15 probably echo Ecclesiasticus 1:2–3: "The sand of the seas, and the drops of rain, and the days of eternity—who can count them? The height of the heavens, and the breadth of the earth, and the deep, and wisdom—who can track them out?"
8. Cf. Psalms 18:10: "[The Lord] rode upon a cherub."
9. Cf. Hebrews 12:11: "Now no chastening for the present seemeth to be joyous, but grievous; nevertheless afterward it yieldeth the peaceable fruit of righteousness unto them which are exercised thereby."
1. As does "Upon Love" (in *Hesperides*), this piece reflects the influence of George Herbert's manner in poetry.

False man would be content   10
    To pay again[2]
What God and Nature lent.

    An hourglass,
In which were sands but few,
    As he did pass,   15
He showed; and told me too
    Mine end near was,
And so away he flew.

His Litany to the Holy Spirit

In the hour of my distress,
When temptations me oppress,
And when I my sins confess,
    Sweet Spirit, comfort me!

When I lie within my bed,   5
Sick in heart and sick in head,
And with doubts discomforted,
    Sweet Spirit, comfort me!

When the house doth sigh and weep,
And the world is drowned in sleep,   10
Yet mine eyes the watch do keep,
    Sweet Spirit, comfort me!

When the artless doctor sees
No one hope, but of his fees,
And his skill runs on the lees,[3]   15
    Sweet Spirit, comfort me!

When his potion and his pill
Has or none or little skill,
Meet for nothing but to kill,
    Sweet Spirit, comfort me!   20

When the passing-bell doth toll,
And the Furies in a shoal[4]
Come to fright a parting soul,
    Sweet Spirit, comfort me!

When the tapers now burn blue,[5]   25
And the comforters are few,
And that number more than true,
    Sweet Spirit, comfort me!

2. I.e., to repay.
3. I.e., his skill is virtually exhausted.
4. Throng.

5. The phenomenon was taken to indicate the presence of evil spirits.

When the priest his last hath prayed,
And I nod to what is said,   30
'Cause my speech is now decayed,
    Sweet Spirit, comfort me!

When, God knows, I'm tossed about,
Either with despair or doubt,
Yet, before the glass be out,   35
    Sweet Spirit, comfort me!

When the Tempter me pursu'th
With the sins of all my youth,
And half damns me with untruth,
    Sweet Spirit, comfort me!   40

When the flames and hellish cries
Fright mine ears and fright mine eyes,
And all terrors me surprise,
    Sweet Spirit, comfort me!

When the Judgment is revealed,   45
And that opened which was sealed,[6]
When to Thee I have appealed,
    Sweet Spirit, comfort me!

A *Thanksgiving to God for His House*

Lord, Thou hast given me a cell
    Wherein to dwell;
A little house, whose humble roof
    Is weather-proof;
Under the spars of which I lie   5
    Both soft and dry;
Where Thou, my chamber for to ward,
    Hast set a guard
Of harmless thoughts, to watch and keep
    Me while I sleep.   10
Low is my porch, as is my fate,
    Both void of state;
And yet the threshold of my door
    Is worn by the poor
Who thither come, and freely get   15
    Good words, or meat.
Like as my parlor, so my hall
    And kitchen's small;
A little buttery, and therein
    A little bin,   20

6. Cf. Revelation 6, 8.

Which keeps my little loaf of bread
    Unchipped, unflead;[7]
Some brittle sticks of thorn or brier
    Make me a fire,
Close by whose living coal I sit,   25
    And glow like it.
Lord, I confess too, when I dine,
    The pulse[8] is Thine,
And all those other bits that be
    There placed by Thee;   30
The worts, the purslane, and the mess[9]
    Of watercress,
Which of Thy kindness Thou hast sent;
    And my content
Makes those, and my belovéd beet,   35
    To be more sweet.
'Tis Thou that crown'st my glittering hearth
    With guiltless mirth,
And giv'st me wassail bowls to drink,
    Spiced to the brink.   40
Lord, 'tis Thy plenty-dropping hand
    That soils[1] my land,
And giv'st me, for my bushel sown,
    Twice ten for one;
Thou mak'st my teeming hen to lay   45
    Her egg each day;
Besides my healthful ewes to bear
    Me twins each year;
The while the conduits of my kine
    Run cream, for wine.   50
All these, and better, Thou dost send
    Me, to this end,
That I should render, for my part,
    A thankful heart;
Which, fired with incense, I resign   55
    As wholly Thine;
But the acceptance, that must be,
    My Christ, by Thee.

To Death

Thou bid'st me come away,
  And I'll no longer stay
Than for to shed some tears
  For faults of former years;
And to repent some crimes   5

---

7. Unbroken.
8. I.e., peas, beans, or lentils.
9. I.e., the herbs (of two kinds) and the supply.
1. Fertilizes.

Done in the present times;
And next, to take a bit
Of bread and wine with it;
To don my robes of love,[2]
Fit for the place above;   10
To gird my loins about
With charity throughout;
And so to travel hence
With feet of innocence:
These done, I'll only cry   15
"God, mercy"; and so die.

To His Saviour, a Child; A Present by a Child

Go, pretty child, and bear this flower
Unto thy little Saviour,
And tell Him, by that bud now blown
He is the *Rose of Sharon*[3] known;
When thou hast said so, stick it there   5
Upon His bib, or stomacher,[4]
And tell Him, for good handsel[5] too,
That thou hast brought a whistle[6] new,
Made of a clean, straight, oaten reed,
To charm His cries, at time of need;   10
Tell Him, for coral, thou hast none,
But if thou hadst, He should have one;
But poor thou art, and known to be
Even as moneyless as He.
Lastly, if thou canst win a kiss   15
From those mellifluous lips[7] of His,
Then never take a second on,
To spoil the first impression.

To His Conscience

Can I not sin, but thou wilt be
My private protonotary?[8]
Can I not woo thee to pass by
A short and sweet iniquity?
I'll cast a mist and cloud upon   5

2. Cf. Isaiah 61:10: "He hath clothed me with the garments of salvation."
3. Cf. Song of Solomon 2:1: "I am the rose of Sharon, and the lily of the valleys."
4. Pinafore (in this context).
5. Pledge, gift.
6. "Small silver whistles seem to have been one of the two *sine qua non* of seventeenth-century babyhood. Trinculo adds the other when [Dryden, *The Tempest*, III. iii] he cries, "It shall be a Whistle for our first Babe, and when the next Shipwrack puts us again to swimming, I'll dive to get a coral to it' " (*Plays and Poems of William Cartwright*, ed. G. Blakemore Evans [Madison, Wis., 1951], p. 694).
7. Cf. Song of Solomon 4:3: "Thy lips are like a thread of scarlet, and thy speech is comely."
8. The protonotary was chief recording clerk in a court of law.

My delicate transgression,
So utter dark as that no eye
Shall see the hugged impiety;
Gifts blind the wise,[9] and bribes do please
And wind[1] all other witnesses,   10
And wilt not thou with gold be tied
To lay thy pen and ink aside,
That in the murk and tongueless night,
Wanton I may, and thou not write?
It will not be; and therefore now,   15
For times to come I'll make this vow:
From aberrations to live free,
So I'll not fear the Judge, or thee.

His Creed

I do believe that die I must,
And be returned from out my dust;
I do believe that when I rise
Christ I shall see with these same eyes;
I do believe that I must come   5
With others to the dreadful Doom;
I do believe the bad must go
From thence to everlasting woe;
I do believe the good, and I,
Shall live with Him eternally;   10
I do believe I shall inherit
Heaven, by Christ's mercies, not my merit;
I do believe the One in Three,
And Three in perfect Unity;
Lastly, that Jesus is a deed   15
Of gift from God. And here's my creed.

Another Grace for a Child

Here a little child I stand,
Heaving up my either hand;
Cold as paddocks[2] though they be,
Here I lift them up to Thee,
For a benison[3] to fall   5
On our meat, and on us all. Amen.

The Bellman

Along the dark and silent night,
With my lantern, and my light,

9. Cf. Deuteronomy 16:19: "A gift doth
blind the eye of the wise."
1. Corrupt.

2. Toads.
3. Blessing.

And the tinkling of my bell,
Thus I walk, and this I tell:
Death and dreadfulness call on   5
To the gen'ral Session,[4]
To whose dismal bar, we there
All accounts must come to clear.
Scores of sins we've made here many;
Wiped out few, God knows, if any.   10
Rise, ye debtors, then, and fall
To make payment, while I call.
Ponder this when I am gone;
By the clock 'tis almost one.

The White Island, or Place of the Blest

In this world, the isle of dreams,
While we sit by sorrow's streams,
Tears and terrors are our themes,
    Reciting;

But when once from hence we fly,   5
More and more approaching nigh
Unto young eternity,
    Uniting

In that whiter island, where
Things are evermore sincere,   10
Candor here and lustre there
    Delighting:

There no monstrous fancies shall
Out of hell an horror call
To create, or cause at all,   15
    Affrighting.

There in calm and cooling sleep
We our eyes shall never steep,
But eternal watch shall keep,
    Attending   20

Pleasures, such as shall pursue
Me immortalized, and you;
And fresh joys, as never, too,
    Have ending.

4. I.e., the Last Judgment.

Thomas Carew

1594–1595	Born, possibly at West Wickham, Kent. His father, Matthew Carew, a lawyer of some distinction, had been a Master in Chancery since 1576, and was knighted by James I in 1603. The family took up residence in London about 1598, but nothing is known of Thomas Carew's early education.
1608	Matriculates at Merton College, Oxford; graduates B.A. in January, 1610/1611.
1612	Incorporated B.A. of Cambridge. Admitted to the Middle Temple, presumably intending to enter the legal profession.
1613	Probably in consequence of his father's financial difficulties, accepts the offer of Sir Dudley Carleton, English ambassador in Venice, to join Carleton's entourage as a secretary.
1615	On completion of the embassy's official business, returns to England with Carleton, in December.
1616	Accompanies Carleton's embassy to the Netherlands. By consequence of some written indiscretions bearing on Carleton's character, returns to England in August, having been discreetly but effectively dismissed from his post.
1616–1618	Unsuccessfully seeking employment from various noblemen; recurrently in attendance at court. Father dies, August, 1618.
1619	Makes one of an embassy to Paris headed by Sir Edward Herbert (later Lord Herbert of Cherbury). Perhaps meets the Italian poet Giambattista Marino, resident in Paris from 1615 to 1623.
1622	First published poem: commendatory verses prefixed to *The Heir*, a comedy by Thomas May. "A Rapture" probably composed between 1622 and 1624. Associating in the early 1620s with Jonson and his circle; frequenting the court and cultivating influential persons there.
1630	Appointed a Gentlemen of the Privy Chamber Extraordinary named Sewer in Ordinary to the King (i.e., a household official in charge of the royal dining arrangements).

1634	Carew's masque, *Coelum Britannicum*, performed at court; published later in the year.
1639	Accompanies Charles I's military expedition against Scotland, brought to a bloodless conclusion at Berwick with the Articles of Pacification, June 18.
1640	Death. Buried in Saint Dunstan's-in-the-West, Westminster, March 23. Publication of *Poems*.
1642	Publication of *Poems*, "the second edition revised and enlarged."

From *POEMS* (1640)

The Spring[1]

Now that the winter's gone, the earth hath lost
Her snow-white robes, and now no more the frost
Candies[2] the grass, or casts an icy cream
Upon the silver lake or crystal stream;
But the warm sun thaws the benumbèd earth,   5
And makes it tender; gives a sacred[3] birth
To the dead swallow; wakes in hollow tree
The drowsy cuckoo and the humble-bee.
Now do a choir of chirping minstrels bring
In triumph to the world the youthful spring.   10
The valleys, hills, and woods in rich array
Welcome the coming of the longed-for May.
Now all things smile; only my love doth lour;
Nor hath the scalding noonday sun the power
To melt that marble ice, which still doth hold   15
Her heart congealed, and makes her pity cold.
The ox, which lately did for shelter fly
Into the stall, doth now securely lie
In open fields; and love no more is made
By the fireside, but in the cooler shade   20
Amyntas now doth with his Chloris sleep

1. While Carew's poetry reflects the shaping influence primarily of models provided by Jonson and Donne (which is not to deny his verse its own individual character), many of his lyrics echo themes and mannerisms favored by French and Italian poets, notably Giambattista Marino (1569–1625). "The Spring" reflects the influence of Pierre de Ronsard (1524–1585); cf. "Amourette" and Amour XXXIII, in *Le Second Livre des Amours*, ed. A. Van Bever, 2 vols. (Paris, 1923), I. pp. 320, 232.
2. I.e., coats with ice.

3. Cf. Textual Notes, p. 379. "Sacred," the reading of both early editions, gains support by the fact that in ancient times the swallow was "held sacred to the gods of the household and to Aphrodite, for she also is one of them" (Aelian, *On the Characteristics of Animals*, ed. A. F. Scholfield, 3 vols. [London, 1959], II, p. 331). A twelfth-century bestiary observes that the swallow "is exalted by an uncommonly devout state of mind" (*The Bestiary: A Book of Beasts*, trans. and ed. T. H. White [New York, 1960], p. 147).

Under a sycamore, and all things keep
Time with the season; only she doth carry
June in her eyes, in her heart January.

A Divine Mistress[4]

In Nature's pieces still I see
Some error, that might mended be;
Something my wish could still remove,
Alter or add; but my fair love
Was framed by hands far more divine,   5
For she hath every beauteous line;
Yet I had been far happier,
Had Nature, that made me, made her.
Then likeness might, that love creates,
Have made her love what now she hates;   10
Yet, I confess, I cannot spare
From her just shape the smallest hair;
Nor need I beg from all the store
Of heaven for her one beauty more.
She hath too much divinity for me;   15
You gods, teach her some more humanity.

A Prayer to the Wind

Go, thou gentle whispering wind,
Bear this sigh, and if thou find
Where my cruel fair doth rest,
Cast it in her snowy breast;
So, inflamed by my desire,   5
It may set her heart afire.
Those sweet kisses thou shalt gain
Will reward thee for thy pain.
Boldly light upon her lip,
There suck odors, and thence skip   10
To her bosom; lastly fall
Down, and wander over all;
Range about those ivory hills,
From whose every part distills
Amber dew; there spices grow,   15
There pure streams of nectar flow;
There perfume thyself, and bring
All those sweets upon thy wing.
As thou return'st, change by thy power
Every weed into a flower;   20
Turn each thistle to a vine,

4. Henry Lawes (1596–1662), who composed the music for Milton's masque *Comus*, set this lyric to music (together with others by Carew) in *Ayres and Dialogues*, published 1653.

Make the bramble eglantine;[5]
For so rich a booty made,
Do but this, and I am paid.
Thou canst with thy powerful blast   25
Heat apace, and cool as fast;
Thou canst kindle hidden flame,
And again destroy the same:
Then, for pity, either stir
Up the fire of love in her,   30
That alike both flames may shine,
Or else quite extinguish mine.

Song: Mediocrity[6] in Love Rejected

Give me more love, or more disdain;[7]
    The torrid or the frozen zone
Bring equal ease unto my pain,
    The temperate affords me none;
Either extreme, of love or hate,   5
Is sweeter than a calm estate.

Give me a storm; if it be love,
    Like Danaë in that golden shower,[8]
I swim in pleasure; if it prove
    Disdain, that torrent will devour   10
My vulture-hopes; and he's possessed
Of heaven, that's but from hell released.
    Then crown my joys, or cure my pain;
    Give me more love, or more disdain.

To My Mistress Sitting by a River's Side: An Eddy[9]

Mark how yon eddy steals away
From the rude stream into the bay;
There locked up safe, she doth divorce
Her waters from the channel's course,
And scorns the torrent that did bring   5
Her headlong from her native spring.
Now doth she with her new love play,
Whilst he runs murmuring away.
Mark how she courts the banks, whilst they
As amorously their arms display,   10
T' embrace and clip her silver waves;
See how she strokes their sides, and craves

---

5. Sweetbrier.
6. Moderation.
7. The theme is a favorite with Carew's contemporaries; cf. especially Godolphin's "Song" ("Or love me less, or love me more"), which may have been modeled

on Carew's lyric.
8. Cf. Herrick, "A Nuptial Song," p. 129, l. 144 and note.
9. The informing conceit of this poem is taken from Donne's Elegy VI ("Oh, let me not serve so"), ll. 21–34.

An entrance there, which they deny;
Whereat she frowns, threat'ning to fly
Home to her stream, and 'gins to swim   15
Backward, but from the channel's brim,
Smiling, returns into the creek,
With thousand dimples on her cheek.
    Be thou this eddy, and I'll make
My breast thy shore, where thou shalt take   20
Secure repose, and never dream
Of the quite forsaken stream;
Let him to the wide ocean haste,
There lose his color, name, and taste;
Thou shalt save all, and, safe from him,   25
Within these arms forever swim.

Song: To My Inconstant Mistress[1]

When thou, poor excommunicate
  From all the joys of love, shalt see
The full reward, and glorious fate,
    Which my strong faith shall purchase me,
    Then curse thine own inconstancy.   5

A fairer hand than thine shalt cure
  That heart which thy false oaths did wound;
And to my soul, a soul more pure
    Than thine shall by Love's hand be bound,
    And both with equal glory crowned.   10

Then shalt thou weep, entreat, complain
  To Love, as I did once to thee;
When all thy tears shall be as vain
    As mine were then, for thou shalt be
    Damned for thy false apostasy.   15

Song: Persuasions to Enjoy

If the quick[2] spirits in your eye
Now languish, and anon[3] must die;
If every sweet, and every grace
Must fly from that forsaken face;
    Then, Celia, let us reap our joys,   5
    Ere Time such goodly fruit destroys.

Or if that golden fleece must grow
Forever, free from aged snow;

1. This poem bears comparison with Donne's "The Apparition."
2. Lively, vital. Cf. Herrick's "His Fare-well to Sack," p. 110, l. 2 and note.
3. Straightway.

If those bright suns must know no shade,
Nor your fresh beauties ever fade;   10
Then fear not, Celia, to bestow
What, still[4] being gathered, still must grow.
   Thus, either Time his sickle brings
   In vain, or else in vain his wings.

A Deposition from Love

I was foretold your rebel sex
   Nor love nor pity knew;
And with what scorn you use to vex
   Poor hearts that humbly sue;
Yet I believed, to crown our pain,   5
   Could we the fortress win,
The happy lover sure should gain
   A paradise within;
I thought love's plagues like dragons sate,[5]
Only to fright us at the gate.   10

But I did enter, and enjoy
   What happy lovers prove;
For I could kiss, and sport, and toy,
   And taste those sweets of love,
Which, had they but a lasting state,   15
   Or if in Celia's breast
The force of love might not abate,
   Jove were too mean[6] a guest.
But now her breach of faith far more
Afflicts, than did her scorn before.[7]   20

Hard fate! to have been once possessed,
   As victor, of a heart,
Achieved with labor and unrest,
   And then forced to depart.
If the stout foe will not resign   25
   When I besiege a town,
I lose but what was never mine;
   But he that is cast down
From enjoyed beauty, feels a woe
Only deposèd kings can know.   30

Ingrateful Beauty Threatened

Know, Celia, since thou art so proud,
   'Twas I that gave thee thy renown;

---

4. Continually.
5. Sat.
6. Humble.

7. Cf. Donne's "The Calme," ll. 3–4:
"The fable is inverted, and far more/A
block afflicts, now, than a stork before."

Thou hadst, in the forgotten crowd
    Of common beauties, lived unknown,
Had not my verse exhaled thy name,   5
And with it imped[8] the wings of fame.

That killing power is none of thine,
    I gave it to thy voice, and eyes;
Thy sweets, thy graces, all are mine;
    Thou art my star, shin'st in my skies;   10
Then dart not from thy borrowed sphere[9]
Lightning on him that fixed thee there.

Tempt me with such affrights no more,
    Lest what I made, I uncreate;
Let fools thy mystic forms adore,   15
    I'll know thee in thy mortal state;
Wise poets that wrapped truth in tales
Knew her themselves, through all her veils.[1]

Disdain Returned

He that loves a rosy cheek,
    Or a coral lip admires,
Or from star-like eyes doth seek
    Fuel to maintain his fires;
As old Time makes these decay,   5
So his flames must waste away.

But a smooth and steadfast mind,
    Gentle thoughts, and calm desires,
Hearts with equal love combined,
    Kindle never-dying fires.   10
Where these are not, I despise
Lovely cheeks, or lips, or eyes.

No tears, Celia, now shall win
    My resolved heart to return;
I have searched thy soul within,   15
    And find nought but pride and scorn;
I have learned thy arts, and now
    Can disdain as much as thou.
Some power,[2] in my revenge, convey
That love to her, I cast away.   20

8. I.e., grafted feathers onto (as falconers repair a bird's injured wing).
9. Cf. Herrick, "A Nuptial Song," p. 128, l. 102 and note. Herrick's "Siren," however, sings sweetly in her sphere; Carew's Celia combines the attributes of a star that sheds malign influence with (by implication) those of the enticing and dangerous Sirens of Homer's *Odys-*

sey, XII. 39–46, 184–200.
1. Renaissance mythographers regularly insist that poetry "veils truth in a fair and fitting garment of fiction" (Boccaccio, *Genealogia Deorum Gentilium, XIV–XV*, ed. C. G. Osgood [Indianapolis, 1956],p. 39).
2. I.e., may some god.

To My Mistress in Absence[3]

Though I must live here, and by force
Of your command suffer divorce;
Though I am parted, yet my mind,
That's more myself, still stays behind.
I breathe in you, you keep my heart;   5
'Twas but a carcass that did part.
Then though our bodies are disjoined,
As things that are to place confined,
Yet let our boundless spirits meet,
And in love's sphere each other greet;   10
There let us work a mystic wreath,
Unknown unto the world beneath;
There let our clasped loves sweetly twin,
There let our secret thoughts unseen
Like nets be weaved and intertwined,   15
Wherewith we'll catch each other's mind.
There whilst our souls do sit and kiss,
Tasting a sweet and subtle bliss
Such as gross lovers cannot know,
Whose hands and lips meet here below,   20
Let us look down, and mark what pain
Our absent bodies here sustain,
And smile to see how far away
The one doth from the other stray;
Yet burn and languish with desire   25
To join, and quench their mutual fire.
There let us joy to see from far
Our emulous flames at loving war,
Whilst both with equal lustre shine,
Mine bright as yours, yours bright as mine.   30
There seated in those heavenly bowers,
We'll cheat the lag and lingering hours,
Making our bitter absence sweet,
Till souls and bodies both may meet.

Song: Eternity of Love Protested

How ill doth he deserve a lover's name,
        Whose pale weak flame
        Cannot retain
His heat, in spite of absence or disdain;
But doth at once, like paper set on fire,   5
        Burn and expire;
True love can never change his seat,
Nor did he ever love, that could retreat.

---

3. Carew's poem recalls, but interestingly diverges from, Donne's "The Ecstasy." Lines 23–24 may owe something to Donne's "A Valediction Forbidding Mourning."

That noble flame which my breast keeps alive
　　　　Shall still survive　　　　　　　10
　　　When my soul's fled;
Nor shall my love die when my body's dead,
That shall wait on me to the lower shade,
　　　　And never fade;
My very ashes in their urn　　　　　　15
Shall, like a hallowed lamp, forever burn.[4]

To Saxham[5]

Though frost and snow locked from mine eyes
That beauty which without door lies,
Thy gardens, orchards, walks, that so
I might not all thy pleasures know,
Yet, Saxham, thou within thy gate　　　　5
Art of thyself so delicate,
So full of native sweets, that bless
Thy roof with inward happiness,
As neither from nor to thy store
Winter takes aught, or spring adds more.　　10
The cold and frozen air had starved[6]
Much poor, if not by thee preserved,
Whose prayers have made thy table blest
With plenty, far above the rest.
The season hardly did afford　　　　　　15
Coarse cates[7] unto thy neighbors' board,
Yet thou hadst dainties, as the sky
Had only been thy volary;[8]
Or else the birds, fearing the snow
Might to another Deluge grow,　　　　　20
The pheasant, partridge, and the lark
Flew to thy house, as to the Ark.[9]
The willing ox of himself came
Home to the slaughter, with the lamb,
And every beast did thither bring　　　　25
Himself, to be an offering.
The scaly herd more pleasure took,
Bathed in thy dish, than in the brook;
Water, earth, air, did all conspire
To pay their tributes to thy fire,　　　　30

4. Sir Thomas Browne inquires, in *Pseudodoxia Epidemica*, "Why some lamps included in close bodies have burned many hundred years, as that discovered in the sepulchre of Tullia the sister of Cicero . . ." (*The Prose of Sir Thomas Browne*, ed. N. J. Endicott [New York, 1967], p. 202). Donne also alludes to the lamp "in Tullia's tomb": cf. "Epithalamion," ll. 215–218.

5. Little Saxham, near Bury Saint Edmunds in Suffolk, was the country residence of Sir John Crofts (1563–1628), with whose family Carew maintained friendly relations. The poem is modeled on Jonson's "To Penshurst."
6. I.e., had caused to die.
7. Victuals, food.
8. Aviary.
9. Cf. Genesis 7:7.

Whose cherishing flames themselves divide
Through every room, where they deride
The night, and cold abroad; whilst they,
Like suns within, keep endless day.
Those cheerful beams send forth their light   35
To all that wander in the night,[1]
And seem to beckon from aloof[2]
The weary pilgrim to thy roof,
Where if, refreshed, he will away,
He's fairly welcome; or if stay,   40
Far more; which he shall hearty find
Both from the master and the hind.[3]
The stranger's welcome each man there
Stamped on his cheerful brow doth wear,
Nor doth this welcome or his cheer   45
Grow less 'cause he stays longer here;
There's none observes, much less repines,
How often this man sups or dines.
Thou hast no porter at the door
T' examine or keep back the poor;   50
Nor locks nor bolts: thy gates have been
Made only to let strangers in;
Untaught to shut, they do not fear
To stand wide open all the year,
Careless who enters, for they know   55
Thou never didst deserve a foe;
And as for thieves, thy bounty's such,
They cannot steal, thou giv'st so much.

Upon a Ribbon

This silken wreath, which circles in mine arm,[4]
Is but an emblem of that mystic charm,
Wherewith the magic of your beauties binds
My captive soul, and round about it winds
Fetters of lasting love. This hath entwined   5
My flesh alone, that hath empaled[5] my mind.
Time may wear out these soft weak bands, but those
Strong chains of brass, Fate shall not discompose.
This holy relic may preserve my wrist,
But my whole frame doth by that power subsist;   10
To that my prayers and sacrifice, to this
I only pay a superstitious kiss.
This but the idol, that's the deity;
Religion there is due; here, ceremony;

---

1. Cf. Matthew 5:16: "Let your light so shine before men, that they may see your good works. . . ."
2. I.e., from a distance.
3. Servant (or farm laborer on the estate).
4. Cf. Donne's "The Funeral" (notably l. 3: "That subtle wreath of hair, which crowns my arm") and "The Relic."
5. Enclosed.

That I receive by faith, this but in trust;   15
Here I may tender duty, there I must;
This order as a layman I may bear,
But I become Love's priest when that I wear.
This moves like air; that as the center[6] stands;
That knot your virtue tied, this but your hands;   20
That, nature framed; but this was made by art;
This makes my arm your prisoner; that, my heart.

A Rapture[7]

I will enjoy thee now, my Celia, come,
And fly with me to Love's Elysium.[8]
The giant, Honor, that keeps cowards out,
Is but a masquer,[9] and the servile rout
Of baser subjects only bend in vain   5
To the vast idol, whilst the nobler train
Of valiant lovers daily sail between
The huge colossus' legs,[1] and pass unseen
Unto the blissful shore. Be bold, and wise,[2]
And we shall enter; the grim Swiss[3] denies   10
Only to tame fools a passage, that not know
He is but form, and only frights in show
The duller eyes that look from far; draw near,
And thou shalt scorn what we were wont to fear.
We shall see how the stalking pageant[4] goes   15
With borrowed legs, a heavy load to those
That made and bear him; not, as we once thought,
The seed of gods, but a weak model wrought
By greedy men, that seek to enclose the common,[5]
And within private arms impale[6] free woman.   20
        Come, then, and mounted on the wings of Love
We'll cut the flitting air, and soar above
The monster's head, and in the noblest seats
Of those blest shades quench and renew our heats.

6. I.e., the earth (by Ptolemaic reckoning situated at the center of the created universe).

7. Carew's poem has some affinity with Donne's Elegy XIX ("Going to Bed"). Not very surprisingly, "The Rapture" excited the admiration of many among Carew's contemporaries; Randolph, Cartwright, John Cleveland, and others composed verses that clearly reflect the influence of its language and tone.

8. I.e., love's paradise. In the Latin poets, Elysium is that part of the underworld reserved for those whose earthly lives had been heroic or markedly righteous (cf. Vergil, *Aeneid*, VI. 637–678).

9. I.e., one who plays a part in a courtly entertainment.

1. The Colossus of Rhodes, one of the seven wonders of the ancient world, was a statue of Apollo, some 120 feet high, made by Chares in the third century B.C.

2. It is not unlikely that Carew ironically recalls that inscription in the House of Busirane, which challenged the wit of chaste Britomart: *"Be bold, be bold, and every where Be bold . . . Be not too bold"* (*The Faerie Queene*, III. xi. 54).

3. The Swiss guards at the Vatican, in Rome, were renowned for their stature.

4. I.e., honor, mere show without substance.

5. I.e., to seize for personal gain that which is properly common to all (as rich men "enclosed" common land for pasturage).

6. I.e., (1) enclose; (2) penetrate.

There shall the Queen of Love, and Innocence,   25
Beauty, and Nature, banish all offence
From our close ivy-twines; there I'll behold
Thy baréd snow and thy unbraided gold;
There my enfranchised hand on every side
Shall o'er thy naked polished ivory slide.   30
No curtain there, though of transparent lawn,[7]
Shall be before thy virgin-treasure drawn;
But the rich mine, to the inquiring eye
Exposed, shall ready still for mintage lie,
And we will coin young Cupids. There a bed   35
Of roses and fresh myrtles shall be spread
Under the cooler shade of cypress groves;
Our pillows, of the down of Venus' doves,[8]
Whereon our panting limbs we'll gently lay,
In the faint respites of our active play;   40
That so our slumbers may in dreams have leisure
To tell the nimble fancy our past pleasure,
And so our souls that cannot be embraced
Shall the embraces of our bodies taste.
Meanwhile the bubbling stream shall court the shore,   45
Th' enamored chirping wood-choir shall adore
In varied tunes the deity of love;
The gentle blasts of western winds shall move
The trembling leaves, and through their close boughs
        breathe
Still music, whilst we rest ourselves beneath   50
Their dancing shade; till a soft murmur, sent
From souls entranced in amorous languishment,
Rouse us, and shoot into our veins fresh fire,
Till we in their sweet ecstasy expire.
    Then, as the empty bee, that lately bore   55
Into the common treasure all her store,
Flies 'bout the painted field with nimble wing,
Deflow'ring the fresh virgins of the spring,
So will I rifle all the sweets that dwell
In my delicious paradise, and swell   60
My bag with honey, drawn forth by the power
Of fervent kisses, from each spicy flower.
I'll seize the rose-buds in their perfumed bed,
The violet knots, like curious mazes spread
O'er all the garden, taste the ripened cherry,   65
The warm, firm apple, tipped with coral berry;
Then will I visit with a wand'ring kiss
The vale of lilies and the bower of bliss;
And where the beauteous region doth divide
Into two milky ways, my lips shall slide   70

7. Fine linen.   no. 4, p. 48, l. 3 and note.
8. Cf. Jonson's "A Celebration of Charis,"

Down those smooth alleys, wearing as I go
A tract[9] for lovers on the printed snow;
Thence climbing o'er the swelling Apennine,
Retire into thy grove of eglantine,[1]
Where I will all those ravished sweets distill   75
Through Love's alembic,[2] and with chemic skill
From the mixed mass one sovereign balm derive,
Then bring that great elixir to thy hive.
    Now in more subtle wreaths I will entwine
My sinewy thighs, my legs and arms with thine;   80
Thou like a sea of milk shalt lie displayed,
Whilst I the smooth, calm ocean invade
With such tempest, as when Jove of old
Fell down on Danaë in a storm of gold;[3]
Yet my tall pine shall in the Cyprian[4] strait   85
Ride safe at anchor, and unlade her freight;
My rudder, with thy bold hand, like a tried
And skillful pilot, thou shalt steer, and guide
My bark into love's channel, where it shall
Dance, as the bounding waves do rise or fall.   90
Then shall thy circling arms embrace and clip
My willing body, and thy balmy lip
Bathe me in juice of kisses, whose perfume
Like a religious incense shall consume,
And send up holy vapors to those powers   95
That bless our loves, and crown our sportful hours,
That with such halcyon[5] calmness fix our souls
In steadfast peace, as no affright controls.
There no rude sounds shake us with sudden starts;
No jealous ears, when we unrip our hearts,   100
Suck our discourse in; no observing spies
This blush, that glance traduce; no envious eyes
Watch our close meetings; nor are we betrayed
To rivals by the bribéd chambermaid.
No wedlock bonds unwreathe our twisted loves;   105
We seek no midnight arbor, no dark groves
To hide our kisses: there the hated name
Of husband, wife, lust, modest, chaste, or shame,
Are vain and empty words, whose very sound
Was never heard in the Elysian ground.   110
All things are lawful there that may delight
Nature or unrestrainéd appetite;
Like and enjoy, to will and act is one:

---

9. Path.
1. Sweetbrier.
2. An alembic was a vessel used in alchemical ("chemic") distillation.
3. Cf. Herrick's "A Nuptial Song," p. 129, 1. 144 and note.
4. The island of Cyprus was a center of the worship of Venus.
5. According to legend, during that period when the halcyon (a sea bird) makes and maintains her nest, the ocean's waves are calm; cf. Ovid, *Metamorphoses*, XI. 415–748.

We only sin when Love's rites are not done.
　The Roman Lucrece[6] there reads the divine 　　　115
Lectures of love's great master, Aretine,[7]
And knows as well as Lais[8] how to move
Her pliant body in the act of love.
To quench the burning ravisher, she hurls
Her limbs into a thousand winding curls, 　　　120
And studies artful postures, such as be
Carved on the bark of every neighboring tree
By learned hands, that so adorned the rind
Of those fair plants, which, as they lay entwined,
Have fanned their glowing fires. The Grecian dame,[9]　125
That in her endless web toiled for a name
As fruitless as her work, doth there display
Herself before the youth of Ithaca,
And th' amorous sport of gamesome nights prefer
Before dull dreams of the lost traveller. 　　　130
Daphne[1] hath broke her bark, and that swift foot,
Which th' angry gods has fastened with a root
To the fixed earth, doth now unfettered run
To meet th' embraces of the youthful sun.
She hangs upon him like his Delphic lyre; 　　　135
Her kisses blow the old, and breathe new fire;
Full of her god, she sings inspiréd lays,
Sweet odes of love, such as deserve the bays,
Which she herself was. Next her, Laura[2] lies
In Petrarch's learned arms, drying those eyes 　　　140
That did in such sweet smooth-paced numbers flow,
As made the world enamored of his woe.
These, and ten thousand beauties more, that died
Slave to the tyrant, now enlarged, deride
His cancelled laws, and for their time misspent 　　　145
Pay into Love's exchequer double rent.
　　Come then, my Celia, we'll no more forbear
To taste our joys, struck with a panic fear,
But will depose from his imperious sway
This proud usurper,[3] and walk free as they, 　　　150
With necks unyoked; nor is it just that he
Should fetter your soft sex with chastity,

6. The name of Lucretia, who took her own life after she had been raped by Tarquin, became a byword for chastity in later times.
7. Pietro Aretino (1492–1556) composed mock-moralistic sonnets to accompany a set of lascivious engravings by Marcantonio Raimondi. Robert Burton notes that "Aretine's Lucretia [in another of Aretino's works] sold her maidenhead a thousand times before she was twenty-four years old" (*Anatomy of Melancholy, ed. cit.*, III, p. 54.)
8. Lais was a beautiful and talented courtesan of Corinth in the fifth century B.C. Cf. Athenaeus, *The Learned Banquet*, XIII, for an account of her career (and of other celebrated courtesans of ancient times).
9. A number of classical writers deny that Penelope, the wife of Odysseus, remained faithful to her husband during his long absence from Ithaca.
1. Cf. Herrick, "The Welcome to Sack," p. 119, l. 92 and note.
2. Petrarch (1304–1374) addressed his celebrated sonnets to Laura.
3. I.e., honor.

Which Nature made unapt for abstinence;
When yet this false imposter can dispense
With human justice and with sacred right,   155
And, maugre[4] both their laws, command me fight
With rivals, or with emulous loves, that dare
Equal with thine their mistress' eyes or hair.
If thou complain of wrong, and call my sword
To carve out thy revenge, upon that word   160
He bids me fight and kill, or else he brands
With marks of infamy my coward hands,
And yet religion bids from bloodshed fly,
And damns me for that act. Then tell me why
This goblin Honor, which the world adores,   165
Should make men atheists, and not women whores.

Epitaph on the Lady Mary Villiers[5]

The Lady Mary Villiers lies
Under this stone; with weeping eyes
The parents that first gave her birth,
And their sad friends, laid her in earth.
If any of them, reader, were   5
Known unto thee, shed a tear;
Or if thyself possess a gem
As dear to thee as this to them,
Though a stranger to this place,
Bewail in theirs, thine own hard case;   10
For thou perhaps at thy return
Mayest find thy darling in an urn.

Another[6]

The purest soul that e'er was sent
Into a clayey tenement
Informed this dust; but the weak mold
Could the great guest no longer hold;
The substance was too pure, the flame   5
Too glorious that thither came;
Ten thousand Cupids brought along
A grace on each wing, that did throng
For place there, till they all oppressed
The seat in which they sought to rest;   10
So the fair model[7] broke, for want
Of room to lodge th' inhabitant.

4. In spite of.
5. Mary Villiers, the daughter of the Earl and Countess of Anglesey (who were Carew's patrons), died on August 4, 1630, about five months after her second birthday.
6. Cf. Textual Notes, p. 380.
7. Mold.

Another

This little vault, this narrow room,
Of love and beauty is the tomb;
The dawning beam that 'gan to clear
Our clouded sky, lies darkened here,
Forever set to us, by death
Sent to inflame the world beneath.
'Twas but a bud, yet did contain
More sweetness than shall spring again;
A budding star that might have grown
Into a sun, when it had blown.[8]
This hopeful beauty did create
New life in Love's declining state;
But now his empire ends, and we
From fire and wounding darts are free;
His brand, his bow, let no man fear:
The flames, the arrows, all lie here.

[*Epitaph for Maria Wentworth*][9]

And here the precious dust is laid;
Whose purely-tempered clay was made
So fine that it the guest betrayed.

Else the soul grew so fast within,
It broke the outward shell of sin,   5
And so was hatched a cherubin.

In height, it soared to God above;
In depth, it did to knowledge move,
And spread in breadth to general love.

Before, a pious duty shined   10
To parents, courtesy behind;
On either side an equal mind.

Good to the poor, to kindred dear,
To servants kind, to friendship clear,
To nothing but herself severe.   15

So, though a virgin, yet a bride
To every grace, she justified
A chaste polygamy, and died.

---

8. Fully opened.
9. The second daughter of Sir Thomas Wentworth (and Anne Wentworth, whose father was Sir John Crofts, of Saxham), Maria died in January, 1633, aged eighteen. The first six verses of Carew's epitaph are inscribed on her tomb in the parish church at Toddington, Bedfordshire.

Learn from hence, reader, what small trust
We owe this world, where virtue must,   20
Frail as our flesh, crumble to dust.

To Ben Jonson: Upon Occasion of His Ode of Defiance Annexed to His Play of The New Inn[1]

'Tis true, dear Ben, thy just chastising hand
Hath fixed upon the sotted age a brand,
To their swoll'n pride and empty scribbling due;
It can nor judge nor write, and yet 'tis true
Thy comic Muse, from the exalted line   5
Touched by thy *Alchemist*, doth since decline
From that her zenith, and foretells a red
And blushing evening, when she goes to bed;
Yet such as shall outshine the glimmering light
With which all stars shall gild the following night.   10
Nor think it much, since all thy eaglets may
Endure the sunny trial,[2] if we say
This hath the stronger wing, or that doth shine
Tricked up in fairer plumes, since all are thine.
Who hath his flock of cackling geese compared   15
With thy tuned choir of swans?[3] or else who dared
To call thy births deformed? But if thou bind
By city-custom, or by gavelkind,[4]
In equal shares thy love on all thy race,
We may distinguish of their sex and place;   20
Though one hand form them, and though one brain strike
Souls into all, they are not all alike.
Why should the follies, then, of this dull age
Draw from thy pen such an immodest rage,
As seems to blast thy (else-immortal) bays,[5]   25
When thine own tongue proclaims thy itch of praise?
Such thirst will argue drouth. No, let be hurled
Upon thy works, by the detracting world,
What malice can suggest; let the rout[6] say,
The running sands, that, ere thou make a play,   30
Count the slow minutes, might a Goodwin[7] frame,
To swallow, when th' hast done, thy shipwrecked name.

---

1. Cf. Jonson's "Ode to Himself," p. 88 and notes.
2. It was believed that eagles confirmed the nature of their young by forcing them to gaze directly at the sun. Cf. *The Bestiary, ed. cit.*, p. 107.
3. "In the Northern parts of the world, once the lute players have tuned up, a great many swans are invited in, and they play a concert together in strict measure" (*The Bestiary, ed. cit.*, p. 119).
4. I.e., according to the London regula-

tion by which a citizen's estate was divided equally among his wife, children, and executors; or the Kentish practice, by which each heir received an equal share of the estate.
5. I.e., the laurel wreath, symbolic of excellence in poetry.
6. Rabble.
7. The notorious Goodwin Sands, near Ramsgate, posed a continual threat to coastal shipping.

Let them the dear expense of oil upbraid,
Sucked by thy watchful lamp, that hath betrayed
To theft the blood of martyred authors, spilt   35
Into thy ink, whilst thou growest pale with guilt.
Repine not at the taper's thrifty waste,
That sleeks thy terser poems; nor is haste
Praise, but excuse;[8] and if thou overcome
A knotty writer, bring the booty home;   40
Nor think it theft, if the rich spoils so torn
From conquered authors be as trophies worn.
Let others glut on the extorted praise
Of vulgar breath; trust thou to after-days:
Thy labored works shall live, when Time devours   45
Th' abortive offspring of their hasty hours.
Thou art not of their rank, the quarrel lies
Within thine own verge;[9] then let this suffice,
The wiser world doth greater thee confess
Than all men else, than thyself only less.   50

An Elegy upon the Death of Dr. Donne, Dean of Paul's[1]

Can we not force from widowed poetry,
Now thou art dead, great Donne, one elegy
To crown thy hearse? Why yet dare we not trust,
Though with unkneaded dough-baked[2] prose, thy dust,
Such as the unscissored[3] churchman, from the flower   5
Of fading rhetoric, short-lived as his hour,
Dry as the sand that measures it, should lay
Upon thy ashes on the funeral day?
Have we no voice, no tune? Didst thou dispense
Through all our language both the words and sense?   10
'Tis a sad truth. The pulpit may her plain
And sober Christian precepts still retain;
Doctrines it may, and wholesome uses, frame,
Grave homilies and lectures, but the flame
Of thy brave[4] soul, that shot such heat and light   15
As burnt our earth, and made our darkness bright,
Committed holy rapes upon our will,
Did through the eye the melting heart distill,
And the deep knowledge of dark truths so teach,

8. Cf. Jonson's distinction between "common rhymers" who "pour forth verses, such as they are, *ex tempore*," and the true poet, who understands the importance of careful revision, in *Timber*, p. 415.
9. Domain.
1. Donne died on March 31, 1631. The text given here is that which appears in *Poems, by J[ohn]. D[onne]. with Elegies on the Authors Death* (1633), 385–388. Cf. Textual Notes, p. 380, for significant variants in the text printed in the 1640 edition of Carew's *Poems*.
2. I.e., tedious and flat. Cf. Donne, "A Letter to the Lady Carey, and Mrs. Essex Riche, from Amiens," ll. 19–21.
3. Unshorn; i.e., with uncut hair.
4. Superior.

As sense might judge what fancy could not reach,   20
Must be desired forever. So the fire
That fills with spirit and heat the Delphic choir,[5]
Which, kindled first by thy Promethean[6] breath,
Glowed here awhile, lies quenched now in thy death.
The Muses' garden, with pedantic weeds   25
O'erspread, was purged by thee; the lazy seeds
Of servile imitation thrown away,
And fresh invention planted. Thou didst pay
The debts of our penurious bankrupt age;
Licentious thefts, that make poetic rage   30
A mimic fury, when our souls must be
Possessed, or with Anacreon's[7] ecstasy,
Or Pindar's, not their own; the subtle cheat
Of sly exchanges, and the juggling feat
Of two-edged words,[8] or whatsoever wrong   35
By ours was done the Greek, or Latin tongue,
Thou hast redeemed, and opened us a mine
Of rich and pregnant fancy; drawn a line
Of masculine expression,[9] which had good
Old Orpheus[1] seen, or all the ancient brood   40
Our superstitious fools admire, and hold
Their lead more precious than thy burnished gold,
Thou hadst been their exchequer, and no more
They each in other's dust had raked for ore.
Thou shalt yield no precedence, but of time,   45
And the blind fate of language, whose tuned chime
More charms the outward sense; yet thou mayst claim
From so great disadvantage greater fame,
Since to the awe of thy imperious wit
Our stubborn language bends, made only fit   50
With her tough thick-ribbed hoops to gird about
Thy giant fancy, which had proved too stout
For their soft melting phrases. As in time
They had the start, so did they cull the prime
Buds of invention many a hundred year,   55
And left the rifled fields, besides the fear
To touch their harvest; yet from those bare lands
Of what is purely thine, thy only hands,

---

5. I.e., the echoing pronouncements of Apollo's oracle at Delphi.
6. Prometheus stole fire from heaven, in spite of Zeus' attempt to conceal it; cf. Hesiod, *Works and Days*, 47–53.
7. For Anacreon, cf. Jonson, Epigram CI, p. 12, 1. 31 and note; for Pindar, cf. Jonson, "To the Immortal Memory [of] Sir Lucius Cary and Sir H. Morison," p. 76, second note.
8. I.e., perhaps, puns and ambiguous terms (although these are often encountered in Donne's poetry).
9. Cf. Jonson, "An Execration Upon Vulcan," p. 69, 1. 78 and note.
1. Cf. Jonson, *The Forest*, XII, p. 38, 1. 77 and note.

(And that thy smallest work) have gleanéd more
Than all those times and tongues could reap before.   60
    But thou art gone, and thy strict laws will be
Too hard for libertines in poetry.
They will repeal[2] the goodly exiled train
Of gods and goddesses, which in thy just reign
Were banished nobler poems; now, with these,   65
The silenced tales o'th' *Metamorphoses*[3]
Shall stuff their lines, and swell the windy page,
Till verse, refined by thee, in this last age
Turn ballad-rhyme,[4] or those old idols be
Adored again with new apostasy.[5]   70
    O pardon me, that break with untuned verse
The reverend silence that attends thy hearse,
Whose awful[6] solemn murmurs were to thee,
More than these faint lines, a loud elegy,
That did proclaim in a dumb eloquence   75
The death of all the arts, whose influence,
Grown feeble, in these panting numbers lies
Gasping short-winded accents, and so dies.
So doth the swiftly turning wheel not stand
In th' instant we withdraw the moving hand,   80
But some small time maintain a faint weak course,
By virtue of the first impulsive force;
And so, whilst I cast on thy funeral pile
Thy crown of bays, oh, let it crack awhile,
And spit disdain, till the devouring flashes   85
Suck all the moisture up, then turn to ashes.
    I will not draw the envy to engross[7]
All thy perfections, or weep all our loss;
Those are too numerous[8] for an elegy,
And this too great to be expressed by me.   90
Though every pen should share a distinct part,
Yet art thou theme enough to 'tire[9] all art;
Let others carve the rest; it shall suffice
I on thy tomb this epitaph incise:
    Here lies a king, that ruled as he thought fit   95
    The universal monarchy of wit;
    Here lie two flamens,[1] and both those the best:
    Apollo's first, at last the true God's priest.

---

2. Call back.
3. Ovid's storehouse of myth and legend, first translated into English by Arthur Golding in 1567, had been translated c. 1621–1626 by George Sandys.
4. I.e., altogether decline into a condition of crude rhyming and versing.
5. I.e., apostasy from Donne's exemplary rule.
6. I.e., awe-struck.
7. I.e., to write large.
8. I.e., too many (also, punningly, "too largely poetical").
9. I.e., to attire, adorn (with a pun on "tire": to wear out).
1. Priests.

In Answer of an Elegiacal Letter, upon the Death of the King of Sweden, from Aurelian Townshend, Inviting Me to Write on that Subject[2]

Why dost thou sound, my dear Aurelian,
In so shrill accents, from thy Barbican,[3]
A loud alarum to my drowsy eyes,
Bidding them wake in tears and elegies
For mighty Sweden's fall? Alas! how may   5
My lyric feet, that of the smooth soft way
Of love, and beauty, only know the tread,
In dancing paces celebrate the dead
Victorious king, or his majestic hearse
Profane with th' humble touch of their low verse?   10
Vergil, nor Lucan,[4] no, nor Tasso more
Than both, nor Donne, worth all that went before,
With the united labor of their wit,
Could a just poem to this subject fit.
His actions were too mighty to be raised   15
Higher by verse; let him in prose be praised,
In modest, faithful story, which his deeds
Shall turn to poems. When the next age reads
Of Frankfort, Leipzig, Würzburg, of the Rhine,
The Lech, the Danube, Tilly, Wallenstein,   20
Bavaria, Pappenheim, Lützen-field,[5] where he
Gained after death a posthume victory,
They'll think his acts things rather feigned than done,
Like our romances of the Knight o' th' Sun.[6]
Leave we him, then, to the grave chronicler,   25
Who, though to annals[7] he cannot refer
His too brief story, yet his journals may
Stand by the Caesars' years, and every day
Cut into minutes, each shall more contain

2. Gustavus II (Gustavus Adolphus), King of Sweden, led the Protestant armies to their first military successes against the forces of the Holy Roman Empire during the Thirty Years' War (1618–1648). He was killed at the battle of Lützen, near Leipzig, on November 16, 1632, although his troops defeated the Catholic army under Wallenstein on that occasion. Aurelian Townshend (c. 1583–c. 1651) was a minor poet who wrote two masques for the court in 1632, *Albion's Triumph* and *Tempe Restored*. The poem to which Carew here responds is printed in Rhodes Dunlap's edition of Carew's poetry, pp. 207–208.
3. Townshend resided for some years in the London parish of Saint Giles, Cripplegate; the Barbican (originally an armed watchtower) is an area within that parish.
4. Marcus Annaeus Lucanus (A.D. 39–65), called Lucan, wrote the heroic poem *Pharsalia*, an account in ten books of the conflict between Pompey and Caesar; Torquato Tasso (1544–1595) was renowned primarily for his epic poem about the Crusades, *Gerusalemme Liberata* (1581).
5. The Catholic generals Tilly, Wallenstein, and Pappenheim, regularly victorious in the early stages of the Thirty Years' War, met their match in Gustavus Adolphus. Tilly died of wounds received at the crossing of the river Lech; Pappenheim was fatally wounded at Lützen, where the imperial army under Wallenstein was defeated. Wallenstein was assassinated in 1634.
6. The Knight of the Sun was the hero of a popular sixteenth-century Spanish romance, translated into English (c. 1580–1601) as *The Mirror of Princely Deeds and Knighthood*.
7. Carew probably alludes to the *Annales* of Tacitus (c. A.D. 59–c. 118).

Of great designment than an emperor's reign.   30
And, since 'twas but his churchyard, let him have
For his own ashes now no narrower grave
Than the whole German continent's vast womb,
Whilst all her cities do but make his tomb.
Let us to supreme providence commit   35
The fate of monarchs, which first thought it fit
To rend the empire from the Austrian grasp;
And next from Sweden's, even when he did clasp
Within his dying arms the sovereignty
Of all those provinces, that men might see   40
The divine wisdom would not leave that land
Subject to any one king's sole command.
Then let the Germans fear if Caesar shall,
Or the united princes, rise and fall;
But let us, that in myrtle bowers sit   45
Under secure shades, use the benefit
Of peace and plenty, which the blessed hand
Of our good king gives this obdurate land;
Let us of revels sing, and let thy breath,
Which filled Fame's trumpet with Gustavus' death,   50
Blowing his name to heaven, gently inspire
Thy past'ral pipe, till all our swains admire
Thy song and subject, whilst they both comprise
The beauties of the *Shepherd's Paradise*.[8]
For who like thee (whose loose discourse is far   55
More neat and polished than our poems are,
Whose very gait's more graceful than our dance)
In sweetly-flowing numbers may advance
The glorious night when, not to act foul rapes
Like birds or beasts, but in their angel-shapes,   60
A troop of deities came down to guide
Our steerless barks in passion's swelling tide
By virtue's card,[9] and brought us from above
A pattern of their own celestial love?
Nor lay it in dark, sullen precepts drowned,   65
But with rich fancy and clear action crowned,
Through a mysterious fable, that was drawn
Like a transparent veil of purest lawn
Before their dazzling beauties, the divine
Venus did with her heavenly Cupid shine.   70
The story's curious web, the masculine style,
The subtle sense, did time and sleep beguile;
Pinioned and charmed they stood to gaze upon
Th'angelic forms, gestures, and motion,
To hear those ravishing sounds that did dispense   75
Knowledge and pleasure to the soul and sense.

8. I.e., Townshend's masque, *Tempe*   1633.
Restored, presented at court in January,   9. Compass.

It filled us with amazement to behold
Love made all spirit, his corporeal mould,
Dissected into atoms, melt away
To empty air, and from the gross allay[1]   80
Of mixtures and compounding accidents,[2]
Refined to immaterial elements.
But when the Queen of Beauty[3] did inspire
The air with perfumes, and our hearts with fire,
Breathing from her celestial organ[4] sweet   85
Harmonious notes, our souls fell at her feet,
And did with humble reverent duty more
Her rare perfections than high state adore.
    These harmless pastimes let my Townshend sing
To rural tunes; not that thy Muse wants wing   90
To soar a loftier pitch, for she hath made
A noble flight, and placed th'heroic shade
Above the reach of our faint flagging rhyme;
But these are subjects proper to our clime: 95
Tourneys, masques, theaters, better become
Our halcyon[5] days. What though the German drum
Bellow for freedom and revenge? The noise
Concerns not us, nor should divert our joys;
Nor ought the thunder of their carabins[6]
Drown the sweet airs of our tuned violins.   100
Believe me, friend, if their prevailing powers
Gain them a calm security like ours,
They'll hang their arms up on the olive bough,
And dance, and revel then, as we do now.

To a Lady that Desired I Would Love Her

Now you have freely given me leave to love,
    What will you do?
Shall I your mirth or pastime move
    When I begin to woo?
Will you torment, or scorn, or love me too?   5

Each petty beauty can disdain, and I,
    Spite of your hate,
Without your leave can see, and die;
    Dispense a nobler fate:
'Tis easy to destroy, you may create.   10

Then give me leave to love, and love me too,
    Not with design

---

1. Alloy.
2. Nonessential qualities.
3. Queen Henrietta Maria took this role in *Tempe Restored*.
4. I.e., throat.
5. Cf. "A Rapture," p. 168, l. 97 and note.
6. Carbines (short firearms).

To raise, as love's curst rebels do
  When puling poets whine,
Fame to their beauty from their blubbered eyne.   15

Grief is a puddle, and reflects not clear
  Your beauty's rays;
Joys are pure streams, your eyes appear
  Sullen in sadder lays;
In cheerful numbers they shine bright with praise,   20

Which shall not mention, to express you fair,
  Wounds, flames, and darts,
Storms in your brow, nets in your hair,
  Suborning all your parts,
Or to bertay or torture captive hearts.   25

I'll make your eyes like morning suns appear,
  As mild and fair,
Your brow as crystal smooth and clear,
  And your disheveled hair
Shall flow like a calm region of the air.   30

Rich nature's store, which is the poet's treasure,
  I'll spend to dress
Your beauties; if your mine of pleasure
  In equal thankfulness
You but unlock, so we each other bless.   35

To My Friend G. N., from Wrest[7]

I breathe, sweet Ghib, the temperate air of Wrest,
Where I no more, with raging storms oppressed,
Wear the cold nights out by the banks of Tweed,[8]
On the bleak mountains where fierce tempests breed,
And everlasting winter dwells; where mild   5
Favonius[9] and the vernal winds exiled
Did never spread their wings, but the wild north
Brings sterile fern, thistles, and brambles forth.
Here, steeped in balmy dew, the pregnant earth
Sends from her teeming womb a flow'ry birth,   10
And cherished with the warm sun's quick'ning heat,
Her porous bosom doth rich odors sweat,

---

7. The identity of "G. N." remains uncertain, although Rhodes Dunlap (*ed. cit.*, p. 256) makes a plausible case for Gilbert North, "who like Carew served Charles I as a gentleman of the privy chamber." The manor of Wrest Park, in Bedfordshire, belonged to Anthony de Grey, Earl of Kent. Carew's poem evidently owes something to Jonson's "To Penshurst."
8. Carew had taken part in Charles I's expedition against the Scots (the "first bishops' war"), an ill-advised venture terminated by the inconclusive Treaty of Berwick, in June, 1639.
9. I.e., Zephyrus, the west wind.

Whose perfumes through the ambient[1] air diffuse
Such native aromatics as we use;
No foreign gums, nor essence fetched from far,   15
No volatile spirits, nor compounds that are
Adulterate, but at nature's cheap expense
With far more genuine sweets refresh the sense.
Such pure and uncompounded beauties bless
This mansion with an useful comeliness,   20
Devoid of art, for here the architect
Did not with curious skill a pile erect
Of carvéd marble, touch,[2] or porphyry,
But built a house for hospitality.
No sumptuous chimney-piece of shining stone   25
Invites the stranger's eye to gaze upon,
And coldly entertains his sight, but clear
And cheerful flames cherish and warm him here;
No Doric nor Corinthian pillars grace
With imag'ry this structure's naked face;   30
The lord and lady of this place delight
Rather to be in act, than seem in sight.
Instead of statues to adorn their wall,
They throng with living men their merry hall,
Where at large tables filled with wholesome meats   35
The servant, tenant, and kind neighbor eats.
Some of that rank, spun of a finer thread,
Are with the women, steward, and chaplain fed
With daintier cates;[3] others of better note,
Whom wealth, parts,[4] office, or the herald's coat[5]   40
Have severed from the common, freely sit
At the lord's table, whose spread sides admit
A large access of friends to fill those seats
Of his capacious circle, filled with meats
Of choicest relish, till his oaken back   45
Under the load of piled-up dishes crack.
Nor think, because our pyramids and high
Exalted turrets threaten not the sky,
That therefore Wrest of narrowness complains,
Or straitened walls, for she more numerous trains   50
Of noble guests daily receives, and those
Can with far more conveniency dispose,[6]
Than prouder piles, where the vain builder spent
More cost in outward gay embellishment
Than real use; which was the sole design   55
Of our contriver, who made things not fine,
But fit for service. Amalthea's horn

---

1. Encompassing.
2. Cf. Jonson, "To Penshurst," p. 21,
l. 2 and note.
3. Viands.

4. Talents, abilities.
5. I.e., noble or gentle lineage.
6. Accommodate.

Of plenty[7] is not in effigy worn
Without the gate, but she within the door
Empties her free and unexhausted store.   60
Nor, crowned with wheaten wreaths, doth Ceres[8] stand
In stone, with a crook'd sickle in her hand;
Nor on a marble tun,[9] his face besmeared
With grapes, is curled unscissored[1] Bacchus reared;
We offer not in emblems to the eyes,   65
But to the taste those useful deities:
We press the juicy god, and quaff his blood,
And grind the yellow goddess into food.
Yet we decline not all the work of art,
But where more bounteous Nature bears a part   70
And guides her handmaid, if she but dispense
Fit matter, she with care and diligence
Employs her skill; for where the neighbor source
Pours forth her waters, she directs their course,
And entertains the flowing streams in deep   75
And spacious channels, where they slowly creep
In snaky windings, as the shelving ground
Leads them in circles, till they twice surround
This island mansion, which i'th'center placed
Is with a double crystal heaven embraced,   80
In which our watery constellations float,
Our fishes, swans, our waterman and boat,
Envied by those above, which wish to slake
Their starburnt limbs in our refreshing lake.
But they stick fast nailed to the barren sphere,[2]   85
Whilst our increase in fertile waters here
Disport, and wander freely where they please
Within the circuit of our narrow seas.
    With various trees we fringe the water's brink,
Whose thirsty roots the soaking moisture drink,   90
And whose extended boughs in equal ranks
Yield fruit, and shade, and beauty to the banks.
On this side young Vertumnus[3] sits, and courts
His ruddy-cheeked Pomona; Zephyr sports
On th'other, with loved Flora, yielding there   95
Sweets for the smell, sweets for the palate here.
But did you taste the high and mighty drink
Which from that fountain flows, you'd clearly think

---

7. According to one version of this myth, Amalthea was a nymph who fed Zeus with goat's milk; in return, Zeus endowed one of the goat's horns with the power of being filled with whatever the nymph might wish. This horn was called the cornucopia, or horn of plenty. Cf., for a basic reference, Apollodorus, *Library*, I. i. 6; but the myth has several variant forms.

8. Ceres is goddess of agriculture and of

the fruits of the earth, as Bacchus is god of wine.

9. Large cask.

1. I.e., with uncut hair.

2. I.e., (by Ptolemaic astronomy), the eighth sphere, containing the fixed stars.

3. Vertumnus, god of the seasons, courted and eventually won the wood nymph Pomona; cf. Ovid, *Metamorphoses*, XIV. 623–771.

The god of wine did his plump clusters bring
And crush the Falerne grape[4] into our spring;　　　　100
Or else disguised in watery robes did swim
To Ceres' bed, and make her big of him,
Begetting so himself on her; for know
Our vintage here in March doth nothing owe
To theirs in autumn, but our fire boils here　　　　105
As lusty liquor as the sun makes there.
　　Thus I enjoy myself, and taste the fruit
Of this blest peace, whilst toiled in the pursuit
Of bucks and stags, th' emblem of war,[5] you strive
To keep the memory of our arms alive.　　　　110

To My Worthy Friend Master George Sandys, On His Translations of the Psalms[6]

I press not to the choir, nor dare I greet
The holy place with my unhallowed feet;
My unwashed Muse pollutes not things divine,
Nor mingles her profaner notes with thine;
Here humbly at the porch she list'ning stays,　　　　5
And with glad ears sucks in thy sacred lays.
So devout penitents of old were wont,
Some without door and some beneath the font,
To stand and hear the Church's liturgies,
Yet not assist the solemn exercise.　　　　10
Sufficeth her that she a lay-place[7] gain,
To trim thy vestments, or but bear thy train;
Though nor in tune nor wing she reach thy lark,
Her lyric feet may dance before the Ark.[8]
Who knows but that her wand'ring eyes, that run　　　　15
Now hunting glowworms, may adore the sun?
A pure flame may, shot by almighty power
Into her breast, the earthy flame devour.
My eyes in penitential dew may steep
That brine which they for sensual love did weep.　　　　20
So, though 'gainst nature's course, fire may be quenched
With fire, and water be with water drenched.
Perhaps my restless soul, tired with pursuit
Of mortal beauty, seeking without fruit
Contentment there, which hath not, when enjoyed,　　　　25
Quenched all her thirst, nor satisfied, though cloyed,

---

4. The "Falernian fields" in Campania were famous for the wine made from grapes grown there.
5. I.e., the hunt.
6. Cf. "An Elegy Upon the Death of Dr. Donne," p. 175, l. 66 and note. Carew's poem was first published in the second edition of Sandys's *A Paraphrase upon the Divine Poems* (1638).
7. I.e., a place appropriate for one not in holy orders.
8. Cf. II Samuel 6:14–15: "David danced before the Lord with all his might. . . . David and all the house of Israel brought up the ark of the Lord with shouting, and with the sound of the trumpet."

Weary of her vain search below, above
In the first Fair[9] may find th' immortal love.
Prompted by thy example then, no more
In molds of clay will I my God adore;   30
But tear those idols from my heart, and write
What His blest Spirit, not fond love, shall indite.
Then I no more shall court the verdant bay,[1]
But the dry leafless trunk on Golgotha,[2]
And rather strive to gain from thence one thorn,   35
Than all the flourishing wreaths by laureates worn.

The Comparison[3]

Dearest, thy tresses are not threads of gold,
Thy eyes of diamonds, nor do I hold
Thy lips for rubies, thy fair cheeks to be
Fresh roses, or thy teeth of ivory;
Thy skin that doth thy dainty body sheathe   5
Not alabaster is, nor dost thou breathe
Arabian odors; those the earth brings forth,
Compared with which would but impair thy worth.
Such may be others' mistresses, but mine
Holds nothing earthly, but is all divine.   10
Thy tresses are those rays that do arise
Not from one sun, but two; such are thy eyes;
Thy lips congealéd nectar are, and such
As, but a deity, there's none dare touch.
The perfect crimson that thy cheek doth clothe,   15
But only that it far exceeds them both,
Aurora's[4] blush resembles, or that red
That Iris struts in when her mantle's spread.
Thy teeth in white do Leda's swan exceed;
Thy skin's a heavenly and immortal weed;[5]   20
And when thou breath'st, the winds are ready
    straight
To filch it from thee, and do therefore wait
Close at thy lips, and snatching it from thence,
Bear it to heaven, where 'tis Jove's frankincense.
Fair goddess, since thy feature[6] makes thee one,   25
Yet be not such for these respects alone;
But as you are divine in outward view,
So be within as fair, as good, as true.

---

9. I.e., God.
1. I.e., the green laurels awarded to poets.
2. I.e., the cross on which Christ was crucified.
3. Cf. Shakespeare's Sonnet 130; also Donne's Elegy VIII ("The Compari-son").
4. Aurora is goddess of the dawn; Iris, goddess of the rainbow. Zeus assumed the form of a swan in order to enjoy Leda; cf. Ovid, *Metamorphoses*, VI. 109.
5. Attire.
6. Physical beauty.

A Song[7]

Ask me no more where Jove bestows,
When June is past, the fading rose;
For in your beauty's orient[8] deep
These flowers, as in their causes,[9] sleep.

Ask me no more whither doth stray   5
The golden atoms of the day;
For in pure love heaven did prepare
Those powders to enrich your hair.

Ask me no more whither doth haste
The nightingale, when May is past;   10
For in your sweet dividing[1] throat
She winters, and keeps warm her note.

Ask me no more where those stars light,
That downwards fall in dead of night;
For in your eyes they sit, and there   15
Fixéd become, as in their sphere.[2]

Ask me no more if east or west
The phoenix[3] builds her spicy nest;
For unto you at last she flies,
And in your fragrant bosom dies.   20

From *POEMS* (1651)

Upon a Mole in Celia's Bosom

The lovely spot which thou dost see
In Celia's bosom was a bee,
Who built her amorous spicy nest
I'th'Hyblas[4] of her either breast;
But from close[5] ivory hives, she flew   5
To suck the aromatic dew

---

7. Like Donne's "Go and catch a falling star," and Herrick's "To Find God," this poem is built about a series of impossible demands. Cf. Textual Notes, p. 380, for variants of language and stanza-arrangement, probably representing earlier drafts of the text given here.
8. Lustrous.
9. Carew probably alludes to Aristotle's "formal cause": "the form or the archetype" of a thing (or, possibly, to the "material cause": "that out of which a thing comes to be and which persists"). Cf. *Physics*, II. ii. 3, in *Basic Works of*

Aristotle, ed. R. McKeon (New York, 1941), p. 240.
1. Harmonious (as in singing).
2. I.e., as in their appropriate place in the heavens.
3. According to Egyptian fable, the phoenix builds her nest of aromatic twigs; every five hundred years she dies by fiery self-immolation, only to be at once reborn from the ashes of her funeral pyre.
4. Mount Hybla, in Sicily, was famous for the quality of the honey produced on its slopes.
5. Secluded.

Which from the neighbor vale distills,
Which parts those two twin-sister hills.
There feasting on ambrosial meat,
A rolling file of balmy sweat,   10
As in soft murmurs before death
Swan-like she sung, choked up her breath;
So she in water did expire,
More precious than the phoenix' fire.
    Yet still her shadow there remains   15
Confined to those Elysian plains,
With this strict law, that who shall lay
His bold lips on that milky way,
The sweet, and smart, from thence shall bring
Of the bee's honey, and her sting.   20

A Fancy

Mark how this polished eastern sheet
Doth with our northern tincture meet,
For though the paper seem to sink,
Yet it receives and bears the ink;
And on her smooth soft brow these spots   5
Seem rather ornaments than blots;
Like those you ladies use to place
Mysteriously about your face,
Not only to set off and break
Shadows and eye-beams, but to speak   10
To the skilled lover, and relate
Unheard his sad or happy fate;
Nor do their characters[6] delight
As careless works of black and white,
But 'cause you underneath may find   15
A sense that can inform the mind;
Divine or moral rules impart,
Or raptures of poetic art;
So what at first was only fit
To fold up silks, may wrap up wit.   20

---

6. Signs, marks.

James Shirley

1596	Born, September 18, in London.
1608–1612	Attends the Merchant Taylors' School in London.
1612	Enters Saint John's College, Oxford; subsequently transfers to Catharine Hall (now Saint Catharine's), Cambridge.
c. 1618	Graduates B.A., Catharine Hall. First poem published: perhaps an early version (no copy survives) of "Narcissus," published in 1646.
c. 1620	Proceeds M.A. About this time, according to Anthony à Wood, "a minister . . . in or near St. Albans in Hertfordshire."
1623–1625	Headmaster of a grammar school in Saint Albans. Converted to Roman Catholicism. Probably married in 1623.
1625	Moves to London and becomes a playwright. First play, *Love Tricks, with Complements*, licensed in February, 1626 (first published play, *The Wedding*, 1629).
1626–1636	Years of greatest success: composes fifteen comedies, four tragedies, two masques (notably "The Triumph of Peace," presented at Whitehall in February, 1634), and a pastoral play, all acted in London. Associating with William Habington, Thomas Randolph, and other poets and playwrights. In high favor with Queen Henrietta Maria.
1636-1640	Living in Dublin and writing plays (two comedies, two tragedies) for production in that city. Returns to London probably before March, 1640.
1641	Shirley's best-known tragedy, *The Cardinal*, licensed in November.
1642	Stage plays suppressed by Parliament. Shirley apparently campaigns with royalist forces led by the Earl of Newcastle until July, 1644, when he returns to London. Befriended and aided by the poet and scholar Thomas Stanley.
1646	Publication of *Poems*. Maintains himself from about this time as a schoolteacher, residing at Whitefriars

in London. Continues to write plays as well as pedagogical texts dealing with grammar.

1666   Shirley's house destroyed in the Great Fire of London.
A few weeks later, he and his wife, homeless and in
straitened circumstances, die on the same day; they
are buried in the churchyard of Saint Giles on
October 29.

From *POEMS* (1646)

Cupid's Call[1]

Ho! Cupid calls; come, lovers, come,
Bring his wanton harvest home;
The west wind blows, the birds do sing,
The earth's enameled, 'tis high spring;
    Let hinds[2] whose soul is corn and hay   5
    Expect their crop another day.

Into Love's spring-garden[3] walk,
Virgins dangle on their stalk,
Full-blown, and playing at fifteen;
Come, bring your amorous sickles then!   10
    See, they are pointing to their beds,
    And call to reap their maidenheads.

Hark, how in yonder shady grove
Sweet Philomel[4] is warbling love,
And with her voice is courting kings;   15
For since she was a bird, she sings,
    "There is no pleasure but in men;
    Oh, come and ravish me again."

Virgins that are young and fair
May kiss, and grow into a pair;   20
Then warm and active use your blood,
No sad thought congeal the flood;
    Nature no med'cine can impart
    When age once snows upon our heart.

---

1. To make this poem, Shirley revised and combined two separate sets of verses, entitled "The Courtesan" and "Another"; cf. Textual Notes, pp. 381–382.
2. Farm laborers, peasants.
3. Lovers' trysts often took place at the "Spring Garden" in London.
4. Philomela, raped and maimed by Tereus, was subsequently turned into a nightingale; cf. Ovid, *Metamorphoses*, VI. 438–670.

To His Mistress

I would the God of Love would die,
And give his bow and shafts to me,
   I ask no other legacy;
This happy fate I then would prove,
That since thy heart I cannot move,   5
   I'd cure and kill my own with love.

Yet why should I so cruel be
To kill myself with loving thee,
   And thou a tyrant still to me?
Perhaps, could'st thou affection show   10
To me, I should not love thee so,
   And that would be my med'cine too.

Then choose to love me, or deny;
I will not be so fond to die
   A martyr to thy cruelty;   15
If thou be'st weary of me, when
Thou art so wise to love again,
   Command, and I'll forsake thee then.

To Odelia[5]

Health to my fair Odelia! Some that know
   How many months are past
Since I beheld thy lovely brow,
   Would count an age at least;
     But unto me,   5
   Whose thoughts are still on thee,
     I vow
By thy black eyes, 'tis but an hour ago.

That mistress I pronounce but poor in bliss,
   That when her servant parts,   10
Gives not as much with her last kiss,
   As will maintain two hearts
     Till both do meet
   To taste what else is sweet.
     Is't fit   15
Time measure love, or our affection it?

Cherish that heart, Odelia, that is mine;
   And if the north thou fear,

---

5. This poem was probably composed in 1642–1644, while Shirley was in northern England with the royalist force, commanded by the Earl of Newcastle. The identity of Odelia has not been established.

Dispatch but from thy southern clime
    A sigh, to warm thine here;   20
       But be so kind
    To send by the next wind:
       'Tis far,
And many accidents do wait on war.

Love's Hue and Cry[6]

In Love's name you are charged: oh, fly
And make a speedy hue and cry
After a face which t'other day
Stole my wand'ring heart away;
To direct you, take in brief   5
These few marks to know the thief.
Her hair a net of beams would prove
Strong enough t'imprison Jove
Dressed in his eagle's shape;[7] her brow
Is a spacious field of snow;   10
Her eyes so rich, so pure a gray,
Every look creates a day,
And if they close themselves (not when
The sun doth set), 'tis night again;
In her cheeks are to be seen   15
Of flowers, both the king and queen,
Thither by all the Graces[8] led,
And smiling in their nuptial bed;
On whom, like pretty nymphs, do wait
Her twin-born lips, whose virgin state   20
They do deplore themselves, nor miss
To blush, so often as they kiss
Without a man. Beside the rest,
You shall know this felon best
By her tongue, for when your ear   25
Once a harmony shall hear
So ravishing, you do not know
Whether you be in heaven or no:
That, that is she! O straight, surprise
And bring her unto Love's assize;[9]   30
But lose no time, for fear that she
Ruin all mankind, like me,
      Fate and philosophy control,
      And leave the world without a soul.

---

6. The ultimate model for this piece is the first Idyl ("Love the Runaway") by the pastoral poet Moschus of Syracuse (fl. 150 B.C.). An earlier version of Shirley's poem appears in his play, *The Witty Fair One*, III. Cf. Textual Notes, pp. 382–383.

7. Ovid refers to the eagle as "the weapon-bearing bird of Jove"; *Metamorphoses*, XV. 386.

8. The three Graces, Euphrosyne, Aglaia, and Thalia, personified grace and beauty to the ancients. Cf. Hesiod, *Theogony*, 908–911.

9. Judicial inquest.

Good-night

Bid me no more good-night; because
  'Tis dark, must I away?
Love doth acknowledge no such laws,
  And Love 'tis I obey,
Which, blind, doth all your light despise,   5
    And hath no need of eyes
      When day is fled;
  Besides, the sun, which you
  Complain is gone, 'tis true,
    Is gone to bed: 10
    Oh, let us do so too.

"Would you know what's soft?"[1]

Would you know what's soft? I dare
Remit you to the down, or air;
The stars we all acknowledge bright,
The snow too is exceeding white;
To please your scent, 'twill not be hard   5
To present you bruiséd nard;[2]
And would you heavenly music hear,
I'll call the orbs to take your ear,
If old Pythagoras[3] sing true.
But ambrosia, heavenly dew,   10
Divinely must affect your taste,
And nectar is your drink at last.
    But would you have all these delights in one,
    Know but the fair Odelia, and 'tis done.

Love for Enjoying

Fair lady, what's your face to me?
I was not only made to see;
Every silent stander-by
May thus enjoy as much as I.
That blooming nature on your cheek   5
Is still inviting me to seek
For unknown wealth; within the ground
Are all the royal metals found.
Leave me to search; I have a thread
Through all the labyrinth shall lead,   10

1. Cf. Jonson, "A Celebration of Charis,"
4, p. 48, ll. 21–30.
2. I.e., spikenard, an aromatic plant from
which a fragrant ointment was derived.
3. The Greek philosopher Pythagoras (fl.
520 B.C.) taught the doctrine of the transmigration of souls. Milton observes, "If
he taught a harmony of the spheres, and
a revolution of the heavens to that sweet
music, he wished to symbolize in a wise
way the intimate relations of the spheres
and their even revolution forever in ac-
cordance with the law of destiny" (Prolusion 2, in *John Milton: Complete Poems
and Major Prose*, ed. M. Y. Hughes (New
York, 1957), p. 603.

And through every winding vein
Conduct me to the golden mine;
Which, once enjoyed, will give me power
To make new Indies every hour.
Look on those jewels that abound   15
Upon your dress: that diamond
No flame, no lustre could impart,
Should not the lapidary's[4] art
Contribute here and there a star;
And just such things ye women are,   20
Who do not in rude quarries shine,
But meeting us y'are made divine.
    Come, let us mix ourselves, and prove
That action is the soul of love;
Why do we coward-gazing stand   25
Like armies in the Netherland,
Contracting fear at either's sight,
Till we both grow too weak to fight?
Let's charge, for shame; and choose you whether
One shall fall, or both together: 30
This is love's war! Whoever dies,
If the survivor be but wise,
He may reduce the spirit fled,
For t'other kiss will cure the dead.

To His Honored Friend Thomas Stanley Esquire, upon His Elegant Poems[5]

A palsy shakes my pen, while I intend
A votive[6] to thy Muse, since to commend
With my best skill will be as short of thee
As thou above all future poesy.
Thou early miracle of wit and art,   5
That hath prodigiously so got the start
Of ages in thy study, Time must be
Old once again in overtaking thee.
I know not where I am, when I peruse
Thy learned loves; how willingly I lose   10
Myself in every grove, and wish to be,
Might it contribute to thy wreath, a tree.
Carew, whose numerous[7] language did before
Steer every genial soul, must be no more
The oracle of love; and might he come   15
But from his own to thy Elysium,[8]

4. A lapidary cuts, polishes, and engraves precious stones.
5. These lines, virtually unchanged, were published also with Stanley's *Poems* (1647). The well-connected Stanley, who called Shirley his "dearest friend," extended support to the elder man throughout the period of the Commonwealth.
6. I.e., an offering to fulfill a vow.
7. Poetical.
8. Cf. Carew, "A Rapture," p. 166, l. 2 and note.

He would repent his immortality,
Given by loose idolaters, and die
A tenant to these shades; and by thy ray
He need not blush to court his Celia.   20
Thy numbers carry height, yet clear, and terse,
And innocent, as becomes the soul of verse;
Poets from hence may add to their great name,
And learn to strike from chastity a flame.
    But I expect some murmuring[9] critic here   25
Should say, "No poems ever did appear
Without some fault." This I must grant a truth;
And, sir, let me deal plainly with your youth,
Not error-proof yet; something may admit
A censure; if you will secure your wit,   30
I know the only way to bring't about:
Accept my love, and leave this copy[1] out.

To the Excellent Pattern of Beauty and Virtue, Lady Elizabeth, Countess of Ormonde[2]

Madam,
Were you but only great, there are some men,
Whose heat is not the Muses', nor their pen
Steered by chaste truth, could flatter you in prose
Or glorious verse; but I am none of those.   5
I never learned that trick of court to wear
Silk at the cost of flattery; or make dear
My pride, by painting a great lady's face
When she had done't before, and swear the grace
Was nature's; anagram upon her name,
And add to her no virtue, my own shame.   10
I could not make this lord a god, then try
How to commit new court idolatry,
And, when he dies, hang on his silent hearse
Wet elegies, and haunt his ghost in verse.
These, some hold witty, thriving garbs; but I   15
Choose (to my loss) a modest poesy,
And place my genius upon subjects fit
For imitation,[3] rather than bold wit;
And such are you, who both in name and blood
Born great, have learned this lesson, to be good.   20
    Armed with this knowledge, madam, I not fear
To hold fair correspondence with the year,

---

9. Grumbling.
1. I.e., this poem.
2. James Butler, twelfth Earl (later, first Duke) of Ormonde (1610–1688), led the royalist armies in Ireland with vigor and skill. He married Elizabeth, only child of the Earl of Desmond, in 1630. Shirley appears to have moved in their social circle during his years in Dublin. With this

poem may be compared Jonson's verse epistle to Lady Aubigny (*The Forest,* XIII, p. 38), which probably served Shirley as a model.
3. I.e., subjects that, by virtue of their intrinsic merit, are appropriate models for poetical imitation (in the Aristotelian sense, as well as in a social context).

And bring my gift, hearty as you are fair;
A servant's wish, for all my wealth is prayer,
Which with the year thus enters.[4] May you be   25
Still the same flowing goodness that we see;
In your most noble lord be happy still,
And heaven chain your hearts into one will;
Be rich in your two darlings of the spring,
Which, as it waits, perfumes their blossoming,   30
The growing pledges of your love and blood;[5]
And may that unborn blessing timely bud,
The chaste and noble treasure of your womb,
Your own, and th'age's expectation come;
And when your days and virtues have made even,[6]   35
Die late, beloved of earth, and change for heaven.

To a Lady upon a Looking-Glass Sent

When this crystal shall present
              Your beauty to your eye,
Think that lovely face was meant
              To dress another by.
        For not to make them proud,   5
        These glasses are allowed
              To those are fair,
              But to compare
The inward beauty with the outward grace,
And make them fair in soul as well as face.[7]   10

Two Gentlemen That Broke Their Promise of a Meeting, Made When They Drank Claret[8]

There is no faith in claret, and it shall
Henceforth with me be held apocryphal.
I'll trust a small-beer[9] promise, nay, a troth
Washed in the Thames, before a French wine oath.
That grape, they say, is binding; yes, 'tis so,   5
And it has made your souls thus costive[1] too.
Circe transformed the Greeks;[2] no hard design,
For some can do as much with claret wine
Upon themselves; witness you two, allowed

4. I.e., which is presented on New Year's Day (1640).
5. Thomas Butler had been born in July, 1634; Richard Butler in June, 1639. A third son ("that unborn blessing" of line 32) was named John.
6. I.e., have harmoniously come to the evening of life.
7. In medieval and Renaissance poetry and pictorial art forms, mirrors regularly symbolize both worldly vanity and discerning self-knowledge: cf. Shakespeare's *Richard II*, IV. i. 276–290. Cf. also, for another kind of example, the painting by Diego de Velázquez (1599–1660), "The Toilet of Venus."
8. Cf. William Habington's reply to this poem, on p. 225 of this edition. For an early version of Shirley's poem, cf. Textual Notes, p. 384.
9. I.e., beer of inferior quality.
1. I.e., reticent, uncommunicative (with a glance at the primary meaning, "constipated").
2. Cf. Homer, *Odyssey*, X.

Once honest, now turned air, and *à la mode*.[3]   10
Begin no health in this, or if by chance
The King's, 'twill question your allegiance;
And men will, after all your ruffling,[4] say
You drink as some do fight, in the French way:
Engage and trouble many, when 'tis known   15
You spread their interest to wave your own.
Away with this false Christian:[5] it shall be
An excommunicate from mirth, and me;
Give me the Catholic[6] diviner flame,
To light me to the fair Odelia's name;   20
'Tis sack that justifies both man and verse,
Whilst you in Lethe-claret still converse.
Forget your own names next; and when you look
With hope to find, be lost in the church-book.[7]

The Garden[8]

This garden does not take[9] my eyes,
Though here you show how art of men
Can purchase nature at a price
Would stock old Paradise again.

These glories while you dote upon,   5
I envy not your spring nor pride,
Nay, boast the summer all your own;
My thoughts with less are satisfied.

Give me a little plot of ground
Where might I with the sun agree,   10
Though every day he walk the round,
My garden he should seldom see.

Those tulips that such wealth display
To court my eye, shall lose their name,
Though now they listen as if they   15
Expected I should praise their flame.

But I would see myself appear
Within the violet's drooping head,
On which a melancholy tear
The discontented morn hath shed.   20

Within their buds let roses sleep,

---

3. I.e., in the fashion.
4. Swaggering.
5. I.e., French claret wine (with an allusion to the "Most Christian" King of France).
6. I.e., Spanish wine, notably sack (with an allusion to the "Most Catholic" King

of Spain).
7. Parish register.
8. Cf. Andrew Marvell's "The Garden," in connection particularly with the first and eighth stanzas of Shirley's poem.
9. Delight.

And virgin lilies on their stem,
Till sighs from lovers glide and creep
Into their leaves to open them.

I'th' center of my ground compose   25
Of bays[1] and yew my summer room,
Which may, so oft as I repose,
Present my arbor and my tomb.

No woman here shall find me out,
Or if a chance do bring one hither,   30
I'll be secure, for round about
I'll moat it with my eyes' foul weather.

No bird shall live within my pale[2]
To charm me with their shames of art,
Unless some wand'ring nightingale   35
Come here to sing, and break her heart.

Upon whose death I'll try to write
An epitaph, in some funeral stone,
So sad and true it may invite
Myself to die, and prove mine own.   40

From *CUPID AND DEATH*[3] (1653)

Song

Victorious men of earth, no more
    Proclaim how wide your empires are;
Though you bind in every shore,
    And your triumphs reach as far
            As night or day,   5
    Yet you, proud monarchs, must obey,
And mingle with forgotten ashes, when
Death calls ye to the crowd of common men.

Devouring famine, plague, and war,
    Each able to undo mankind,   10
Death's servile emissaries are;
    Nor to these alone confined,
            He hath at will
    More quaint and subtle ways to kill:
A smile or kiss, as he will use the art,   15
Shall have the cunning skill to break a heart.

1. Laurels.
2. Enclosure.
3. This masque, "presented before His Excellency the Ambassador of Portugal," in March, 1653, is based on the fancy that the arrows of Cupid and those of Death were, through a trick, temporarily exchanged.

From THE CONTENTION OF AJAX AND
ULYSSES FOR THE ARMOR OF ACHILLES[4]
(1659)

Dirge

The glories of our blood and state
    Are shadows, not substantial things;
There is no armor against fate;
    Death lays his icy hand on kings;
        Scepter and crown   5
        Must tumble down,
And in the dust be equals made
With the poor crooked scythe and spade.

Some men with swords may reap the field,
    And plant fresh laurels where they kill;   10
But their strong nerves at last must yield,
    They tame but one another still;
        Early or late,
        They stoop to fate,
And must give up their murmuring breath,   15
When they, pale captives, creep to death.

The garlands wither on your brow,
    Then boast no more your mighty deeds;
Upon death's purple altar now,
    See where the victor-victim bleeds;   20
        Your heads must come
        To the cold tomb;
Only the actions of the just
Smell sweet, and blossom in their dust.

4. Cf. Ovid, *Metamorphoses*, XIII. 1–398. This poem, Shirley's most celebrated lyric, concludes the drama.

Mildmay Fane,
Earl of Westmorland

c. 1600   Born, probably in Kent. His father, Francis Fane, first Earl of Westmorland, descended from a powerful Kentish family, had augmented his fortune and influence by his marriage, in 1599, to Mary, the granddaughter of Sir Walter Mildmay, Queen Elizabeth's Treasurer and the founder of Emmanuel College, Cambridge. The Mildmays held large estates in Northamptonshire.

c. 1615–
1617   Attends Emmanuel College, Cambridge.

1620–1621   Member of Parliament for Peterborough (and again in 1626–1628).

1625   Member of Parliament for Kent.

1626   Created a Knight of the Bath at the time of Charles I's coronation.

1628   Marries Grace Thornhurst, of Herne, Kent, who subsequently bore a son, Charles, and five daughters; she died in 1637 or 1638.

1638   Marries Mary Townshend (daughter of Sir Horace Vere), who bore a son, Vere, and four daughters.

1642   Having sided with Charles I at the outbreak of the civil war, imprisoned in the Tower of London, by Parliamentary order, until April, 1643; for some months thereafter restricted to an area within five miles around London. Fined £2,000.

1644   Set at liberty, having subscribed to the (Presbyterian) covenant, probably to save his property from appropriation by the Parliamentary government.

1648   Publication of *Otia Sacra*.

1660   At the Restoration, appointed Lord Lieutenant of Northamptonshire.

1666   Death, February 12.

From *OTIA SACRA*[1] (1648)

My Country Audit[2]

Blest privacy! Happy retreat, wherein
I may cast up my reck'nings,[3] audit sin,
Count o'er my debts, and how arrears increase
In nature's book, towards the God of peace;
What through perverseness hath been waived,[4] or done   5
To my first covenant's contradiction;
How many promised resolutions broke
Of keeping touch,[5] almost as soon as spoke.
    Thus, like that tenant who, behind-hand cast,[6]
    Entreats so oft forbearance till at last   10
    The sum surmounts his hopes, and then no more
    Expects, but mercy to strike off the score,[7]
So here, methinks, I see the Landlord's grace
Full of compassion to my drooping case,
Bidding me be of comfort, and not grieved: 15
My rent His Son should pay if I believed.

My Carol

    Arise, arise,
Dull fancy, from the bed of earth,
    And that low strain
    Besots thy vein,
That so thou may'st devise   5
Some record of that famous birth,
Which about this time, as our date will have,
One Son for all the rest the Father gave.

    Leave to the bee
To set a valuation   10
    On this or that
    Fair garden-plat,[8]

---

1. The title subtly combines two meanings: "sacred poems" (cf. Ovid, *Tristia*, II. 224) and "the poetical fruits of leisure" (cf. *Tristia*, IV. x. 19). The poems in Book I of *Otia Sacra* are, in fact, predominantly devotional in character; the greater number of those in Book II are concerned with secular matters and the simple pleasures of life in the country. The collection includes a number of "emblematic" poems, which have some affinity with Francis Quarles's *Emblems* (1635); of the "metaphysical" poets it is Marvell, however, with whose outlook Fane is most clearly in sympathy. Robert Herrick may perhaps have persuaded Fane to publish his verses; cf. "To the Right Honorable Mildmay, Earl of Westmorland," on p. 133 of this edition.
2. This poem and "To Retiredness" were probably composed at Fane's country estate of Apthorpe, Northamptonshire, which had belonged to his mother's family. The Fanes were originally a Kentish family, having settled in and around Tonbridge in c. 1425.
3. I.e., calculate my accounts.
4. I.e., either (1) put aside, neglected; or (2) flaunted.
5. I.e., keeping agreements sealed by clasping of hands.
6. I.e., fallen into debt.
7. Account.
8. Garden plot.

There t' browse some flower or tree;
And to some foreign nation
To crown their annals with the pelican,   15
Or far-fetched cordial, myrobalan.[9]

Here's comfort more:
A gift that's far beyond all worth
The curious mind
Could ever find   20
In what a plant e'er bore,
Or barren wilderness brought forth;
Sweetness[1] excels the bee's bag, and such good
As proved our strong restorative by's blood.

My Observation At Sea

Though every thing we see or hear may raise
The Maker's praise,
For without lightning or thunder,
His works are all of wonder;
Yet amongst those there's none   5
Like to the ocean,

Where, not a catalogue to keep
Of several shapes inhabiting the deep,
Let but our thoughts confer[2]
With what once graveled[3] the philosopher;   10
And we must straight confess
Amazement more, but apprehension less.

The fire for heat and light
Most exquisite;
And the all-temp'ring air   15
Beyond compare;
Earth, composition and solidity,
Bountiful mixéd with humidity;
But here, for profit and content,
Each must give place to th' liquid element,   20

Whose admirable course, that steers
Within twelve hours[4] mariners

9. I.e., to boast that the (relatively exotic) pelican is indigenous to that land, or that myrobalan (an astringent Oriental fruit, at one time used medicinally) may be obtained there. That the pelican is traditionally a symbol of the Eucharist lends emphasis to Fane's irony.
1. I.e., such sweetness as.
2. Compare.
3. Baffled. Ancient philosophers (not merely Aristotle, known as "The Philosopher") were unable to account satisfactorily for the regular ebb and flow of the tides, although by the first century A.D. the connection between tidal motion and the action of sun and moon was generally recognized.
4. The tide ebbs and flows twice in each lunar day.

Outwards and homewards bound,
May be sufficient ground
To raise conclusion from thence   25
At once of mighty power and providence.

For as the Cynthian queen[5]
Her bounty less or more vouchsafes be seen,
So by her wane she brings
The tides to neaps, and by her full to springs;[6]   30
Yet not but as He please
Who set her there, chief governess of seas;

Which understood
Truly by such would seek for traffic good,
They must their anchors weigh   35
Out of the oozy dirt and clay,
Earth's contemplations yield,
And hoisting sails, they'll straightway have them filled
With a fresh-mackerel gale,[7] whose blast
May port them in true happiness at last.   40

There th'in a bay of bliss,
Where a sweet calm our welcome is,
Let us at length the cables veer[8]
Fore and abaft, that may our moorage clear
From warp[9] or winding, so ride, fixed upon   45
Our hope's sheet-anchor of salvation.

To Kiss God's Rod; Occasioned upon a Child's Sickness

Whatever God's divine
Decree
Awardeth unto mine
Or me,
Though't may seem ill,   5
With patience
I am resolved to undergo,
Nor to His Purpose once say no,
But moderate both mind and will;
And, conquering th' rebellions of sense,   10
Place all content in true obedience.

Thus I create it good[1]
When His

---

5. I.e., the moon.
6. Neap tides, the lowest high tide in a lunar month, occur when the moon is at first or third quarter; spring tides, highest tide in a lunar month, occur when the moon is full or new.
7. I.e., "a strong breeze, such as mackerel are best caught in" (*OED*).
8. Pay out.
9. Twist, tangle.
1. I.e., effectively recognize that, according to God's plan, "all things work together for good."

Correction's understood,
                Which is   15
            Not to destroy,
            But to reclaim,
    And t'cause me turn a new leaf o'er,
    Count all an error writ before,
    So find the sting of flatt'ring joy;   20
Making the scope of all my future aim
To reverence and glorify His name.

    Thus when our God will frown, if we weigh it
    In judgment's scales, we make't a benefit.

Man Leavens the Batch[2]

God makes all things for good; 'tis man
Sours and worsts creation:
Who, leavened by his father,[3] thence
Becomes all disobedience;
No thought, no word, no action he   5
Contrives, can own integrity
To Him that made him, for by deeds,
As words and heart, his growth's in weeds,
Which, whilst neglected, do express
God's grace, but man's unfruitfulness.   10
    Now if again man would bear corn,
    He must himself a weeder turn.

A Dedication of My First Son[4]

Is it not fit the mold and frame
Of man should dedicate the same
To God, Who first created it; and t' give
To Him the first fruit of that span we live?

In the world's infancy, could Hannah tell   5
She ought to offer her son Samuel
    To Him that made him, and refine
    That sacrifice with flour and wine?[5]

---

2. Literally, to "leaven the batch" is to add leavening to a quantity of dough in order to produce fermentation before baking; figuratively, the expression signifies "to change profoundly by inward operation." Fane employs the phrase in the sense of Matthew 16:11-12, i.e., "to debase or corrupt by additives."
3. I.e. (ultimately), Adam.
4. Fane married twice; his first wife, Grace· Thornhurst, who died in April, 1640, bore him a son, Charles (the subject of this poem), and five daughters.
5. Hannah, the barren wife of Elkanah, prayed that she might bear a son, vowing that the child should be dedicated to God's service; when Samuel was born, she brought him (together with "three bullocks, and one ephah of flour, and a bottle of wine") to the priest Eli, in fulfillment of her vow. Cf. I. Samuel 1:11, 24–28.

Was Abram's long-expected seed
From Sarah's womb condemned to bleed?[6]   10
And shall the times, now they grow old, conclude
In faithlessness, and in ingratitude?

Let shame awake us, and where blessings fall,
Let everyone become a prodigal
    In paying vows of thanks, and bring   15
    The first and best for offering.[7]

Where am I, then, whom God hath deigned to bless
With hopes of a succeeding happiness
    Unto my house? Why is't I stand
    At th' altar with an empty hand?   20

    Have I no herds, no flocks, no oil,
    No incense-bearing Sheba-soil?[8]
Is not my granary stored with flour that's fine?
Are not my strutted[9] vessels full of wine?

What temporal blessing's wanting to suffice   25
And furnish out a lively sacrifice,
    Save only this, to make a free-
    Will-offering of an infancy?

    Which if I should not do, that piled-
    Up wood, whereon lay Sarah's child,   30
The Temple would accuse me, where the son
Of Elk'na first had dedication.

    Wherefore accept, I pray Thee, this
    Thou'st given, and my first son is;
Let him be Thine, and from his cradling,   35
Begin his service's first reckoning.

Grant, with his days, Thy grace increase, and fill
His heart, or leave there room to harbor ill,
    That in the progress of his years,
    He may express Whose badge he wears.   40

Upon the Times

Awake, thou best of sense,
Intelligence,
And let no fancy-vapor steer

---

6. Cf. Genesis 20:1–14.
7. Cf. Luke 15:11–32.
8. Shebam (Hebrew ''balsam'') was lo-

cated in the center of the Moabite vineyards; cf. Numbers 32:3.
9. Distended.

Thy contemplation t'think that peace is near,
    Whilst war in words we do bemoan,   5
There's nothing less left in invention.

    England that was, not is,
    Unless in metamorphosis,
    Changed from the bower of bliss and rest,
To become now Bellona's interest,[1]   10
    In danger of a funeral pile,
Unless some happy swift means reconcile.

    Which how to bring to pass,
    Beyond man's hopes, alas!
    Therefore be pleased, Thou who didst make   15
    Atonement for his sake,
    To silence this unnatural spell,
As Thou didst once the Delphian Oracle.[2]

My Close-Committee[3]

    How busied's man
    To seek and find
  An accusation
    Against all those
He deems his body's good, or goods oppose;   5
And winks at such as hazard soul and mind.

    Nothing, of late,
    Is done or spoke
  But either king or state
    Concernéd are,   10
The while each 'gainst his neighbor wages war;
So 're all the bonds of love and friendship broke.

    And how comes this,
    But that we do
  Or utter what's amiss   15
    In every thing,
Making each fancy lord, each will a king,
And all that checks not reason, treason too?

    Were't not more wise
    To lay about   20

1. Bellona was the Roman goddess of war.
2. In *De Defectu Oraculorum* ("On the Cessation of the Oracles"), Plutarch (c. 50–c. 120) alludes to a mysterious voice that, about the time of Christ's crucifixion, cried that the great Pan was dead. The tradition was elaborated by many Christian poets.
3. I.e., a committee meeting in private session.

Which way for to surprise
That trait'rous band
Of sins, that in our bosoms bear command,
And, entertaining grace, t' cause those march out?

Our lust, our pride,   25
Ambition,
Or whatsoe'er beside,
Seems to give way
To that unjust militia and array,
Bring we t' our close-committee's inquisition: 30
    Thus, when our hearts these for malignants brand,
    Commit them not, but banish them thy land.

Occasioned by Seeing a Walk of Bay Trees

No thunder blasts Jove's plant,[4] nor can
Misfortune warp an honest man;
Shaken he may be by some one
Or other gust, unleaved by none;
Though tribulation's sharp and keen,   5
His resolutions keep green;
And whilst integrity's his wall,
His year's all spring, and hath no fall.

In Praise of Fidelia

Get thee a ship well-rigged and tight,
With ordnance[5] stored, and manned for fight,
Snug in her timbers' mold for th' seas,
Yet large in hold for merchandise;
Spread forth her cloth, and anchors weigh,   5
And let her on the curled waves play
Till, fortune-towed, she chance to meet
Th' Hesperian[6] home-bound western fleet;
Then let her board 'em, and for price
Take gold ore, sugar-canes, and spice: 10
    Yet when all these sh'hath brought ashore,
    In my Fidelia I'll find more.

---

4. Although the bay, or laurel, is sacred rather to Apollo (cf. Ovid, *Metamorphoses*, I. 557–565), "victorious [Roman] generals celebrating a triumph . . . wore the costume of Jupiter . . . in the right hand they bore a branch of laurel . . . a wreath of laurel crowned their brows" (Sir James G. Frazer, *The Golden Bough*, abr. ed. [New York, 1948], p. 148).
5. Guns, ammunition.
6. I.e. (in this context), West Indian; whence Spanish fleets brought home spices and precious metals.

A Happy Life[7]

That which creates a happy life
Is substance left, not gained by strife,
A fertile and a thankful mold,[8]
A chimney always free from cold;
Never to be the client, or   5
But seldom times the counselor.
A mind content with what is fit,
Whose strength doth most consist in wit;[9]
A body nothing prone to be
Sick; a prudent simplicity.   10
Such friends as of one's own rank are;
Homely fare, not sought from far;
The table without art's help spread;
A night in wine not buriéd,
Yet drowning cares; a bed that's blest   15
With true joy, chastity, and rest;
Such short, sweet slumber as may give
Less time to die in't, more to live:
    Thine own estate whate'er commend,
    And wish not for, nor fear thine end.   20

[On Ben Jonson]

He who began from brick and lime[1]
    The Muses' hill to climb,
And whilom[2] busied in laying stone,
    Thirsted to drink of Helicon,[3]
      Changing his trowel for a pen,   5
Wrote straight the temper not of dirt, but men.

Now, since that he is turned to clay, and gone,
    Let those remain of th'occupation
He honored once, square him a tomb may say
    His craft exceeded far a dauber's way;[4]   10
Then write upon 't: *He could no longer tarry,*
But was returned again unto the quarry.

7. "The happy country life [was] the most typical expression of the Royalist and Anglican spirit of the seventeenth century" (Maren-Sofie Røstvig, *The Happy Man,* 2 vols. [Oslo-Oxford, 1954], I, p. 22). Cf. Earl Miner, *op. cit.,* pp. 88–99, for a discussion of the appeal, in this regard, made by Horace to the Cavalier poets.
8. Soil; also, perhaps, man's corporeal form.
9. I.e., in sound wisdom.
1. After leaving Westminster School, Jonson was apprenticed as a bricklayer.
2. While.
3. Mount Helicon in Boeotia, site of the Hippocrene spring, was sacred to the Muses and to Apollo, god of poetry and song.
4. I.e., that of an inexpert workman.

To Retiredness[5]

Next unto God, to whom I owe
What e'er I here enjoy below,
I must indebted stand to thee,
Great patron of my liberty;
For in the cluster of affairs,   5
Whence there are dealing[6] several shares,
As in a trick thou hast conveyed
Into my hand what can be said;
Whilst he who doth himself possess,
Makes all things pass[7] him seem far less.   10

Riches and honors that appear,
Rewards to the adventurer,
On either tide of court or seas,
Are not attained nor held with ease,
But, as unconstancy bears sway,   15
Quickly will fleet and ebb away;
And oft when fortune those confers,
She gives them but for torturers;
When, with a mind ambition-free,
These, and much more, come home to me.   20

Here I can sit; and sitting under
Some portions of His works of wonder,
Whose all are such, observe by reason
Why every plant obeys its season;
How the sap rises, and the fall   25
Wherein they shake off leaves and all;
Then how again they bud and spring,
Are laden for an offering;
Which whilst my contemplation sees,
I am taught thankfulness from trees.   30

Then, turning over nature's leaf,
I mark the glory of the sheaf,
For every field's a several[8] page
Deciphering the Golden Age;
So that without a miner's pains,   35
Or Indies' reach, here plenty reigns;
Which, watered from above, implies
That our acknowledgments should rise
To Him that thus creates a birth
Of mercies for us out of earth.   40

Here is no other case in law

---

5. Cf. Andrew Marvell, "The Garden."
6. Contending (with a punning allusion to cardplay).
7. I.e., (1) that surpass; (2) that pass by.
8. Separate, distinct.

But what the sunburnt hat of straw
With crooked sickle reaps and binds
Up into sheaves to help the hinds;[9]
Whose arguing alone's in this,   45
Which cop[1] lies well, and which amiss,
How the hock-cart[2] with all its gear
Should be tricked up, and what good cheer
Bacon with cook's reports express,
And how to make the tenth go less.[3]   50

There are no other wars or strifes,
Encouragers, shrill trumpets, fifes,
Or horrid drums, but what excels
All music, nature's minstrels
Piping and chirping, as they sit   55
Embower'd in branches, dance to it;
And if at all those do contest,
It is in this, but which sings best;
And when they have contended long,
I, though unseen, must judge the song.   60

Thus out of fears or noise of war,
Crowds, and the clamorings at bar,
The merchant's dread, th' unconstant tides,
With all vexations besides,
I hug my quiet, and alone   65
Take thee for my companion,
And deem, in doing so, I've all
I can true conversation[4] call;
For so my thoughts by this retreat
Grow stronger, like contracted heat.   70

Whether on nature's book I muse,
Or else some other writes on 't use
To spend the time in,[5] every line
Is not eccentric but divine;
And though all others[6] downward tend,   75
These look to heaven, and ascend
From when they came; where, pointed high,
They ravish into mystery,
To see the footsteps here are trod
Of mercy by a gracious God.   80

---

9. Farm laborers.
1. Sheaf.
2. I.e., the wagon bringing in the last load of the harvest.
3. I.e., how to reduce the tithe (the tenth part of one's produce, paid over to ec-clesiastical authorities).
4. I.e., social intercourse.
5. I.e., or else employ my time in reading another man's writings about nature.
6. I.e., all artificial constructs.

Thomas Randolph

1605	Born, Newnham-cum-Badby, Northamptonshire; baptized on June 15. His father, William Randolph, was steward (i.e., estate manager) to Lord Zouch.
c. 1614	Writes a verse "History of our Saviour's Incarnation" (no longer extant).
c. 1618–1623	Educated at Westminster School, London, as a "King's Scholar."
1623	Attains the highest rating among those Westminster schoolboys competing for places at Cambridge and Oxford.
1624	Matriculates at Trinity College, Cambridge.
1628	Graduates B.A.; created a "minor fellow" in 1629.
1630	First published work in English: *Aristippus, or the Joviall Philosopher*, a dramatic satire in prose and verse on university education, the pleasures of drinking, and other matters. Probably makes the acquaintance of Ben Jonson at about this time.
1631	Proceeds M.A. at Cambridge. Incorporated M.A. at Oxford.
1632	His blank-verse drama, *The Jealous Lovers*, presented at Cambridge, in March, on the occasion of the visit to the University by Charles I and Henrietta Maria: a great success. The play is published later in the year by Cambridge University.
1633	*Amyntas*, Randolph's pastoral play, presented at Whitehall. Health and fortunes in decline from this time by consequence of his "irregular" life.
1635	Dies, while visiting his friend William Stafford in Blatherwick, Northamptonshire; buried in the Stafford vault in Blatherwick Church on March 17.
1638	Publication of *Poems, with The Muses' Looking-Glass and Amyntas*.

From *POEMS, WITH THE MUSES'*
LOOKING-GLASS AND AMYNTAS (1638)

A *Gratulatory*[1] *to Mr. Ben Jonson for His Adopting*
of Him To Be His Son

I was not born to Helicon,[2] nor dare
Presume to think myself a Muse's heir.
I have no title to Parnassus hill,
Nor any acre of it by the will
Of a dead ancestor, nor could I be   5
Ought but a tenant unto poetry.
But thy adoption quits me of all fear,
And makes me challenge a child's portion there.
I am akin to heroes, being thine,
And part of my alliance is divine.   10
Orpheus, Musaeus,[3] Homer too, beside
Thy brothers by the Roman mother's side,
As Ovid, Vergil, and the Latin lyre
That is so like thee, Horace: the whole choir
Of poets are by thy adoption all   15
My uncles; thou hast given me pow'r to call
Phoebus[4] himself my grandsire; by this grant
Each sister of the Nine is made my aunt.
Go, you that reckon from a large descent
Your lineal honors, and are well content   20
To glory in the age of your great name,
Though on a herald's faith you build the same;
I do not envy you, nor think you blest,
Though you may bear a gorgon on your crest
By direct line from Pegasus;[5] I will boast   25
No farther than my father; that's the most
I can or should be proud of, and I were
Unworthy his adoption if that here
I should be dully modest; boast I must,
Being son of his adoption, not his lust.   30

1. I.e., an expression of gratitude. For an account (possibly apocryphal) of the circumstances leading to Randolph's "adoption," which took place in c. 1630, cf. W. Winstanley, *Lives of the Most Famous English Poets* [1687], ed. W. R. Parker (Gainesville, Fla., 1963), pp. 143–144. Being "somewhat addicted to libertine indulgences," Randolph never fulfilled the promise of his early years, when he had given "proof of an amazing quickness of parts" (D. E. Baker, *Biographia Dramatica* . . . , 2 vols. [London, 1792], I, p. 366).
2. Mount Helicon, in Boeotia, and Mount Parnassus, near Delphi, were sacred to the nine Muses and to Apollo, god of poetry and song.
3. For Orpheus, cf. Jonson, *The Forest*, XII, p. 38, l. 77 and note. The Musaeus referred to is probably not the fifth-century author of "Hero and Leander," but the mythical singer to whom Aristophanes alludes in his comedy *The Frogs* (ll. 1032–1033).
4. Phoebus Apollo.
5. The winged horse Pegasus sprang from the blood of the gorgon Medusa, when Perseus struck off her head; cf. Ovid, *Metamorphoses*, IV. 785–786.

And to say truth, that which is best in me
May call you father; 'twas begot by thee.
Have I a spark of that celestial flame
Within me, I confess I stole the same,
Prometheus-like,[6] from thee; and may I feed   35
His vulture when I dare deny the deed.
Many more moons thou hast, that shine by night,
All bankrupts, were't not for a borrowed light,
Yet can forswear it; I the debt confess
And think my reputation ne'er the less.   40
For, father, let me be resolved by you:
Is't a disparagement from rich Peru
To ravish gold; or theft, for wealthy ore
To ransack Tagus', or Pactolus' shore?[7]
Or does he wrong Alcinous,[8] that for want   45
Doth take from him a sprig or two, to plant
A lesser orchard? Sure it cannot be;
Nor is it theft to steal some flames from thee.
Grant this, and I'll cry guilty, as I am,
And pay a filial reverence to thy name.   50
For when my Muse upon obedient knees
Asks not a father's blessing, let her leese
The fame of this adoption; 'tis a curse
I wish her 'cause I cannot think a worse.
And here, as piety bids me, I entreat   55
Phoebus to lend thee some of his own heat,
To cure thy palsy,[9] else I will complain
He has no skill in herbs; poets in vain
Make him the god of physic. 'Twere his praise
To make thee as immortal as thy bays,[1]   60
As his own Daphne; 'twere a shame to see
The god not love his priest more than his tree.
 But if heaven take thee, envying us thy lyre,
 'Tis to pen anthems for an angels' choir.

Upon the Loss of His Little Finger[2]

Arithmetic nine digits, and no more,
Admits of; then I still have all my store.
For what mischance hath ta'en from my left hand,
It seems did only for a cipher stand.

---

6. Cf. Jonson, "Ode to Himself" (on p. 63 of this edition), l. 27 and note.
7. The Spanish river Tagus and the Lydian river Pactolus (in western Turkey) were celebrated for the gold ore in their sands.
8. The garden of Alcinous, king of the Phaeacians, is described in Homer, *Odyssey*, VII. 112–134.
9. Cf. Jonson, "Ode to Himself," p. 89,

l. 50 and note.
1. Laurels. Cf. Herrick, "The Welcome to Sack, p. 119, l. 92 and note.
2. According to Winstanley (p. 142), the finger was cut off during a violent quarrel that took place while Randolph was drinking in "gentlemen's company." In line 16, the expression "made a hand of" means "done away with."

But this I'll say for thee, departed joint,   5
Thou wert not given to steal, nor pick, nor point
At any in disgrace; but thou didst go
Untimely to thy death only to show
The other members what they once must do:
Hand, arm, leg, thigh, and all must follow too.   10
Oft didst thou scan my verse, where, if I miss
Henceforth, I will impute the cause to this.
A finger's loss (I speak it not in sport)
Will make a verse a foot too short.
Farewell, dear finger: much I grieve to see   15
How soon mischance hath made a hand of thee.

An Elegy[3]

Love, give me leave to serve thee, and be wise,
To keep thy torch in but restore blind eyes.
I will a flame into my bosom take
That martyrs court when they embrace the stake:
Not dull and smoky fires, but heat divine,   5
That burns not to consume but to refine.
I have a mistress for perfections rare
In every eye, but in my thoughts most fair,
Like tapers on the altar shine her eyes;
Her breath is the perfume of sacrifice.   10
And wheresoe'er my fancy would begin,
Still her perfection lets religion in.
I touch her like my beads with devout care,
And come unto my courtship as my prayer.
We sit, and talk, and kiss away the hours,   15
As chastely as the morning dews kiss flowers.
Go, wanton lover, spare thy sighs and tears,
Put on the livery which thy dotage wears,
And call it love; where heresy gets in,
Zeal's but a coal to kindle greater sin.   20
We wear no flesh, but one another greet,
As blessed souls in separation meet.
Were't possible that my ambitious sin
Durst commit rapes upon a cherubin,
I might have lustful thoughts to her, of all   25
Earth's heav'nly choir the most angelical.
Looking into my breast, her form I find

3. This poem, entitled "A Platonic Elegy" in later editions, reflects that fashionable concern with "Platonic love." which was encouraged by Queen Henrietta Maria and her circle. James Howell, writing in the last year of Randolph's life, remarks, "The court affords little news at present, but that there is a love called Platonic love, which much sways there of late. It is a love abstracted from all corporal gross impressions and sensual appetite, but consists in contemplations and ideals of the mind, not in any carnal fruition" (*Epistolae Ho-Elianae, or Familiar Letters,* ed. J. Jacobs [London, 1890], p. 317).

That like my guardian angel keeps my mind
From rude attempts; and when affections stir,
I calm all passions with one thought of her.   30
Thus they whose reasons love, and not their sense,
The spirits love; thus one intelligence
Reflects upon his like, and by chaste loves
In the same sphere this and that angel moves.
Nor is this barren love; one noble thought   35
Begets another, and that still is brought
To bed of more; virtues and grace increase,
And such a numerous issue ne'er can cease,
Where children, though great blessings, only be
Pleasures reprieved to some posterity.   40
Beasts love like men, if men in lust delight,
And call that love which is but appetite.
When essence meets with essence, and souls join
In mutual knots, that's the true nuptial twine:
Such, lady, is my love, and such is true;   45
All other love is to your sex, not you.

Upon His Picture

When age hath made me what I am not now,
And every wrinkle tells me where the plow
Of time hath furrowed; when an ice shall flow
Through every vein, and all my head wear snow;
When death displays his coldness in my cheek,   5
And I myself in my own picture seek,
Not finding what I am, but what I was,
In doubt which to believe, this, or my glass:
Yet though I alter, this remains the same
As it was drawn, retains the primitive frame   10
And first complexion; here will still be seen
Blood on the cheek and down upon the chin;
Here the smooth brow will stay, the lively eye,
The ruddy lip, and hair of youthful dye.
Behold what frailty we in man may see,   15
Whose shadow is less given to change than he.

An Ode to Mr. Anthony Stafford[4] to Hasten Him into the Country

Come, spur away,
I have no patience for a longer stay,
But must go down,

---

4. Anthony Stafford (1857–1645), author
of various moral and historical works,
is described by Anthony à Wood as "a
good scholar . . . well read in ancient
history, poets and other authors" (*Athe-
nae Oxoniensis* [1691–1692; ed. P. Bliss,
4 vols., Oxford, 1813], 4 vols. [New
York, 1967], III, pp. 33–34).

And leave the chargeable[5] noise of this great town.
>> I will the country see,   5
>> Where old simplicity,
>>> Though hid in gray,
>>> Doth look more gay
> Than foppery in plush and scarlet clad.
>> Farewell, you city-wits that are   10
>>> Almost at civil war;
> 'Tis time that I grow wise, when all the world grows mad.

>>> Most of my days
I will not spend to gain an idiot's praise,
>>>> Or to make sport   15
For some slight puny[6] of the Inns of Court.
>>> Then, worthy Stafford, say,
>>> How shall we spend the day;
>>>> With what delights
>>>> Shorten the nights?   20
When from this tumult we are got secure
> Where mirth with all her freedom goes,
>> Yet shall no finger lose,[7]
Where every word is thought, and every thought is pure.

>>> There from the tree   25
We'll cherries pluck, and pick the strawberry,
>>>> And every day
Go see the wholesome country girls make hay,
>>> Whose brown hath lovelier grace
>>> Than any painted face   30
>>>> That I do know
>>>> Hyde Park can show;
Where I had rather gain a kiss than meet,
> Though some of them in greater state
>> Might court my love with plate,   35
The beauties of the Cheap, and wives of Lombard Street.[8]

>>> But think upon
Some other pleasures, these to me are none;
>>>> Why do I prate
Of women, that are things against my fate?   40
>>> I never mean to wed
>>> That torture to my bed.
>>>> My Muse is she
>>>> My love shall be.
Let clowns[9] get wealth, and heirs; when I am gone,   45

5. Burdensome.
6. Puisne—i.e., a first-year law student.
7. Cf. Randolph's poem, "Upon the Loss of His Little Finger," p. 210.
8. Hyde Park, given to the people of London by Charles I in 1637, was a fashionable promenade; Lombard Street was predominantly given over to merchants' offices; Cheapside and Eastcheap were known for their markets and shops.
9. I.e. (in this context), crass fellows.

And this great bugbear, grisly death,
    Shall take this idle breath,
If I a poem leave, that poem is my son.

        Of this, no more;
We'll rather taste the bright Pomona's[1] store;   50
        No fruit shall 'scape
Our palates, from the damson[2] to the grape.
    Then, full, we'll seek a shade
    And hear what music's made;
        How Philomel[3]   55
        Her tale doth tell,
And how the other birds do fill the choir;
    The thrush and blackbird lend their throats,
        Warbling melodious notes;
We will all sports enjoy, which others but desire.   60

        Ours is the sky,
Where at what fowl we please our hawk shall fly;
        Nor will we spare
To hunt the crafty fox or timorous hare,
        But let our hounds run loose   65
        In any ground they'll choose;
        The buck shall fall,
        The stag and all;
Our pleasures must from their own warrants be,
    For to my Muse, if not to me,   70
        I'm sure all game is free;
Heaven, earth, are all but parts of her great royalty.

        And when we mean
To taste of Bacchus' blessings now and then,
        And drink by stealth   75
A cup or two to noble Berkeley's[4] health,
        I'll take my pipe and try
        The Phrygian[5] melody,
        Which he that hears
        Lets through his ears   80
A madness to distemper all the brain,
    Then I another pipe will take
    And Doric music make,
To civilize with graver notes our wits again.

---

1. The wood nymph Pomona was the Roman divinity of fruit trees; cf. Carew, "To My Friend G. N. From Wrest," p. 181, 1. 93 and note.
2. Small plum.
3. Cf. Shirley, "Cupid's Call," p. 187, 1. 14 and note.
4. Stafford dedicated *The Guide of Honor* (1634) to George, eighth Baron Berkeley (1601–1658).

5. In ancient Greek music, the Phrygian mode was that suited "to express peaceful action under no stress of hard necessity"; the Dorian mode was appropriate rather for the "brave man in warlike action or in any hard and dangerous task" (Plato, *Republic*, III. 378–399 [ed. F. M. Cornford, Oxford, 1941]). Randolph seems to be using the terms to suggest Oriental abandon and Greek control.

An Answer to Mr. Ben Jonson's Ode,[6]
to Persuade Him Not to Leave the Stage

Ben, do not leave the stage
    'Cause 'tis a loathsome age,
For pride and impudence will grow too bold
    When they shall hear it told
They frighted thee; stand high, as is thy cause,   5
    Their hiss is thy applause.
    More just were thy disdain
    Had they approved thy vein.
So thou for them, and they for thee were born:
They to incense, and thou as much to scorn.   10

    Wilt thou engross thy store
    Of wheat, and pour no more,
Because their bacon-brains have such a taste
    As more delight in mast?[7]
No, set 'em forth a board of dainties, full   15
    As thy best Muse can cull;
    While they the while do pine
    And thirst, 'midst all their wine;
What greater plague can hell itself devise
Than to be willing thus to tantalize?[8]   20

    Thou canst not find them stuff
    That will be bad enough
To please their palates; let 'em thine refuse
    For some pie-corner[9] Muse;
She is too fair an hostess, 'twere a sin   25
    For them to like thine *Inn*:
    'Twas made to entertain
    Guests of a nobler strain.
Yet, if they will have any of thy store,
Give 'em some scraps, and send them from thy door.   30

    And let those things in plush,
    Till they be taught to blush,
Like what they will, and more contented be
    With what Broome swept from thee;[1]
I know thy worth, and that thy lofty strains   35
    Write not to clothes but brains.
    But thy great spleen doth rise
    'Cause moles will have no eyes;

6. Cf. Jonson's "Ode to Himself," on p. 88 of this edition; also Carew's "To Ben Jonson" (p. 172).
7. I.e., in food for hogs.
8. For deceiving the gods Tantalus was condemned to thirst in the underworld, standing up to his chin in water which forever eluded his effort to drink: cf. Ovid, *Metamorphoses*, IV. 458, X. 41.
9. I.e., confused and obscure.
1. Cf. Jonson, "Ode to Himself," l. 27 and note.

This only in my Ben I faulty find,
He's angry they'll not see him that are blind.   40

    Why should the scene be mute
    'Cause thou canst touch a lute
And string thy Horace? Let each Muse of nine
    Claim thee, and say, "Thou art mine!"
'Twere fond[2] to let all other flames expire,   45
    To sit by Pindar's[3] fire;
    For by so strange neglect
    I should myself suspect
The palsy[4] were as well thy brain's disease,
If they could shake thy Muse which way they please.   50

    And though thou well canst sing
    The glories of thy king,
And on the wings of verse his chariot bear
    To heaven, and fix it there,
Yet let thy Muse as well some raptures raise   55
    To please him him, as to praise.
    I would not have thee choose
    Only a treble Muse,[5]
But have this envious, ignorant age to know
Thou that canst sing so high, canst reach as low.   60

On the Death of a Nightingale[6]

Go, solitary wood, and henceforth be
Acquainted with no other harmony
Than the pies'[7] chattering, or the shrieking note
Of boding owls, and fatal raven's throat.
Thy sweetest chanter's dead, that warbled forth   5
Lays that might tempests calm, and still the north,
And call down angels from their glorious sphere[8]
To hear her songs, and learn new anthems there.
That soul is fled, and to Elysium[9] gone;
Thou a poor desert left; go then and run,   10
Beg there to stand a grove, and if she please
To sing again beneath thy shadowy trees;
The souls of happy lovers crowned with blisses
Shall flock about thee, and keep time with kisses.

---

2. Foolish.
3. Cf. Jonson, "To the Immortal Memory of . . . Sir Lucius Cary and Sir H. Morison," p. 76, and notes.
4. Cf. Jonson, "Ode to Himself," 1. 50 and note.
5. I.e., a Muse that dictates exclusively the highest poetic strain.

6. Cf. Henry Vaughan, "To My Ingenuous Friend, R. W.," p. 350, ll. 33–36.
7. Magpies'.
8. Cf. Herrick, "A Nuptial Song," p. 128, l. 102 and note.
9. Cf. Carew, "A Rapture," p. 166, l. 2 and note.

A Mask for Lydia

Sweet Lydia, take this mask, and shroud
Thy face within the silken cloud,
    And veil those powerful skies;
For he whose gazing dares so high aspire
    Makes burning-glasses of his eyes,   5
And sets his heart on fire.

Veil, Lydia, veil, for unto me
There is no basilisk[1] but thee:
    Thy very looks do kill.
Yet in those looks so fixed is my delight,   10
    Poor soul, alas, I languish still
In absence of thy sight.

Close up those eyes, or we shall find
Too great a lustre strike us blind;
    Or if a ray so good   15
Ought to be seen, let it but then appear
    When eagles do produce their brood
To try their young ones there.[2]

Or if thou would'st have me to know
How great a brightness thou canst show   20
    When they have lost the sun,
Then do thou rise, and give the world this theme:
    Sol from th'Hesperides[3] is run,
And back hath whipped his team.

Yet through the Goat when he shall stray,   25
Thou through the Crab must take thy way;[4]
    For should you both shine bright
In the same tropic, we poor moles should get
    Not so much comfort by the light,
As torment by the heat.   30

Where's Lydia now? Where shall I seek
Her charming lip, her tempting cheek
    That my affections bowed?
So dark a sable hath eclipsed my fair,
    That I can gaze upon the cloud   35
That durst not see the star.

1. According to legend, the glance or breath of the basilisk (a monstrous serpent or dragon) was fatal.
2. Cf. Carew, "To Ben Jonson," p. 172, l. 12 and note.
3. I.e., from the legendary garden of golden apples, in the west.
4. Capricorn, the goat, is the sign of the zodiac for the wintry period from December 23 to January 20; Cancer, the Crab, is the zodiacal sign for the midsummer period from June 22 to July 23.

But yet methinks my thoughts begin
To say there lies a white within,
　　Though black her pride control;
And what care I how black a face I see,　　　　40
　　So there be whiteness in the soul,
Still such an Ethiope be.

Upon Love Fondly[5] Refused for Conscience's Sake

Nature, creation's law, is judged by sense,
　　Not by the tyrant conscience.
Then our commission[6] gives us leave to do
　　What youth and pleasure prompts us to,
For we must question, else, heaven's great decree,　　　5
　　And tax it with a treachery,
If things made sweet to tempt our appetite
　　Should with a guilt stain the delight.
Higher powers rule us, ourselves can nothing do;
　　Who made us love made't lawful too.　　　　10
It was not love, but love transformed to vice,
　　Ravished by envious avarice,
Made women first impropriate;[7] all were free;
　　Enclosures man's inventions be.
I'th' Golden Age no action[8] could be found　　　15
　　For trespass on my neighbor's ground;
'Twas just with any fair to mix our blood;
　　The best is most diffusive good.
She that confines her beams to one man's sight
　　Is a dark-lantern[9] to a glorious light.　　　20
Say, does the virgin-spring less chaste appear
　　'Cause many thirsts are quenchéd there?
Or have you not with the same odors met
　　When more have smelt your violet?
The phoenix[1] is not angry at her nest　　　25
　　'Cause her perfumes make others blest:
Though incense to th' eternal gods be meant,
　　Yet mortals revel in the scent.
Man is the lord of creatures, yet we see
　　That all his vassals' loves are free;　　　30
The severe wedlock's fetters do not bind
　　The pard's[2] inflamed and amorous mind,

---

5. Foolishly. The argument and "witty" rhetoric of Randolph's poem may be compared with those of Leander's persuasive address to Hero, in Marlowe's "Hero and Leander"; also with the extended appeal made by Comus to the Lady, in Milton's *Comus*.
6. Warrant (by implication, "assigned task").
7. I.e., assigned to be the property of particular men.
8. I.e., no basis for legal proceedings.
9. I.e., a lantern with an opening that may be closed to conceal the light.
1. Cf. Carew, "A Song," p. 184, l. 18 and note.
2. Leopard's.

But that he may be like a bridegroom led
    Even to the royal lion's bed.
The birds may for a year their loves confine,   35
    But make new choice each Valentine.
If our affections then more servile be
    Than are our slaves', where's man's sovereignty?
Why, then, by pleasing more should you less please,
    And spare the sweets, being more sweet than these?   40
If the fresh trunk have sap enough to give
    That each insertive[3] branch may live,
The gard'ner grafts not only apples there,
    But adds the warden[4] and the pear;
The peach and apricot together grow,   45
    The cherry and the damson too,
Till he hath made by skilful husbandry
    An entire orchard of one tree.
So, lest our paradise perfection want,
    We may as well inoculate as plant.   50
What's conscience but a beldame's[5] midnight theme,
    Or nodding nurse's idle dream?
So feigned, as are the goblins, elves, and fairies,
    To watch their orchards and their dairies,
For who can tell when first her reign begun?   55
    I'th' state of innocence was none;
And since large conscience, as the proverb shows,
    In the same sense with bad one goes,[6]
The less the better, then, whence this will fall:
    'Tis to be perfect to have none at all.   60
Suppose it be a virtue, rich and pure,
    'Tis not for spring or summer, sure,
Nor yet for autumn: love must have his prime,
    His warmer heats, and harvest time.
Till we have flourished, grown, and reaped our wishes,   65
    What conscience dares oppose our kisses?
But when time's colder hand leads us near home,
    Then let that winter-virtue come;
Frost is till then prodigious;[7] we may do
    What youth and pleasure prompts us to.   70

---

3. Grafted.
4. A variety of baking pear.
5. I.e., an elderly matron's.
6. I.e., pliable. Cf., for example, in Shakespeare's *Henry VIII*, the Old Lady's suggestion (at II. iii. 29–33) that Anne Boleyn should (by acceding to the king's desire for her) gain "eminence, wealth, sovereignty,"

        which gifts
  (Saving your mincing) the capacity
  Of your soft cheveril conscience
    would receive,
  If you might please to stretch it.
7. I.e., unnatural.

William Habington

1605	Born, November 4 or 5, at Hindlip, Worcestershire. The Habingtons were Roman Catholics: William's uncle had been executed in 1586 for his connection with the Babington Plot against Queen Elizabeth's life; his father had been imprisoned for six years at that time. Educated at Saint Omer and at Paris, Habington subsequently resides at Hindlip, where his father indulges a passion for antiquarian research.
1630–1633	At some time during this period marries Lucy Herbert ("Castara"), youngest daughter of William Herbert, first Baron Powis.
1634	Publication of *Castara*.
1635	Second (enlarged) edition of *Castara*.
1640	Third (further enlarged) edition of *Castara*. Also publishes a tragicomedy, *The Queen of Aragon*, which appears to have been acted at court.
1641	Publication of *Observations Upon History*.
c. 1644–1650	According to Anthony à Wood, "not unknown to Oliver the usurper."
1654	Death, November 30; buried at Hindlip.

From CASTARA[1] (1640)

To Roses in the Bosom of Castara

Ye blushing virgins happy are
In the chaste nunn'ry of her breasts,
For he'd profane so chaste a fair,
Whoe'er should call them Cupid's nests.

1."Chaste altar." The third (augmented) edition of *Castara*, published in 1640, is divided into three parts: three prose "characters" ("A Mistress," "A Wife," "A Holy Man") successively introduce and in some sense epitomize the central emphasis of each part. The first grouping includes fifty-seven poems; the second, fifty (together with the prose "character," "A Friend," and eight elegies to the memory of Habington's friend George Talbot); the third, twenty-two, of which a majority are based on passages in the Psalms and the Book of Job. In his preface to the collection, Habington observes that when poetry "is wholly employed in the soft strains of love, his soul who entertains it loseth much of that strength which should confirm him man"; he offers rather "the innocency of a chase Muse." "In all those flames in which I burnt, I never felt a wanton heat, nor was my invention ever sinister [i.e., corrupted away] from the strait way of chastity. And when love builds upon that rock, it may safely contemn the battery of the waves and threatenings of the wind."

Transplanted thus, how bright ye grow,   5
How rich a perfume do ye yield!
In some close[2] garden cowslips so
Are sweeter than i' th' open field.

In these white cloisters live secure
From the rude blasts of wanton breath,   10
Each hour more innocent and pure,
Till you shall wither into death.

Then that which living gave you room,
Your glorious sepulcher shall be;
There wants no marble for a tomb,   15
Whose breast hath marble been to me.

To Castara

Do not their profane orgies hear,
Who but[3] to wealth no altars rear;
The soul's oft poisoned through the ear.

Castara, rather seek to dwell
I' th' silence of a private cell;   5
Rich discontent's a glorious hell.

Yet Hindlip[4] doth not want extent
Of room, though not magnificent,
To give free welcome to content.

There shalt thou see the early spring   10
That wealthy stock of nature bring,
Of which the Sybil's books did sing.[5]

From fruitless palms shall honey flow,
And barren winter harvest show,
While lilies in his bosom grow;   15

No north wind shall the corn infest,[6]
But the soft spirit of the east
Our scent with perfumed banquets feast.

A satyr here and there shall trip,
In hope to purchase leave to sip
Sweet nectar from a fairy's lip.   20

2. Secluded.
3. Except.
4. Hindlip Hall, near Worcester, was the country estate of the Habington family.

5. Cf. Herrick, "To the Right Honorable Mildmay, Earl of Westmorland," p. 133, l. 4 and note.
6. Disturb.

The nymphs with quivers shall adorn
Their active sides, and rouse the morn
With the shrill music of their horn.   25

Wakened with which, and viewing thee,
Fair Daphne[7] her fair self shall free
From the chaste prison of a tree,

And with Narcissus[8] to thy face
Who humbly will ascribe all grace
Shall once again pursue the chase.   30

So they whose wisdom did discuss
Of these as fictions, shall in us
Find they were more than fabulous.

To a Wanton

In vain, fair sorceress, thy eyes speak charms,
In vain thou mak'st loose circles with thy arms,
I'm 'bove thy spells. No magic him can move
In whom Castara hath inspired her love.
As she, keep thou strict sent'nel o'er thy ear,   5
Lest it the whispers of soft courtiers hear;
Read not his raptures,[9] whose invention must
Write journeywork, both for his patron's lust
And his own plush; let no admirer feast
His eye o' th' naked banquet of thy breast.   10
If[1] this fair precedent, nor yet my want
Of love to answer thine, make thee recant
Thy sorc'ries, pity shall to justice turn,
And judge thee, witch, in thy own flames to burn.

A Dialogue Between Araphil[2] and Castara

Araph. Doth not thou, Castara, read
        Am'rous volumes in my eyes?
        Doth not every motion plead
        What I'd show, and yet disguise?
            Senses act each other's part;   5
            Eyes, as tongues, reveal the heart.

Cast.   I saw love as lightning break
        From thy eyes, and was content

---

7. Cf. Ovid, *Metamorphoses*, I, 452–567.
8. The story of Narcissus, who fell in love with his own image reflected in the water and who was eventually changed into the flower that bears his name, appears in Ovid, *Metamorphoses*, III, 339–510.

9. Habington perhaps alludes to Carew's poem, "A Rapture" (p. 166).
1. I.e., if neither.
2. "The lover of the [chaste] altar."

Oft to hear thy silence speak;
Silent love is eloquent.
  So the sense of learning hears   10
  The dumb music of the spheres.[3]

Araph. Then there's mercy in your kind,
List'ning to an unfeigned love;
Or strives he to tame the wind,
Who would your compassion move?   15
  No, you're piteous as you're fair;
  Heaven relents, o'ercome by prayer.

Cast. But loose man too prodigal
Is in the expense of vows,   20
And thinks to him kingdoms fall
When the heart of woman bows;
  Frailty to your arms may yield;
  Who resists you, wins the field.

Araph. Triumph not to see me bleed,   25
Let the boar chased from his den
On the wounds of mankind feed.[4]
Your soft sex should pity men:
  Malice well may practise art,
  Love hath a transparent heart.   30

Cast. Yet is love all one deceit,
A warm frost, a frozen fire;[5]
She within herself is great
Who is slave to no desire.
  Let youth act, and age advise,   35
  And then love may find his eyes.

Araph. Hymen's torch[6] yields a dim light
When ambition joins our hands;
A proud day, but mournful night,
She sustains who marries lands.   40
  Wealth slaves man; but for their ore,
  Th'Indians[7] had been free, though poor.

Cast. And yet wealth the fuel is
Which maintains the nuptial fire,

---

3. According to the Greek philosopher Pythagoras, the "music of the spheres" could be heard only by those of particular virtue and insight. Cf. Shirley, "Would you know what's soft?," p. 190, l. 9 and note.
4. Habington may perhaps allude to the "wild boar" that is penned in a cave beneath the "Mount" of Venus, in the Gardens of Adonis (*The Faerie Queene*, III. vi. 48). Spenser signifies, by the boar, animal passion and the instinct for disorder and violence.
5. The conceit of love's paradoxical oppositions is conventional in Petrarchan poetry.
6. Hymen, god of marriage, is conventionally represented carrying a torch.
7. I.e., the natives of those South and Central American lands where Spanish explorers found gold.

And in honor there's a bliss;   45
They're immortal who aspire.
　　　But truth says, "No joys are sweet,
　　　But where hearts united meet."

Araph.　Roses breathe not such a scent
　　　To perfume the neighb'ring groves   50
　　　As when you affirm content
　　　In no sphere of glory moves.
　　　　　Glory narrow souls combines;
　　　　　Noble hearts love only joins.

Upon Castara's Absence

'Tis madness to give physic[8] to the dead;
Then leave me, friends. Yet haply[9] you'd here read
A lecture; but I'll not dissected be,
T'instruct your art by my anatomy.[1]
But still you trust your sense, swear you descry   5
No difference in me. All's deceit o' th'eye:
Some spirit hath a body framed in th'air
Like mine, which he doth, to delude you, wear;
Else heaven by miracle makes me survive
Myself, to keep in me poor love alive.   10
But I am dead; yet let none question where
My best part rests, and with a sigh or tear
Profane the pomp, when they my corpse inter;
My soul[2] imparadised, for 'tis with her.

To the World. The Perfection of Love[3]

You who are earth, and cannot rise
　　Above your sense,
Boasting the envied wealth which lies
Bright in your mistress' lips or eyes,
Betray a pitied eloquence.   5

That which doth join our souls, so light
　　And quick doth move,
That like the eagle in his flight
It doth transcend all human sight,
Lost in the element of love.   10

You poets reach not this, who sing
　　The praise of dust

8. Medicine.
9. Perchance.
1. Cf. Donne's "The Dampe."
2. I.e., my soul is.

3. Cf., with reference especially to lines 19–21 and 23–30, Donne's "The Ecstasy." This poem first appears in the 1635 edition of *Castara*.

But kneaded, when by theft you bring
The rose and lily from the spring
T'adorn the wrinkled face of lust.   15

When we speak love, nor art nor wit
    We gloss upon:
Our souls engender, and beget
Ideas, which you counterfeit
In your dull propagation.   20

While time seven ages[4] shall disperse,
    We'll talk of love,
And when our tongues hold no commerce,[5]
Our thoughts shall mutually converse,
And yet the blood no rebel prove.   25

And though we be of several kind
    Fit for offence,
Yet are we so by love refined,
From impure dross we are all mind;
Death could not more have conquered sense.   30

How suddenly those flames expire
    Which scorch our clay;
Prometheus-like, when we steal fire
From heaven, 'tis endless and entire:
It may know age, but not decay.   35

To a Friend, Inviting Him to a Meeting upon Promise[6]

May you drink beer, or that adult'rate wine
Which makes the zeal of Amsterdam divine,[7]
If you make breach of promise. I have now
So rich a sack that even yourself will bow
T'adore my Genius.[8] Of this wine should Prynne[9]   5
Drink but a plenteous glass, he would begin

4. It was believed that the world would pass through six "Ages" (i.e., eras), and that the Last Judgment would usher in the seventh, and final, Age. Cf. S. C. Chew, *The Pilgrimage of Life* (New Haven, 1962), ch. VI. "Aristotle had made three divisions [in the history of the world] . . . ; St. Augustine . . . and the Venerable Bede, six; Hippocrates [the Greek physician, c. 460–c. 357 B.C.], the famous seven" (*op. cit.*, p. 146).
5. I.e., are silent.
6. This piece and the four that follow are drawn from the second grouping of poems that comprise *Castara*. Habington here responds to Shirley's poem, "Two Gentlemen That Broke Their Promise of a Meeting, Made When They Drank Claret," on p. 193 of this edition.
7. Habington alludes sardonically to those English Puritans who had fled to the Netherlands to escape persecution by the Anglican authorities.
8. I.e., my protecting spirit.
9. William Prynne (1600–1669) was a Puritan pamphleteer whose fierce attacks on contemporary mores (notably stage plays and the theaters in London, in *Histriomastix*, published in 1623) led at length to savage reprisals by the government, which imposed fines amounting to £10,000, and sentenced him to have his ears cut off and to be branded on both shoulders.

A health to Shakespeare's ghost. But you may bring
Some excuse forth, and answer me, the King
Today will give you audience, or that on
Affairs of state you and some serious Don[1]   10
Are to resolve, or else, perhaps, you'll sin
So far as to leave word you're not within.
    The least of these will make me only think
Him subtle who can in his closet[2] drink,
Drunk even alone; and, thus made wise, create   15
As dangerous plots as the Low Country state,
Projecting for such baits[3] as shall draw o'er
To Holland all the herrings from our shore.
    But you're too full of candor, and I know
Will sooner stones at Sal'sbury casements throw,[4]   20
Or buy up for the silenced Levites[5] all
The rich impropriations, than let pall
So pure Canary, and break such an oath,
Since charity is sinned against in both.
    Come, therefore, blest even in the Lollards'[6] zeal,   25
Who canst with conscience safe, 'fore hen and veal,
Say grace in Latin, while I faintly sing
A penitential verse in oil and ling.[7]
Come, then, and bring with you, prepared for fight,
Unmixed Canary; Heaven send both prove right!   30
This I am sure: my sack will disengage
All human thoughts, inspire so high a rage
That Hippocrene[8] shall henceforth poets lack,
Since more enthusiasms are in my sack.
    Heightened with which, my raptures shall commend   35
How good Castara is, how dear my friend.

To Castara, upon Beauty

Castara, see that dust the sportive wind
So wantons with; 'tis haply all you'll find
Left of some beauty; and how still[9] it flies,
To trouble, as it did in life, our eyes.
Oh, empty boast of flesh! Though our heirs gild   5
The far-fetched Phrygian[1] marble, which shall build
A burden to our ashes, yet will death

1. I.e., some solemn Spanish grandee.
2. Private chamber.
3. I.e., devising such alluring temptations.
4. Church windows in Salisbury, Wiltshire, had been broken (in 1630) by a local official of Puritanical inclinations.
5. I.e., Puritan ministers who had been officially removed from their parishes.
6. The Lollards (from Dutch, "mumblers") were followers of the English
reformer John Wycliffe (c. 1320–1384).
7. A North Sea fish, ling somewhat resembles cod. Habington is making game of Puritan asceticism.
8. The Hippocrene spring, created when the winged horse Pegasus struck the ground with his hoof, was situated on the slopes of Mount Helicon, in Boeotia.
9. Continually.
1. Phrygia was located in Asia Minor.

Betray them to the sport of every breath.
Dost thou, poor relic of our frailty, still
Swell up with glory? Or is it thy skill   10
To mock weak man, whom every wind of praise
Into the air doth 'bove his center raise?
　　If so, mock on, and tell him that his lust
　　To beauty's[2] madness; for it courts but dust.

Against Them Who Lay Unchastity to the Sex of Women[3]

　　They meet but with unwholesome springs,
　　And summers which infectious are,[4]
　　They hear but when the mermaid sings,
　　And only see the falling star,
　　　　Whoever dare   5
　　Affirm no woman chaste and fair.

　　Go, cure your fevers, and you'll say
　　The dog-days[5] scorch not all the year;
　　In copper mines no longer stay,
　　But travel to the west,[6] and there   10
　　　　The right ones see;
　　And grant all gold's not alchemy.

　　What madman, 'cause the glowworm's flame
　　Is cold, swears there's no warmth in fire?
　　'Cause some make forfeit of their name,   15
　　And slave themselves to man's desire,
　　　　Shall the sex, free
　　From guilt, damned to the bondage be?

　　Nor grieve, Castara, though 'twere frail,
　　Thy virtue then would brighter shine,   20
　　When thy example should prevail,
　　And every woman's faith be thine;
　　　　And were there none,
　　'Tis majesty to rule alone.

To Castara, upon an Embrace

　　'Bout th' husband oak the vine
　　Thus wreathes to kiss his leafy face;
　　　Their streams thus rivers join,
　　And lose themselves in the embrace.

---

2. I.e., beauty is.
3. The poem responds to the challenges posed by Donne in his lyric, "Go and catch a falling star."
4. Bubonic plague was a particular threat during the hot summer months.
5. I.e., the most sultry weeks of the summer.
6. I.e., to Worcestershire, Habington's county of residence.

But trees want sense when they enfold,   5
And waters, when they meet, are cold.

Thus turtles[7] bill, and groan
Their loves into each other's ear;
Two flames thus burn in one,
When their curled heads to heaven they rear;   10
But birds want soul, though not desire,
And flames material soon expire.

If not profane, we'll say
When angels close, their joys are such;
For we not love obey   15
That's bastard to[8] a fleshly touch.
Let's close, Castara, then, since thus
We pattern[9] angels, and they us.

To Castara

Give me a heart where no impure
    Disordered passions rage,
Which jealousy doth not obscure,
    Nor vanity t'expense engage,
Nor wooed to madness by quaint oaths,   5
    Or the fine rhetoric of clothes,
Which not the softness of the age
    To vice or folly doth decline;
Give me that heart, Castara, for 'tis thine.

Take thou a heart where no new look   10
    Provokes new appetite,
With no fresh charm of beauty took
    Or wanton stratagem of wit;
Not idly wand'ring here and there,
    Led by an am'rous eye or ear,   15
Aiming each beauteous mark to hit,
    Which virtue doth to one confine;
Take thou that heart, Castara, for 'tis mine.

And now my heart is lodged with thee,
    Observe but how it still   25
Doth listen how thine doth with me;
    And guard it well, for else it will
Run hither back, not to be where
    I am, but 'cause thy heart is here.

7. Turtledoves.
8. I.e., that is the illegitimate conse-   quence of.
                                             9. Imitate.

But without discipline or skill   20
Our hearts shall freely 'tween us move;
Should thou or I want hearts, we'd breathe by love.

Nox Nocti Indicat Scientiam.[1] *David*

When I survey the bright
        Celestial sphere,
So rich with jewels hung that night
Doth like an Ethiop bride appear,

My soul her wings doth spread   5
        And heavenward flies,
Th'Almighty's mysteries to read
In the large volumes of the skies.

For the bright firmament
        Shoots forth no flame   10
So silent, but is eloquent
In speaking the Creator's name.

No unregarded star
        Contracts its light
Into so small a character,[2]   15
Removed far from our human sight,

But if we steadfast look,
        We shall discern
In it, as in some holy book,
How man may heavenly knowledge learn.   20

It tells the conqueror
        That far-stretched power
Which his proud dangers traffic for,[3]
Is but the triumph of an hour.

That from the farthest north   25
        Some nation may,
Yet undiscovered, issue forth,
And o'er his new-got conquest sway.

Some nation yet shut in
        With hills of ice   30
May be let out to scourge his sin,
Till they shall equal him in vice.

1. "Night unto night sheweth knowledge" (Psalms 19:2). This poem makes
part of the third and final section of
Castara.

2. Sign, symbol.
3. I.e., undertake to maintain (in the
sense of sordid commercial enterprise).

And then they likewise shall
    Their ruin have,
For as yourselves, your empires fall,   35
And every kingdom hath a grave.

Thus those celestial fires,
    Though seeming mute,
The fallacy of our desires
And all the pride of life confute.   40

For they have watched since first
    The world had birth;
And found sin in itself accurst,
And nothing permanent on earth.

Edmund Waller

1606	Born, March 3, at Coleshill, Hertfordshire; baptized March 9 at Amersham. Eldest son of a wealthy landowner.
1616	Father dies.
1616–1620	Attends Eton, and (from March, 1620) King's College, Cambridge, as a fellow commoner. Leaves without taking a degree.
1621	Represents Amersham in Parliament.
1622	Admitted to Lincoln's Inn.
1624–1628	Member of Parliament for Ilchester in the last Parliament of James I; for Chipping Wycombe and Amersham in the first and third Parliaments of Charles I.
1631	Enabled by the intervention of Charles I to marry the wealthy heiress Anne Banks, without her guardians' consent, in July.
1634	Death of his wife.
1635	From about this time, associated with Lucius Cary, Lord Falkland, and the group of philosophers and poets meeting at Great Tew. Becomes acquainted with Lady Dorothy Sidney ("Sacharissa"), whom he intermittently courts in verse until 1638.
1640	Member of Parliament for Amersham in the "Short Parliament," and for Saint Ives in the "Long Parliament," convened in November.
1643	Centrally active in a conspiracy designed to secure London for the King, while serving as one of the Parliamentary commission designated to reach an agreement with the sovereign; subsequently (the plot discovered) betrays his associates, two of whom are hanged. Imprisoned in the Tower of London from September, 1643, until November, 1644; fined £10,000 and banished from the realm. For some years thereafter lives comfortably with his second wife in France and Italy.
1645	Publication of first, second (augmented), and third editions of *Poems*. Later editions appear in 1664, 1668, 1682, 1686.

1651	Chiefly by consequence of his mother's influence with Cromwell, receives a pardon; returns to England in the year following.
1653	Death of his mother.
1661	Member of Parliament for Hastings; regularly in Parliament until his death. Welcomed and respected in courtly and literary circles.
1687	Death, October 21; buried at his estate in Beaconsfield, Hertfordshire.
1690	*The Second Part of Mr. Waller's Poems* published.

From POEMS[1] (1686)

To the King, on His Navy[2]

Where'er thy navy spreads her canvas wings,
Homage to thee, and peace to all she brings;
The French and Spaniard, when thy flags appear,
Forget their hatred, and consent to fear.
So Jove from Ida did both hosts survey,   5
And when he pleased to thunder, part the fray.[3]
Ships heretofore in seas like fishes sped,
The mighty still upon the smaller fed;
Thou on the deep imposest nobler laws,
And by that justice hast removed the cause   10
Of those rude tempests, which for rapine sent,
Too oft, alas, involved the innocent.
Now shall the ocean, as thy Thames, be free

1. Waller's character is fairly summarized by Edward Hyde, Earl of Clarendon, who acknowledges "the excellence and power of his wit, and pleasantness of his conversation," but chiefly emphasizes, with cold disdain, "a narrowness in his nature to the lowest degree, an abjectness and want of courage to support him in any virtuous undertaking, an insinuation and servile flattery to the height the vainest and most imperious nature could be contented with." In old age, Clarendon remarks, "his company was acceptable, where his spirit was odious, and he was at least pitied, where he was most detested" (*Life of Edward Earl of Clarendon*, 2 vols. [Oxford, 1760], I, p. 38). Nevertheless, Waller's poetry was extravagantly admired in his own lifetime and in the eighteenth century: Dryden wrote, in 1664, that "the excellence and dignity of rhyme were never fully known till Mr. Waller taught it; he first made writing easily an art" (*Essays of John Dryden*, ed. W. P. Ker, 2 vols. [Oxford, 1926], I, p. 7). His employment of the pentameter couplet served (with Denham's "Cooper's Hill") as a model for Dryden, Pope, and the poets of the Augustan Age. Cf. Ruth Wallerstein, "The Development of the Rhetoric and Metre of the Heroic Couplet, Especially in 1625–1645," *PMLA*, L (1935). 166–209; and G. Williamson, "The Rhetorical Pattern of Neo-Classical Wit," in *Seventeenth Century Contexts* (Chicago, 1969), pp. 240–271.

2. Noting the allusion in line 4 to a period of truce, in 1627, between France and Spain, G. Thorn-Drury assigns the poem to that year, when the Earl of Buckingham was making the English fleet ready for sea (*Poems of Edmund Waller*, 2 vols. [London, 1893], II, pp. 160–161).

3. In Homer's *Iliad*, the gods look on from Mount Ida as Greeks and Trojans engage in battle on the plain below.

From both those fates, of storms and piracy;
But we most happy, who can hear no force   15
But wingéd troops, or Pegasean horse.[4]
'Tis not so hard for greedy foes to spoil
Another nation, as to touch our soil.
Should nature's self invade the world again,
And o'er the center spead the liquid main,   20
Thy power were safe, and her destructive hand
Would but enlarge the bounds of thy command;
Thy dreadful fleet would style thee lord of all,
And ride in triumph o'er the drownéd ball;[5]
Those towers of oak o'er fertile plains might go,   25
And visit mountains where they once did grow.
    The world's Restorer never could endure
That finished Babel[6] should those men secure,
Whose pride designed that fabric to have stood
Above the reach of any second flood;[7]   30
To thee, His chosen, more indulgent, He
Dares trust such power with so much piety.

To Mr. Henry Lawes,[8]
Who Had Then Newly Set a Song of Mine, in the Year 1635

Verse makes heroic virtue live;
But you can life to verses give.
As when in open air we blow,
The breath, though strained, sounds flat and low;
But if a trumpet take the blast,   5
It lifts it high, and makes it last:
So in your airs our numbers[9] dressed,
Make a shrill sally from the breast
Of nymphs, who, singing what we penned,
Our passions to themselves commend;   10
While love, victorious with thy art,
Governs at once their voice and heart.
    You by the help of tune and time
Can make that song that was but rhyme.
Noy[1] pleading, no man doubts the cause;   15
Or questions verses set by Lawes.
    As a church window, thick with paint,
Lets in a light but dim and faint;
So others, with division, hide

---

4. Cf. Randolph, "A Gratulatory," p. 209, 1. 25 and note.
5. Globe.
6. I.e., the Tower of Babel.
7. Cf. Genesis 11:1–9.
8. Cf. the note on Carew's "A Divine Mistress," p. 158; several of Waller's poems, set to music by Lawes, appear in *Ayres and Dialogues* (1653).
9. Verses.
1. William Noy (1577–1634), who became Attorney General in 1631, was noted for his legal abilities. Cf. James Howell, *Epistolae Ho-Elianae, ed. cit.*, pp. 319–320.

The light of sense, the poet's pride;[2]   20
But you alone may truly boast
That not a syllable is lost;
The writer's and the setter's skill
At once the ravished ears do fill.
Let those which only warble long,   25
And gargle in their throats a song,
Content themselves with *ut, re, mi:*[3]
Let words, and sense, be set by thee.

Upon Ben Jonson[4]

Mirror of poets! Mirror of our age!
Which her whole face beholding on thy stage,
Pleased, and displeased, with her own faults, endures
A remedy like those whom music cures.
Thou hast alone those various inclinations   5
Which nature gives to ages, sexes, nations,
So tracéd with thy all-resembling pen,[5]
That whate'er custom has imposed on men,
Or ill-got habit (which deforms them so
That scarce a brother can his brother know),   10
Is represented to the wondering eyes
Of all that see, or read, thy comedies.
Whoever in those glasses[6] looks may find
The spots returned, or graces, of his mind;
And by the help of so divine an art,   15
At leisure view, and dress, his nobler part.
Narcissus,[7] cozened by that flattering well,
Which nothing could but of his beauty tell,
Had here, discovering the deformed estate
Of his fond mind, preserved himself with hate.   20
But virtue too, as well as vice, is clad
In flesh and blood so well, that Plato had
Beheld what his high fancy once embraced,
Virtue with colors, speech, and motion graced.[8]
The sundry postures of thy copious Muse   25

---

2. I.e., others devise musical settings
inappropriate to the words and meaning
of the poems set.
3. I.e., with meaningless sound alone
(*ut, re, mi* are the first three syllables of
the scale).
4. This poem was first published in
Jonsonus Virbius (1638), a collection of
tributes in Greek, Latin, and English,
dedicated to Jonson's memory. Of the
authors represented in the present edition, Habington, Godolphin, and Cartwright also contributed English verses to
the memorial volume.
5. I.e., thy pen, which can represent

every aspect of nature.
6. Mirrors.
7. Cf. Habington, "To Castara," p. 222,
n. 8.
8. Waller perhaps has in view Plato's
account of "the poet and taleteller who
would imitate the action of the good man
and would tell his tale in the [virtuous]
patterns" that appropriately match the
austere principles of Plato's ideal state.
Cf. *Republic*, III. 398b; II. 378 c–e; in
Collected Dialogues of Plato, ed. Edith
Hamilton and H. Cairns (New York,
1961), pp. 643, 625.

Who would express, a thousand tongues must use;
Whose fate's no less peculiar[9] than thy art;
For as thou couldst all characters impart,
So none could render thine, which still escapes,
Like Proteus,[1] in variety of shapes;   30
Who was not this, nor that, but all we find,
And all we can imagine, in mankind.

At Penshurst[2] [1]

Had Sacharissa[3] lived when mortals made
Choice of their deities, this sacred shade
Had held an altar to her power, that gave
The peace and glory which these alleys have;
Embroidered so with flowers where she stood,   5
That it became a garden of a wood.
Her presence has such more than human grace,
That it can civilize the rudest place;
And beauty too, and order, can impart,
Where nature ne'er intended it, nor art.   10
The plants acknowledge this, and her admire,
No less than those of old did Orpheus' lyre;[4]
If she sit down, with tops all towards her bowed,
They round about her into arbors crowd;
Or if she walk, in even ranks they stand,   15
Like some well-marshaled and obsequious band.
Amphion so made stones and timber leap
Into fair figures from a confused heap;[5]
And in the symmetry of her parts is found
A power like that of harmony in sound.   20
   Ye lofty beeches, tell this matchless dame,
That if together ye fed all one flame,
It could not equalize the hundredth part
Of what her eyes have kindled in my heart.
Go, boy, and carve this passion on the bark   25
Of yonder tree, which stands the sacred mark
Of noble Sidney's birth;[6] when such benign,
Such more than mortal-making stars did shine,
That there they cannot but forever prove
The monument and pledge of humble love;   30

9. Distinctive.
1. Proteus, old man of the sea, could change into every kind of shape: cf. Homer, *Odyssey*, IV. 456–458.
2. Cf. Jonson, "To Penshurst," pp. 21–23 and notes.
3. "The name is derived from the Latin appellation of *sugar*" (cf. Dr. Johnson's remarks on Waller, on pp. 429–432 of this edition); i.e., Lady Dorothy Sidney (b. 1617), eldest daughter of the Earl of Leicester, whom Waller vainly courted in verse from 1635 until her marriage to Lord Spencer in 1639.
4. Cf. Jonson, *The Forest*, XII, p. 38, l. 77 and note.
5. Amphion's skill in music was such that, moved by his lyre, stones of their own accord formed the walls of Thebes; cf. Homer, *Odyssey*, XI. 260.
6. Cf. Jonson, "To Penshurst," l. 14 and note.

His humble love whose hope shall ne'er rise higher
Than for a pardon that he dares admire.

At Penshurst [2]

While in the park I sing, the listening deer
Attend my passion, and forget to fear.
When to the beeches I report my flame,
They bow their heads, as if they felt the same.
To gods appealing, when I reach their bowers   5
With loud complaints, they answer me in showers.
To thee[7] a wild and cruel soul is given,
More deaf than trees, and prouder than the heaven!
Love's foe professed, why dost thou falsely feign
Thyself a Sidney? from which noble strain   10
He[8] sprung, that could so far exalt the name
Of love, and warm our nation with his flame,
That all we can of love or high desire
Seems but the smoke of amorous Sidney's fire.
Nor call her mother, who so well does prove   15
One breast may hold both chastity and love.
Never can she, that so exceeds the spring
In joy and bounty, be supposed to bring
One so destructive. To no human stock
We owe this fierce unkindness, but the rock,[9]   20
That cloven rock produced thee, by whose side
Nature, to recompense the fatal pride
Of such stern beauty, placed those healing springs,
Which not more help than that destruction brings.
Thy heart no ruder than the rugged stone   25
I might, like Orpheus, with my numerous moan
Melt to compassion; now, my trait'rous song
With thee conspires to do the singer wrong,
While thus I suffer not myself to lose
The memory of what augments my woes,   30
But with my own breath still foment the fire
With flames as high as fancy can aspire.
    This last complaint the indulgent ears did pierce
Of just Apollo, president[1] of verse;
Highly concernéd that the Muse should bring   35
Damage to one whom he had taught to sing,
Thus he advised me: "On yon agéd tree
Hang up thy lute, and hie thee to the sea,
That there with wonders thy diverted mind
Some truce, at least, may with this passion find."   40

---

7. I.e., "Sacharissa," Lady Dorothy Sidney.
8. I.e., Sir Philip Sidney.
9. Lady Dorothy Sidney was born at Sion House; from a nearby hill, Mount Sion, spring the mineral waters of Tunbridge Wells.
1. I.e., presiding deity.

Ah, cruel nymph! from whom her humble swain
Flies for relief unto the raging main,
And from the winds and tempests does expect
A milder fate than from her cold neglect;
Yet there he'll pray that the unkind may prove   45
Blest in her choice; and vows this endless love
Springs from no hope of what she can confer,
But from those gifts which heaven has heaped on her.

The Battle of the Summer Islands[2]

CANTO I

What fruits they have, and how heaven smiles
Upon those late-discovered isles.

Aid me, Bellona![3] while the dreadful fight
Betwixt a nation and two whales I write.
Seas stained with gore I sing, adventurous toil,
And how these monsters did disarm an isle.
  Bermudas, walled with rocks, who does not know?   5
That happy island where huge lemons grow,
And orange trees, which golden fruit do bear,
The Hesperian garden[4] boasts of none so fair;
Where shining pearl, coral, and many a pound,
On the rich shore, of ambergris[5] is found.   10
The lofty cedar, which to heaven aspires,
The prince of trees, is fuel for their fires;
The smoke by which their loaded spits do turn,
For incense might on sacred altars burn;
Their private roofs on odorous timber borne,   15
Such as might palaces for kings adorn.
The sweet palmettos a new Bacchus yield,
With leaves as ample as the broadest shield,
Under the shadow of whose friendly boughs
They sit, carousing where their liquor grows.   20
Figs there unplanted through the fields do grow,
Such as fierce Cato[6] did the Romans show,
With the rare fruit inviting them to spoil
Carthage, the mistress of so rich a soil.
The naked rocks are not unfruitful there,   25
But, at some constant seasons, every year

2. I.e., the Bermudas, named for the Spanish navigator Juan de Bermúdez, who discovered them in 1515. They became known in England as the Somers (or "Summer") Islands, after the ships of Sir George Somers, en route for Virginia, were wrecked there in 1609.
3. The Roman goddess of war.
4. Cf. Herrick, *Hesperides*, p. 104 and first note.
5. A waxy substance derived from the sperm whale, ambergris is used in making perfume.
6. Marcus Porcius Cato (234–149 B.C.), known for his austerity, regularly called for the destruction of Carthage, Rome's rival in the Mediterranean world. He was the author of *De Agri Cultura*.

Their barren tops with luscious food abound,
And with the eggs of various fowl are crowned.
Tobacco is the worst of things[7] which they
To English landlords, as their tribute, pay.   30
Such is the mold, that the blest tenant feeds
On precious fruits, and pays his rent in weeds.
With candied plantains, and the juicy pine,[8]
On choicest melons, and sweet grapes, they dine,
And with potatoes fat their wanton swine.   35
Nature these cates[9] with such a lavish hand
Pours out among them, that our coarser land
Tastes of that bounty, and does cloth return,
Which not for warmth but ornament is worn;
For the kind spring, which but salutes us here,   40
Inhabits there, and courts them all the year.
Ripe fruits and blossoms on the same trees live;
At once they promise what at once they give.
So sweet the air, so moderate the clime,
None sickly lives, or dies before his time.   45
Heaven sure has kept this spot of earth uncursed
To show how all things were created first.
The tardy plants in our cold orchards placed
Reserve their fruit for the next age's taste.
There a small grain in some few months will be   50
A firm, a lofty, and a spacious tree.
The palma-christi, and the fair papaw,[1]
Now but a seed, preventing[2] nature's law,
In half the circle of the hasty year
Project a shade, and lovely fruit do wear.   55
And as their trees, in our dull region set,
But faintly grow, and no perfection get,
So in this northern tract our hoarser throats
Utter unripe and ill-constrainéd notes,
Where the supporter of the poets' style,   60
Phoebus, on them eternally does smile.
Oh! how I long my careless limbs to lay
Under the plantain's shade, and all the day
With amorous airs my fancy entertain,
Invoke the Muses, and improve my vein!   65
No passion there in my free breast should move,
None but the sweet and best of passions, love.
There while I sing, if gentle love be by,
That tunes my lute, and winds the strings so high;
With the sweet sound of Sacharissa's name   70
I'll make the listening savages grow tame.
But while I do these pleasing dreams indite,
I am diverted from the promised fight.

7. I.e., tobacco (by implication delightful and desirable) is the most common
commodity.
8. Pineapple.

9. Delicacies.
1. I.e., the castor-oil plant and the pa-
paya.
2. Anticipating.

CANTO II

Of their alarm, and how their foes
Discovered were, this Canto shows.

Though rocks so high about this island rise
That well they may the numerous Turk despise,
Yet is no human fate exempt from fear,
Which shakes their hearts, while through the isle they hear
A lasting noise, as horrid and as loud   5
As thunder makes before it breaks the cloud.
Three days they dread this murmur, ere they know
From what blind cause th' unwonted sound may grow.
At length two monsters of unequal size,
Hard by the shore, a fisherman espies: 10
Two mighty whales! which swelling seas had tossed,
And left them prisoners on the rocky coast.
One as a mountain vast; and with her came
A cub, not much inferior to his dam.
Here in a pool, among the rocks engaged,   15
They roared, like lions caught in toils, and raged.
The man knew what they were, who heretofore
Had seen the like lie murdered on the shore,
By the wild fury of some tempest cast,
The fate of ships and shipwrecked men to taste.   20
As careless dames, whom wine and sleep betray
To frantic dreams, their infants overlay,[3]
So there, sometimes, the raging ocean fails,
And her own brood exposes; when the whales
Against sharp rocks, like reeling vessels quashed,[4]   25
Though huge as mountains, are in pieces dashed;
Along the shore their dreadful limbs lie scattered,
Like hills with earthquakes shaken, torn, and shattered.
Hearts sure of brass they had, who tempted first
Rude seas that spare not what themselves have nursed.   30
The welcome news through all the nation spread,
To sudden joy and hope converts their dread;
What lately was their public terror, they
Behold with glad eyes as a certain prey,
Dispose already of th' untaken spoil,   35
And, as the purchase of their future toil,
These share the bones, and they divide the oil.
So was the huntsman by the bear oppressed,
Whose hide he sold—before he caught the beast!
   They man their boats, and all their young men arm   40
With whatsoever may the monsters harm:
Pikes, halberds, spits, and darts that wound so far,
The tools of peace, and instruments of war.

3. I.e., lie upon (and smother) their   4. Crushed.
young ones.

Now was the time for vigorous lads to show
What love or honor could invite them to;   45
A goodly theater, where rocks are round
With reverend age, and lovely lasses, crowned.
Such was the lake which held this dreadful pair
Within the bounds of noble Warwick's[5] share,
Warwick's bold earl! than which no title bears   50
A greater sound among our British peers;
And worthy he the memory to renew
The fate and honor, to that title due,
Whose brave adventures have transferred his name,
And through the new world spread his growing fame.   55
  But how they fought, and what their valor gained,
Shall in another Canto be contained.

CANTO III

The bloody fight, successful toil,
And how the fishes sacked the isle.

The boat which on the first assault did go
Struck with a harping-iron[6] the younger foe,
Who, when he felt his side so rudely gored,
Loud as the sea that nourished him he roared.
As a broad bream,[7] to please some curious taste,   5
While yet alive in boiling water cast,
Vexed with unwonted heat, bounds, flings about
The scorching brass, and hurls the liquor out,
So with the barbed javelin stung, he raves,
And scourges with his tail the suffering waves.   10
Like Spenser's Talus with his iron flail,[8]
He threatens ruin with his ponderous tail,
Dissolving at one stroke the battered boat,
And down the men fall, drenchéd in the moat;
With every fierce encounter they are forced   15
To quit their boats, and fare like men unhorsed.
  The bigger whale like some huge carrack[9] lay,
Which wanteth sea-room with her foes to play;
Slowly she swims, and when, provoked, she would
Advance her tail, her head salutes the mud;   20
The shallow water doth her force infringe,
And renders vain her tail's impetuous swinge;[1]
The shining steel her tender sides receive,
And there, like bees, they all their weapons leave.
  This sees the cub, and does himself oppose   25

5. Robert Rich, second Earl of Warwick
(1587–1658), was one of the principal
proprietors of the English colony in the
Bermudas.
6. Harpoon.
7. The bream is a fresh-water fish of the
carp family.
8. Talus, "made of yron mould," is
Artegall's squire in *The Faerie Queene*.
9. Galleon.
1. Sweep.

Betwixt his cumbered mother and her foes;
With desperate courage he receives her wounds,
And men and boats his active tail confounds.
Their forces joined, the seas with billows fill
And make a tempest, though the winds be still.   30
    Now would the men with half their hopéd prey
Be well content, and wish this cub away;
Their wish they have: he, to direct his dam
Unto the gap through which they thither came,
Before her swims, and quits the hostile lake,   35
A prisoner there, but for his mother's sake.
She, by the rocks compelled to stay behind,
Is by the vastness of her bulk confined.
They shout for joy! and now on her alone
Their fury falls, and all their darts are thrown.   40
Their lances spent, one bolder than the rest
With his broadsword provoked the sluggish beast;
Her oily side devours both blade and haft,
And there his steel the bold Bermudian left.
Courage the rest from his example take,   45
And now they change the color of the lake;
Blood flows in rivers from her wounded side,
As if they would prevent the tardy tide,
And raise the flood to that propitious height
As might convey her from this fatal strait.   50
She swims in blood, and blood does spouting throw
To heaven, that heaven men's cruelties might know.
Their fixéd javelins in her side she wears,
And on her back a grove of pikes appears:
You would have thought, had you the monster seen   55
Thus dressed, she had another island been.
Roaring, she tears the air with such a noise,
As well resembled the conspiring voice
Of routed armies, when the field is won,
To reach the ears of her escapéd son.   60
He, though a league removéd from the foe,
Hastes to her aid; the pious Trojan[2] so,
Neglecting for Creusa's life his own,
Repeats the danger of the burning town.
The men, amazéd, blush to see the seed   65
Of monsters human piety exceed.
Well proves this kindness what the Grecians sung,
That Love's bright mother from the ocean sprung.[3]
Their courage droops, and, hopeless now, they wish
For composition with th' unconquered fish,   70
So she their weapons would restore again;
Through rocks they'd hew her passage to the main.

---

2. Aeneas returned to burning Troy to seek his wife Creusa (*Aeneid*, II. 749–794).

3. Venus was reputed to have sprung from the sea foam: cf. Ovid, *Metamorphoses*, IV. 537.

But how instructed in each other's mind,
Or what commerce can men with monsters find?
Not daring to approach their wounded foe,   75
Whom her courageous son protected so,
They charge their muskets, and with hot desire
Of fell revenge, renew the fight with fire;
Standing aloof, with lead they bruise the scales
And tear the flesh of the incensèd whales.   80
But no success their fierce endeavors found,
Nor this way could they give one fatal wound.
Now to their fort they are about to send
For the loud engines which their isle defend;
But what those pieces, framed to batter walls,   85
Would have effected on those mighty whales,
Great Neptune will not have us know, who sends
A tide so high that it relieves his friends.
And thus they parted with exchange of harms:
Much blood the monsters lost, and they their arms.   90

To Phyllis

Phyllis! why should we delay
Pleasures shorter than the day?
Could we (which we never can)
Stretch our lives beyond their span,
Beauty like a shadow flies,   5
And our youth before us dies.
Or, would youth and beauty stay,
Love hath wings, and will away.
Love hath swifter wings than Time;
Change in love to heaven does climb.   10
Gods, that never change their state,
Vary oft their love and hate.
    Phyllis! to this truth we owe
All the love betwixt us two.
Let not you and I inquire   15
What has been our past desire;
On what shepherds you have smiled,
Or what nymphs I have beguiled;
Leave it to the planets too,
What we shall hereafter do;   20
For the joys we now may prove,[4]
Take advice of present love.

On a Girdle

That which her slender waist confined
Shall now my joyful temples bind;

---

4. Experience.

No monarch but would give his crown,
His arms might do what this has done.

It was my heaven's extremest sphere,   5
The pale[5] which held that lovely deer;
My joy, my grief, my hope, my love,
Did all within this circle move!

A narrow compass! and yet there
Dwelt all that's good, and all that's fair;   10
Give me but what this ribbon bound,
Take all the rest the sun goes round.

To the Mutable Fair

Here, Celia! for thy sake I part
With all that grew so near my heart:
The passion that I had for thee,
The faith, the love, the constancy!
And, that I may successful prove,   5
Transform myself to what you love.
   Fool that I was! so much to prize
Those simple virtues you despise;
Fool! that with such dull arrows strove,
Or hoped to reach a flying dove;   10
For you, that are in motion still,
Decline our force, and mock our skill,
Who like Don Quixote do advance
Against a windmill our vain lance.
   Now will I wander through the air,   15
Mount, make a stoop[6] at every fair;
And with a fancy unconfined,
As lawless as the sea or wind,
Pursue you wheresoe'er you fly,
And with your various thoughts comply.   20
   The formal stars do travel so
As we their names and courses know,
And he that on their changes looks
Would think them governed by our books;
But never were the clouds reduced   25
To any art; the motions used
By those free vapors are so light,
So frequent, that the conquered sight
Despairs to find the rules that guide
Those gilded shadows as they slide;   30
And therefore of the spacious air

5. Enclosure.   "stoops" on its prey).
6. I.e., swoop down (as a falcon

Jove's royal consort[7] had the care,
And by that power did once escape,
Declining bold Ixion's rape;
She with her own resemblance graced   35
A shining cloud, which he embraced.
   Such was that image, so it smiled
With seeming kindness, which beguiled
Your Thyrsis lately, when he thought
He had his fleeting Celia caught.   40
'Twas shaped like her, but, for the fair,
He filled his arms with yielding air.
   A fate for which he grieves the less
Because the gods had like success;
For in the story, one, we see,   45
Pursues a nymph, and takes a tree;
A second, with a lover's haste,
Soon overtakes whom he had chased,
But she that did a virgin seem,
Possessed, appears a wandering stream;   50
For his supposéd love, a third
Lays greedy hold upon a bird,
And stands amazed to find his dear
A wild inhabitant of th'air.[8]
   To these old tales such nymphs as you   55
Give credit, and still make them new;
The amorous now like wonders find
In the swift changes of your mind.
   But, Celia, if you apprehend
The Muse of your incenséd friend,   60
Nor would that he record your blame
And make it live, repeat the same;
Again deceive him, and again,
And then he swears he'll not complain;
For still to be deluded so   65
Is all the pleasure lovers know,
Who, like good falconers, take delight
Not in the quarry, but the flight.

To a Lady in a Garden

Sees not my love how time resumes
The glory which he lent these flowers?
Though none should taste of their perfumes,

---

7. I.e., Juno (Hera). Ixion aspired to ravish her; but, far gone with wine, he was deceived by Zeus, who made a false Hera from a cloud. Ixion was subsequently bound to a flaming wheel which rolled eternally through the heavens. Cf. Ovid, *Metamorphoses*, IV. 461, for an allusion to the story.

8. Lines 45–54 allude successively to Apollo and Daphne (Ovid, *Metamorphoses*, I. 452–568); Alpheus and Arethusa (*ibid.*, V. 572–636), and (possibly) Tereus and Procne (*ibid.*, VI. 438–670).

Yet must they live but some few hours;
Time what we forbear devours!   5

Had Helen or th' Egyptian queen[9]
Been ne'er so thrifty of their graces,
Those beauties must at length have been
The spoil of age, which finds out faces
In the most retiréd places.   10

Should some malignant planet bring
A barren drought, or ceaseless shower,
Upon the autumn or the spring,
And spare us neither fruit nor flower,
Winter would not stay an hour.   15

Could the resolve of love's neglect
Preserve you from the violation
Of coming years, then more respect
Were due to so divine a fashion,
Nor would I indulge my passion.   20

Song

Stay, Phoebus, stay;
The world to which you fly so fast,
Conveying day
From us to them, can pay your haste
With no such object, nor salute your rise   5
With no such wonder, as de Mornay's[1] eyes.

Well does this prove
The error[2] of those antique books,
Which made you move
About the world; her charming looks   10
Would fix your beams, and make it ever day,
Did not the rolling earth snatch her away.

"While I listen to thy voice"

While I listen to thy voice,
Chloris, I feel my life decay;
That powerful noise[3]
Calls my flitting soul away.
Oh! suppress that magic sound,   5
Which destroys without a wound.

9. I.e., Cleopatra.
1. The lady's identity has not been established, although it is reasonable to suppose that she may have been one of Queen Henrietta Maria's attendants.
2. By Ptolemaic reckoning, the planets (including the sun) rotated about the stationary earth, located at the center of the universe.
3. I.e., that harmonious (and so powerful) sound.

Peace, Chloris, peace! or singing die,
    That together you and I
    To heaven may go;
For all we know   10
Of what the blessed do above
Is, that they sing and that they love.

Song

    Go, lovely rose!
Tell her that wastes her time and me
    That now she knows,
When I resemble her to thee,
    How sweet and fair she seems to be.   5

    Tell her that's young,
And shuns to have her graces spied,
    That hadst thou sprung
In deserts where no men abide,
    Thou must have uncommended died.   10

    Small is the worth
Of beauty from the light retired;
    Bid her come forth,
Suffer herself to be desired,
    And not blush so to be admired.   15

    Then die, that she
The common fate of all things rare
    May read in thee;
How small a part of time they share,
    That are so wondrous sweet and fair!   20

On St. James's Park, As Lately Improved by His Majesty[4]

Of the first Paradise there's nothing found;
Plants set by Heaven are vanished, and the ground;
Yet the description lasts; who knows the fate
Of lines that shall this paradise relate?
    Instead of rivers rolling by the side   5
Of Eden's garden, here flows in the tide;[5]

4. Immediately following his accession to the throne in 1660, Charles II set about making improvements in Saint James's Park in London. "Advised . . . by André Le Nôtre, Louis XIV's garden designer, he planted it with fruit trees, stocked it with deer, made a lake on which he could feed his ducks and round which he could walk his spaniels, and built an avenue, lined with trees and covered with powdered cockleshells, where he could play pall mall, a game something like croquet that had originated in Italy as *palla a maglio* (ball to mallet) and had become a fashionable craze in France" (C. Hibbert, *London, The Biography of a City* [New York, 1969], p. 81).

5. Among his other improvements, Charles had arranged to divert into the park a stream of water from the Thames.

The sea, which always served his empire, now
Pays tribute to our Prince's pleasure too.
Of famous cities we the founders know;
But rivers, old as seas, to which they go,   10
Are nature's bounty; 'tis of more renown
To make a river than to build a town.
    For future shade, young trees upon the banks
Of the new stream appear in even ranks;
The voice of Orpheus, or Amphion's hand,[6]   15
In better order could not make them stand;
May they increase as fast, and spread their boughs,
As the high fame of their great owner grows!
May he live long enough to see them all
Dark shadows cast, and as his palace tall!   20
Methinks I see the love that shall be made,
The lovers walking in that amorous shade,
The gallants dancing by the river's side;
They bathe in summer, and in winter slide.
Methinks I hear the music in the boats,   25
And the loud echo which returns the notes;
Whilst overhead a flock of new-sprung fowl
Hangs in the air, and does the sun control,
Darkening the sky; they hover o'er, and shroud
The wanton sailors with a feathered cloud.   30
Beneath, a shoal of silver fishes glides,
And plays about the gilded barges' sides;
The ladies, angling in the crystal lake,
Feast on the waters with the prey they take;
At once victorious with their lines and eyes,   35
They make the fishes, and the men, their prize.
A thousand Cupids on the billows ride,
And sea-nymphs enter with the swelling tide,
From Thetis[7] sent as spies, to make report,
And tell the wonders of her sovereign's court.   40
All that can, living, feed the greedy eye,
Or dead, the palate, here you may descry;
The choicest things that furnished Noah's ark,
Or Peter's sheet,[8] inhabiting this park;
All with a border of rich fruit-trees crowned,   45
Whose loaded branches hide the lofty mound.
Such various ways the spacious alleys lead,
My doubtful Muse knows not what path to tread.
Yonder, the harvest of cold months laid up,
Gives a fresh coolness to the royal cup;   50

6. Cf. "At Penshurst [1]," p. 235, ll.
12 and 18 and notes.
7. Thetis, a sea nymph, was the mother
of Achilles.
8. Simon Peter "saw heaven opened, and
a certain vessel descending unto him, as
it had been a great sheet knit at the four
corners, and let down to the earth:
Wherein were all manner of fourfooted
beasts of the earth, and wild beasts, and
creeping things, and fowls of the air"
(Acts 10:11–12).

There ice, like crystal firm, and never lost,
Tempers hot July with December's frost;
Winter's dark prison, whence he cannot fly
Though the warm spring, his enemy, draws nigh.
Strange! that extremes should thus preserve the snow,　　55
High on the Alps, or in deep caves below.
　　Here, a well-polished Mall[9] gives us the joy
To see our Prince his matchless force employ;
His manly posture, and his graceful mien,
Vigor and youth, in all his motions seen;　　60
His shape so lovely, and his limbs so strong,
Confirm our hopes we shall obey him long.
No sooner has he touched the flying ball,
But 'tis already more than half the Mall;
And such a fury from his arm has got,　　65
As from a smoking culverin[1] 'twere shot.
　　Near this my Muse, what most delights her, sees
A living gallery of aged trees;
Bold sons of earth that thrust their arms so high,
As if once more they would invade the sky.[2]　　70
In such green palaces the first kings reigned,
Slept in their shades, and angels entertained;
With such old counsellors they did advise,
And, by frequenting sacred groves, grew wise.
Free from th' impediments of light and noise,　　75
Man, thus retired, his nobler thoughts employs.
Here Charles contrives the ordering of his states,
Here he resolves his neighboring princes' fates;
What nation shall have peace, where war be made,
Determined is in this oraculous shade;[3]　　80
The world, from India to the frozen north,
Concerned in what this solitude brings forth.
His fancy, objects from his view receives;
The prospect, thought and contemplation gives.
That seat of empire here salutes his eye,　　85
To which three kingdoms[4] do themselves apply;
The structure by a prelate[5] raised, Whitehall,
Built with the fortune of Rome's capitol;
Both, disproportioned to the present state
Of their proud founders, were approved by Fate.　　90
From hence he does that antique pile[6] behold
Where royal heads receive the sacred gold;
It gives them crowns, and does their ashes keep;

---

9. Cf. n. 4, above.
1. Cannon.
2. Waller perhaps has in mind the revolt against the gods made by the giants, earth's children, who "darted rocks and burning oaks at the sky" (Apollodorus, *Library*, I. vi. 1).

3. I.e., grove where royal decisions, like the oracles' utterances in ancient times, are made.
4. I.e., England, Scotland, and Ireland.
5. I.e., Cardinal Wolsey (1472–1530), Lord Chancellor to Henry VIII.
6. I.e., Westminster Abbey.

There made like gods, like mortals there they sleep,
Making the circle of their reign complete,   95
Those suns of empire; where they rise, they set.
When others fell, this, standing, did presage
The crown should triumph over popular rage;
Hard by that house[7] where all our ills were shaped,
Th' auspicious temple stood, and yet escaped.   100
So snow on Etna does unmelted lie,
Whence rolling flames and scattered cinders fly;
The distant country in the ruin shares
What falls from heaven the burning mountain spares.
Next, that capacious hall[8] he sees, the room   105
Where the whole nation does for justice come;
Under whose large roof flourishes the gown,
And judges grave, on high tribunals, frown.
Here, like the people's pastor he does go,
His flock subjected to his view below;[9]   110
On which reflecting in his mighty mind,
No private passion does indulgence find;
The pleasures of his youth suspended are,
And made a sacrifice to public care.
Here, free from court compliances, he walks,   115
And with himself, his best adviser, talks;
How peaceful olive may his temples shade,
For mending laws, and for restoring trade;
Or how his brows may be with laurel charged,[1]
For nations conquered, and our bounds enlarged.   120
Of ancient prudence here he ruminates,
Of rising kingdoms, and of falling states;
What ruling arts gave great Augustus fame,
And how Alcides[2] purchased such a name.
His eyes, upon his native palace bent,   125
Close by, suggest a greater argument.
His thoughts rise higher, when he does reflect
On what the world may from that star[3] expect
Which at his birth appeared to let us see
Day, for his sake, could with the night agree;   130
A prince, on whom such different lights did smile,
Born the divided world to reconcile!
Whatever Heaven or high extracted blood

---

7. I.e., the Houses of Parliament, within the precincts of the Palace of Westminster. The Commons met in Saint Stephen's Chapel; the Lords in the Parliament Chamber. These buildings, save for Westminster Hall, were destroyed by fire in 1834.
8. I.e., Westminster Hall.
9. At the coronation of Charles II, a medal was struck representing the king as a shepherd tending his flock.

1. I.e., crowned with the laurel garland, emblematic (in this context) of power and victory. In heraldry, to "charge" is to assume as an armorial bearing.
2. Hercules.
3. In 1630, as Charles I was returning, at midday, from Saint Paul's, after having given thanks for the birth of his son, the future Charles II, a star was widely reported to have been observed in the sky.

Could promise or foretell, he will make good;
Reform these nations, and improve them more   135
Than this fair park, from what it was before.

Of English Verse

Poets may boast, as safely vain,
Their work shall with the world remain;
Both, bound together, live or die,
The verses and the prophecy.

But who can hope his lines should long   5
Last in a daily changing tongue?
While they are new, envy prevails;
And as that dies, our language fails.

When architects have done their part,
The matter may betray their art;   10
Time, if we use ill-chosen stone,
Soon brings a well-built palace down.

Poets that lasting marble seek
Must carve in Latin or in Greek;[4]
We write in sand, our language grows,   15
And, like the tide, our work o'erflows.

Chaucer his sense can only boast,
The glory of his numbers lost;[5]
Years have defaced his matchless strain,
And yet he did not sing in vain.   20

The beauties which adorned that age,
The shining subjects of his rage,
Hoping they should immortal prove,
Rewarded with success his love.

This was the generous poet's scope,   25
And all an English pen can hope,
To make the fair approve his flame,
That can so far extend their fame.

Verse, thus designed, has no ill fate
If it arrive but at the date   30

4. The traditional view that poetry written in Greek or (especially) Latin would survive that written in the vernacular tongues of Europe had been very generally abandoned by the end of the seventeenth century.

5. Chaucer's technical mastery of his medium was generally obscured throughout the sixteenth and seventeenth centuries, in part because of a failure to recognize the principles of Chaucerian pronunciation.

Of fading beauty; if it prove
But as long-lived as present love.

Of the Last Verses in the Book[6]

When we for age could neither read nor write,
The subject made us able to indite;
The soul, with nobler resolutions decked,
The body stooping, does herself erect.
No mortal parts are requisite to raise   5
Her that, unbodied, can her Maker praise.

    The seas are quiet when the winds give o'er;
So, calm are we when passions are no more,
For then we know how vain it was to boast
Of fleeting things, so certain to be lost.   10
Clouds of affection from our younger eyes
Conceal that emptiness which age descries.

    The soul's dark cottage, battered and decayed,
Lets in new light through chinks that time has made;
Stronger by weakness, wiser, men become,   15
As they draw near to their eternal home.
Leaving the old, both worlds at once they view,
That stand upon the threshold of the new.
                —*Miratur Limen Olympi.*
                        Vergil.[7]

6. I.e., of the "Divine Poems," first published in 1685.
7. Cf. Vergil, *Eclogues,* v. 56: *Candidus insuetum miratur limen Olympi* ("Arrayed in dazzling white, he stands enraptured at Heaven's unfamiliar threshold").

Sir John Suckling

1609	Born in Twickenham, Middlesex; baptized February 10. His father, descended from a prominent Norfolk family, was appointed Comptroller of James I's Household in 1622; his mother (deceased, 1613) was the sister of Lionel Cranfield, who became the Lord Treasurer.
1623	Matriculates at Trinity College, Cambridge; leaves in 1626 without taking a degree.
1627	On his father's death, inherits extensive estates in Suffolk, Lincoln, and Middlesex. Probably accompanies Buckingham's expedition to the Île de Ré.
1629–1630	With Lord Wimbledon's regiment in the Low Countries until May, 1630; subsequently studying astrology at the University of Leyden. Knighted, September, 1630.
1631–1632	In Germany, with Sir Henry Vane's embassy to Gustavus Adolphus.
1633–1634	Devotes himself to gambling on a grand scale, and to the (unsuccessful) courtship of Anne Willoughby, a wealthy heiress.
1637	Writes the prose *Account of Religion by Reason*.
1638	Publication of his play, *Aglaura*, presented before Charles I and Henrietta Maria in February and again in April. First separately published poems: commendatory verses to Lord Lepington's translation of Malvezzi's *Romulus and Tarquin*, and to Davenant's *Madagascar, With Other Poems*.
1639	Recruits and equips a troop of cavalrymen for the King's expedition against the Scots.
1640	Member of Parliament for Bramber. Takes part in the unsuccessful action against the Scots at Newburn Ford, near Newcastle, August 28.
1641	Involved with royalist plans to make use of the army on behalf of Charles I. Pressed by Parliament to account for his movements, flees to Dieppe on May 6; arrives in Paris on May 14. Apparently takes his own life, by poison, in late July or shortly thereafter.

1646   Publication of *Fragmenta Aurea.*
1659   Publication of *The Last Remains of Sir John Suckling.*

From *FRAGMENTA AUREA*[1] (1646)

Loving and Beloved

There never yet was honest man
   That ever drove the trade of love;
It is impossible, nor can
   Integrity our ends promove;[2]
For kings and lovers are alike in this,   5
That their chief art in reign dissembling is.

Here we are loved, and there we love;
   Good nature now and passion strive
Which of the two should be above,
   And laws unto the other give.   10
So we false fire with art sometimes discover,
And the true fire with the same art do cover.

What rack[3] can fancy find so high?
   Here we must court, and here engage,
Though in the other place we die.   15
   Oh, 'tis torture all, and cozenage,[4]
And which the harder is I cannot tell,
To hide true love, or make false love look well.

Since it is thus, God of Desire,
   Give me my honesty again,   20
And take thy brands back, and thy fire;
   I'm weary of the state I'm in:
Since (if the very best should now befall)
Love's triumph must be Honor's funeral.

---

1. "Golden remains." John Aubrey's account of Suckling's character and career (not to mention the poet's description of himself in "A Sessions of the Poets," p. 256, ll. 83–88) tends to reinforce the popular conception of Suckling as gallant, gamester, and libertine; and as a poet whose best work is charming but trivial. Congreve's Millamant, however, meant more than this when she spoke of "natural, easy Suckling (*The Way of the World*, IV. i); and it is of interest that Pope explicitly placed Suckling in "another school" from that including Waller and Carew, while Joseph Spence drew attention to the formal "purity" of Suckling's verse (J. Spence, *Observations, Anecdotes, and Characters of Books and Men,* ed. J. M. Osborn, 2 vols. [Oxford, 1966], I, pp. 196, 274). Many of Suckling's lyrics, in fact, "brilliantly fulfill a seventeenth-century standard of wit in language and thought," as L. A. Beaurline remarks in his analysis of "Why So Pale and Wan" (*TSLL,* IV [1962–63], 553–563).
2. Promote. The line, however, punningly reinforces the brutal realism informing line 2.
3. The rack was an instrument of torture devised to stretch (and, if need be, pull apart) the bodies of those bound upon it.
4. Trickery.

A *Sessions*[5] of the Poets

A sessions was held the other day,
And Apollo[6] himself was at it, they say;
The laurel that had been so long reserved,
Was now to be given to him best deserved.

           And   5

Therefore the wits of the town came thither;
'Twas strange to see how they flocked together.
Each strongly confident of his own way,
Thought to gain the laurel away that day.

There was Selden,[7] and he sat hard by the chair;   10
Wenman not far off, which was very fair;
Sandys with Townshend, for they kept no order;
Digby and Chillingworth a little further.

           And

There was Lucan's translator[8] too, and he   15
That makes God speak so big in's poetry;
Selwin and Waller, and Berkeleys both the brothers;
Jack Vaughan and Porter, and divers others.

The first that broke silence was good old Ben,
Prepared before with Canary wine,   20
And he told them plainly he deserved the bays,
For his were called *Works*, where others' were but plays.[9]

5. The poem, composed in 1637, seems originally to have been entitled "The Wits"; the title given here, by which the piece is generally known, was probably of editorial origin, in 1648. Thomas Clayton, citing Dr. Johnson in support, observes that the poem "introduced a much-imitated minor genre—'the trial for the bays'—into English poetry" (*Works of Sir John Suckling: The Non-Dramatic Works*, ed. T. Clayton [Oxford, 1971], pp. 266, 268). The complicated textual problems are discussed by L. A. Beaurline in *SB*, XVI (1963), 43–60; cf. Textual Notes, pp. 388–389 for the most significant variants. The text given here conforms generally to that in Clayton's edition: "the sense of the poem argues for a structure based on octaves, and the graphic pattern of a number of the witnesses proves that octaves with single words suspended between their quatrains in a form of bob and wheel was the original design" (*ed. cit.*, p. 274).
6. Excellence in the art of poetry was traditonally rewarded with the garland of laurel ("bays"), which was sacred to Apollo, god of poetry and song. Ben Jonson and his admirers habitually foregathered in the "Apollo Room" of the Devil Tavern, near Temple Bar, in London; in this room, it appears, a bust of Apollo was set over Jonson's place.
7. I.e., John Selden (1584–1654); cf. Jonson, "Epistle to Master John Selden,"
p. 59 and notes. The other persons named in this stanza include Sir Francis Wenman (fl. 1615–1640); George Sandys (1577–1644), whose translation of the Psalms was praised in verse by Carew; Aurelian Townshend (c. 1583–c. 1651), whose "Elegiacal Letter" had elicited Carew's diffident but characteristic response; Sir Kenelm Digby (1603–1665), general editor of the 1640–1641 edition of Jonson's *Works*; and William Chillingworth (1602–1644), Protestant theologian and, with Wenman, one of Lord Falkland's circle at Great Tew.
8. I.e., Thomas May (1595–1650), who had translated Lucan's epic poem *Pharsalia* in 1626–1627. "He that makes God speak so big in's poetry" is unidentified, as is "Selwin." Other persons named in this stanza are Samuel Waller; Sir William Berkeley (d. 1677), and his brother John, first Baron Berkeley of Stratton (d. 1678); Selden's friend Sir John Vaughan (1605–1674); and Endymion Porter (1587–1649), for whom cf. Herrick, "The Country Life," p. 137 and notes.
9. Jonson, the first English poet to publish his *Works* (1616), was widely criticized on that account. A contemporary gibe, "Pray tell me, Ben, where does the mystery lurk,/What others call a play you call a work?" drew this anonymous response: "The author's friend thus for the author says:/Ben's plays are works, when others' works are plays."

And

Bid them remember how he had purged the stage
Of errors that had lasted many an age;   25
And he hoped they did not think *The Silent Woman*,
The Fox, and *The Alchemist* outdone by no man.

Apollo stopped him there, and bade him not go on,
'Twas merit, he said, and not presumption
Must carry 't; at which Ben turned about,   30
And in great choler offered to go out;

But

Those that were there thought it not fit
To discontent so ancient a wit;
And therefore Apollo called him back again,   35
And made him mine host of his own New Inn.[1]

Tom Carew was next, but he had a fault
That would not well stand with a laureate;
His Muse was hard bound,[2] and th'issue of 's brain
Was seldom brought forth but with trouble and pain.   40

And

All that were present there did agree,
A laureate's Muse should be easy and free;
Yet sure 'twas not that, but 'twas thought that his grace
Considered, he was well he had a cup-bearer's place.[3]   45

Will Davenant,[4] ashamed of a foolish mischance
That he had got lately travelling in France,
Modestly hoped the handsomeness of 's Muse
Might any deformity about him excuse.

And   50

Surely the company would have been content,
If they could have found any precedent;
But in all their records, either in verse or prose,
There was not one laureate without a nose.

To Will Berkeley sure all the wits meant well,   55
But first they would see how his snow would sell;[5]
Will smiled and swore in their judgments they went less
That concluded of merit upon success.

So

1. Jonson's play, *The New Inn*, had been poorly received in 1629. Cf. Jonson's "An Ode to Himself," p. 88.
2. I.e., Carew composed his verses slowly and with some painstaking revision. Evidence of his concern to revise and polish his work is provided by the variant texts of the lyric "Ask me no more" (cf. Textual Notes, p. 380).
3. Carew had been appointed "Sewer in Ordinary" (i.e., an honorary steward at the royal dining table) in c. 1630.

4. The poet and playwright Sir William Davenant (1606–1688), who in fact became poet laureate in 1637, had "got a terrible clap of a black handsome wench that lay in Axe Yard, Westminster . . . which cost him his nose, with which mischance many wits were too cruelly bold" (John Aubrey, *Brief Lives, ed. cit.,* p. 76).
5. This allusion has not been definitively explained.

Suddenly taking his place again,   60
He gave way to Selwin, who straight stepped in,
But alas! he had been so lately a wit
That Apollo hardly knew him yet.

Tobie Matthew[6] (pox on him, how came he there?)
Was whispering nothing in somebody's ear,   65
When he had the honor to be named in court;
But, sir, you may thank my Lady Carlisle for't;
                                                             For
Had not her care furnished you out
With something of handsome, without all doubt   70
You and your sorry Lady Muse had been
In the number of those that were not let in.

In haste from the court two or three came in,
And they brought letters, forsooth, from the Queen;
'Twas discreetly done, too, for if th' had come   75
Without them, th' had scarce been let into the room.
                                                            This
Made a dispute, for 'twas plain to be seen
Each man had a mind to gratify the Queen;
But Apollo himself could not think it fit;   80
There was difference, he said, betwixt fooling and wit.

Suckling next was called, but did not appear,
But straight one whispered Apollo i' th' ear,
That of all men living he cared not for't,
He loved not the Muses so well as his sport;   85
                                                             And
Prized black eyes, or a lucky hit
At bowls, above all the trophies of wit;
But Apollo was angry, and publicly said,
'Twere fit that a fine were set upon 's head.   90

Wat Montague[7] now stood forth to his trial,
And did not so much as suspect a denial;
But witty Apollo asked him first of all,
If he understood his own pastoral.
                                                      For   95
If he could do it, 'twould plainly appear
He understood more than any man there,
And did merit the bays above all the rest;
But the Monsieur[8] was modest, and silence confessed.

---

6. Sir Tobie Mathew (1577–1655), son of
the Archbishop of Canterbury, had become a Roman Catholic priest in 1614. He
assiduously courted the favor of Lucy
Hay, Countess of Carlisle (1599–1660), a
reigning beauty and wit at the court of

Charles I.
7. Walter Montagu (c. 1603–1677) was
the author of a pastoral comedy, *The
Shepherd's Paradise*, performed at court
in 1633.
8. I.e., the Frenchified fellow.

During these troubles, in the crowd was hid   100
One that Apollo soon missed, little Sid;[9]
And having spied him, called him out of the throng,
And advised him in his ear not to write so strong.
                    Then

Murray[1] was summoned, but 'twas urged that he   105
Was chief already of another company.

Hales,[2] set by himself, most gravely did smile
To see them about nothing keep such a coil;[3]
Apollo had spied him, but knowing his mind
Passed by, and called Falkland[4] that sat just behind.   110
                    But

He was of late so gone with divinity,[5]
That he had almost forgot his poetry;
Though to say the truth (and Apollo did know it)
He might have been both his priest and his poet.   115

At length who but an alderman[6] did appear,
At which Will Davenant began to swear;
But wiser Apollo bade him draw nigher,
And when he was mounted a little higher,
                    He   120
Openly declared that 'twas the best sign
Of good store of wit to have good store of coin;[7]
And without a syllable more or less said,
He put the laurel on the alderman's head.

At this all the wits were in such a maze   125
That for a good while they did nothing but gaze
One upon another; not a man in the place
But had discontent writ in great[8] in his face.
                    Only

The small poets cleared up again,   130
Out of hope, as 'twas thought, of borrowing;
But sure they were out, for he forfeits his crown,
When he lends any poets about the town.

---

9. I.e., Sidney Godolphin (1610–1643); cf. p. 273 of this edition.
1. William Murray (c. 1600–1651), subsequently first Earl of Dysart, made one of the circle of courtly advisers to Charles I.
2. John Hales (1584–1656) was one of Lord Falkland's circle at Great Tew.
3. I.e., became so excited.
4. I.e., Lucius Cary, second Viscount Falkland (c. 1610–1643). Cf. Jonson's poem "To the Immortal Memory . . . of

. . . Sir Lucius Cary and Sir H. Morison," p. 76 and first note.
5. I.e., so concerned with theological disputation (explicitly with the role of reason in theology).
6. I.e., the chief officer of a city ward, concerned primarily with the material well-being of the citizenry.
7. Proverbs on this theme abound in every literature; cf., for example, Pope, *Imitations of Horace*, Epistle I. i. 81.
8. I.e., in large letters.

Sonnets[9]

I

Dost see how unregarded now
    That piece of beauty passes?
There was a time when I did vow
    To that alone;
    But mark the fate of faces: 5
The red and white[1] works now no more on me,
Than if it could not charm, or I not see.

And yet the face continues good,
    And I have still desires,
Am still the selfsame flesh and blood,   10
        As apt to melt
    And suffer from those fires;
Oh! some kind power unriddle where it lies,
Whether my heart be faulty, or her eyes?

She every day her man does kill,   15
    And I as often die;
Neither her power, then, nor my will
        Can questioned be;
    What is the mystery?
Sure beauties' empires, like to greater states,   20
Have certain periods set, and hidden fates.

II

Of thee, kind boy,[2] I ask no red and white,
    To make up my delight;
    No odd becoming graces,
Black eyes, or little know-not-whats,[3] in faces;
Make me but mad[4] enough, give me good store   5
Of love for her I court;
    I ask no more,
'Tis love in love that makes the sport.

There's no such thing as that we beauty call,
    It is mere cozenage[5] all;   10
    For though some, long ago,

---

9. I.e., short lyrics. Musical settings of Sonnets I and II appear in *Select Ayres and Dialogues* (London, 1659), and in other mid-century song collections.
1. I.e., the lady's complexion. The Petrarchan convention of praising "red and white" female beauty, regularly a feature of Elizabethan poetry, was largely repudiated, for various reasons, by seventeenth-century English poets. Cf. Marvell's "The Garden," ll. 17–18: "No white nor red was ever seen/So am'rous as this lovely green."
2. I.e., Cupid.
3. I.e. (perhaps), beauty patches.
4. Frantic.
5. Trickery.

Liked certain colors mingled so and so,
That doth not tie me now from choosing new;
If I a fancy take
    To black and blue,   15
That fancy doth it beauty make.

'Tis not the meat, but 'tis the appetite
    Makes eating a delight,
    And if I like one dish
More than another, that a pheasant is;   20
What in our watches, that in us is found:[6]
So to the height and nick
    We up be wound,
No matter by what hand or trick.

III

Oh! for some honest lover's ghost,
    Some kind unbodied post[7]
    Sent from the shades below:
    I strangely long to know
Whether the nobler chaplets[8] wear,   5
Those that their mistress' scorn did bear,
    Or those that were used kindly.

For whatsoe'er they tell us here
    To make those sufferings dear,
    'Twill there, I fear, be found,   10
    That to the being crowned
T'have loved alone will not suffice,
Unless we also have been wise,
    And have our loves enjoyed.

What posture can we think him in,   15
    That here unloved again
    Departs, and's thither gone
    Where each sits by his own?
Or how can that Elysium[9] be,
Where I my mistress still must see   20
    Circled in others' arms?

6. The conceit of man's likeness to a timepiece occurs in Suckling's verse with some frequency. Thomas Hobbes, in the Introduction to *Leviathan* (1651), inquired, "What is the heart, but a spring; and the nerves, but so many strings; and the joints, but so many wheels, giving motion to the whole body, such as was intended by the artificer?"
7. Messenger. The opening lines may glance at those of Donne's lyric "Love's Usury."
8. Garlands.
9. Cf. Carew, "A Rapture," p. 166, 1. 2 and note.

For there the judges all are just,
    And Sophonisba[1] must
    Be his whom she held dear,
    Not his who loved her here;   25
The sweet Philoclea,[2] since she died,
Lies by her Pyrocles his side,
    Not by Amphialus.

Some bays, perchance, or myrtle bough,
    For difference crowns the brow   30
    Of those kind souls that were
    The noble martyrs here;
And if that be the only odds
(As who can tell?), ye kinder gods,
    Give me the woman here.   35

Against Fruition [1]

Stay here, fond[3] youth, and ask no more; be wise:
Knowing too much long since lost paradise.
The virtuous joys thou hast, thou would'st should still
Last in their pride; and would'st not take it ill,
If rudely from sweet dreams (and for a toy)   5
Thou wert waked? he wakes himself, that does enjoy.

Fruition adds no new wealth, but destroys,
And while it pleaseth much the palate, cloys;
Who thinks he shall be happier for that,
As reasonably might hope he might grow fat   10
By eating to a surfeit; this once past,
What relishes? even kisses lose their taste.

Urge not 'tis necessary: alas! we know
The homeliest thing which mankind does is so;
The world is of a vast extent, we see,   15
And must be peopled; children there must be;
So must bread too; but since there are enough
Born to the drudgery, what need we plough?

Women enjoyed, whate'er before they've been,
Are like romances read, or sights once seen;   20
Fruition's dull, and spoils the play much more
Than if one read or knew the plot before.
'Tis expectation makes a blessing dear;
Heaven were not heaven, if we knew what it were.

1. Sophonisba, daughter of the Carthaginian general Hasdrubal, loved the Numidian prince Masinissa; when, in 204 B.C., Scipio Africanus demanded that she should be surrendered to Rome, she took her life by poison.
2. Philoclea, Pyrocles, and Amphialus are characters in Sir Philip Sidney's romance, *Arcadia*.
3. Foolish.

And as in prospects we are there pleased most   25
Where something keeps the eye from being lost,
And leaves us room to guess, so here restraint
Holds up delight, that with excess would faint.
They who know all the wealth they have, are poor;
He's only rich that cannot tell his store.[4]

Song

I prithee spare me, gentle boy,[5]
Press me no more for that slight toy,
That foolish trifle of an heart;
I swear it will not do its part,
Though thou dost thine, employ'st thy power and art.   5

For through long custom it has known
The little secrets, and is grown
Sullen and wise, will have its will,
And, like old hawks, pursues that still
That makes least sport, flies only where't can kill.   10

Some youth that has not made his story
Will think, perchance, the pain's the glory,
And mannerly sit out love's feast;
I shall be carving of the best,
Rudely call for the last course 'fore the rest.   15

And, oh! when once that course is past,
How short a time the feast doth last;
Men rise away, and scarce say grace,
Or civilly once thank the face
That did invite, but seek another place.   20

Upon My Lady Carlisle's[6] *Walking in Hampton Court Garden*
Dialogue
T.C.   J.S.[7]

THOM.

Didst thou not find the place inspired,
And flowers, as if they had desired
No other sun, start from their beds,
And for a sight steal out their heads?

---

4. Suckling glances at Ovid, *Metamorphoses*, III. 466: *inopem me copia fecit*
("plenty makes me poor").
5. I.e., Cupid.
6. Cf. "A Sessions of the Poets," p. 256,
l. 64 and note. Suckling's cynical view
of Lady Carlisle is at odds with the ad-

miring note struck in poems addressed to
her by Herrick, Waller, and Carew (who
wrote two New Year's poems to the
lady).
7. I.e., Thomas Carew and Sir John
Suckling.

Heard'st thou not music when she talked?   5
And didst not find that, as she walked,
She threw rare perfumes all about,
Such as bean-blossoms newly out
Or chaféd[8] spices give—?

J.S.

I must confess those perfumes, Tom,   10
I did not smell; nor found that from
Her passing by, ought sprung up new;
The flowers had all their birth from you,
For I passed o'er the selfsame walk,
And did not find one single stalk   15
Of anything that was to bring
This unknown after after-spring.

THOM.

Dull and insensible, could'st see
A thing so near a deity
Move up and down, and feel no change?   20

J.S.

None and so great were alike strange.
I had my thoughts, but not your way;
All are not born, sir, to the bay.[9]
Alas! Tom, I am flesh and blood,
And was consulting how I could   25
In spite of masks and hoods descry
The parts denied unto the eye;
I was undoing all she wore;
And, had she walked but one turn more,
Eve in her first state had not been   30
More naked, or more plainly seen.

THOM.

'Twas well for thee she left the place,
There is great danger in that face;
But hadst thou viewed her leg and thigh
And, upon that discovery,   35
Searched after parts that are more dear
(As fancy seldom stops so near),

8. Warmed.
9. I.e., to poetical excellence, symbolized by the laurel (or "bays"); by implica-tion, with highly developed imaginative powers.

No time or age had ever seen
So lost a thing as thou hadst been.[1]

J.S.[2]

'Troth, in her face I could descry   40
No danger, no divinity.
But since the pillars were so good
On which the lovely fountain stood,
Being once come so near, I think
I should have ventured hard to drink.   45
What ever fool like me had been
If I'd not done as well as seen?
There to be lost why should I doubt
When fools with ease go in and out?

"That none beguiléd be by time's quick flowing"

That none beguiléd be by time's quick flowing,
Lovers have in their hearts a clock still going;
For, though time be nimble, his motions
Are quicker
And thicker   5
Where love hath his notions.

Hope is the mainspring on which moves desire,
And these do the less wheels, fear, joy, inspire;
The balance is thought, evermore
Clicking   10
And striking,
And ne'er giving o'er.

Occasion's the hand which still's moving round,
Till by it the critical hour may be found;
And, when that falls out, it will strike   15
Kisses,
Strange blisses,
And what you best like.

" 'Tis now, since I sat down before"

'Tis now, since I sat down before
That foolish fort, a heart
(Time strangely spent), a year and more,
And still I did my part:

1. The stanza recalls the story of Actaeon, who chanced to see the goddess Diana naked; he was consequently transformed into a stag and torn to pieces by his own hounds: cf. Ovid, *Metamorphoses*, III. 155–252.
2. This final stanza appears only in manuscript.

Made my approaches,[3] from her hand   5
    Unto her lip did rise,
And did already understand
    The language of her eyes;

Proceeded on with no less art,
    My tongue was engineer;   10
I thought to undermine the heart
    By whispering in the ear.

When this did nothing, I brought down
    Great cannon-oaths, and shot
A thousand thousand to the town;   15
    And still it yielded not.

I then resolved to starve the place
    By cutting off all kisses,
Praising and gazing on her face,
    And all such little blisses.   20

To draw her out, and from her strength,
    I drew all batteries in;
And brought myself to lie at length
    As if no siege had been.

When I had done what man could do,   25
    And thought the place mine own,
The enemy lay quiet too,
    And smiled at all was done.

I sent to know from whence and where
    These hopes and this relief;   30
A spy informed, Honor was there,
    And did command in chief.

"March, march," quoth I, "the word straight give;
    Let's lose no time, but leave her;
That giant[4] upon air will live,   35
    And hold it out forever.

"To such a place our camp remove,
    As will no siege abide;
I hate a fool that starves her love,
    Only to feed her pride."   40

---

3. I.e., entrenchments constructed in progressive diagonals, by which those besieging a town might gradually "approach" its walls.
4. I.e., honor. Cf. Carew, "A Rapture," p. 166, l. 3.

Against Fruition [2]

Fie upon hearts that burn with mutual fire!
I hate two minds that breathe but one desire.
Were I to curse th' unhallowed sort of men,
I'd wish them to love, and be loved again.
Love's a chameleon, that lives on mere air,[5]   5
And surfeits when it comes to grosser fare;
'Tis petty jealousies, and little fears,
Hopes joined with doubts, and joys with April tears,
That crowns our love with pleasures: these are gone
When once we come to full fruition,   10
Like waking in a morning, when all night
Our fancy hath been fed with true delight.
Oh, what a stroke 'twould be! Sure I should die,
Should I but hear my mistress once say, "Aye."
That monster expectation feeds too high   15
For any woman e'er to satisfy;
And no brave spirit ever cared for that
Which in down beds with ease he could come at.
She's but an honest whore that yields, although
She be as cold as ice, as pure as snow;   20
He that enjoys her hath no more to say
But keep us fasting, if you'll have us pray.[6]
Then, fairest mistress, hold the power you have,
By still denying what we still do crave;
In keeping us in hopes strange things to see,   25
That never were, nor are, nor e'er shall be.

A Ballad upon a Wedding[7]

I tell thee, Dick, where I have been,
Where I the rarest things have seen,
    Oh, things without compare!
Such sights again cannot be found
In any place on English ground,   5
    Be it at wake[8] or fair.

At Charing Cross,[9] hard by the way

---

5. This popular belief is often encountered in literature of the period; cf., for example, *Hamlet*, III. ii. 91–92.
6. I.e., beg for more.
7. The poem probably celebrates the wedding of John Lord Lovelace to Lady Anne Wentworth, on July 11, 1638; cf. *Works of Suckling, ed. cit.*, pp. 280–281. "Dick" may be the poet Richard Lovelace, brother to the groom; but this identification need not be insisted upon since the speaker and his companion are evidently rustics (presumably from the West Country, Devonshire or Somerset). Clayton observes that Suckling's poem initiates "a minor genre, that of the 'rusticated epithalamion,' a gently burlesqued version of the traditional pastoral epithalamion" (*ed. cit.*, p. 279).
8. Parish festival.
9. Originally the site of a stone cross erected by Edward I in memory of his consort, Queen Eleanor, Charing Cross had at an early date become a busy center in the city of Westminster. The Haymarket is situated nearby.

Where we, thou know'st, do sell our hay,
 There is a house with stairs;
And there did I see coming down   10
Such folk as are not in our town,
 Forty, at least, in pairs.

Amongst the rest, one pest'lent fine[1]
(His beard no bigger, though, than thine)
 Walked on before the rest: 15
Our landlord looks like nothing to him;
The King (God bless him!), 'twould undo him,
 Should he go still[2] so dressed.

At course-a-park,[3] without all doubt,
He should have first been taken out   20
 By all the maids i' th' town,
Though lusty Roger there had been,
Or little George upon the Green,
 Or Vincent of the Crown.[4]

But wot[5] you what? the youth was going 25
To make an end of all his wooing;
 The parson for him stayed;
Yet by his leave, for all his haste,
He did not so much wish all past,
 Perchance, as did the maid.   30

The maid (and thereby hangs a tale,
For such a maid no Whitsun-ale[6]
 Could ever yet produce):
No grape that's kindly[7] ripe could be
So round, so plump, so soft as she,   35
 Nor half so full of juice.

Her finger was so small, the ring
Would not stay on which they did bring,
 It was too wide a peck;[8]
And to say truth (for out it must),   40
It looked like the great collar (just)
 About our young colt's neck.

---

1. I.e., exceptionally fine.
2. Continually.
3. "A country game, in which a girl called out one of the other sex to choose her" (*OED*).
4. "As good as George of Green" was an English proverb or folk saying; it seems that the other names refer also to generalized types of male prowess.
5. Know.
6. I.e., no Whitsuntide festival. Held on the seventh Sunday after Easter, to commemorate Pentecost (cf. Acts 2:1–4), these celebrations were characterized by merrymaking, and drinking on an heroic scale.
7. Naturally.
8. I.e., it was much too large.

Her feet beneath her petticoat
Like little mice stole in and out,
 As if they feared the light;   45
But oh! she dances such a way,
No sun upon an Easter day
 Is half so fine a sight.[9]

He would have kissed her once or twice,
But she would not, she was so nice,[1]   50
 She would not do't in sight;
And then she looked as who should say,
I will do what I list today,
 And you shall do't at night.

Her cheeks so rare a white was on,   55
No daisy makes comparison
 (Who sees them is undone[2]),
For streaks of red were mingled there,
Such as are on a Katherine pear[3]
 (The side that's next the sun).   60

Her lips were red, and one was thin,
Compared to that was next her chin
 (Some bee had stung it newly);
But, Dick, her eyes so guard her face,
I durst no more upon them gaze   65
 Than on the sun in July.

Her mouth so small, when she does speak,
Thou'dst swear her teeth her words did break,
 That they might passage get;
But she so handled still the matter,   70
They came as good as ours, or better,
 And are not spent a whit.

If wishing should be any sin,
The parson himself had guilty been
 (She looked that day so purely);   75
And did the youth so oft the feat
At night, as some did in conceit,[4]
 It would have spoiled him, surely.

Passion, oh me! how I run on!
There's that that would be thought upon,   80
 I trow,[5] besides the bride:

---

9. Cf. Herrick, "Ceremonies for Candlemas Eve," p. 145, l. 7 and note.
1. Demure.
2. I.e., is overcome.

3. I.e., a small and early variety of pear.
4. Fancy.
5. Reckon.

The business of the kitchen's great,
For it is fit that men should eat,
    Nor was it there denied.

Just in the nick the cook knocked thrice,   85
And all the waiters in a trice
    His summons did obey;
Each servingman, with dish in hand,
Marched boldly up, like our trained band,[6]
    Presented, and away.   90

When all the meat was on the table,
What man of knife or teeth was able
    To stay to be entreated?
And this the very reason was,
Before the parson could say grace,   95
    The company was seated.

Now hats fly off, and youths carouse;
Healths first go round, and then the house,
    The bride's came thick and thick;
And when 'twas named another's health,   100
Perhaps he made it hers by stealth;
    And who could help it, Dick?

O' th' sudden up they rise and dance;
Then sit again, and sigh, and glance;
    Then dance again and kiss;   105
Thus several ways the time did pass,
Whilst every woman wished her place,
    And every man wished his.

By this time all were stol'n aside
To counsel and undress the bride,   110
    But that he must not know;
But yet 'twas thought he guessed her mind,
And did not mean to stay behind
    Above an hour or so.

When in he came, Dick, there she lay   115
Like new-fall'n snow melting away
    ('Twas time, I trow, to part);
Kisses were now the only stay,
Which soon she gave, as who would say,
    "Good Boy!" with all my heart.[7]   120

---

6. I.e., our village militia (trained in the rudiments of close-order drill and the use of firearms).

7. Cf. Textual Notes, p. 390.

But just as heav'ns would have, to cross it,
In came the bridesmaids with the posset;[8]
    The bridegroom eat[9] in spite,
For had he left the women to't,
It would have cost two hours to do't,   125
    Which were too much that night.

At length the candle's out, and now
All that they had not done, they do:
    What that is, who can tell?
But I believe it was no more   130
Than thou and I have done before
    With Bridget and with Nell.

"My dearest rival, lest our love"

My dearest rival, lest our love
Should with eccentric motion move,[1]
Before it learn to go astray
We'll teach and set it in a way,
And such directions give unto't   5
That it shall never wander foot.[2]
Know first, then, we will serve as true
For one poor smile, as we would do
If we had what our higher flame
Or our vainer wish could frame.   10
Impossible shall be our hope,
And love shall only have his scope
To join with fancy now and then,
And think what reason would condemn;
And on these grounds we'll love as true,   15
As if they were most sure t'ensue;
And chastely for these things we'll stay,
As if tomorrow were the day.
Meantime we two will teach our hearts
In love's burdens bear their parts:[3]   20
Thou first shall sigh, and say, "She's fair";
And I'll still answer, "Past compare."
Thou shalt set out each part o' th' face
While I extol each little grace;
Thou shalt be ravished at her wit,   25
And I, that she so governs it;
Thou shalt like well that hand, that eye,
That lip, that look, that majesty,
And in good language them adore;

8. Cf. Herrick, "A Nuptial Song," p.
125, 1. 132 and note.
9. Ate.
1. I.e., deviate.

2. I.e., go astray.
3. I.e., in love's choral refrains sing
their individual melodies.

While I want words, and do it more.   30
Yea, we will sit and sigh a while,
And with soft thoughts some time beguile,
But straight again break out and praise
All we had done before, new ways.
Thus will we do till paler death   35
Come with a warrant for our breath;
And then whose fate shall be to die
First of us two, by legacy
Shall all his store bequeath, and give
His love to him that shall survive;   40
For no one stock[4] can ever serve
To love so much as she'll deserve.

Song[5]

Why so pale and wan, fond lover?
    Prithee, why so pale?
Will, when looking well can't move her,
    Looking ill prevail?
    Prithee, why so pale?   5

Why so dull and mute, young sinner?
    Prithee, why so mute?
Will, when speaking well can't win her,
    Saying nothing do't?
    Prithee, why so mute?   10

Quit, quit, for shame; this will not move,
    This cannot take her;
If of herself she will not love,
    Nothing can make her:
    The devil take her!   15

Song[6]

No, no, fair heretic, it needs must be
    But an ill love in me,
    And worse for thee.
For were it in my power
To love thee now, this hour,   5
    More than I did the last,
'Twould then so fall
I might not love at all;
    Love that can flow, and can admit increase,
    Admits as well an ebb, and may grow less.   10

4. Lineage.
5. First printed in Suckling's play *Aglaura*
(IV. ii. 15–29) in 1638, this most famous
of the poet's lyrics was set to music by
William Lawes.
6. First printed in *Aglaura* (IV. iv. 4–23),
this lyric was set to music by Henry
Lawes in 1659.

True love is still the same; the torrid zones,
    And those more frigid ones,
      It must not know;
For love grown cold or hot,
Is lust or friendship, not   15
      The thing we have;
For that's a flame would die,
Held down, or up too high;
   Then think I love more than I can express,
   And would love more, could I but love thee less.   20

From *THE LAST REMAINS OF SIR JOHN SUCKLING* (1659)

"Out upon it! I have loved"[7]

Out upon it! I have loved
   Three whole days together;[8]
And am like to love three more,
   If it prove fair weather.

Time shall molt away his wings   5
   Ere he shall discover
In the whole wide world again
   Such a constant lover.

But the spite on't is, no praise
   Is due at all to me: 10
Love with me had made no stay,
   Had it any been but she.

Had it any been but she,
   And that very very face,
There had been at least ere this   15
   A dozen dozen in her place.

A Song to a Lute[9]

Hast thou seen the down i' th'air
   When wanton blasts have tossed it,
Or the ship on the sea
   When ruder winds have crossed it?

---

7. Cf. Textual Notes, p. 390.
8. The poem may have been based on a proverb, "After three days men grow weary of a wench, a quest, and weather rainy" (*Works of Suckling, ed. cit.,* p. 254).
9. This lyric makes part of Suckling's play *The Sad One* (IV. iii. 47–56). Cf. Jonson, "A Celebration of Charis," 4, p. 48, ll. 21–30.

Hast thou marked the crocodile's weeping,   5
   Or the fox's sleeping?
Or hast viewed the peacock in his pride,
   Or the dove by his bride,
    When he courts for his lechery?
Oh, so fickle, oh, so vain, oh, so false, so false, is she!   10

Sidney Godolphin

1610	Born at Godolphin Hall, near Helston, Cornwall; baptized January 15.
1613	Orphaned by his father's death (his mother had died in 1612); inherits lands in Norfolk. Reared by his uncle, Francis Godolphin; probably educated initially by private tutors.
1623	Contributes a poetical fragment to *Carolus Redux*, printed to celebrate the return of Prince Charles from Spain.
1624	Matriculates at Exeter College, Oxford, in June. Leaves in 1627 without taking a degree.
1627–1628	Perhaps attends one of the Inns of Court. Associating from this time with Lucius Cary, Lord Falkland, and the group congregating at Great Tew. Acquainted with Ben Jonson. Member of Parliament for Helston, 1628.
1632	Probably in Denmark, with an embassy headed by Robert Sidney, Earl of Leicester.
1638	Contributes a poem to the Jonson memorial volume, *Jonsonus Virbius*, and commendatory verses to George Sandys' *Paraphrase Upon the Divine Poems*.
1640	Member of Parliament for Helston in the "Short Parliament," which convened in April, and in the "Long Parliament," which convened in November.
1642	Joins royalist forces commanded by Sir Ralph Hopton in Devonshire.
1643	Killed in a skirmish with Parliamentary forces at Chagford, Devonshire, on February 9. Buried on the following day in the nearby village of Okehampton.

From *POEMS*[1] (ed. W. Dighton, 1931)

Constancy

Love unreturned, howe'er the flame
Seem great and pure, may still admit
Degrees of more, and a new name
And strength acceptance gives to it.

Till then, by honor there's no tie   5
Laid on it, that it ne'er decay;
The mind's last act by constancy
Ought to be sealed, and not the way.[2]

Did ought but love's perfection bind
Who should assign at what degree   10
Of love, faith ought to fix the mind,
And in what limits we are free.

So hardly[3] in a single heart
Is any love conceived,
That fancy still supplies one part,   15
Supposing it received.

When undeceived such love retires,
'Tis but a model lost;
A draught of what might be expires,
Built but at fancy's cost.   20

Yet if the ruin one tear move,
From pity, not love, sent,
Though not a palace, it will prove
The most wished monument.

1. Thomas Hobbes, in the dedicatory letter preceding his *Leviathan*, speaks admiringly of Godolphin's character; but the brief account of the poet given by the Earl of Clarendon is of particular interest to students of Godolphin's work. With his customary discernment, Clarendon recognizes that "it may be, the very remarkableness of his little person [cf. Suckling's allusion to "little Sid" in "A Sessions of the Poets," p. 257, l. 101] made the sharpness of his wit and the composed quickness of his judgment and understanding the more notable"; nevertheless, "there was never . . . so large an understanding, and so unrestrained a fancy, in so very small a body." At court he was "very acceptable. . . . Everybody loved his company very well, yet he loved very much to be alone, being in his constitution inclined somewhat to melancholy, and to retirement amongst his books. . . . Of so nice and tender a composition that a little rain or wind would disorder him, and divert him from any short journey, [yet] he put himself into the first troops which were raised in the west for the king, and bore the uneasiness and fatigue of winter marches with an exemplar courage and alacrity; until by too brave a pursuit of the enemy [he was shot down] in an obscure village in Devonshire" (*Life, ed. cit.*, I, pp. 36–37).

2. I.e., not by the particular circumstances of the act (but by the principles of constancy informing it).

3. I.e., wtih such difficulty.

Song[4]

Or love me less, or love me more,
    And play not with my liberty,
Either take all, or all restore,
    Bind me at least, or set me free.
Let me some nobler torture find   5
    Than of a doubtful wavering mind;
Take all my peace, but you betray
    Mine honor too this cruel way.

'Tis true that I have nursed before
    That hope of which I now complain;   10
And having little, sought no more,
    Fearing to meet with your disdain.
The sparks of favor you did give,
    I gently blew to make them live;
And yet have gained by all this care   15
    No rest in hope, nor in despair.

I see you wear that pitying smile
    Which you have still vouchsafed my smart,[5]
Content thus cheaply to beguile
    And entertain an harmless heart;   20
But I no longer can give way
    To hope, which doth so little pay;
And yet I dare no freedom owe[6]
    Whilst you are kind, though but in show.

Then give me more, or give me less,   25
    Do not disdain a mutual sense,
Or your unpitying beauties dress
    In their own free indifference;
But show not a severer eye
    Sooner to give me liberty,   30
For I shall love the very scorn
    Which for my sake you do put on.

Song

'Tis affection but dissembled,
    Or dissembled liberty,
To pretend thy passion changéd
      With change of thy mistress' eye,
      Following her inconstancy;   5

---

4. Cf. Carew, "Song: Mediocrity In Love Rejected," p. 159.   5. Pain.
6. Own; i.e., acknowledge.

Hopes which do from favor flourish
   May perhaps as soon expire
As the cause which did them nourish;
   And disdained they may retire:
   But love is another fire.[7]   10

For if beauty cause thy passion,
   If a fair, resistless eye
Melt thee with its soft impression,
   Then thy hopes will never die,
   Nor be cured by cruelty.   15

'Tis not scorn that can remove thee,
   For thou either wilt not see
Such loved beauty not to love thee,
   Or wilt else consent that she
   Judges as she ought of thee.   20

Thus thou either canst not sever
   Hope from what appears so fair,
Or, unhappier, thou canst never
   Find contentment in despair,
   Nor make love a trifling care.   25

There are seen but few retiring
   Steps in all the paths of love
Made by such, who, in aspiring,
   Meeting scorn, their hopes remove;
   Yet even these ne'er change their love.   30

"No more unto my thoughts appear"

No more unto my thoughts appear,
   At least appear less fair,
For crazy tempers[8] justly fear
   The goodness of the air.

Whilst your pure image hath a place   5
   In my impurer mind,
Your very shadow is the glass
   Where my defects I find.

Shall I not fly that brighter light
   Which makes my fires look pale,   10
And put that virtue out of sight
   Which makes mine none at all?

---

7. Cf. "As you came from the holy land of Walsingham," attributed to Sir Walter Raleigh, ll. 41–44:
   But true love is a durable fire
     In the mind ever burning;
   Never sick, never old, never dead,
     From itself never turning.

8. I.e., frail, infirm temperaments.

No, no, your picture doth impart
    Such value, I not wish
The native worth to any heart   15
    That's unadorned with this.

Though poorer in desert I make
    Myself, whilst I admire,
The fuel which from hope I take
    I give to my desire.   20

If this flame lighted from your eyes
    The subject do calcine,[9]
A heart may be your sacrifice,
    Too weak to be your shrine.

"Chloris, it is not thy disdain"
To The Tune Of, *In Faith, I Cannot Keep My Father's Sheep*[1]

Chloris, it is not thy disdain
    Can ever cover with despair
    Or in cold ashes hide that care
Which I have fed with so long pain;
I may perhaps mine eyes refrain,   5
And fruitless words no more impart,
But yet still serve, still serve thee in my heart.

What though I spend my hapless days
    In finding entertainments out,
    Careless of what I go about,   10
Or seek my peace in skilful ways,
Applying to my eyes new rays
Of beauty, and another flame
Unto my heart? My heart is still the same.

'Tis true that I could love no face   15
    Inhabited by cold disdain,
    Taking delight in others' pain.
Thy looks are full of native grace;
Since then, by chance, scorn there hath place,
'Tis to be hoped I may remove   20
This scorn one day, one day by endless love.

"Lord, when the wise men came from far"

Lord, when the wise men came from far,
Led to Thy cradle by a star,

---

9. I.e., turn to powder (by heat).
1. The tune is printed in John Playford's *The Treasury of Musick* (London, 1669), bk. I, p. 42.

Then did the shepherds too rejoice,
Instructed by Thy angel's voice;[2]
Blest were the wise men in their skill,[3]   5
And shepherds in their harmless will.

Wise men, in tracing nature's laws,
Ascend unto the highest cause;
Shepherds with humble fearfulness
Walk safely, though their light be less;   10
Though wise men better know the way,
It seems no honest heart can stray.

There is no permit in the wise
But love, the shepherds' sacrifice;
Wise men, all ways of knowledge passed,   15
To th'shepherds' wonder come at last.
To know can only wonder breed,
And not to know is wisdom's seed.[4]

A wise man at the altar bows,
And offers up his studied vows,   20
And is received; may not the tears
Which spring too from a shepherd's fears
And sighs upon his frailty spent,
Though not distinct, be eloquent?

'Tis true, the object sanctifies   25
All passions which within us rise;
But since no creature comprehends
The Cause of causes, End of ends,
He who himself vouchsafes to know
Best pleases his Creator so.   30

When then our sorrows we apply
To our own wants and poverty,
When we look up in all distress,
And our own misery confess,
Sending both thanks and prayers above,   35
Then, though we do not know, we love.

---

2. Cf. Matthew 2:1–10; Luke 2:8–18.
3. Wisdom.
4. The outlook informing these lines is perhaps most explicitly phrased by Cornelius Agrippa von Nettesheim (c. 1486–1535), whose work Godolphin very probably knew: "How can one perceive truth? Is it by scientific speculations, by the pressing witness of sensation, by the artificial arguments of logic, by evident proofs, by demonstrative syllogisms, by the light and efforts of human reason? Bah! Get rid of all that: the only means of discerning truth is faith" (*Of the Vanity and Uncertainty of Arts and Sciences* [London, 1659], p. 222). Cf. also Fulke Greville, "A Treatie of Humane Learning," and Sir Thomas Browne, *Religio Medici*, I. 9.

From *JONSONUS VIRBIUS*[5] (1638)

On Ben Jonson

The Muses' fairest light in no dark time,
The wonder of a learned age; the line
Which none can pass; the most proportioned wit
To nature; the best judge of what was fit;
The deepest, plainest, highest, clearest pen;   5
The voice most echoed by consenting men,
The soul which answered best to all well said
By others, and which most requital made;
Tuned to the highest key of ancient Rome,
Returning all her music with his own;   10
In whom, with nature, study claimed a part,
And yet who to himself owed all his art:
   Here lies Ben Jonson. Every age will look
   With sorrow here, with wonder on his book.

From *POEMS, BY J[OHN]. D[ONNE].* (1635)

Elegy on D. D.[6]

Now, by one year, time and our frailty have
Lessened our first confusion, since the grave
Closed thy dear ashes, and the tears which flow
In these have no springs but of solid woe;
Or they are drops which cold amazement froze   5
At thy decease, and will not thaw in prose.
All streams of verse which shall lament that day
Do truly to the ocean tribute pay,
But they have lost their saltness, which the eye,
In recompense of wit, strives to supply.   10
Passion's excess for thee we need not fear,
Since first by thee our passions hallowed were;
Thou mad'st our sorrows, which before had been
Only for the success, sorrows for sin;
We owe thee all those tears, now thou art dead,   15
Which we shed not, which for ourselves we shed.
Nor didst thou only consecrate our tears,
Give a religious tincture to our fears,
But even our joys had learned an innocence:
Thou didst from gladness separate offence;   20

---

5. This volume, a collection of poems in memory of Jonson, also includes English verses by Habington, Waller, and Cartwright (of the poets represented in this edition). The poem has been ascribed to John Cleveland (1613–1658); but cf. *The Poems of Sidney Godolphin*, ed. W. Dighton (Oxford, 1931), p. xxxviii.
6. I.e., Dr. Donne.

All minds at once sucked grace from thee, as where,
The curse revoked, the nations had one ear.[7]
Pious dissector! thy one hour did treat
The thousand mazes of the heart's deceit;
Thou didst pursue our loved and subtle sin   25
Through all the foldings we had wrapped it in,
And in thine own large mind finding the way
By which ourselves we from ourselves convey,[8]
Didst in us, narrow models, know the same
Angles, though darker, in our meaner frame.   30
How short of praise is this? My Muse, alas,
Climbs weakly to that truth which none can pass;[9]
He that writes best may only hope to leave
A character[1] of all he could conceive,
But none of thee, and with me must confess   35
That fancy finds some check from an excess
Of merit; most, of nothing, it hath spun,
And truth, as reason's task and theme, doth shun.
She makes a fairer flight in emptiness
Than when a bodied truth doth her oppress.   40
Reason, again, denies her scales because
Hers are but scales; she judges by the laws
Of weak comparison; thy virtue sleights[2]
Her feeble beam and her unequal weights.
What prodigy of wit and piety   45
Hath she else known, by which to measure thee?
Great soul! We can no more the worthiness
Of what you were, than what you are, express.

---

7. Cf. Revelation 22: 2–3.
8. Steal away (i.e., hypocritically conceal).
9. Surpass (or, perhaps, "express").
1. Description.
2. Disdains.

William Cartwright

1611	Born in Northway, Gloucestershire, on or about December 23. Financial reverses may account for family's subsequent move to Cirencester, where father becomes an innkeeper and Cartwright receives his early education.
1623–1624	Enters Westminster School, London, as a King's Scholar. Probably comes to the attention of Ben Jonson at this period.
1628	Elected to a studentship (i.e., recognized as a potentially outstanding scholar) at Christ Church, Oxford.
1629	Leader of a student protest against certain disciplinary arrangements at Christ Church.
1632	Receives the B.A. degree.
1635	Proceeds M.A. First published English poem: commendatory verses to Francis Kynaston's *Amorum Troili et Cresseidae*. Two plays, *The Lady-Errant* and *The Ordinary*, probably composed about this time.
1636	*The Royal Slave* presented on the occasion of a royal visit to Oxford in August, and again in November at Hampton Court.
1638	Takes holy orders. Contributes a poem to the Jonson memorial volume, *Jonsonus Virbius*.
1639	Publication of *The Royal Slave*.
1642	Appointed succentor (a choral leader) in Salisbury Cathedral. Preaches the "victory sermon" on the king's return to Oxford after the Battle of Edgehill. Appointed Reader in Metaphysic at Oxford University; serves as a member of the academic "Council of War," which co-operates with the royal military authorities in the city of Oxford.
1643	Appointed Junior Proctor in Oxford University. Dies of a fever, November 29; buried in Christ Church.
1651	Publication of *Comedies, Tragi-Comedies, With Other Poems*.

From COMEDIES, TRAGI-COMEDIES, WITH OTHER POEMS[1] (1651)

To Mr. W. B.,[2] at the Birth of His First Child

You're now transcribed, and public view
Perusing finds the copy true,
Without erratas new crept in,
Fully complete and genuine,
And nothing wanting can espy   5
But only bulk and quantity;
The text in letters small we see,
And the arts in one epitome.
Oh, what pleasure do you take
To hear the nurse discovery make,   10
How the nose, the lip, the eye,
The forehead full of majesty,
Shows the father; how to this
The mother's beauty added is;
And after all, with gentle numbers,[3]   15
To woo the infant into slumbers.

    And these delights he yields you now,
The swathe[4] and cradle this doth show;
But hereafter, when his force
Shall wield the rattle and the horse,   20
When his vent'ring tongue shall speak
All synalaephaes,[5] and shall break
This word short off, and make that two,
Prattling as obligations[6] do,
'Twill ravish the delighted sense   25
To view these sports of innocence,
And make the wisest dote upon
Such pretty imperfection.
    Those hopeful cradles promise such

---

1. According to Humphrey Moseley, who published the 1651 edition of Cartwright's plays and poems, Ben Jonson once said, "My Son Cartwright writes all like a man." The poetical reputation of this Son of Ben declined rapidly after his untimely death in 1643, but the poems selected here indicate something of the grace and ingenuity that Cartwright, looking to Donne as well as to Jonson, could bring to bear on a variety of themes. His occasional verse, sometimes merely facile, can strike notes appropriate to the birth of a child and also to the plight of a beleaguered king; his contribution to *Jonsonus Virbius,* the collection of poems honoring Jonson's memory (by reason of its length, not included in this edition), gives clear evidence of Cartwright's critical powers. Academic and courtly connections no doubt contributed to his success as preacher and lecturer at Oxford; yet, as his modern editor observes, he was evidently "a person of engaging charm and force," for whom (according to John Aubrey) "the king [Charles I] dropped a tear at the news of his death" (*Plays and Poems of William Cartwright,* ed. G. Blakemore Evans [Madison, Wis., 1951], p. 21).

2. The identity of this person has not been established.

3. I.e., lullabies.

4. Swaddling band.

5. I.e., confused sounds: "the coalescence or contraction of two syllables into one" (*OED*).

6. I.e., as legal documents (which include conventionally abbreviated fragments of Latin terms).

Future goodness, and so much,   30
That they prevent[7] my prayers, and I
Must wish but for[8] formality.
    I wish religion timely be
Taught him with his A B C.
I wish him good and constant health,   35
His father's learning, but more wealth,
And that to use, nor hoard; a purse
Open to bless, not shut to curse.
May he have many and fast friends,
Meaning good will, not private ends,   40
Such as scorn to understand,
When they name love, a piece of land.
May the swathe and whistle[9] be
The hardest of his bonds. May he
Have no sad cares to break his sleep,   45
Nor other cause, than now, to weep.
May he ne'er live to be again
What he is now, a child; may pain,
If it do visit, as a guest
Only call in, not dare to rest.   50

Beauty and Denial[1]

No, no, it cannot be; for who e'er set
A blockhouse to defend a garden yet?
Roses ne'er chide my boldness when I go
To crop their blush; why should your cheeks do so?
The lilies ne'er deny their silk to men;   5
Why should your hands push off, and draw back, then?
The sun forbids me not his heat; then why
Comes there to earth an edict from your eye?
I smell perfumes, and they ne'er think it sin:
Why should your breath not let me take it in?   10
A dragon kept the golden apples, true;[2]
But must your breasts be therefore kept so too?
All fountains else flow freely, and ne'er shrink;
And must yours cheat my thirst when I would drink?
Where nature knows no prohibition,   15
Shall art prove anti-nature, and make one?
    But oh, we scorn the proffered lip and face,
And angry frowns sometimes add quicker grace
Than quiet beauty; 'tis that melting kiss
That truly doth distill immortal bliss,   20

---

7. Anticipate.
8. I.e., merely to satisfy.
9. Cf. Herrick, "To His Saviour, a Child," p. 153, l. 8 and note.
1. Cf. Randolph, "Upon Love Fondly Refused," p. 218 and first note.
2. A hundred-headed dragon, offspring of Typhon and Echidna, guarded the golden apples in the Garden of the Hesperides: cf. Apollodorus, *Library,* II. v. 11.

Which the fierce-struggling youth by force, at length,
Doth make the purchase of his eager strength;
Which, from the rifled weeping virgin scant
Snatched, proves a conquest rather than a grant.
    Believe't not; 'tis the paradox of someone   25
That in old time did love an Amazon,
One of so stiff a temper that she might
Have called him spouse upon the marriage night;
Whose flames consumed him lest someone might be
Seduced hereafter by his heresy.[3]   30
    That you are fair and spotless makes you prove
Fitter to fall a sacrifice to love;
On towards his altar, then, vex not the priest,
'Tis ominous[4] if the sacrifice resist.
Who conquers still, and ransacks, we may say   35
Doth not affect, but rather is in pay.
But if there must be real lists of love,
And our embracing a true wrestling prove,
Bare, and anoint you, then; for if you'll do
As wrestlers use, you must be naked too.[5]   40

Women[6]

Give me a girl, if one I needs must meet,
Or in her nuptial or her winding sheet;
I know but two good hours that women have,
One in the bed, another in the grave.
Thus of the whole sex all I would desire   5
Is, to enjoy their ashes, or their fire.

To Chloe, Who Wished Herself Young Enough For Me[7]

Chloe, why wish you that your years
    Would backwards run till they meet mine,
That perfect likeness, which endears
    Things unto things, might us combine?
Our ages so in date agree   5
That twins do differ more than we.

There are two births: the one when light
    First strikes the new-awakened sense;

3. The Athenian youth Soloon fell desperately in love with Antiope, queen of the Amazons; when she rejected him, he drowned himself. Cf. Plutarch's *Lives of the Noble Grecians and Romans* ("Theseus").
4. I.e., a bad omen.
5. Cf. Donne, Elegy XIX, ll. 47–48.
6. This poem is based on an epigram in the Greek Anthology (A.D. 980): "Every woman is a source of annoyance, but she has two good seasons: the one in her bridal chamber, the other when she is dead" (XI. 381).
7. The thought and expression of this poem may be compared wtih those of Donne's lyric "The Good-morrow."

The other when two souls unite,
    And we must count our life from thence;   10
When you loved me and I loved you,
Then both of us were born anew.

Love then to us did new souls give,
    And in those souls did plant new pow'rs;
Since when another life we live,   15
    The breath we breathe is his, not ours;
Love makes those young men whom age doth chill,

And whom he finds young, keeps young still.
Love, like that angel that shall call
    Our bodies from the silent grave,   20
Unto one age doth raise us all,
    None too much, none too little have;
Nay, that the difference may be none,
He makes two not alike, but one.[8]

And now, since you and I are such,   25
    Tell me what's yours and what is mine?
Our eyes, our ears, our taste, smell, touch,
    Do, like our souls, in one combine;
So by this, I as well may be
Too old for you, as you for me.   30

A Valediction

Bid me not go where neither suns nor showers
    Do make or cherish flowers,
Where discontented things in sadness lie,
    And nature grieves as I;
  When I am parted from those eyes,   5
  From which my better day doth rise,
    Though some propitious power
    Should plant me in a bower,
Where amongst happy lovers I might see
    How showers and sunbeams bring   10
    One everlasting spring,
Nor would those fall, nor these shine forth to me;
    Nature herself to him is lost
    Who loseth her he honors most.
Then fairest to my parting view display   15
    Your graces all in one full day,
Whose blessed shapes I'll snatch and keep, till when
    I do return and view again;

8. Cf. Donne, "The Good-morrow," ll. 20–21: "If our two loves be one, or, thou and I/Love so alike, that none do slacken, none can die."

So by this art fancy shall fortune cross,[9]
And lovers live by thinking on their loss.   20

No Platonic Love[1]

Tell me no more of minds embracing minds,
 And hearts exchanged for hearts;
That spirits spirits meet, as winds do winds,
 And mix their subtlest parts;
That two unbodied essences may kiss,   5
And then, like angels, twist and feel one bliss.

I was that silly[2] thing that once was wrought
 To practise this thin love;
I climbed from sex to soul, from soul to thought;
 But thinking there to move,   10
Headlong I rolled from thought to soul, and then
From soul I lighted at the sex again.

As some strict down-looked men pretend to fast
 Who yet in closets[3] eat,
So lovers who profess they spirits taste   15
 Feed yet on grosser meat;
I know they boast they souls to souls convey,
Howe'er they meet, the body is the way.

Come, I will undeceive thee: they that tread
 Those vain aerial ways   20
Are, like young heirs and alchemists, misled
 To waste their wealth and days;
For searching thus to be forever rich,
They only find a med'cine for the itch.

A New Year's Gift[4]

Although propriety be crossed
 By those that cry't up most,[5]
No vote hath yet passed to put down
 The pious fires
 Of good desires;   5
Our wishes are as yet our own.

Blest be the day then, 'tis New Year's:
 Nature knows no such fears

9. Thwart.
1. Cf. Randolph, "An Elegy," p. 211 and first note.
2. Witless (also, "innocent").
3. I.e., in private rooms.
4. The poem seems to be addressed to Charles I.
5. I.e., be flouted by those who pretend to hold it in especially high regard.

As those which do our hearts divide;
      In spite of force,   10
      Times keep their course;
The seasons run not on their side.

I send, my Muse, to one that knows
      What each relation owes,
One who keeps waking in his breast   15
      No other sense
      But conscience;
That only is his interest.

Though to be moderate, in this time,
      Is thought almost a crime,   20
That virtue yet is his so much,
      That they who make
      All whom they take
Guilty, durst never call him such.

He wishes peace, that public good,   25
      Dry peace, not bought with blood,
Yet such as honor may maintain,
      And such the crown
      Would gladly own.[6]
Wish o'er that wish to him again.   30

He wishes that this storm subside,
      Hushed by a turn of tide,
That one fixed calm would smooth the main,
      As winds relent
      When fury's spent.   35
Oh, wish that wish to him again.

The joys that solemn victories crown,
      When we not slay our own,
Joys that deserve a general song,
      When the day's gained   40
      And no sword stained,
Press on and round him in a throng.

Thoughts rescue,[7] and his danger kissed,
      Being found as soon as missed,
With him not taken as before,   45
      Hazard can ne'er
      Make him more dear.
We must not fear so long once more.

6. Acknowledge.   7. Cf. Textual Notes. p. 391.

Twist then in one most glorious wreath
    All joys you can bequeath,   50
And see them on the kingdom thrown;
      When there they dwell,
      He's pleased as well
As if they sat on him alone.

Go, and return, and for his sake   55
    Less noise and tumult make
Than stars when they do run their rounds;
      Though swords and spears
      Late filled his ears,
He silence loves, or gentle sounds.   90

James Graham, Marquis of Montrose

1612	Born, probably in October, at Montrose, on the east coast of Scotland; the only son of the fourth Earl of Montrose and of Lady Margaret Ruthven (deceased, 1618).
1624–1626	Attends school in Glasgow. Father dies, 1626.
1627–1628	Attends Saint Andrew's University.
1629	Marries Magdalene Carnegie, November.
1633–1636	Traveling on the continent.
1638–1639	Actively supports the Scottish Covenanters in opposition to efforts by Charles I and Archbishop Laud to impose uniformity of worship on Scotland. Campaigns successfully in the vicinity of Aberdeen.
1640–1643	Increasingly disenchanted with the presbyterian principles of the Covenanters, and with their leader, the Duke of Argyll, offers his services to Charles I. "My dear and only love" probably composed in this period.
1644	Appointed Lieutenant General in Scotland by Charles I; created Marquis of Montrose.
1644–1646	Defeats Covenanter armies in six battles between September, 1644 (Tippermuir), and August, 1645 (Kilsyth). Subsequently defeated at Philiphaugh in September 1645, by superior forces under Leslie; obliged to leave Scotland in September, 1646.
1646–1649	After various unsuccessful efforts to raise money and troops, commissioned Lieutenant Governor of Scotland in March 1649, by Charles II at the Hague.
1650	Sails in March from Bergen, Norway, to Kirkwall, in the Orkney Islands. Crosses into northern Scotland with a small force, which is crushed by Leslie's troops at Carbisdale, northwest of Inverness, on April 27. Betrayed to the government by Neil Macleod of Assynt, he is hanged, drawn, and quartered in Edinburgh, on May 21. His head, impaled on a spike on the Tollbooth, is not taken down until 1661.

From A *CHOICE COLLECTION OF COMIC AND SERIOUS SCOTS POEMS* (1711)

"My dear and only love, I pray"[1]

My dear and only love, I pray
    This noble world of thee
Be governed by no other sway
    But purest monarchy;
For if confusion have a part,   5
    Which virtuous souls abhor,
And hold a synod[2] in thy heart,
    I'll never love thee more.

Like Alexander I will reign,
    And I will reign alone: 10
My thoughts shall evermore disdain
    A rival on my throne.
He either fears his fate too much,
    Or his deserts are small,
That puts it not unto the touch[3]   15
    To win or lose it all.

But I must rule and govern still,
    And always give the law,
And have each subject at my will,
    And all to stand in awe.   20
But 'gainst my battery, if I find
    Thou shunn'st the prize so sore
As that thou sett'st me up a blind,[4]
    I'll never love thee more.

Or in the empire of thy heart,   25
    Where I should solely be,
Another do pretend a part
    And dares to vie with me;
Or if committees thou erect,
    And go on such a score,[5]   30

1. "As a soldier Montrose ranks by common consent with the greatest of his age" (John Buchan, *Montrose* [London, 1928], p. 389); as a poet, although he wrote a few other pieces, he is remembered almost exclusively for this lyric. Whether the loyalties it affirms are given to an unnamed mistress or to a political ideal, "the stanzas are typical of the Cavaliers of the mid-seventeenth century, in their passionate, at times incoherent loyalty" (*Poems of James Graham, Marquis of Montrose (1612–1650)*, ed. J. L. Weir [London, 1938], p. 51). Critical opinion generally concurs with Buchan's view that the poem, written c. 1642, "is a political and not a love poem" (*op. cit.*, p. 152n); it is of interest that Montrose wrote to the future Charles II, on January 28, 1649 (two days before the execution of Charles I), "I never had passion upon earth so strong as to do the King, your father, service" (Buchan, *op. cit.*, p. 328).
2. I.e., an assembly of ecclesiastics.
3. Touchstone; i.e., that shrinks from a challenge.
4. I.e., that you are deceitful.
5. I.e., and proceed in that fashion.

I'll sing and laugh at thy neglect,
   And never love thee more.

But if thou wilt be constant then,
   And faithful of thy word,
I'll make thee glorious by my pen   35
   And famous by my sword:
I'll serve thee in such noble ways
   Was never heard before;
I'll crown and deck thee all with bays,[6]
   And love thee evermore.   40

6. I.e., with laurel garlands (in this context, the emblem of victory).

Sir John Denham

1615	Born in Dublin; brought to England, 1617, and educated initially in London. His father was Lord Chief Justice of the King's Bench in Ireland, 1612–1616; his mother, daughter of an Irish peer, died in 1619.
1631–1634	Attending Trinity College, Oxford; apparently leaves without taking a degree. Marries Anne Cotton, June, 1634.
1634–1636	Studying law at Lincoln's Inn. Given to obsessive gambling, but writes a prose essay against that vice, *The Anatomy of Play* (published, 1651), to calm his father's concern. Translates Book II of Vergil's *Aeneid*, in heroic couplets (published, 1656).
1639	On the death of his father, inherits a large fortune and extensive lands; takes up residence at Egham, Surrey. Called to the bar.
1641	First draft of "Cooper's Hill" perhaps written in this year. His blank-verse tragedy, *The Sophy*, acted at Blackfriars.
1642	Publication of *The Sophy* and of the first edition of "Cooper's Hill." As Sheriff of Surrey, attempts to defend Farnham Castle against Parliamentary forces, but resists only briefly before surrendering to Sir William Waller. His estates confiscated by Parliament.
1643–1647	Employed in various capacities for the royalist cause. First wife dies in this period.
1648–1652	Living abroad, in attendance on the future Charles II.
1655–1656	Working for the royalist cause in England and Wales. Fourth (revised) edition of "Cooper's Hill" published.
1658	Given permission by Cromwell to reside in Bury Saint Edmunds, Suffolk.
1660	At the Restoration, appointed Surveyor of the Works (the post once held by Inigo Jones); knighted, and given various offices and lands by Charles II.
1661	Member of Parliament for Old Sarum, Wiltshire; in Parliament until his death.
1663	Elected to the Royal Society.
1665	Marries Margaret Brooke, a beauty of twenty-three,

who shortly becomes the publicly acknowledged mistress of the Duke of York.

1666   Apparently insane (by consequence of paresis) for some months.

1667   Death of Lady Denham, January 6; various highly placed personages, including Denham himself, suspected of having poisoned the lady.

1668   Publication of *Poems and Translations, with The Sophy*.

1669   Death, March 10. Buried in Westminster Abbey.

From POEMS AND TRANSLATIONS (1668)

Cooper's Hill[1]

Sure there are poets which did never dream
Upon Parnassus, nor did taste the stream
Of Helicon;[2] we therefore may suppose
Those made not poets, but the poets those.
And as courts make not kings, but kings the court,   5
So where the Muses and their train resort,
Parnassus stands: if I can be to thee
A poet, thou Parnassus art to me.
Nor wonder, if (advantaged in my flight,
By taking wing from thy auspicious[3] height)   10
Through untraced ways and airy paths I fly,
More boundless in my fancy than my eye:
My eye, which swift as thought contracts the space
That lies between, and first salutes the place
Crowned with that sacred pile, so vast, so high,   15
That whether 'tis a part of earth or sky
Uncertain seems, and may be thought a proud
Aspiring mountain, or descending cloud,

1. Cooper's Hill is a rise of ground near Egham, Surrey. Denham's poetical reputation rests almost entirely upon this "topographical-reflective" poem, which Dr. Johnson called "the work that confers upon him the rank and dignity of an original author" (cf. Johnson's remarks on Denham, p.432). Dryden, in the dedicatory epistle to his play, *The Rival Ladies* (1664), observed that the poem, "for the majesty of the style is, and ever will be, the exact standard of good writing"; in the dedication of his translation of the *Aeneid* (1697), he remarked particularly the "sweetness" of the most famous couplet in the poem (ll. 191–192), adding that few "can find the reason of that sweetness." For a discussion of the poem's "topographical dialectic," cf. the essay by Earl Wasserman, pp. 555–570. For variant readings in the (pirated) edition of 1642 and in the first authorized edition of 1655, cf. Textual Notes, pp. 391–395. A full account of the complicated textual problems is given in Brendan O Hehir, *Expans'd Hieroglyphicks: A Study of Sir John Denham's "Coopers Hill," with a Critical Edition of the Poem* (Berkeley, 1969).

2. In ancient Greece, Mount Parnassus and Mount Helicon were sacred to the Muses and to Apollo, god of poetry and song.

3. I.e., favorable for augury.

Paul's, the late theme of such a Muse whose flight
Has bravely reached and soared above thy height;[4]   20
Now shalt thou stand though sword, or time, or fire,
Or zeal[5] more fierce than they, thy fall conspire,
Secure, whilst thee the best of poets sings,
Preserved from ruin by the best of kings.
Under his proud survey the city lies,   25
And like a mist beneath a hill doth rise,
Whose state and wealth, the business and the crowd,
Seems at this distance but a darker cloud;
And is to him who rightly things esteems
No other in effect than what it seems;   30
Where, with like haste, through several ways they run,
Some to undo and some to be undone;
While luxury and wealth, like war and peace,
Are each the other's ruin and increase,
As rivers lost in seas, some secret vein   35
Thence reconveys, there to be lost again.[6]
Oh, happiness of sweet retired content!
To be at once secure and innocent.
Windsor[7] the next (where Mars with Venus dwells,
Beauty with strength) above the valley swells   40
Into my eye, and doth itself present
With such an easy and unforced ascent
That no stupendous precipice denies
Access, no horror turns away our eyes;
But such a rise as doth at once invite   45
A pleasure and a reverence from the sight.
Thy mighty master's emblem, in whose face
Sat meekness, heightened with majestic grace;
Such seems thy gentle height, made only proud
To be the basis of that pompous load,   50
Than which a nobler weight no mountain bears,
But Atlas only that supports the spheres.[8]
When nature's hand this ground did thus advance,
'Twas guided by a wiser power than chance,
Marked out for such a use as if'twere meant   55
T'invite the builder, and his choice prevent.[9]
Nor can we call it choice when what we choose,
Folly or blindness only could refuse.
A crown of such majestic towers doth grace

---

4. These lines refer to Samuel Waller's poem "Upon His Majesty's Repairing of Paul's" (c. 1640).
5. I.e., the zeal of those Puritans who considered the decorative and ceremonial aspects of Anglican worship to be idolatrous.
6. Cf. Donne's lyric, "The Triple Foole," ll. 6–7.
7. Charles I and his consort Henrietta Maria dwelt intermittently at the royal residence of Windsor Castle, westward from Cooper's Hill.
8. The Titan Atlas, brother to Prometheus, was condemned by Zeus to bear the heavens on his back (cf. Hesiod, *Theogony*, 517–520).
9. Anticipate.

The gods' great mother[1] when her heavenly race   60
Do homage to her; yet she cannot boast
Amongst that numerous and celestial host
More heroes than can Windsor, nor doth fame's
Immortal book record more noble names.
Not to look back so far, to whom this isle   65
Owes the first glory of so brave a pile,
Whether to Caesar, Albanact, or Brute,
The British Arthur, or the Danish Canute[2]
(Though this of old no less contest did move
Than when for Homer's birth seven cities strove;[3]   70
Like him in birth, thou should'st be like in fame,
As thine his fate, if mine had been his flame),
But whosoe'er it was, nature designed
First a brave place, and then as brave a mind.
Not to recount those several kings, to whom   75
It gave a cradle, or to whom a tomb,
But thee, great Edward, and thy greater son[4]
(The lilies which his father wore, he won),
And thy Bellona,[5] who the consort came
Not only to thy bed, but to thy fame;   80
She to thy triumph led one captive king
And brought that son, which did the second bring.[6]
Then didst thou found that Order;[7] whether love
Or victory thy royal thoughts did move,
Each was a noble cause, and nothing less   85
Than the design has been the great success,
Which foreign kings and emperors esteem
The second honor to their diadem.
Had thy great destiny but given thee skill
To know, as well as power to act her will,   90
That from those kings, who then thy captives were,
In after-times should spring a royal pair[8]
Who should possess all that thy mighty power,
Or thy desires more mighty, did devour,
To whom their better fate reserves whate'er   95
The victor hopes for, or the vanquished fear;

1. I.e., the Asian goddess Cybele, known to the Greeks as Rhea.
2. According to Geoffrey of Monmouth (c. 1100–1154), Brute, the (legendary) descendant of Aeneas, founded London; his son Albanact ruled Scotland after the death of Brute (*Historia Regum Britanniae*, I. xvii, II. 1). The Danish King Canute ruled England from 1018 to 1035.
3. Homer was probably born in Chios or Smyrna; Rhodes, Colophon, Salamis, Argos, and Athens also claimed the honor.
4. Edward III, who claimed France through his mother's lineage, was the father of the Black Prince, victor at Poitiers in 1356.
5. Bellona was the Roman goddess of war; the term here refers to Philippa of Hainault, consort of Edward III.
6. King David II of Scotland was taken prisoner at Neville's Cross in 1346; King John II of France was captured (by the Black Prince) at Poitiers.
7. I.e., the Order of the Garter, founded by Edward III in 1349; its badge is the red-cross shield of Saint George and England, surrounded by a blue garter inscribed "honi soit qui mal ye pense" ("evil be to him that evil thinks").
8. I.e., Charles I and Henrietta Maria.

That blood which thou and thy great grandsire[9] shed,
And all that since these sister nations bled,
Had been unspilt, had happy Edward known
That all the blood he spilt had been his own.   100
When he that patron[1] chose in whom are joined
Soldier and martyr, and his arms confined
Within the azure circle, he did seem
But to foretell and prophesy of him[2]
Who to his realms that azure round hath joined,   105
Which nature for their bound at first designed;
That bound, which to the world's extremest ends,
Endless itself, its liquid arms extends:
Nor doth he need those emblems which we paint,
But is himself the soldier and the saint.[3]   110
Here should my wonder dwell, and here my praise;
But my fixed thoughts my wandering eye betrays,
Viewing a neighboring hill,[4] whose top of late
A chapel crowned, till in the common fate
The adjoining Abbey fell (may no such storm   115
Fall on our times, where ruin must reform).
Tell me, my Muse, what monstrous dire offense,
What crime could any Christian king incense
To such a rage? Was't luxury, or lust?
Was he so temperate, so chaste, so just?   120
Were these their crimes? They were his own much more;
But wealth is crime enough to him that's poor,
Who having spent the treasures of his crown,
Condemns their luxury to feed his own.
And yet this act, to varnish o'er the shame   125
Of sacrilege, must bear devotion's name.
No crime so bold but would be understood
A real, or at least a seeming good.
Who fears not to do ill, yet fears the name,
And free from conscience, is a slave to fame.   130
Thus he the church at once protects and spoils;
But princes' swords are sharper than their styles.[5]
And thus to th' ages past he makes amends,
Their charity destroys, their faith defends.
Then did religion in a lazy cell,   135
In empty, airy contemplations dwell,
And like the block, unmovéd, lay; but ours,

---

9. I.e., Edward I.
1. I.e., Saint George of Cappadocia. For an interesting account of this figure, cf. Ralph Waldo Emerson, *English Traits*, IX.
2. I.e., Charles I.
3. Peter Paul Rubens (1577–1640) had painted Charles I in the figure of Saint George.
4. I.e., Saint Anne's Hill, southeast from Cooper's Hill, the site of Chertsey Abbey, seized for the Crown when the monasteries were dissolved in the reign of Henry VIII.
5. I.e., (1) sharper than their pens; (2) sharper than their titles. Some years before Henry VIII broke with Rome, the Pope had conferred upon him the title "Defender of the Faith."

As much too active, like the stork devours.[6]
Is there no temperate region can be known
Betwixt their frigid and our torrid zone?   140
Could we not wake from that lethargic dream
But to be restless in a worse extreme?
And for that lethargy was there no cure
But to be cast into a calenture?
Can knowledge have no bound, but must advance   145
So far, to make us wish for ignorance?
And rather in the dark to grope our way
Than led by a false guide to err by day?
Who sees these dismal heaps, but would demand
What barbarous invader sacked the land?   150
But when he hears no Goth, no Turk did bring
This desolation, but a Christian king,
When nothing but the name of zeal[7] appears
'Twixt our best actions and the worst of theirs,
What does he think our sacrilege would spare,   155
When such th' effects of our devotions are?
Parting from thence 'twixt anger, shame, and fear,
Those for what's past, and this for what's too near,[8]
My eye, descending from the hill, surveys
Where Thames amongst the wanton[9] valleys strays.   160
Thames, the most loved of all the ocean's sons
By his old sire, to his embraces runs,
Hasting to pay his tribute to the sea,
Like mortal life to meet eternity.
Though with those streams he no resemblance hold,   165
Whose foam is amber and their gravel gold;[1]
His genuine, and less guilty wealth to explore,
Search not his bottom, but survey his shore,
O'er which he kindly spreads his spacious wing,
And hatches plenty for th' ensuing spring.   170
Nor then destroys it with too fond a stay,
Like mothers which their infants overlay;[2]
Nor with a sudden and impetuous wave,
Like profuse kings, resumes the wealth he gave.
No unexpected inundations spoil   175
The mower's hopes, nor mock the plowman's toil;
But God-like his unwearied bounty flows;
First loves to do, then loves the good he does.
Nor are his blessings to his banks confined,

---

6. The fable, from Aesop, appears also in Donne's "The Calme," ll. 3–4. It is of interest that in that poem Donne also alludes to "the calenture" (cf. l. 144), a delirious fever "incident to sailors within the tropics" (*OED*).
7. Cf. l. 22 and note.
8. I.e., anger and shame for what's past, and fear for what's too immediately threatening.
9. Fertile.
1. I.e., the Spanish river Tagus and the Lydian river Pactolus, famous for their ore-bearing sands. Cf. Randolph, "A Gratulatory," p. 210, l. 44.
2. Cf. Waller, "The Battle of the Summer Islands," II, p. 239, ll. 21–22.

But free and common as the sea or wind;   180
When he to boast, or to disperse his stores,
Full of the tributes of his grateful shores,
Visits the world, and in his flying towers[3]
Brings home to us, and makes the Indies ours;
Finds wealth where 'tis, bestows it where it wants,   185
Cities in deserts, woods in cities plants,
So that to us no thing, no place is strange,
While his fair bosom is the world's exchange.
O could I flow like thee, and make thy stream
My great example, as it is my theme!   190
Though deep, yet clear, though gentle, yet not dull,
Strong without rage, without o'er-flowing full.[4]
Heaven her Eridanus[5] no more shall boast,
Whose fame in thine, like lesser currents lost,
Thy nobler streams shall visit Jove's abodes,   195
To shine amongst the stars and bathe the gods.
Here nature, whether more intent to please
Us or herself with strange varieties
(For things of wonder give no less delight
To the wise Maker's, than beholder's sight,   200
Though these delights from several causes move;
For so our children, thus our friends we love),
Wisely she knew the harmony of things,
As well as that of sounds, from discords springs.
Such was the discord which did first disperse   205
Form, order, beauty through the universe.
While dryness moisture, coldness heat resists,[6]
All that we have, and that we are, subsists;
While the steep horrid roughness of the wood
Strives with the gentle calmness of the flood,   210
Such huge extremes when nature doth unite,
Wonder from thence results, from thence delight.
The stream is so transparent, pure, and clear,
That had the self-enamored youth[7] gazed here,
So fatally deceived he had not been,   215
While he the bottom, not his face had seen.
But his proud head the airy mountain hides
Among the clouds; his shoulders and his sides
A shady mantle clothes; his curléd brows
Frown on the gentle stream, which calmly flows,   220
While winds and storms his lofty forehead beat,
The common fate of all that's high or great.
Low at his foot a spacious plain[8] is placed,

3. I.e., tall-masted sailing ships.
4. Lines 189–192, the famous "Thames couplets," were unendingly praised and imitated by poets in the eighteenth century; cf. the observations of Dr. Johnson, p. 433. Cf. also Pope, *The Dunciad*, III. 169–172.

5. I.e., the Milky Way (also a classical name for the Italian river Po).
6. Cf. Ovid, *Metamorphoses*, I. 17–20.
7. I.e., Narcissus.
8. I.e., Egham Mead, or Runnymede, where the Magna Charta was signed in 1215.

Between the mountain and the stream embraced,
Which shade and shelter from the hill derives,   225
While the kind river wealth and beauty gives;
And in the mixture of all these appears
Variety, which all the rest endears.
This scene had some bold Greek, or British bard
Beheld of old, what stories had we heard   230
Of fairies, satyrs, and the nymphs, their dames,
Their feasts, their revels, and their amorous flames.
'Tis still the same, although their airy shape
All but a quick poetic sight escape.
There Faunus and Sylvanus keep their courts,   235
And thither all the hornéd host resorts
To graze the ranker mead; that noble herd
On whose sublime and shady fronts is reared
Nature's great masterpiece, to show how soon
Great things are made, but sooner are undone.   240
Here have I seen the King,[9] when great affairs
Give leave to slacken and unbend his cares,
Attended to the chase by all the flower
Of youth, whose hopes a nobler prey devour.
Pleasure with praise and danger they would buy,   245
And wish a foe that would not only fly.
The stag now conscious of his fatal growth,
At once indulgent to his fear and sloth,
To some dark covert his retreat had made,
Where nor man's eye, nor heaven's, should invade   250
His soft repose; when th' unexpected sound
Of dogs and men his wakeful ear doth wound.
Roused with the noise, he scarce believes his ear,
Willing to think th' illusions of his fear
Had given this false alarm; but straight his view   255
Confirms that more than all he fears is true.
Betrayed in all his strengths, the wood beset,
All instruments, all arts of ruin met,
He calls to mind his strength and then his speed,
His wingéd heels, and then his arméd head;   260
With these t' avoid, with that his fate to meet;
But fear prevails and bids him trust his feet.
So fast he flies that his reviewing[1] eye
Has lost the chasers, and his ear the cry;
Exulting, till he finds their nobler sense   265
Their disproportioned speed does recompense;
Then curses his conspiring feet, whose scent
Betrays that safety which their swiftness lent.
Then tries his friends: among the baser herd,
Where he so lately was obeyed and feared,   270

9. The allegorical significance of the stag hunt described in lines 241–328 is discussed in detail by Earl Wasserman (cf. p. 570), and also by Brendan O Hehir, *ed. cit.*, pp. 244–250.
1. I.e., backward-looking.

His safety seeks; the herd, unkindly[2] wise,
Or chases him from thence, or from him flies.
Like a declining statesman, left forlorn
To his friends' pity and pursuers' scorn,
With shame remembers, while himself was one   275
Of the same herd, himself the same had done.
Thence to the coverts and the conscious[3] groves,
The scenes of his past triumphs and his loves,
Sadly surveying where he ranged alone,
Prince of the soil, and all the herd his own,   280
And like a bold knight errant did proclaim
Combat to all, and bore away the dame,
And taught the woods to echo to the stream
His dreadful challenge and his clashing beam;[4]
Yet faintly now declines the fatal strife,   285
So much his love was dearer than his life.
Now every leaf and every moving breath
Presents a foe, and every foe a death.
Wearied, forsaken, and pursued, at last
All safety in despair of safety placed,   290
Courage he thence resumes, resolved to bear
All their assaults, since 'tis in vain to fear.
And now too late he wishes for the fight;
That strength he wasted in ignoble flight.
But when he sees the eager chase renewed,   295
Himself by dogs, the dogs by men pursued,
He straight revokes his bold resolve, and more
Repents his courage than his fear before;
Finds that uncertain ways unsafest are,
And doubt a greater mischief than despair.   300
Then to the stream, when neither friends, nor force,
Nor speed, nor art avail, he shapes his course;
Thinks not their rage so desperate t' assay
An element more merciless than they.
But fearless they pursue, nor can the flood   305
Quench their dire thirst; alas, they thirst for blood.
So towards a ship the oar-finned galleys ply,
Which wanting sea to ride, or wind to fly,
Stands but to fall revenged on those that dare
Tempt the last fury of extreme despair.   310
So fares the stag among th' enragéd hounds,
Repels their force, and wounds returns for wounds.
And as a hero, whom his baser foes
In troops surround, now these assails, now those,
Though prodigal of life, disdains to die   315
By common hands; but if he can descry
Some nobler foe's approach, to him he calls
And begs his fate, and then contented falls;

2. Unnaturally.   4. Antlers.
3. Sympathetic.

So when the king a mortal shaft lets fly
From his unerring hand, then glad to die,   320
Proud of the wound, to it resigns his blood
And stains the crystal with a purple flood.
This a more innocent and happy chase
Than when of old, but in the self-same place,[5]
Fair liberty pursued, and meant a prey   325
To lawless power, here turned and stood at bay,
When in that remedy all hope was placed
Which was, or should have been at least, the last.
Here was that Charter sealed wherein the crown
All marks of arbitrary power lays down.   330
Tyrant and slave, those names of hate and fear,
The happier style of king and subject bear:
Happy when both to the same center move,
When kings give liberty, and subjects love.
Therefore not long in force this Charter stood;   335
Wanting that seal, it must be sealed in blood.
The subjects armed, the more their princes gave,
Th' advantage only took the more to crave,
Till kings by giving, give themselves away,
And even that power that should deny, betray.   340
"Who gives constrained, but his own fear reviles,
Not thanked, but scorned; nor are they gifts, but spoils."[6]
Thus kings, by grasping more than they could hold,
First made their subjects by oppression bold;
And popular sway, by forcing kings to give   345
More than was fit for subjects to receive,
Ran to the same extremes; and one excess
Made both, by striving to be greater, less.
When a calm river, raised with sudden rains,
Or snows dissolved, o'erflows the adjoining plains,   350
The husbandmen with high-raised banks secure
Their greedy hopes, and this he can endure.
But if with bays[7] and dams they strive to force
His channel to a new or narrow course,
No longer then within his banks he dwells;   355
First to a torrent, then a deluge swells;
Stronger and fiercer by restraint he roars,
And knows no bound, but makes his power his shores.

On Mr. Abraham Cowley
His Death and Burial Amongst the Ancient Poets[8]

Old Chaucer, like the morning star,
To us discovers day from far;

---

5. I.e., Runnymede.
6. The author of the quoted lines is unidentified.
7. Embankments.

8. Cowley, who died on July 28, 1667, was accorded a magnificent funeral in Westminster Abbey; his remains lie near those of Chaucer and Spenser.

His light those mists and clouds dissolved,
Which our dark nation long involved;[9]
But he descending to the shades,   5
Darkness again the age invades.
Next, like Aurora, Spenser rose,
Whose purple blush the day foreshows;
The other three with his own fires
Phoebus, the poets' god, inspires: 10
By Shakespeare's, Jonson's, Fletcher's lines
Our stage's lustre Rome's outshines.
These poets near our princes sleep,
And in one grave their mansion keep.[1]
They lived to see so many days,   15
Till time had blasted all their bays;[2]
But cursèd be the fatal hour
That plucked the fairest, sweetest flower
That in the Muses' garden grew,
And amongst withered laurels threw!   20
Time, which made them their fame outlive,
To Cowley scarce did ripeness give.
Old mother wit and nature gave
Shakespeare and Fletcher all they have;
In Spenser, and in Jonson, art   25
Of slower nature got the start;
But both in him so equal are,
None knows which bears the happiest share;
To him no author was unknown,
Yet what he wrote was all his own.   30
He melted not the ancient gold,
Nor, with Ben Jonson, did make bold
To plunder all the Roman stores
Of poets and of orators;
Horace his wit, and Vergil's state,   35
He did not steal, but emulate;
And when he would like them appear,
Their garb, but not their clothes, did wear.
He not from Rome alone, but Greece,
Like Jason brought the golden fleece;   40
To him that language, though to none
Of th' others, as his own was known.
On a stiff gale, as Flaccus[3] sings,
The Theban swan[4] extends his wings,
When through th' ethereal clouds he flies;   45
To the same pitch our swan doth rise:
Old Pindar's flights by him are reached,

---

9. Enshrouded.
1. Ben Jonson was buried in Westminster Abbey; Shakespeare, however, was buried in Holy Trinity Church in Stratford, and John Fletcher (1579–1625) in Saint Saviour's, Southwark.

2. Laurels; i.e., poetical reputation.
3. I.e., Horace (Quintus Horatious Flaccus); cf. *Odes*, IV. ii. 25–27.
4. I.e., Pindar, Greek lyric poet of the fifth century B.C.

When on that gale his wings are stretched.
His fancy and his judgment such,
Each to the other seemed too much;   50
His severe judgment, giving law,
His modest fancy kept in awe,[5]
As rigid husbands jealous are
When they believe their wives too fair.
His English stream so pure did flow   55
As all that saw and tested know;
But for his Latin vein, so clear,
Strong, full, and high, it doth appear
That were immortal Vergil here,
Him, for his judge, he would not fear;   60
Of that great portraiture, so true
A copy pencil never drew.
My Muse her song had ended here,
But both their Genii[6] straight appear;
Joy and amazement her did strike,   65
Two twins she never saw so like.
'Twas taught by wise Pythagoras,[7]
One soul might through more bodies pass;
Seeing such transmigration here,
She thought it not a fable there,   70
Such a resemblance of all parts,
Life, death, age, fortune, nature, arts;
Then lights her torch at theirs, to tell
And show the world this parallel.
Fixed and contemplative their looks,   75
Still turning over nature's books;
Their works chaste, moral, and divine,
Where profit and delight combine;
They, gilding dirt, in noble verse
Rustic philosophy rehearse.[8]   80
When heroes, gods, or god-like kings
They praise, on their exalted wings
To the celestial orbs they climb,
And with the harmonious spheres keep time.
Nor did their actions fall behind   85
Their words, but with like candor[9] shined;
Each drew fair characters, yet none
Of those they feigned excels their own.
Both by two generous princes loved,[1]
Who knew and judged what they approved;   90
Yet having each the same desire,
Both from the busy throng retire;

5. Cf. Thomas Hobbes's observations on the relationship of judgment and fancy in *Leviathan*, I. 8.
6. I.e., those of Vergil and Cowley.
7. The Greek philosopher Pythagoras (fl. 525 B.C.) believed in the transmigration of souls.
8. Denham alludes to Vergil's *Georgics* and, perhaps, to Cowley's *Anacreontics*.
9. Purity.
1. Caesar Augustus sponsored Vergil; Charles II, Cowley.

Their bodies to their minds resigned,
Cared not to propagate their kind;
Yet, though both fell before their hour,   95
Time on their offspring hath no power:
Nor fire nor fate their bays shall blast,
Nor death's dark veil their day o'ercast.

A Song[2]

Somnus,[3] the humble god, that dwells
In cottages and smoky cells,
Hates gilded roofs and beds of down,
And, though he fears no prince's frown,
Flies from the circle of a crown.   5

Come, I say, thou powerful god,
And thy leaden charming[4] rod
Dipped in the Lethean lake,[5]
O'er his wakeful temples shake,
Lest he should sleep and never wake.   10

Nature, alas, why art thou so
Obligéd to thy greatest foe?
Sleep, that is thy best repast,
Yet of death it bears a taste,
And both are the same thing at last.   15

---

2. These verses also appear in Act V of
Denham's play, *The Sophy*.
3. The god of sleep; cf. Textual Notes,
p. 395.

4. Spellbinding.
5. I.e., in Lethe, the river of Hades from
which the shades of the dead drink to forget the past, Cf. Plato, *Republic*, 621a–b.

Richard Lovelace

1618   Born in Woolwich, in the outskirts of London (or possibly born in Holland); the eldest son of Sir William Lovelace, who had served in the Low Countries under Sir Horace Vere and who was killed in action near Assen, Holland, in 1627. By royal warrant, receives his early education at Charterhouse School by virtue of his father's death on active service.

1634   Matriculates at Gloucester Hall (now Worcester College), Oxford, as a gentleman commoner.

1636   His comedy, *The Scholar*, acted at Oxford. Awarded the M.A. degree, apparently at the request of one of Queen Henrietta Maria's ladies in waiting, on the occasion of a royal visit to Oxford.

1637   Incorporated M.A. at Cambridge. At court, gains the support of Lord Goring, subsequently Earl of Norwich and, from 1647, general in the royalist army.

1638   First published poems: "An Elegy," printed in *Musarum Oxoniensis Charisteria Pro Serenissima Regina Maria*; and commendatory verses prefixed to Anthony Hodges's translation of *Clitophon and Leucippe* (a Greek romance of the third century A.D.).

1639–1640   As ensign in Goring's regiment, takes part in the King's military expeditions against Scotland. Writes a tragedy, *The Soldier*. Presumably makes Sir John Suckling's acquaintance at this time.

1640–1641   Residing at his estate in Kent.

1642   In April, presents the Kentish Petition (a royalist manifesto) to Parliament; consequently imprisoned in the Gatehouse Prison in Westminster for some two months. Writes "To Althea. From Prison" during this time. Following his release, resides briefly in London; then follows Goring to the Low Countries. Remains in Holland and France until 1646.

1646–1647   Returns to England; living in London.

1648   In October, committed by Parliament to Peterhouse Prison, Aldersgate (probably for his connection with disturbances in Kent).

1649   Released from prison, April. Publication of *Lucasta*. Financially ruined by his outlay in behalf of the royalist cause, exists thereafter in miserable circumstances, maintained by charity.

1657 or
1658   Death, in London. Buried in Saint Bride's Church.
1659   Publication of *Lucasta: Posthume Poems*.

From LUCASTA[1] (1649)

To *Lucasta. Going Beyond the Seas.*
Song. Set by Mr. Henry Lawes[2]

If to be absent were to be
    Away from thee;
  Or that when I am gone,
    You or I were alone;
Then, my Lucasta, might I crave   5
Pity from blust'ring wind or swallowing wave.

But I'll not sigh one blast or gale
    To swell my sail,
  Or pay a tear to 'suage[3]
    The foaming blue-god's[4] rage;   10
For whether he will let me pass
Or no, I'm still as happy as I was.

Though seas and land betwixt us both,
    Our faith and troth,
  Like separated souls,   15
    All time and space controls;
Above the highest sphere we meet
Unseen, unknown, and greet as angels greet.

So then we do anticipate
    Our after-fate,   20

1. Lovelace and Suckling have traditionally been paired as in some sense archetypally representative of the "Cavalier" spirit. There is a measure of truth in this view, but the two poets are not, after all, much alike. If Suckling's verse is often lighthearted, his friend's poems are regularly serious and thoughtful, struck through with somber undertones. Suckling as a rule employs relatively simple diction, while that of Lovelace's poetry is often hard to disentangle. John Aubrey's portrait of Suckling is triumphantly anecdotal; that of Lovelace effectively amounts to one telling sentence: "He was an extraordinary handsome man, but proud" (*ed. cit.*, p. 65). Much of Lovelace's verse, in fact, reflects its author's deter-

mination to present a cool and unruffled countenance to the world, betraying little of the inner terror, even hysteria, induced by the spectacle of a disintegrating society. To come to grips with Lovelace, one needs to set over against "The Grasshopper" such poems as "The Vintage to the Dungeon," or, especially, "A Loose Saraband."
2. The identity of Lucasta ("chaste light") has not been established. Henry Lawes (1596–1662) composed the music for Milton's *Comus* in 1634, and for Carew's masque, *Coelum Britannicum*, presented at Whitehall in the same year.
3. Assuage.
4. I.e., Neptune's.

And are alive i' the skies,
   If thus our lips and eyes
Can speak like spirits unconfined
In heaven, their earthy bodies left behind.

To Lucasta. Going to the Wars.
Song. Set by Mr. John Lanière[5]

Tell me not, sweet, I am unkind,
   That from the nunnery
Of thy chaste breast, and quiet mind,
   To war and arms I fly.

True, a new mistress now I chase,   5
   The first foe in the field;
And with a stronger faith embrace
   A sword, a horse, a shield.

Yet this inconstancy is such,
   As you too shall adore;   10
I could not love thee, dear, so much,
   Loved I not honor more.

To Amarantha, That She Would Dishevel Her Hair.
Song. Set by Mr. Henry Lawes[6]

   Amarantha sweet and fair,
Ah, braid no more that shining hair!
   As my curious hand or eye,
Hovering round thee, let it fly.

   Let it fly as unconfined   5
As its calm ravisher, the wind,
   Who hath left his darling, th' East,
To wanton o'er that spicy nest.

   Ev'ry tress must be confessed
But neatly tangled at the best,   10
   Like a clue[7] of golden thread,
Most excellently raveléd.

   Do not then wind up that light
In ribbons, and o'ercloud in night;
   Like the sun in's early ray,
But shake your head and scatter day.   15

5. The Lanière family had been musicians to the royal household for several generations; John Lanière died in 1650. The literary tradition in which this poem takes its place is discussed by G. F. Jones, *CL*, XI (1959), 131–143.
6. Lawes's musical setting was printed in his collection *Ayres and Dialogues* (1653).
7. Ball.

See, 'tis broke! Within this grove,
The bower and the walks of love,
    Weary lie we down and rest,
And fan each other's panting breast.   20

Here we'll strip and cool our fire
In cream below, in milk-baths higher;
    And when all wells are drawn dry,
I'll drink a tear out of thine eye.

Which our very joys[8] shall leave,   25
That sorrows thus we can deceive;
    Or our very sorrows weep,
That joys so ripe, so little keep.

Ode. To Lucasta. The Rose.
Set by Dr. John Wilson[9]

Sweet, serene, sky-like flower,
Haste to adorn her bower;
    From thy long cloudy bed,
    Shoot forth thy damask head.

New-startled blush of Flora!   5
The grief of pale Aurora,
    Who will contest no more;[1]
    Haste, haste, to strew her floor.

Vermilion ball that's given
From lip to lip in heaven,   10
    Love's couch's coverled;[2]
    Haste, haste, to make her bed.

Dear offspring of pleased Venus,
And jolly plump Silenus;[3]
    Haste, haste, to deck the hair   15
    Of th'only sweetly fair.

See! rosy is her bower,
Her floor is all this flower;
    Her bed a rosy nest
    By a bed of roses pressed.   20

---

8. I.e., our deepest and truest joys.
9. Known as the most accomplished lutenist in England, John Wilson (1595–1674) was appointed musician to Charles I in 1635 and chamber musician to Charles II in 1661.
1. I.e., Aurora, goddess of the dawn, will contest no more with the rose, whose hue matches the blush of Flora, goddess of flowers and the spring.
2. Coverlet.
3. The satyr Silenus was the foster father of Bacchus.

But early as she dresses,
Why fly you her bright tresses?
   Ah, I have found, I fear:
   Because her cheeks are near.

Gratiana Dancing and Singing

See! with what constant motion,
Even and glorious as the sun,
   Gratiana steers that noble frame,
Soft as her breast, sweet as her voice,
That gave each winding law and poise,   5
   And swifter than the wings of fame.

She beat the happy pavement
By such a star made firmament,
   Which now no more the roof envies,
But swells up high with Atlas even,   10
Bearing the brighter, nobler heaven,
   And in her all the deities.

Each step trod out a lover's thought
And the ambitious hopes he brought;
   Chained to her brave feet with such arts,   15
Such sweet command and gentle awe,
As when she ceased, we sighing saw
   The floor lay paved with broken hearts.

So did she move; so did she sing
Like the harmonious spheres that bring   20
   Unto their rounds their music's aid;
Which she perfor`med such a way
As all th'enamored world will say
The Graces danced, and Apollo played.

The Scrutiny. Song.
Set by Mr. Thomas Charles[4]

Why should you swear I am forsworn,
   Since thine I vowed to be?
Lady, it is already morn,
   And' twas last night I swore to thee
That fond[5] impossibility.   5

---

4. First printed by John Playford in *Select Musical Ayres and Dialogues* (London, 1652), this song also appears in Playford's *Select Ayres and Dialogues* (1659), where the setting is attributed to Henry Lawes. The poem is discussed by N. H. Holland in *Literature and Psychology*, XIV (1964), 43–55.
5. Foolish.

Have I not loved thee much and long,
    A tedious twelve hours' space?
I must all other beauties wrong,
    And rob thee of a new embrace,
Could I still dote upon thy face.   10

Not but all joy in thy brown hair
    By others may be found;
But I must search the black and fair,
    Like skillful mineralists that sound[6]
For treasure in unplowed-up ground.   15

Then, if when I have loved my round,
    Thou prov'st the pleasant she,
With spoils of meaner beauties crowned
    I laden will return to thee,
Ev'n sated with variety.   20

The Grasshopper. Ode.
To My Noble Friend, Mr. Charles Cotton[7]

O thou that swing'st upon the waving hair
    Of some well-filléd oaten beard,
Drunk every night with a delicious tear
    Dropped thee from heav'n, where now th'art reared;

The joys of earth and air are thine entire,   5
    That with thy feet and wings dost hop and fly;
And, when thy poppy works, thou dost retire
    To thy carved acorn bed to lie.

Up with the day, the sun thou welcom'st then,
    Sport'st in the gilt plats[8] of his beams,   10
And all these merry days mak'st merry men,
    Thyself, and melancholy streams.[9]

But ah, the sickle! golden ears are cropped;
    Ceres and Bacchus bid good-night;
Sharp frosty fingers all your flow'rs have topped,   15
    And what scythes spared, winds shave off quite.

6. Probe, explore.
7. Lovelace apparently addresses, not Charles Cotton the poet (1630–1687), but his father (d. 1658). Clarendon says of the elder Cotton that he had "such a pleasantness and gaiety of humor, such a sweetness and gentleness of nature, and such a civility and delightfulness in conversation that no man in the court or out of it appeared a more accomplished person" (*Life, ed. cit.*, I, p. 25). The poem is based on verses by the Greek lyric poet Anacreon, whom Abraham Cowley also follows in his *Anacreontics* on this subject. Cf. D. C. Allen's essay on the background and structure of Lovelace's poem, pp. 570-577.
8. I.e., golden braids.
9. I.e., makes men, thyself, and melancholy streams merry.

Poor verdant fool! and now green ice! thy joys,
 Large and as lasting as thy perch of grass,
Bid us lay in 'gainst winter, rain, and poise[1]
 Their floods with an o'erflowing glass.   20

Thou best of men and friends! we will create
 A genuine summer in each other's breast,
And spite of this cold time and frozen fate,
 Thaw us a warm seat to our rest.

Our sacred hearths shall burn eternally   25
 As vestal flames,[2] the north wind, he
Shall strike[3] his frost-stretched wings, dissolve, and fly
 This Etna in epitome.

Dropping December shall come weeping in,
 Bewail th' usurping of his reign;   30
But when in show'rs of old Greek we begin,
 Shall cry, he hath his crown again![4]

Night as clear Hesper[5] shall our tapers whip
 From the light casements where we play,
And the dark hag from her black mantle strip,   35
 And stick there everlasting day.

Thus richer than untempted kings are we,
 That asking nothing, nothing need:
Though lord of all what seas embrace, yet he
 That wants[6] himself is poor indeed.   40

The Vintage to the Dungeon. A Song.
Set by Mr. William Lawes[7]

Sing out, pent souls, sing cheerfully!
Care shackles you in liberty,
Mirth frees you in captivity;
    Would you double fetters add?
    Else why so sad?   5
Besides your pinioned arms you'll find
Grief, too, can manacle the mind.

Live then pris'ners uncontrolled,
Drink o' th' strong, the rich, the old,

---

1. Counterbalance.
2. The temple of Vesta, Roman goddess of the hearth, was attended by "Vestal Virgins" (appointed for a period of years), who swore to retain their virginity while they guarded the sacred flame.
3. I.e., shall abruptly spread.
4. Cf. the remarks of D. C. Allen, *op.*

cit., on this stanza.
5. The evening star.
6. Lacks.
7. If this song is to be connected with Lovelace's own career, it may relate to his imprisonment in the Gatehouse of Westminster in 1642.

Till wine too hath your wits in hold;   10
  Then if still your jollity
      And throats are free,
Triumph in your bonds and pains,
And dance to th' music of your chains.

To Lucasta. From Prison. An Epode[8]

Long in thy shackles, liberty
  I ask, not from these walls but thee[9]
(Left for awhile another's bride),
  To fancy all the world beside.

Yet ere I do begin to love,   5
  See! how I all my objects prove;[1]
Then my free soul to that confine
  'Twere possible I might call mine.

First I would be in love with Peace,
  And her rich swelling breasts' increase;   10
But how, alas! how may that be,
  Despising earth, will she love me?

Fain would I be in love with War,
  As my dear just avenging star;
But War is loved so ev'rywhere,   15
  Ev'n he disdains a lodging here.

Thee and thy wounds I would bemoan,
  Fair thorough-shot[2] Religion;
But he lives only that kills thee,
  And whoso binds thy hands is free.   20

I would love a Parliament
  As a main prop from Heaven sent;
But ah! who's he that would be wedded
  To th' fairest body that's beheaded?[3]

Next would I court my Liberty,   25
  And then my birthright, Property;
But can that be, when it is known
  There's nothing you can call your own?

---

8. This poem was presumably composed while Lovelace was confined in Peterhouse Prison, from June, 1648, until April, 1649.
9. I.e., Lucasta.
1. Test; i.e., consider carefully.
2. Shot through.
3. On December 6, 1648, by Cromwell's order, 141 members of Parliament were arrested or prevented from taking their seats ("Pride's Purge," so called because a Colonel Pride directed the operation); the remaining 78 members constituted the "Rump" Parliament. Charles I was executed on January 30, 1649.

A Reformation I would have,
    As for our griefs a sov'reign salve;   30
That is, a cleansing of each wheel
    Of state that yet some rust doth feel;

But not a Reformation so
    As to reform were to o'erthrow;
Like watches by unskillful men   35
    Disjointed, and set ill again.

The Public Faith[4] I would adore,
    But she is bankrupt of her store;
Nor how to trust her can I see,
    For she that cozens[5] all, must me.   40

Since then none of these can be
    Fit objects for my love and me,
What then remains but th' only spring
    Of all our loves and joys, the King?

He who, being the whole ball   45
    Of day on earth, lends it to all;
When seeking to eclipse his right,
    Blinded, we stand in our own light.

And now an universal mist
    Of error is spread o'er each breast,   50
With such a fury edged as is
    Not found in th' inwards of th' abyss.

Oh, from thy glorious starry wain,[6]
    Dispense on me one sacred beam,
To light me where I soon may see   55
    How to serve you, and you trust me.

To Althea. From Prison.
Song. Set by Dr. John Wilson[7]

When Love with unconfinéd wings
    Hovers within my gates,
And my divine Althea brings
    To whisper at the grates;

---

4. The government habitually borrowed money on the "public faith," a practice widely derided by royalist sympathizers.
5. Cheats.
6. Wagon. The seven brightest stars in the constellation Ursa Major (i.e., the stars of the Big Dipper) were known as "Charles's Wain." Cf. also Jonson, "Ode to Himself," p. 89, l. 60.
7. This most famous of Lovelace's poems was probably written while he was confined in the Gatehouse in 1642; Wilson's setting appears in Playford's *Select Ayres and Dialogues* (1659).

When I lie tangled in her hair 5
  And fettered to her eye,
The gods that wanton in the air
  Know no such liberty.

When flowing cups run swiftly round,
  With no allaying Thames,[8] 10
Our careless heads with roses bound,[9]
  Our hearts with loyal flames;
When thirsty grief in wine we steep,
  When healths and draughts go free,
Fishes that tipple in the deep 15
  Know no such liberty.

When, like committed[1] linnets, I
  With shriller throat shall sing
The sweetness, mercy, majesty,
  And glories of my King; 20
When I shall voice aloud how good
  He is, how great should be,
Enlargéd winds that curl the flood
  Know no such liberty.

Stone walls do not a prison make, 25
  Nor iron bars a cage:
Minds innocent and quiet take
  That for an hermitage.
If I have freedom in my love,
  And in my soul am free, 30
Angels alone, that soar above,
  Enjoy such liberty.

Lucasta's World. Epode

Cold as the breath of winds that blow
To silver shot descending snow,

  Lucasta sighed, when she did close
    The world in frosty chains!
  And then a frown to rubies froze 5
    The blood boiled in our veins;

Yet cooléd not the heat her sphere
Of beauties first had kindled there.

---

8. I.e., no water.
9. Cf. Herrick, "When He Would Have

His Verses Read," p. 105, l. 9 and note.
1. I.e., equal.

Then moved, and with a sudden flame
Impatient to melt all again,   10

> Straight from her eyes she lightning hurled,
>   And earth in ashes mourns;
> The sun his blaze denies the world,
>   And in her luster burns;

Yet warmèd not the hearts her nice[2]   15
Disdain had first congealed to ice.

And now her tears nor grieved desire
Can quench this raging, pleasing fire;

> Fate but one way allows; behold
>   Her smiles' divinity!   20
> They fanned this heat, and thawed that cold,
>   So framed up a new sky.

Thus earth from flames and ice reprieved,
E'er since hath in her sunshine lived.

La Bella Bona Roba[3]

I cannot tell who loves the skeleton
Of a poor marmoset,[4] nought but bone, bone.
Give me a nakedness with her clothes on.[5]

Such whose white satin upper coat of skin,
Cut upon velvet rich incarnadine,   5
Has yet a body (and of flesh) within.

Sure it is meant good husbandry in men
Who do incorporate with airy lean,
T' repair their sides, and get their rib again.[6]

Hard hap unto that huntsman that decrees   10
Fat joys for all his sweat, whenas he sees,
After his 'say, nought but his keeper's fees.[7]

---

2. Fastidious.

3. "Bona roba" was a common term for a prostitute; cf. Shakespeare's Justice Shallow, "We knew where the bona robas were and had the best of them at commandment" (*Henry IV, Part II*, III. ii. 22–23).

4. Ordinarily implying playful endearment, the term in this context means "wanton."

5. I.e., give me a well-rounded (i.e., plump) nakedness.

6. Cf. Genesis 2:21–22.

7. I.e., after his assay (of the fatness of a slain deer's flesh), nothing but the meager portion allotted to a gamekeeper. Cf. Beaumont and Fletcher, *Philaster*, IV. ii. 10–20.

Then Love, I beg, when next thou tak'st thy bow,
Thy angry shafts, and dost heart-chasing go,
Pass rascal[8] deer, strike me the largest doe.   15

The Fair Beggar

Commanding asker, if it be
   Pity that you fain would have,
Then I turn beggar unto thee,
   And ask the thing that thou dost crave;
I will suffice thy hungry need   5
So thou wilt but my fancy feed.

In all ill years, wast ever known
   On so much beauty such a dearth,
Which in that thrice-bequeathéd gown
   Looks like the sun eclipsed with earth,   10
Like gold in canvas, or with dirt
Unsoiléd ermines close begirt?

Yet happy he that can but taste
   This whiter skin, who thirsty is;
Fools dote on satin motions laced,   15
   The gods go naked in their bliss;
At th' barrel's head there shines the vine,
There only relishes the wine.

There quench my heat, and thou shalt sup,
   Worthy the lips that it must touch,   20
Nectar from out the starry cup;
   I beg thy breath not half so much;
So both our wants supplied shall be,
You'll give for love, I, charity.

Cheap, then, are pearl-embroideries   25
   That not adorn but cloud thy waist;
Thou shalt be clothed above all price
   If thou wilt promise me embraced;
We'll ransack neither chest nor shelf,
I'll cover thee with mine own self.   30

But, cruel, if thou dost deny
   This necessary alms to me,
What soft-souled man but with his eye
   And hand will hence be shut to thee?
Since all must judge you more unkind,   35
I starve your body, you my mind.

8. Lean.

From LUCASTA. POSTHUME POEMS (1659)

A *Black Patch On Lucasta's Face*[9]

Dull as I was, to think that a court fly
  Presumed so near her eye,
   When 'twas th' industrious bee
Mistook her glorious face for paradise;
To sum up all his chemistry of spice,   5
  With a brave pride and honor led,
  Near both her suns he makes his bed,
And though a spark struggles to rise as red;[1]
   Then emulates the gay
    Daughter of day,   10
   Acts the romantic phoenix' fate;[2]
When now, with all his sweets laid out in state,
  Lucasta scatters but one heat,
And all the aromatic pills do sweat,
And gums calcined,[3] themselves to powder beat;   15
   Which a fresh gale of air
   Conveys into her hair;
   Then chaste he's set on fire,
And in these holy flames doth glad expire;
   And that black marble tablet there   20
  So near her either sphere[4]
   Was placed; nor foil, nor ornament,
But the sweet little bee's large monument.

The Snail[5]

Wise emblem of our politic world,
Sage snail, within thine own self curled;
Instruct me softly to make haste,
Whilst these my feet go slowly fast.
  Compendious snail! thou seem'st to me   5
Large Euclid's[6] strict epitome;
And in each diagram, dost fling
Thee from the point unto the ring.
A figure now triangular,
An oval now, and now a square,   10

---

9. Small patches of black silk or court plaster were worn by fashionable ladies (and some men) to set off and enhance their beauty, and also to mask facial defects.
1. I.e., to match the dazzling brightness (of those "suns," her eyes).
2. The legendary phoenix was said to end its life by self-immolation on a pyre of aromatic woods, from which it arose again to new life.
3. Changed to powder (by heat).
4. I.e., her eyes.
5. This poem is discussed in detail by R. L. Wadsworth in *MLR*, LXV (1970), 750–760.
6. Euclid (fl. c. 300 B.C.) systematized and effectively founded the mathematical science of geometry.

And then a serpentine dost crawl,
Now a straight line, now crook'd, now all.
    Preventing[7] rival of the day,
Th'art up and openest thy ray,
And ere the morn cradles the moon,   15
Th' art broke into a beauteous noon.
Then when the sun sups in the deep,
Thy silver horns ere Cynthia's peep;
And thou from thine own liquid bed,
New Phoebus, heav'st thy pleasant head.   20
    Who shall a name for thee create,
Deep riddle of mysterious state?
Bold nature, that gives common birth
To all products of seas and earth,
Of thee, as earthquakes, is afraid,   25
Nor will thy dire deliv'ry aid.
    Thou thine own daughter then, and sire,
That son and mother art entire,
That big still with thyself dost go,
And liv'st an aged embryo;   30
That like the cubs of India,[8]
Thou from thyself a while dost play;
But frightened with a dog or gun,
In thine own belly thou dost run,
And as thy house was thine own womb,   35
So thine own womb concludes thy tomb.
    But now I must, analyzed king,
Thy economic virtues sing;
Thou great staid husband[9] still within,
Thou thee, that's thine, dost discipline;   40
And when thou art to progress bent,
Thou mov'st thyself and tenement;
As warlike Scythians traveled,[1] you
Remove your men and city too;
Then after a sad dearth and rain,   45
Thou scatterest thy silver train;
And when the trees grow nak'd and old,
Thou clothest them with cloth of gold,
Which from thy bowels thou dost spin,
And draw from the rich mines within.   50
    Now hast thou changed thee saint; and made
Thyself a fane[2] that's cupola'd,
And in thy wreathéd cloister thou

7. Anticipating.
8. Lovelace may here recall Edward Topsell's account (based on that of Conrad Gesner) of the "Semivulpa or Apish-Fox," a denizen of "the country of Payran," which carries its young in "a skin like a bag or scrip . . . neither do they come forth of that receptacle, except it be to suck milk, or sport themselves" (Edward Topsell, *History of Four-Footed Beasts and Serpents and Insects*, ed. W. Ley, 3 vols. [New York, 1967], I, p. 16).
9. Steward.
1. Cf. Herodotus, *Histories*, IV. 1–142.
2. Temple.

Walkest thine own gray friar too;
Strict, and locked up, th'art hood all o'er   55
And ne'er eliminat'st thy door.
On salads thou dost feed severe,
And 'stead of beads thou drop'st a tear,
And when to rest, each calls the bell,
Thou sleep'st within thy marble cell,   60
Where in dark contemplation placed,
The sweets of nature thou dost taste;
Who now with time thy days resolve,
And in a jelly thee dissolve
Like a shot star,[3] which doth repair   65
Upward, and rarefy the air.

A Loose Saraband[4]

Nay prithee, dear, draw nigher,
    Yet closer, nigher yet,
Here is a double fire,
    A dry one and a wet;
True lasting heavenly fuel   5
Puts out the vestal jewel,
When once we twining marry
Mad love with wild Canary.

Off with that crownéd Venice[5]
    Till all the house doth flame,   10
We'll quench it straight in Rhenish,
    Or what we must not name;
Milk lightning still assuageth,
So when our fury rageth,
As th' only means to cross it,   15
We'll drown it in love's posset.[6]

Love never was well-willer
    Unto my nag or me,
Ne'er watered us i' th' cellar,[7]
    But the cheap buttery;   20
At th'head of his own barrels,
Where broached are all his quarrels,
Should a true noble master
Still make his guest his taster.

---

3. It was thought that falling (shooting) stars became jellies on reaching the earth. Cf. Donne, "Epithalamion," ll. 204–205.
4. Originally a stately Spanish dance, the saraband in seventeenth-century England was regarded somewhat differently. In Ben Jonson's play, *The Staple of News*, for instance, Old Pennyboy observes, "How they are tickled / With a light air, the bawdy saraband" (IV. ii).
5. I.e., that goblet of Venetian glass.
6. I.e., in milky sperm.
7. I.e., in the wine cellar (as distinct from the buttery, where beer and ale were stored).

See! all the world how't staggers,   25
  More ugly drunk than we,
As if far gone in daggers
  And blood it seemed to be;
We drink our glass of roses
Which nought but sweets discloses,   30
Then in our loyal chamber
Refresh us with love's amber.

Now tell me, thou fair cripple,
  That dumb canst scarcely see
Th'almightiness of tipple,   35
  And th'odds 'twixt thee and thee,
What of Elysium's[8] missing?
Still drinking and still kissing,
Adoring plump October;
Lord! what is man and sober?   40

Now, is there such a trifle
  As honor, the fool's giant?[9]
What is there left to rifle
  When wine makes all parts pliant?
Let others glory follow,   45
In their false riches wallow,
And with their grief be merry;
Leave me but love and sherry.

Love Made in the First Age. To Chloris

In the nativity of time,
Chloris, it was not thought a crime
  In direct Hebrew for to woo.[1]
Now we make love as all on fire,
Ring retrograde our loud desire,   5
  And court in English backward too.

Thrice happy was that golden age,
When compliment was construed rage,
  And fine words in the center hid;
When cursèd *No* stained no maid's bliss,   10
And all discourse was summed in *Yes,*
  And nought forbade, but to forbid.

Love then unstinted, love did sip,
And cherries plucked fresh from the lip,
  On cheeks and roses free he fed;   15
Lasses like autumn plums did drop,

8. Cf. Carew, "A Rapture," p. 166, l. 2 and note.
9. Cf. Carew, "A Rapture," l. 3.
1. It was believed (partly on the evidence of Genesis 11:1) that Hebrew, which reads from right to left, was the original language of mankind.

And lads indifferently[2] did crop
A flower and a maidenhead.

Then unconfinéd each did tipple
Wine from the bunch, milk from the nipple,   20
   Paps tractable as udders were;
Then equally the wholesome jellies
Were squeezed from olive trees and bellies,
   Nor suits of trespass did they fear.

A fragrant bank of strawberries,   25
Diapered[3] with violet's eyes
   Was table, tablecloth, and fare;
No palace to the clouds did swell,
Each humble princess then did dwell
   In the piazza[4] of her hair.   30

Both broken faith and th' cause of it,
All-damning gold, was damned to th' pit;
   Their troth, sealed with a clasp and kiss,
Lasted until that extreme day
In which they smiled their souls away,   35
   And, in each other, breathed new bliss.

Because no fault, there was no tear;
No groan did grate the granting ear;
   No false foul breath their del'cate smell:
No serpent kiss poisoned the taste,   40
Each touch was naturally chaste,
   And their mere sense a miracle.

Naked as their own innocence,
And unembroidered from offense
   They went, above poor riches, gay;   45
On softer than the cygnet's down,
In beds they tumbled of their own;
   For each within the other lay.

Thus did they live; thus did they love,
Repeating only joys above;   50
   And angels were, but with clothes on,
Which they would put off cheerfully,
To bathe them in the galaxy,
   Then gird them with the heavenly zone.

Now, Chloris, miserably crave   55
The offered bliss you would not have,
   Which evermore I must deny,

2. Impartially.
3. Patterned, strewn.

4. Arcade (hence, "delicately artful structure").

Whilst ravished with these noble dreams,
And crownéd with mine own soft beams,
  Enjoying of myself I lie.   60

A Mock-Song

  Now Whitehall's in the grave,
  And our head is our slave,[5]
The bright pearl in his close shell of oyster;
  Now the miter is lost,
  The proud prelates, too, crossed,   5
And all Rome's confined to a cloister;
  He that Tarquin was styled,[6]
  Our white land's exiled,
   Yea undefiled,
Not a court ape's left to confute us;   10
  Then let your voices rise high,
  As your colors did fly,
   And flourishing cry,
"Long live the brave Oliver-Brutus."

  Now the sun is unarmed,   15
  And the moon by us charmed,
All the stars dissolved to a jelly;[7]
  Now the thighs of the crown
  And the arms are lopped down,
And the body is all but a belly;   20
  Let the Commons go on,
  The town is our own,
   We'll rule alone;
For the knights have yielded their spent gorge;[8]
  And an order is ta'en   25
  With *honi soit* profane,[9]
   Shout forth amain,
For our dragon hath vanquished the St. George.

A Fly Caught in a Cobweb

Small type of great ones, that do hum
Within this whole world's narrow room,
That with a busy hollow noise
Catch at the people's vainer voice,

---

5. With the execution of Charles I, in 1649, outside his own palace of Whitehall, Cromwell (considered by royalists to be a low fellow without breeding or culture) became master of England.
6. I.e., Charles II, regularly so described in the official newspaper of the Commonwealth, *Mercurius Politicus*.

7. Cf. "The Snail," p. 317, l. 65 and note.
8. I.e. (perhaps), for the privileged aristocracy has been destroyed.
9. The motto on the royal coat of arms is *honi soit qui mal y pense* ("evil be to him who evil thinks").

And with spread sails play with their breath,   5
Whose very hails new christen death,
Poor fly, caught in an airy net,
Thy wings have fettered now thy feet;
Where like a lion in a toil,[1]
Howe'er thou keep'st a noble coil[2]   10
And beat'st thy gen'rous breast, that o'er
The plains thy fatal buzzes roar,
Till thy all-bellied foe , round elf,
Hath quartered thee within himself.
    Was it not better once to play   15
I' th' light of a majestic ray?
Where though too near and bold, the fire
Might singe thy upper down attire,
And thou i' th' storm to lose an eye,
A wing, or a self-trapping thigh,   20
Yet hadst thou fall'n like him, whose coil
Made fishes in the sea to broil;
When now th' hast 'scaped the noble flame,
Trapped basely in a slimy frame;
And free of air, thou art become   25
Slave to the spawn of mud and loam.
    Nor is't enough thyself dost dress
To thy swol'n lord a num'rous mess,[3]
And by degrees thy thin veins bleed,
And piecemeal dost his poison feed;   30
But now devoured, art like to be
A net spun for thy family,
And straight expanded in the air
Hang'st for thy issue too a snare.
Strange witty death, and cruel ill,   35
That killing thee, thou thine dost kill!
Like pies[4] in whose entombéd ark
All fowl crowd downward to a lark,
Thou art thine en'mies' sepulcher,
And in thee buriest too thine heir.   40
    Yet Fates a glory have reserved
For one so highly hath deserved;
As the rhinoceros doth die
Under his castle[5] enemy,
As through the crane's trunk[6] throat doth speed   45
The asp doth[7] on his feeder feed;
Fall yet triumphant in thy woe,
Bound with the entrails of thy foe.

---

1. Net.
2. Tumult.
3. I.e., a large meal.
4. Magpies.
5. Elephant (known as the "carry-castle" from the howdah or pavilion on his back). Topsell observes that there is between rhinoceros and elephant "a natural . . . enmity" (*ed. cit.*, I, p. 463).
6. I.e., tubular.
7. I.e., that doth.

324 · *Richard Lovelace*

Advice To My Best Brother, Colonel Francis Lovelace[8]

Frank, wilt live handsomely? Trust not too far
Thyself to waving[9] seas, for what thy star
Calculated by sure event must be,
Look in the glassy epithet[1] and see.

Yet settle here your rest, and take your state,   5
And in calm halcyon's nest[2] ev'n build your fate;
Prithee lie down securely, Frank, and keep
With as much no noise the inconstant deep
As its inhabitants; nay, steadfast stand,
As if discovered were a Newfoundland   10
Fit for plantation here; dream, dream still,
Lulled in Dione's cradle,[3] dream, until
Horror awake your sense, and you now find
Yourself a bubbled pastime for the wind,
And in loose Thetis'[4] blankets torn and tossed;   15
Frank, to undo thyself why art at cost?

Nor be too confident, fixed on the shore,
For even that too borrows from the store
Of her rich neighbor, since now wisest know,
And this to Galileo's judgment owe,[5]   20
The palsy earth itself is every jot
As frail, inconstant, waving as that blot
We lay upon the deep; that sometimes lies
Changed, you would think, with's bottom's properties,
But this eternal strange Ixion's wheel[6]   25
Of giddy earth, ne'er whirling leaves to reel
Till all things are inverted, till they are
Turned to that antic confused state they were.

Who loves the golden mean, doth safely want
A cobwebbed cot, and wrongs entailed upon't;   30
He richly needs a palace for to breed
Vipers and moths, that on their feeder feed;
The toy that we (too true) a mistress call,

8. Colonel Francis Lovelace (c. 1618–c. 1675) commanded the royalist garrison at Carmarthen, in Wales, from June, 1644, until October, 1645. After the Restoration, he shipped over with his regiment to America, where it appears that he became (in 1668) the Governor of New York, serving in that capacity for some time. Cf. *Poems of Richard Lovelace*, ed. C. H. Wilkinson, 2 vols. (Oxford, 1925), I, pp. 4–6. This poem is based on Horace, *Odes*, II, x.
9. Rolling.
1. I.e., crystal ball. But cf. *Poems, ed. cit.*, I, p. 102.

2. Cf. Carew, "The Rapture," p. 168, l. 97 and note.
3. I.e., in Aphrodite's cradle, the sea. Dione was the mother of Aphrodite (Venus), who is hence called Dionaea, and occasionally Dione.
4. The sea nymph Thetis was the mother of Achilles.
5. The telescopic observations of the heavens made by Galileo Galilei (1564–1642) were instrumental for change in man's conception of the universe.
6. Cf. Waller, "To the Mutable Fair," p. 244, l. 34 and note.

Whose looking-glass and feather weighs up all;
And clothes which larks would play with in the sun,[7]   35
That mock him in the night when's course is run.

To rear an edifice by art so high
That envy should not reach it with her eye,
Nay, with a thought come near it, would'st thou know
How such a structure should be raised? build low.   40
The blust'ring wind's invisible rough stroke
More often shakes the stubborn'st, proper'st oak,
And in proud turrets we behold withal,
'Tis the imperial top declines to fall;
Nor does heav'n's lightning strike the humble vales,   45
But high aspiring mounts batters and scales.

A breast of proof defies all shocks of fate,
Fears in the best, hopes in the worser state;
Heaven forbid that, as of old, time ever
Flourished in spring, so contrary, now never;   50
That mighty breath which blew foul winter hither
Can eas'ly puff it to a fairer weather.
Why dost despair then, Frank? Aeolus has
A Zephyrus as well as Boreas.[8]

'Tis a false sequel, solecism, 'gainst those   55
Precepts by fortune giv'n us, to suppose
That, 'cause it is now ill, 'twill e'er be so;
Apollo doth not always bend his bow;
But oft uncrownéd of his beams divine,
With his soft harp awakes the sleeping Nine.[9]   60

In strictest things magnanimous appear,
Greater in hope, howe'er thy fate, than fear;
Draw all your sails in quickly, though no storm
Threaten your ruin with a sad alarm;
For tell me how they differ, tell me, pray,   65
A cloudy tempest, and a too fair day.

---

7. Falconers used pieces of scarlet cloth (or mirrors) to attract and entrap birds. Cf. Shakespeare's *Henry VIII*, III. ii. 276–279.
8. I.e., the god of the winds has at command a (mild) west wind as well as a (harsh) north wind.
9. Phoebus Apollo combined with other attributes those of the god who punishes, the sun god, and (in conjunction with the nine Muses) the god of poetry and song.

Abraham Cowley

1618	Born in London, the posthumous son of a stationer.
1629	Admitted to Westminster School, in London, as a King's Scholar.
1633	Publication of *Poetical Blossoms* (five poems).
1636	Second (augmented) edition of *Poetical Blossoms*; third edition published in 1637.
1637	Matriculates at Trinity College, Cambridge.
1638	Publication of *Love's Riddle*, a pastoral drama, and of *Naufragium Joculare*, a Latin comedy (acted at Cambridge in this year).
1639	Takes the B.A. degree.
1641	A comedy, *The Guardian* (rewritten in 1658 as *The Cutter of Coleman Street*), presented at Cambridge before Prince Charles.
1642	Proceeds M.A.
1643	Publication of *The Puritan and the Papist*, a satire. In April, having been removed from Cambridge by official fiat, takes up residence at Saint John's College, Oxford, where he associates with Lord Falkland and other moderate royalists.
1646–1656	In France, actively employed by Queen Henrietta Maria and exiled members of the court.
1647	Publication of *The Mistress*.
1656	On return to England, arrrested and (briefly) imprisoned; released on bail, but remains under bail until 1660. Publication of *Poems*.
1657	Incorporated M.D. at Oxford.
1659–1660	Living in France.
1661	Publication of *A Proposition for the Advancement of Experimental Philosophy*, and of *A Discourse by Way of Vision, Concerning the Government of Oliver Cromwell*. *The Cutter of Coleman Street* acted at Lincoln's Inn Fields.
1662	Publication of *A Couleii Plantarum Libri Duo*.
1663	Publication of *Verses lately Written upon Several Occasions*. Retirement to Barn Elms, Kent.
1665	Moves to Chertsey.
1667	Death, July 28. Buried in Westminster Abbey.

1668   Publication of *The Works Of Mr. Abraham Cowley*, edited by Thomas Sprat.

From THE WORKS OF MR. ABRAHAM COWLEY[1] (1668)

From *Miscellanies*

The Motto
Tentanda via est, etc.[2]

What shall I do to be forever known,
   And make the age to come my own?
I shall like beasts or common people die,
   Unless you write my elegy,
Whilst others great by being born are grown,   5
   Their mothers' labor, not their own.
In this scale gold, in th'other fame does lie,
   The weight of that mounts this so high.
These men are fortune's jewels, molded bright,
   Brought forth with their own fire and light;   10
If I her vulgar stone, for either look,
   Out of myself it must be strook.
Yet I must on: what sound is't strikes mine ear?
   Sure I Fame's trumpet hear;
It sounds like the last trumpet, for it can   15
   Raise up the buried man.
Unpassed Alps stop me, but I'll cut through all
   And march, the Muses' Hannibal.[3]
Hence, all the flattering vanities that lay
   Nets of roses in the way;   20
Hence, the desire of honors or estate
   And all that is not above fate;

1. As Dr. Johnson remarked, Cowley "has been at one time too much praised and too much neglected at another" (cf. p. 433). Dryden's youthful enthusiasm, for instance, gave place at last to gloomy reflections on Cowley's "want . . . of judgment," while Pope, in 1737, spoke for his own generation: "Who now reads Cowley? if he pleases yet,/His moral pleases, not his pointed wit" (*Imitations of Horace*, Epistle II. i. 75–76). But if Johnson deplored the "metaphysick style" of the poems that comprise *The Mistress*, he admired the ode "Of Wit," thought well of Cowley's elegies and Anacreontic pieces, and allowed the *Pindaric Odes* to be "not without a just claim to praise." These are precisely the poems which (with some few others) effectively illus-trate Douglas Bush's assessment of Cowley as "a mirror . . . of the new rationalism of the English and the European mind," in whose work the traditions of Christian humanism fuse with an emergent faith in scientific progress, under the aegis of "neoclassical good sense" (*English Literature in the Earlier Seventeenth Century*, ed. cit., p. 165).
2. Cf. Vergil, *Georgics*, III. 8–9: "A path must be found out whereby I too may rise from earth and fly in triumph on the lips of men."
3. The Carthaginian general Hannibal (247–c. 183 B.C.) led his troops across the Alps in the spring of 218 B.C., subsequently annihilating the Roman forces led by Flaminius at Lake Trasimene.

Hence, Love himself, the tyrant of my days,
    Which intercepts my coming praise.
Come, my best friends, my books, and lead me on: 25
    'Tis time that I were gone.
Welcome, great Stagirite,[4] and teach me now
    All I was born to know;
Thy scholar's vict'ries thou dost far outdo,
    He conquered th'earth, the whole world you.   30
Welcome, learn'd Cicero,[5] whose blest tongue and wit
    Preserve Rome's greatness yet:
Thou art the first of orators; only he
    Who best can praise thee, next must be.
Welcome the Mantuan swan,[6] Vergil the wise,   35
    Whose verse walks highest, but not flies;
Who brought green poesy to her perfect age,
    And made that art which was a rage.[7]
Tell me, ye mighty three, what shall I do
    To be like one of you?   40
But you have climbed the mountain's top, there sit
    On the calm flour'shing head of it,
And whilst with wearied steps we upward go,
    See us and clouds below.

Ode. Of Wit[8]

Tell me, O tell, what kind of thing is wit,
    Thou[9] who master art of it,
For the first matter[1] loves variety less;
Less women love't, either in love or dress.
    A thousand different shapes it bears,   5
    Comely in thousand shapes appears.
Yonder we saw it plain; and here 'tis now,
Like spirits in a place, we know not how.

London, that vents[2] of false ware so much store,
    In no ware deceives us more,   10
For men led by the color and the shape,

---

4. I.e., Aristotle (384–322 B.C.), born in the Macedonian town of Stagira. Alexander the Great (356–323 B.C.) was his pupil from 342–335 B.C.
5. Marcus Tullius Cicero (106–43 B.C.), orator and philosopher, was widely admired for the range, clarity, and style of his writings.
6. Vergil (70–19 B.C.) was born near Mantua.
7. I.e., the frenzied and uncontrolled expression of poetic inspiration.
8. "As true wit consists in the resemblance of ideas, and false wit in the resemblance of words, there is another kind of wit, which consists partly in the resemblance of ideas, and partly in the resemblance of words; which, for distinction's sake, I shall call mixed wit. This kind of wit is that which abounds in Cowley more than in any author that ever wrote" (Dr. Johnson, *The Spectator*, 62). Cf. also T. S. Eliot's remarks on some aspects of Cowley's wit (pp. 578–584).
9. It seems probable that Cowley's poem is not addressed to an actual person.
1. I.e., the original matter from which all things were created.
2. Vends, sells.

Like Zeuxis' birds fly to the painted grape;[3]
    Some things do through our judgment pass
    As through a multiplying[4] glass,
And sometimes, if the object be too far,   15
We take a falling meteor for a star.

Hence 'tis a wit, that greatest word of fame,
    Grows such a common name;
And wits by our creation they become,
Just so, as tit'lar bishops[5] made at Rome.   20
    'Tis not a tale, 'tis not a jest
    Admired with laughter at a feast,
Nor florid talk, which can that title gain;
The proofs of wit forever must remain.

'Tis not to force some lifeless verses meet   25
    With their five gouty feet;
All ev'rywhere, like man's, must be the soul,
And reason the inferior powers control.
    Such were the numbers which could call
    The stones into the Theban wall;[6]   30
Such miracles are ceased; and now we see
No towns or houses raised by poetry.

Yet 'tis not to adorn and gild each part;
    That shows more cost than art.
Jewels at nose and lips but ill appear;   35
Rather than all things wit, let none be there.
    Several[7] lights will not be seen
    If there be nothing else between;
Men doubt, because they stand so thick i' th' sky,
If those be stars which paint the galaxy.   40

'Tis not when two like words make up one noise,
    Jests for Dutch men and English boys,
In which who finds out wit, the same may see
In an'grams and acrostics, poetry.
    Much less can that have any place   45
    At which a virgin hides her face:
Such dross the fire must purge away; 'tis just
The author blush, there where the reader must.

'Tis not such lines as almost crack the stage
    When Bajazet[8] begins to rage,   50

3. The Greek painter Zeuxis (fl. c. 400 B.C.) was accounted a master of realistic effect (*trompe l'oeil*).
4. Magnifying.
5. I.e., bishops who bear the title but have no see.
6. Cf. Waller, "At Penshurst" [1], p. 235, l. 17 and note.
7. Separate, distinct.
8. Cowley alludes not to the actual Turkish Sultan Bajazet (1347–1403), but to the dramatic character in Marlowe's play *Tamburlaine*, whose speeches are marked by bombast and rant.

Nor a tall metaphor in the bombast way,
Nor the dry chips of short-lunged Seneca,[9]
    Nor upon all things to obtrude,
    And force some odd similitude.
What is it, then, which like the Power Divine   55
We only can by negatives define?

In a true piece of wit all things must be,
    Yet all things there agree;
As in the ark, joined without force or strife,
All creatures dwelt, all creatures that had life;   60
    Or as the primitive forms of all,
    If we compare great things with small,
Which without discord or confusion lie
In that strange mirror of the Deity.

But love, that molds one man up out of two,   65
    Makes me forget and injure you;
I took you for myself, sure, when I thought
That you in anything were to be taught.
    Correct my error with thy pen;
    And if any ask me then,   70
What thing right wit and height of genius is,
I'll only show your lines, and say, *'Tis this.*

On the Death of Mr. William Hervey
Immodicis brevis est aetas, et rara senectus.[1]

It was a dismal and a fearful night;
Scarce could the morn drive on th' unwilling light,
When sleep, death's image, left my troubled breast
    By something liker death possessed.
My eyes with tears did uncommanded flow,   5
    And on my soul hung the dull weight
    Of some intolerable fate.
What bell was that? Ah me! Too much I know.

My sweet companion, and my gentle peer,
Why hast thou left me thus unkindly here,   10
Thy end forever, and my life to moan?
    Oh, thou hast left me all alone!
Thy soul and body, when death's agony
    Besieged around thy noble heart,
    Did not with more reluctance part   15
Than I, my dearest friend, do part from thee.

---

9. The literary style of Lucius Annaeus
Seneca (d. A.D. 65) was terse and curt, in
contrast to the urbane and balanced style
associated with Cicero.
1. "To the extraordinarily gifted, life is
brief and old age rare" (Martial, *Epigrams*, VI. xxix. 7). William Hervey
(1616–1642), Cowley's close friend, attended Pembroke College, Cambridge.

My dearest friend, would I had died for thee!
Life and this world henceforth will tedious be:
Nor shall I know hereafter what to do
    If once my griefs prove tedious too.   20
Silent and sad I walk about all day,
    As sullen ghosts stalk speechless by
      Where their hid treasures lie.
Alas, my treasure's gone, why do I stay?

He was my friend, the truest friend on earth;   25
A strong and mighty influence joined our birth.
Nor did we envy the most sounding name
    By friendship giv'n of old to fame.
None but his brethren he, and sisters, knew,
    Whom the kind youth preferred to me;   30
      And ev'n in that we did agree,
For much above myself I loved them too.

Say, for you saw us, ye immortal lights,
How oft unwearied have we spent the nights?
Till the Ledaean stars,[2] so famed for love,   35
    Wondered at us from above.
We spent them not in toys, in lusts, or wine,
    But search of deep philosophy,
      Wit, eloquence, and poetry,
Arts which I loved, for they, my friend, were thine.   40

Ye fields of Cambridge, our dear Cambridge, say,
Have ye not seen us walking every day?
Was there a tree about which did not know
    The love betwixt us two?
Henceforth, ye gentle trees, forever fade;   45
    Or your sad branches thicker join,
      And into darksome shades combine,
Dark as the grave wherein my friend is laid.

Henceforth no learned youths beneath you sing,
Till all the tuneful birds to your boughs they bring;   50
No tuneful birds play with their wonted cheer,
    And call the learned youths to hear;
No whistling winds through the glad branches fly,
    But all with sad solemnity,
      Mute and unmovéd be,   55
Mute as the grave wherein my friend does lie.

To him my Muse made haste with every strain
Whilst it was new, and warm yet from the brain.

2. I.e., Castor and Pollux (known also as the Dioscuri), Leda's twin sons, who were stellified as the constellation Gemini. Cf. Jonson, "To the Immortal Memory . . . of . . . Sir Lucius Cary and Sir H. Morison," pp. 78–79, ll. 89–99.

He loved my worthless rhymes, and like a friend
    Would find out something to commend.   60
Hence now, my Muse, thou canst not me delight;
    Be this my latest verse
    With which I now adorn his hearse,
And this my grief without thy help shall write.

Had I a wreath of bays about my brow,   65
I should contemn³ that flourishing honor now,
Condemn it to the fire, and joy to hear
    It rage and crackle there.
Instead of bays, crown with sad cypress me,
    Cypress which tombs does beautify;   70
    Not Phoebus grieved so much as I
For him, who first was made that mournful tree.⁴

Large was his soul; as large a soul as e'er
Submitted to inform a body here.
High as the place 'twas shortly in heav'n to have,   75
    But low and humble as his grave;
So high that all the virtues there did come
    As to their chiefest seat,
    Conspicuous and great;
So low that for me, too, it made a room.   80

He scorned this busy world below, and all
That we, mistaken mortals, pleasure call;
Was filled with innocent gallantry and truth,
    Triumphant o'er the sins of youth.
He, like the stars to which he now is gone,   85
    That shine with beams like flame,
    Yet burn not with the same,
Had all the light of youth, of the fire none.

Knowledge he only sought, and so soon caught,
As if for him knowledge had rather sought;   90
Nor did more learning ever crowded lie
    In such a short mortality.
Whene'er the skillful youth discoursed or writ,
    Still did the notions throng
    About his eloquent tongue,   95
Nor could his ink flow faster than his wit.

So strong a wit did nature to him frame
As all things but his judgment overcame;
His judgment like the heav'nly moon did show,
    Temp'ring that mighty sea below.   100

---

3. Scorn.
4. The remorse of Cyparissus at having accidentally killed his favorite stag was such that he prayed for death. Phoebus Apollo transformed him into a cypress tree (Ovid, *Metamorphoses*, X. 106–142).

Oh, had he lived in learning's world, what bound
    Would have been able to control
    His overpowering soul?
We have lost in him arts that not yet are found.

His mirth was the pure spirits of various wit,   105
Yet never did his God or friends forget,
And, when deep talk and wisdom came in view,
    Retired and gave to them their due.
For the rich help of books he always took,
    Though his own searching mind before   110
    Was so with notions written o'er
As if wise nature had made that her book.

So many virtues joined in him, as we
Can scarce pick here and there in history;
More than old writers' practice e'er could reach,   115
    As much as they could ever teach.
These did religion, queen of virtues, sway,
    And all their sacred motions steer,
    Just like the first and highest sphere,[5]
Which wheels about, and turns all heav'n one way.   120

With as much zeal, devotion, piety,
He always lived, as other saints do die.
Still with his soul severe account he kept,
    Weeping all debts out ere he slept.
Then down in peace and innocence he lay,   125
    Like the sun's laborious light,
    Which still in water sets at night,
Unsullied with his journey of the day.

Wondrous young man, why wert thou made so good,
To be snatched hence ere better understood?   130
Snatched before half of thee enough was seen!
    Thou ripe, and yet thy life but green!
Nor could thy friends take their last sad farewell,
    But danger and infectious death
    Maliciously seized on that breath   135
Where life, spirit, pleasure always used to dwell.

But happy thou, ta'en from this frantic age,
Where ignorance and hypocrisy does rage!
A fitter time for heav'n no soul e'er chose,
    The place now only free from those.   140
There 'mong the blest thou dost forever shine,
    And wheresoe'er thou casts thy view

---

5. I.e., the *primum mobile*, the outermost sphere by which all others in the Ptolemaic system were thought to be moved.

Upon that white and radiant crew,
See'st not a soul clothed with more light than thine.

And if the glorious saints cease not to know   145
Their wretched friends who fight with life below,
Thy flame to me does still the same abide,
  Only more pure and rarefied.
There whilst immortal hymns thou dost rehearse,
  Thou dost with holy pity see   150
  Our dull and earthly poesy,
Where grief and misery can be joined with verse.

On the Death of Mr. Crashaw[6]

Poet and saint! to thee alone are given
The two most sacred names of earth and heaven,
The hard and rarest union which can be,
Next that of Godhead with humanity.
Long did the Muse's banished slaves abide,   5
And built vain pyramids to mortal pride;
Like Moses thou, though spells and charms withstand,
Hast brought them nobly home back to their Holy Land.
  Ah wretched we, poets of earth! but thou
Wert, living, the same poet which thou'rt now   10
Whilst angels sing to thee airs divine,
And joy in an applause so great as thine.
Equal society with them to hold,
Thou need'st not make new songs, but say the old;
And they (kind spirits!) shall all rejoice to see   15
How little less than they exalted man may be.
  Still the old heathen gods in numbers dwell,
The heav'nliest thing on earth still keeps up hell.
Nor have we yet quite purged the Christian land;
Still idols here like calves at Bethel stand.[7]   20
And though Pan's death long since all oracles broke,
Yet still in rhyme the fiend Apollo spoke;[8]
Nay, with the worst of heathen dotage we
(Vain men!) the monster woman deify;
Find stars, and tie our fates there in a face,[9]   25

---

6. The poet Richard Crashaw (c. 1612–1649) became Cowley's friend at Cambridge, where he was a Fellow of Peterhouse from 1635 to 1643. He subsequently removed to Paris, then to Rome. Converted to the Roman Catholic faith in about 1645, he was granted an ecclesiastical post at Loreto, Italy, shortly before his death.
7. Jeroboam, King of Israel, set up two golden calves in Bethel and in Dan, which the Israelites were induced to worship with sacrifice and feasting (1 Kings 12:25–33).
8. In the essay "On the Cessation of the Oracles," Plutarch tells of the voice that cried that the great Pan was dead. Christians associated this account with Christ's mission on earth. Cowley suggests that, while the Oracle of Apollo at Delphi has been silenced, the pagan deity continues to speak through the medium of love poetry (the "numbers" of l. 17).
9. Cf., for example, Sidney's sonnet sequence, *Astrophil and Stella*.

And Paradise in them by whom we lost it, place.
What different faults corrupt our Muses thus?
Wanton as girls, as old wives fabulous![1]
    Thy spotless Muse, like Mary, did contain
The boundless Godhead; she[2] did well disdain   30
That her eternal verse employed should be
On a less subject than eternity;
And for a sacred mistress scorned to take
But her whom God Himself scorned not His spouse
      to make.
It, in a kind, her miracle did do;   35
A fruitful mother was, and virgin too.
    How well, blest swan, did fate contrive thy death,
And made thee render up thy tuneful breath
In thy great mistress' arms, thou most divine
And richest off'ring of Loreto's shrine!   40
Where, like some holy sacrifice t' expire,
A fever burns thee, and love lights the fire.
Angels, they say, brought the famed chapel there,
And bore the sacred load in triumph through the air.
'Tis surer much they brought thee there, and they,   45
And thou, their charge, went singing all the way.
    Pardon, my mother church,[3] if I consent
That angels led him when from thee he went,
For even in error sure no danger is
When joined with so much piety as his.   50
Ah, mighty God, with shame I speak't, and grief,
Ah, that our greatest faults were in belief!
And our weak reason were ev'n weaker yet,
Rather than thus our wills too strong for it.
His faith perhaps in some nice[4] tenets might   55
Be wrong; his life, I'm sure, was in the right.
And I myself a Catholic will be,
So far at least, great saint, to pray to thee.
    Hail, bard triumphant! and some care bestow
On us, the poets militant below!   60
Opposed by our old enemy, adverse chance,
Attacked by envy and by ignorance,
Enchained by beauty, tortured by desires,
Exposed by tyrant love to savage beasts and fires,
Thou from low earth in nobler flames didst rise,   65
And, like Elijah, mount alive the skies.[5]
Elisha-like (but with a wish much less,
More fit thy greatness and my littleness)
Lo, here I beg (I whom thou once didst prove

---

1. I.e., given to recounting fables and legends.
2. I.e., Crashaw's muse.
3. I.e., the Church of England.
4. Oversubtle.

5. Cf. 2 Kings 2:11: "Elijah went up by a whirlwind into heaven." His successor Elisha prayed that "a double portion" of Elijah's spirit should be allotted to him (*ibid.*, 2:9).

So humble to esteem, so good to love) 70
Not that thy spirit might on me doubled be,
I ask but half thy mighty spirit for me;
And when my Muse soars with so strong a wing,
'Twill learn of things divine, and first of thee to sing.

From *Anacreontics; Or, Some Copies of Verses Translated Periphrastically out of Anacreon*[6]

I. *Love*

I'll sing of heroes and of kings;
In mighty numbers,[7] mighty things;
Begin, my Muse; but lo, the strings
To my great song rebellious prove;
The strings will sound of nought but love. 5
I broke them all, and put on new;
'Tis this or nothing sure will do.
"These sure," said I, "will me obey,
These sure heroic notes will play."
Straight I began with thund'ring Jove 10
And all th'immortal pow'rs but Love.
Love smiled, and from my enfeebled lyre
Came gentle airs, such as inspire
Melting love, soft desire.
Farewell, then, heroes, farewell kings, 15
And mighty numbers, mighty things;
Love tunes my heart just[8] to my strings.

II. *Drinking*

The thirsty earth soaks up the rain,
And drinks, and gapes for drink again.
The plants suck in the earth, and are
With constant drinking fresh and fair.
The sea itself, which one would think 5
Should have but little need of drink,
Drinks ten thousand rivers up,
So filled that they o'erflow the cup.
The busy sun (and one would guess
By's drunken, fiery face no less) 10
Drinks up the sea, and when he's done,
The moon and stars drink up the sun.
They drink and dance by their own light,
They drink and revel all the night.
Nothing in nature's sober found, 15

6. Cowley translated and grouped together eleven poems attributed to the
Greek lyric poet Anacreon of Teos (born
c. 550 B.C.).
7. Verses.
8. Precisely.

But an eternal health goes round.
Fill up the bowl then, fill it high,
Fill all the glasses there, for why
Should every creature drink but I,
Why, man of morals, tell me why?   20

VIII. *The Epicure*

Fill the bowl with rosy wine,
Around our temples roses twine,
And let us cheerfully awhile
Like the wine and roses smile.
Crowned with roses, we contemn   5
Gyges'[9] wealthy diadem.
Today is ours; what do we fear?
Today is ours; we have it here.
Let's treat it kindly, that it may
Wish, at least, with us to stay.   10
Let's banish business, banish sorrow;
To the gods belongs tomorrow.

X. *The Grasshopper*[1]

Happy insect, what can be
In happiness compared to thee?
Fed with nourishment divine,
The dewy morning's gentle wine!
Nature waits upon thee still,   5
And thy verdant cup does fill;
'Tis filled wherever thou dost tread,
Nature self's thy Ganymede.[2]
Thou dost drink and dance and sing,
Happier than the happiest king!   10
All the fields which thou dost see,
All the plants belong to thee,
All that summer hours produce,
Fertile made with early juice.
Man for thee does sow and plow,   15
Farmer he, and landlord thou!
Thou dost innocently joy,
Nor does thy luxury destroy;
The shepherd gladly heareth thee,
More harmonious than he.   20
Thee country hinds with gladness hear,
Prophet of the ripened year!
Thee Phoebus loves, and does inspire;

9. The wealth of the Lydian King Gyges, who reigned in the seventh century B.C., inspired the proverbial expression, "the riches of Gyges."

1. Cf. the poem by Lovelace (p. 310), who also looks to Anacreon's original.
2. I.e., Nature herself is thy Ganymede (Jove's cupbearer).

Phoebus is himself thy sire.
To thee of all things upon earth,   25
Life is no longer than thy mirth.
Happy insect, happy thou,
Dost neither age nor winter know.
But when thou'st drunk, and danced, and sung
Thy fill, the flow'ry leaves among   30
(Voluptuous, and wise withal,
Epicurean[3] animal!),
Sated with thy summer feast,
Thou retir'st to endless rest.

From *The Mistress*

The Spring[4]

Though you be absent here, I needs must say
The trees as beauteous are, and flowers as gay
    As ever they were wont to be;
    Nay, the birds' rural music too
    Is as melodious and free   5
    As if they sung to pleasure you:
I saw a rosebud ope this morn; I'll swear
The blushing morning opened not more fair.

How could it be so fair, and you away?
How could the trees be beauteous, flowers so gay?   10
    Could they remember but last year,
    How you did them, they you delight,
    The sprouting leaves which saw you here
    And called their fellows to the sight,
Would, looking round for the same sight in vain,   15
Creep back into their silent barks again.

Where'er you walked, trees were as reverent made
As when of old gods dwelt in every shade;
    Is't possible they should not know
    What loss of honor they sustain,   20
    That thus they smile and flourish now,
    And still their former pride retain?
Dull creatures! 'tis not without cause that she
Who fled the god of wit was made a tree.[5]

In ancient times sure they much wiser were,   25
When they rejoiced the Thracian verse to hear;

---

3. The Greek philosopher Epicurus (342–270 B.C.) in fact taught his followers to seek not merely sensual gratification but (and chiefly) that peace of mind that is the consequence of a virtuous life.

4. This poem may profitably be compared wih Carew's "The Spring," p. 157.
5. Cowley alludes to Daphne, who was pursued by Apollo, the god of poetry. She was transformed into a laurel.

In vain did nature bid them stay,
When Orpheus[6] had his song begun;
They called their wond'ring roots away
And bade them silent to him run.   30
How would those learned trees have followed you?
You would have drawn them, and their poet too.

But who can blame them now? for, since you're gone,
They're here the only fair, and shine alone.
    You did their natural rights invade;   35
    Wherever you did walk or sit,
    The thickest boughs could make no shade,
    Although the sun had granted it;
The fairest flowers could please no more, near you,
Than painted flowers set next to them could do.   40

Whene'er then you come hither, that shall be
The time, which this to others is, to me.
    The little joys which here are now,
    The name of punishments do bear,
    When by their sight they let us know   45
    How we deprived of greater are.
'Tis you the best of seasons with you bring;
This is for beasts, and that for men, the spring.

Platonic Love[7]

    Indeed I must confess,
    When souls mix 'tis an happiness;
But not complete till bodies too combine,
And closely as our minds together join.
But half of heaven the souls in glory taste,   5
    Till by love in heaven at last
        Their bodies too are placed.

    In thy immortal part
    Man, as well as I, thou art.
But something 'tis that differs thee and me,   10
And we must one even in that difference be.
I thee, both as a man and woman prize;
    For a perfect love implies
        Love in all capacities.·

    Can that for true love pass   15
    When a fair woman courts her glass?
Something unlike must in love's likeness be,
His wonder is one and variety.

6. Cf. Jonson, *The Forest*, XII, p. 38, l. 77 and note.   7. Cf. Randolph, "An Elegy," p. 211 and first note.

For he, whose soul nought but a soul can move,
  Does a new Narcissus[8] prove,   20
    And his own image love.

That souls do beauty know,
  'Tis to the body's help they owe;
If when they know't they straight abuse that trust,
And shut the body from't, 'tis as unjust   25
As if I brought my dearest friend to see
  My mistress, and at th' instant he
    Should steal her quite from me.

Against Fruition[9]

No; thou'rt a fool, I'll swear, if e'er thou grant;
Much of my veneration thou must want,[1]
When once thy kindness puts my ignorance out,
For a learn'd age is always least devout.
Keep still thy distance; for at once to me   5
Goddess and woman too thou canst not be;
Thou'rt queen of all that sees thee, and as such
Must neither tyrannize nor yield too much;
Such freedom give as may admit command,
But keep the forts and magazines in thine hand.   10
Thou'rt yet a whole world to me, and dost fill
My large ambition; but 'tis dang'rous still,
Lest I like the Pellaean prince[2] should be,
And weep for other worlds, having conquered thee.
When Love has taken all thou hast away,   15
His strength by too much riches will decay.
Thou in my fancy dost much higher stand
Than women can be placed by Nature's hand;
And I must needs, I'm sure, a loser be,
To change thee, as thou'rt there, for very thee.   20
Thy sweetness is so much within me placed,
That shouldst thou nectar give, 'twould spoil the taste.
Beauty at first moves wonder and delight;
'Tis Nature's juggling trick to cheat the sight;
We admire it, whilst unknown, but after more   25
Admire ourselves for liking it before.
Love, like a greedy hawk, if we give way,
Does overgorge himself with his own prey;
Of very[3] hopes a surfeit he'll sustain
Unless by fears he cast them up again: 30
His spirit and sweetness dangers keep alone;
If once he lose his sting, he grows a drone.

---

8. Cf. Ovid, *Metamorphoses*, III. 341–510.
9. Cf. the two poems by Sir John Suckling on this theme (pp. 260, 265).

1. Lack.
2. I.e., Alexander the Great, born at Pella, in Macedonia.
3. Absolute.

From *Pindaric Odes*[4]

To Mr. Hobbes[5]

Vast bodies of philosophy
  I oft have seen, and read,
  But all are bodies dead;
  Or bodies by art fashionéd;
I never yet the living soul could see,   5
    But in thy books and thee.
  'Tis only God can know
Whether the fair idea thou dost show
Agree entirely with his own or no.
      This I dare boldly tell,   10
'Tis so like truth 'twill serve our turn as well.
Just,[6] as in nature, thy proportions be,
As full of concord their variety,
As firm the parts upon their center rest,
And all so solid are that they at least   15
As much as nature emptiness detest.

Long did the mighty Stagirite[7] retain
The universal intellectual reign,
Saw his own country's short-lived leopard slain;[8]
The stronger Roman eagle did outfly,[9]   20
Oft'ner renewed his age, and saw that die.
Mecca itself, in spite of Mahomet possessed,[1]
And chased by a wild deluge from the East,
His monarchy new planted in the West.
But as in time each great imperial race   25
Degenerates, and gives some new one place,
    So did this noble empire waste,
    Sunk by degrees from glories past,

4. Cowley gives some account of his purposes in undertaking to render the Pindaric mode in English verse in his Preface to *Pindaric Odes*, first published in 1656. Cf. also H. D. Goldstein, *"Anglorum Pindarus:* Model and Milieu," *CL,* XVII (1965), 299–310.

5. The philosopher Thomas Hobbes (1588–1679), known primarily for his treatise of political philosophy, *Leviathan* (1651), published a number of other important works in the fields of history, law, and science, not to mention his translations of Thucydides (1629) and Homer (1673–1676). For an intriguing account of Hobbes's character and career, cf. John Aubrey, *Brief Lives, ed. cit.,* pp. 237–262.

6. Precise, exact.

7. I.e., Aristotle.

8. "Outlasted the Grecian Empire, which in the Visions of Daniel is represented by a Leopard, with four wings upon the back, and four heads, vii.6" (Cowley's note).

9. "Was received even beyond the bounds of the Roman Empire, and outlived it" (Cowley's note).

1. "For Aristotle's philosophy was in great esteem among the Arabians or Saracens, witness those many excellent books upon him, or according to his principles, written by Averroes, Avicenna, Avempace, and divers others. *In spite of Mahomet,* because his law, being adapted to the barbarous humour of those people he had first to deal with, and aiming only at greatness of empire by the sword, forbids all the studies of learning; which (nevertheless) flourished admirably under the Saracen monarchy, and continued so, till it was extinguished with that empire, by the inundation of the Turks, and other nations" (Cowley's note).

And in the schoolmen's hands[2] it perished quite at last.
      Then nought but words it grew,   30
      And those all barb'rous too.
   It perished, and it vanished there,
The life and soul breathed out, became but empty air.

The fields which answered well the ancients' plow,
Spent and outworn return no harvest now,   35
In barren age wild and unglorious lie,
      And boast of past fertility,
The poor relief of present poverty.
      Food and fruit we now must want
      Unless new lands we plant.   40
We break up tombs with sacrilegious hands;
      Old rubbish we remove;
To walk in ruins, like vain ghosts, we love,
      And with fond[3] divining wands
      We search among the dead   45
      For treasures buriéd,
   Whilst still the liberal earth does hold
So many virgin mines of undiscovered gold.

The Baltic, Euxin,[4] and the Caspian,
And slender-limbed Mediterranean,   50
Seem narrow creeks to thee, and only fit
For the poor wretched fisher-boats of wit.
Thy nobler vessel the vast ocean tries,
      And nothing sees but seas and skies,
      Till unknown regions it descries,   55
Thou great Columbus of the golden lands of new
      philosophies.
      Thy task was harder much than his,
      For thy learned America is
   Not only found out first by thee,
And rudely left to future industry,   60
      But thy eloquence and thy wit
Has planted, peopled, built, and civilized it.

      I little thought before
      (Nor being my own self so poor,
      Could comprehend so vast a store),   65
   That all the wardrobe of rich eloquence
      Could have afforded half enough
      Of bright, of new, and lasting stuff
To clothe the mighty limbs of thy gigantic sense;
Thy solid reason, like the shield from heaven   70
      To the Trojan hero given,[5]

---

2. I.e., in the hands of medieval scholasticism.
3. Foolish, futile.
4. The Black Sea.

5. At the request of Venus, Vulcan forged a magnificently engraved shield for her son Aeneas; cf. *Aeneid*, VIII, 600–731.

Too strong to take a mark from any mortal dart,
Yet shines with gold and gems in every part,
And wonders on it graved by the learn'd hand of art;
    A shield that gives delight   75
    Even to the enemies' sight,
Then when they're sure to lose the combat by 't.

Nor can the snow which now cold age does shed
    Upon thy reverend head
Quench or allay the noble fires within,   80
    But all which thou hast been,
    And all that youth can be, thou'rt yet,
    So fully still dost thou
Enjoy the manhood, and the bloom of wit,
And all the natural heat, but not the fever too.   85
So contraries on Etna's top conspire,
Here hoary frosts, and by them[6] breaks out fire.
A secure peace the faithful neighbors keep,
Th' emboldened snow next to the flame does sleep.
    And if we weigh, like thee,   90
    Nature and causes, we shall see
    That thus it needs must be,
To things immortal time can do no wrong,
And that which never is to die, forever must be young.

From *Verses Written On Several Occasions*

To The Royal Society[7]

Philosophy, the great and only heir
    Of all that human knowledge which has been
Unforfeited by man's rebellious sin,
    Though full of years he do appear,
(Philosophy, I say, and call it *he*,   5
For whatsoe'er the painter's fancy be,
    It a male virtue seems to me),
Has still been kept in nonage[8] till of late,
Nor managed or enjoyed his vast estate:
Three or four thousand years, one would have thought,   10
To ripeness and perfection might have brought
    A science so well bred and nursed,

6. I.e., near them. Cowley gives Claudian, *De Raptu Proserpine,* as his source for this "description of fire and snow upon Etna (but not the application of it)."
7. The Royal Society received its official charter from Charles II in 1662; its activities had really begun some seventeen years before, with the meetings at Gresham College, in London, of a group of scholars interested primarily in "experimental philosophy" (i.e., science). The range and character of the future Society's interests were rather more broadly defined in the decade from 1648, when activities were carried on chiefly at Oxford; but the Baconian ideal of co-operative research continued to inform the work of these scientists, historians, and men of letters. Bishop Thomas Sprat (1635–1713) published *The History of the Royal Society* in 1667; Cowley's ode, composed for the occasion, was included in that volume.
8. I.e., treated as a legal minor (cf. l. 34).

And of such hopeful parts, too, at the first.
But, oh, the guardians and the tutors then
(Some negligent, and some ambitious men)   15
    Would ne'er consent to set him free,
Or his own natural powers to let him see,
Lest that should put an end to their authority.

That his own business he might quite forget,
They amused him with the sports of wanton wit;   20
With the desserts of poetry they fed him,
Instead of solid meats t' increase his force;
Instead of vigorous exercise, they led him
Into the pleasant labyrinths of ever fresh discourse;[9]
    Instead of carrying him to see   25
The riches which do hoarded for him lie
    In nature's endless treasury,
    They chose his eye to entertain
    (His curious but not covetous eye)
With painted scenes, and pageants of the brain.   30
Some few exalted spirits this latter age has shown,
That labored to assert the liberty
(From guardians who were now usurpers grown)
Of this old minor still, captived philosophy;
    But 'twas rebellion called to fight   35
    For such a long-oppresséd right.
Bacon[1] at last, a mighty man, arose,
    Whom a wise King, and nature, chose
    Lord Chancellor of both their laws,
And boldly undertook the injured pupil's cause.   40

Authority, which did a body boast,
Though 'twas but air condensed, and stalked about
Like some old giant's more gigantic ghost,
    To terrify the learned rout
With the plain magic of true reason's light,   45
    He chased out of our sight,
Nor suffered living men to be misled
    By the vain shadows of the dead:
To graves, from whence it rose, the conquered phantom
    fled.
    He broke that monstrous god which stood   50
In midst of th' orchard, and the whole did claim,
    Which, with an useless scythe of wood,

9. Cowley perhaps recalls the description of Gargantua's early education (directed by pedants), in Book I of *Gargantua and Pantagruel*, by the French humanist François Rabelais (c. 1494–1553).
1. Francis Bacon (1561–1626), first Baron Verulam and Viscount Saint Albans, appointed Attorney General in 1613, became Lord Chancellor in 1618; three years later, convicted of bribery and embezzlement (cf. ll. 105–106), his political career collapsed in ruins. He devoted his remaining years primarily to philosophical works intended to make part of his (never completed) large system of experimental philosophy.

And something else[2] not worth a name
(Both vast for show, yet neither fit
Or to defend, or to beget: 55
Ridiculous and senseless terrors!) made
Children and superstitious men afraid.
    The orchard's open now, and free;
Bacon has broke that scarecrow deity:
    Come, enter, all that will,   60
Behold the ripened fruit, come gather now your fill.
    Yet still, methinks, we fain would be
    Catching at the forbidden tree;
    We would be like the Deity,
When truth and falsehood, good and evil, we   65
Without the senses' aid within ourselves would see;
    For 'tis God only who can find
    All nature in His mind.

From words, which are but pictures of the thought
(Though we our thoughts from them perversely drew),   70
To things, the mind's right object, he it brought;
Like foolish birds to painted grapes we flew;[3]
He sought and gathered for our use the true;
And when on heaps the chosen bunches lay,
He pressed them wisely the mechanic way,[4]   75
Till all their juice did in one vessel join,
Ferment into a nourishment divine,
    The thirsty soul's refreshing wine.
Who to the life an exact piece would make,
Must not from other's work a copy take;   80
    No, not from Rubens or Van Dyck;[5]
Much less content himself to make it like
Th' ideas and the images which lie
In his own fancy, or his memory.
    No, he before his sight must place   85
    The natural and living face;
    The real object must command
Each judgment of his eye, and motion of his hand.

From these and all long errors of the way
In which our wandering predecessors went,   90
And like th' old Hebrews many years did stray
    In deserts but of small extent,
Bacon, like Moses, led us forth at last;
    The barren wilderness he passed,

2. I.e., a phallus (cf. 1. 55).
3. Cf. "Ode. Of Wit," p. 329, 1. 12 and note.
4. I.e., employing a machine.
5. Portraits painted by the Flemish artists Peter Paul Rubens (1577–1640) and Sir Anthony Vandyck (1599–1641) were extravagantly admired in Cowley's time; Vandyck painted many portraits of Charles I and various members of the royal household.

Did on the very border stand 95
Of the blest promised land,
And from the mountain's top of his exalted wit,
    Saw it himself, and showed us it.
But life did never to one man allow
Time to discover worlds, and conquer too; 100
Nor can so short a line sufficient be
To fathom the vast depths of nature's sea.
    The work he did we ought t'admire,
And were unjust if we should more require
From his few years, divided 'twixt th' excess 105
Of low affliction and high happiness.
For who on things remote can fix his sight,
That's always in a triumph or a fight?

From you, great champions, we expect to get
These spacious countries but discovered yet; 110
Countries where yet instead of nature we
Her images and idols worshipped see.
These large and wealthy regions to subdue,
Though learning has whole armies at command,
    Quartered about in every land, 115
A better troop she ne'er together drew.
    Methinks, like Gideon's little band,[6]
    God with design has picked out you,
To do those noble wonders by a few:
When the whole host He saw, "They are," said He, 120
"Too many to o'ercome for Me."
    And now He chooses out His men,
    Much in the way that He did then;
    Not those many whom He found
    Idly extended on the ground, 125
    To drink with their dejected head
The stream just so as by their mouths it fled;
    No, but those few who took the waters up,
And made of their laborious hands the cup.

Thus you prepared; and in the glorious fight 130
    Their wondrous pattern, too, you take:
Their old and empty pitchers first they brake,
And with their hands then lifted up the light.
    Io![7] sound too the trumpets here!
Already your victorious lights appear; 135
New scenes of heaven already we espy,
And crowds of golden worlds on high,
Which, from the spacious plains of earth and sea,
    Could never yet discovered be
By sailor's or Chaldaean's[8] watchful eye.

---

6. Cf. Judges 7:4–8.
7. "Io!" in classical literature is a cry
of joy and exultation.

8. The Chaldeans (intellectually a dominant force in ancient Babylonia) were
famous for their study of astrology.

Nature's great works no distance can obscure;
No smallness her near objects can secure;
   You've taught the curious sight to press
   Into the privatest recess
Of her imperceptible littleness.   145
   You've learned to read her smallest hand,[9]
And well begun her deepest sense to understand.

Mischief and true dishonor fall on those
Who would to laughter or to scorn expose
So virtuous and so noble a design,   150
So human for its use, for knowledge so divine.
The things which these proud men despise, and call
   Impertinent, and vain, and small,
Those smallest things of nature let me know,
Rather than all their greatest actions do.   155
Whoever would deposéd truth advance
   Into the throne usurped from it,
Must feel at first the blows of ignorance,
   And the sharp points of envious wit.
So when, by various turns of the celestial dance,   160
   In many thousand years
   A star, so long unknown, appears,
Though heaven itself more beauteous by it grow,
   It troubles and alarms the world below,
Does to the wise a star, to fools a meteor show.   165

With courage and success, you the bold work begin;
   Your cradle has not idle been:
None e'er but Hercules[1] and you could be
At five years' age worthy a history.
   And ne'er did fortune better yet   170
   Th' historian[2] to the story fit:
   As you from all old errors free
And purge the body of philosophy,
   So from all modern follies he
Has vindicated eloquence and wit.   175
His candid[3] style like a clean stream does slide,
   And his bright fancy all the way
   Does like the sunshine in it play;
It does like Thames, the best of rivers, glide,
Where the god does not rudely overturn,   180
   But gently pour the crystal urn,
And with judicious hand does the whole current guide.
'T has all the beauties nature can impart,
And all the comely dress without the paint of art.

---

9. I.e., her handwriting; Cowley alludes to the microscope.
1. When he was eight months old, Hercules strangled two serpents (sent by the goddess Hera) in his cradle; cf. Apollodorus, *Library*, II. iv. 8.
2. I.e., Bishop Sprat; cf. first note, above.
3. Pure, clear.

Henry Vaughan

1621 or 1622	Born (the twin of Thomas Vaughan) in Newton, in the parish of Llansantfraed, Breconshire, Wales. Initially educated by a local clergyman.
1638–1640	Probably at Jesus College, Oxford, where Thomas Vaughan matriculates in December, 1638. Does not take a degree.
1640–1642	Studying law in London.
1642–1646	Law clerk to Sir Marmaduke Lloyd, Chief Justice of the Brecon circuit court. Probably serving with royalist forces, 1645–1646.
1646	Marries Catherine Wise; settles at Newton. Publication of *Poems, With the Tenth Satire of Juvenal Englished*.
1647	Writes dedicatory epistle later published with *Olor Iscanus*.
1650	First edition of *Silex Scintillans* published.
1651	Publication of *Olor Iscanus*. Practicing medicine from about this time.
1652	Publication of *The Mount of Olives: Or, Solitary Devotions*.
1654	Publication of *Flores Solitudinis* (including three prose translations, *Of Temperance and Patience, Of Life and Death*, and *The World Contemned*, and a life of Saint Paulinus of Nola). Wife dies about this time.
1655	Marries his wife's sister, Elizabeth Wise. Second (augmented) edition of *Silex Scintillans* published. Translates Henry Nollius's *Hermetical Physick*, a treatise dealing with the medical aspects of Hermetic doctrine.
1657	Translates Nollius's *The Chymists Key*, published by "Eugenius Philalethes" (Thomas Vaughan).
1666	Death of Thomas Vaughan.
1678	*Thalia Rediviva* published.
1695	Death, April 23. Buried in Llansantfraed churchyard.

From *POEMS, WITH THE TENTH SATIRE OF JUVENAL ENGLISHED*[1] (1646)

To My Ingenuous Friend, R. W.[2]

When we are dead, and now no more
Our harmless mirth, our wit, and score[3]
Distracts the town; when all is spent
That the base niggard world hath lent
Thy purse or mine; when the loathed noise   5
Of drawers, 'prentices, and boys
Hath left us, and the clam'rous bar
Items no pints i' th' Moon or Star;[4]
When no calm whisp'rers wait the doors
To fright us with forgotten scores,   10
And such aged, long bills[5] carry
As might start an antiquary;
When the sad tumults of the Maze,[6]
Arrests, suits, and the dreadful face
Of sergeants[7] are not seen, and we   15
No lawyers' ruffs or gowns must see;
When all these mulcts[8] are paid, and I
From thee, dear wit, must part, and die:
We'll beg the world would be so kind
To give's one grave, as we'd one mind;   20
There (as the wiser few suspect
That spirits after death affect)
Our souls shall meet, and thence will they,
Freed from the tyranny of clay,
With equal wings and ancient love   25
Into the Elysian fields[9] remove,
Where in those blessed walks they'll find
More of thy genius, and my mind.
    First, in the shade of his own bays,[1]

1. Vaughan takes his place in literary history among the "metaphysical" poets, as the meditative and Neoplatonic heir of George Herbert; anthologists as a rule draw selections of his verse primarily from *Silex Scintillans*, where Vaughan's particular genius is fully displayed. The *Poems* of 1646 and *Olor Iscanus* (1651), however, each very considerably given over to translations from Latin poetry, hint at the poetical direction in which Vaughan will move. More to the point in the context of this edition, they indicate the poet's early affinities with at least some aspects of the Cavalier temperament: the claims and rewards of friendship, the social function of gracefully figured compliment, the decorous and tender response to the death of a child. Some incisive observations on these early poems will be found in Earl Miner, *op. cit.*, pp. 179–180, 254–255.
2. The identity of "R. W." has not been definitively established. "Ingenuous," in this context, has the force of "honorable and open."
3. Tally of debts.
4. These names presumably refer to taverns or to rooms in taverns.
5. I.e., lists of debts extending over a long period of time.
6. The Maze was a building adjacent to an alehouse on the south bank of the Thames, in a raffish quarter of London.
7. Attorneys.
8. Fines.
9. Cf. Carew, "A Rapture," p. 166, l. 2 and note.
1. Laurels.

Great Ben they'll see, whose sacred lays   30
The learned ghosts admire, and throng
To catch the subject of his song.
Then Randolph, in those holy meads,
His *Lovers*, and *Amyntas* reads,[2]
Whilst his nightingale close by   35
Sings his and her own elegy.
From thence dismissed by subtle roads,
Through airy paths and sad abodes,
They'll come into the drowsy fields
Of Lethe,[3] which such virtue yields   40
That (if what poets sing be true)
The streams all sorrow can subdue.
Here on a silent, shady green,
The souls of lovers oft are seen,
Who in their lives' unhappy space   45
Were murdered by some perjured face.
All these th'enchanted streams frequent,
To drown their cares and discontent,
That th'inconstant, cruel sex
Might not in death their spirits vex.   50
    And here our souls, big with delight
Of their new state, will cease their flight;
And now the last thoughts will appear
They'll have of us, or any here;
But on those flow'ry banks will stay,   55
And drink all sense and cares away.
    So they that did of these discuss
Shall find their fables true in us.

To Amoret, *Walking in a Starry Evening*

If, Amoret, that glorious eye,
    In the first birth of light,
      And death of night,
Had, with those elder fires you spy
    Scattered so high,   5
      Receivéd form and sight,

We might suspect in the vast ring,
    Amidst these golden glories
      And fiery stories,[4]
Whether the sun had been the king   10
    And guide of day,
      Or your brighter eye should sway.

---

2. Randolph's comedy, *The Jealous Lovers*, was presented at Oxford in 1631; his pastoral *Amyntas* (published 1638) was acted at Whitehall in 1632–1633. The allusion in line 35 is to his poem, "On the Death of a Nightingale" (q.v., p. 216).

3. Lethe was the river of forgetfulness in the classical underworld.

4. Tiers.

But, Amoret, such is my fate,
  That if thy face a star
    Had shined from far,   15
I am persuaded in that state
    'Twixt thee and me,
  Of some predestined sympathy.

For sure such two conspiring minds,
  Which no accident or sight   20
    Did thus unite,
Whom no distance can confine,
    Start, or decline,⁵
  One for another were designed.

To Amoret Gone From Him

Fancy and I last evening walked,
And, Amoret, of thee we talked;
The west just then had stol'n the sun,
And his last blushes were begun.
We sat, and marked how everything   5
Did mourn his absence: how the spring
That smiled, and curled about his beams,
Whilst he was here, now checked her streams;
The wanton eddies of her face
Were taught less noise, and smoother grace,   10
And in a slow, sad channel went,
Whisp'ring the banks their discontent;
The careless ranks of flowers that spread
Their perfumed bosoms to his head,
And with an open, free embrace   15
Did entertain his beamy face,
Like absent friends point to the west,
And on that weak reflection feast.
If creatures, then, that have no sense
But the loose tie of influence,   20
Though fate and time each day remove
Those things that element their love,
At such vast distance can agree,
    Why, Amoret, why should not we?

A Rhapsody.

*Occasionally written upon a meeting with some of his friends
at the Globe Tavern⁶ in a chamber painted overhead with a
cloudy sky and some few dispersed stars, and on the sides
with landscapes, hills, shepherds, and sheep.*

Darkness and stars i' th' midday! They invite
Our active fancies to believe it night;

5. I.e., disturb, or weaken.
6. The tavern in question is thought to be the Globe in Fleet Street, not that in Southwark.

For taverns need no sun, but for a sign
Where rich tobacco and quick tapers shine,
And royal, witty sack, the poet's soul,   5
With brighter suns than he doth gild the bowl,
As though the pot and poet did agree
Sack should to both illuminator be.
That artificial cloud with its curled brow
Tells us 'tis late, and that blue space below   10
Is filled with many stars; mark, how they break
In silent glances o'er the hills, and speak
The evening to the plains, where, shot from far,
They meet in dumb salutes, as one great star.
  The room, methinks, grows darker, and the air   15
Contracts a sadder[7] color, and less fair;
Or is 't the drawer's skill, hath he no arts
To blind us so, we can't know pints from quarts?
No, no, 'tis night: look where the jolly clown[8]
Musters his bleating herd and quits the down.   20
Hark! how his rude pipe frets the quiet air,
While every hill proclaims Lycoris fair.
Rich, happy man! that canst thus watch, and sleep,
Free from all cares but thy wench, pipe, and sheep.
  But see, the moon is up: view where she stands   25
Sentinel o'er the door, drawn by the hands
Of some base painter, that for gain hath made
Her face the landmark to the tippling trade.
This cup to her, that to Endymion[9] give;
'Twas wit at first, and wine that made them live.   30
Choke may the painter! and his box disclose
No other colors than his fiery nose,
And may we no more of his pencil see
Than two churchwardens,[1] and mortality.
  Should we go now a-wand'ring, we should meet   35
With catchpoles,[2] whores, and carts in every street;
Now when each narrow lane, each nook and cave,
Signposts and shop-doors pimp for every knave,
When riotous, sinful plush and tell-tale spurs
Walk Fleet Street and the Strand, when the soft stirs   40
Of bawdy ruffled silks turn night to day,
And the loud whip, and coach scolds all the way;
When lust of all sorts, and each itchy blood,
From the Tower wharf to Cymbeline and Lud,[3]
Hunts for a mate, and the 'tired footman reels   45

---

7. More gloomy.
8. Rustic.
9. The shepherd Endymion's beauty was such that, as he slept beside his flocks on Mount Latmos, Selene (the moon) came down from the heavens to kiss him; cf. Apollodorus, *Library*, I. vii. 5.

1. Honorary parish officials.
2. Sheriff's officers.
3. I.e., from Tower Wharf, at the south-eastern corner of London, to Ludgate (in the western wall of the city), where statues of the legendary British Kings Lud and Cymbeline were set up.

'Twixt chair-men,[4] torches, and the hackney wheels.
    Come, take the other dish; it is to him[5]
That made his horse a Senator. Each brim
Look big as mine; the gallant, jolly beast
Of all the herd (you'll say) was not the least.   50
    Now crown the second bowl, rich as his worth
I'll drink it to: he[6] that like fire broke forth
Into the Senate's face, crossed Rubicon,
And the state's pillars with their laws thereon,
And made the dull graybeards and furred gowns fly   55
Into Brundisium to consult and lie.
    This to brave Sulla![7] Why should it be said
We drink more to the living than the dead?
Flatt'rers and fools do use it; let us laugh
At our own honest mirth, for they that quaff   60
To honor others do like those that sent
Their gold and plate to strangers to be spent.
    Drink deep! This cup be pregnant, and the wine
Spirit of wit, to make us all divine,
That, big with sack and mirth, we may retire   65
Possessors of more souls and nobler fire;
And, by the influx[8] of this painted sky
And labored forms, to higher matters fly;
So, if a nap shall take us, we shall all
    After full cups have dreams poetical.   70

Let's laugh now, and the pressed grape drink
    Till the drowsy day-star wink;
And in our merry, mad mirth run
Faster and further than the sun;
And let none his cup forsake   75
Till that star again doth wake:
So we men below shall move
    Equally with the gods above.

To Amoret, of the Difference 'Twixt Him and Other Lovers, and What True Love Is

Mark, when the evening's cooler wings
    Fan the afflicted[9] air, how the faint sun,
        Leaving undone
        What he begun,

---

4. I.e., footmen carrying sedan chairs.
5. I.e., the Roman Emperor Gaius Caligula; cf. Suetonius, *The Twelve Caesars*, "Gaius Caligula," lv.
6. I.e., Julius Caesar. When, in 49 B.C., Caesar led his army across the Rubicon and marched on Rome, Pompey and the Senate fled to Brundisium (Brindisi) in southern Italy.
7. Vaughan probably alludes to Lucius Cornelius Sulla (138–78 B.C.), Roman dictator in the period 82–79 B.C.
8. Influence.
9. I.e. (probably), changed, darkened.

Those spurious flames sucked up from slime and earth[1]   5
      To their first, low birth,
      Resigns, and brings.

They shoot their tinsel beams, and vanities,
    Threading with those false fires their way;
        But as you stay   10
        And see them stray,
You lose the flaming track, and subtly they
      Languish away,
      And cheat your eyes.

Just so,[2] base sublunary lovers' hearts,   15
    Fed on loose, profane desires,
        May for an eye
        Or face comply;
But those removed, they will as soon depart,
      And show their art,   20
      And painted fires.

Whilst I by pow'rful love, so much refined,
    That my absent soul the same is,
        Careless to miss
        A glance or kiss,   25
Can with those elements of lust and sense
      Freely dispense,
      And court the mind.

Thus to the north the lodestones move,
    And thus to them th'enamored steel aspires;   30
        Thus, Amoret,
        I do affect;[3]
And thus, by wingéd beams and mutual fire,
      Spirits and stars conspire;
      And this is love.   35

Upon the Priory Grove,[4] His Usual Retirement

Hail, sacred shades! cool, leafy house!
Chaste treasurer of all my vows
And wealth! on whose soft bosom laid
My love's fair steps I first betrayed.
      Henceforth no melancholy flight,   5
No sad wing, or hoarse bird of night

1. I.e. (probably), the glimmerings of the will-o'-the-wisp. Cf. *Works of Henry Vaughan*, ed. L. C. Martin, 2nd ed. (Oxford, 1957), p. 701.
2. I.e., in the manner of those spurious flames. This and the following stanza clearly recall Donne's "Valediction For-bidding Mourning."
3. I.e., I (also) am moved.
4. Brecon Priory, in Brecknock, Wales, was the home of Colonel Herbert Price, a friend of the family of Catherine Wise, Vaughan's first wife.

Disturb this air, no fatal throat
Of raven, or owl, awake the note
Of our laid echo, no voice dwell
Within these leaves but Philomel.[5]   10
The poisonous ivy here no more
His false twists on the oak shall score,
Only the woodbine here may twine
As th'emblem of her love, and mine;
The amorous sun shall here convey   15
His best beams, in thy shades to play;
The active air, the gentlest show'rs,
Shall from his wings rain on thy flow'rs,
And the moon from her dewy locks
Shall deck thee with her brightest drops;   20
Whatever can a fancy move,
Or feed the eye, be on this grove.
        And when at last the winds and tears
Of heaven, with the consuming years,
Shall these green curls bring to decay,   25
And clothe thee in an aged gray
(If ought a lover can foresee,
Or if we poets prophets be),
From hence transplanted, thou shalt stand
A fresh grove in th'Elysian land,   30
Where (most blest pair!), as here on earth
Thou first didst eye our growth, and birth,
So there again thou'lt see us move
In our first innocence and love;
And in thy shades, as now, so then,   35
We'll kiss, and smile, and walk again.

From *OLOR ISCANUS*[6] (1651)

An Epitaph Upon the Lady Elizabeth,[7]
Second Daughter to His Late Majesty

Youth, beauty, virtue, innocence,
Heav'n's royal and select expense,
With virgin-tears, and sighs divine,
Sit here, the Genii[8] of this shrine,
Where now (thy fair soul winged away)   5
They guard the casket where she lay.
        Thou hadst, ere thou the light couldst see,
Sorrows laid up and stored for thee;

---

5. I.e., the nightingale. Cf. Shirley, "Cupid's Call," p. 187, l. 14 and note.
6. "The swan of Usk"; the river Usk flows through Brecknock.

7. Elizabeth, second daughter of Charles I, died on September 8, 1650, in her fifteenth year.
8. I.e., the guardian spirits.

Thou suck'dst in woes, and the breasts lent
Their milk to thee but to lament;   10
Thy portion here was grief; thy years
Distilled no other rain but tears,
Tears without noise, but, understood,
As loud and shrill as any blood;[9]
Thou seem'st a rosebud born in snow,   15
A flower of purpose sprung to bow
To headless tempests, and the rage
Of an incenséd, stormy age.
Others, ere their afflictions grow,
Are timed and seasoned for the blow,   20
But thine, as rheums the tend'rest part,[1]
Fell on a young and harmless heart.
And yet as balm-trees[2] gently spend
Their tears for those that do them rend,
So mild and pious thou wert seen,   25
Though full of suff'rings, free from spleen,
Thou didst not murmur nor revile,
But drank'st thy wormwood with a smile.
        As envious eyes blast, and infect,
And cause misfortunes by aspect,   30
So thy sad stars dispensed to thee
No influx but calamity;
They viewed thee with eclipséd rays,
And but the back-side[3] of bright days.

These were the comforts she had here,   35
As by an unseen hand, 'tis clear,
Which now she reads, and smiling wears
A crown with Him who wipes off tears.[4]

---

9. French Fogle notes that in Genesis
4:10, Abel's blood is said to cry from the
ground (*Complete Poetry of Henry
Vaughan,* ed. F. Fogle [New York, 1964],
p. 88).
1. Cf. George Herbert, "Outlandish Proverbs," no. 475: "Wealth is like rheum,
it falls on the weakest parts."

2. I.e., as trees yielding balsam.
3. I.e., the dark side. Following line 34,
some lines are omitted in the 1651 edition.
4. Cf. Revelation 7:13–17, concluding,
"and God shall wipe away all tears from
their eyes."

Thomas Stanley

1625	Born at Cumberlow, Hertfordshire; baptized, September 8. The only son of Sir Thomas Stanley and his wife Mary, a cousin to Richard Lovelace. Initially educated by the classical scholar William Fairfax, son of Edward Fairfax, the translator of Tasso's *Gerusalemme Liberata*.
1639	Admitted to Pembroke Hall, Cambridge, as a gentleman commoner.
1642	Takes M.A. degree. At the outbreak of the civil war, leaves England; resides in France until 1646.
1646	Returns to England; takes up residence in the Middle Temple, London. Befriends and assists James Shirley; also, probably, Lovelace and Herrick.
1647	*Poems and Translations* published. Marries Dorothy Enyon, heiress of a titled and wealthy Northamptonshire family.
1648–1649	Working on translations of poetrry by classical and contemporary authors. Following the execution of Charles I in January, 1649, retires to Cumberlow.
1651	Publication of *Poems*. Turns his attention primarily to classical scholarship.
1655	Publication of *A History of Philosophy*, volume I; subsequent volumes appear in 1656, 1660, and 1662.
1661	Elected a charter member of the Royal Society.
1663	Publishes a scholarly edition of Aeschylus. Named a Fellow of the Royal Society.
1678	Death, April 12. Buried in Saint Martin-in-the-Fields, London.

From *POEMS*[1] (1651)

The Glowworm

Stay, fairest Charissa, stay and mark
This animated gem, whose fainter spark
Of fading light its birth had from the dark.

A star thought by the erring passenger,[2]
Which falling from its native orb dropped here,   5
And makes the earth, its center, now its sphere.

Should many of these sparks together be,
He that the unknown light far off should see
Would think it a terrestrial galaxy.

Take't up, fair saint; see how it mocks thy fright;   10
The paler flame doth not yield heat, though light,
Which thus deceives thy reason through thy sight.

But see how quickly it, ta'en up, doth fade,
To shine in darkness only being made,
By th'brightness of thy light turned to a shade;   15

And burnt to ashes by thy flaming eyes,
On the chaste altar of thy hand it dies,
As to thy greater light a sacrifice.

Changed, Yet Constant[3]

Wrong me no more
In thy complaint,
Blamed for inconstancy;
I vowed t'adore

1. If Stanley is not the most famous of the poets whose work is represented in this edition, it is nonetheless appropriate that some examples of his art should conclude a collection of seventeenth-century poems in the Cavalier mode. Among his contemporaries, Carew and Lovelace are the figures whose work his poetry most often recalls; yet the many drafts and revisions of several among these poems indicate his artistic affinity with Ben Jonson, while such pieces as "The Bracelet" reflect the influence of Donne. Stanley's linguistic facility enabled him to exploit the resources of Continental verse to a degree not equaled by most of his contemporaries. Graceful translations from Marino, Guarini, Lope de Vega, and others stand together in the *Poems* of 1651 with his English verses. The urbane sophistication of Stanley's poetry is matched by his character and career. Naturally sympathetic to the royalist cause, well connected and independently wealthy, he appears to gave gotten on with Englishmen of every political persuasion, keeping clear of the time-server's role while extending support to less fortunate literary men, whatever their politics. After 1651 he turned away from poetry, bringing his considerable attainments as a classical scholar to bear rather on philosophy and history, in the fashion of one who recognized the power of time and change and who would have regretfully acknowledged the force of the concluding lines in John Dryden's *The Secular Masque* (1700):

'Tis well an old age is out,
And time to begin a new.

2. I.e., the wandering wayfarer.

3. Cf. Lovelace, "The Scrutiny," p. 309.

The fairest saint, 5
Nor changed whilst thou wert she;
But if another thee outshine,
Th'inconstancy is only thine.

To be by such
Blind fools admired 10
Gives thee but small esteem,
By whom as much
Thou'dst be desired
Didst thou less beauteous seem;
Sure why they love they know not well, 15
Who why they should not cannot tell.

Women are by
Themselves betrayed,
And to their short joys cruel,
Who foolishly 20
Themselves persuade
Flames can outlast their fuel;
None, though Platonic their pretense,[4]
With reason love unless by sense.

And he, by whose 25
Command to thee
I did my heart resign,
Now bids me choose
A deity
Diviner far than thine; 30
No power can love from beauty sever;
I'm still love's subject, thine was never.

The fairest she
Whom none surpass
To love hath only right, 35
And such to me
Thy beauty was
Till one I found more bright;
But 'twere as impious to adore
Thee now, as not t'have done't before. 40

Nor is it just
By rules of love
Thou should'st deny to quit
A heart that must
Another's prove, 45
Ev'n in thy right to it;
Must not thy subjects captives be
To her who triumphs over thee?

4. Cf. Randolph, "An Elegy," p. 211, and first note.

Cease then in vain
To blot my name 50
With forged apostasy;
Thine is that stain
Who dar'st to claim
What others ask of thee.
Of lovers they are only true 55
Who pay their hearts where they are due.

Celia Singing

Roses in breathing forth their scent,
Or stars their borrowed ornament;
Nymphs in the watery sphere that move,
Or angels in their orbs above;
The wingéd chariot of the light, 5
Or the slow, silent wheels of night;
The shade which from the swifter sun
Doth in a circular motion run;
Or souls that their eternal rest do keep,
Make far more noise than Celia's breath in sleep. 10

But if the angel which inspires
This subtle frame with active fires
Should mold this breath to words, and those
Into a harmony dispose,
The music of this heavenly sphere 15
Would steal each soul out at the ear,
And into plants and stones infuse
A life that cherubins[5] would choose;
And with new powers invert the laws of fate,
Kill those that live, and dead things animate. 20

The Repulse[6]

Not that by this disdain
I am released,
And freed from thy tyrannic chain,
Do I myself think blest;

Nor that thy flame shall burn 5
No more; for know
That I shall into ashes turn,
Before this fire doth so;

Nor yet that unconfined
I now may rove, 10

5. I.e., the highest among the orders of angels. 6. Cf. Carew, "A Deposition from Love," p. 161.

And with new beauties please my mind;
    But that thou ne'er didst love:

    For since thou hast no part
        Felt of this flame,
I only from thy tyrant heart   15
    Repulsed, not banished, am.

    To lose what once was mine
        Would grieve me more
Than those inconstant sweets of thine
    Had pleased my soul before.   20

    Now I have lost the bliss
        I ne'er possessed;
And spite of fate am blest in this,
    That I was never blest.

Love's Innocence

See how this ivy strives to twine
Her wanton arms about the vine,
And her coy lover thus restrains,
Entangled in her amorous chains;
See how these neighb'ring palms do bend   5
Their heads, and mutual murmurs send,
As whisp'ring with a jealous fear
Their loves into each other's ear.
Then blush not such a flame to own[7]
As like thyself no crime hath known: 10
Led by these harmless guides, we may
Embrace and kiss as well as they.
    And like those blessed souls above,
Whose life is harmony and love,
Let us our mutual thoughts betray   15
And in our wills our minds display;
This silent speech is swifter far
Than the ears' lazy species are,
And the expression it affords
(As our desires) 'bove reach of words.   20
    Thus we, my dear, of these may learn
A passion others not discern;
Nor can it shame or blushes move,
Like plants to live, like angels love;
    Since all excuse with equal innocence   25
    What above reason is, or beneath sense.

7. Acknowledge.

Speaking And Kissing

The air which thy smooth voice doth break
    Into my soul like lightning flies,
My life retires whilst thou dost speak,
    And thy soft breath its room supplies.

Lost in this pleasing ecstasy,   5
    I join my trembling lips to thine,
And back receive that life from thee,
    Which I so gladly did resign.

Forbear, Platonic fools, t'inquire
    What numbers do the soul compose;   10
No harmony can life inspire
    But that which from these accents flows.

La Belle Confidente[8]

You earthly souls that court a wanton flame,
    Whose pale weak influence
Can rise no higher than the humble name
    And narrow laws of sense,
        Learn by our friendship to create   5
        An immaterial fire,
        Whose brightness angels may admire,
        But cannot emulate.

Sickness may fright the roses from her cheek,
    Or make the lilies fade,   10
But all the subtle ways that death doth seek
    Cannot my love invade;
        Flames that are kindled by the eye
        Through time and age expire;
        But ours, that boast a reach far higher.   15
        Cannot decay or die.

For when we must resign our vital breath,
    Our loves by fate benighted,
We by this friendship shall survive in death,
    Even in divorce united.   20
        Weak love, through fortune or distrust,
        In time forgets to burn,
        But this pursues us to the urn
        And marries either's dust.

8. I.e., intimate female friend.

The Bracelet[9]

Rebellious fools that scorn to bow
    Beneath love's easy sway,
Whose stubborn wills no laws allow,
    Disdaining to obey,
Mark but this wreath of hair, and you shall see,   5
None that might wear such fetters would be free.

I once could boast a soul like you,
    As unconfined as air;
But mine, which force could not subdue,
    Was caught within this snare;   10
And, by myself betrayed, I, for this gold,
A heart that many storms withstood have sold.

No longer now wise art inquire,
    With this vain search delighted,
How souls that human breasts inspire   15
    Are to their frames united;
Material chains such spirits well may bind,
When this soft braid can tie both arm and mind.

Now, beauties, I defy your charm,
    Ruled by more powerful art;   20
This mystic wreath which crowns my arm
    Defends my vanquished heart;
And I, subdued by one more fair, shall be
Secured from conquest by captivity.

The Exequies[1]

Draw near,
You lovers that complain[2]
Of fortune or disdain,
And to my ashes lend a tear;
Melt the hard marble with your groans,   5
And soften the relentless stones,
Whose cold embraces the sad subject hide
Of all love's cruelties, and beauty's pride.

No verse,
No epicedium[3] bring,   10
Nor peaceful requiem sing
To charm the terrors of my hearse;

---

9. Cf. Donne, "The Funeral."
1. Funeral ceremonies.
2. Lament.
3. Dirge.

No profane numbers[4] must flow near
The sacred silence that dwells here;
Vast griefs are dumb; softly, oh, softly mourn,   15
Lest you disturb the peace attends my urn.

Yet strew
Upon my dismal grave
Such offerings as you have,
Forsaken cypress and sad yew;   20
For kinder flowers[5] can take no birth
Or growth from such unhappy earth.
Weep only o'er my dust, and say, "Here lies
To love and fate an equal sacrifice."

Song

I prithee let my heart alone,
    Since now 'tis raised above thee;
Not all the beauty thou dost own
    Again can make me love thee.

He that was shipwrecked once before   5
    By such a siren's[6] call,
And yet neglects to shun that shore,
    Deserves his second fall.

Each flatt'ring kiss, each tempting smile
    Thou dost in vain bestow,   10
Some other lovers might beguile
    Who not thy falsehood know.

But I am proof against all art,
    No vows shall e'er persuade me
Twice to present a wounded heart   15
    To her that hath betrayed me.

Could I again be brought to love
    Thy form, though more divine,
I might thy scorn as justly move
    As thou now sufferest mine.   20

The Relapse

Oh, turn away those cruel eyes,
    The stars of my undoing,
Or death, in such a bright disguise,
    May tempt a second wooing.

4. Verses.
5. I.e., roses.
6. I.e., an enticing woman. In Homer's *Odyssey*, the Sirens were sea nymphs who, by their song, lured men to destruction.

Punish their blindly impious pride,   5
    Who dare contemn[7] thy glory;
It was my fall that deified
    Thy name, and sealed thy story.

Yet no new sufferings can prepare
    A higher praise to crown thee;   10
Though my first death proclaim thee fair,
    My second will unthrone thee.

Lovers will doubt thou canst entice
    No other for thy fuel,
And if thou burn one victim twice,   15
    Both think thee poor and cruel.

On Mr. Shirley's Poems[8]

When, dearest friend, thy verse doth re-inspire
Love's pale decaying torch with brighter fire,
Whilst everywhere thou dost dilate thy flame,
And to the world spread thy Odelia's name,
The justice of all ages must remit   5
To her the prize of beauty, thee of wit.
    Then, like some skilful artist, that to wonder[9]
Framing a piece, displeased, takes it asunder,
Thou beauty dost depose, her charms deny,
And all the mystic chains of love untie;   10
Thus thy diviner Muse a power 'bove fate
May boast, that can both make and uncreate.
    Next thou call'st back to life that love-sick boy,[1]
To the kind-hearted nymphs less fair than coy,
Who, by reflex beams burnt with vain desire,   15
Did phoenix-like in his own flames expire;
But should he view his shadow drawn by thee,
He with himself once more in love would be.
    Echo (who though she words pursue, her haste
Can only overtake and stop the last)   20
Shall her first speech and human veil obtain
To sing thy softer numbers o'er again.
Thus, into dying poetry, thy Muse
Doth full perfection and new life infuse;
Each line deserves a laurel, and thy praise   25
Asks not a garland, but a grove of bays;
Nor can ours raise thy lasting trophies higher,

---

7. Scorn.
8. Stanley and Shirley were close **friends**; cf. Shirley's poem "To His Honored Friend Thomas Stanley Esquire, upon His Elegant Poems," p. 191.
9. I.e., that in a manner exciting others'

wonder.
1. Stanley alludes to Shirley's long poem, "Narcissus, or The Self-Lover," a reworking of an earlier poem entitled "Echo, or The Infortunate Lovers." Cf. Ovid, *Metamorphoses*, III. 341–510.

Who only reach at merit to admire.
  But I must chide thee, friend: how canst thou be
A patron, yet a foe to poetry?   30
For while thou dost this age to verse restore,
Thou dost deprive the next of owning more;
And hast so far e'en future aims surpassed
That none dare write: thus being[2] first and last,
All their abortive Muses will suppress,   35
And poetry by this increase grow less.

From *POEMS AND TRANSLATIONS* (1647)

Expectation

Chide, chide no more away
The fleeting daughters of the day,
Nor with impatient thoughts outrun
    The lazy sun,
Or think the hours do move too slow;   5
   Delay is kind,
  And we too soon shall find
That which we seek, yet fear to know.

The mystic dark decrees
Unfold not of the destinies,   10
Nor boldly seek to antedate
    The laws of fate;
Thy anxious search awhile forbear;
   Suppress thy haste,
  And know that time at last   15
Will crown thy hope, or fix thy fear.

2. I.e., thus, since you are.

Textual Notes

The texts of the poems in this edition are based on those of the most authoritative early editions. For the majority of those poets represented here, this means that the text is based on that of the first edition in which each poem appears; however, where the particular authority of an edition other than the first has been clearly established, the present text is based upon that edition. Thus, the third (second augmented) edition of Habington's *Castara* (1640) takes precedence over the earlier editions of 1634 and 1635; the edition of Waller's *Poems* published in 1686 (the last to appear during the poet's lifetime) has been preferred to the earlier editions of 1645 and 1664; while the text of Denham's "Cooper's Hill" is based on that in the first collected edition, *Poems and Translations* (1668). The texts of poems by Sidney Godolphin (in the absence of any early edition) follow those in William Dighton's edition of 1931, which makes use of manuscript materials previously unavailable to scholars. The provenance of individual editions consulted is indicated separately, by the author, in the list of variants.

The texts in this Critical Edition have been "updated" in several particulars, notably spelling and punctuation. Spelling has been consistently modernized throughout, save where such "updating" would outrage rhyme or meter, or obscure meaning. The "updating" of punctuation is another matter. In certain respects, to be sure, there is no difficulty: thus, (1) italicized proper names are given in roman type; (2) the use of *i*, *u*, and *v* is regularized to conform with modern practice; (3) the ampersand is replaced by *and*; (4) diphthongs are replaced by separate characters; (5) quotations are punctuated in accord with modern practice; (6) the silent *e* is substituted for the apostrophe in such words as *annoy'd* and *abandon'd*; (7) accents are inserted over final *-ed* to indicate the sounding of the extra syllable.

Problems arise, however, in the larger contexts of punctuational consistency. To bring the punctuation of the work of one seventeenth-century poet into reasonable accord with modern practice without altering the original meaning is itself a challenge; to undertake that task with the work of eighteen writers as various as those represented here, and to impose upon all a uniformly consistent standard of modernization in this regard, appears to the present editor to be neither feasible nor proper. In the most general terms, the punctuation of poems in this Critical Edition is somewhat lighter than that of the early texts. Throughout, the editor's silent punctuational emendations reflect an effort to clarify the poem for modern readers, while preserving the meaning (and, as far as may be possible, the emphases) of the original texts. Again, where the punctuation of early texts apparently reflects an unusually erratic or careless compositior's hand (as, intermittently, with the 1648 edition of Herrick's *Hesperides* or the 1649 edition of Lovelace's *Lucasta*), the present editor has silently adjusted punctuation to support meaning. Yet each poet is in some sense his own man. An editor intent on "updating" the punctuation of Jonson's second epigram to Donne (XCVI), for instance, soon perceives that the original punctuation must substantially stand if the poem's subtle ambiguities are to be preserved. The balanced couplets of Waller and Denham, turning so often on a centrally placed caesura, resist too cavalier an "updating" of the original punctuation, which supports and emphasizes the rhythmical movement of the verse. And yet again, the poets represented here are far from consistent (to say nothing of the complications introduced by compository error or whim) in their capitalization of such terms as *Nature, Fate, Love, the Muse*, and so on, or in their use of the apostrophe in such forms as *should'st, tak'st, didst*, etc. In this Critical Edition, *Muse* is regularly capitalized; *Nature, Love*, etc., are capitalized only when personification significantly contributes to the poem's metaphoric structure; *King* and *Queen* are capitalized, as a rule, only when particular monarchs are so denoted. As for the vexed question of the apostrophe, one might risk the suggestion that it appears in such forms as those noted above with relatively less frequency as the century wears on; but no one of the poets represented here, I believe, is absolutely consistent in this regard. Accordingly, the editor has felt obliged (given the decision to prefer punctuation generally lighter than that which typically marks the original texts) to take note of each poet's usual punctuational practice, and to make some serious effort to preserve the features of that practice. As A. L. Clements observes, with reference to the textual principles followed in his Critical Edition of Donne, "If strict consistency has been sacrificed it has been . . . for the sake of better, special purposes."

The list of variants is not intended to provide a complete critical apparatus such as that provided in Herford and Simpson's edition of Ben Jonson or in the definitive modern editions of other poets represented here. That the texts in this Critical Edition are modernized in some particulars evidently bears on this matter. Variants noted include substantive departures from the basic texts, together with significant substantive variants in other early editions and manuscripts. A few of the most helpful emendations proposed by scholars and editors are also included. Semisubstantive and inconsequential departures from the text are not included. Owing to limitations of space, the complex and extensive variants in manuscripts of Herrick's "A Nuptial Song . . . on Sir Clipsby Crew and His Lady" and the manuscript variants of Denham's "Cooper's Hill" (i.e., those not reproduced in the printed editions) are excluded from the list of variants. As a rule, spelling in manuscript variants has been modernized; original punctuation is retained. Where significant variants occur in a single manuscript, the document is initially identified; "MSS" means "two or more manuscripts."

Ben Jonson

The text of the *Epigrams* and *The Forest* in this edition is based on that in a copy of the 1616 edition of the *Works* in the Cambridge University Library; the texts of poems in *Underwood* and (with one exception) those of the songs from Jonson's plays and masques are based on a copy of the 1640–1641 edition of the *Works* in the same library. The text of "To the Memory of . . . Mr. William Shakespeare" is based on a microfilm copy of the text in *Mr. William Shakespeare's Comedies, Histories, and Tragedies* (1623) in the Folger Shakespeare Library; that of "Ode to Himself" ("Come leave the loathéd stage") on a microfilm copy of the text in *Ben Jonson's Execration Against Vulcan* (1640, noted as Q in the list of variants) in the British Museum; that of the song, "It was a beauty that I saw," on a microfilm copy of the text in *The New Inn* (1631), in the British Museum. Manuscript information (together with variants in the 1640 duodecimo edition of *Ben Jonson's Execration Against Vulcan* [noted as D in the list of variants]) is obtained from *Ben Jonson*, ed. C. H. Herford and P. and E. M. Simpson, 11 vols. (Oxford, 1925–1952), VIII. A few of the emendations made by editors of Jonson's *Works* (notably Peter Whalley, 1756; William Gifford, 1816; Francis Cunningham, 1871; and Herford and Simpson) are included among the variants.

EPIGRAMS

XXIII: To John Donne
2/ one 1616; own *Bodleian MS. Ashmole 47.*

XCI: To Sir Horace Vere
9/ leave thy acts, 1616; leave, then, acts; *B.M. MS. Add. 23229.*

CI: Inviting a Friend to Supper
16/ think 1616; say *B.M. MS. Harleian 6917.*
17/ lie 1616; buy *MS.*
19–20/ and godwit, if we can,/Knat, rail, and ruff too 1616; and perhaps if we can/A duck and mallard *MS.*
36/ Pooly, or Parrot 1616; fool, or parrot *MS.*

CXX: Epitaph on S. P. . . .
7/ seemed to 1616; both did *Bodleian MS. Ashmole 38.*
11/ three filled 1616; thrice past *MS.*
20–22/ They have repented,/And have sought, to give new birth,/In baths to steep him 1616; since have repented/and would have given new breath/Nay they desire (not able) to give birth/In charms to sleep him *MS.*

CXXIV: Epitaph on Elizabeth, L. H.
6/ virtue than 1616; beauty than *Bodleian MS. Rawl. poet. 160*; beauty that *B.M. MS. Harleian 6057.*
7/ all 1616; most *Harleian MS.*
11/ where 1616; when *Harleian MS.*

CXXXIII: On the Famous Voyage
30/ the 1640; thee 1616.
161/ is *Gifford 1816*; are 1616.
177/ Holborn 1616; Holborn-height *Gifford 1816*; Holborn bridge *Cunningham 1871*; Holborn (the three *H & S 1947.*

THE FOREST

III: To Sir Robert Wroth

6/ sheriff's . . . mayor's 1616; sergeants . . . sheriff MSS.

9/ when 1616; where *Bodleian MS. Rawl. poet. 31*.

24/ house 1616; lodge MSS.

28/ gladder 1616; welcome MSS. sight 1616; right *B.M. MS. Harleian 4064*.

41 ears, yet humble in their height 1616; ears cut down in their most height MSS.

43/ that doth longer last 1616; and ploughed lands up cast MSS.

46/ lent MSS.; lend 1616, 1640.

55/ grace 1616; place MSS.

60/ *After this line, some MSS. read:* The milk nor oil, did ever flow so free/Nor yellow honey from the tree

66/ live 1616; be MSS.

77/ Let him than hardest sires more disinherit 1616; Than hardest let him more disherit MSS.

87/ glad 1616; proud MSS.

98/ knows 1616; thinks *B.M. MS.*

99/ be thou 1616; art thou MSS.

100/ Thy . . . thy 1616; Whose . . . whose MSS.

101/ Be 1616; Is MSS. and 1616, 1640; an *B.M. MS.*

V: Song: To Celia

1/ my 1616; sweet MSS.

2/ may 1616; can *Volpone*.

4/ good 1616; bliss *B.M. MS. Add. 10309*.

14/ So removéd by our wile 1616; So removed by many a mile MSS.

15/ fruit 1616; fruits *Volpone*, MSS.

16/ theft 1616; thefts *Volpone*.

VI: To the Same

15/ Thames 1616; streams *B.M. MS. Add. 10309*.

16/ his streams 1616; the Thames MS.

19/ may 1616; shall *Volpone*, MS.

VIII: To Sickness

11/ store 1616; score *Bodleian MS. Rawl. poet. 31*.

27/ yea, 1616; and MSS.

38/ stew 1616; crank MSS.

41/ thee 1616; that *Bodleian MS.*

IX: Song: To Celia

Another version, in B.M. MS. Sloane 1446, reads:

> Drink to me Celia with thine eyes
> > And I'll pledge thee with mine
> > Leave but a kiss within the cup
> > And I'll expect no wine
> The thirst that from the soul proceeds   5
> > Doth ask a drink divine
> But might I of love's nectar sup
> I would not change for thine

I sent to thee a rosy wreath
Not so to honor thee   10
But being well assured that there
It would not withered be
And thou thereon didst only breathe
 And sent'st it back to me
Since when it lives and smells I swear   15
 Not of itself but thee

XI: Epode
29/ passions 1616, 1640; passions still *MSS.*
39/ 'tis 1616; he's *MSS.*
45/ far more gentle 1616; most gentle and *MSS.*
67/ we 1616; I *MSS.*
68/ we 1616; I *MSS.*
72/ we 1616; I *MSS.*
75/ ourselves 1616; myself *MSS.*
76/ We 1616; I *MSS.*
83/ we 1616; I *MSS.*
84/ filled 1616; graced *MSS.*
85/ we 1616; I *MSS.*
91/ we propose 1616; I conceive *MSS.* our 1616; my *MSS.*

XII: Epistle to Elizabeth, Countess of Rutland
15/ buys great 1616; gets *MSS.*
22/ nor 1616; not *MSS.*
25/ in 1616; on *Bodleian MS. Rawl. poet.* 31.
63/ only 1616; holy *MSS.* rage 1616; sense *MSS.*
76/ to notes 1616; the notes *Bodleian MS.*
77/ act 1616; arts *Bodleian MS.*
79/ Muse 1616; verse *MSS.* least 1616; less *Bodleian MS.*
84/ Borne up by 1616; beset with *MSS.*
87/ tickling 1616; tinkling *MSS.*
The concluding lines in MSS. read:

   Who, wheresoe'er he be, on what dear coast,
   Now thinking on you, though to England lost,
   For that firm grace he holds in your regard,
   I, that am grateful for him, have prepared
   This hasty sacrifice, wherein I rear
   A vow as new and ominous as the year;
   Before his swift and circled race be run,
   My best of wishes: may you bear a son.

XIII: Epistle to Katharine, Lady Aubigny
100/ about 1616; above 1640.

UNDERWOOD

A Hymn to God the Father
14/ Rarely 1640; cannot *Bodleian MS. Rawl. poet.* 23.
20/ To free 1640; to be *B.M. MS. Egerton* 2013.

22/ With all since *H & S* 1947; Withall since *1640*; with all sins *Bodleian MS.*

30/ Me farther toss *1640*; And now begin *MSS.*

32/ Under His *1640*; Beneath Thy *Bodleian MS.*

A Celebration of Charis

2. How He Saw Her

22/ with *Gifford 1816*; which *1640.*

3. What He Suffered

11/ draught. *Hunter 1963*; draught *1640*; draught, *H & S* 1947.

12/ Arméd *Hunter 1963*; Aimed, *1640*; Aimed *H & S 1947.* shaft *1640*; shaft. *H & S* 1947.

4. Her Triumph

4/ car *1640*; coach *B.M. MS. Add. 15227.*

11/ light *1640*; delight *B.M. MS. Harleian 6057.*

21/ bright *1640*; white *B.M. MS. Add. 15227.*

7. Begging Another, on Color of Mending the Former

2/ long *1640*; beg *Bodleian MS. Ashmole 38.* beg *1640*; ask *MSS.*

6/ touch *1640*; suck *MSS.*

17/ whilst our tongues *1640*; while we thus *MSS.*

9. Her Man Described by Her Own Dictamen

4/ greater *1640*; greatest *B.M. MS. Harleian 4955.*

18/ Front, an ample field of *1640*; forehead large, and white as *MS.*

32/ school *1640*; art *MS.*

37/ him; *MS.*; him *1640.*

The Musical Strife . . .

3/ each *1640*; one *Trinity College, Dublin MS. G.2.21.*

8/ but must lose *1640*; doth not want *Trin. Coll. MS.*

9/ then your *1640*; we our *MSS.*

15/ No tunes are sweet *1640*; no voice is sweet *MSS*; no ear hath sound *MSS.*

16/ those *1640*; your *MSS.*

19/ pleasure *1640*; passion *MSS.*

20/ On what they viewing know *1640*; On what they see or know *MSS*; Themselves with what they know *Trin. Coll. MS.*

21/ O sing not you, then *1640*; Sing we no more then *MSS.*

25/ souls *1640*; notes *MSS.*

27/ state *1640*; seat *Trin. Coll. MS.*

28/ May *1640*; Shall *MSS.*

My Picture Left in Scotland

1/ now think *1640*; doubt that *Drummond, Conversations, 1619.*

5/ love *1640*; suit *Drummond, B.M. MS. Harleian 4955.*

6/ was *1640*; is *Drummond.*

7/ every close did *1640*; all my closes *Drummond, MS.*

8/ sentence *1640*; numbers *Drummond, MS.*

9/ hath *1640*; makes *Drummond, MS.* youngest *1640*; wisest *D, Q.*

13/ Tell *1640*; prompt *Drummond.*

14/ hundreds *1640, MS., D, Q*; hundred *Drummond.*

15/ seven *1640*; six *Drummond, MS., D, Q.*

16/ cannot *1640, Drummond*; could not *D, Q.*

An Epitaph on Master Vincent Corbett
1/ have *1640*; hope *B.M. MS. Sloane 1792.*
14/ All *1640*; At *MS.*
20/ specious *1640*; spacious *MS.*
The following lines, perhaps not part of the preceding poem, are printed after l. 36, in 1640:

> Reader, whose life, and name, did e'er become
>   An epitaph, deserved a tomb:
> Nor wants it here through penury, or sloth,
>   Who makes the one, so't be first, makes both.

An Epistle to Master John Selden
4/ Truth . . . naked *1640*; Since, naked, best Truth, and the Graces *Selden, "Titles of Honor," 1614.*
17/ far otherwise *1640*; far from this fault *1614.*
37/ T'instruct *1640*; To inform *1614.*
56/ manly elocution, *1640*; masculine elocution; *1614.*
66/ thine *1614*; their *1640.*
76/ same *1640*; rich *1614.*
81/ gain *1614*; grain *1640.*

An Elegy ["Though beauty be the mark of praise"]
29/ off-spring *1640*; offering *Whalley 1756.*

An Ode to Himself ["Where dost thou careless lie"]
4/ security *1640*; obscurity *B. M. MS. Egerton 923.*
6/ and destroys *1640*; and oft destroys *MSS., H & S.*
12/ defaced *1640*; displaced *Egerton MS.*
13/ thy silence *1640*; they silent *B.M. MS. Rawl. poet. 31.*
16/ great *1640*; quick *Egerton MS.*
29/ give *1640*; guide *Egerton MS.*
30/ him *1640*; them *MSS.*

An Ode ["High-spirited friend"]
20/ same *1640*; fame *Newdigate 1936.*

A Fit of Rhyme Against Rhyme
15/ art *Gifford 1816*; are *1640.*

An Execration Upon Vulcan
3/ thus to devour *1640*; thus in an hour *MSS.*
4/ in an hour *1640*; to devour *MSS.*
14/ any . . . the *1640*; every . . . her *D, Q.*
26/ some *1640*; lewd *MSS., D, Q.*
33/ Or . . . tomes *1640*; or spent my wretched paper or my time *MSS.*
34/ Of . . . palindromes *1640*; in weaving riddles in more wretched rhyme *MSS.*
35/ hard *1640*; fine *Bodleian MS. Engl. poet. e.14.*
45/ moneys *1640*; maskings *MSS.*
48/ Or . . . power *1640*; Or if thou wouldst enforce the power from her *MSS.*
50/ more thrift and more variety *1640*; more change, and taste of tyranny *MSS.*; more thirst and more variety *D, Q.*

51/ me 1640; them MSS.

53/ Singe . . . eyes 1640; Cloth spices, or guard sweetmeats from the flies MSS. poor 1640; crisp D, Q.

54/ me 1640; them MSS., D, Q.

55/ me 1640; them MSS.

56/ Not . . . rage 1640; Not snatched them hence in one poor minute's rage B.M. MS. *Sloane* 1792.

58/ consumption 1640; *propter viam* MSS.

61–62/ that . . . ream 1640; many a ream/Had filled your large nostrils with the steam *Sloane MS.*

73/ seals 1640; charms D, Q.

74/ bright 1640; the MSS.

77/ Pasquil's 1640; Breton's MSS.

82/ Ball 1640; Baal D, Q.

88/ mast'ry 1640; mystery D, Q.

95–97/ not afraid . . . To our own 1640; not amiss/Revealed (if some can judge) of Argenis,/for our own MSS.

99–100/ Wherein . . . lent 1640; Wherein (besides the noble aids were lent,/of Carew, Cotton, Selden, oils were spent) *Sloane MS.*

104/ faction 1640; fashion *Bodleian MS.* drawn 1640; taught MSS.

110/ 'Cause . . . fire! 1640; Cause thou canst do these halting tricks in fire? MSS.

119/ against the pageant 1640; upon the next Mayor's MSS.

120/ Vulcanale 1640; pagan prayer MSS.

124/ My 1640; Our MSS., D, Q.

134/ Flanked . . . forced 1640; Fenced . . . forked Q.

139/ The . . . news 1640; There were, that straight did nose it out for news B.M. MS. *Harleian* 4955; There were, that straight did noise it out for news MSS.

142/ locked 1640; raked MSS., D, Q.

144/ the 1640; in MSS.

146/ And cried it was 1640; 'Twas verily D, Q.

147/ accursèd 1640; profaner MSS. Paris D, Q; *Parish-* 1640.

148/ Nay, (sighed a sister) D, Q; Nay sighed a Sister MSS.; Nay, sighed, ah Sister 1640.

152/ place 1640; plot MSS.

157/ his 1640; thy MSS., D, Q.

159/ He is 1640; Thou art MSS. He did 1640; thou didst MSS.

160/ his 1640; thy MSS., D, Q.

171/ chroniclers MSS., D, Q; chronicles 1640, MSS.

173/ But say, all six good men *Harleian MS.*; But say all six good men MSS., D, Q; But, say all six, good men 1640.

183/ brick-kilns *Bodleian MS.*; brick-kills 1640; brick-hills *Harleian MS.*, D, Q.

183–185/ or some . . . blaze about 1640; or a forge/some 4 miles hence and have him there disgorge/or else in penny fagots blaze about MSS.

191/ your flameship, Vulcan; if it be 1640; the fireworks, Vulcan, if they be MSS.

202/ Who . . . beget 1640; who with the' devil did ordnance beget MSS.

205–208/ Blow . . . many ways 1640; Blow up and ruin and enjoy the praise/Of murdering of mankind many ways *Sloane MS.*; Blow up and ruin, and enjoy with praise/of massacring mankind so many ways *Bodleian MS.*

212/ places 1640; fortunes *Harleian MS.*

216/ B. B.'s 1640; Bess Broughton's MSS., D, Q.

An Epistle . . . Tribe of Ben

62/ thence *Gifford* 1816; then 1640.

To the Immortal Memory . . . of . . . Cary and . . . Morison

Title/ To . . . Morison 1640; ODE PINDARICK To the Noble Sir Lucius Cary D, *Edinburgh Univ. MS. Dc. 7.94*; ODE PINDARICK On the Death of Sir Henry Morison Q; To Sir Lucius Cary, on the death of his Brother Morison B.M. MS. *Harleian 4955.*

The Turn 1640; The turn of ten D.

10/ deepest 1640; secret *Bodleian MS. Ashmole 36–7.*

The Counter-turn 1640; The Counter-turn of ten D.

11/ wiser 1640; wisest MSS.

15/ hurried 1640; harried *Bodleian MS.*

The Stand 1640; The Stand, of twelve D.

41/ So 1640; Too D, Q.

44/ fall'st 1640; tripst MSS., D, Q.

50/ measure 1640; fashion *Bodleian MS.*

123/ in deed *Bodleian MS.*; indeed 1640, D, Q.

126/ lines 1640; lives MSS.

Epithalamion . . .

28/ (perfection at 1640; perfection, (at B.M. MS. *Harleian 4955.*

46/ she 1640; they MS.

166/ find 1640; feel MS.

171/ Francis 1640; sister MS.

184/ So . . . shade 1640; So large: his body then, not boughs, project his shade MS.

187–188/ yet . . . pay 1640; and the more/gently he asketh, she will pay MS.

BEN JONSON'S EXECRATION AGAINST VULCAN

Ode to Himself ["Come leave the loathéd stage"]

27/ Broome's Q, *Bodleian MS. Ashmole 38*; There, *New Inn 1631.*

28/ There as his master's meal D, Q, MSS.; As the best ordered meal *New Inn.*

33/ scene clothes D, Q; stage-clothes *New Inn.*

36/ stuffing D, Q, MSS.; larding *New Inn.*

37/ With rage of D, Q; with rags of MSS.; With their foul *New Inn.*

39/ foul D, Q, MSS.; turned *New Inn.*

53/ of D, Q, *Ashmole MS.*; o'er *New Inn.*

54/ may . . . then D, Q; may, blood-shaken, then *New Inn.*

56/ That no tuned harp D, Q; As they shall cry, *New Inn.*

58/ Shall truly D, Q, MSS.; No harp e'er *New Inn.*

59–60/ When . . . triumph D, Q, MSS.; In tuning forth the acts of his sweet reign;/And raising Charles his chariot *New Inn.*

Richard Corbett

Texts in this edition are based, with one exception, either on those in a copy of *Certain Elegant Poems, Written by Dr. Corbet, Bishop of Norwich* (1647) in the Cambridge University Library, or on those in a microfilm copy of *Poetica Stromata or a Collection of Sundry Pieces in Poetry* (1648) in the Newberry Library. The text of Corbett's epitaph on Donne is based on that in the Scolar Press facsimile (Menston, 1970) of *Poems, by J. D. with Elegies on the Authors Death* (1633). Manuscript and related information is obtained from *The Poems of Richard Corbett*, ed. J. A. W. Bennett and H. R. Trevor-Roper (Oxford, 1955).

CERTAIN ELEGANT POEMS

A Proper New Ballad . . .
13/ sprung 1648; stol'n 1647.
23/ merrily 1647; merrily merrily 1648.
47/ need 1647; want 1648.
51/ can preserve 1647; looketh to 1648.
57–64/ *omitted in 1647.*

An Elegy Upon the Death of His Own Father
6/ his 1648; one 1647.
16/ the age before 1647; their age beyond 1648.
18/ plainness 1648; feignedness 1647.
20/ Add too 1648; Adding 1647.
28/ soon-sprung *B & T-R from MSS.*; some spring 1647; some sprung 1648.
40/ their 1648; fed 1647.
42/ literal 1648; liberal 1647.
45–48/ *omitted in 1648.*
46/ saved *B & T-R from MSS.*; said 1647.
53–56/ *omitted in 1647.*

To His Son, Vincent Corbett [*not in 1648*]
6/ Too *B & T-R from MSS.*; so 1647.
8/ But truly *B & T-R from MSS.*; Enough for 1647.
14/ up but to *B & T-R from MSS.*; on, but 1647.

POETICA STROMATA

Upon Fairford Windows [*not in 1647*]
1–2/ glass . . . brass *B & T-R from "Parnassus Biceps, or several choice pieces"* 1656; brass/With you is shorter lived than glass 1648.
10/ what *B & T-R from* 1656; that 1648.

Robert Herrick

The text is based on that in a copy of *Hesperides* and *His Noble Numbers* (1648) in the Library of Trinity College, Cambridge. A microfilm of another copy in the Huntington Library has also been consulted. Manuscript and related information is obtained from *The Poetical Works of Robert Herrick*, ed. L. C. Martin (Oxford, 1956), and, for certain poems, from *The Complete Poetry of Robert Herrick*, ed. J. Max Patrick (New York, 1963).

HESPERIDES

The Vine

3/ Which . . . and 1648; Spreading his branches *The Garden of Delight* 1658.

5/ long small 1648; cedary 1658.

9–12/ About . . . So that my 1648; Her curious parts I so did twine/With the rich clusters of my vine,/That my sweet 1658.

16–17/ could . . . one 1648; lay and could not stir,/But yield her self my 1658.

His Farewell to Sack

1/ known, so 1648; true and *Recreation for Ingenious Headpieces* 1650.

3/ man 1648; or MSS.

6/ resigning, yet resisting 1648; yet chaste, and undefiled 1650.

15/ shagged 1648; sad *some* MSS.; sage *some* MSS.

19/ above 1648; loved MSS. divinest 1648; diviner MSS.

27/ flashing 1648; striking MSS.; stretching 1650.

38/ eye of admiration 1648; eyes of adoration MSS.

43/ made 1648; forged MSS.

45/ not smile 1648; draw in MSS.

46/ MSS. *and* 1650 *insert (with minor variants)*:

> Thy glaring fires, lest in their sight the sin
> Of idolatry steal upon me, and
> I turn apostate to the strict command
> Of Nature; bid me now farewell, or smile
> More inly, lest thy tempting looks beguile

To a Gentlewoman . . .

2/ dare swear 1648; believe MSS.

4–11/ *Most* MSS. *read (with minor variants)*:

> And night will come, when men will swear
> Time has spilt snow upon your hair:
> Then when in your glass you seek
> But find no rosebud in your cheek,
> No, nor the bed to give the shew
> Where such a rare carnation grew,
> And such a smiling tulip too.

The Lily in a Crystal

12/ fine . . . to 1648; soft shade, which gleams *Harvard MS. Eng. 626 F.*

13/ draws . . . thereto 1648; doth the sight renew MS.

14/ that . . . with 1648; uniting unto MS.

20/ darts his radiant 1648; shoots his pointed MS.

50–51/ have . . . men 1648; like a Paphian dove/May charm the soul MS.

The Welcome to Sack

3/ likeness 1648; liking *Rosenbach MS.* 1083/16.

4/ natures 1648; waters MSS.

6/ fierce 1648; hot *Rosenbach MS.* wished 1648; stol'n *Rosenbach MS.*

12/ Outshine 1648; Dash forth MSS.

17/ betray 1648; display MSS.

25/ Why frowns . . . confer 1648; O then no longer let my sweet defer MSS.

26/ Favors . . . idolater? 1648; Her buxom smiles from me her worshipper MSS.

27/ are those looks, those looks 1648; are those happy looks *some MSS.*; are those amber looks *some MSS.*

29/ Tell . . . fault 1648; tell me hath my soul/Profaned in speech or done an act that's foul/Against thy purer essence, for that fault MSS. (*with minor variants*).

40/ In . . . wine 1648; Or quench my thirst upon some other wine *some MSS.* (*with minor variants*); or quench my lust upon some other wine *some MSS.*

46/ possibility 1648; probability MSS.

47/ When . . . lack 1648; When all the world may know the vines shall lack MSS.

After l. 48 most MSS. read:

> Sack is my life, my leaven, salt to all
> My dearest dainties, 'tis the principal
> Fire to all my functions, gives me blood
> An active spirit full marrow and what is good

50/ Iphiclus . . . corn 1648; Ixions upon the top of corn *Rosenbach MS.*

53/ And ride 1648; Amid *Rosenbach MS.*

63/ Small . . . he 1648; Full chalice of thy purer nectar, he MSS.

65/ Jove's 1648; Juno's *Rosenbach MS.* brave 1648; vast MSS.

67/ gen'rous blood, his 1648; blood, his lustful MSS.

71/ fate to break us 1648; hate to sunder MSS.

75/ carriage 1648; visage MSS.

77/ nerves with spirit 1648; feeble sinews MSS.

83/ fires 1648; blessings MSS.

89/ may my numbers 1648; let my verses MSS.

To the Virgins, to Make Much of Time

11–12/ But . . . former 1648; Expect not then the last and worst/Time still succeeds the former MSS. (*with minor variants*).

To the Rose. Song

4/ flowing 1648; peevish *Recreation for Ingenious Headpieces* 1650.

How Violets Came Blue

1–2/ Love . . . spent 1648; The violets, as poets tell,/With Venus wrangling went *Recreation for Ingenious Headpieces* 1650.

A Nuptial Song . . .

Cf. Poetical Works, ed. Martin, pp. 476–480, for complete list of variants.

Oberon's Feast

8/ short prayers 1648; the dance MSS.

9/ A moon-parched grain 1648; A yellow corn MSS. purest 1648; perky MSS.

10/ glitt'ring 1648; sandy *MSS.*
16/ spleen, the chirring 1648; fire the pittering *MSS.*
After 1. 18 *MSS. read:*
> The humming dorr, the dying swan
> And each a choice musician.

27/ and tastes 1648; but with *MSS.*
28/ Of that we call 1648; Neat-cool allay *MSS.*
31–33/ then . . . sag 1648; he not spares/To feed upon the candid hairs/
   Of a dried canker with a sag *MSS.*
35/ Gladding 1648; Stroking *MSS.*
38/ A bloated . . . fly 1648; A pickled maggot and a dry *MSS.*
41/ *After* "tooth" *MSS. read (with minor variants):*
> and with the fat
> A well-boiled inkpin of a bat.
> A bloated earwig with the pith
> Of sugared rush he glads him with.
> But most of all the glowworm's fire
> As much betickling his desire
> To know his queen mixed with the far-
> Fetched binding jelly of a star
> The silk-worm's seed, a little moth

51/ dainty daisy 1648; daisy chalice *MSS.*

Thomas Carew

Texts are based, with one exception, on those in copies of *Poems* (1640)
and *Poems. With a Maske* (1651) in the Cambridge University Library.
The text of Carew's "Elegy" on Donne is based on that in *Poems, By J. D.*
(1633). A microfilm of another copy of the 1640 edition in the Huntington Library has also been consulted. Manuscript and other textual information is obtained principally from *The Poems of Thomas Carew*, ed. Rhodes
Dunlap (Oxford, 1949). The facsimile of portions of the Wyburd MS.
(Bodleian MS. Don. b. 9), reproduced in the Scolar Press facsimile of the
1940 edition of Carew's *Poems* (Menston, 1969), has been consulted as
well.

POEMS (1640)

The Spring
6/ sacred 1640; second *MSS.*

A Prayer to the Wind
5–6/ So . . . afire 1640; *omitted in Huntington Library MS.* 116.
9–24/ Boldly . . . paid 1640; *Huntington MS. substitutes the following:*
> Taste her lips and then confess
> If Arabia doth possess
> Or the Hybla honored hill
> Sweet like these that thence distill
> Having got so rich a fee,
> Do another boon for me

27–28/ Thou . . . same *1640*; *omitted in Huntington MS.*

A Rapture

25/ Queen *1642*, MSS.; Queens *1640*.

65/ cherry *1640*; cherries MSS.

66/ apple, tipped with coral berry *1640*; apples, tipped with crimson berries MSS.

92/ willing *1640*; naked MSS.

101/ spies *1640*; eyes MSS.

102/ envious eyes *1640*; politic spies MSS.

Another ["The purest soul that e'er was sent"]

5–10/ *C. L. Powell, in MLR, XI (1916), 286–287, proposes the following alternative version, based on B.M. MS. Harleian 6917:*

> The substance was too pure, the frame
> So glorious that thither came
> Ten thousand Cupids, bringing along
> A grace on each wing, that did throng
> For place there, till they all oppressed
> The seat in which they thought to rest.

To Ben Jonson . . .

19/ on *1640*; to MSS.

21/ form *1640*; shape MSS.

An Elegy upon the Death of Dr. Donne . . .

3/ dare *Poems, By J. D. 1633*; did *1640*.

5/ churchman *1633*; lect'rer *1640*.

7/ should *1633*; might *1640*.

17/ our will *1633*; the will *1640*.

44/ dust had raked *1633*; dung had searched *1640*.

50/ stubborn *1633*; troublesome *1640*.

58/ is purely *1633*; was only *1640*.

59/ thy *1633*; their *1640*.

63/ repeal *1633*; recall *1640*.

65/ Were *1633*; Was *1640*.

74/ faint *1633*; rude *1640*.

81/ small *1633*; short *1640*. maintain *1633*; retain *1640*.

88/ our *1633*; the *1640*.

89/ an *1633*; one *1640*.

91–92/ *omitted in 1640.*

94/ tomb *1633*; grave *1640*.

95–98/ *not italicized in 1640.*

97/ lie *1633*; lies *1640*.

To . . . Sandys . . .

5/ list'ning stays Sandys' *Paraphrase upon the Divine Poems 1638*; stays *1640*.

A Song ["Ask me no more where Jove bestows"]

Some MS. versions arrange the stanzas 2, 3, 1, 4, 5. B.M. MS. Add 23229, in Dunlap's view "an early draft," reads:

Ask me no more where Jove bestows
When June is past, the damask rose
For on your cheeks and lips they be
Fresher than on any tree.

Ask me no more where those stars light   5
That downwards fall in dark of night,
For in your eyes they sit and there
Fixed become, as in their sphere.

Ask me no more where nightingale
When June is past puts forth her tale,   10
For in your sweet dividing throat
She winters and keeps warm her note.

Nor ask me whether east or west,
The phoenix builds her spiced nest
For unto you she always flies,   15
And in your fragrant bosom dies.

*Two MS. versions that arrange the stanzas 2, 3, 1, 4, 5 conclude with a
(nearly identical) sixth stanza:*

Ask me no more whether north or south
These vapors come from out thy mouth
For unto heaven they are sent from hence
And there are made Jove's frankincense.

POEMS (1651)

Upon a Mole in Celia's Bosom
5/ close *1642, 1651*; those *Bodleian MS. Don. b. 9.*

James Shirley

The text is based on that in a copy of *Poems, &c.* (1646) in the Cambridge University Library. The Scolar Press facsimile of a copy of this
edition in the Bodleian Library, together with poems by Shirley in Bodleian
MS. Rawl. poet. 88 (Menston, 1970), has also been consulted. Further
textual information is obtained from *The Poems of James Shirley*, ed.
R. L. Armstrong (New York, 1941), and from *The Dramatic Works and
Poems of James Shirley*, ed. W. Gifford and A. Dyce, 6 vols. (London,
1833).

POEMS

Cupid's Call
*The poem derives from two separate lyrics, given in Bodleian MS. Rawl.
poet. 88 as follows:*

THE COURTESAN

Cupid calls o young men come,
Bring his wanton, wanton harvest home.
  When the birds most sweetly sing,
  And flowers are in their prime,
  No season, but the spring,   5
  Is Cupids harvest time.

Into Love's field, or garden walk,
Virgins dangle, dangle on their stalk,
  Blown, and playing at fifteen,
  And pointing to their beds,   10
  Come bring your sickles then,
  And reap their maidenheads.

ANOTHER

Hark, hark how in every grove,
Nightingales do sing of love,
They have lost their sullen note,
Warbling with a merry throat,
  There is no bliss to men   5
O let them ravish me again.

Virgins, that are young and fair,
Kiss yourselves into a pair.
Warm, and active keep your blood,
Let no thought congeal the flood,   10
  In youth refuse no art,
For age will snow upon your heart.

To His Mistress
Another version of st. 1 (in MS.) reads:
        O would to God, the god of Love would die,
        And give his bow, and arrows unto me,
        Then should I see to hit, (for love is blind)
        Her heart that to my vows is so unkind,
        And armed thus, this happiness I would prove,   5
        To wound her heart, or kill my own with love.

Love's Hue and Cry
*Another version, in Shirley's play, "The Witty Fair One" (1632–3), III. ii,
reads:*
        In Loves name you are charged hereby
        To make a speedy hue and cry,
        After a face, who t'other day
        Came and stole my heart away;
        For your directions in brief   5
        These are best marks to know the thief:
        Her hair a net of beams would prove,

Strong enough to capture Jove,
Playing the eagle: her clear brow
Is a comely field of snow.   10
A sparkling eye, so pure a gray
As when it shines it needs no day.
Ivory dwelleth on her nose;
Lilies, married to the rose,
Have made her cheek the nuptial bed;   15
Lips betray their virgin red,
As they only blushed for this,
That they one another kiss;
But observe, beside the rest,
You shall know this felon best   20
By her tongue; for if your ear
Shall once a heavenly music hear,
Such as neither gods nor men
But from that voice shall hear again,
That, that is she, oh, take her t'ye,   25
None can rock heaven asleep but she.

"Would you know what's soft?"
Another version, in several MSS., reads:

Would you know what's soft? I dare
Not bring you to the down, or air;
Nor to a star to show what's bright,
Nor to the snow to teach you white,
Nor if you would music hear,   5
Call the orbs to take your ear,
Nor to please your scent, bring forth
Bruised nard, or what's more worth
Or on food were your thoughts placed
Bring ambrosia for a taste.   10
Would you have all others in one?
Name my mistress, and 'tis done.

Love for Enjoying
Another version, in Bodleian MS. Rawl. poet. 88, reads:

Lady: what's your face to me?
I was not only made to see;
Every silent stander by
Thus enjoys, as much, as I.
Your rose and lilies are not mine,   5
By praising them into divine;
Natures wealth upon your brow,
On your cheek, or lip, doth show
That within are to be found,
Rocks of pearl, and diamond,   10
To which, a lapidary's art
Must richness and the price impart.
Here a vein with golden threads,
To the mine of pleasure leads,

Which who once enjoys, has power   15
To make more Indies every hour.
Come let us mix our selves, and prove
'Tis action, that perfects love.
Your smiles, and kisses; fruitless toying,
Stay me not, but tempt enjoying.   20
Shall we on either gazing stand,
Like armies in the Netherland,
Taking fear, at eithers sight,
Till we grow too weak to fight?
Give the signal, let us try   25
Who shall fall, yourself or I;
'Tis loves war, if either yield
We both lose, and win the field.

Two Gentlemen That Broke Their Promise . . .
An early version, in Bodleian MS Rawl. poet. 88, reads:

TO E. H. AND W. H.

There is no faith in claret, now I see
That blushing wine doth merely frenchify,
Can promises in wine, and wine, that should
Having no color, best agree with blood,
Make men so cold, that after, they appear   5
As dull as they which compliment in beer?
But 'tis no wonder, for we do not seek
A Christian, where there is no Catholic.
'Tis sack that justifies; and had you both
Promised in sack, each word had been an oath.   10

The Garden
Another version, in B.M. MS. Add. 33998, reads:

CHLORINDA'S GARDEN

Fain would I have a plot of ground
    Which the sun did never see,
Nor by wanton lover found,
    That alone my garden be.

No curious flowers do I crave,   5
    To tempt my smelling, or my eye,
A little heart's ease let me have
    But to look on, ere I die.

In the violet's drooping head
    Will my counterfeit appear,   10
A little thyme, but withered;
    But no woodbine shall grow there.

Weave a pretty robe of willow,
   On each side let blackthorn grow,
Raise a bank, where for my pillow,   15
   Wormwood, rue, and poppy strow.

No bird sing here but Philomel,
   Or the orphan turtle groan,
Either of these two can tell
   My sad story, by their own.   20

Here let no man find me out,
   Or, if chance shall bring one hither,
I'll be secure, when round about
   'Tis moated with my eyes' foul weather.

Thus let me sigh my heart away,   25
   At last to one as sad as I,
I'll give my garden, that he may,
   By my example, love and die.

Mildmay Fane, Earl of Westmorland

The text is based on that in a microfilm of a copy of *Otia Sacra* (1648) in the University of Illinois Library. *The Poems of Mildmay, Second Earl of Westmoreland* (1648), ed. A. B. Grosart (Manchester, 1879), and the versions of Fane's poems included in *Rare Poems of the Seventeenth Century*, ed. L. B. Marshall (Cambridge, 1936), have also been consulted.

OTIA SACRA

My Country Audit
1/ privacy!; privacy, *1648*.
5/ waived; wav'd *1648*.
My Observation At Sea
6/ ocean,; ocean. *1648*.
To Kiss God's Rod . . .
18/ new leaf; new-leaf *1648*.
19/ error writ; error-writ *1648*.
A Dedication of My First Son
8/ flour; flowre *1648*.
In Praise of Fidelia
2/ stored; store *1648*.
To Retiredness
72/ on't use; on't, use *1648*.

Thomas Randolph

The text is based on that in a copy of *Poems, with the Muses' Looking-Glass and Amyntas* (1638), in the Cambridge University Library. A microfilm of another copy of this edition, in the British Museum, has also been consulted. Manuscript and further textual information is obtained from *The Poems and Amyntas of Thomas Randolph*, ed. J. J. Parry (New Haven, Conn., 1917), and *The Poems of Thomas Randolph*, ed. G. Thorn-Drury (London, 1929).

POEMS, WITH THE MUSES' LOOKING-GLASS AND AMYNTAS

A Gratulatory to Mr. Ben Jonson . . .
6/ tenant unto 1638; poor tenant to B.M. MS. Add. 22602.
14/ thee, Horace *Parry* 1917; thy Horace 1638. whole 1638; full MS.
27/ can or should 1638; should or dare MS.
28/ adoption 1638; election MS.

Upon the Loss of His Little Finger
3/ what mischance hath ta'en 1638; that which chance did cut *Bodleian MS. Firth i.4.*
8/ death 1638; grave MSS.
11/ verse 1638; rhymes MSS.

An Elegy
2/ blind 1638; thine *Bodleian MS. Firth i.4.*
3/ my 1638; thy MS.
8/ most 1638; more MS.
12/ her perfection 1638; my affection MS.
15–16/ MS. *substitutes:* And when I send her verse, those that might be/ Termed sonnets in the loose, are hymns in me.
After l. 20 MS inserts: My mistress' face is fair, but soul divine,/And I adore the saint above the shrine.
23/ my 1638; mans MS.
26/ Earth's 1638; The MS.

Upon His Picture
5/ coldness 1638; colors *Bodleian MS. Firth i.4.*
15–16/ MS. *substitutes:* How shall it move my tears, when I shall see/My shadow is less giv'n to change than me.

An Answer to Mr. Jonson's Ode . . .
19/ plague can 1638; pain could *Bodleian MS. Firth i.4.*
30/ scraps, and send them from thy 1638; alms and serve them at the MS.
32/ Till they be taught to 1638; Whose follies cannot MS.
33/ and more 1638; I will MS.
39/ This only in my Ben I faulty 1638; And this alone in thee I guilty MS.
45/ fond 1638; sin MS.
50/ Muse 1638; quill MS.
53/ the wings of verse 1638; thy Uzzahs wing MS.
54/ fix it there 1638; make't a star MS.
57/ I would not have thee 1638; I know thou wouldst not MS.
59/ age 1638; eye MS.

William Habington

The text is based on that in a microfilm of a copy of *Castara* (1640) in the Yale University Library. Microfilms of copies of the 1634 and 1635 editions in the Huntington Library have also been consulted. Full textual apparatus is provided in K. Allott's edition of *Castara* (Liverpool, 1948).

CASTARA

A Dialogue Between Araphil and Castara
26/ chased *1634*, *1635*; chafed *1640*.

To a Friend, Inviting Him to a Meeting upon Promise
23/ pure *1640*; sure *1635*.

Edmund Waller

The text is based on that in a copy of the 1686 edition of *Poems, &c.* in the Cambridge University Library. Other editions consulted include the first ("Works," pub. for T. Walkley) and second issues of the 1645 edition (in a microfilm of the Huntington Library copy, and in the Scolar Press facsimile of a copy in the British Museum [Menston, 1971], respectively), and a copy of the "first authorized" edition of 1664 in the Cambridge University Library. The Scolar Press facsimile of Bodleian M.S. Don d 55 has also been consulted. Further information is obtained from *The Poems of Edmund Waller*, ed. G. Thorn-Drury, 2 vols. (London, 1905).

POEMS

To the King, on His Navy
8/ mighty . . . smaller *1686*; mightiest . . . smallest *Bodleian MS. Don d 55*, *1645*, *1664* .

9/ nobler *1664*, *1686*; stricter *MS.*, *1645*.

29/ designed that fabric to have stood *MS.*, *1664*, *1686*; designed, that fabrics should have stood *1645*.

To Mr. Henry Lawes . . .
17/ As a church window *1686*; For as a window *Ayres and Dialogues* *1653*.

Upon Ben Jonson
5/ Thou hast alone *MS.*, *1645*, *1664*, *1686*; Thou not alone *Jonsonus Virbius* *1638*.

7/ So tracéd *1664*, *1686*; Hast tracked *MS.*, *1645*; Hast traced *1638*.

8/ That whate'er *1664*, *1686*; What ever *MS.*, *1645*; But all that *1638*.

9/ habit *1645*, *1664*, *1686*; habits *MS.*, *1638*. deforms *1664*, *1686*; distorts *MS.*; distort *1638*; deserts *1645*.

10/ a brother can his brother *1664*, *1686*; one brother can the brother *MS.*, *1645*; the brother can the brother *1638*.

11/ represented *1638*, *1664*, *1686*; representing *MS.*, *1645*.

29/ which *1686*; who *MS.*, *1638*, *1645*, *1664*.

At Penshurst [1]
1/ Sacharissa *1664*, *1668*; Dorothea *MS.*, *1645*.

22/ fed all one *1686*; feed all on *MS.*; feed all on one *1645*; fed all on one *1664*.

At Penshurst [2]
40/ this passion *1664*, *1686*; affection *MS.*, *1645*.

The Battle of the Summer Islands
II, Proem, 1/ alarm 1664, 1686; affright MS., 1645.
36/ as the MS., 1664, 1686; as if 1645.
III, 7/ bounds MS.; boils 1645, 1664, 1686.
11/ Spenser's 1664, 1686; fairy MS., 1645.
29/ forces 1664, 1686; furies MS.; surges 1645.

On a Girdle
5/ was 1664, 1686; is 1645.
8/ Did 1664, 1686; Do 1645.
10/ Dwelt 1664, 1686; Dwells 1645.
11/ bound 1664, 1686; tied 1645.
12/ Take . . . round 1664, 1686; Take all the sun goes round beside 1645.

To the Mutable Fair
26/ motions MS.; motion 1645, 1664, 1686.

To a Lady in a Garden
In MS. and 1645 the title reads "To a Lady in Retirement"
3/ of their 1686; their sweet MS., 1645.
17/ you 1686; thee MS.; ye 1645.

"While I listen to thy voice"
4/ flitting 1645, 1664, 1686; fleeting MS.

On St. James's Park . . .
54/ draws 1664, 1686; grows *A Poem on St. James Park* 1661.
61/ lovely 1664, 1686; comely 1661.
89–90/ state . . . Fate 1664, 1686; state . . . Fates 1661.
95–96/ *omitted in* 1661.
109/ Here . . . go 1664, 1686; Here he does like the people's pastor go 1661.
121/ ruminates 1664, 1686; meditates 1661.

Sir John Suckling

The text is based on that in copies of *Fragmenta Aurea* (1646) and *The Last Remains of Sir John Suckling* (1659) in the Cambridge University Library. A microfilm of a copy of the 1646 edition of *Fragmenta Aurea* in the Yale University Library has also been consulted. Manuscript and other textual information is obtained from *The Works of Sir John Suckling: The Non-Dramatic Works*, ed. T. Clayton (Oxford, 1971).

FRAGMENTA AUREA

A Sessions of the Poets
The arrangement of "suspensions" (single words suspended between quatrains), imperfect in the 1646 edition of Fragmenta Aurea, follows that of Clayton's edition.
Title/ A Sessions of the Poets 1646; The Wits MSS.
9/ Thought . . . day 1646; That day thought to carry the laurel away MSS., *Fragmenta Aurea* 1648.
17/ Berkeleys *two* MSS.; Bartlets *most* MSS., 1646, 1648.

26/ did not 1646; did MSS., 1648.

39/ hard 1646; hide 1648.

55/ Berkeley *two MSS.*; Bartlet *most MSS.*, 1646, 1648.

60/ Suddenly *two MSS.*, 1646; Sullenly *some MSS.*

63/ Apollo 1646; Apollo himself MSS., 1648.

64/ on him 1646; on't MSS., 1648. how came 1646; what made 1648.

65/ whispering nothing 1646, 1648; busily whispering *most MSS.*

69/ care 1646; character MSS., 1648.

72/ let in 1646; to come in MSS., 1648.

77–81/ *omitted in 1646.*

83/ But 1646; And MSS., 1648.

93/ But witty 1646; But wise 1648; Wise MSS. asked 1646; then asked MSS., 1648.

99/ silence *some MSS.*, 1646, 1648; silent *some MSS.*

100/ crowd MSS., 1648; court 1646.

121/ that 'twas MSS., 1648; that 1646.

122/ wit MSS., 1648; wit's 1646.

128/ in great MSS., 1646; at large 1648.

130/ poets MSS., 1646; ones 1648. cleared *some MSS.*, 1646; cheered *some MSS.*, 1648.

133/ poets 1646; poet MSS., 1648.

Sonnet I

14/ my heart be faulty, or her eyes 1646; her face be guilty, or my eyes MSS.

Against Fruition [1]

10/ might grow 1646, *some MSS.*; should grow *some MSS.*

16/ there 1646, *some MSS.*; then *some MSS.*

24/ Heaven were 1646, *most MSS.*; It were *some MSS.*

Upon My Lady Carlisle's Walking . . .

7–8/ all . . . out 1646; everywhere/Such as Arabian gumtrees bear *Bodleian MS. Rawl. poet. 199.*

13/ had all their birth from 1646; were wholly made by MS.

16–17/ was . . . after-spring 1646; came to bring/News of this unknown after-spring MS.

26/ masks and hoods 1646; silks and lawn MS.

36/ Searched after 1646; Pressed on to MS.

37/ seldom stops 1646; hardly steps MS.

40–49/ *omitted in 1646.*

A Ballad upon a Wedding

3/ without 1646; beyond MSS., *Fragmenta Aurea* 1648.

5/ In any place on 1646; In any part of MSS., 1648.

12/ Forty MSS., 1648; Vorty 1646.

46/ But oh! MSS., 1646; But Dick 1648.

61–72/ *The order of these two stanzas is reversed in some MSS.*

65/ them 1646; her MSS., 1648.

72/ spent a 1646; spoiled one MSS.

79–84/ In 1646, *this stanza, with first three and last three lines transposed, follows l. 96.*

107/ Whilst MSS., 1648; Till 1646.

120/ Good Boy 1646; God b'w'y' *MSS.*, 1648; Good b'w'y' *Bodleian MS. Rawl. poet.* 37.

THE LAST REMAINS OF SIR JOHN SUCKLING

"Out Upon It! . . ."
4/ prove 1659; hold *MSS.*
5/ molt 1659; melt *MSS.*
6/ shall *some MSS.*, 1659; can *some MSS.*
9/ the spite on't 1659; a pox upon't *MSS.*
10/ Is due 1659; There is due *MSS.*
14/ very very *MSS*; very 1659.

A Song to a Lute
4/ winds 1659 (*Poems*); waves 1659 (*The Sad One*).

Sidney Godolphin

With two exceptions, the text is based on that in *Poems of Sidney Godolphin*, ed. William Dighton (Oxford, 1931), from which manuscript information is obtained. The text of Godolphin's epitaph on Jonson is based on that in a microfilm of a copy of *Jonsonus Virbius* (1638) in the British Museum; that of the elegy on Donne is based on the text in *Poems, by J. D.* (1635), in *The Poems of John Donne*, ed. Sir H. J. C. Grierson (London, 1933). The texts of Godolphin's poems reproduced in *Minor Poets of the Caroline Period*, ed. G. Saintsbury, 3 vols. (Oxford, 1906), II, have also been consulted.

POEMS

Song (" 'Tis affection but dissembled")
6/ favor *Bodleian MS. Malone* 13; favors *Drinkwater MS.*

"Chloris, it is not thy disdain"
8/ hapless *Malone MS.*; hopeless *Drinkwater MS.*

"Lord, when the wise men came from far"
16/ come *Malone MS*; came *Drinkwater MS.*

William Cartwright

The text is based on a copy of *Comedies, Tragi-Comedies, With Other Poems* (1651), in the Cambridge University Library. Manuscript and other textual information is obtained from *The Plays and Poems of William Cartwright*, ed. G. Blakemore Evans (Madison, Wis., 1951).

COMEDIES, TRAGI-COMEDIES, WITH OTHER POEMS

No Platonic Love
15/ profess 1651; protest *The Marrow of Compliments* 1655.
19/ Come . . . tread 1651; Let all believe this truth that those that tread 1655.

A New Year's Gift
43/ Thoughts rescue *1651*; Though he's rescued *Evans conj. 1951*.

James Graham, Marquis of Montrose

The text is based on that in a copy of James Watson, *A Choice Collection of Comic and Serious Scots Poems* (Edinburgh, 1711), in the Cambridge University Library. Additional textual information is available in *The Poems of James Graham, Marquis of Montrose (1612–1650)*, ed. J. L. Weir (London, 1938). The poem first appeared, c. 1660, in broadside form, with the title, "An Excellent New Ballad to the Tune of 'I'll never love thee more.' "

Sir John Denham

The text is based on that in a copy of *Poems and Translations* (1668) in the Cambridge University Library. Microfilms of a copy of *Cooper's Hill* (1642) in the British Museum and of a copy of *Poems and Translations* (1668) in the Huntington Library have also been consulted. Other textual information is obtained from *The Poetical Works of Sir John Denham*, ed. T. H. Banks, 2nd ed. (New Haven, 1969), and B. O Hehir, *Expans'd Hieroglyphicks: A Critical Edition of Sir John Denham's Coopers Hill* (Berkeley, 1969).

POEMS AND TRANSLATIONS

Cooper's Hill
1/ Sure . . . which *1668*; Sure we have poets, that *1642*; If there be poets, which *1655*.
3/ we . . . may *1668*; and therefore I *1642*; we justly may *1655*.
6/ train *1655, 1668*; troops *1642*.
13–18/ In *1655* and *1668* *these lines replace the following couplet in* *1642*:
        Exalted to this height, I first look down
        On Paul's, as men from thence upon the town.
18/ descending *1668*; a falling *1655*.
25–30/ Under . . . seems *1655, 1668*; *1642 reads*:
        As those who raised in body, or in thought
        Above the earth, or the air's middle vault,
        Behold how winds, and storms, and meteors grow,
        How clouds condense to rain, congeal to snow,
        And see the thunder formed, before it tear
        The air, secure from danger and from fear,
        So raised above the tumult and the crowd
        I see the city in a thicker cloud
        Of business, than of smoke, where men like ants
        Toil to prevent imaginary wants;
        Yet all in vain, increasing with their store,
        Their vast desires, but make their wants the more.

As food to unsound bodies, though it please
The appetite, feeds only the disease,

36/ *After this line, 1642 reads:*

Some study plots, and some those plots t'undo,
Others to make 'em, and undo 'em too,
False to their hopes, afraid to be secure
Those mischiefs only which they make, endure,
Blinded with light, and sick of being well,
In tumults seek their peace, their heaven in hell.

41–60/ *Into . . . race 1655, 1668; 1642 reads:*

Into my eye, as the late married dame,
(Who proud, yet seems to make that pride her shame)
When nature quickens in her pregnant womb
Her wishes past, and now her hopes to come:
With such an easy, and unforced ascent,
Windsor her gentle bosom doth present;
Where no stupendous cliff, no threat'ning heights
Access deny, no horrid steep affrights,
But such a rise, as doth at once invite
A pleasure, and a reverence from the sight.
Thy master's emblem, in whose face I saw
A friend-like sweetness, and a king-like awe,
Where majesty and love so mixed appear,
Both gently kind, both royally severe.
So Windsor, humble in itself, seems proud,
To be the base of that majestic load,
Than which no hill a nobler burden bears,
But Atlas only, that supports the spheres.
Nature this mount so fitly did advance,
We might conclude, that nothing is by chance
So placed, as if she did on purpose raise
The hill, to rob the builder of his praise.
For none commends his judgement, that doth choose
That which a blind man only could refuse;
Such are the towers which th'hoary temples graced
Of Cybele, when all her heavenly race

79–82/ *And thy . . . bring 1655, 1668; 1642 reads:*

He that the lilies wore, and he that won,
And thy Bellona who deserves her share
In all thy glories, of that royal pair
Which waited on thy triumph, she brought one,
Thy son the other brought, and she that son
Nor of less hopes could her great offspring prove,
A royal eagle cannot breed a dove.

85–86/ *Each was . . . success 1655, 1668; 1642 reads:*

Each was a noble cause, nor was it less
I'th'institution, than the great success,
Whilst every part conspires to give it grace,
The King, the cause, the patron, and the place,

101–113/ *When he . . . of late 1655, 1668; 1642 reads:*

Thou hadst extended through the conquered East
Thine and the Christian name, and made them blest
To serve thee, while that loss this gain would bring,
Christ for their God, and Edward for their King;
When thou that saint thy patron didst design,
In whom the martyr, and the soldier join;
And when thou didst within the azure round,
(Who evil thinks may evil him confound)
The English arms encircle, thou didst seem
But to foretell, and prophesy of him
Who has within that azure round confined
These realms, which nature for their bound designed.
That bound which to the worlds extremest ends,
Endless herself, her liquid arms extends;
In whose heroic face I see the saint
Better expressed than in the liveliest paint,
That fortitude which made him famous here,
That heavenly piety, which saints him there,
Who when this Order he forsakes, may he
Companion of that sacred order be.
Here could I fix my wonder, but our eyes,
Nice as our tastes, affect varieties;
And though one please him most, the hungry guest
Tastes every dish, and runs through all the feast;
So having tasted Windsor, casting round
My wand'ring eye, an emulous hill doth bound,
My more contracted sight, whose top of late

122/ But . . . poor, *1655, 1668*; But they, alas, were rich, and he was poor, *1642*.

127–33/ No crime . . . amends *1655, 1668; 1642 reads:*

    And he might think it just, the cause and time
    Considered well, for none commits a crime
    Appearing such, but as 'tis understood
    A real or at least a seeming good.
    While for the church his learned pen disputes,
    His much more learned sword his pen confutes;
    Thus to the ages past he makes amends

149–156/ Who sees . . . are? *1655, 1668; omitted in 1642.*

165–166/ Though with . . . gold; *1655, 1668*; And though his clearer sand no golden veins,/Like Tagus and Pactolus streams contains *1642*.

171–172/ Nor then . . . overlay *1655, 1668; omitted in 1642.*

173/ sudden and impetuous *1655, 1668*; furious and unruly *1642*.

177–186/ But God-like . . . plants *1655, 1668; 1642 reads:*

    Then like a lover he forsakes his shores,
    Whose stay with jealous eye his spouse implores,
    Till with a parting kiss he saves her tears,
    And promising return, secures her fears;
    As a wise king first settles fruitful peace
    In his own realms, and with their rich increase
    Seeks wars abroad, and then in triumph brings

The spoils of kingdoms, and the crowns of kings;
So Thames to London doth at first present
Those tributes which the neighboring countries sent;
But at his second visit from the east,
Spices he brings, and treasures from the west;
Finds wealth where 'tis, and gives it where it wants,
Cities in deserts, woods in cities plants;
Rounds the whole globe, and with his flying towers
Brings home to us and makes both Indies ours.

189–196/ O could . . . gods 1668; 1655 *omits* 193–196; 1642 *reads:*
O could my verse freely and smoothly flow,
As thy pure flood, heaven should no longer know
Her old Eridanus, thy purer stream
Should bathe the gods, and be the poet's theme.

217–233/ But his . . . shape 1655, 1668; 1642 *reads:*
And such the roughness of the hill, on which
Diana her toils, and Mars his tents might pitch.
And as our surly, supercilious lords,
Big in their frowns, and haughty in their words,
Look down on those, whose humble fruitful pain
Their proud, and barren greatness must sustain:
So looks the hill upon the stream, between
There lies a spacious, and a fertile green;
Where from the woods, the Dryades oft meet
The Naiades, and with their nimble feet
Soft dances lead, although their airy shape

236/ hornéd 1655, 1668; horrid 1642. *After l.* 236, 1642 *reads:*
(When like the elixir, with his evening beams,
The sun has turned to gold the silver streams)

240/ are undone 1655, 1668; much undone 1642.

241/ the King 1655, 1668; our Charles 1642.

243–271/ Attended to . . . unkindly wise 1655, 1668; 1642 *reads:*
Chasing the royal stag, the gallant beast,
Roused with the noise 'twixt hope and fear distressed,
Resolves 'tis better to avoid, than meet
His danger, trusting to his winged feet:
But when he sees the dogs, now by the view
Now by the scent his speed with speed pursue,
He tries his friends, amongst the lesser herd,
Where he but lately was obeyed, and feared,
Safety he seeks, the herd unkindly wise,

275–288/ With shame . . . death 1655, 1668; *omitted in* 1642.

293–294/ And now . . . flight 1655, 1668; *omitted in* 1642.

297–303/ He straight . . . t'assay 1655, 1668; 1642 *reads:*
When neither speed, nor art, nor friends, nor force
Could help him towards the stream he bends his course;
Hoping those lesser beasts would not assay

307–312/ So towards . . . wounds 1655, 1668; *omitted in* 1642.

316/ common 1655, 1668; vulgar 1642.

319–322/ So when . . . flood 1655, 1668; 1642 *reads:*

> So the tall stag, amids the lesser hounds
> Repels their force, and wounds returns for wounds,
> Till Charles from his unerring hand lets fly
> A mortal shaft, then glad, and proud to die
> By such a wound he falls, the crystal flood
> Dying he dies, and purples with his blood:

326/ lawless power 1655, 1668; tyranny 1642.

328/ *After this line 1642 reads:*

> For armed subjects can have no pretence
> Against their princes, but their just defence,
> And whether then, or no, I leave to them
> To justify, who else themselves condemn:
> Yet might the fact be just, if we may guess
> The justness of an action from success

343–348/ Thus kings . . . less 1655, 1668; 1642 *reads:*

> And they, whom no denial can withstand,
> Seem but to ask, while they indeed command.
> Thus all to limit royalty conspire,
> While each forgets to limit his desire.
> Till kings like old Antaeus by their fall,
> Being forced, their courage from despair recall.

After 358, 1642 *reads:*

> Thus kings by grasping more than they can hold,
> First made their subjects by oppressions bold,
> And popular sway by forcing kings to give
> More, than was fit for subjects to receive,
> Ran to the same extreme, and one excess
> Made both, by stirring to be greater, less;
> Nor any way, but seeking to have more,
> Makes either lose, what each possessed before.
> Therefore their boundless power tell princes draw
> Within the channel, and the shores of law,
> And may that law, which teaches kings to sway
> Their scepters, teach their subjects to obey.

On . . . Cowley . . .
In the first edition of this poem (1667), ll. 67–70, 81–84, and 87–88 are omitted.

A Song ["Somnus, the humble god, that dwells"]
1/ Somnus 1668; Morpheus *The Sophy* 1642, *Poems and Translations* 1671, 1684.

Richard Lovelace

The text is based on that in a copy of *Lucasta* (1649) in the Library of Emmanuel College, Cambridge, and a copy of *Lucasta. Posthume Poems* (1659) in the Library of Trinity College, Cambridge. A microfilm of a copy of the 1659 volume in the Huntington Library has also been consulted. Manuscript and other textual information is obtained from *The Poems of Richard Lovelace*, ed. C. H. Wilkinson, 2 vols. (Oxford, 1925).

LUCASTA

The Scrutiny . . .
7/ hours' 1649, 1659; months *Wits Interpreter* 1655.
8/ must 1649, 1659; should *Select Musicall Ayres and Dialogues* 1653, *Wits Interpreter* 1655.
11/ Not but all joy 1649, 1659; Not that all joys *Select Musicall Ayres and Dialogues* 1652, *Wits Interpreter* 1655.
12/ By 1649, 1659; In 1655.
13/ I must 1649, 1659; I will 1652, 1655.
18/ With spoils 1649, 1659; In spoil 1652, 1655.

To Lucasta. From Prison . . .
12/ will she 1659; she will 1649.

To Althea. From Prison . . .
Cf. *Wilkinson's edition, I, pp. 47–60, for full account of variants.*
7/ gods 1649, 1659; birds MSS.
18/ throat 1649, 1659; notes *B.M. MS. Add.* 22603; note MSS.
27/ Minds innocent and quiet take 1649, 1659; The spotless soul and innocent MSS.; A spotless mind and innocent MSS.
32/ Enjoy MSS., 1649, 1659; Know no *Bodleian MS.* 1267 *Rawl. D.*

Abraham Cowley

The text is based on that in a copy of *The Works Of Mr. Abraham Cowley* (1668) in the Cambridge University Library. A microfilm of another copy of that edition in the British Museum has also been consulted. Further textual information is obtained from A. R. Waller's edition of Cowley's *Poems* (Cambridge, 1905).

THE WORKS OF MR. ABRAHAM COWLEY

Ode. Of Wit.
51/ the bombast 1668; th'Oxford *Poems* 1656.

On the Death of Mr. Crashaw
21/ broke 1668; breaks 1656.
22/ spoke 1668; speaks 1656.

Anacreontics I: Love
14/ soft 1668; and soft 1656.

Platonic Love
3–4 too combine . . . join 1668; too do join,/And both our wholes into one whole combine *The Mistress* 1647, *Poems* 1656.

To the Royal Society
In the first version of this poem (in Sprat's History of the Royal Society, 1667), the following lines appear after l. 145:
>   She with much stranger art than his who put
>   All th'Iliads in a nut,
>   The numerous work of life does into atoms shut.

Henry Vaughan

The text is based on that in a microfilm of a copy of *Poems, With the Tenth Satire of Juvenal Englished* (1646) in the University of Illinois Library, and (for "An Epitaph upon the Lady Elizabeth") a microfilm of a copy of *Olor Iscanus* (1651) in the British Museum. Further textual information is obtained from *The Works of Henry Vaughan*, ed. L. C. Martin (Oxford, 1963), and from *The Complete Poetry of Henry Vaughan*, ed. French Fogle (Garden City, New York, 1964).

POEMS, WITH THE TENTH SATIRE OF JUVENAL ENGLISHED

To Amoret, Walking in a Starry Evening
8–9/ Amidst . . . stories 1646; Which rolls those fiery spheres/Thro' years and years *B.M. MS. C. 56.b.16.*
18/ Of some predestined 1646; There would be perfect *MS.*

Thomas Stanley

The text is based on that in a copy of *Poems* (1651) in the Cambridge University Library; the text of "Expectation" is based on that in a microfilm of a copy of *Poems and Translations* (1647) in the University of Illinois Library. Manuscript and further textual information is obtained from *Poems and Translations of Thomas Stanley*, ed. G. M. Crump (Oxford, 1962). *Minor Poems of the Caroline Period*, ed. G. Saintsbury, 3 vols. (Oxford, 1921), has also been consulted.

POEMS

The Glowworm
2/ animated gem 1651; living star of earth *MSS.*, 1647.
4/ erring 1651; deceived *MSS.*, 1647.
11/ paler 1647, 1651; purer *Bodleian MS. Mus. b.1.*
15/ thy 1651; the 1647.
Changed, Yet Constant
12–13/ By whom . . . desired 1651; Who would as much/With love be fired *Cambs. Univ. Lib. MS. Add. 7514.*
17–24/ *In MS. this stanza reads:* She thats most fair/Exacts above/The rest obedience/For none there are/With reason love/But they that love by sense/Nor think allegiance I decline/Who was love's subject never thine
31–32 Now power . . . never 1651; 'Twere the same sin should I adore/Thee now or not have done't before *MS.*
33–48/ *Omitted in MS.*
For another distinctive MS. version of the poem, cf. Crump's edition, pp. 7–9.
Celia Singing
Title/Celia Singing 1651; Celia sleeping or singing 1647.

10/ more 1647; less 1651.

12/ frame *Cambs MS.*, 1647; flame 1651.

19/ powers 1651; power 1647.

The Repulse

21/ have *Gardner 1957, Crump 1962*; have not *Cambs MS.*, 1647, 1651.

Love's Innocence

1/ strives to 1651; (Dear) doth *Cambs MS.*, 1647.

7/ As . . . fear 1651; To one another, whisp'ring there MS., 1647.

9–11/ such a . . . guides 1651; (Fair) that flame to show/Which like thyself no crime can know:/Thus led by those chaste guides MS., 1647.

12/ well 1651; free MS., 1647.

20/ (As our desires) 1651; (As are our flames) MS., 1647.

21/ we, my dear 1651; Doris, we MS., 1647.

La Belle Confidente

15/ But ours, that boast a reach 1647, 1651; Ours that a being boast *Cambs MS.*

17/ For 1651; And MS., 1647.

18/ Our . . . benighted 1651; (Even in divorce delighted) MS., 1647.

20/ Even in divorce 1651; Still in the grave MS., 1647.

The Bracelet

7/ soul 1651; heart MSS., 1647.

12/ A heart . . . sold 1651; Have to mine enemy my freedom sold MSS., 1647.

15/ human breasts 1651; do our life MSS., 1647.

22/ Defends my vanquished 1651; Guards and defends my MSS., 1647.

The Exequies

5/ hard marble with your 1647, 1651; the marble with sad *Bodleian MS.*

7/ the sad subject 1651; do a victim MSS., 1647.

8/ Of all . . . pride 1651; That (paid to beauty) on love's altar died MSS., 1647.

21/ flowers 1647, 1651; trees *Bodleian MS.*

22/ such 1647, 1651; this *Bodleian MS.*

23/ only 1647, 1651; *omitted Bodleian MS.*

The Relapse

5/ blindly impious 1651; irreligious *Cambs MS.*; blind, and impious 1647.

16/ Both think 1647, 1651; Both speak *Cambs MS.* and 1647, 1651; or *Cambs MS.*

On Mr. Shirley's Poems

19/ words 1651; speech 1647.

30/ foe 1651; friend 1647.

31–32/ *omitted in 1647.*

33/ And hast . . . surpassed 1651; Thou hast so far all future times surpassed 1647.

Criticism

Seventeenth-Century Criticism

BEN JONSON

From *Timber, or Discoveries*†

[*Man, Nature, and the Ancients*][1]

Natures that are hardened to evil, you shall sooner break, than make straight; they are like poles that are crooked, and dry: there is no attempting them. * * *

The two chief things that give a man reputation in counsel, are the opinion of his honesty, and the opinion of his wisdom. The authority of those two will persuade, when the same counsels, uttered by other persons less qualified, are of no efficacy, or working.

Wisdom without honesty is mere craft, and cozenage. And therefore the reputation of honesty must first be gotten; which cannot be, but by living well. A good life is a main argument.

Next a good life, to beget love in the persons we counsel, by dissembling our knowledge of ability in ourselves, and avoiding all suspicion of arrogance, ascribing all to their instruction, as an ambassador to his master, or a subject to his sovereign; seasoning all with humanity and sweetness, only expressing care and solicitude. And not to counsel rashly, or on the sudden, but with advice and meditation: *Dat nox consilium.*[2] For many foolish things fall from wise men, if they speak in haste, or be extemporal. It therefore behooves the giver of counsel to be circumspect; especially to beware of those with whom he is not thoroughly acquainted, lest any spice of rashness, folly, or self-love appear, which will be marked by new persons, and men of experience in affairs. * * *

A man should so deliver himself to the nature of the subject,

---

† *Timber, or Discoveries* (included in the third volume of Jonson's *Works*, published in 1640–1641) is a "commonplace book," i.e., a collection of pithy observations on manners, men, and art. While Jonson draws on Greek and Latin authors and on sixteenth-century humanists for much of his material, he has extensively reworked his source materials, combining them with anecdotes and opinions that reflect his own experience. The text is based on that in *Ben Jonson*, ed. C. H. Herford, P. and E. M. Simpson, 11 vols. (Oxford, 1925–1952), VIII (hereafter cited as *H&S*).
1. The observations in this section are, save for the first sentence, based on various writings by the Spanish humanist Juan Luis Vives (1492–1540) [*Editor*].
2. "Night gives counsel" [*Editor*].

whereof he speaks, that his hearer may take knowledge of his discipline with some delight: and so apparel fair, and good matter, that the studious of elegancy be not defrauded; redeem arts from their rough, and braky seats, where they lay hid, and overgrown with thorns, to a pure, open, and flowery light: where they may take the eye, and be taken by the hand.

I cannot think Nature is so spent, and decayed, that she can bring forth nothing worth her former years. She is always the same, like herself: and when she collects her strength, is abler still. Men are decayed, and studies: she is not.

I know nothing can conduce more to letters, than to examine the writings of the ancients, and not to rest in their sole authority, or take all upon trust from them, provided the plagues of judging, and pronouncing against them be away; such as are envy, bitterness, precipitation, impudence, and scurrile scoffing. For to all the observations of the ancients, we have our own experience: which, if we will use, and apply, we have better means to pronounce. It is true they opened the gates, and made the way, that went before us; but as guides, not commanders: *Non domini nostri, sed duces fuere.* Truth lies open to all: it is no man's several. *Patet omnibus veritas; nondum est occupata. Multum ex illa, etiam futuris relictum est.*[3]

If in some things I dissent from others, whose wit, industry, diligence, and judgement I look up at, and admire: let me not therefore hear presently of ingratitude, and rashness. For I thank those, that have taught me, and will ever: but yet dare not think the scope of their labour, and enquiry, was to envy their posterity, what they also could add, and find out.

If I err, pardon me: *Nulla ars simul et inventa est, et absoluta.*[4] I do not desire to be equal to those that went before; but to have my reason examined with theirs, and so much faith to be given them, or me, as those shall evict. I am neither author, or fautor[5] of any sect. I will have no man addict himself to me; but if I have anything right, defend it as truth's, not mine (save as it conduceth to a common good.) It profits not me to have any man fence, or fight for me, to flourish, or take a side. Stand for truth, and 'tis enough. * * *

[Poets and "Wits"]

Nothing in our age, I have observed, is more preposterous, than the running judgments upon poetry, and poets; when we shall hear those things commended, and cried up for the best writings,

---

3. "Much of it is left also for those to come" [*Editor*].

4. "No art is complete the moment it is discovered" [*Editor*].

5. Advocate [*Editor*].

which a man would scarce vouchsafe to wrap any wholesome drug in; he would never light his tobacco with them. And those men almost named for miracles, who yet are so vile, that if a man should go about to examine and correct them, he must make all they have done, but one blot. Their good is so entangled with their bad, as forcibly one must draw on the other's death with it. A sponge dipped in ink will do all: *Comitetur punica librium spongia. Et paulo post, Non possunt . . . multae, una litura potest.*[6]

Yet their vices have not hurt them: nay, a great many they have profited; for they have been loved for nothing else. And this false opinion grows strong against the best men: if once it take root with the ignorant. Cestius,[7] in his time, was preferred to Cicero; so far, as the ignorant durst; they learned him without book, and had him often in their mouths. But a man cannot imagine that thing so foolish, or rude, but will find, and enjoy an admirer; at least, a reader, or spectator. The puppets are seen now in despite of the players; Heath's *Epigrams*,[8] and the Sculler's poems have their applause. There are never wanting that dare prefer the worst preachers, the worst pleaders, the worst poets; not that the better have left to write, or speak better, but that they that hear them judge worse: *Non illi peius dicunt, sed hi corruptius judicant.* Nay, if it were put to the question of the Water-rhymer's works, against Spenser, I doubt not, but that they would find more suffrages; because the most favor common vices, out of a prerogative the vulgar have, to lose their judgments, and like that which is naught.

Poetry, in this latter age, hath proved but a mean mistress, to such as have wholly addicted themselves to her, or given their names up to her family. They who have but saluted her on the by, and now and then tendered their visits, she hath done much for, and advanced in the way of their own professions (both the Law, and the Gospel) beyond all they could have hoped, or done for themselves, without her favor. Wherein she doth emulate the judicious, but preposterous bounty of the time's grandees: who accumulate all they can upon the parasite, or freshman in their friendship; but think an old client, or honest servant, bound by his place to write, and starve.

Indeed, the multitude commend writers, as they do fencers, or wrestlers; who if they come in robustiously, and put for it, with a deal of violence, are received for the braver fellows: when many times their own rudeness is a cause of their disgrace; and a slight

6. "Let a Punic sponge go with the book"; (and, a little farther on) "No amount [of erasures] will serve; a general blotting-out is needed" (Martial, *Epigrams*, IV. x) [*Editor*].
7. Cestius of Smyrna was a Greek rhetorician who responded to several of Cicero's orations [*Editor*].
8. John Heath's *Epigrams* were published in 1610; the Thames waterman John Taylor (1580–1653), known as "the water-poet," published his verses in 1630 [*Editor*].

touch of their adversary, gives all that boisterous force the foil. But in these things, the unskillful are naturally deceived, and judging wholly by the bulk, think rude things greater than polished; and scattered more numerous, than composed: nor think this only to be true in the sordid multitude, but the neater sort of our gallants: for all are the multitude; only they differ in clothes, not in judgment or understanding.

I remember, the players have often mentioned it as an honor to Shakespeare, that in his writing (whatsoever he penned), he never blotted out line. My answer hath been, would he had blotted a thousand. Which they thought a malevolent speech. I had not told posterity this, but for their ignorance, who choose that circumstance to commend their friend by, wherein he most faulted. And to justify mine own candor (for I loved the man, and do honor his memory, on this side idolatry, as much as any.) He was (indeed) honest, and of an open, and free nature: had an excellent fancy; brave notions, and gentle expressions: wherein he flowed with that facility, that sometimes it was necessary he should be stopped: *Sufflaminandus erat*, as Augustus said of Haterius.[9] His wit was in his own power; would the rule of it had been so too. Many times he fell into those things, could not escape laughter: as when he said in the person of Caesar, one speaking to him, "Caesar, thou dost me wrong." He replied, "Caesar did never wrong, but with just cause,"[1] and such like; which were ridiculous. But he redeemed his vices, with his virtues. There was ever more in him to be praised, than to be pardoned.

In the difference of wits,[2] I have observed; there are many notes: and it is a little mastery to know them: to discern, what every nature, every disposition will bear: for before we sow our land, we should plough it. There are no fewer forms of minds, than of bodies amongst us. The variety is incredible; and therefore we must search. Some are fit to make divines, some poets, some lawyers, some physicians; some to be sent to the plough, and trades.

There is no doctrine will do good, where nature is wanting. Some wits are swelling, and high; others low and still: some hot and fiery; others cold and dull: one must have a bridle, the other a spur.

There be some that are forward, and bold; and these will do every little thing easily: I mean, that is hard by, and next them: which they will utter, unretarded, without any shamefastness. These

9. The remark ("What he needed was a brake") occurs in Marcus Annaeus Seneca, *Controversiae*, IV. The Roman rhetorician Quintus Haterius died in A.D. 26 [*Editor*].

1. Cf. *Julius Caesar*, III i. 47–48 [*Edi-*

tor].

2. The remainder of this section is largely based on Books I and II of Quintilian's *Institutio Oratoria* and Seneca's *Controversiae*, III [*Editor*].

never perform much, but quickly. They are, what they are on the sudden; they show presently, like grain, that, scattered on the top of the ground, shoots up, but takes no root; has a yellow blade, but the ear empty. They are wits of good promise at first, but there is an *Ingenistitium*.[3] They stand still at sixteen, they get no higher.

You have others, that labor only to ostentation; and are ever more busy about the colors, and surface of a work, than in the matter, and foundation: for that is hid, the other is seen.

Others that in composition are nothing, but what is rough and broken: *Quae per salebras, altaque, saxa cadunt*.[4] And if it would come gently, they trouble it of purpose. They would not have it run without rubs,[5] as if that style were more strong and manly, that struck the ear with a kind of unevenness. These men err not by chance, but knowingly, and willingly; they are like men that affect a fashion by themselves, have some singularity in a ruff, cloak, or hat-band; or their beards, specially cut to provoke beholders, and set a mark upon themselves. They would be reprehended, while they are looked on. And this vice, one that is in authority with the rest, loving, delivers over to them to be imitated: so that oft-times the faults which he fell into, the others seek for: this is the danger, when vice becomes a precedent.

Others there are, that have no composition at all; but a kind of tuning, and rhyming fall, in what they write. It runs and slides, and only makes a sound. Women's poets they are called: as you have women's tailors.

> They write a verse, as smooth, as soft, as cream;
> In which there is no torrent, nor scarce stream.

You may sound these wits, and find the depth of them, with your middle finger. They are cream-bowl, or but puddle deep.

Some that turn over all books, and are equally searching in all papers, that write out of what they presently find or meet, without choice: by which means it happens, that what they have discredited, and impugned in one work, they have before, or after, extolled the same in another. Such are all the essayists, even their master Montaigne. These, in all they write, confess still what books they have read last; and therein their own folly, so much, that they bring it to the stake raw, and undigested: not that the place did need it neither; but that they thought themselves furnished, and would vent it.

Some again, who (after they have got authority, or, which is less, opinion, by their writings, to have read much) dare presently to

3. "A wit-stand" [Jonson's note].
4. "Which fall over rough places and high rocks" (Martial, *Epigrams,* XI, xc.

2) [*Editor*].
5. I.e., uneven places in the surface of a bowling green [*Editor*].

feign whole books, and authors, and lie safely. For what never was, will not easily be found; not by the most curious.

And some, by a cunning protestation against all reading, and false venditation of their own naturals,[6] think to divert the sagacity of their readers from themselves, and cool the scent of their own fox-like thefts; when yet they are so rank, as a man may find whole pages together usurped from one author, their necessities compelling them to read for present use, which could not be in many books; and so come forth more ridiculously, and palpably guilty, than those, who, because they cannot trace, they yet would slander their industry.

But the wretcheder are the obstinate contemners of all helps, and arts: such as presuming on their own naturals (which perhaps are excellent) dare deride all diligence, and seem to mock at the terms, when they understand not the things; thinking that way to get off wittily, with their ignorance. These are imitated often by such, as are their peers in negligence, though they cannot be in nature: and they utter all they can think, with a kind of violence, and indisposition; unexamined, without relation, either to person, place, or any fitness else; and the more willful, and stubborn, they are in it, the more learned they are esteemed of the multitude, through their excellent vice of judgment: who think those things the stronger, that have no art: as if to break, were better than to open; or to rent asunder, gentler than to loose.

It cannot but come to pass, that these men, who commonly seek to do more than enough, may sometimes happen on something that is good, and great; but very seldom: and when it comes, it doth not recompense the rest of their ill. For their jests, and their sentences (which they only, and ambitiously seek for) stick out, and are more eminent; because all is sordid, and vile about them; as lights are more discerned in a thick darkness, than a faint shadow. Now because they speak all they can (however unfitly) they are thought to have the greater copy;[7] where the learned use ever election, and a mean;[8] they look back to what they intended at first, and make all an even, and proportioned body. The true artificer will not run away from nature, as he were afraid of her; or depart from life, and the likeness of truth; but speak to the capacity of his hearers. And though his language differ from the vulgar somewhat; it shall not fly from all humanity, with the Tamerlanes, and Tamer-Chams[9] of the late age, which had nothing in them but the scenical strutting, and furious vociferation, to warrant them to the ignorant gapers. He knows it is his only art, so to carry it, as

6. I.e., display of their natural gifts [*Editor*].
7. Abundance [*Editor*].
8. I.e., selection and moderation [*Editor*].
9. *Tamer-Cham*, a lost play, appears to have been an imitation of Marlowe's *Tamburlaine* [*Editor*].

none but artificers perceive it. In the meantime perhaps he is called barren, dull, lean, a poor writer (or by what contumelious word can come in their cheeks) by these men, who without labor, judgment, knowledge, or almost sense, are received, or preferred before him. He gratulates them, and their fortune. Another age, or juster men, will acknowledge the virtues of his studies: his wisdom, in dividing:[1] his subtlety, in arguing: with what strength he doth inspire his readers; with what sweetness he strokes them: in inveighing, what sharpness; in jest, what urbanity he uses. How he doth reign in men's affections; how invade, and break in upon them; and makes their minds like the thing he writes. Then in his elocution to behold, what word is proper: which hath ornament: which height: what is beautifully translated: where figures are fit: which gentle, which strong to show the composition manly. And how he hath avoided faint, obscure, obscene, sordid, humble, improper, or effeminate phrase; which is not only praised of the most, but commended (which is worse), especially for that it is naught.

[*Knowledge and Ignorance*]

I know no disease of the soul, but ignorance; not of the arts and sciences, but itself; yet relating to those, it is a pernicious evil: the darkener of man's life, the disturber of his reason, and common confounder of truth; with which a man goes groping in the dark, no otherwise than if he were blind. Great understandings are most racked and troubled with it; nay, sometimes they will rather choose to die, than not to know the things they study for. Think then what an evil it is; and what good the contrary.

Knowledge is the action of the soul; and is perfect without the senses, as having the seeds of all science and virtue in itself; but not without the service of the senses: by those organs, the soul works. She is a perpetual agent, prompt and subtle; but often flexible, and erring; entangling herself like a silkworm; but her reason is a weapon with two edges, and cuts through. In her indagations[2] oft-times new scents put her by; and she takes in errors into her, by the same conduits she doth truths. * * *

[*English "Wits"*]

Cicero is said to be the only wit, that the people of Rome had equalled to their empire. *Ingenium par imperio*.[3] We have had many, and in their several ages (to take in but the former *seculum*).[4] Sir Thomas More, the elder Wyatt; Henry, Earl of Surrey;

---

1. I.e., in rhetorical *divisio* [*Editor*].
2. Investigations [*Editor*].

3. "Character is power" [*Editor*].
4. Age [*Editor*].

Sir Thomas Chaloner,[5] Sir Thomas Smith, Sir Thomas Elyot, Bishop Gardiner, were for their times admirable: and the more, because they began eloquence with us. Sir Nicholas Bacon[6] was singular, and almost alone, in the beginning of Queen Elizabeth's times. Sir Philip Sidney, and Mr. Hooker[7] (in different matter) grew great masters of wit, and language; and in whom all vigor of invention, and strength of judgment met. The Earl of Essex, noble and high; and Sir Walter Raleigh, not to be contemned, either for judgment, or style. Sir Henry Savile[8] grave, and truly lettered; Sir Edwin Sandys, excellent in both: Lord Egerton, the Chancellor, a grave, and great orator; and best, when he was provoked. But his learned, and able (though unfortunate) successor[9] is he, who hath filled up all numbers; and performed that in our tongue, which may be compared, or preferred, either to insolent Greece, or haughty Rome. In short, within his view, and about his times, were all the wits born, that could honor a language, or help study. Now things daily fall: wits grow downward, and eloquence grows backward: so that he may be named, and stand as the mark, and $ἀκμή$[1] of our language. * * *

[The Prince and the Poet][2]

Wise, is rather the attribute of a prince, than learned, or good. The learned man profits others, rather than himself; the good man, rather himself than others; but the prince commands others, and doth himself. The wise Lycurgus gave no law but what himself kept. Sylla and Lysander did not so: the one, living extremely dissolute himself, enforced frugality by the laws; the other permitted those licenses to others, which himself abstained from. But the prince's prudence is his chief art and safety. In his counsels and deliberations, he foresees the future times. In the equity of his judgment, he hath remembrance of the past; and knowledge of what is to be done, or avoided for the present. Hence the Persians

5. The scholarly diplomat Sir Thomas Chaloner (1521–1565) translated Erasmus's *The Praise of Folly*; Sir Thomas Smith (1513–1577), Elizabeth's Secretary of State for some years, was widely known for his study of English government, *De Republica Anglorum*; Sir Thomas Elyot (c. 1490–1546) wrote the educational and political treatise *The Governour*; Bishop Stephen Gardiner (c. 1483–1555), Lord Chancellor under Mary Tudor, wrote several books defending the Roman Catholic faith [*Editor*].
6. Sir Nicholas Bacon (1509–1579), Lord Keeper of the Seal in Elizabeth's reign, was the father of Sir Francis Bacon [*Editor*].

7. Richard Hooker (1533–1600) wrote *Of the Laws of Ecclesiastical Polity* [*Editor*].
8. Sir Henry Savile (1549–1622), Provost of Eton, "was perhaps the most learned Englishman of his time" (*H & S*, XI, p. 19); Sir Edwin Sandys (1561–1629) wrote learnedly on religious topics; Thomas Egerton (c. 1540–1617) was Lord Chancellor under James I [*Editor*].
9. I.e., Sir Francis Bacon [*Editor*].
1. "Acme" [*Editor*]. .
2. The first part of this section is based on passages in the work of two Renaissance political theorists, Franciscus Patricius and H. Farnese; the second part draws on Quintilian's *Institutio Oratoria* [*Editor*].

gave out their Cyrus to have been nursed by a bitch, a creature to encounter ill, as of sagacity to seek out good; showing that wisdom may accompany fortitude, or it leaves to be, and puts on the name of rashness.

There be some men are born only to suck out the poison of books: *Habent venenum pro victu: imo, pro deliciis.*[3] And such are they that only relish the obscene and foul things in poets; which makes the profession taxed. But by whom? Men that watch for it, and (had they not had this hint) are so unjust valuers of letters as they think no learning good, but what brings in gain. It shows, they themselves would never have been of the professions they are, but for the profits and fees. But if another learning, well used, can instruct to good life, inform manners, no less persuade and lead men than they threaten and compel; and have no reward; is it therefore the worse study? I could never think the study of wisdom confined only to the philosopher; or of piety to the divine; or of state to the politique. But that he which can feign a commonwealth (which is the poet), can govern it with counsels, strengthen it with laws, correct it with judgments, inform it with religion and morals; is all these. We do not require in him mere elocution; or an excellent faculty in verse; but the exact knowledge of all virtues and their contraries; with ability to render the one loved, the other hated, by his proper embattling them. The philosophers did insolently, to challenge only to themselves that which the greatest generals and gravest councillors never durst. For such had rather do, than promise the best things. * * *

[The Art of Teaching][4]

I take this labor in teaching others, that they should not be always to be taught; and I would bring my precepts into practise. For rules are ever of less force, and value, than experiments. Yet with this purpose, rather to show the right way to those that come after, than to detect any that have slipped before by error, and I hope it will be more profitable. For men do more willingly listen, and with more favor, to precept, than reprehension. Among diverse opinions of an art, and most of them contrary in themselves, it is hard to make election; and therefore, though a man cannot invent new things after so many, he may do a welcome work yet to help posterity to judge rightly of the old. But arts and precepts avail nothing, except nature be beneficial, and aiding. And therefore these things are no more written to a dull disposition, than rules of husbandry to a barren soil. No precepts will profit a fool; no

3. "They have poison for their food; even for their delicacies" [*Editor*].

4. This section is based on passages in Quintilian, *op. cit.*, I–II [*Editor*].

more than beauty will the blind, or music the deaf. As we should take care, that our style in writing, be neither dry, nor empty: we should look again it be not winding, or wanton with farfetched descriptions; either is a vice. But that is worse which proceeds out of want, than that which riots out of plenty. The remedy of fruitfulness is easy, but no labor will help the contrary: I will like, and praise some things in a young writer; which yet if he continue in, I cannot but justly hate him for the same. There is a time to be given all things for maturity; and that even your country-husbandman can teach; who to a young plant will not put the pruning knife, because it seems to fear the iron, as not able to admit the scar. No more would I tell a green writer all his faults, lest I should make him grieve and faint, and at last despair. For nothing doth more hurt, than to make him so afraid of all things, as he can endeavor nothing. Therefore youth ought to be instructed betimes, and in the best things: for we hold those longest, we take soonest. As the first scent of a vessel lasts: and that tinct the wool first receives. Therefore a master should temper his own powers, and descend to the other's infirmity. If you pour a glut of water upon a bottle, it receives little of it; but with a funnel, and by degrees, you shall fill many of them, and spill little of your own; to their capacity they will all receive, and be full. And as it is fit to read the best authors to youth first, so let them be of the openest, and clearest. As Livy before Sallust,[5] Sidney before Donne: and beware of letting them taste Gower, or Chaucer at first, lest falling too much in love with antiquity, and not apprehending the weight, they grow rough and barren in language only. When their judgments are firm, and out of danger, let them read both, the old and the new: but no less take heed, that their new flowers, and sweetness do not as much corrupt, as the others' dryness, and squalor, if they choose not carefully. Spenser, in affecting the ancients, writ no language: yet I would have him read for his matter; but as Vergil read Ennius.[6] The reading of Homer and Vergil is counselled by Quintilian, as the best way of informing youth, and confirming man. For besides, that the mind is raised with the height, and sublimity of such a verse, it takes spirit from the greatness of the matter, and is tincted with the best things. Tragic, and lyric poetry is good too: and comic with the best, if the manners of the reader be once in safety. In the Greek poets, as also in Plautus, we shall see the economy, and disposition of poems, better observed than in Terence, and the later: who thought the sole grace, and virtue of

5. The style of the Roman historian Titus Livius (59 B.C.–A.D. 17) is clear and forthright; that of Gaius Crispus Sallustius (86–34 B.C.) relatively concise and terse [Editor].

6. Quintus Ennius (239–169 B.C.) was the author of Annales, a history of Rome in dactylic hexameters [Editor].

their fable, the sticking in of sentences, as ours do the forcing in of jests. * * *

[*Language and Learning*][7]

Language most shows a man: speak that I may see thee. It springs out of the most retired, and inmost parts of us, and is the image of the parent of it, the mind. No glass renders a man's form, or likeness, so true as his speech. Nay, it is likened to a man; and as we consider feature, and composition in a man; so words in language: in the greatness, aptness, sound, structure, and harmony of it. Some men are tall, and big, so some language is high and great. Then the words are chosen, their sound ample, the composition full, the absolution plenteous,[8] and poured out, all grave, sinewy and strong. Some are little, and dwarfs: so of speech it is humble, and low, the words poor and flat; the members and periods, thin and weak, without knitting, or number. The middle are of a just stature. There the language is plain, and pleasing: even without stopping, round without swelling; all well-turned, composed, elegant, and accurate. The vicious language is vast, and gaping, swelling, and irregular; when it contends to be high, full of rock, mountain, and pointedness: as it affects to be low, it is abject, and creeps, full of bogs, and holes. And according to their subject, these styles vary, and lose their names: for that which is high and lofty, declaring excellent matter, becomes vast and tumorous,[9] speaking of petty and inferior things: so that which was even, and apt in a mean and plain subject, will appear most poor and humble in a high argument. Would you not laugh, to meet a great counsellor of state in a flat cap, with his trunk hose, and a hobbyhorse cloak,[1] his gloves under his girdle, and yond haberdasher in a velvet gown, furred with sables? There is a certain latitude in these things, by which we find the degrees. The next thing to the stature, is the figure and feature in language: that is, whether it be round, and straight, which consists of short and succinct periods, numerous, and polished; or square and firm, which is to have equal and strong parts, every where answerable, and weighed. The third is the skin, and coat, which rests in the well-joining, cementing, and coagmentation[2] of words; when as it is smooth, gentle, and sweet: like a table, upon which you may run your finger without rubs, and your nail cannot find a joint; not horrid, rough, wrinkled, gaping, or chapped. After these the flesh, blood, and bones come in question. We say it

---

7. The first part of this section is based on a passage from Vives's *De Ratione Dicendi*; the second part on Bacon's *Advancement of Learning*, I. iv [*Editor*].
8. I.e., the delivery free [*Editor*].

9. Swollen [*Editor*].
1. I.e., a long cloak like that worn by the "hobby horse" performers in morris dances [*Editor*].
2. Combination [*Editor*].

is a fleshy style, when there is much periphrasis, and circuit of words; and when with more than enough, it grows fat and corpulent; *arvina orationis*,[3] full of suet and tallow. It hath blood, and juice, when the words are proper and apt, their sound sweet, and the phrase neat and picked. *Oratio uncta, et bene pasta.*[4] But where there is redundancy, both the blood and juice are faulty, and vicious. *Redundant sanguine, quae multo plus dicit, quam necesse est.*[5] Juice in language is somewhat less than blood; for if the words be but becoming, and signifying, and the sense gentle, there is juice: but where that wanteth, the language is thin, flagging, poor, starved, scarce covering the bone; and shows like stones in a sack. Some men, to avoid redundancy, run into that; and while they strive to have no ill blood, or juice, they lose their good. There be some styles, again, that have not less blood, but less flesh, and corpulence. These are bony, and sinewy: *Ossa habent, et nervos.*

It was well noted by the late L. St. Alban,[6] that the study of words is the first distemper of learning: vain matter the second: and a third distemper is deceit, or the likeness of truth; imposture held up by credulity. All these are the cobwebs of learning, and to let them grow in us, is either sluttish or foolish. Nothing is more ridiculous, than to make an author a dictator, as the schools have done Aristotle. The damage is infinite, knowledge receives by it. For to many things a man should owe but a temporary belief, and a suspension of his own judgment, not an absolute resignation of himself, or a perpetual captivity. Let Aristotle, and others have their dues; but if we can make farther discoveries of truth and fitness than they, why are we envied? Let us beware while we strive to add, we do not diminish, or deface; we may improve, but not augment. By discrediting falsehood, truth grows in request. We must not go about like men anguished, and perplexed, for vicious affectation of praise: but calmly study the separation of opinions, find the errors have intervened, awake antiquity, call former times into question; but make no parties with the present, nor follow any fierce undertakers, mingle no matter of doubtful credit, with the simplicity of truth, but gently stir the mold about the root of the question, and avoid all digladiations,[7] facility of credit, or superstitious simplicity; seek the consonancy, and concatenation of truth; stoop only to point of necessity, and what leads to convenience. Then make exact animadversion where style hath degenerated, where flourished, and thrived in choiceness of phrase, round and clean composition of sentence, sweet falling of the clause, varying an illustration by tropes and figures, weight of matter, worth of sub-

---

3. "The fat of speech" [*Editor*].
4. "Speech sleek and well-fed" [*Editor*].
5. "That style which says more than is strictly required has too much blood in it" [*Editor*].
6. I.e., Sir Frances Bacon [*Editor*].
7. Disputations [*Editor*].

ject, soundness of argument, life of invention, and depth of judgment. This is *monte potiri*, to get the hill. For no perfect discovery can be made upon a flat or a level. * * *

[Poets and Poetry]

WHAT IS A POET?

A poet is that, which by the Greeks is called κατ' ἐξοχὴν, ὁ ποιητής, a maker, or a feigner: his art, an art of imitation, or feigning; expressing the life of man in fit measure, numbers, and harmony, according to Aristotle: from the word ποιεῖν, which signifies to make or feign. Hence, he is called a poet, not he which writeth in measure only; but that feigneth and formeth a fable, and writes things like the truth. For, the fable and fiction is (as it were) the form and soul of any poetical work, or poem.

WHAT MEAN YOU BY A POEM?

A poem is not alone any work, or composition of the poet's in many, or few verses; but even one alone verse sometimes makes a perfect poem. As, when Aeneas hangs up, and consecrates the arms of Abas, with this inscription: *Aeneas haec de Danais victoribus arma.*[8] And calls it a poem, or *carmen.* Such as those in Martial. *Omnia, Castor, emis: sic fiet, ut omnia vendas.*[9] And, *Pauper videri cinna vult, et est pauper.*[1]

So were Horace his *Odes* called, *Carmina;* his lyric songs. And Lucretius designs a whole book, in his sixth: *Quod in primo quoque carmine claret.*[2] And anciently, all the oracles were called, *Carmina;* or, whatever sentence was expressed, were it much, or little, it was called, an epic, dramatic, lyric, elegiac, or epigrammatic poem.

BUT, HOW DIFFERS A POEM FROM WHAT WE CALL POESY?

A poem, as I have told you, is the work of the poet; the end, and fruit of his labor, and study. Poesy is his skill, or craft of making: the very fiction itself, the reason, or form of the work. And these three voices differ, as the thing done, the doing, and the doer; the thing feigned, the feigning, and the feigner: so the poem, the poesy, and the poet. Now, the poesy is the habit, or the art: nay, rather the

8. "Aeneas [won] these arms from the conquering Greeks" (*Aeneid,* III. 288) [*Editor*].
9. "Castor, you buy everything; by the same token, you will sell everything" (Martial, *Epigrams,* VII. xcviii) [*Editor*].
1. "Cinna wishes to appear a pauper, and is a pauper" (*ibid.,* VIII. xix) [*Editor*].
2. "Which is set forth in the first part of my poem" [*Editor*].

queen of arts, which had her original from heaven, received thence from the Hebrews, and had in prime estimation with the Greeks, transmitted to the Latins, and all nations, that professed civility. The study of it (if we will trust Aristotle) offers to mankind a certain rule, and pattern of living well, and happily; disposing us to all civil offices of society. If we will believe Tully,[3] it nourisheth, and instructeth our youth; delights our age; adorns our prosperity; comforts our adversity; entertains us at home; keeps us company abroad, travels with us; watches; divides the times of our earnest, and sports; shares in our country recesses, and recreations; insomuch as the wisest and best learned have thought her the absolute mistress of manners, and nearest of kin to virtue. And, whereas they entitle philosophy to be a rigid, and austere poesy: they have (on the contrary) styled poesy, a dulcet, and gentle philosophy, which leads on, and guides us by the hand to action, with a ravishing delight, and incredible sweetness. But, before we handle the kinds of poems, with their special differences; or make court to the art itself, as a mistress, I would lead you to the knowledge of our poet, by a perfect information, what he is, or should be by nature, by exercise, by imitation, by study; and so bring him down through the disciplines of grammar, logic, rhetoric, and the ethics, adding somewhat, out of all, peculiar to himself, and worthy of your admittance, or reception.

1. *Ingenium*.[4] First, we require in our poet, or maker (for that title our language affords him, elegantly, with the Greek), a goodness of natural wit. For, whereas all other arts consist of doctrine, and precepts: the poet must be able by nature, and instinct, to pour out the treasure of his mind; and, as Seneca saith, *Aliquando secundum Anacreontem insanire, jucundum esse*,[5] by which he understands, the poetical rapture. And according to that of Plato; *Frustra Poeticas fores sui compos pulsavit*.[6] And of Aristotle: *Nullum magnum ingenium sine mixtura dementiae fuit. Nec potest grande aliquid, et supra caeteros loqui, nisi mota mens*.[7] Then it riseth higher, as by a divine instinct, when it contemns common, and known conceptions. It utters somewhat above a mortal mouth. Then it gets aloft, and flies away with his rider, whether, before, it was doubtful to ascend. This the poets understood by their Helicon, Pegasus, or Parnassus; and this made Ovid to boast:

---

3. I.e., Cicero [*Editor*].

4. I.e., "genius," or natural character [*Editor*].

5. "According to Anacreon, occasionally it is pleasing to be seized with madness" (Seneca, *De Tranquilitate Animi*, xvii) [*Editor*].

6. "A man in his senses knocks vainly at the gates of poetry" (*Phaedrus*, 245a) [*Editor*].

7. "There was never a great genius without a touch of madness. Nor may the mind achieve or express anything great unless emotion plays a part" [*Editor*].

Est, Deus in nobis; agitante calescimus illo:
Sedibus aethereis spiritus ille venit.[8]

And Lipsius, to affirm; *Scio, Poetam neminem praestantem fuisse, sine parte quadam uberiore divinae aurae.*[9] And, hence it is, that the coming up of good poets (for I mind not *mediocres*, or *imos*),[1] is so thin and rare among us; every beggarly corporation affords the state a mayor, or two bailiffs, yearly: but, *Solus Rex, aut Poeta, non quotannis nascitur.*[2]

2. *Exercitatio.* To this perfection of nature in our poet, we require exercise of those parts, and frequent. If his wit will not arrive suddenly at the dignity of the ancients, let him not yet fall out with it, quarrel, or be overhastily angry: offer, to turn it away from study, in a humor; but come to it again upon better cogitation; try another time, with labor. If then it succeed not, cast not away the quills, yet: nor scratch the wainscot, beat not the poor desk; but bring all to the forge, and file, again; turn it anew. There is no statute law of the kingdom bids you be a poet, against your will; or the first quarter.[3] If it come, in a year, or two, it is well. The common rhymers pour forth verses, such as they are *(ex tempore)*, but there never comes from them one sense, worth the life of a day. A rhymer, and a poet, are two things. It is said of the incomparable Vergil, that he brought forth his verses like a bear, and after formed them with licking. Scaliger, the father,[4] writes it of him, that he made a quantity of verses in the morning, which afore night he reduced to a less number. But, that which Valerius Maximus[5] hath left recorded of Euripides, the tragic poet, his answer to Alcestis, another poet, is as memorable, as modest: who, when it was told to Alcestis, that Euripides had in three days brought forth but three verses, and those with some difficulty, and throes; Alcestis, glorying he could with ease have sent forth a hundred in the space; Euripides roundly replied, "Like enough. But, here is the difference; thy verses will not last those three days; mine will to all time." Which was, as to tell him, he could not write a verse. I have met many of these rattles, that made a noise, and buzzed. They had their hum; and, no more. Indeed, things, wrote with labor, deserve to be so read, and will last their age.

---

8. "There is a god in us, by whose movement we are kept warm; that spirit comes from the heavenly realms" (cf. *Fasti*, vi. 5–6, and *Ars Amatoria*, iii. 549–550) [*Editor*].
9. "I know there has never been a great poet without a richer share than most possess of divine inspiration." Justus Lipsius (1547–1606) was a Flemish scholar and translator [*Editor*].

1. I.e., the ordinary or inferior [*Editor*].
2. "It is only a king or a poet that is not born every year" [*Editor*].
3. I.e., three months (relatively soon) [*Editor*].
4. I.e., J. C. Scaliger (1484–1558), Italian humanist [*Editor*].
5. Valerius Maximus (fl. c. A.D. 35) compiled an anthology of historical anecdotes [*Editor*].

3. *Imitatio*. The third requisite in our poet, or maker, is imitation, to be able to convert the substance, or riches of another poet, to his own use. To make choice of one excellent man above the rest, and so to follow him, till he grow very he: or, so like him, as the copy may be mistaken for the principal. Not, as a creature, that swallows, what it takes in, crude, raw, or undigested; but, that feeds with an appetite, and hath a stomach to concoct,[6] divide, and turn all into nourishment. Not, to imitate servilely, as Horace saith, and catch at vices, for virtue: but, to draw forth out of the best, and choicest flowers, with the bee, and turn all into honey, work it into one relish, and savor: make our imitation sweet: observe, how the best writers have imitated, and follow them. How Vergil, and Statius[7] have imitated Homer; how Horace, Archilochus; how Alcæus, and the other lyrics: and so of the rest.

4. *Lectio*. But, that, which we especially require in him is an exactness of study, and multiplicity of reading, which maketh a full man, not alone enabling him to know the history, or argument of a poem, and to report it: but so to master the matter, and style, as to show, he knows, how to handle, place, or dispose of either, with elegancy, when need shall be. And not think, he can leap forth suddenly a poet, by dreaming he hath been in Parnassus, or, having washed his lips (as they say) in Helicon. There goes more to his making, than so.

Ars corona.[8] For to nature, exercise, imitation, and study, art must be added, to make all these perfect. And, though these challenge to themselves much, in the making up of our maker, it is art only can lead him to perfection, and leave him there in possession, as planted by her hand. It is the assertion of Tully, If to an excellent nature, there happen an accession, or conformation of learning, and discipline, there will then remain somewhat noble, and singular. For, as Simylus saith in Stobaeus:[9]

Οὖτε φύσις ἱκανὴ γίνεται τέχνης ἄτερ,
οὖτε πᾶν τέχνη μὴ φύσιν κεκτημένη·

without art, nature can never be perfect; and, without nature, art can claim no being. But, our poet must beware, that his study be not only to learn of himself; for, he that shall affect to do that, confesseth his ever having a fool to his master. He must read many; but, ever the best, and choicest: those, that can teach him anything, he must ever account his masters, and reverence: among whom Horace, and

---

6. Digest [*Editor*].

7. The epic poet Statius (c. A.D. 61–c. 96) composed the *Thebaid*; Archilocus was a Greek lyric poet of the seventh century B.C.; the Greek poet Alcaeus flourished late in the same century [*Editor*].

8. "Art [is] the crown" [*Editor*].

9. Stobaeus, about A.D. 500, compiled an anthology of Greek writings, including passages from the work of Simylus, who flourished in the fourth century B.C. [*Editor*].

(he that taught him) Aristotle, deserve to be the first in estimation. Aristotle was the first accurate critic, and truest judge; nay, the greatest philosopher, the world ever had: for, he noted the vices of all knowledges, in all creatures, and out of many men's perfections in a science, he formed still one art. So he taught us two offices[1] together, how we ought to judge rightly of others, and what we ought to imitate specially in ourselves. But all this in vain, without a natural wit, and a poetical nature in chief.

BEN JONSON

From *Conversations With William Drummond of Hawthornden*†

That he had an intention to perfect an epic poem entitled *Heroologia*, of the worthies of his country roused by fame, and was to dedicate it to his country; it is all in couplets, for he detesteth all other rhymes. Said he had written a discourse of poesy both against Campion and Daniel, especially this last, where he proves couplets to be the bravest sort of verses, especially when they are broken, like hexameters; and that cross rhymes and stanzas (because the purpose would lead him beyond 8 lines to conclude) were all forced.

He recommended to my reading Quintilian (who, he said, would tell me the faults of my verses as if he had lived with me) and Horace, Plinius Secundus' *Epistles*, Tacitus, Juvenal, Martial, whose epigram . . . he hath translated.[1]

His censure of the English poets was this: That Sidney did not keep a decorum in making everyone speak as well as himself. Spenser's stanzas pleased him not, nor his matter, the meaning of which allegory he had delivered in papers to Sir Walter Raleigh. Samuel Daniel was a good honest man, had no children, but no poet.

That Michael Drayton's *Polyolbion* (if he had performed what he promised to write, the deeds of all the worthies) had been excellent; his long verses pleased him not.

That Silvester's translation of Du Bartas was not well done, and that he wrote his verses before it ere he understood to confer.

---

1. Duties [*Editor*].

† During Jonson's visit to Scotland in 1618–1619, he stayed in Edinburgh (for some three weeks) with the Scottish poet and man of letters William Drummond (1585–1649), who recorded in note form his guest's opinions on literary and other matters. The text is based on that in *H & S*, I, pp. 132–151.

1. Cf. Martial, *Epigrams*, X. xlvii [*Editor*].

Nor that of Fairfax's.[2]

That the translations of Homer and Vergil in long Alexandrines were but prose.

That John Harington's Ariosto, under all translations, was the worst.

* * *

That Donne's *Anniversary* was profane and full of blasphemies.

That he told Mr. Donne, if it had been written of the Virgin Mary, it had been something. To which he answered that he described the idea of a woman and not as she was. That Donne for not keeping of accent deserved hanging.

That Shakespeare wanted art.

That Sharpham, Day, Dekker were all rogues, and that Minshew was one.[3]

That Abram Francis[4] in his English hexameters was a fool.

That next himself, only Fletcher and Chapman could make a masque.

* * *

His censure of my verses was that they were all good, especially my epitaph of the prince, save that they smelled too much of the schools and were not after the fancy of the time. For a child, says he, may write after the fashion of the Greeks and Latin verses in running;[5] yet that he wished, to please the king, that piece of *Forth Feasting* had been his own.

He esteemeth John Donne the first poet in the world in some things. His verses of the lost chain,[6] he hath by heart; and that passage of *The Calm*: that dust and feathers do not stir, all was so quiet. Affirmeth Donne to have written all his best pieces ere he was 25 years old. Sir Edward Wotton's verses of a happy life[7] he hath by heart, and a piece of Chapman's translation of the 13 of the *Iliad*, which he thinketh well done.

That Donne said to him he wrote that *Epitaph on Prince Henry*

---

2. I.e., the translation of Tasso's epic poem *Gerusalemme Liberata,* by Edward Fairfax (c. 1575–1635) [*Editor*].
3. Edward Sharpham (1576–1608) and John Day (fl. 1606) were contemporary playwrights of no particular mark; Thomas Dekker (1570–1632), the author of *The Shoemakers' Holiday,* also wrote a number of prose pamphlets on social conditions in London; the lexicographer John Minsheu published a polyglot dictionary in 1617 [*Editor*].
4. Abraham Fraunce (c. 1587–1633), author of *The Arcadian Rhetorike,* was known in his day primarily for his translations of Thomas Watson's Latin play

Amyntas [*Editor*].
5. Samuel Daniel, in *A Defence of Ryme* (1603), objects to "those continual cadences of couplets used in long and continued poems," adding that "to beguile the ear with a running out, and passing over the rhyme . . . is rather graceful than otherwise" (*Poems and a Defence of Ryme,* ed. A. C. Sprague [Chicago, 1965], pp. 155–156) [*Editor*].
6. I.e., Elegy XI ("The Bracelet") [*Editor*].
7. I.e., the lyric beginning, "How happy is he born or taught," by Sir Henry Wotton (1568–1639) [*Editor*].

("Look to me, faith") to match Sir Edward Herbert[8] in obscureness.

He hath by heart some verses of Spenser's *Calender*, about wine, between Colin and Pierce.[9]

* * *

That Petronius, Plinius Secundus, Tacitus speak best Latin; that Quintilian's 6. 7. 8. books were not only to be read but altogether digested. Juvenal, Persius, Horace, Martial for delight, and so was Pindar. For health, Hippocrates. Of their nation, Hooker's *Ecclesiastical History* (whose children are now beggars) for church matters.

* * *

For a heroic poem, he said there was no such ground as King Arthur's fiction, and that Sir Philip Sidney had an intention to have transformed all his *Arcadia* to the stories of King Arthur.

His acquaintance and behavior with poets living with him.

Daniel was at jealousies with him.

That Francis Beaumont loved too much himself and his own verses.

That Sir John Roe[1] loved him, and when they two were ushered by my Lord Suffolk from a masque, Roe wrote a moral epistle to him, which began that next to plays the court and the state were the best: God threateneth kings, kings lords, and lords do us.

He beat Marston and took his pistol from him.

* * *

Ned Field[2] was his scholar and he had read to him the satires of Horace and some epigrams of Martial.

That Markham[3] (who added his *English Arcadia*) was not of the number of the faithful (i.e., poets) and but a base fellow.

That such were Day and Middleton.

That Chapman and Fletcher were loved of him.

Overbury[4] was first his friend, then turned his mortal enemy.

* * *

That in that paper Sir Walter Raleigh had of the allegories of

8. Douglas Bush describes Lord Herbert of Cherbury (1582–1648) as "the first disciple of Donne on the secular side" (*English Literature in the Earlier Seventeenth Century, op. cit.*, p. 160) [*Editor*].
9. The allusion is to *The Shepheardes Calender*, "October," ll. 109–114 [*Editor*].
1. The "moral epistle" by Sir John Roe, the brother of that William Roe to whom Jonson's Epigram CXXVIII is addressed, appears in *The Poems of John Donne*, ed. Sir H. J. C. Grierson (London, 1933), pp. 383–384 [*Editor*].
2. Nathaniel Field (1587–1633) was a playwright and actor who took roles in plays by Jonson and Shakespeare [*Editor*].
3. Gervase Markham (1568–1637), who wrote voluminously on several subjects, is distinguished chiefly for having been the first to import an Arabian stallion into England [*Editor*].
4. Sir Thomas Overbury (1581–1613), known to literary history for his Theophrastian *Characters*, met his death by poison, administered over a lengthy period of time by agents of Lady Essex [*Editor*].

his [Spenser's] *Fairie Queene,* by the Blatant Beast the Puritans were understood; by the false Duessa, the Queen of Scots.

That Southwell was hanged; yet, so he had written that piece of his *The Burning Babe,* he would have been content to destroy many of his.

* * *

That Donne himself, for not being understood, would perish.

That Sir Walter Raleigh esteemed more of fame than conscience: the best wits of England were employed for making of his history; Ben himself had written a piece to him of the Punic War, which he altered and set in his book.

* * *

Marston wrote his father-in-law's preachings, and his father-in-law his comedies.

Shakespeare in a play brought in a number of men saying they had suffered shipwreck in Bohemia, where there is no sea near by some 100 miles.

Daniel wrote *Civil Wars,* and yet hath not one battle in his book.

* * *

His opinion of verses.

That he wrote all his first in prose, for so his master Camden had learned him.

That verses stood by sense without either colors or accent, which yet other times he denied.

A great many epigrams were ill, because they expressed in the end what should have been understood by what was said.

* * *

He was better versed and knew more in Greek and Latin than all the poets in England and quintessenced their brains.

* * *

He is a great lover and praiser of himself, a contemner and scorner of others, given rather to lose a friend than a jest; jealous of every word and action of those about him (especially after drink, which is one of the elements in which he liveth); a dissembler of ill parts which reign in him, a bragger of some good that he wanteth; thinketh nothing well but what either he himself, or some of his friends and countrymen, hath said or done. He is passionately kind and angry; careless either to gain or keep; vindicative,[5] but, if he be well answered, at himself.

5. Vindictive [*Editor*].

FRANCIS BEAUMONT

[A Letter to Ben Jonson]†

The sun, which doth the greatest comfort bring
To absent friends (because the self-same thing
They know, they see, however absent), is
Here our best hay-maker (forgive me this;
It is our country's style); in this warm shine   5
I lie, and dream of your full Mermaid wine.
Oh, we have water mixed with claret lees,
Drink apt to bring in drier heresies
Than beer, good only for the sonnet's strain,
With fustian metaphors to stuff the brain;   10
So mixed that, given to the thirstiest one,
'Twill not prove alms, unless he have the stone.
I think with one draught man's invention fades,
Two cups had quite spoiled Homer's *Iliads*;
'Tis liquor that will find out Sutcliffe's wit,[1]   15
Lie where he will, and make him write worse yet.
Filled with such moisture, in most grievous qualms,
Did Robert Wisdom write his singing psalms;[2]
And so must I do this; and yet I think
It is a potion sent us down to drink   20
By special providence, keeps us from fights,
Makes us not laugh when we make legs[3] to knights;
'Tis this that keeps our minds fit for our states,
A med'cine to obey our magistrates.
For we do live more free than you; no hate,   25
No envy at another's happy state
Moves us, we are all equal, every whit;
Of land, that God gives men here, is their wit,
If we consider fully; for our best
And gravest man will, with his main house-jest   30
Scarce please you; we want subtlety to do
The city tricks: lie, hate, and flatter too.
Here are none that can bear a painted show,
Strike when you wink, and then lament the blow,
Who, like mills set the right way to grind,   35
Can make their gains alike with every wind.
Only some fellow with the subtlest pate

---

† Francis Beaumont (1584–1616) is known chiefly for the plays he wrote in collaboration with John Fletcher (1579–1625). The text follows the version appended to *The Nice Valour*, in Beaumont and Fletcher, *Comedies and Tragedies* (London, 1647).
1. Dr. Matthew Sutcliffe (c. 1550–1629), Dean of Exeter, contributed to the literature of theological controversy in the first decade of the seventeenth century [*Editor*].
2. Robert Wisdom (d. 1568), Archdeacon of Ely, had composed a number of metrical translations of the Psalms [*Editor*].
3. I.e., when we bow [*Editor*].

Amongst us, may perchance equivocate
At selling of a horse, and that's the most.
Methinks the little wit I had is lost   40
Since I saw you; for wit is like a rest[4]
Held up at tennis, which men do the best
With the best gamesters. What things have we seen
Done at the Mermaid! heard words that have been
So nimble and so full of subtle flame,   45
As if that everyone from whence they came
Had meant to put his whole wit in a jest,
And had resolved to live a fool the rest
Of his dull life; then when there has been thrown
Wit able enough to justify the town   50
For three days past, wit that might warrant be
For the whole city to talk foolishly
Till that were cancelled; and when that was gone,
We left an air behind us, which alone
Was able to make the two next companies   55
Right witty; though but downright fools, mere[5] wise.
When I remember this, and see that now
The country gentlemen begin to allow
My wit for dry-bobs,[6] then I needs must cry,
I see my days of ballading[7] grow nigh;   60
I can already riddle, and can sing
Catches, sell bargains, and I fear shall bring
Myself to speak the hardest words I find
Over as fast as any, with one wind
That takes no med'cines. But one thought of thee   65
Makes me remember all these things to be
The wit of our young men, fellows that show
No part of good, yet utter all they know;
Who like trees of the guard have growing souls[8]
Only; strong destiny, which all controls,   70
I hope hath left a better fate in store
For me, thy friend, than to live ever poor,
Banished unto this home; fate once again
Bring me to thee, who canst make smooth and plain
The way of knowledge for me, and then I,   75
Who have no good but in thy company,
Protest it will my greatest comfort be
To acknowledge all I have to flow from thee.
Ben, when these scenes are perfect, we'll taste wine;
I'll drink thy Muse's health, thou shalt quaff mine.   80

---

4. I.e., an extended rally [*Editor*].
5. I.e., absolutely [*Editor*].
6. Taunting jests [*Editor*].

7. I.e., writing doggerel verse ⌈*Editor*⌉ .
8. I.e., vegetable (not rational) souls [*Editor*].

EDMUND BOLTON

From *Hypercritica*†

* * * [Proposes to name those poets] among us whose English hath in my conceit most propriety, and is nearest to the phrase of court, and to the speech used among the noble, and among the better sort in London; the two sovereign seats, and as it were Parliament tribunals, to try the question in.

* * *

[Names, among others, Surrey, Wyatt, Raleigh, Donne, and Fulke Greville.] But if I should declare mine own rudeness rudely, I should then confess, that I never tasted English more to my liking, nor more smart, and put to the height of use in poetry, than in that vital, judicious, and most practicable language of Benjamin Jonson's poems.

JAMES HOWELL

From *Epistolae Ho-Elianae*‡

To Sir Thomas Hawk[ins], Knight[1]
Sir,
I was invited yesternight to a solemn supper by B. J., where you were deeply remembered. There was good company, excellent cheer, choice wines, and jovial welcome. One thing intervened which almost spoiled the relish of the rest, that B. began to engross all the discourse, to vapor extremely of himself, and by vilifying others to magnify his own Muse. T. Ca.[2] buzzed me in the ear that, though Ben had barrelled up a great deal of knowledge, yet it seems he had not read the *Ethics*,[3] which, among other precepts of morality, forbid self-commendation, declaring it to be an ill-favored solecism in good manners. It made me think upon the lady (not very young) who, having a good while given her guests neat enter-

---

† Edmund Bolton (c. 1575–c. 1633) included Jonson's name in a list of prospective members for the Royal Academy of Letters proposed by Bolton in 1616; the project was eventually abandoned in the reign of Charles I. The text of *Hypercritica* (c. 1618) follows that given in *Ancient Critical Essays on English Poets and Poesy*, ed. Joseph Haslewood, 2 vols. (London, 1815), II, p. 251.
‡James Howell (c. 1594–1666), committed in 1643 to the Fleet Prison (probably for his royalist sympathies), remained there for eight years; during that time, he composed the greater part of *Epistolae Ho-Elianae*, a series of epistolary essays based in part on events in his life prior to 1643. The text follows that in J. Jacobs's edition (London, 1890), 403–404.
1. The poet and translator Sir Thomas Hawkins (d. 1640) was one of the eighty-four persons nominated by Edmund Bolton to be charter members of the proposed Royal Academy of Letters [*Editor*].
2. I.e., Thomas Carew [*Editor*].
3. I.e., Aristotle's *Nicomachaean Ethics* [*Editor*].

tainment, a capon being brought upon the table, instead of a spoon she took a mouthful of claret and spouted it into the poop of the hollow bird. Such an accident happened in this entertainment, you know. . . . But for my part I am content to dispense with the Roman infirmity of B., now that time hath snowed upon his *pericranium.* You know Ovid and (your) Horace were subject to his humor. . . . As also Cicero. . . . There is another reason that excuseth B., which is, that if one be allowed to love the natural issue of his body, why not that of the brain, which is of a spiritual and more noble extraction? I preserve your manuscript safe for you till you return to London. What news the times affords this bearer will impart unto you. So I am, sir, your very humble and most faithful servitor,

J. H.

Westminster, 5 April 1636.

THOMAS FULLER

From *The Worthies of England*†

Benjamin Jonson was born in this city. Though I cannot, with all my industrious inquiry, find him in his cradle, I can fetch him from his long-coats.[1] When a little child, he lived in Hartshorn Lane near Charing Cross, where his mother married a bricklayer for her second husband.

He was first bred in a private school in Saint Martin's church; then in Westminster school; witness his own epigram;

> 'Camden, most reverend head, to whom I owe
> All that I am in arts, all that I know;
> How nothing's that to whom my country owes
> The great renown and name wherewith she goes,' etc.

He was statutably admitted into Saint John's College in Cambridge (as many years after incorporated an honorary member of Christ Church in Oxford) where he continued but few weeks for want of further maintenance, being fain to return to the trade of his father-in-law. And let them blush not that have, but those who have not, a lawful calling. He helped in the new structure of Lincoln's Inn, when, having a trowel in his hand, he had a book in his pocket.

Some gentlemen, pitying that his parts should be buried under the rubbish of so mean a calling, did by their bounty manumise[2] him freely to follow his own ingenious inclinations. Indeed his

† The text is that of John Freeman's edition (London, 1951).

1. I.e., infants' garments [*Editor*].
2. Liberate [*Editor*].

parts were not so ready to run of themselves, as able to answer the spur; so that it may be truly said of him, that he had an elaborate wit wrought out by his own industry. He would sit silent in a learned company, and suck in (besides wine) their several humours into his observation. What was *ore* in others, he was able to refine to himself.

He was paramount in the dramatic part of poetry, and taught the stage an exact conformity to the laws of comedians. His comedies were above the *volge*[3] (which are only tickled with downright obscenity), and took not so well at the first stroke as at the rebound, when beheld the second time; yea, they will endure reading, and that with due commendation, so long as either ingenuity or learning are fashionable in our nation. If his later be not so spriteful and vigorous as his first pieces, all that are old will, and all that desire to be old should, excuse him therein.

He was not very happy in his children, and most happy in those which died first, though none lived to survive him. This he bestowed as part of an epitaph on his eldest son, dying in infancy:

'Rest in soft peace; and, ask'd, say here doth lye,
Ben Jonson his best piece of poetry.'

He died anno Domini 1638; and was buried about the belfry, in the abbey church at Westminster.

* * *

Many were the wit-combats betwixt him [William Shakespeare] and Ben Jonson; which two I behold like a Spanish great galleon and an English man-of-war: master Jonson (like the former) was built far higher in learning; solid, but slow in his performances. Shakespeare, with the English man-of-war, lesser in bulk, but lighter in sailing, could turn with all tides, tack about, and take advantage of all winds, by the quickness of his wit and invention.

EDWARD HYDE, EARL OF CLARENDON

From *The Life of Edward, Earl of Clarendon*†

Whilst he[1] was only a student of the law, and stood at gaze, and irresolute what course of life to take, his chief acquaintance were Ben Jonson, John Selden, Charles Cotton, John Vaughan, Sir

3. I.e., above the capacities of the commoner sort of spectator [*Editor*].
† The text is that of the edition published at Oxford in 1760.
1. I.e., Edward Hyde (subsequently Earl of Clarendon). For Selden, cf. Jonson, "An Epistle to Master John Selden," p. 59, and first note for Vaughan, Digby, and May, cf. Suckling, "A Sessions of the Poets," p. 254 and notes [*Editor*].

Kenelm Digby, Thomas May, and Thomas Carew, and some others of eminent faculties in their several ways. Ben Jonson's name can never be forgotten, having by his very good learning, and the severity of his nature and manners, very much reformed the stage; and indeed the English poetry itself. His natural advantages were, judgment to order and govern fancy, rather than excess of fancy, his productions being slow and upon deliberation, yet then abounding with great wit and fancy and will live accordingly; and surely as he did exceedingly exalt the English language in eloquence, propriety, and masculine expressions; so he was the best judge of, and fittest to prescribe rules to poetry and poets, of any man who had lived with, or before him, or since: if Mr. Cowley had not made a flight beyond all men, with that modesty yet, to ascribe much of this, to the example and learning of Ben Jonson. His conversation was very good, and with the men of most note; and he had for many years an extraordinary kindness for Mr. Hyde, till he found he betook himself to business, which he believed ought never to be preferred before his company. He lived to be very old, and till the palsy made a deep impression upon his body, and his mind.

SAMUEL BUTLER

From *Criticisms Upon Books and Authors*†

Men of the quickest apprehensions, and aptest geniuses to anything they undertake, do not always prove the greatest masters in it. For there is more patience and phlegm required in those that attain to any degree of perfection, than is commonly found in the temper of active, and ready wits, that soon tire and will not hold out; as the swiftest race-horse will not perform a long journey so well as a sturdy dull jade. Hence it is that Vergil, who wanted much of that natural easiness of wit that Ovid had, did nevertheless with hard labor and long study in the end arrive at a higher perfection than the other with all his dexterity of wit, but less industry, could attain to: the same we may observe of Jonson, and Shakespeare. For he that is able to think long and study well, will be sure to find out better things than another man can hit upon suddenly, though of more quick and ready parts, which is commonly but chance, and the other art and judgment.

---

† The text is that of *Characters and Passages from Note-Books*, ed. A. R. Waller (Cambridge, 1908).

JOHN DRYDEN

[Observations on Jonson's Art]†

I must desire you to take notice, that the greatest man of the last age, Ben Jonson, was willing to give place to them in all things: he was not only a professed imitator of Horace, but a learned plagiary of all the others; you track him everywhere in their snow: if Horace, Lucan, Petronius Arbiter, Seneca, and Juvenal, had their own from him, there are few serious thoughts which are new in him: you will pardon me, therefore, if I presume he loved their fashion, when he wore their clothes.

* * *

As for Jonson, to whose character I am now arrived, if we look upon him while he was himself (for his last plays were but his dotages), I think him the most learned and judicious writer which any theatre ever had. He was a most severe judge of himself, as others. One cannot say he wanted wit, but rather that he was frugal of it. In his works you find little to retrench or alter. Wit and language, and humor also in some measure, we had before him; but something of art was wanting to the drama, till he came. He managed his strength to more advantage than any who preceded him. You seldom find him making love in any of his scenes, or endeavoring to move the passions; his genius was too sullen and saturnine to do it gracefully, especially when he came after those who had performed both to such an height. Humor was his proper sphere; and in that he delighted most to represent mechanic people. He was deeply conversant in the ancients, both Greek and Latin, and he borrowed boldly from them: there is scarce a poet or historian among the Roman authors of those times, whom he has not translated in *Sejanus* and *Catiline*. But he has done his robberies so openly, that one may see he fears not to be taxed by any law. He invades authors like a monarch; and what would be theft in other poets, is only victory in him. With the spoils of these writers he so represents old Rome to us, in its rites, ceremonies, and customs, that if one of their poets had written either of his tragedies, we had seen less of it than in him. If there was any fault in his language, it was, that he weaved it too closely and laboriously, in his comedies especially: perhaps, too, he did a little too much

† The first three passages are excerpted from *An Essay of Dramatick Poesie*; the text follows that in vol. XVII of *The Works of John Dryden*, ed. S. H. Monk (Berkeley, 1971). The fourth passage is excerpted from the Preface to *An Evening's Love*, and follows the text in vol. X of *The Works of John Dryden*, ed. M. E. Novak (Berkeley, 1970).

Romanize our tongue, leaving the words which he translated almost as much Latin as he found them: wherein, though he learnedly followed their language, he did not enough comply with the idiom of ours. If I would compare him with Shakespeare, I must acknowledge him the more correct poet, but Shakespeare the greater wit. Shakespeare was the Homer, or father of our dramatic poets; Jonson was the Vergil, the pattern of elaborate writing; I admire him, but I love Shakespeare. To conclude of him; as he has given us the most correct plays, so in the precepts which he has laid down in his *Discoveries,* we have as many and profitable rules for perfecting the stage, as any wherewith the French can furnish us.

* * *

And as for your instance of Ben Jonson, who, you say, writ exactly without the help of rhyme; you are to remember, it is only an aid to a luxuriant fancy, which his was not: as he did not want imagination, so none ever said he had much to spare.

* * *

But Ben Jonson is to be admired for many excellencies; and can be taxed with fewer failings than any English poet. I know I have been accused as an enemy of his writings; but without any other reason, than that I do not admire him blindly, and without looking into his imperfections. For why should there be *ipse dixit*[1] in our poetry, any more than there is in our philosophy? I admire and applaud him where I ought: those who do more, do but value themselves in their admiration of him; and, by telling you they extol Ben Jonson's way, would insinuate to you that they can practise it. For my part, I declare that I want judgment to imitate him; and should think it a great impudence in myself to attempt it. To make men appear pleasantly ridiculous on the stage, was, as I have said, his talent; and in this he needed not the acumen of wit but that of judgment. For the characters and representations of folly are only the effects of observation; and observation is an effect of juudgment.* * * I think there is no folly so great in any poet of our age, as the superfluity and waste of wit was in some of our predecessors: particularly we may say of Fletcher and of Shakespeare, what was said of Ovid, *In omni ejus ingenio, facilius quod rejici, quam quod adjici potest, invenies:*[2] The contrary of which was true in Vergil, and our incomparable Jonson. . . .

---

1. "He himself has said it" [*Editor*].
2. "In any case, as in regard to all the manifestations of his genius [his detrac-

tors will] find it easier to detect superfluities than deficiencies" (Quintilian, *Institutio Oratoria,* VI. iii. 5) [*Editor*].

The Eighteenth
and Nineteenth Centuries

DR. SAMUEL JOHNSON

From *Lives of The English Poets*†

[*Waller*]

Waller was not one of those idolaters of praise who cultivate their minds at the expence of their fortunes. Rich as he was by inheritance, he took care early to grow richer by marrying Mrs. Banks, a great heiress in the city, whom the interest of the court was employed to obtain for Mr. Crofts. Having brought him a son, who died young, and a daughter, who was afterwards married to Mr. Dormer of Oxfordshire, she died in childbed, and left him a widower of about five and twenty, gay and wealthy, to please himself with another marriage.

Being too young to resist beauty, and probably too vain to think himself resistible, he fixed his heart, perhaps half fondly and half ambitiously, upon the Lady Dorothea Sidney, eldest daughter of the Earl of Leicester, whom he courted by all the poetry in which Sacharissa is celebrated: the name is derived from the Latin appellation of *sugar*, and implies, if it means any thing, a spiritless mildness and dull good-nature, such as excites rather tenderness than esteem, and such as, though always treated with kindness, is never honoured or admired.

Yet he describes Sacharissa as a sublime predominating beauty, of lofty charms and imperious influence, on whom he looks with amazement rather than fondness, whose chains he wishes, though in vain, to break, and whose presence is 'wine that inflames to madness.'

His acquaintance with this high-born dame gave wit no opportunity of boasting its influence; she was not to be subdued by the powers of verse, but rejected his addresses, it is said, with disdain, and drove him away to solace his disappointment with Amoret or Phillis. She married in 1639 the Earl of Sunderland, who died

† The text is that of G. Birkbeck Hill's editions, 3 vols. (Oxford, 1905).

at Newberry in the king's cause; and, in her old age, meeting somewhere with Waller, asked him when he would again write such verses upon her; 'When you are as young, Madam,' said he, 'and as handsome, as you were then.'

In this part of his life it was that he was known to Clarendon, among the rest of the men who were eminent in that age for genius and literature; but known so little to his advantage, that they who read his character[1] will not much condemn Sacharissa that she did not descend from her rank to his embraces, nor think every excellence comprised in wit.

* * *

The poem on the death of the Protector[2] seems to have been dictated by real veneration for his memory. Dryden and Sprat[3] wrote on the same occasion; but they were young men, struggling into notice, and hoping for some favour from the ruling party. Waller had little to expect; he had received nothing but his pardon from Cromwell, and was not likely to ask any thing from those who should succeed him.

Soon afterwards the Restauration supplied him with another subject; and he exerted his imagination, his elegance, and his melody with equal alacrity for Charles the Second.[4] It is not possible to read, without some contempt and indignation, poems of the same author, ascribing the highest degree of 'power and piety' to Charles the First, then transferring the same 'power and piety' to Oliver Cromwell; now inviting Oliver to take the Crown, and then congratulating Charles the Second on his recovered right. Neither Cromwell nor Charles could value his testimony as the effect of conviction, or receive his praises as effusions of reverence; they could consider them but as the labour of invention and the tribute of dependence.

Poets, indeed, profess fiction, but the legitimate end of fiction is the conveyance of truth; and he that has flattery ready for all whom the vicissitudes of the world happen to exalt must be scorned as a prostituted mind that may retain the glitter of wit, but has lost the dignity of virtue.

The *Congratulation* was considered as inferior in poetical merit to the *Panegyrick*,[5] and it is reported that when the king told Waller of the disparity he answered, 'Poets, Sir, succeed better in fiction than in truth.'

---

1. Cf. p. 232 of this edition [*Editor*].
2. I.e., "Upon the Late Storm, and Of the Death of His Highness [Oliver Cromwell] Ensuing the Same" (not included in this edition) [*Editor*].
3. I.e., Bishop Thomas Sprat, the historian of the Royal Society [*Editor*].
4. Johnson alludes to the poem, "To the King, Upon His Majesty's Happy Return" (not included in this edition) [*Editor*].
5. I.e., Waller's "Panegyric to my Lord Protector" [*Editor*].

*   *   *

The characters, by which Waller intended to distinguish his writings, are spriteliness and dignity: in his smaller pieces he endeavours to be gay; in the larger, to be great. Of his airy and light productions the chief source is gallantry; that attentive reverence of female excellence which has descended to us from the Gothick ages.[6] As his poems are commonly occasional and his addresses personal, he was not so liberally supplied with grand as with soft images; for beauty is more easily found than magnanimity.

The delicacy which he cultivated restrains him to a certain nicety and caution, even when he writes upon the slightest matter. He has therefore in his whole volume nothing burlesque, and seldom any thing ludicrous or familiar. He seems always to do his best, though his subjects are often unworthy of his care.

*   *   *

As much of Waller's reputation was owing to the softness and smoothness of his numbers, it is proper to consider those minute particulars to which a versifier must attend.

He certainly very much excelled in smoothness most of the writers who were living when his poetry commenced. The poets of Elizabeth had attained an art of modulation, which was afterwards neglected or forgotten. Fairfax[7] was acknowledged by him as his model; and he might have studied with advantage the poem of Davis,[8] which, though merely philosophical, yet seldom leaves the ear ungratified.

But he was rather smooth than strong; of 'the full resounding line,' which Pope attributes to Dryden, he has given very few examples. The critical decision has given the praise of strength to Denham, and of sweetness to Waller.

*   *   *

The general character of his poetry is elegance and gaiety. He is never pathetick, and very rarely sublime. He seems neither to have had a mind much elevated by nature, nor amplified by learning. His thoughts are such as a liberal conversation and large acquaintance with life would easily supply. They had however then, perhaps, that grace of novelty, which they are now often supposed to want by those who, having already found them in later books, do not know or enquire who produced them first. This treatment is unjust. Let not the original author lose by his imitators.

*   *   *

He borrows too many of his sentiments and illustrations from

6. I.e., the Middle Ages [*Editor*].
7. Edward Fairfax (c. 1575–1635) translated Tasso's epic *Gerusalemme Liberata* [*Editor*].
8. I.e., "Nosce Teipsum," by Sir John Davies (1569–1626) [*Editor*].

the old mythology, for which it is vain to plead the example of ancient poets: the deities which they introduced so frequently were considered as realities, so far as to be received by the imagination, whatever sober reason might even then determine. But of these images time has tarnished the splendor. A fiction, not only detected but despised, can never afford a solid basis to any position, though sometimes it may furnish a transient allusion, or slight illustration. No modern monarch can be much exalted by hearing that, as Hercules had had his *club*, he has his *navy*.[9]

But of the praise of Waller, though much may be taken away, much will remain, for it cannot be denied that he added something to our elegance of diction, and something to our propriety of thought; and to him may be applied what Tasso said, with equal spirit and justice, of himself and Guarini,[1] when, having perused the *Pastor Fido*, he cried out, 'If he had not read *Aminta*, he had not excelled it.'

[Denham]

Denham is deservedly considered as one of the fathers of English poetry. 'Denham and Waller,' says Prior, 'improved our versification, and Dryden perfected it.[2] He has given specimens of various composition, descriptive, ludicrous, didactick, and sublime.

* * *

His poem on the death of Cowley was his last, and among his shorter works his best performance: the numbers are musical, and the thoughts are just.

Cooper's Hill is the work that confers upon him the rank and dignity of an original author. He seems to have been, at least among us, the author of a species of composition that may be denominated *local poetry*, of which the fundamental subject is some particular landscape to be poetically described, with the addition of such embellishments as may be supplied by historical restrospection or incidental meditation.

To trace a new scheme of poetry has in itself a very high claim to praise, and its praise is yet more when it is apparently copied by Garth and Pope;[3] after whose names little will be gained by an enumeration of smaller poets, that have left scarce a corner of the island not dignified either by rhyme or blank verse.

9. The allusion is to Waller's "To the King" (not included in this edition) [*Editor*].
1. *Il Pastor Fido*, a pastoral drama by Giovanni Battista Guarini (1537–1612), was widely admired in the seventeenth century [*Editor*].

2. Matthew Prior (1664–1721), in the Preface to his poem "Solomon," refers in fact not to Denham but to Sir William Davenant [*Editor*].
3. The allusion is to "Claremont," by Samuel Garth (1661–1719), and to Pope's "Windsor Forest" [*Editor*].

Cooper's Hill if it be maliciously inspected will not be found without its faults. The digressions are too long, the morality too frequent, and the sentiments sometimes such as will not bear a rigorous enquiry.

The four verses, which, since Dryden has commended them, almost every writer for a century past has imitated, are generally known:

> 'O could I flow like thee, and make thy stream
> My great example, as it is my theme!
> Though deep, yet clear; though gentle, yet not dull;
> Strong without rage, without o'erflowing full.'

The lines are in themselves not perfect, for most of the words thus artfully opposed are to be understood simply on one side of the comparison, and metaphorically on the other; and if there be any language which does not express intellectual operations by material images, into that language they cannot be translated. But so much meaning is comprised in so few words; the particulars of resemblance are so perspicaciously collected, and every mode of excellence separated from its adjacent fault by so nice a line of limitation; the different parts of the sentence are so accurately adjusted; and the flow of the last couplet is so smooth and sweet— that the passage however celebrated has not been praised above its merit. It has beauty peculiar to itself, and must be numbered among those felicities which cannot be produced at will by wit and labour, but must arise unexpectedly in some hour propitious to poetry.

[*Cowley*]

Cowley, like other poets who have written with narrow views and, instead of tracing intellectual pleasure to its natural sources in the mind of man, paid their court to temporary prejudices, has been at one time too much praised and too much neglected at another.

Wit, like all other things subject by their nature to the choice of man, has its changes and fashions, and at different times takes different forms. About the beginning of the seventeenth century appeared a race of writers that may be termed the metaphysical poets, of whom in a criticism on the works of Cowley it is not improper to give some account.

The metaphysical poets were men of learning, and to shew their learning was their whole endeavor; but, unluckily resolving to shew it in rhyme, instead of writing poetry they only wrote verses, and very often such verses as stood the trial of the finger better than of the ear; for the modulation was so imperfect that they were only found to be verses by counting the syllables.

If the father of criticism[4] has rightly denominated poetry τέχνη μιμητική, *an imitative art*, these writers will without great wrong lose their right to the name of poets, for they cannot be said to have imitated any thing: they neither copied nature nor life; neither painted the forms of matter nor represented the operations of intellect.

Those however who deny them to be poets allow them to be wits. Dryden confesses of himself and his contemporaries that they fall below Donne in wit, but maintains that they surpass him in poetry.

If wit be well described by Pope as being 'that which has been often thought, but was never before so well expressed,'[5] they certainly never attained nor ever sought it, for they endeavoured to be singular in their thoughts, and were careless of their diction. But Pope's account of wit is undoubtedly erroneous; he depresses it below its natural dignity, and reduces it from strength of thought to happiness of language.

If by a more noble and more adequate conception that be considered as wit which is at once natural and new, that which though not obvious is, upon its first production, acknowledged to be just; if it be that, which he that never found it, wonders how he missed; to wit of this kind the metaphysical poets have seldom risen. Their thoughts are often new, but seldom natural; they are not obvious, but neither are they just; and the reader, far from wondering that he missed them, wonders more frequently by what perverseness of industry they were ever found.

But wit, abstracted from its effects upon the hearer, may be more rigorously and philosophically considered as a kind of *discordia concors*; a combination of dissimilar images, or discovery of occult resemblances in things apparently unlike. Of wit, thus defined, they have more than enough. The most heterogeneous ideas are yoked by violence together; nature and art are ransacked for illustrations, comparisons, and allusions; their learning instructs, and their subtilty surprises; but the reader commonly thinks his improvement dearly bought, and though he sometimes admires, is seldom pleased.

From this account of their compositions it will be readily inferred that they were not successful in representing or moving the affections. As they were wholly employed on something unexpected and surprising they had no regard to that uniformity of sentiment, which enables us to conceive and to excite the pains and the pleasure of other minds: they never enquired what on any occasion

4. I.e., Aristotle [*Editor*].   [*Editor*].
5. Cf. "An Essay on Criticism," l. 297

they should have said or done, but wrote rather as beholders than partakers of human nature; as beings looking upon good and evil, impassive and at leisure; as Epicurean deities making remarks on the actions of men and the vicissitudes of life, without interest and without emotion. Their courtship was void of fondness and their lamentation of sorrow. Their wish was only to say what they hoped had been never said before.

Nor was the sublime more within their reach than the pathetick; for they never attempted that comprehension and expanse of thought which at once fills the whole mind, and of which the first effect is sudden astonishment, and the second rational admiration. Sublimity is produced by aggregation, and littleness by dispersion. Great thoughts are always general, and consist in positions not limited by exceptions, and in descriptions not descending to minuteness. It is with great propriety that subtlety, which in its original import means exility[6] of particles, is taken in its metaphorical meaning for nicety of distinction. Those writers who lay on the watch for novelty could have little hope of greatness; for great things cannot have escaped former observation. Their attempts were always analytick: they broke every image into fragments, and could no more represent by their slender conceits and laboured particularities the prospects of nature or the scenes of life, than he who dissects a sun-beam with a prism can exhibit the wide effulgence of a summer noon.

What they wanted however of the sublime they endeavored to supply by hyperbole; their amplification had no limits: they left not only reason but fancy behind them, and produced combinations of confused magnificence that not only could not be credited, but could not be imagined.

Yet great labour directed by great abilities is never wholly lost: if they frequently threw away their wit upon false conceits, they likewise sometimes struck out unexpected truth: if their conceits were far-fetched, they were often worth the carriage. To write on their plan it was at least necessary to read and think. No man could be born a metaphysical poet, nor assume the dignity of a writer by descriptions copied from descriptions, by imitations borrowed from imitations, by traditional imagery and hereditary similes, by readiness of rhyme and volubility of syllables.

In perusing the works of this race of authors the mind is exercised either by recollection or inquiry; either something already learned is to be retrieved, or something new is to be examined. If their greatness seldom elevates, their acuteness often surprises; if the imagination is not always gratified, at least the powers of reflection and comparison are employed; and in the mass of materials, which

6. Thinness [*Editor*].

ingenious absurdity has thrown together, genuine wit and useful knowledge may be sometimes found, buried perhaps in grossness of expression, but useful to those who know their value, and such as, when they are expanded to perspicuity and polished to elegance, may give lustre to works which have more propriety though less copiousness of sentiment.

This kind of writing, which was, I believe, borrowed from Marino and his followers, had been recommended by the example of Donne, a man of very extensive and various knowledge, and by Jonson, whose manner resembled that of Donne more in the ruggedness of his lines than in the cast of his sentiments.

When their reputation was high they had undoubtedly more imitators than time has left behind. Their immediate successors, of whom any remembrance can be said to remain, were Suckling, Waller, Denham, Cowley, Cleveland,[7] and Milton. Denham and Waller sought another way to fame, by improving the harmony of our numbers. Milton tried the metaphysick style in his lines upon Hobson the Carrier. Cowley adopted it, and excelled his predecessors; having as much sentiment and more musick. Suckling neither improved versification nor abounded in conceits. The fashionable style remained chiefly with Cowley: Suckling could not reach it, and Milton disdained it.

* * *

His *Miscellanies* contain a collection of short compositions, written some as they were dictated by a mind at leisure, and some as they were called forth by different occasions; with great variety of style and sentiment, from burlesque levity to awful grandeur. Such an assemblage of diversified excellence no other poet has hitherto afforded. To choose the best among many good is one of the most hazardous attempts of criticism. I know not whether Scaliger himself has persuaded many readers to join with him in his preference of the two favourite odes, which he estimates in his raptures at the value of a kingdom. I will however venture to recommend Cowley's first piece,[8] which ought to be inscribed *To my Muse*, for want of which the second couplet is without reference. . . .

The ode on wit is almost without a rival. It was about the time of Cowley that *Wit*, which had been till then used for *Intellection* in contradistinction to *Will*, took the meaning whatever it be which it now bears.

Of all the passages in which poets have exemplified their own precepts none will easily be found of greater excellence than that in which Cowley condemns exuberance of wit:

7. The poet John Cleveland (1613–1658) combined a fervent royalism with a taste for exaggerated metaphor [*Editor*].
8. I.e., "The Motto" [*Editor*].

'Yet 'tis not to adorn and gild each part;
  That shews more cost than art.
Jewels at nose and lips but ill appear;
Rather than all things wit, let none be there.
    Several lights will not be seen,
    If there be nothing else between.
Men doubt, because they stand so thick i' th' sky,
If those be stars which paint the galaxy.'

* * *

In his poem on the death of Hervey there is much praise, but little passion, a very just and ample delineation of such virtues as a studious privacy admits, and such intellectual excellence as a mind not yet called forth to action can display. He knew how to distinguish and how to commend the qualities of his companion, but when he wishes to make us weep he forgets to weep himself, and diverts his sorrow by imagining how his crown of bays, if he had it, would *crackle* in the *fire*. It is the odd fate of this thought to be worse for being true. The bay-leaf crackles remarkably as it burns; as therefore this property was not assigned it by chance, the mind must be thought sufficiently at ease that could attend to such minuteness of physiology. But the power of Cowley is not so much to move the affections, as to exercise the understanding.

* * *

Cowley seems to have had, what Milton is believed to have wanted, the skill to rate his own performances by their just value, and has therefore closed his *Miscellanies* with the verses upon Crashaw, which apparently[9] excel all that have gone before them, and in which there are beauties which common authors may justly think not only above their attainment, but above their ambition.

To the *Miscellanies* succeed the *Anacreontiques*, or paraphrastical translations of some little poems, which pass, however justly, under the name of Anacreon. Of those songs dedicated to festivity and gaiety, in which even the morality is voluptuous, and which teach nothing but the enjoyment of the present day, he has given rather a pleasing than a faithful representation, having retained their spriteliness, but lost their simplicity. The Anacreon of Cowley, like the Homer of Pope, has admitted the decoration of some modern graces, by which he is undoubtedly made more amiable to common readers, and perhaps, if they would honestly declare their own perceptions, to far the greater part of those whom courtesy and ignorance are content to style the learned.

These little pieces will be found more finished in their kind than

9. Clearly [*Editor*].

any other of Cowley's works. The diction shews nothing of the mould of time, and the sentiments are at no great distance from our present habitudes of thought. Real mirth must be always natural, and nature is uniform. Men have been wise in very different modes; but they have always laughed the same way.

Levity of thought naturally produced familiarity of language, and the familiar part of language continues long the same: the dialogue of comedy, when it is transcribed from popular manners and real life, is read from age to age with equal pleasure. The artifice of inversion, by which the established order of words is changed, or of innovation, by which new words or new meanings of words are introduced, is practised, not by those who talk to be understood, but by those who write to be admired.

The *Anacreontiques* therefore of Cowley give now all the pleasure which they ever gave. If he was formed by nature for one kind of writing more than for another, his power seems to have been greatest in the familiar and the festive.

The next class of his poems is called *The Mistress*, of which it is not necessary to select any particular pieces for praise or censure. They have all the same beauties and faults, and nearly in the same proportion. They are written with exuberance of wit, and with copiousness of learning; and it is truly asserted by Sprat that the plenitude of the writer's knowledge flows in upon his page, so that the reader is commonly surprised into some improvement. But, considered as the verses of a lover, no man that has ever loved will much commend them. They are neither courtly nor pathetick, have neither gallantry nor fondness. His praises are too far-sought and too hyperbolical, either to express love or to excite it: every stanza is crowded with darts and flames, with wounds and death, with mingled souls, and with broken hearts.

* * *

In the general review of Cowley's poetry it will be found that he wrote with abundant fertility, but negligent or unskilful selection; with much thought, but with little imagery; that he is never pathetick, and rarely sublime, but always either ingenious or learned, either acute or profound.

It is said by Denham in his elegy:

> 'To him no author was unknown;
> Yet what he writ was all his own.'

This wide position requires less limitation when it is affirmed of Cowley than perhaps of any other poet: he read much, and yet borrowed little.

His character of writing was indeed not his own: he unhappily adopted that which was predominant. He saw a certain way to present praise; and not sufficiently enquiring by what means the ancients have continued to delight through all the changes of human manners he contented himself with a deciduous laurel, of which the verdure in its spring was bright and gay, but which time has been continually stealing from his brows.

He was in his own time considered as of unrivalled excellence. Clarendon represents him as having taken a flight beyond all that went before him,[1] and Milton is said to have declared that the three greatest English poets were Spenser, Shakespeare, and Cowley.[2]

* * *

It may be affirmed without any encomiastick[3] fervour that he brought to his poetick labours a mind replete with learning, and that his pages are embellished with all the ornaments which books could supply; that he was the first who imparted to English numbers the enthusiasm of the greater ode, and the gaiety of the less; that he was equally qualified for spritely sallies and for lofty flights; that he was among those who freed translation from servility, and, instead of following his author at a distance, walked by his side; and that if he left versification yet improvable, he left likewise from time to time such specimens of excellence as enabled succeeding poets to improve it.

WILLIAM HAZLITT

[Suckling, Denham, and Cowley]†

It should appear, in tracing the history of our literature, that poetry had, at the period of which we are speaking, in general declined, by successive gradations, from the poetry of imagination, in the time of Elizabeth, to the poetry of fancy (to adopt a modern distinction) in the time of Charles I; and again from the poetry of fancy to that of wit, as in the reign of Charles II, and Queen Anne. It degenerated into the poetry of mere common places, both in style and thought, in the succeeding reigns; as in the latter part of the last century, it was transformed, by means of the French Revolution, into the poetry of paradox.

* * *

1. Cf. Edward Hyde, Earl of Clarendon, *Life of Edward Earl of Clarendon*, 2 vols. (Oxford, 1740), I, p. 30 [*Editor*].
2. Cf. John Milton, *Paradise Lost*, ed. T. Newton, 4 vols. (Dublin, 1773), I, pp. 49–50 [*Editor*].
3. Laudatory [*Editor*].

† The first two passages are excerpted from "Lectures on the English Poets" (1818–1819); the others from "Lectures on the English Comic Writers" (1819). The text follows that in P. P. Howe's edition of Hazlitt's *Works*, 21 vols. (London, 1930).

Sir John Suckling was of the same mercurial stamp,[1] but with a greater fund of animal spirits; as witty, but less malicious. His Ballad on a Wedding is perfect in its kind, and has a spirit of high enjoyment in it, of sportive fancy, a liveliness of description, and a truth of nature, that never were surpassed. It is superior to either Gay[2] or Prior; for with all their naïveté and terseness, it has a Shakspearian grace and luxuriance about it, which they could not have reached.

Denham and Cowley belong to the same period, but were quite distinct from each other: the one was grave and prosing, the other melancholy and fantastical. There are a number of good lines and good thoughts in the Cooper's Hill. And in Cowley there is an inexhaustible fund of sense and ingenuity, buried in inextricable conceits, and entangled in the cobwebs of the schools. He was a great man, not a great poet.

*   *   *

Suckling is also ranked,[3] without sufficient warrant, among the metaphysical poets. Sir John was of 'the court, courtly;' and his style almost entirely free from the charge of pedantry and affectation. There are a few blemishes of this kind in his works, but they are but few. His compositions are almost all of them short and lively effusions of wit and gallantry, written in a familiar but spirited style, without much design or effort. His shrewd and taunting address to a desponding lover will sufficiently vouch for the truth of this account of the general cast of his best pieces. [Quotes "Why so pale and wan?"]

The two short poems against fruition, that beginning, 'There never yet was woman made, nor shall, but to be curst,'—the song, 'I pr'ythee, spare me, gentle boy, press me no more for that slight toy, that foolish trifle of a heart,'—another, ' 'Tis now, since I sat down before, that foolish fort, a heart,'—Lutea Alanson[4]—the set of similes, 'Hast thou seen the down in the air, when wanton winds have tost it,'—and his 'Dream,' which is a more tender and romantic cast, are all exquisite in their way. They are the origin of the style of Prior and Gay in their short fugitive verses, and of the songs in the Beggar's Opera. His Ballad on a Wedding is his masterpiece, and is indeed unrivalled in that class of composition, for the voluptuous delicacy of the sentiments, and the luxuriant richness of the images.

*   *   *

Cowley had more brilliancy of fancy and ingenuity of thought

---

1. I.e., as John Wilmot, Earl of Rochester (1648–1680) [Editor].
2. John Gay (1685–1732) wrote The Beggar's Opera [Editor].

3. I.e., by Dr. Johnson, in the Life of Cowley [Editor].
4. I.e., the poem, "Lutea Allison" [Editor].

than Donne, with less pathos and sentiment. His mode of illustrating his ideas differs also from Donne's in this: that whereas Donne is contented to analyze an image into its component elements, and resolve it into its most abstracted species; Cowley first does this, indeed, but does not stop till he has fixed upon some other prominent example of the same general class of ideas, and forced them into a metaphorical union, by the medium of the generic definition. Thus . . . he talks in the Motto, or Invocation to his Muse, of 'marching the Muse's Hannibal' into undiscovered regions. That is, he thinks first of being a leader in poetry, and then he immediately, by virtue of this abstraction, becomes a Hannibal; though no two things can really be more unlike in all the associations belonging to them, than a leader of armies and a leader of the tuneful Nine. . . . The best of his poems are the translations from Anacreon, which remain, and are likely to remain unrivalled. The spirit of wine and joy circulates in them; and though they are lengthened out beyond the originals, it is by fresh impulses of an eager and inexhaustible feeling of delight. [Quotes "Drinking."] This is a classical intoxication; and the poet's imagination, giddy with fancied joys, communicates its spirit and its motion to inanimate things, and makes all nature reel round with it. It is not easy to decide between these choice pieces, which may be reckoned among the *delights of human kind*; but that to the Grasshopper is one of the happiest as well as most serious [quotes the poem].

ALGERNON CHARLES SWINBURNE

[Jonson's Poetry]†

The book of epigrams published by Jonson in the collected edition of his select works up to the date of the year 1616 is by no means an attractive introduction or an alluring prelude to the voluminous collection of miscellanies which in all modern editions it precedes. 'It is to be lamented,' in Gifford's[1] opinion, 'on many accounts,' that the author has not left us 'a further selection.' It is in my opinion to be deplored that he should have left us so large a selection—if that be the proper term—as he has seen fit to bequeath to a naturally and happily limited set of readers. 'Sunt bona, sunt quædam mediocria, sunt mala plura':[2] and the worst are so bad, so foul if not so dull, so stupid if not so filthy, that the stu-

---

† From *A Study of Ben Jonson* (London, 1889).
1. William Gifford edited Jonson's *Works* in 1816 [*Editor*].

2. "There are good things and a certain number that are mediocre; most are bad" [*Editor*].

dent stands aghast with astonishment at the self-deceiving capacity
of a writer who could prefix to such a collection the vaunt that his
book was 'not covetous of least self-fame'— 'much less' prone to
indulgence in 'beastly phrase.' No man can ever have been less
amenable than Sir Walter Scott to the infamous charge of Puritan-
ism or prudery; and it is he who has left on record his opinion that
'surely that coarseness of taste which tainted Ben Jonson's powerful mind is proved from his writings. Many authors of that age are
indecent, but Jonson is filthy and gross in his pleasantry, and
indulges himself in using the language of scavengers and night-
men.'[3] I will only add that the evidence of this is flagrant in certain
pages which I never forced myself to read through till I had undertaken to give a full and fair account—to the best of my ability—of
Ben Jonson's complete works. How far poetry may be permitted
to go in the line of sensual pleasure or sexual emotion may be de-
batable between the disciples of Ariosto and the disciples of Milton; but all English readers, I trust, will agree with me that coprol-
ogy[4] should be left to Frenchmen. Among them—that is, of
course, among the baser sort of them—that unsavoury science will
seemingly never lack disciples of the most nauseous, the most abject, the most deliberate bestiality. It is nothing less than lament-
able that so great an English writer as Ben Jonson should ever have
taken the plunge of a Parisian diver into the cesspool: but it is as
necessary to register as it is natural to deplore the detestable fact
that he did so. The collection of his epigrams which bears only too
noisome witness to this fact is nevertheless by no means devoid
of valuable and admirable components. The sixty-fifth,[5] a palinode
or recantation of some previous panegyric, is very spirited and vigorous; and the verses of panegyric which precede and follow it are
wanting neither in force nor in point. The poem 'on Lucy Countess
of Bedford'[6] . . . would be worthy of very high praise if the texture
of its expression and versification were unstiffened and undisfigured
by the clumsy license of awkward inversions. . . .

The epitaph on little Salathiel Pavy, who had acted under his
own name in the induction to *Cynthia's Revels,* is as deservedly
famous as any minor work of Jonson's; for sweetness and simplicity it has few if any equals among his lyrical attempts.

Of the fifteen lyric or elegiac poems which compose *The Forest,*
there is none that is not worthy of all but the highest praise; there
is none that is worthy of the highest. To come so near so often and
yet never to touch the goal of lyric triumph has never been the
fortune and the misfortune of any other poet. Vigour of thought,

3. Cf. Scott's *Life of John Dryden,* ed.
B. Kreissman (Lincoln, Neb., 1963), p.
227 [*Editor*].
4. Concern with excrement [*Editor*].

5. "To My Muse" (not included in this
edition) [*Editor*].
6. Epigram LXXVI [*Editor*].

purity of phrase, condensed and polished rhetoric, refined and appropriate eloquence, studious and serious felicity of expression, finished and fortunate elaboration of verse, might have been considered as qualities sufficient to secure a triumph for the poet in whose work all these excellent attributes are united and displayed; and we cannot wonder that younger men who had come within the circle of his personal influence should have thought that the combination of them all must ensure to their possessor a place above all his possible compeers. But among the humblest and most devout of these prostrate enthusiasts was one who had but to lay an idle and reckless hand on the instrument which hardly would answer the touch of his master's at all, and the very note of lyric poetry as it should be—as it was in the beginning, as it is, and as it will be for ever—responded on the instant to the instinctive intelligence of his touch. As we turn from Gray to Collins, as we turn from Wordsworth to Coleridge, as we turn from Byron to Shelley, so do we turn from Jonson to Herrick; and so do we recognize the lyric poet as distinguished from the writer who may or may not have every gift but one in higher development of excellence and in fuller perfection of power, but who is utterly and absolutely transcended and shone down by his probably unconscious competitor on the proper and peculiar ground of pure and simple poetry.

But the special peculiarity of the case now before us is that it was so much the greater man who was distanced and eclipsed; and this not merely by a minor poet, but a humble admirer and a studious disciple of his own. Herrick, as a writer of elegies, epithalamiums, panegyrical or complimentary verses, is as plainly and as openly an imitator of his model as ever was the merest parasite of any leading poet, from the days of Chaucer and his satellites to the days of Tennyson and his. No Lydgate or Lytton[7] was ever more obsequious in his discipleship; but for all his loving and loyal protestations of passionate humility and of ardent reverence, we see at every turn, at every step, at every change of note, that what the master could not do the pupil can. When Chapman set sail after Marlowe, he went floundering and lurching in the wake of a vessel that went straight and smooth before the fullest and the fairest wind of song; but when Herrick follows Jonson the manner of movement or the method of progression is reversed. Macaulay, in a well-known passage, has spoken of Ben Jonson's 'rugged rhymes';[8] but rugged is not exactly the most appropriate epithet.

7. John Lydgate (c. 1370–c. 1451) wrote, among other works, *The Falls of Princes* (1494); the novelist Edward Bulwer-Lytton (1803–1873) is best known for *The Last Days of Pompeii* (1834) [*Editor*].

8. Thomas Babington Macaulay, "The Life and Writings of Addison," in *Literary Essays . . .* (London, 1937), pp. 610–611. What Macaulay actually says is, "Ben's heroic couplets resemble blocks rudely hewn out by an unpracticed hand, with a blunt hatchet" [*Editor*].

Donne is rugged: Jonson is stiff. And if ruggedness of verse is a damaging blemish, stiffness of verse is a destructive infirmity. Ruggedness is curable; witness Donne's *Anniversaries*: stiffness is incurable; witness Jonson's *Underwoods*. In these, as in the preceding series called *The Forest*, there is so lavish a display of such various powers as cannot but excite the admiration they demand and deserve. They have every quality, their author would undoubtedly have maintained, that a student of poetry ought to expect and to applaud. What they want is that magic without which the very best verse is as far beneath the very best prose as the verse which has it is above all prose that ever was or ever can be written. . . . In 'the admirable Epode,' as Gifford calls it, which concludes Ben Jonson's contributions to *Love's Martyr*, though there is remarkable energy of expression, the irregularity and inequality of style are at least as conspicuous as the occasional vigour and the casual felicity of phrase. But if all were as good as the best passages this early poem of Jonson's would undoubtedly be very good indeed. Take for instance the description or definition of true love:

> That is an essence far more gentle, fine,
>> Pure, perfect, nay divine;
> It is a golden chain let down from heaven,
>> Whose links are bright and even,
> That falls like sleep on lovers.

Again:

> O, who is he that in this peace enjoys
>> The elixir of all joys,
> (A form more fresh than are the Eden bowers
>> And lasting as her flowers;
> Richer than time, and as time's virtue rare,
>> Sober as saddest care,
> A fixed thought, an eye untaught to glance;)
>> Who, blest with such high chance,
> Would at suggestion of a steep desire
>> Cast himself from the spire
> Of all his happiness?

And few of Jonson's many moral or gnomic passages are finer than the following:

> He that for love of goodness hateth ill
>> Is more crown-worthy still
> Than he which for sin's penalty forbears;
>> His heart sins, though he fears.

This metre, though very liable to the danger of monotony, is to my ear very pleasant; but that of the much admired and doubtless admirable address to Sir Robert Wroth is much less so. This poem is as good and sufficient an example of the author's ability and inability as could be found in the whole range of his elegiac or lyric works. It has excellent and evident qualities of style; energy and purity, clearness and sufficiency, simplicity and polish; but it is wanting in charm. Grace, attraction, fascination, the typical and essential properties of verse, it has not. . . .

The spirit of persuasive enchantment, the goddess of entrancing inspiration, kept aloof from him alone of all his peers or rivals. To men far weaker, to poets not worthy to be named with him on the score of creative power, she gave the gift which from him was all but utterly withheld. And therefore it is that his place is not beside Shakespeare, Milton, or Shelley, but merely above Dryden, Byron, and Crabbe. The verses on Penshurst are among his best, wanting neither in grace of form nor stateliness of sound, if too surely wanting in the indefinable quality of distinction or inspiration: and the farewell to the world has a savour of George Herbert's style about it which suggests that the sacred poet must have been a sometime student of the secular. Beaumont, again, must have taken as a model of his lighter lyric style the bright and ringing verses on the proposition 'that women are but men's shadows.' The opening couplet of the striking address 'to Heaven' has been, it seems to me, misunderstood by Gifford; the meaning is not—'Can I not think of God without its making me melancholy?' but 'Can I not think of God without its being imputed or set down by others to a fit of dejection?' The few sacred poems which open the posthumous collection of his miscellaneous verse are far inferior to the best of Herrick's *Noble Numbers*; although the second of the three must probably have served the minor poet as an occasional model. . . .

The miscellaneous verses collected under the pretty and appropriate name of *Underwoods* comprise more than a few of Ben Jonson's happiest and most finished examples of lyric, elegiac, and gnomic or didactic poetry; and likewise not a little of such rigid and frigid work as makes us regret the too strenuous and habitual application of so devoted a literary craftsman to his professional round of labour. The fifth of these poems, *A Nymph's Passion*, is not only pretty and ingenious, but in the structure of its peculiar stanza may remind a modern reader of some among the many metrical experiments or inventions of a more exquisite and spontaneous lyric poet, Miss Christina Rossetti. The verses 'on a lover's dust, made sand for an hour-glass,' just come short of excellence in their fantastic way; those on his picture are something more than smooth and neat; those against jealousy are exceptionally sweet and spontaneous, again recalling the manner of the poetess just mentioned; with a touch of something like Shelley's—

> I wish the sun should shine
> On all men's fruits and flowers, as well as mine—

and also of something like George Herbert's at his best. *The Dream* is one of Jonson's most happily expressed fancies; the close of it is for once not less than charming.

Of the various elegies and epistles included in this collection it need only be said that there is much thoughtful and powerful writing in most if not in all of them, with occasional phrases or couplets of rare felicity, and here and there a noble note of enthusiasm or a masterly touch of satire. . . . The 'epistle answering to one that asked to be sealed of the tribe of Ben' is better in spirit than in execution; manful, straightforward, and upright. . . . Ben Jonson's views regarding womanhood in general were radically cynical though externally chivalrous: a charge which can be brought against no other poet or dramatist of his age. He could pay more splendid compliments than any of them to this or that particular woman; the deathless epitaph on 'Sydney's sister, Pembroke's mother,' is but the crowning flower of a garland, the central jewel of a set; but no man has said coarser (I had well-nigh written, viler) things against the sex to which these exceptionally honoured patronesses belonged. . . .

The memorial ode on the death of Sir Henry Morison has thoughtful and powerful touches in it, as well as one stanza so far above the rest that it gains by a process which would impair its effect if the poem were on the whole even a tolerably good one. The famous lines on 'the plant and flower of light' can be far better enjoyed when cut away from the context. The opening is as eccentrically execrable as the epode of the solitary strophe which redeems from all but unqualified execration a poem in which Gifford finds 'the very soul of Pindar'—whose reputation would in that case be the most inexplicable of riddles. Far purer in style and far more equable in metre is the 'ode gratulatory' to Lord Weston; and the 'epithalamion' on the marriage of that nobleman's son, though not without inequalities, crudities, and platitudes, is on the whole a fine and dignified example of ceremonial poetry.

* * *

Twentieth-Century Criticism

PATRICK CRUTTWELL

The Classical Line†

The dramatic and metaphysical way of writing was not the only way of the early seventeenth century, though by far the most fruitful. Along with it was the tradition which can be called the classical: a kind of poetry, that is, clearly and more or less directly derived from classical models. Not that this way can be rigidly separated from the other—all divisions between kinds of writing, after all, like all divisions into "ages", are not much more than artificial conveniences. Often, indeed, the two overlapped, and the same man was capable of both. Ben Jonson especially: the only writer who was completely a native both of the living theatre and of the world of classical learning and doctrine. But even in him the two worlds seem not quite in harmony: when the latter is too dominant, as in *Catiline* and *Sejanus*, the virtues of the former are lost, and the verdict of contemporary audiences, as reported by Leonard Digges—

> . . . they would not brooke a line
> Of tedious (though well-labour'd) *Catiline*[1]

has become the judgment of posterity.[2]

Of this classical poetry, the origin was of course Renaissance classicism: the group of doctrines which can be summed up as maintaining that one should take the classics as models, and on those models make an English poetry by adapting their forms and catching their tones. When one says the "classics", what one should really mean, certainly for the sixteenth and seventeenth centuries, is Latin. Greek, then as always, counted for very little: it was the possession of a small minority, never backed up by the enormous weight of educational monopoly which Latin enjoyed. One ought, indeed, to narrow it still farther: it was not so much

---

† From *The Shakespearean Moment and Its Place in the Poetry of the Seventeenth Century* (New York, 1955).

1. Verses prefixed to the Second Folio.
2. Cf. Jonson's *Ode* "Come leave the loathed stage", in which, disgusted with the bad taste of the playhouse (which

had hissed *The New Inn*), he turns for consolation to the classics and to verse written by their lights:

> Leave things so prostitute,
> And take the *Alcaick* lute,
> Or thine own *Horace* or *Anacreons* lyre;
> Warme thee by *Pindares* fire . . .

Latin, as "classical" Latin. By way of demonstrating their superiority to the monkish barbarism of the Middle Ages, which had had the bad taste to keep Latin a living language, the scholars and humanists of the Renaissance performed that curious trick from which some of us have still suffered in twentieth-century school: they extracted some hundred years of Latin literature, pronounced this to be "pure" and "classical", and condemned the rest to darkness. This tract of literature became the raw material for Renaissance education and a standard unquestioned by classicist taste. Thus the only kind of classical "influence" which, as critics of poetry, we are really concerned with—the direct action of one language on another—was limited to that particular age of Latin poetry which centres round the age of Augustus.

To be "Augustan" is not only an eighteenth century ambition; it can be seen operating as an ideal all through the classical tradition from the Renaissance onwards. Ben Jonson, commenting on Shakespeare's excessive fluency, finds it natural to enforce his reprimand with an Augustan example: "*sufflaminandus erat*; as *Augustus* said of *Haterius*." The same standard Waller finds appropriate for the praise of Cromwell—

> As the vex'd World to find repose at last
> It self into *Augustus* arms did cast;
> So *England* now does with like toyle opprest,
> Her weary Head upon your Bosome rest[3]

Dryden for the celebration of Charles II's restoration—

> Oh Happy Age! Oh times like those alone,
> By Fate reserv'd for great *Augustus* throne!
> When the joint growth of Arms and Arts foreshew
> The World a Monarch, and that Monarch *You*[4]

and Dr. Johnson for the praise of Dryden's achievement:

> What was said of Rome, adorned by Augustus, may be applied by an easy metaphor to English poetry embellished by Dryden, "lateritiam invenit, marmoream reliquit." He found it brick, and he left it marble.
>
> (*Life of Dryden*)

Both for political and literary judgments, the Augustan standard would serve.

Why the Augustan age should have exerted such an attraction, is not hard to see. Whether or not justified by the reality, an ideal picture was formed of a court at once powerful and tasteful ("*joint* growth of Arms and Arts"), both favouring poets and favoured by them. It provided them with something worth singing *about*—in

---

3. *Panegyrick to my Lord Protector.*   4. *Astraea Redux.*

the shape of great men who were not arrant scoundrels and great deeds which extended civilization—and provided them also with something worth singing *for*. To fit this picture certain adjustments, no doubt unconscious, had to be made: the "rebels" and individualists of Roman poetry, such as Catullus and Lucretius, were comparatively depreciated; the equivocal aspects of Horace—his irony and cynicism—and of Virgil—his deep melancholy—were little dwelt on, if indeed they were felt at all. They did not fit. Horace had to be an urbane and contented celebrator of the golden mean and the Augustan achievement, Virgil a highly-polished, untormented praiser of rusticity and prophet of imperialism. These two, above all others, were the influences, and these views of them—not wrong, perhaps, but certainly inadequate—coloured a great deal of the English poetry written in the classical vein.

Especially, perhaps, those poems which celebrate great men and great occasions. Their tradition starts from the success of the Renaissance humanists in persuading their "princes" that literary fame was a desirable possession and themselves the right persons to supply it. Poetry, it was generally agreed, had a State function to perform: it should elevate, magnify, and preserve. * * *

Together with panegyric, as a "public" kind of poetry, was elegy. This, of course, is one of the mass-produced forms of the seventeenth century: there is no better illustration both of the naturalness with which the age turned to poetry—its feeling that poetry was a proper and inevitable thing—and of the remoteness of much of its poetry from what we would call genuine "feeling", than the whole bookfuls of elegies called forth by the deaths of such persons as Prince Henry, Edward King, Lord Hastings, *et alii*. Here, at least, the age is as far as it can be from the romantic conviction (or heresy) that true poetry can be made only from "spontaneous expression" and "powerful emotion". Still, it can be said that such elegies-to-order achieve poetry only in two ways. If they follow the classical mode, they must have some true feeling of personal sorrow. If they follow the metaphysical, they make their poetry by that process, observed in Donne's *Anniversaries*, of using the ostensible subject as nothing more than a centre round which to move in an orbit as wide as the poet fancies. (And if they follow the Miltonic, as in *Lycidas*, they must be concerned with John Milton.) * * * [Discusses Dryden's *Eleonora* and *To the Memory of Mr. Oldham*.]

Both in State panegyric and in elegy, the presence of Horace counts for much. On the whole, indeed, if we exclude epic and pastoral as special kinds, and therefore Virgil, the standard for both, it is Horace who seems to be the strongest power over all this classical poetry. (Ovid, his only rival, the true classicists regarded with some disdain: his luscious eroticism and verbal conceits appealed more to the world of the "sugared sonnets" and mythological sensualities.) The manner of the Horace who is not lyricist—the Horace of the *Satires* and *Epistles,* familiar and talkative—is overwhelmingly the presiding tone of two other kinds of seventeenth century verse: the friendly, unbuttoned discourse and the literary causerie.

The tone which the former sets itself to render is that of the cultured but unpedantic gentleman, living in comfort but not in luxury, knowing the great world but not tied to it, amiably chatting with a friend of equal status and similar type. Horace on his Sabine farm—dearest and most durable literary daydream of those who enjoyed their classical educations—is always there in the background. Jonson's *Inviting a Friend to Supper,* for example, with its opening of modest confidence and decent, not lavish hospitality.

> To-night, grave sir, both my poore house, and I
>> Doe equally desire your companie:
> Not that we thinke us worthy such a guest,
>> But that your worth will dignifie our feast,
> With those that come; whose grace may make that seeme
>> Something, which, else, could hope for no esteeme.
> It is the faire acceptance, Sir, creates
>> The entertaynment perfect: not the cates . . .

When the "culture" comes along, it is (as it ought to be in this kind of context) exclusively Latin:

> How so e'er, my man
> Shall reade a piece of Virgil, Tacitus,
>> Livie, or of some better booke to us,
> Of which wee'll speake our minds, amidst our meate.

If one encountered nowadays that tone of serene classical superiority, one would probably find it thoroughly infuriating, for one would expect it, justifiably or not, to be allied to a taste essentially dead. At the safe distance of three hundred years (and when uttered by a man of Jonson's creative achievement) it rings true and evokes no protest. This tone of familiar talk is responsible for some of the most delightful verse of the seventeenth century; another such is Drayton's epistle to Henry Reynolds:

> My dearely loved friend how oft have we,
> In winter evenings (meaning to be free,)
> To some well-chosen place us'd to retire;
> And there with moderate meate, and wine, and fire,
> Have past the howres contentedly with chat,
> Now talk'd of this, and then discours'd of that,
> Spoke our owne verses 'twixt our selves, if not

> Other mens lines, which we by chance had got,
> Or some Stage pieces famous long before,
> Of which your happy memory had store . . .

The poem goes on to Drayton's endearing picture of his own schooldays:

> In my small selfe I greatly marveil'd then,
> Amongst all other, what strange kinde of men
> These Poets were; And pleased with the name,
> To my milde Tutor merrily I came,
> (For I was then a proper goodly page,
> Much like a Pigmy, scarse ten yeares of age)
> Clasping my slender armes about his thigh.
> O my deare master! cannot you (quoth I)
> Make me a Poet, doe it if you can,
> And you shall see, I'll quickly bee a man.
> Who me thus answered smiling, boy quoth be,
> If you'll not play the wag, but I may see
> You ply your learning, I will shortly read
> Some Poets to you; *Phoebus* be my speed . . .

This kind of verse has a very clear connection with that of the eighteenth century; the line runs straight—with the Horatian influence always present and keeping it recognizably the same—from such poems as these, through Dryden's epistle to his kinsman John Driden, to Pope's *Imitations of Horace* and *Epistle to Dr. Arbuthnot*. Pope gives it the final perfection, raises it from the level of delightful verse to that of great poetry; he does it by letting himself go a good deal more, widening the range so that real passions—anger and venom and moral solemnity—can be brought within it: but the essential tone, the familiar talking voice, is never lost.

The literary causerie comes very close to it. Behind it, as a rule, are the grand exemplars, Horace's *Ars Poetica* and the first epistle of his second book, which takes one on a rapid gallop through his Roman literary past. Drayton's epistle, already cited, follows the latter model: it lays down what was beginning to be the conventional view of the history of English poetry—that Chaucer began it, doing remarkably well considering the limitations of the language in his benighted times—

> That noble *Chaucer*, in those former times,
> The first inrich'd our *English* with his rimes,
> And was the first of ours, that ever brake,
> Into the *Muses* treasure, and first spake
> In weighty numbers, delving in the Mine
> Of perfect knowledge, which he could refine,
> And coyne for current, and as much as then

> The *English* language could expresse to me,
> He made it doe . . .

—Gower came next; Surrey and Wyatt, Spenser and Sidney, continued it. Drayton deals also with his contemporaries: with Marlowe, among others, whom he sees as the type of "poetic madness", and with Shakespeare, whom he seems to think of as solely a writer of comedy—betraying in this, perhaps, a kind of inadequacy not rarely found in this sort of verse. Still, in such poems as this will be found a remarkably high proportion of what is really alive and interesting in the literary criticism of the early seventeenth century. * * *

Of all this seventeenth century verse in the classical line, the common feature is that it is always, in varying senses, a public kind of poetry. Even when it is not "occasional"—celebrating some great occasion or great person—it always assumes the existence of a listener, a sympathetic listener usually, on good terms of understanding with the writer. By that assumption this poetry is precluded from dealing with depths and extremes of emotion, of analysis or subtlety. For this is a poetry in which *communication* is the first consideration; it must limit itself to what the other man is sure both to understand and to appreciate. State poems, by their very nature, can hardly afford themselves the luxury of original ideas or unexpected sentiments—the commonplace is of their essence—and the poems of familiar discourse are also limited—limited by their Horatian convention of quiet good sense and easy good breeding. "We know, of course—talker and listener—we *both* know what sensible well-bred gentlemen don't talk about": that is the standard implied. This classical verse thus shows a self-consciousness very different from that of metaphysical or Shakespearean. The latter's self-consciousness is dramatic, that of the actor, who can let himself go—to all appearances—completely, because he knows that in reality the part he is playing need not be identified with his self: and because of that, his parts can always be changed, his range is infinite. But the self-consciousness of the classical verse is that of someone obliged to behave according to a certain code, who would feel himself disgraced or humiliated if he went outside it.

This is the real point at which such verse has an affinity to the poetic ideals and practice of the eighteenth century, and here too is the point at which it is radically different from the poetry of the Shakespearean moment. For the latter, as earlier chapters have argued, has as one of its vital characteristics the willingness to include everything, the refusal to leave out anything, whether on grounds of relevance or morality or taste. The classicist taste—reinforced by that "refining" on moral grounds in which the eighteenth century carried on the work of the Puritans—was more than anything else a system of pruning and selecting: it rejected some things in the hope of achieving a more manageable and comprehensible order out of what was left. This pruning and selecting, which, when the time came (after the Restoration), it was going to apply to English, it already applied, as we have noted, to the raw material on which its judgments were based: to the classics themselves. And between the two—between the principles behind the two selections, English and Latin—there is a real likeness: between the poetry of Catullus and Lucretius on the one hand, and that of the Roman Augustans, especially the two most influential, Virgil and Horace, on the other hand, there is a difference not at all unlike that which came over English poetry between the age of Shakespeare and Donne and that of Dryden and Pope. The language of the earlier poets in both is much richer, more flexible and uninhibited, more natural, nearer to the speaking voice, than that of their successors, which has been subjected to a process of refinement, to a pruning of vocabulary, a chastening of material, and a standardizing of rhythm.[5] Coleridge—or Coleridge's headmaster—perceived that difference where the Roman poets were concerned, as *Biographia Literaria* tells us:

> He habituated me to compare Lucretius (in such extracts as I then read), Terence, and above all the chaster poems of Catullus, not only with the Roman poets of the, so called, silver and brazen ages; but with even those of the Augustan aera; and on grounds of plain sense and universal logic to see and assert the superiority of the former in the truth and nativeness both of their thoughts and diction.

Whether Coleridge recognized that the taste which his head-master protested against in Latin was the same as that which he himself scarified in English—the false kind of poetic diction, as exemplified by Gray—is not quite clear; he probably did, since he certainly recognized that the traditional kind of classical education, with as its finest flower that absurd bi-lingual acrostic known as "Latin Verses", was largely responsible for bad taste in English poetry; and *that* sort of education was the pedagogical infant of Roman and English Augustan taste.

Coleridge and his master put their fingers on the quality which the earlier poetry had, and the later lost, in the word "nativeness". This is the quality which keeps the language of poetry in an un-selfconscious, probably unconscious, harmony and kinship with the current colloquial speech of the age; and this is what was partly lost when classicism became the dominant standard for English poetry, and would have been entirely lost if its victory had been total instead of partial. For classicist doctrine works by imposing a set of principles created for one language on to another: it is thus

5. What Dr. Johnson remarks of Pope, that he was "a master of poetical prudence", in that he virtually confined himself to one metre, could be said equally of Virgil.

the negation of "negativeness". In this too there is a certain parallel between English and Latin: with, for the latter, Greek models
performing the function that Latin performed for the English
classicists. As Horace advises in the *Ars Poetica*:

> vos exemplaria Graeca
> nocturna versate manu, versate diurna.[6]

"Nativeness" almost goes; and its loss is most intimately connected with the final, post-Restoration collapse of the quality of
poetic drama; perhaps it was really the same thing, since the existence of a drama both popular and poetic had been by far the most
effective bridge for the linking of poetic and popular language.
Once this bridge ceased to be effective, the connection could be
kept only by individual *tours de force*, such as Pope continually ac-
complishes in such works as the *Imitations of Horace*; but writers
of lesser genius had to take refuge in the easier resource of a pre-
fabricated diction. The last forty years of the seventeenth century—
the years after the Restoration—show the confused beginnings of
this process; they show English poetry still struggling to keep the
drama as its centre and front of its life, but more and more aware
of the vast inferiority of its own achievements in that sphere to
those of the drama before the Civil War, and more and more, in
consequence, tending to find its real bent in other spheres. They
show, too, an effort on the part of criticism to excuse this inferiority by claiming some compensatory gains. They are, for poetry,
confused and unsatisfactory years, these last decades of the seventeenth century; the old way has been irretrievably lost, the new has
not yet been conclusively found. But the classical tradition which
this chapter has examined was one of the new way's parents. The
other was Milton, whose true nature is much more justly seen if he
is taken as the first of the Augustans than as a poet whose lifetime
overlapped those of Shakespeare and Donne. And in the decades
after the Restoration the new way is born.

JOSEPH SUMMERS

[Donne and Jonson]†

The most important distinctions between the poetry of Donne
and the poetry of Jonson approximate the differences which John
Buxton has recently described between the kinds of poetry circu-

---

6. "Take you the Greeks' examples . . . /
In hand, and turn them over day and
night" (Jonson's translation) [*Editor*].

† From *The Heirs of Donne and Jonson*
(New York, 1970).

lated in manuscripts among literary coteries in the 1590's and the kinds intended for publication:[1] poetry imitating private voices in contrast to poetry imitating public voices, poetry written by conscious amateurs in contrast to poetry written by professionals. Donne was the man who wrote, shortly after the publication of his 'Second Anniversary' in 1612, 'Of my Anniversaries, the fault that I acknowledge in my self, is to have descended to print any thing in verse, which though it have excuse even in our times, by men who professe, and practise much gravitie; yet I confesse I wonder how I declined to it, and do not pardon my self . . .,[2] and Jonson was the man who shocked and amused his contemporaries by disclosing his literary seriousness and ambition when, four years after Donne's remark, he published some of his plays and poems as his *Works*.

From the major contrast implied, one can easily move to the popular contrast between 'colloquial' and 'formal' styles. But that formulation can be misleading. It may seem to postulate a single, completely unselfconscious, 'natural' (and therefore for some readers 'good') style, so close to an abstraction called 'reality' as to be its inevitable voice, and another, 'artful,' 'artificial,' 'rhetorical,' completely removed from any spoken language—and therefore 'bad.' I doubt that things have ever been that simple; at any rate, such a distinction is too crude for an age as rhetorically aware as the late sixteenth and early seventeenth centuries. It is possible to hold theoretically that 'real,' 'essential' man is man utterly alone, with no thought of others or of an audience, but it is hardly possible to talk sensibly about such a notion. Once we admit the use of language, that incorrigibly social medium, we are involved, willy-nilly, with matters of audiences, stances, purposes, and all the rest. *Every* use of language is more or less 'artful' or 'formal' as its user is more or less conscious of what he is doing and successful in doing it; and every use of language has also some relation (although sometimes a sadly remote one) to language as it has been either spoken or sung. 'Formal' and 'colloquial' alone strike me as too vague to be very useful: 'colloquial' for whom? what kind of speakers in what mood? speaking directly to whom? overheard by whom? for what purposes? And what kind of 'formality'? inviting what sorts of recognitions or participations from what readers or hearers? I do not mean to imply that these are easy questions or that I have the answers to them. (What *can* one determine about the 'audience' and 'purposes' of a persuasion to love, written both in a middle style and in the form of a strict Italian sonnet, addressed to a real lady but published by the poet?) But they are questions which we might keep in mind when we read Donne and Jonson and the rest. And it may be

1. *Elizabethan Taste* (London, 1963), pp. 317–318.   2. Quoted by Buxton, *Elizabethan Taste*, pp. 317–318.

helpful also to question some of our perhaps unconscious assumptions about colloquialism and linguistic 'realism' in general. Is the heightened speech of a passionate persuasion to love more 'colloquial' than the fairly neutral conversation of old lovers—or of a husband and wife? Is speech addressed to one hearer necessarily more 'realistic' than speech addressed to several hearers? Is language expressing anger or impatience intrinsically more 'authentic' than meditative language—or even social chatter? Is harshness always more 'real' or even 'colloquial' than euphony? * * *

There are advantages in beginning with the epigrams and 'Paradoxes and Problems,' particularly since that seems to be about where Donne and Jonson began. Donne's few epigrams are off-hand squibs, most of them only two-lines long and many of them very funny; such as 'Antiquary':

> If in his study Hammon hath such care
> To'hang all old strange things, let his wife beware.

Or, 'A Selfe Accuser':

> Your mistress, that you follow whores, still taxeth you:
> 'Tis strange she should confess it, though'it be true.

In his recent edition, W. Milgate attributes to Donne 'Manliness':

> Thou call'st me effeminate, for I love women's joys;
> I call not thee manly, though thou follow boys.[3]

Jonson, by contrast, called his 'Epigrams' the 'ripest of my studies,' and published one-hundred-three; he included complimentary and elegiac as well as satiric epigrams and even expanded the term to include a scabrous mock-heroic of almost two-hundred lines, 'The Famous Voyage.' Jonson was usually serious about imitating (and attempting to surpass) Martial. In most of his epigrams he seems to have wanted a density, a deliberate and weighty judgement, a public and permanent status close to that of an actual inscription, even when they, too, contained only a single couplet:

> To Alchemists
> If all you boast of your great art be true;
> Sure, willing poverty lives most in you. (No. VI)

More characteristic (and more impressive) are epigrams of eight or ten lines, such as 'On some-thing, that walks some-where':

> At court I met it, in clothes brave enough,
> To be a courtier; and looks grave enough,
> To seem a statesman: as I near it came,
> It made me a great face, I asked the name.

---

3. *The Satires, Epigrams, and Verse Letters* (Oxford, 1967), p. 52.

'A lord,' it cried, 'buried in flesh, and blood,
And such from whom let no man hope least good,
For I will do none: and as little ill,
For I will dare none.' Good Lord, walk dead still.
                                        (No. XI)

What we are invited to admire here is less the cleverness of the observer than the justice and precision of his observation. The symmetries of the poem ('brave enough' and 'grave enough,' 'To be' and 'to seem,' 'good' and 'ill,' 'do' and 'dare'), carefully climaxed by the implied contrast between walking dead and being alive, help convince us that private judgement has, in fact, correctly observed public reality. Jonson often gains something of that effect, even in his most personal and moving epitaphs. He seems to have begun, if not as an aged eagle, at least with the tone of a sober and fully mature citizen. One could almost deduce his admiration for Francis Bacon and Selden.

The witty, mercurial, 'interesting' young man who speaks Donne's epigrams is, I think, more clearly defined in 'Paradoxes and Problems,' those prose juvenilia to which Donne devoted a good deal more care. He is, literally and quite intentionally, dazzling. He knows all the old arguments and can stand them on their heads. He is a master of wild analogy, semi-arcane lore, and false logic. He cannot only play the usual young man's game of hooting at generally accepted conventions and the graybeards (by, for example, defending women's inconstancy or their duty to paint), but he can have even more sport in hoisting other such young men with their own petards: what fun to *defend* as paradoxes the notions that virginity is a virtue or that 'it is possible to find some virtue in some women'! And he is wonderfully inventive in thinking up multiple solutions for 'problems' such as 'Why Hath the Common Opinion Afforded Women Souls?' and 'Why doth the Pox so much Affect to Undermine the Nose?' The 'Paradoxes and Problems' are virtuoso performances. Our chief pleasure is in the agility of the intellectual footwork, the fertility of the invention, the gaiety of all that energy. The usual pose is sceptical, satirical, endlessly knowing; but if the young speaker has any settled or serious convictions it is all to his present purpose that they should not show. The last thing he wishes is to give a sense of mature, public, and permanent judgement. Donne's young speaker could not possibly be imagined as the author of any of Jonson's epigrams—only, perhaps, as the subject of one. Although both poets went on to different and more ambitious kinds of poetry, I think one can continue to catch glimpses in the poems of these early speakers' stances and assumptions and values.

The most substantial third of Jonson's epigrams are eulogistic.

They evidence Jonson's conviction that part of the poet's duty was to provide the voice of fame for his worthy contemporaries (Jonson told Drummond that he meant to perfect 'an Epic Poem intitled Heroölogia,' a praise of the worthies of England) as well as his attempt to make eulogy more believable and more interesting than it often was. One way to praise a quality was to imitate or echo it. When Jonson addressed the usually mellifluous Francis Beaumont, for example, he used end-stopped couplets whose balanced construction conveys the compliment almost as clearly as does their meaning: [Quotes Epigram LV.] The three poems which concern Donne (largely as satirist and elegist) are very different. One addressed to Donne seems an allusion to, if not a parody of, Donne's 'masculine persuasive force,' with its reversed feet, harsh alliterations, arbitrary elisions, enjambment, and its blunt imperative: [Quotes Epigram XCVI.]

One does not have to believe that Jonson ever for a minute thought his title to poet depended on Donne's opinion to recognize the seriousness of the poetic ambition which such epigrams imply. Jonson seems to have believed that a poet should know and be able to imitate the best contemporary poets and styles. Furthermore, as the most thoroughgoing classicist England had yet produced, he believed that 'the true artificer' should be mastercraftsman enough to provide a demonstration of Milton's ideal of the well-educated man, by performing 'justly, skilfully, and magnanimously all the [*poetic*] offices, both private and public, of peace and war.' For Jonson such a demonstration included the composition of the epigrams, the verse-letters, the odes, the songs, the epithalamiums, the tragedies, the comedies, and those masques which combined entertainment and compliment, mythical fictions and social realities, as well as most of the beautiful arts. It seems inevitable that Jonson should have translated Horace's *Art of Poetry*. It is hard to imagine Donne's doing so.* * *

If Jonson held in theory that a poet should be able to write exhaustively about almost everything, Donne came near to fulfilling such an ideal in practice on the one subject of the psychology of love. In his *Love Elegies* and *Songs and Sonnets*, the individual speaker sometimes loves all women and sometimes he curses or despairs of all or announces that he is through with love. Sometimes he says that he can love any woman, or any woman so long as she is true, or any woman so long as she is untrue. Sometimes he cares only for the woman's body and the physical act of love; on at least one occasion he claims to love only one woman's virtuous soul. In some of the best poems, he insists that love is properly fulfilled only when it embraces both body and soul. But before we conclude that these poems are direct reflections of one unusually varied sexual autobiography, we should notice that two of the poems are written in the voice of a woman, one of them arguing wittily for absolute female promiscuity ('Good is not good, unless / A thousand it possess').[4] In addition to their varied attitudes and speakers, the poems explore various forms of address (often, as Helen Gardner has suggested, owing something to Ovid, the classical epigrams, Petrarch, or the English drama): a lover advises other lovers on how best to begin an affair; he satirizes the foulness of another lover's mistress; he celebrates his new day of love as the beginning of a new life; he celebrates a full year of love; he imagines the future canonization of himself and his mistress as saints of a new religion of love; he laments the death of his loved one; he imagines his own burial; he makes his will. And he frequently explores the technically metaphysical (Neoplatonic or scholastic) subtleties concerning the nature and number of the new being which results from the perfect union of lovers. There are, however, some limitations. Helen Gardner has remarked that Donne 'never speaks in the tone of a man overwhelmed by what he feels to be wholly undeserved good fortune.'[5] I should think, too, that we value the note of simple tenderness in 'Sweetest love, I do not go' partly because it is so rare in Donne. And 'The Flea' is memorable, among other reasons, because it is one of the few occasions in which Donne used (and, I think, parodied) the traditional persuasion to love. It is almost as if Donne wished to explore all the possibilities of personal love poetry except the sort that had been most popular in the vernacular; the poem which declares initial passion or devotion and attempts to persuade the lady to respond. In nearly all of Donne's best love poems (and a number of them are surely among the best poems in the language), the speaker is either passionately engaged or outrageously witty and playful or both.

The contrast with Jonson is precise. Jonson began *The Forest* with 'Why I write not of Love':

> Some act of Love's bound to rehearse,
> I thought to bind him, in my verse:
> Which when he felt, 'Away' (quoth he)
> 'Can Poets hope to fetter me?
> It is enough, they once did get
> Mars, and my Mother, in their net:
> I wear not these my wings in vain.'
> With which he fled me: and again,
> Into my ri'mes could ne'er be got
> By any art. Then wonder not,
> That since, my numbers are so cold,
> When Love is fled, and I grow old.

4. "Confined Love." The other poem is "Break of Day."

5. John Donne, *The Elegies and the Songs and Sonnets* (Oxford, 1965), p. xvii.

The personal love poem, addressed by a recognizably individual speaker to a specific mistress (fictional or otherwise), is the realm of the amateur in more than etymology, and Jonson seems almost embarrassed by it. When he infrequently attempts such poems, he often presents himself as a ruefully comic figure. In 'My Picture Left in Scotland' (*The Underwood*, IX), for example, he attributes his failure in love to the notion that 'Love is rather deaf, than blind'; despite the excellence of his poems, he fears his mistress has seen

> My hundreds of gray hairs,
> Told seven and forty years,
> Read so much wast, as she cannot imbrace
> My mountain belly, and my rocky face,
> And all these through her eyes, have stopt her ears.

Even within his remarkable sequence 'A Celebration of Charis' Jonson presents himself as conscious that others see him as

> Cupid's Statue with a Beard,
> Or else one that played his Ape,
> In a Hercules-his shape.   (No. 3)

But a major Renaissance poet who could not write of love is almost inconceivable. The three Celia poems (*The Forest*, V, VI, IX) may economically suggest something of the way Jonson was able to write 'objective,' 'classical,' and also very English love poems. 'Drink to me, only, with thine eyes' may owe a great deal to Philostratus, but it is most remarkable in its successful anonymity. It is *the* English poem declaring a lover's secret pledge. As in many genuinely popular love poems, the speaker is characterized only by his emotion; any number of readers have been able to identify with him. The poem so completely expresses its situation that, as with the madrigals and lute songs and some popular modern songs, we feel little sense of impropriety if it is sung by a woman or by more than one voice. 'Come my Celia, let us prove,/While we may, the sports of love' is almost equally the type of the cynical persuasion to love. The *carpe diem* theme is even older than Catullus, but Jonson places and criticizes the traditional arguments by the final lines:

> 'Tis no sin, love's fruit to steal,
> But the sweet theft to reveal:
> To be taken, to be seen,
> These have crimes accounted been.

Once the concepts of 'sin' and 'crimes' are openly introduced into such a context, they cannot be easily dismissed. That Jonson hardly intended the poem to be 'persuasive' is suggested by its ironic context within *Volpone*, where it first appeared: like Volpone's appeals

to erotic conspicuous consumption, the song is precisely calculated
to offend rather than to seduce a heavenly Celia. 'Kiss me, sweet' is
another matter still. Although Catallus may again have furnished a
point of departure, the poem's request for a kiss expands to include
a magnificent enumeration of local, natural, and English detail; and
when Jonson uses that sort of 'matter of England' in his lyrics, we
are usually invited not to judge but to rejoice:

> First give a hundred,
> Then a thousand, then another
> Hundred, then unto the other
> Add a thousand, and so more:
> Till you equal with the store,
> All the grass that Rumney yields,
> Or the sands in Chelsey fields,
> Or the drops in silver Thames,
> Or the stars, that guild his streams,
> In the silent summer-nights,
> When youths ply their stol'n delights.

The first stanza of 'Her Triumph,' that metrical *tour de force*
from 'A Celebration of Charis' (*The Underwood*, II), suggests the
other chief area of Jonson's success in love poetry: the masque,
with all its visual, musical, and mythological resources:

> See the Chariot at hand here of Love
>   Wherein my Lady rideth!
> Each that draws, is a Swan or a Dove,
>   And well the Car Love guideth.
> As she goes, all hearts do duty
>   Unto her beauty;
> And enamour'd, do wish, so they might
>   But enjoy such a sight,
> That they still were to run by her side,
> Thorough Swords, thorough Seas, whither she would ride.

As some of their titles indicate (*Love Freed from Ignorance and
Folly, Lovers made Men,* and *Love's Triumph through Callipolis,*
for example), it is within the masques that Jonson used much of
the traditional Renaissance lore concerning the 'philosophy of love.'
It was Jonson who identified twelve types of depraved lovers and
fifteen sorts of virtuous lovers (the latter number probably partly
determined by the number of courtiers available for the occasion),
and it was Jonson who anticipated both Milton and Dryden by
occasionally writing of love in a new way:

> So love, emergent out of *Chaos*, brought
>   The world to light!

> And gently moving on the water, wrought
> All form to sight![6]

* * *

Donne's [public poems] are not central to his work as most of Jonson's public poems are to his. It is within those poems that one can see, firmly related, Jonson's chief moral and poetic concerns. 'To Penshurst,' for example, like so many of Jonson's poems, is fundamentally a celebration of an ideal mean and measure—not merely an avoidance of extremes (whether of decoration or riches or emotion or individuality), but an orderly fulfillment of responsible actions within society, within the family, within the time of a human life. And the natural symbols for such a fulfillment come, of course, from the fruitful harvest of the elements and the year's cycle.

> The early cherry, with the later plum,
>   Fig, grape, and quince, each in his time doth come:
> The blushing apricot, and wooly peach
>   Hang on thy walls, that every child may reach.
> And though thy walls be of the country stone,
>   They're rear'd with no man's ruin, no man's groan,
> There's none, that dwell about them, wish them down;
>   But all come in, the farmer and the clown:
> And no one empty-handed, to salute
>   Thy lord, and lady, though they have no suit:
> Some bring a capon, some a rural cake,
>   Some nuts, some apples; some that think they make
> The better cheeses, bring 'hem; or else send
>   By their ripe daughters, whom they would commend
> This way to husbands; and whose baskets bear
>   An emblem of themselves, in plum, or pear.
>   (*The Forest*, II, ll. 41–56)

'To Penshurst' creates, simultaneously, a moral ideal and an aesthetic which, relating value firmly to function rather than rarity or display, should have satisfied the theoreticians of the Bauhaus. The work of art is valued less for its memorial preservation of the past or its formal finish or completeness than for its continuing contribution to life:

> Now, Penshurst, they that will proportion thee
>   With other edifices, when they see
> Those proud, ambitious heaps, and nothing else,
>   May say, their lords have built, but thy lord dwells.
>   (ll. 99–102)

6. 'Euclia's Hymn' from *Love's Triumph Through Callipolis*, Ben Jonson, ed. C. H. Herford and Percy and Evelyn Simpson, VII (Oxford, 1941), 740.

It is within such a context that we can best understand Jonson's remarks about language and style in *Timber*. 'Pure and neat Language I love, yet plain and customary.' '*Metaphors* farfet hinder to be understood, and affected, lose their grace.' 'The chief virtue of a style is perspicuity, and nothing so vicious in it, as to need an Interpreter.' 'That I call Custom of speech, which is the consent of the Learned; as Custom of life, which is the consent of the good.' Jonson attempted one of the most difficult things a poet can conceive in any age: to present an ideal of the mean, of rational control and fulfilled public function, so that it seizes the imagination of the reader and stirs his emotions. The clarity, the learning, and the labour were necessary for the successful communication of such an ideal; they also reflected it. Moreover, some glimpses we get of Jonson's temperament and actions (irascible, sometimes violent or drunken, dictatorial, professionally jealous, occasionally crude in personal relations, saturnine, enjoying the exposure of the sordid) suggest that he may have embraced both his ideal and the means to attain it less because they were easily congenial than because they were necessary to his survival. Jonson may have been more temperamentally inclined to a despairing pessimism than Donne. He seems to have found in his combination of a roughly neo-stoic ethic and a neo-classic aesthetic a major sustaining force analogous to what Donne discovered within the church. * * *

Jonson's Pindaric ode on Cary and Morison . . . seems to me one of the best and most 'serious' poems of the age. I would even defend its horrendous opening about the 'Infant of Saguntum' who, during the siege of Hannibal, when half-born returned to his mother's womb to die. That bit of Senecan violence and even the fustian of 'Sword, fire, and famine, with fell fury met' both provide an analogy to Cary's and Jonson's and 'our' initial horror and near despair at the fact of the young Morison's death and help us to correct that response. For it is placed firmly with, 'could they but life's miseries fore-see,/No doubt all Infants would return like thee.' It *is* the proper response for infants; but the poem's primary concern is with an astonishing maturity which does not retreat from a world of violence and destruction and with a definition of life 'by the act' rather than 'the space' or simple duration. With the aid of negative examples (the old man who 'did no good' 'For three of his fourscore' years, the one who makes his days seem years by repeating his fears and miseries, showing that he has 'been long,/Not lived') the poem leads us at last to rejoice in a vital triumph and fulfilment which time cannot touch. The central formulations of the moral measurement of life are presented triumphantly in terms which apply equally to the craftsman's successfully articulated poem:

All Offices were done
By him, so ample, full, and round,
In weight, in measure, number, sound,
As though his age imperfect might appear,
His Life was of Humanity the Sphere.   (ll. 48–52

      . . . for life doth her great actions spell,
By what has done and wrought
In season, and so brought
To light: her measures are, how well
Each syllab'e answered, and was formed, how fair;
These make the lines of life, and that's her ayre.
                           (ll. 59–64)

In small proportions, we just beauties see:
And in short measures, life may perfect be.
                          (ll. 73–74

And such a force the faire example had,
As they that saw
The good, and durst not practise it, were glad
That such a Law
Was left yet to Man-kind;
Where they might read, and find
Friendship, in deed, was written, not in words:
And with the heart, not pen,
  Of two so early men,
Whose lines her rolls were, and recórds.
Who e'er the first down bloomèd on the chin,
Had sowed these fruits, and got the harvest in.
                        (ll. 117–28)

At the center of the formal celebration of this most neo-classic poem, Jonson was able to place himself, in person as well as name, almost playfully and more fully than he ever could have in a frankly confessional mode.

Considering these last poems and also some of Donne's finest *Songs and Sonnets and Divine Poems*, one is tempted to characterize the poetry of Donne and Jonson in terms of a whole series of seemingly opposed ideals and practices. Besides the private and the public, the amateur and the professional, the individual and the general, one thinks of extravagance and sobriety, excess and measure, spontaneity and deliberation, immediacy and distance, daring and propriety, roughness and elegance, tension and balance, agility and weight. And one can go on to expression and function, ecstasy and ethics, experience and thought, energy and order, the genius and the craftsman—ending with those inevitable seventeenth-century pairs, passion and reason, wit and judgement, nature and art. But such a marshalling of abstractions can be misleading. So arranged, the members of those pairs may seem more fully antagonistic than they really are; and such an account obscures how much Donne and Jonson had in common. We should remember that three love elegies perhaps written by neither were attributed by contemporaries to both. A sentence from Douglas Bush suggests succinctly why such confusion was possible: 'Both poets rebelled, in their generally different ways, against pictorial fluidity, decorative rhetorical patterns, and half-medieval idealism, and both, by their individual and selective exploitation of established doctrines and practices, created new techniques, a new realism of style (or new rhetoric), sharp, condensed, and muscular, fitted for the intellectual and critical realism of their thought.'[7] Among a number of the things that Jonson said about Donne was the remark that he was 'the first poet in the world in some things'; and Donne addressed Jonson in a Latin poem as *Amicissimo et Meritissimo* and praised him as a unique kind of classicist, a follower of the ancients who dared to do new things. I think that each was correct in those judgements.

EARL MINER

[The Cavalier Ideal of the Good Life]†

The social character of Cavalier poetry affords one kind of testimony to the cohesive civilization behind the work. To say so much is not to say that all Cavalier poets were alike, any more than to say that all parts of England were then alike. More than that, the same men and poets changed with the times. The question of just what changes took place is one still exercising social historians. Simply put, however, Cavalier social values are those of an aristocracy and gentry that two centuries before might have struggled against the throne but that now sought to protect the King, for all his faults (Elizabeth, James I, Charles I, Charles II) against his enemies, and to preserve crown, mitre, estates, and what was often termed "our liberties." But social values often conflicted with family interests, religious belief, and ambition. There was much changing of sides, and in fact much of what happened in the century remains beyond our reach. But I see no need to worry our problems hair by hair or to subtlize them out of existence. When, on "that memorable Scene," as Marvell put it, Charles I "with his keener Eye/The Axes edge did try," he presumably found time to consider that he had enemies. And these enemies are precisely those who threw the name

7. *English Literature in the Earlier Seventeenth Century,* p. 107.

† From *The Cavalier Mode from Jonson to Cotton* (Princeton, 1971).

"Cavalier" at the King's supporters, as many of them had thrown "Puritan" at the other side. Not all who supported the King, however, were Cavalier poets. Some men turned to the more intimate alternative of Metaphysical poetry. Very many more were led by piety or indifference to disregard poetry. What deserves remark, therefore, is the variety of those who shared Cavalier poetic and human values, and the degree of agreement among them as to what their values were.

The foremost Cavalier ideal expressed in poetry is what we may call the good life, and in a sense that is the subject of all else following in this book as well as of the preceding chapter. This ideal reflects many things: a conservative outlook, a response to a social threat, classical recollections, love of a very English way of life, and a new blending of old ideas. The ideal is not necessarily Christian or pagan, this worldly or otherworldly. But by comparison with Metaphysical and Restoration poetry, it probably does seem more secular and classical, pagan, or Horatian in some ways than do the other two great modes of seventeenth-century poetry. In itself, Cavalier poetry reveals a consistent urge to define and explore the features of what constituted human happiness, and of which kind of man was good.

One of the best introductions to the idea of the good life may be found in *The Compleat Angler*, whether in Izaak Walton's first part (1653 *et seq.*) or Charles Cotton the Younger's second (1676 *et seq.*).[1] The charm attributed to this work testifies not to a measurability of charm, but to a conviction of decent pleasure that Walton and Cotton carry straight to the heart of even the most indifferent fisherman. Here Walton speaks in the guise of the "angler," Piscator.

> I'll now lead you to an honest Ale-house, where we shall find a cleanly room, Lavender in the windowes, and twenty Ballads stuck about the wall; there my Hostis (which I may tel you, is both cleanly and conveniently handsome) has drest many a [chub] for me, and shall now dress it after my fashion, and I warrant it good meat. (1, ch. ii; 1653, p. 49)

England is one of the handsomest and pleasantest countries of the world, when the sun shines, and there is a real sense in which the sun shines always in *The Compleat Angler*, even when Peter tells of a rainy day.

> *Peter* . . . indeed we went to a good honest Ale-house, and there we plaid at shovel-board half the day; all the time that it rained

---

1. Walton especially revised his work for reprintings. Some of the best things I quote derive entirely or in their quoted form from later editions. His "naturalness" was both genuine and artistic.

we were there, and as merry as they that fish'd, and I am glad we are now with a dry house over our heads, for heark how it rains and blows. Come Hostis, give us more Ale, and our Supper with what haste you may, and when we have sup'd, let us have your Song, *Piscator*, and the [catch] that your Scholar promised us, or else *Coridon* will be dogged . . .
[Viator]. And I hope the like [i.e., to be perfect] for my [song], which I have ready too, and therefore lets go merrily to Supper, and then have a gentle touch at singing and drinking; but the last with moderation. (1. ch. xi; 1653, pp. 208–09)

Walton stresses certain elements more heavily, and others more lightly, than a Jonson or a Herrick would; and what he writes turns upon the subject of angling. But his very English book does bring to view a good life, a world in which man's life possesses fullness, and satisfaction is realized.

Walton's small group of anglers exemplifies the usual social microcosm of the Cavaliers. Such another, and more properly poetic, group we find in the famous Tribe of Ben, with Jonson like Piscator the good father figure inculcating virtue, self-knowledge, and poetry (Jonson's mysterious trinity) in his Sons, as they express their praise, happiness, and devotion. And their disagreement. One of the wonderful things we discover about Jonson in his relations with his Tribe is his ability to take criticism. His Sons show the complete devotion expected of sons and the frankness expected (in theory, usually) of friends. The evidence, although implicit, drives again and again to show that Jonson expected his Sons to be honest (in not just the modern sense, but also in Walton's and the usual Roman senses). Here is James Howell, writing "To my Father, Mr. Ben Johnson":

> Father *Ben Nullum fit magnum ingenium sine mixtura dementiae*, there's no great Wit without some Mixture of Madness . . . it is verified in you, for I find that you have been oftentimes mad! you were mad when you writ your [*Volpone*], and madder when you writ your *Alchymist*; you were mad when you writ *Catalin*, and stark mad when you writ *Sejanus*; but when you writ your *Epigrams*, and the *Magnetic Lady*, you were not so mad; insomuch that I perceive there be Degrees of Madness in you. Excuse me that I am so free with you.[2]

Free he is, but he spent the next six months hunting out a Welsh grammar for his Father Ben. Jonson's world is, then, a tougher, more verisimilar world than Walton's, so that the goodness and grace that he won for his poetry represent victories far greater than those achieved in Walton's semipastoral world. His tone, his frank,

2. Howell, *Epistolae Ho-Elianae*, 11th edition (London, 1754), I. V. 1 (27 June 1629).

manly, ethical note that led his Sons to respond so forthrightly, can be heard in that poem celebrating the rites of admission to the Tribe.

> Men that are safe, and sure, in all they doe,
>   Care not what trials they are put unto;
> They meet the fire, the Test, as Martyrs would;
>   And though Opinion stampe them not, are gold . . .
>
>   First give me faith, who know
>   My selfe a little. I will take you so,
> As you have writ your selfe. Now stand, and then,
>   Sir, you are Sealed of the Tribe of Ben.[3]

A true and complete man, inviolate in his central integrity, although passionate enough, Jonson conveys as no other English poet does that sense of *integer vitae*. Reading his ethical poetry, we sense that his central claim (and one that animates us as we read) simply comes to this: "I am a man, and I am true."

Whether or not Jonson's poem just quoted from was addressed to Thomas Randolph, I cannot say, but by what seems a coincidence we have a poem by Randolph offering his gratitude for admittance to the Tribe: "A gratulatory to Mr Ben. Johnson for his adopting of him to be his Son." His gratitude is partly personal and loyal, partly derived from the debt of an artistic "mystery"—whether angling or poetry—that the yonng owe to their masters.

> I was not borne to *Helicon*, nor dare
> Presume to thinke my selfe a *Muses* heire.
> I have no title to *Parnassus* hill,
> Nor any acre of it by the will
> Of a dead Ancestour, nor could I bee
> Ought but a tenant unto Poëtrie,
> But thy Adoption quits me of all feare,
> And makes me challenge a childs portion there.
> I am a kinne to *Hero's* being thine,
> And part of my alliance is divine.
> *Orpheus, Musaeus, Homer* too; beside
> Thy Brothers by the *Roman* Mothers side;
> As *Ovid, Virgil*, and the *Latine Lyre*,
> That is so like thy *Horace*.   (1–14)

Randolph's grateful awe conveys part of the good life: its definition of what is good in terms of relations with contemporaries and with the immortal men of the past. Herrick, addressing Jonson, treats a different aspect of the good life, its relaxed pleasure (with, he insists, moderation, although no doubt he and Walton meant different limits by that).

3. *An Epistle Answering to One That Asked to Be Sealed of the Tribe of Ben*, ll. 1–4, 75–78.

> Ah *Ben*!
> Say how, or when
> Shall we thy Guests
> Meet at those *Lyrick* Feasts,
> Made at the *Sun*,
> The *Dog*, the triple *Tunne*?
> Where we such clusters had,
> As made us nobly wild, not mad . . .[4]

Whether it is Jonson, Walton, Howell, Randolph, or Herrick—or others—certain elements are shared. Most important is the premise of the good life, which involves social intercourse with like-minded people. Very frequently that relation turns on the band of friends, male equals joined in fraternal affection and esteem. But the relation may be paternal and filial, as we see in the anglers and the Tribe of Ben. Two other groups make up the four chief kinds: men and women, lord and vassal. The latter relation usually involves prince and subject, but it may be patron and artist. Since all four resemble each other in involving relationship and in representing value, they may be substituted for each other: the woman loved may be a queen, her lover her subject. In due course we shall have cause to observe that such bonds were formed as much by rites and ceremonies as by ethical concerns. We must acknowledge that on occasion some thought that there was just cause for breaking the bonds: Suckling debated the code of love in his lyrics, and most Cavaliers treated the vices of kings and even questions of justifiable regicide in their tragedies. But the usual alignment that imparts Cavalier literature its special flavor is friendship or love or small groups, in each case a relation with a code that implicitly agrees with those in the world whose opinion and principle one values. The limits of the good life and the strength of the social bonds were tested by the Cavalier poets themselves and by events. And we sometimes encounter those moments that make us believe that we are advancing at one step toward pleasure and heaven. A sentence added to later editions of *The Compleat Angler* expresses such anti-Puritanical wisdom in little.

> None of these [trout] have been known to be taken with an Angle, unless it were one that was caught by Sir *George Hastings* (an excellent Angler, now with God).[5]

It is of course the parenthesis that strikes us, a conjunction of many things, but especially of a recreation with divinity, that we may fairly grant to Walton and the Cavaliers as their discovery. Walton's pastoral notes and warmth of heart will be found, with

4. Herrick, "An Ode for him," ll. 1–8.   of 1750, ed. Browne, p. 49.
5. Walton, I. iv; quoted from the edition

many of the very same details we have noticed, in Cavalier religious poetry. Here is Herrick, in "A Thanksgiving to God, for his House."

> Lord, Thou hast given me a cell
>   Wherein to dwell;
> An little house, whose humble Roof
>   Is weather-proof;
> Under the sparres of which I lie
>   Both soft, and drie . . .
> Lord, I confesse too, when I dine,
> . The Pulse is Thine,
> And all those other Bits, that bee
>   There plac'd by Thee;
> The Worts, the Purslain, and the Messe
>   Of Water-cresse,
> Which of Thy kindnesse Thou hast sent; . . .
> 'Tis thou that crown'st my glittering Hearth
>   With guiltlesse mirth;
> And giv'st me Wassaile Bowles to drink,
>   Spic'd to the brink. . . .
> All these, and better Thou dost send
>   Me, to this end,
> That I should render, for my part,
>   A thankfull heart;
> Which, fir'd with incense, I resigne,
>   As wholly Thine;
> But the acceptance, that must be,
>   My Christ, by Thee.[6]

The snug house (the fire loved by the Cavaliers comes in a passage omitted), the good food and abundant drink, and the heart, "fir'd with incense," for sacrifice to Christ—all these things make up the good life for which Herrick pays God due thanks. Many will feel that there is more of the *Hesperides* in *The Noble Numbers* than of the latter in the former. There is truth in such a belief. But it is also true that in his secular poems Herrick tends to substitute pagan religious detail for Christian,[7] and that is precisely one of the things that humanists were about (and for which they were criticized by the more austerely pious). In Herrick as well as in Walton, we discover a lively strain of pleasure and joy of life.

"Sir *George Hastings* (an excellent Angler, now with God)." Walton names a name, adding a title and what is in some sense an

6. Lines 1–6, 27–33, 37–40, 51–58.

7. Some of the most valuable specialized studies of Cavalier poets are the essays touching Herrick by Robert H. Deming: "Robert Herrick's Classical Ceremony," *ELH: A Journal of English History*, XXXIV (1967), 327–48; "Herrick's Funeral Poems," *Studies in English Lit-* *rature, IX* (1969), 153–67; and his dissertation, 'The Classical Ceremonial in the Poetry of Robert Herrick" (Wisconsin, 1965). These studies deal with subjects important in themselves, relevant to other poets, and intimate to some of my concerns here and in ch. iv.

occupation. Once again the implication is social: we have our associates, our band of choice, like spirits. And if we seek as before for confirmation in Ben Jonson's poetry, we find him consoling Sir Lucius Cary (later Lord Falkland) for the death of their mutual friend, Sir Henry Morison.

> Call, noble *Lucius,* then for Wine,
> And let thy lookes with gladnesse shine:
> Accept this garland, plant it on thy head,
> And thinke, nay know, thy *Morison's* not dead.
> Hee leap'd the present age,
> Possest with holy rage,
> To see that bright eternall Day:
> Of which we *Priests,* and *Poëts* say
> Such truths, as we expect for happy men,
> And there he lives with memorie; and *Ben* . . .[8]

Wine and a poetic garland, priests and poets, the named members of a fraternal society—these make up the good life, these provide the marks of "happy men." Unless I am mistaken, Jonson's "happy" is a reverse Latinism of that kind peculiar to him, as when he uses "running judgements" for "current judgements." "Happy" must mean *beati,* and "happy" both in the secular sense and the religious sense of glorification. Above all, Jonson's view presumes a unity of the like-minded and a unity within individual character, *integer vitae.* And for this moral vision, he became the arbiter of his age and "lives with memorie" ever since.* * *

Our next step must be to Jonson himself: man and poet. To try to say it all at once, it is moral integrity that marks the firm center of his poetic compass. Of course we have evidence and to spare showing that Jonson was physically gross, "rocky" as he said, excessive, combative, and (by politer standards) coarse. The evidence also shows that he possessed delicacy, an element of surpassing fancifulness; that he inculcated moderation; that he was a loyal friend; that he possessed a seemingly unerring sense of decorum, beauty, and justice; and that he was admired. Without his massive animal strength, his very virtues might have been insipid. But without his consistent ideals, his integrity, he might have aroused our dislike.

What a poet praises (or criticizes) in others usually tells us something of his own ideals. When Jonson acclaimed someone for being "alwayes himselfe and even," we see very clearly the ideal of *integer vitae.* In a few lines already quoted, we see that self-knowledge is as essential to Jonson as to Socrates.

8. *To the Immortall Memorie, and Friendship of That Noble Paire, Sir Lucius Cary, and Sir H. Morison,* ll. 75–84. *Caveat emptor:* I shall be quoting the passage, and a few others, more than once.

> First give me faith, who know
> My selfe a little. I will take you so,
> As you have writ your selfe.[9]

Knowing oneself and others implies a capacity to trust oneself and others. It also implies that one will remain oneself with constancy in a world of threat and change.

> Well, with mine owne fraile Pitcher, what to doe
> I have decreed; keepe it from waves, and presse;
> Lest it be justled, crack'd, made nought, or lesse:
> Live to the point I will, for which I am man,
> And dwell as in my Center, as I can.[1]

The traditional emblems are here: the vessel of the soul, the threatening waves, the center for constancy, and the circle for perfection. And what such emblems help portray is precisely a good man defining his place in the world.

In that world, and as part of the moral landscape of Jonson's poetry, there rise shapes and forces threatening the constant man. As Milton said, we are no longer capable of defining good without a knowledge of evil, and Jonson often provides ample shadowing for his bright ideals. Even his panegyrics bear warnings for princes and kingdoms.

> Who, *Virtue*, can thy power forget,
> That sees these live, and triumph yet?
> Th' *Assyrian* pompe, the *Persian* pride,
> *Greekes* glory, and the *Romanes* dy'de:
> And who yet imitate
> Theyr noyses, tary the same fate.
> Force Greatnesse, all the glorious wayes
> You can, it soon decayes;
> But so *good Fame* shall, never:
> Her triumphs, as theyr Causes, are for ever.[2]

Merlin gives to Chivalry a Jonsonian caution in matters of praising kings, in a passage coming at its end to the high ideal of integrity which Jonson set.

> Nay, stay your valure, 'tis a wisdome high
> In Princes to use fortune reverently.
> He that in deedes of *Armes* obeyes his blood
> Doth often tempt his destinie beyond good.
> Looke on this throne, and in his temper view
> The light of all that must have grace in you:

9. Jonson, *An Epistle . . . the Tribe of Ben,* ll. 75–77.
1. *Ibid.,* ll. 56–60.
2. Jonson, *The Masque of Queens,* ll. 764–73.

His equall *Justice*, upright *Fortitude*
And settled *Prudence*, with that *Peace* indued
Of face, as minde, always himselfe and even.
So HERCULES, and good men beare up *heaven*.[3]

The legend of Hercules relieving Atlas of his burden of the world
worked throughout the century as a political type for kings.[4] What
set off Jonson's use of the type is the dominance of political and
other concerns by the moral. To me, the moral element lives in
Jonson's very cadence and syntax. To others, I can point to the cau-
tioning of princes to moderate courses, the insistence on integrity
("alwayes himselfe and even"), and the equation of "good men"
with the Hercules/king typology. The regal is assimilated in the
individual, in the very manhood of the good man.

The good life finds definition, then, in terms of other lives,
whether those of kings or of commoners. But the act of defining
involves the discovery of self-knowledge, and in order to be defined
as a good man one must be constant. On assumptions such as
these, Jonson creates an artistic fiction no less imaginative than that
of the writer of love lyrics. And his fiction enables him to laugh at
himself, to drop the adventitious in human life, in order to stress
what is central to goodness. As he conceded in addressing Sir William Burlase ("My Answer. The Poet to the Painter"):

> Why? though I seeme of a prodigious wast,
> I am not so voluminous, and vast
> But there are lines, wherewith I might b'embrac'd. . . .
>
> But, you are he can paint; I can but write:
> A Poet hath no more but black and white,
> Ne knowes he flatt'ring Colours, or false light.
>
> Yet when of friendship I would draw the face,
> A letter'd mind, and a large heart would place
> To all posteritie; I will write *Burlase*.   (1–3, 19–24)

He draws himself good humoredly as a gross man, so that what he
says about himself as writer and about Burlase is accepted as truth.
(Jonson also plays with the two "sister arts," of course.) By such
means he creates a fiction of himself, his friends, and his King as
good men. It must be stressed that that fiction is as much something made, or rather, as much a transformation of reality, as anything in Donne. But like every good fiction, it carries the stamp of
artistic currency within the perfect ring of its own coinage. All these
considerations join in Jonson's self-awareness.

3. Jonson, *Prince Henries Barriers*, 405–
14.
4. In *Mystagogus Poeticus*, p. 116, Ross
writes that Hercules can be "The type of
a good king." (Alexander Ross published
this work in 1647 [*Editor*]).

> Let me be what I am, as *Virgil* cold,
>> As *Horace* fat; or as *Anacreon* old;
> No Poets verses yet did ever move,
>> Whose Readers did not thinke he was in love.[5]

The conviction is necessary. Jonson convinces us that, like his Prince, James I, he was a good judge of good men. More than that, and unlike James, he also had good judgment of bad men and of himself. And if the portrait I have been getting Jonson to draw of himself makes him seem too bluff, let me refer to the word "thinke" in the last line quoted, or ask if there is not some fun in the first two lines, and wonder if it might not be worthwhile to be cold, fat, and old if one could also be an English poet combining the geniuses of Virgil, Horace, and Anacreon? My aim has been to emphasize the strength of Jonson's moral architecture, because that is, to my view, the essential, the functional aspect of his art.

* * *

The good man has one further function besides knowing himself, improving himself, and conquering his passions with equanimity. He must judge good and evil in other men. Many of Jonson's poems judge evil through the resources of satire, and others judge good through panegyric. How conscious Jonson was of the role of the good man as judge can be seen from his praise of one of the most learned men of the day in "An Epistle to Master John Selden."

> What fables have you vext! what truth redeem'd!
> Antiquities search'd! Opinions dis-esteem'd!
> Impostures branded! And Authorities urg'd!
> What blots and errours, have you watch'd and purg'd
> Records, and Authors of! how rectified,
> Times, manners, customes!   (39–44)

Jonson possessed many poetic and human virtues, and some of them are at least implied there. He prized learning that brought moral experience, wisdom. He may cleverly adapt the old proverb that a wise man is at home in all countries, including Selden among those "that have beene/Ever at home: yet, have all Countries seene" (29–30). But he does not stop there, adding that his friend is

> . . . like a Compasse keeping one foot still
> Upon your Center, doe your Circle fill
> Of generall knowledge; watch'd men, manners too,
> Heard what times past have said, seene what ours doe.
>   (31–34)

A quiet wit voices itself in the distinction between hearing what is remote and seeing what is at hand. It is as though Selden has talked

5. Jonson, *An Elegie*, ll. 1–4.

with the wise men of the past. The compass image conveys a virtue important to Jonson, constancy,[6] and the circle emblem of course perfection.

These many aspects of the Cavalier conception of *vir bonus* and of *vita bona* seem all to come together in Jonson's regular pindaric ode, *To the Immortall Memorie, and Friendship of That Noble Paire, Sir Lucius Cary, and Sir H. Morison*. As the poem tells us, Sir Henry Morison died (*aet.* about twenty) in battle. Sir Lucius Cary, later Viscount Falkland, also later to fall in battle, was as much an ideal courtier as the legendary Sir Philip Sidney (who also died in the field). Falkland married Morison's sister and styled himself a "brother" of Ben Jonson. Such adoption of relationships enables Jonson to write with great feeling and integrity about his subject, which, in its initial stages, consists of the negative contrast (1–42) and then the positive value represented by Morison.

> Hee stood, a Souldier to the last right end,
> A perfect Patriot, and a noble friend,
> But most a vertuous Sonne.
> All Offices were done
> By him, so ample, full, and round,
> In weight, in measure, number, sound,
> As though his age imperfect might appeare,
> His life was of Humanitie the Spheare.   (45–52)

Like the circle, the sphere is an emblem of perfection and here is suggestive of the macrocosm. Words less obvious in import provide the crucial, distinctive features of Jonson's vision of the good man, however. "Hee stood"—the simple declaration implies constancy and self-sufficiency in a world of strife, *mens immota manet*. How meaningful this seemingly passive or defensive posture may seem to a world with values other than our own can best be judged by recalling the climax of *Paradise Regained*:

> To whom thus Jesus. Also it is written,
> Tempt not the Lord thy God; he said and stood.
> But Satan smitten with amazement fell. (IV, 560–62)

Repeatedly in the seventeenth century the moral crisis centers on standing or falling, or, in another version, of fleeing from the doomed city: Whither shall I fly? What shall I do to be saved? "Hee stood." That this does not mean merely passive or defensive action can be shown by what follows: Morison performed "All

6. See Rosemary Freeman, *English Emblem Books* (London, 1948); there is a very full discussion of lore associated with compasses in John Freccero's essay, "Donne's 'Valediction Forbidding Mourning,' " *ELH: A Journal of English Literary History*, XXX (1963), 335–76, which touches on Jonson at n. 43. Since Jonson took for himself the emblem of the broken compass, we see that he possessed humility, after all. In my view, that image is appropriate for the world of the plays but not for the poet's vision of that world.

Offices." This, the central word of the passage, derives from the Stoic word for obligations or duties, and to anyone in the century who could understand such things it would immediately call to mind "Tully's *Offices*," the very popular *De Officiis* by Cicero.

We may recall, "For he, that once is good, is ever great," in reviewing the best known stanza of the poem, which now contrasts falling with another image.

> It is not growing like a tree
> In bulke, doth make a man better bee;
> Or standing long an Oake; three hundred yeare,
> To fall a logge, at last, dry, bald, and seare:
> A Lillie of a Day,
> Is fairer farre, in May,
> Although it fall, and die that night;
> It was the Plant, and flowre of light.
> In small proportions, we just beauties see:
> And in short measures, life may perfect bee.
>
> (65–74)

The "flowre of light," that supererogatory image, runs through numerous versions in the next three stanzas, culminating in "Two names of friendship, but one Starre:/Of hearts the union" (98–99). The old trope for friendship, one heart in bodies twain, is altered here into the stellar apotheosis that emerges in Jonson's handling of the light imagery radiating from the lily. But the stanza's formal properties also deserve attention. In the central two lines (the fifth and sixth) we see the "Lillie of a Day," and these two short lines represent the "small proportions," "just beauties," and "short measures" that Jonson speaks of in the last two lines. More than that, there is a circularity of rhyme scheme, with the rhyme sounds of the first and last couplets being the same. The circularity is complete in the shift from "better bee" (66) to "perfect bee" (74). The stanza almost seems an unspoken version of Jonson's compass conceit.

The elegiac reconciliation completes itself in such perfection, so that what remains is the celebration we have partly read on earlier pages.

> Call, noble *Lucius*, then for Wine,
> And let thy lookes with gladnesse shine:
> Accept this garland, plant it on thy head,
> And thinke, nay know, thy *Morison's* not dead.
> Hee leap'd the present age,
> Possest with holy rage,
> To see that bright eternall Day:
> Of which we *Priests*, and *Poëts* say
> Such truths, as we expect for happy men,
> And there he lives with memorie; and *Ben*

Johnson, who sung this of him, e're he went
Himselfe to rest,
Or taste a part of that full joy he meant
To have exprest,
In this bright *Asterisme*.   (75–89)

The imagistic development from the "flowre of light" must strike
every reader, and so too the introduction of the poet's name. In
fact, seventeenth-century elegies from Donne's *Anniversaries* to
Dryden's *Eleonora* usually do not allow names, unless pastoral
appellations, in the text of the poem, Jonson is not so "classical,"
but he does employ the oratorical device of "ethical proof" or personal testimony in that remarkable division of his name between
two stanzas. Toward the end of the second of these stanzas, Jonson
speaks of Falkland's *"Harry,"* that is, Sir Henry. At the beginning
of the joined stanzas there appears "noble *Lucius*," at the end "his
Harry." What bridges the two is *"Ben / Johnson"*—the man who
identifies himself as priest and poet saying "Such truths, as we expect for happy men" (82–83).

Without a forfeit of social relationships, the sense of personality
runs throughout the poem, and indeed throughout Jonson's poetry.
No shrinking violet, he extolls himself among the flowers of light.
The conviction—and the imagistic resources enabling the reader
to relive the conviction—of the good man and the good life provide
the firm ethical center of Cavalier poetry. Loyalty to the King, and
to "the Church and the laws," as Sir Philip Warwick put it, provided Cavalier poetry with the social basis for its integrity. In a
nearer concentric of that sphere there lay ideals of integrity, constancy, self-sufficiency and, if need be, self-sacrifice. The Cavaliers could not make exclusive claim to such ideals, any more than
could the Puritans to faith and service in a providential cause. In
fact, Falkland later went off to the wars with divided mind and
with what has seemed to many a deliberate, almost suicidal excess
of bravery. Such men did not return from their Battles of Newbury:
Falkland was not a friend whom one needed "to Perswade . . . to
the Warres." Whether to stand, to fly to death in what one knew
or hoped to be a good cause, or to brighten like the "flowre of
light," it was important that one be oneself and be good. As Jonson's learned friend Selden put it concerning books,

> I would call *Books* onely those which have in them either of the
> two objects of Mans best part, V*erum* or *Bonum*, and to an
> instructing purpose handled.[7]

We recognize Jonson's tone in those words, and even more wholly
in a distinction Selden draws at length.

7. Selden, *Titles of Honor* (London, 1614), sig. a2^r-v.

So Generous, so Ingenuous [sincere], so proportion'd to good,
such Fosterers of Vertue, so Industrious, of such Mould are the
Few: so Inhuman, so Blind, so Dissembling, so Vain, so justly
Nothing, but what's Ill disposition, are the *Most*.[8]

And it was of Jonson, to whom the Cavaliers owed their rich ethical
patrimony, that Selden could write: that is, of

> my beloved friend that singular Poet M. *Ben: Jonson*, whose
> speciall Worth in Literature, accurat Judgement, and Perform-
> ance, known only to that *Few* which are truly able to know him,
> hath had from me, ever since I began to learn, an increasing
> admiration.[9]

Sir John Beaumont caught the accent in his poem on Jonson's
death, saying of him,

> Since then, he made our Language pure and good,
> To teach us speake, but what we understood . . .
> And though He in a blinder age could change
> Faults to perfections, yet 'twas farre more strange
> To see (how ever times, and fashions frame)
> His wit and language still remaine the same
> In all mens mouths . . .
> Could I have spoken in his language too,
> I had not said so much, as now I doe,
> To whose cleare memory, I this tribute send
> Who Dead's my wonder, Living was my Friend.[1]

Jonson would have taken pride in that identification with himself
and goodness and right language, just as he would have recognized
the imagery and the friendship of Falkland's poem in *Jonsonus
Virbius.*

> I then but aske fit Time to smooth my Layes,
> (And imitate in this the Pen I praise)
> Which by the Subjects Power embalm'd, may last,
> Whilst the Sun Light, the Earth doth shadows cast,
> And feather'd by those Wings fly among men,
> Farre as the Fame of Poetry and BEN.[2]

O Rare Ben Jonson! Neither the first nor the last English poet to
think that his poetry was a moral as well as a beautiful art, he alone
put the good man at the center of his poetry and made us believe
that he was such, for all his follies. His imagination was fanciful
enough to create new forms for the stage or to present to him as he

8. *Ibid.*, sigs. a2^v–a3^r.
9. *Ibid.*, sig. d1^r; I have reversed roman
and italic usage.
1. "To the Memory of him who can
never be forgotten, Master Benjamin
Jonson," ll. 41 ff. from the collection
made by Falkland, *Jonsonus Virbius*; in
Ben Jonson, ed. C. H. Herford, Percy and
Evelyn Simpson, 11 vols. (Oxford, 1925–
1952), XI, 438–39.
2. *An Eglogue*, ll. 285–90; *Ben Jonson*,
XI, 437.

lay abed the Romans and Carthaginians doing battle about his great toe. His humanity was such that he grieved as a father for the loss of son and daughter and yet could adopt others to his Tribe. But with his learning it was his conviction of the centrality of the good life to poetry that won him the unparalleled respect of his contemporaries.

GEOFFREY WALTON

The Tone of Ben Jonson's Poetry†

It is well known that Pope imitated the opening couplet of Jonson's *Elegie on the Lady Jane Pawlet, Marchion: of Winton*:

> What gentle ghost, besprent with *April* deaw,
> Hayles me, so solemnly, to yonder Yewgh?

in his own opening couplet of the *Elegy to the Memory of an Unfortunate Lady*:

> What beck'ning ghost, along the moonlight shade
> Invites my steps, and points to yonder glade?

The similarity and the difference between the grand style of Pope and the slightly Spenserian language of Jonson on this occasion are obvious. I have chosen to begin with a reference to this piece of plagiarism, however, because these two poems may be taken to mark, in so far as there are any beginnings and ends in literature, the limits of my study, and because the debt draws pointed attention to the dignified and courteous tone of Jonson's poetry, especially in his occasional verses. Several lines of elegy, which often intersect and blend, run between Jonson's epitaphs and formal eulogies and Pope's poem, which seems to gather up into itself all the various threads, the earlier Metaphysical and philosophic meditation of Donne, the formality of Cowley on Crashaw, the tenderness of Cowley on Hervey, the satire of Dryden in the ode on Anne Killigrew and the elegiac of Milton on the same Lady Jane.[1] Pope inherited a large measure of Metaphysical wit coming from Donne, but the predominant aspect of his genius, the Augustan decorum, can be traced back to Donne's contemporary, Jonson.

Although Jonson's greatness as a poet is generally recognized, very little has been written on his lyric and other non-dramatic poems. There is room for a detailed consideration of certain aspects of this

† From *Metaphysical to Augustan: Studies in Tone and Sensibility in the Seventeenth Century* (London: Bowes & Bowes, 1955), pp. 23–44.

1. Dr. F. R. Leavis has analysed Pope's poem in *Revaluation,* Chap. III.

work and for some redirection of attention towards poems hitherto neglected. Making a limited approach, I want to try to locate and define as clearly as possible his characteristic tone and civilized quality.

One often finds oneself trying, with a certain sense of frustration, to reconcile Professor C. H. Herford's morose rough diamond "with no native well-spring of verse music" and the kind of seventeenth-century Mallarmé implied by Mr. Ralph Walker.[2] The coarse side of Jonson must not be forgotten. He was rooted in the English life of tavern and workshop in his life and in his art, besides being the friend of Selden and Lord Aubigny. We have to take into account *The Voyage* as well as the *Hymn to Diana,* and remember the last line of *A Celebration of Charis.* Dr. Leavis places the odes to himself at the central point, as showing us both the independent, forthright working dramatist and the learned Horatian who brought out his plays annotated in folio.[3]

I disagree with Dr. Leavis about the odes. "The racy personal force" and the "weighty and assertive personal assurance" are indeed present. The poems are eminently successful in the sense that they communicate their content without hesitation or vagueness. One can accept and applaud the fiercely contemptuous satire on dullness and ill will, but the final effect, I think, embarrasses still, as it seems to have embarrassed the "Tribe" and as the author in person had earlier embarrassed Drummond of Hawthornden.[4] These odes are too personal and self-regarding. It is not the self-pity of a Shelley that is forced upon us, but self-assertion and unseemly pride:

> 'Twere simple fury still thyselfe to waste
>   On such as have no taste. . . .
> 'Tis crowne enough to vertue still, her owne applause.

This is not redeemed by the finer aspiration of:

> Strike that disdaine-full heate
> Throughout, to their defeate,
> As curious fooles, and envious of thy straine,
> May, blushing, sweare no palsey's in thy braine.

Though Cartwright, Randolph and Cleveland approved, one can sympathize with that excellent literary critic, Thomas Carew, when he expostulates:

> 'Tis true (dear Ben) thy just chastizing hand
> Hath fixed upon the sotted Age a brand
> To their swolne pride, and empty scribbling due . . .
>   . . . but if thou bind,

2. See *Ben Jonson,* ed. Herford and Simpson, Vol. II, p. 340; and R. Walker, "Ben Jonson's Lyric Poetry," *The Cri-* *terion,* Vol. XIII, 1934.
3. *Revaluation,* Chap. I.
4. *Conversations,* 19.

By Citie, or by *Gavell-kind,*
In equall shares thy love on all thy race,
We may distinguish of their sexe and place;
Though one hand form them and though one brain strike
Souls into all, they are not all alike.
Why should the follies then of this dull age
Draw from thy Pen such an immodest rage,
As seems to blast thy (else immortall) Bayes,
When thine owne hand proclaims thy ytch of praise?
The wiser world doth greater Thee confesse
Than all men else, than Thyself only lesse.

Along with his mastery of the irregular Donnean couplet, Carew
shows here a fineness of feeling and a regard for his poetic father, a
polish of tone and an integrity of character, which represent all that
was best in the class and way of life from which he came. Carew
feels that the great intellectual leader has been ungentlemanly in a
very deep sense; that ideal demanded a measure of humility; it was
something rooted in the traditional code and which became oblit-
erated in the more superficial, if more formally polite, Augustan age.
In an ode on the same theme, not published until the present
century, Jonson expresses a proud but far more admirable attitude
towards the public:

Yet since the bright and wise
    Minerva deignes
Uppon this humbled earth to cast hir eyes,
    Wee'l rip our ritchest veynes
And once more strike the Eare of tyme with those fresh straynes:
    As shall besides delight
    And Cuninge of their grounde
Give cause to some of wonder, some despight;
But unto more despaire to imitate their sounde. . . .

    Cast reverence if not feare
    Throughout their generall brests
And by their taking let it once appeare
Who worthie come, who not, to be witts Pallace guests.[5]

However, the point to be emphasized is that Jonson at his best
has a superlatively civilized tone, and it was, in fact, in him that
Carew found models for the expression of such a tone in poetry. In
Jonson it springs, of course, mainly from his classical culture, that
culture which Carew and his class shared in a way corresponding
to Jonson's participation in the social activities which produced the
manners and the tone of their world. The tone which issues in

---

5. This ode (not included in the present edition) is printed in *Ben Jonson, ed. cit.,*
VIII, pp. 419–421 [*Editor*].

Jonson's poetry from this double source is best exemplified in the following ode:

> High-spirited friend,
> I send nor Balmes, nor Cor'sives to your wound,
> Your fate hath found
> A gentler, and more agile hand, to tend
> The Cure of that, which is but corporall,
> And doubtful Dayes, (which were nam'd *Criticall*,)
> Have made their fairest flight,
> And now are out of sight.
> Yet doth some wholesome Physick for the mind,
> Wrapt in this paper lie,
> Which in the taking if you misapply
> You are unkind.
>
> Your covetous hand,
> Happy in that faire honour it hath gain'd
> Must now be rayn'd.
> True valour doth her owne renowne command
> In one full Action; nor have you now more
> To doe, then to be husband of that store.
> Thinke but how deare you bought
> This same which you have caught,
> Such thoughts wil make you more in love with truth.
> 'Tis wisdom, and that high
> For men to use their fortune reverently,
> Even in youth.

This is no mere pindaric experiment. To whoever is addressed Jonson is giving extremely intimate personal advice, analysing a situation and a character instead of writing a conventional epithalamium, but his delicate movement and hesitating phrases, using the opportunities of the formal pattern, keep it free of all suggestion of patronage or importunity. There is great strength in the total effect of mature wisdom. Jonson is appealing to an ideal of human dignity and reasonable behaviour held in common with his reader which inspires frankness and at the same time sincere mutual respect. The ultimate basis is again the old idea of courtesy. This was a quality of the spirit which made it possible to consider serious moral matters in a social context without losing sight of their seriousness or doing anything in what would later be called "bad form." This ode by itself seems to me a refutation of Professor Herford's opinion that Jonson "for all his generous warmth lacked the finer graces of familiarity." It has both.

The wit of Jonson, like that of Donne, manifests itself in many ways. As an intellectual force it has a disciplinary and clarifying rather than a free-ranging and elaborating effect, but the relationship between the two poets is shown in Jonson's admiration for Donne and in the common features of that group of elegies whose authorship has long been in dispute between them.[6] In discussing the more social aspect of Jonson's wit, the tone that he handed on to his "sons," usually in the form of an economy and polish of technique, I think that one can claim that these "finer graces" form one of Jonson's great qualities as a poet. "High-spirited friends . . ." and "Fair friend . . ."[7] that elegant, but closely reasoned and firmly phrased lyric, equally expressive of his distinctive classical urbanity, together give us the quintessence of Jonson's attitude towards his friends and fellow poets, his patrons and patronesses. It is not the formal decorum of a large polite world—such, in any case, did not yet exist—but one feels it to be, I think, the tone of small circles in which aristocratic and cultivated people knew each other intimately. One can back up these deductions by a short survey of Jonson's occasional and certain other verses and of imitations by his "sons." They have the kind of tone I have just noted, and they describe the life that contributed to produce that tone. Beside these poems much of the social verse, even of Pope, sounds brassy. One knows that life at Whitehall, particularly in the reign of James I, was often disorderly, not to say squalid, and that sports and pastimes on the best-ordered country estate were rough and cruel, but the refinement was also there, sometimes in the same people. In the poetry it is preserved for ever.

The epigram, *Inviting a Friend to Supper*, is admirable social verse, besides being a document of the Jonson world, an offering of scholarly conversation with simple but good food and wine—Virgil and Tacitus with canary. A long series of epigrams and complimentary verses sketch in the type of men with whom Jonson liked to associate and the qualities that for him made up a civilized life. *An Epistle, answering one that asked to be Sealed of the Tribe of BEN* is unfortunately little more than satire on smart London life and the masques of Inigo Jones. *An Epistle to a Friend, to persuade him to the Warres* with its finely realized opening:

> Wake, friend, from forth thy Lethargie: the Drum
> Beates brave and loude in Europe and bids come
> All that dare rowse . . .

6. Praise outweighs blame in the *Conversations*, and, if one takes these remarks along with the two epigrams to the poet and that to Lady Bedford "with Mr. Donne's Satires," the whole forms a brief but apposite critical estimate.

With regard to the disputed authorship of the four elegies, I think that Mrs. Simpson gives good reasons for what should be a final division of responsibility, allotting *The Expostulation* to Donne and the others to Jonson (*Jonson and Donne, R.E.S.,* Vol. XV).

7. Professor Herford and Mr. and Mrs. Simpson give this poem to Godolphin (*Ben Jonson,* Vol. VIII, p. 265). If it is his, it not only shows his distinction as a poet, but also the remarkable homogeneity of tone within the "Tribe."

is again mainly negative, a vigorous and racy denunciation of loose sexual morality and excessive drinking, but the ending sets up a heroic ideal of moral and physical valour, temperate, stoical and devout, the very reverse of the Renaissance braggart:

> Goe, quit 'hem all. And take along with thee
> Thy true friends wishes, *Colby*, which shall be
> That thine be just, and honest; that thy Deeds
> Not wound thy conscience, when thy body bleeds;
> That thou dost all things more for truth, then glory
> And never but for doing wrong be sory
> That by commanding first thyselfe, thou mak'st
> Thy person fit for any charge thou tak'st;
> That fortune never make thee to complaine,
> But what shee gives, thou dar'st give her againe;
> That whatsoever face thy fate puts on,
> Thou shrinke or start not, but be always one;
> That thou thinke nothing great, but what is good,
> And from that thought strive to be understood.
> So, 'live so dead, thou wilt preserve a fame
> Still pretious, with the odour of thy name.
> And last, blaspheme not, we did never heare
> Man thought the valianter, 'cause he durst sweare. . . .

The two poems to the brilliant young Earl of Newcastle, exalting his horsemanship and his fencing, show a kindred enthusiasm. As Professor Herford remarks, admiration for virility "gives eloquence to his verse." Vincent Corbet stands for graver and gentler virtues:

> His Mind was pure, and neatly kept,
>   As were his Nourceries; and swept
> So of uncleannesse, or offence,
> That never came ill odour thence:
>   And add his Actions unto these,
>   They were as specious as his Trees.
> 'Tis true, he could not reprehend,
> His very Manners taught to 'mend,
>   They were so even, grave, and holy;
>   No stubbornnesse so stiffe, nor folly
> To licence ever was so light
> As twice to trespasse in his sight,
>   His looks would so correct it, when
>   It chid the vice, yet not the Men.
> Much from him I confesse I wonne,
> And more, and more, I should have done,
>   But that I understood him scant.
>   Now I conceive him by my want. . . .

The poet's self-criticism emphasizes the respectfulness of his atti-tude and deserves particular notice in this essay. In addressing Selden his verse is less distinguished, but it must be quoted for the attitude to himself shown in:

> Though I confesse (as every Muse hath err'd,
> and mine not least) . . .

and for the conception of scholarship and the literary life described:

> Stand forth my Object, then, you that have beene
> Ever at home: yet, have all Countries seene;
> And like a Compasse keeping one foot still
> Upon your Center, doe your circle fill
> Of generall knowledge; watch'd men, manners too,
> Heard what times past have said, seene what ours doe:
> Which Grace shall I make love to first? your skill,
> Or faith in things? or is't your wealth and will
> T'instruct and teach? or your unweary'd paine
> Of Gathering? Bountie'in pouring out againe?
> What fables have you vext! what truth redeem'd!
> Antiquities search'd! Opinions dis-esteem'd!
> Impostures branded! and Authorities urg'd! . . .

In writing to Drayton, Jonson notes that they have not followed the custom of exchanging verses and continues:

> And, though I now begin, 'tis not to rub
> Hanch against Hanch, or raise a rhyming *Club*
> About the towne.

"Butter reviewers," said Mr. Nixon to the young Hugh Selwyn Mauberley.

This quotation rounds off my references to Jonson's verses on himself as a writer and his relation to the literary world. One does not take everything in seventeenth-century commendatory verses at its face value. Drayton was no Homer, but it is worth studying what Jonson says—and, more important, does not say—about the lesser figures whom he honours. The most interesting lines in the eulogy of Shakespeare are those calling upon the shades of the Greek tragedians. Jonson's critical acumen here breaks through all his own and the age's prejudices. Sir Henry Savile was somewhat above the Jonson circle and receives a formal epigram, but the ideals admired as embodied in him correspond to those of the epistle to Selden, literary skill joined to integrity of character[8]—a very solemn conception of the philosopher and the gentleman, to recall deliberately Addison's famous phrase:

---

8. Courthope notes that in dedicating to Savile a translation of Cicero, *De Oratore*, Lib. II, 62–3, Jonson reverses the order of qualities, making moral strength more important than literary skill (*History of English Poetry*, Vol. III, p. 181); it is typical of him.

> We need a man that knows the severall graces
> Of historie, and how to apt their places;
> Where brevitie, where splendour, and where height,
> Where sweetnesse is requir'd and where weight;
> We need a man, can speake of the intents,
> The councells, actions, orders and events
> Of state, and censure them: we need his pen
> Can write the things, the causes, and the men.
> But most we need his faith (and all have you)
> That dares nor write things false, nor hide things true.

One sees in these poems the positive moral and intellectual values which are more usually merely implicit in the plays: young Wittipol in the *Devil is an Ass* emerges as a personality of some solidity and life, but the majestic Cicero is never an adequate dramatic foil to the political gangsters in *Catiline*. In the poems one can observe, described and felt in the texture of the poetry itself, the cultural ideals that gave Jonson his assurance and intellectual dignity and at the same time his feeling for civilized personal relationships. His tone only fails him when personal bitterness or excessive indignation causes him to lose his bearings and his sense of fellowship in the republic of letters.

Jonson was, however, conscious of a larger community than that meeting at the Devil Tavern with connections at the universities. Some of his finest verse celebrates this social scene and the characters who inhabited it and, in fact, led the nation. Courthope remarks that in this mode "Jonson is unequalled by any English poet, except perhaps Pope at his best."[9] We know from the plays what he thought of the projectors and of other pioneers of nascent capitalism. He held older ideals of social justice and responsibility.[1] He saw the values he believed in embodied in certain noblemen and squires, and in statesmen and lawgivers such as Burleigh and Sir Edward Coke. The greatest document, and also the finest poem, in this connection is, of course, *To Penshurst*:

> Thou are not, PENSHURST, built for envious show,
> Of touch, or marble, nor canst boast a row
> Of polish'd pillars, or a roofe of gold:
> Thou hast no lanthorne, whereof tales are told;
> Or stayre, or courts; but stand'st an ancient pile,
> And these grudg'd at, are reverenc'd the while.

It is a medieval house—it happens to have been built about the year of Chaucer's birth. For Jonson a new genius presides over it from:

9. Ibid., p. 179.
1. For the background of what follows I am much indebted to Professor Trevelyan's *England under the Stuarts*, Chaps.

I–II, and Professor L. C. Knights's *Drama and Society in the Age of Ben Jonson*, Chaps. I–IV.

> That taller tree, which of a nut was set,
> At his great birth, where all the *Muses* met.

It was now the seat of Sir Philip Sidney's brother, and Sidney appears several times in similar poems as the representative of civilization.[2] He brings the culture of *Il Cortegiano* to bear on the more active traditional idea of the gentleman expressed in, say, Langland's:

> Kings and knightes · sholde kepe it by resoun,
> Riden and rappe down · the reumes aboute,
> And taken transgressores · and tyen hem faste,
> Till treuthe had ytermyned · her trespas to ende,
> That is the profession appertly · that appendeth for knightes,
> And nought to fasten on Fryday · in fyvescore wynter,
> But holden with him and with her · that wolden al treuthe,
> And never leue hem for loue · ne for lacchying of syluer.[3]

Penshurst is surrounded by all the beauty and wealth of nature, but it is much more than a house:

> And though thy walls be of the countrey stone,
>   They'are rear'd with no mans ruine, no mans grone,
> There's none, that dwell about them, wish them downe. . . .
> Where comes no guest, but is allow'd to eate,
>   Without his feare, and of thy lords own meate:
> Where the same beere, and bread, and self-same wine,
>   That is his Lordships, shall be also mine.
> And I not faine to sit (as some, this day,
>   At great mens tables) and yet dine away.

Jonson sees it is an active centre of a patriarchal community in which duties and responsibilities are as important as rights, and of a way of life in which all classes, including the poet—Jonson intimates that for him and for others such hospitality is becoming a thing of the past—yet live in close personal contact. *To Sir Robert Wroth* describes a very similar scene at Durance with rather more emphasis on the sporting life of the great estate—an aspect less likely to be forgotten [quotes ll. 21–58]. The Golden Age is thus naturalized in the hall of an English mansion in a real agricultural setting, and we

2. Cf. *To Sir Edward Sacvile, To the Countess of Rutland* and *To Lady Mary Wroth.*

3. *Piers Plowman,* B., Passus I, 94–101. I am indebted to Mr. Dawson's *The Vision of Piers Plowman in Medieval Religion* for this quotation. I quote Langland as a representative spokesman. I do not wish to suggest that seventeenth-century noblemen made a habit of reading him; Peacham refers to "that bitter Satyre of Piers Plowman" (*Compleat Gentleman,* ed. Gordon, p. 95), but he may mean one of the imitations, as he attributes it to Lydgate.

In the matter of culture Peacham lays down a scheme of literary, musical and artistic studies for the gentleman and suggests a suitable blend of pride and condescension in manners; similarly Lord Herbert ends his educational recommendations: "I could say much more . . . and particularly concerning the discreet civility which is to be observed in communication either with friends or strangers . . . many precepts conducing there unto may be had in *Guazzo de la Civile Conversation,* and *Galateus de Moribus*" (*Life,* ed. Lee, p. 42).

end with an almost Homeric scene of feasting, in which bounty and humanity have temporarily overthrown the whole social hierarchy. Other contemporary moralists and commentators lamented that this old-fashioned "house-keeping" was dying out. In Selden's *Table Talk* the account of the Hall is significantly in the past tense:

> The Hall was the Place where the great Lord used to eat, (wherefore else were Halls made so big?), where he saw all his Servants and Tenants about him. He eat not in private, except in time of sickness: when he became a thing cooped up, all his greatness was spilled. Nay, the King himself used to eat in the Hall, and his Lords sat with him, and then he understood Men.

Inigo's Jones's Double Cube Room at Wilton, say, would not have lent itself to such a life. It may sound cheap to say that Jonson made the most of two worlds; he certainly wrote at a time when a highly cultivated society still kept in close contact with the community which supported it and still preserved traditions which encouraged it to maintain this kind of give and take, social, economic and cultural.

Nevertheless, despite changing architecture and changing habits of life, the ideal persisted. Jonson initiated an extremely interesting line of what, borrowing a modern analogy, one may call documentary poetry. It deserves a brief exploration. The most obvious imitations of his poems are Carew's *To Saxham* and *To my Friend G. N., from Wrest*. No one is going to claim that Carew shared his master's powers of social observation. The first poem is a light and fanciful thing; the other, less well known, which gives a detailed picture of the scene and of the social organization represented there, illustrates a number of points already made [quotes ll. 19–24, 31–44, 61–69]. The picture of the wine-press carries us away from the thoroughly English scene; it shows the Cavalier taking his eye off the object in order to classicize. But the mere fact that a man like Carew, derivative as he clearly is, recognized the existence—and the value—of such a scheme of things to the point of writing about it shows that the rather artificial culture of Charles I's court with its extravagant masques and its Italian pictures and Flemish painters had also not lost touch with its roots. Vandyck perhaps overdoes the elegance and refinement in his portrait of Carew and Killigrew, but when William Dobson paints Endymion Porter he shows us a florid country squire with beautiful laces and also dog and gun, leaning on a relief of muses and with a classical bust of a poet in the background; it is a superb and highly revealing work. Similarly Herrick in *The Hock-Cart* starts on the shores of the Mediterranean and then hurries home [quotes ll 1–6, 26–29, 32–39]. As a whole it is, with its colloquial language, a vivid picture of a Devon harvest festival, and Herrick has suggested, in the reference to the plough, the deeper meaning. Lovelace shows us that he was something of a naturalist as well as a chivalrous Kentish squire in those fanciful and moralized descriptions of insects and in *The Falcon* for whom he laments:

> Ah Victory, uphap'ly wonne!
> Weeping and Red is set the Sun,
> Whilst the whole Fields floats in one tear,
> And all the Air doth mourning wear:
> Close-hooded all thy kindred come
> To pay their Vows upon thy Tombe;
> The *Hobby* and the *Musket* too,
> Do march to take their last adieu.
>
> The *Lanner* and the *Lanneret*,
> Thy Colours bear as Banneret;
> The *Goshawk* and her *Tercel*, rous'd
> With Tears attend thee as new bows'd,
> All these are in their dark array
> Led by the various *Herald-Jay*.
>
> But thy eternal name shall live
> Whilst Quills from Ashes fame reprieve,
> Whilst open stands Renown's wide dore,
> And Wings are left on which to soar:
> Doctor *Robbin*, the Prelate *Pye*
> And the poetick *Swan* shall dye,
> Only to sing thy Elegie.

Whatever personal significance this may have had for Lovelace—it would seem to express a haunting regret for lost causes—its interest for us in the present context lies in his charming blend of the gentleman's knowledge of field sports and heraldry with poetic traditions—one thinks inevitably of the *Parlement of Foules*.[4] The idiom of these poems is, as Sir Herbert Grierson has put it, "that of an English gentleman of the best type, natural, simple, occasionally careless, but never diverging into vulgar colloquialism . . . or into conventional, tawdry splendour."[5] Several contributors to *Jonsonus Virbius* make plain the influence of Jonson in favour of "right and natural language." This is a stream of English poetry, the gentleman writing as a gentleman about his position and responsibilities, his interests and pleasures, which, if we omit Byron who is in any case often both vulgar and tawdry, now for better or worse dries up.

Early Stuart governments made several attempts to arrest the decay of the patriarchal household and the drift to London. Sir

4. As regards Chaucer's position in the early seventeenth century, it is, I think, worth recalling that, though Jonson strongly discourages the uses of "Chaucerisms," Peacham encourages his gentleman to "account him among the best of [his] English books in [his] library. . . . He saw in those times without his spectacles" (*The Compleat Gentleman*, ed. Gordon, p. 94).

5. *Metaphysical Poetry*, p. xxxi.

Richard Fanshawe wrote *An Ode, upon His Majesties Proclamation in the Year 1630. Commanding the Gentry to reside upon their Estates in the Countrey.* He sees what Jonson sees, and expresses the anxiety of those who realized how times were changing:

> Nor let the Gentry grudge to go
> Into those places whence they grew,
> But think them blest they may do so
>   Who would pursue.
>
> The smoky glory of the Town,
> That may go till his native Earth,
> And by the shining Fire sit down
>   Of his own hearth. . . .
>
> The Countrey too ev'n chops for rain:
> You that exhale it by your power,
> Let the fat drops fall down again
>   In a full shower. . . .

One thus sees embodied in verse of considerable distinction a picture of a social order, its natural setting and its occupations, and a sense of some of the dangers threatening it. The fact that it was written by men of very varying distinction of character and intelligence shows how widely the ideals expressed were held. That they were not always lived up to one may take for granted, though the enthusiasm of the verse seems to be more than merely literary. And as regards cultural standards there must have been, for a small number of houses like Penshurst, Wrest, Wilton, Great Tew or Bolsover, a very large number like that of Mrs. Henry Hastings[6] or of far less individuality and long forgotten. The scheme of knightly prowess, literary and musical interests and public spirit set forth by Peacham in *The Compleat Gentleman* was not universally followed; he bitterly reproaches those who waste their substance in London, "appearing but as Cuckoes in the Spring, one time in the yeare to the Countrey and their tenants, leaving the care of keeping good houses at Christmas, to the honest Yeomen of the Countrey."[7] However, one finds in this verse evidence of a climate of social opinion and, more important, feelings and habits which, with all their imperfections, were civilized in the narrower artistic sense, and also in the wider sense of having a foundation of social justice. This world provided Jonson with his larger *milieu*, or rather *milieux*, for its being made up of small groups is an important feature; he had lived in the house of Lord Aubigny and was a visitor at several others. One does not find this scene in English poetry after the Restoration. Though English noblemen never became, as Fanshawe feared they might, mere

6. See *Characters of the Seventeenth Century*, ed. Nichol Smith, p. 44.   7. Op. cit., p. 220.

court sycophants or men about town, manners in the widest sense changed in the era of the coffee-house. Life became more formally decorous. Pope, in the *Epistle to Boyle*, presents an ideal vision comparable to Jonson's:

> His Father's Acres who enjoys in peace,
> Or makes his Neighbours glad if he increase:
> Whose chearful Tenants bless their yearly toil,
> Yet to their Lord owe more than to the soil;
> Whose ample Lawns are not asham'd to feed
> The milky heifer and deserving steed;
> Whose rising Forests, not for pride or show,
> But future Buildings, future Navies grow:
> Let his plantations stretch from down to down,
> First shade a Country, and then raise a Town.

But fine as it is, and central to Pope's work, it does not imply so intimate and personal a relationship between the classes as the earlier poetry. The whole domestic layout had altered as ideas changed, and the lord was benevolent from the portico or the church steps rather than from the dais in the hall. Nevertheless one finds the spirit still alive in the age of "Squire Allworthy," of Coke of Norfolk and of Dr. Johnson's Club, and it was the tradition of culture that died first.

It need hardly be said that Jonson used an independent tone towards his patrons—except when he was in extreme financial straits. He had opinions about his rightful place at table in an age when all knew their own degrees and had their rightful places by birth or merit; "my Lord," he says that he said to the Earl of Salisbury, evidently a more remote patron than Sir William Sidney, "you promised I should dine with you, but I do not."[8] *An Epistle to Sir Edward Sacvile, now Earl of Dorset* treats, after Seneca, of the question of patronage and gratitude:

> You cannot doubt, but I, who freely know
> This Good from you, as freely will it owe;
> And though my fortune humble me, to take
> The smallest courtesies with thankes, I make
> Yet choyce from whom I take them; and would shame
> To have such doe me good, I durst not name:
> They are the Noblèst benefits, and sinke
> Deepest in Man, of which when he doth thinke,
> The memorie delights him more, from whom
> Then what he hath receiv'd. Gifts stinke from some,
> They are so long a coming, and so hard;
> Where any Deed is forc't, the Grace is mard.

---

8. *Conversations,* 13.

He goes on to analyse the characters of niggardly and ungracious patrons and those who sponge upon them. Jonson thought he knew who deserved his respect and why. In *Timber* he defines his conception of manners by implication, in the act of defining Courtesy in its euphemistic sense:

> *Nothing* is a courtesie, unless it be meant us; and that friendly, and lovingly. Wee owe no thankes to *Rivers*, that they carry our boats. . . It is true, some man may receive a Courtesie, and not know it; but never any man received it from him, that knew it not. . . . No: The doing of *Courtesies* aright, is the mixing of the respects for his owne sake, and for mine. He that doth them meerly for his owne sake, is like one that feeds his Cattell to sell them: he hath his Horse well drest for *Smithfield*.

Good manners for Jonson were something that, while adorning the upper tiers of the social hierarchy, should yet permeate through it. He expected the same kind of consideration from a patron as he showed towards his "high-spirited friend," and he admired similar qualities in his friends in every sense.

The grace of Jonson's manner comes out in his addresses to noble ladies, especially the Countesses of Rutland, Montgomery, and Bedford, and Lady Mary Wroth. A consideration of them will form a conclusion to this study, for, though he flatters splendidly, he does not cringe. There were certain fixed viewpoints in Jonson's outlook.

He praises his patronesses partly for their beauty and their taste, partly for deeper qualities. He writes to Lady Mary Wroth with full Renaissance exuberance:

> Madame, had all antiquities beene lost,
>   All historie seal'd up, and fables crost;
> That we had left us, nor by time, nor place,
>   Least mention of a *Nymph*, a *Muse*, a *Grace*,
> But even their names were to be made a-new,
>   Who could not but create them all, from you?
> He, that but saw you weare the wheaten hat,
>   Would call you more than Ceres, if not that:
> And, drest in shepherds tyre, who would not say:
>   You were the bright Oenone, Flora, or *May?*
> If dancing, all would cry th'*Idalian* Queene,
>   Were leading forth the *Graces* on the greene:
> And, armed for the chase, so bare her brow
>   Diana' alone, so hit, and hunted so.[9]

Lady Montgomery is a new Susanna, and in Lady Bedford he bows before qualities of character which belong peculiarly to his own vision [quotes Epigram LXXVI]. This beautifully polished epigram is a suitable vehicle for the presentation of a vision of aristocratic

9. Epigram CV (not included in this edition) [*Editor*].

elegance, charm, virtue and intelligence—one notices the emphatic
and subtle rhythm of the third quatrain—and the poet's admiration
for them. One is reminded of the undirected, and possibly therefore
more perfect, *Elegie:*

> Though Beautie be the Marke of Praise,
>   And yours of whom I sing be such
>   As not the Word can praise too much,
> Yet is't your vertue now I raise,

where the sense of the rarity and fragility of such qualities is delicately realized in the cadence of:

> His falling Temples you have rear'd,
>   The withered Garlands tane away;
>   His Altars kept from the Decay,
> That envie wish'd, and Nature fear'd.

The dangers and difficulties besetting his ideals of the lady are
magnificently argued out in "Not to know vice at all . . ." and *To
the World. A farewell for a Gentle-woman, vertuous and noble:*

> No, I doe know that I was borne
>   To age, misfortune, sicknesse, griefe:
> But I will beare these, with that scorne,
>   As shall not need thy false reliefe.

This is the simple but dignified Stoicism which conditions of the age
made both necessary and desirable. Jonson admired it in others and
possessed it himself. This moral strength and perception, along with
his erudition and conscious art, discoursed on in *Timber,* and an
ever-present sense of the whole gamut of living, combine with the
tone of the Jacobean noble household, "curteous, facile, sweet,"
where in season "freedome doth with degree dispense," to support
the brilliance of the famous lyrics. Like his gentlewoman he could
say,

> Nor for my peace will I goe farre,
>   As wandrers doe, that still doe rome,
> But make my strengths, such as they are,
>   Here in my bosome, and at home.

The end of it all is realized with unerring taste in such things as:

> Would'st thou heare, what man can say
>   In a little? Reader, stay.
> Under-neath this stone doth lye.
>   As much beautie, as could dye:
> Which in life did harbour give
>   To more vertue, then doth live.

> If, at all, shee had a fault
>> Leave it buryed in this vault.
> One name was ELIZABETH,
>> Th' other let it sleepe with death:
> Fitter, where it dyed, to tell,
>> Then that it liv'd at all. Farewell.

I am brought back to my starting point, the *Elegie on the Lady Jane Pawlet*, through which the urbanity of Jonson links up directly with that of Pope, Jonson thought "couplets be the bravest sort of verses, especially when they are broken like hexameters,"[1] and he has an important place in their development, but, as regards regularity, he broke them with a caesura in varied places, and the following lines from one of his livelier occasional poems are worth remembering:

> To hit in angles, and to clash with time:
>> As all defence, or offence, were a chime!
> I hate such measur'd, give me metall'd fire. . . .[2]

He liked a varied movement in poetry as well as fencing. The *Elegie*, like the other poems in couplets, bears this out:

> I doe obey you, Beautie! for in death
>> You seeme a faire one! O that you had breath,
> To give your shade a name! Stay, stay, I feele
>> A horrour in mee! all my blood is steele!
> Stiffe! starke! My joynts 'gainst one another knock!
>> Whose Daughter? ha? Great *Savage* of the Rock? . . .
> Her Sweetnesse, Softnesse, her faire Courtesie,
>> Her wary guardes, her wise simplicitie,
> Were like a ring of Vertues, 'bout her set,
>> And pietie the Center, where all met.
> A reverend State she had, an awful Eye,
>> A dazling, yet inviting, Majestie:
> What Nature, Fortune, Institution, Fact
>> Could summe to a perfection, was her Act!
> How did she leave the world? with what contempt?
>> Just as she in it liv'd! and so exempt
> From all affection! when they urg'd the Cure
>> Of her disease, how did her soule assure
> Her suffrings, as the body had beene away!
>> And to the Torturers (her Doctors) say,
> Stick on your Cupping-glasses, feare not, put
>> Your hottest Causticks to, burne, lance, or cut:
> 'Tis but a body which you can torment,
>> And I, into the world, all Soule, was sent!
> Then comforted her Lord! and blest her Sonne!
>> Chear'd her faire Sisters in her race to runne!

1. *Conversations*, 1.   Newcastle.
2. *An Epigram. To William Earle of*

With gladness temper'd her sad Parents teares!
   Made her friends joyes to get above their feares!
And, in her last act, taught the Standers-by,
   With admiration, and applause to die!
Let angels sing her glories, who can call
   Her spirit home, to her originall! . . .

It combines a slightly naïve declamatory manner at the start with Jonson's characteristic blend of urbanity, shrewd observation and simplicity in the description of the Marchioness's personality and an anticipation of the more formal high decorum of the Augustans towards the end; but no Augustan would have written her words to the doctors, overflowing as they are with "enthusiasm." Here in a lady at the top of the social hierarchy one notes the hierarchy of virtues. They correspond fairly to the qualities of men we have already seen portrayed. Together Jonson's lords and ladies form a brilliant, dignified, benevolent and gracious society, "dazling, yet inviting." We can see from the poems, and other evidence corroborates, that there was no impassable gap between the world of the poet's vision and Jacobean and Caroline England. *Eupheme* on the Lady Venetia Digby is usually held up as an example of hyperbole; a passage in a quiet key on the character of the Lady, whether true to life in this particular case or not, shows, with a characteristic note of irony, a picture of deportment which would be appropriate to any of the scenes or characters discussed:

All Nobilitie,
  (But pride, that schisme of incivilitie)
She had, and it became her! she was fit
   T'have knowne no envy, but by suffring it!
She had a mind as calme, as she was faire;
   Not tost or troubled with light Lady-aire;
But, kept an even gate, as some streight tree
   Mov'd by the wind, so comely moved she.
And by the awfull manage of her Eye
   She swaid all bus'nesse in the Familie!

Jonson himself, as we have seen at the start, was sometimes guilty of "that schisme of incivilitie." He probably needed the stimulus of good company to bring out the full refinement of his literary culture. But it is brought out over and over again, and was, and is, a model of its kind. It is impossible finally to separate the qualities presented in the poems from the poet's attitude towards them; social manner and manners are infectious and the one seems to have evoked the other. We should need more biographical information than we possess to take the matter further but I do not think it is base to attribute to Jonson what might be called poetic "party manners."

One cannot sum up an achievement such as Jonson's in a word. I have only touched in passing on his trenchancy and seriousness as a satirist and his strength and delicacy as a lyric poet. I wanted to deal at some length with his tone and accent because, in considering the meaning of wit, I believe that, though it changed from an intellectual to a social spirit as the century wore on, nevertheless a social spirit of a clear and peculiarly noble kind was present in poetry from the start and that this spirit is exemplified particularly in Ben Jonson. His poetry, even more than his plays, links seventeenth-century culture and the polite civilization of the Augustans to the better features of the medieval social order and to the half-religious ideal of Courtesy.

HUGH MACLEAN

[The Social Function of Jonson's Complimentary Verse]†

* * * It has often been the fate of the poems to be praised chiefly (sometimes exclusively) for their formal virtues, while the best criticism of the comedies, more than ever since L. C. Knights's *Drama and Society in the Age of Jonson* has kept steadily in view Jonson's comment that "the Study of [Poesy] (if wee will trust *Aristole*) offers to mankind a certain rule, and Patterne of living well, and happily; disposing us to all Civil Offices of Society."[1] That is rather curious, too. The comedies, by their nature, present this "certaine rule, and Patterne" indirectly, appealing (as Knights says) to the "sardonic contemplation" of an audience characterized by "a lively sense of human limitations."[2] The epigrams, as a rule, repeat that method; but a significant number of poems, particularly in *The Forrest*, deal explicitly and directly with "high and noble matter," with "the mysteries of manners, armes, and arts." Geoffrey Walton, following Leavis, remarks on Jonson's regular attention, in the poems, to "serious moral matters in a social context."[3] I suggest

† From "Ben Jonson's Poems: Notes on the Ordered Society," in *Essays in English Literature from the Renaissance to the Victorian Age, Presented to A. S. P. Woodhouse,* eds. Millar MacLure and F. Watt (Toronto, 1964), pp. 43–68.

1. *Ben Jonson,* ed. C. H. Herford and P. Simpson (11 vols.; Oxford, 1925–52), VIII, 636. All references to Jonson's poetry and prose are made to this edition, hereafter cited as *H&S*. Critical works that attend to the "total achievement" of Jonson's poems include G. B. Johnston, *Ben Jonson: Poet* (New York, 1945); W.

Trimpi, *Ben Jonson's Poems: A Study of the Plain Style* (Stanford, 1962), and the articles by G. R. Hibbard, Paul Cubeta, and Geoffrey Walton referred to in this essay. I am particularly indebted to the studies by Johnston and Trimpi and to Hibbard's article.

2. L. C. Knights, *Drama and Society in the Age of Jonson* (London, 1937), 208, 198.

3. Geoffrey Walton, "The Tone of Ben Jonson's Poetry," in *Seventeenth Century English Poetry,* ed. W. R. Keast, 2nd ed. (New York, 1971), 135.

that, while the plays deal principally in the satiric recognition and descriptions of the factors that contribute to social disorder, we find in the poems (with the *Discoveries* behind, as theory to practice), not an explicit and detailed outline of the social order Jonson admired, but rather "notes" on particular elements that ought to mark a society properly ordered, as well as suggestions for conduct in the midst of a disordered one. The negative strictures of the comedies, accordingly, are supplemented and completed by positive advices in the poetry and the *Discoveries*.

One must be careful not to claim too much: no integrated grand design for society emerges from the "lesser theatre" of these poems, so often committed to compliment. But the recurrence of three related themes is striking. In brief, the poems lay stress on the virtue of friendship between good men, who are receptive by nature to the free exchange of opinion and counsel, and on the strong resource such friendships constitute for the ordered society and the secure state. They reflect also Jonson's views on the relationship that ought ideally to obtain between prince and poet, in the interest of the people at large. Finally, they indicate the social attitudes and actions befitting a "ruling class" which thoroughly understands the nature of its responsibilities and desires to make them effective. It is relevant to observe here also that, when Jonson speaks to this third question, he is apt to select the verse-epistle as a vehicle peculiarly suited to the poet who outlines, for the benefit of those in high place, "holy lawes/Of nature, and societie." In this, as in much else, "there must be a Harmonie, and concent of parts."[4]

* * *

[Notes that Jonson addresses relatively few poems to royalty]; even if wisdom had not checked the impulse to counsel a king, Jonson was not the man to lavish his talents on this particular variety of panegyric. But an attractive alternative remained. One could, if one were reasonably decorous, address a ruling class instead. Those members of aristocratic families who extended their patronage and support to Jonson, especially those with whom the poet could consider himself to be on terms at least relatively informal, must in any event be honoured in the poet's verse. While he could not ordinarily expect to be as candid (or blunt) as with his own colleagues, he could claim with some justice to have attained something like friendship with a number of highly placed individuals. Relatively free, therefore, from the limitations imposed where princes were in question, yet still addressing or chiefly complimenting persons regularly concerned, in various spheres, with the maintenance of order in social and political life, Jonson could counsel while appearing chiefly

4. *H&S*, VIII, 617.

to praise. For young Sir William Sidney, the poet might assume an oracular tone; with others, the note of approbation or reminder would often be more fitting. Particularly in *The Forrest*, but elsewhere too, he incorporates in gracefully complimentary verse those principles of social responsibility which the actions of a ruling class ought in his view to reflect. The poet, in short, transfers his advisory function (properly directed to a prince) to that class from which, as a rule, the monarch will draw his counsellors; and he can address some of them, at least, in a manner formal and "easy" at once.

Jonson's attitude to his patrons is conditioned primarily by three factors. He needed their support, of course, but that is in some ways the least important of the three. Poems that openly request or acknowledge financial support appear only in the last years, when the poet's fortunes were palled. As a rule, Jonson chose to ignore the subject, or to make it the occasion for a lecture on the art of giving and receiving, as in the "Epistle to . . . Sacville" (*Und.* XIII), which strikes a characteristic note.

> You . . . whose will not only, but desire
> To succour my necessities, tooke fire,
> Not at my prayers, but your sense; which laid
> The way to meet, what others would upbraid;
> And in the Act did so my blush prevent,
> As I did feele it done, as soone as meant:
> You cannot doubt, but I, who freely know
> This Good from you, as freely will it owe;
> And though my fortune humble me, to take
> The smallest courtesies with thankes, I make
> Yet choyce from whom I take them. . . .(7–17)

The lines reflect a cast of mind also apparent in Aubrey's allusion to "Mr. Benjamin Johnson (who ever scorned an unworthy patrone)."[5] No doubt unworthiness might consist in the refusal to honour a promise of support, as Epigram LXV ("To my Muse") may indicate. But the poem hints at deeper causes of scorn; and Epigram X ("To my lord Ignorant") is perhaps relevant:

> Thou call'st me *Poet*, as a terme of shame:
> But I have my revenge made, in thy name.

While the episode at Salisbury's table is familiar, there were others of the sort:

> Ben one day being at table with my Lady Rutland [Drummond writes], her husband comming in, accused her that she keept table to poets, of which she wrott a letter to him which he answered. My Lord intercepted the letter, but never challenged him.[6]

5. John Aubrey, *Brief Lives*, ed. A.   6. *H&S*, I, 142.
Powell (London, 1949), 371.

A patron may be "unworthy" on several counts, but his failure to acknowledge the poet's right to a privileged place in society is particularly reprehensible. Finally, Jonson expected the patron and his class to exemplify virtuous conduct, and so to persuade a society and secure a state. The *Epigrams* are dedicated to Pembroke, "Great Example of Honor and Vertue"; and whatever Jonson thought of the man described by Clarendon as "immoderately given up to women," Epigram CII illustrates the poet's ideal.

> . . . thou, whose noblesse keeps one stature still,
> And one true posture, though besieg'd with ill
> Of what ambition, faction, pride can raise;
> Whose life, ev'n they, that envie it, must praise;
> That art so reverenc'd, as thy comming in,
> But in the view, doth interrupt their sinne;
> Thou must draw more: and they, that hope to see
> The common-wealth still safe, must studie thee.

More specifically (as the poems reveal), Jonson expected a patron to pay more than lip-service to the ideal of fraternity; to illustrate in thought and action the continuing virtue of ancient traditions; to renew in each age, by the wise application of inherited talent, the life and force of those traditions. When hard circumstance closed every other avenue, there remained an obligation to exemplify (if need be, "farre from the maze of custome, error, strife") the ideal of virtuous life appropriate to one's station.

Jonson, accordingly, looked for a good deal more than financial support from the highly placed persons who could sponsor him. And he "counselled" his patrons, directly, and indirectly, in a good many genres, from the epigram to the ode. The verse-epistle in particular he found well suited to his personality and his purposes. As Trimpi shows,[7] the genre by Jonson's time combined regard for a continuing stylistic tradition with an attitude toward the range of matter proper to the verse-epistle considerably more liberal than that of classical practice. Cicero's observations on the characteristics of the plain style in oratory, and the view of Demetrius that, in genres suited to the plain style (i.e., comedy, satire, epigram, epistle), "the diction throughout [will be] current and familiar," particularly that the epistle should "obey the laws of friendship, which demand that we should 'call a spade a spade,' as the proverb has it," contributed to a tradition of epistolary style endorsed by Lipsius, Vives, and John Hoskyns.[8] On the other hand, Demetrius' opinion that "there are epistolary topics, as well as an epistolary style," and that "in the case of the plain style, we can no doubt point to subject matter which is homely and appropriate to the style itself," had gradually

7. Trimpi, *Poems*, 60–75.   8. *Ibid.*, 6–9.

given way to the view that the range of topics proper to the epistle may extend to "all public, private, and domestic concerns."[9]

A verse form at once traditional and evolving in this way suited Jonson very well. The manner of any one epistle will certainly vary with the occasion; one does not address a noble lord as one might ask a friend to dinner. Nor are we to expect advice directly given so much as the counsel implicit in the poet's approbation of the action and character he describes; for "it . . . behooves the giver of counsell to be circumspect."[1] Still, the humanist who allowed Aristotle his due while insisting on the right to "make further Discoveries of truth and fitnesse," and who thought rules less forceful than experiments, recognized the suitability of the verse-epistle for precepts turning on the principle, "Newness of Sense, Antiquitie of voyce!"[2] Again, it was an appropriate medium for the poet concerned to remind society and its leaders of the dangerous temptation to "rest/On what's deceast": rather (*Und.* XIII, 131–4),

> 'Tis by degrees that men arrive at glad
> Profit in ought; each day some little adde,
> In time 'twill be a heape; This is not true
> Alone in money, but in manners too.

And, of course, for one whose sense of injur'd merit lay always ready to hand, the relatively plain-spoken style of the verse-epistle might usefully reinforce expressions hinting at an equality of merit, or even at actual friendship, between poet and the highly placed person addressed.[3]

Evidently Jonson employs forms other than the verse-epistle proper to endorse or counsel the social actions of his patrons. It may be observed, however, that while XII and XIII in *The Forrest* are explicitly termed "epistles," III ("To Sir Robert Wroth") is surely one also. The "Ode: To Sir William Sydney" gives advice as directly as does the "Epistle to a Friend, to perswade him to the Warres" (*Und.* XV), or even the "Epistle to . . . Sacvile." And the *Epi-grams* (among which appears "Inviting a friend to supper") include several pieces not obviously representative of Jonson's taut standards for the epigram. Jonson was fond of mingling literary kinds, and in any event he had good classical precedents for the prac-tice.[4] That various formal labels are attached to these poems should not obscure the fact that they all reflect his conviction that the poet has a clear right, a duty even, to speak out to his patron in a manly fashion. Perhaps one may risk the suggestion that Jonson found the

9. *Ibid.*, 68, 70.
1. *H&S*, VIII, 566.
2. "An Epistle to Master John Selden" (*Und.* XIV), 60: *H&S*, VIII, 160.
3. In this connection, see J. A. Levine,

"The Status of the Verse Epistle before Pope," *SP*, LIX (1962), 658–84, esp. 675–6.
4. See Trimpi, *Poems*, 159–60.

verse-epistle especially congenial and that something of its character and tone often echoes in poems not formally so described. If he employs the verse-epistle to remind a ruling group of the constant standard it must uphold and of the continual adjustment to circumstance this will require, and to insist besides on the essential fraternity of a healthy society, poems called "odes" or "epigrams" reflect those elements too.

"To Penshurst," formally both ode and "country-house poem," has been rather thoroughly examined by G. R. Hibbard (and others),[5] but since Jonson here explicitly considers the role of an aristocratic dynasty (in terms of one with which he felt particular sympathy), one or two points need emphasis. Penshurst, apt symbol of the Sidney line, instructively illustrates Jonson's social ideal in one aspect at least: the contrast with those more magnificent ancestral piles that betray pride and ambition points up Penshurst's vitality and their lack of it. But we are not regularly made aware of "the world outside" Penshurst in this poem, although opening and conclusion remind us of that world's existence: Jonson's emphasis falls deliberately on the positive ideal exemplified at Penshurst. That nature is everywhere compliant, even eager to serve man, effectively supplements the fraternal atmosphere prevailing in this household, where all classes are as welcome as the poet (45–50; 61–4):

> . . . though thy walls be of the countrey stone,
> They'are rear'd with no mans ruine, no mans grone,
> There's none, that dwell about them, wish them downe;
> But all come in, the farmer, and the clowne:
> And no one empty-handed, to salute
> Thy lord, and lady, though they have no sute. . . .
> [There] comes no guest, but is allow'd to eate,
> Without his feare, and of thy lords owne meate:
> Where the same beere, and bread, and self-same wine,
> That is his Lordships, shall be also mine.

And while the family that acknowledges its social responsibilities spreads general influence on all sides, so too it prepares for its successors, those aristocratic patrons of the next age, by properly educating and directing offspring who (96–8) may

> every day,
> Reade, in their vertuous parents noble parts,
> The mysteries of manners, armes, and arts.[6]

If this is how a great family ought to act, Jonson remarks also on the conduct appropriate to individual members of that family. Of

5. G. R. Hibbard, "The Country House Poem of the Seventeenth Century," *Journal of the Warburg and Courtauld Institute,* XIX (1956), 159 ff.; and see Paul Cubeta, "A Jonsonian Ideal: 'To Penshurst,' " *PQ* XLII (1963), 14–24.
6. See also "An Epigram on . . . Burleigh" (*Und.* XXX), 13–19.

the various poems addressed to members of the clan, the "Ode: To Sir William Sydney, on his Birth-day" is of special interest; since the person addressed is at the point of transition from youth to manhood, his responsibilities to a noble line and to society at large are emphasized in conjunction. Jonson thought that "no perfect Discovery can bee made upon a flat or a levell"; also that "to many things a man should owe but a temporary beliefe, and a suspension of his owne Judgement, not an absolute resignation of himselfe, or a perpetuall captivity."[7] These principles underlie his advice to the young Sidney [quotes *The Forrest*, XIV, ll. 27–50].

These poems clearly reflect important elements in Jonson's "theory of social order"; they are guide-lines for a ruling class that collectively and individually cares about its responsibilities. But they lack a dimension. The bright perfection of a Sidney-world obscures the sombre social backdrop that requires to be regulated by Sidneys and those like them. Leaders cannot forever prevent the incursions of vice, after all, by exemplifying virtue at a cool remove; they must often descend into the arena and actively wrestle with the enemy. Perhaps Jonson felt some reluctance, for reasons of decorum, to present Sidneys in postures other than serene: one recalls the "Epode" (*Forrest*, XI):

> Not to know vice at all, and keepe true state,
>   Is vertue, and not *Fate:*
> Next, to that vertue, is to know vice well,
>   And her blacke spight expell.   (1–4)

In any case, other poems not addressed to members of the Sidney clan complement and amplify the views approved in "Penshurst" and counselled in the "Ode." And each presumes a context appropriate to the second couplet of the "Epode."

Epigram LXXVI ("On Lucy Countesse of Bedford") has often attracted the admiration of critics: "How to be" may be suggested as the theme of this poem, which wittily translates ideal into fact. Less often noticed, but more significant here, is Epigram XCIV ("To Lucy, Countesse of Bedford, with Mr. Donnes Satyres"), an equally polished piece, with the theme, "How to act." [Quotes the poem.] Here is a poem decorously circular in design, turning on the role appropriate to patrons and exemplified by Lucy, who is not simply "Life of the *Muses* day," but who has the wit to discern and distinguish: to be, in fact, one of those "rare friends" that "rare poems" demand, patrons who, by extending favour to the poet, acknowledge the quality of the poetry—one might say, pay court to it. Far from assuming an attitude of aloofness and hauteur, his patroness, who deliberately seeks out satirical poems for their "matter," is concerned with the moral character of all levels of society, not merely her own. As true aristocrat, the Countess of Bedford justifies her place in the social order by gaining knowledge, through the mirror held up to nature by the poet, of social conditions upon which she may then (Jonson seems to imply) bring her beneficent influence to bear. But even if she does not act in that way, her refusal to turn away from unpleasant or disturbing aspects of society, her insistence on a full view, indicate the completeness of her own nature, one fit to be described as evening and morning star both: a "full constant light," in fact, perfectly exemplifying the recognition that ancient privilege never exempts from present responsibility.

"To Sir Robert Wroth" (*The Forrest*, III) parallels "To Penshurst" in its emphasis on the acquiescence of external nature in the pursuits of man ("A serpent river leades/To some coole, courteous shade"), and on the mingling in this household, when occasion arises, of all classes (53–8):

> The rout of rurall folke come thronging in,
>   (Their rudeness then is thought no sinne)
> Thy noblest spouse affords them welcome grace;
>   And the great *Heroes*, of her race,
> Sit mixt with losse of state, or reverence.
>   Freedome doth with degree dispense.

However, unlike the other, this poem continually reminds the reader of threatening and vicious forces at court and in the world environing Wroth's home; the "thousands" who (85–8)

> . . . goe flatter vice, and winne,
>   By being organes to great sinne,
> Get place, and honor, and be glad to keepe
>   The secrets, that shall breake their sleepe. . . .

The natural surroundings of Durrants provide, not a permanent haven, but merely a "securer rest," to which Wroth may intermittently retreat for spiritual refreshment and moral strength, before returning to the task Jonson considers appropriate to every leader: "To doe thy countrey service, thy selfe right." Further, while divine power and natural influences may direct Wroth and his highly placed fellows to peace of mind, and enable them to meet the temptations of city and court with equanimity, still (93–4)

> . . . when man's state is well,
>   'Tis better, if he there can dwell.

These tentative expressions point to the fact that the life even of the good man is one of continual and rigorous struggle, to shore up or regulate social order, and also, through self-examination, to guard against the "subtle traines" (as the "Epode" has it) by which "severall" passions invade the minde,/And strike our reason blinde."

The "Epistle to . . . Sacvile" (*Und.* XIII), in which social vice and disorder are once again extensively detailed, with special attention to "hunters of false fame," adds a final note of counsel to the active leader. It is not enough merely to hold at bay the forces making for disorder in society and in oneself. The point of struggle is to secure virtue or to alter a vicious situation: to make something happen. At the very least, one may demonstrate in one's own person what others may also achieve (135–44). ("They are ever good men, that must make good the times").

> . . . we must more than move still, or goe on,
> We must accomplish; 'Tis the last Key-stone
> That makes the Arch. The rest that there were put
> Are nothing till that comes to bind and shut.
> Then stands it a triumphall marke! then Men
> Observe the strength, the height, the why, and when,
> It was erected; and still walking under
> Meet some new matter to looke up and wonder!
> Such Notes are vertuous men! they live as fast
> As they are high; are rooted and will last.

All these poems counsel or approve social actions befitting persons responsible for the maintenance and direction of social order. But what if society, hardened in bad moulds, too toughly resists the efforts of dedicated leaders to re-direct its course? For Jonson had read his Seneca: "Wee will rather excuse [a vice] then be rid of it. That wee cannot, is pretended; but that wee will not, is the true reason. . . . It was impossible to reforme these natures; they were dry'd, and hardned in their ill.[8] The "Epistle: To Katherine, Lady Aubigny" (*The Forrest*, XIII) gives counsel for just such a situation. Not surprisingly, Jonson advises his patroness to profit by the poet's example: fortitude in adversity and confidence to endure in the midst of trial will both be required. The poem opens with a warning:

> 'Tis growne almost a danger to speake true
> Of any good minde, now: There are so few.
> The bad, by number, are so fortified,
> As what th'have lost t'expect, they dare deride.
> So both the prais'd, and praisers suffer. . . .

But the poet, "at fewd/With sinne and vice, though with a throne endew'd" does not recoil. "Though forsooke/Of *Fortune*," Jonson proudly claims (15–20)

> [I] have not alter'd yet my looke,
> Or so my selfe abandon'd, as because

8. *H&S*, VIII, 580.

> Men are not just, or keepe no holy lawes
> Of nature, and societie, I should faint. . . .

The character of Lady Aubigny, "perfect, proper, pure and naturall"
(for so her "beauties of the mind" are shown in the poet's mirror),
enables her to take a stand analogous to that of the beleagured poet.
Even friendship may fail (53–58); but the individual's responsibility to virtue remains constant (51–2):

> 'Tis onely that can time, and chance defeat:
> For he, that once is good, is ever great.

In an unregenerate world that "cannot see/Right, the right way,"
the virtuous individual may continue to influence others merely by
being true to herself, as Jonson reminds Lady Aubigny (110–12),

> . . . since you are truly that rare wife,
> Other great wives may blush at: when they see
> What your try'd manners are, what theirs should bee.

But this, he knew, was rather to be wished than expected; and since
even a poet might sing, in fierce adversity, "high, and aloofe," the
key passage of the poem (59–63; 121–4) advocates the pursuit of
virtue in a larger context. When the times defy moral redemption,
and friends fall off,

> This makes, that wisely you decline your life,
> Farre from the maze of custome, error, strife,
> And keepe an even, and unalter'd gaite;
> Not looking by, or backe (like those, that waite
> Times, and occasions, to start forth, and seeme) . . .

> Live that one, still; and as long yeeres doe passe,
> *Madame*, be bold to use this truest glasse:
> Wherein, your forme, you still the same shall finde;
> Because nor it can change, nor such a minde.

Exemplary action, therefore, may now and again be matched by an
exemplary endurance that conquers time and circumstance.

The "Epistle to Elizabeth Countesse of Rutland" (*The Forrest*,
XII), to conclude, draws together a number of views already noted,
now with special reference to the poet's central role. The epistle
touches on the "credentials" of the poet-counsellor and on the conditions most favourable for the exercise of his gifts. As Hercules,
Helen, gods and men owed their lives beyond life "onely [to] *Poets*,
rapt with rage divine," so Jonson's poetry (89–91) will undertake

> . . . high, and noble matter, such as flies
> From braines entranc'd, and fill'd with extasies;
> Moodes, which the god-like Sydney oft did prove. . . .

In an age when

> ... almightie gold ...
> Solders crackt friendship; makes love last a day;
> Or perhaps lesse,

Sidney's daughter can be trusted to

> ... let this drosse carry what price it will
> With noble ignorants, and let them still,
> Turne, upon scorned verse, their quarter-face:
> With you, I know, my offring will find grace.
> For what a sinne 'gainst your great fathers spirit,
> Were it to thinke, that you should not inherit
> His love unto the *Muses*, when his skill
> Almost you have, or may have, when you will?

But the poem intends more than this: by spelling out the nature of that fame awaiting patrons fortunate enough to hold a place in Jonson's verse, it establishes the claim of the poet to a seat among the highest ranks of the social community. Jonson can promise "strange *poems*, which, as yet,/Had not their forme touch'd by an English wit"; poems, however, that also recall and confirm the powers of Orphic song. Ancient truth will live again in modes newly suited to contemporary conditions and taste. This poet can, of course, assure the worthy patron of earthly fame, "like a rich, and golden *pyramede*,/Borne up by statues." But Jonson's commitment is more explicit (86–7): to

> ... show, how, to the life, my soule presents
> Your forme imprest there. ...

The exemplary form of virtue embodied in the Countess of Rutland while she lived will not merely be remembered through Jonson's verse, but truly re-created in it; as "god-like Sidney" had given the mark of the right poet to be his capacity so to create another nature. "To flatter my good Lord," we recall, is "To lose the formes, and dignities of men." False friendship destroys life; but the poet, like a true friend, preserves the "formes" of the men and women he addresses in his poems. The true poet gives life, in fact, as kings can "create new men" (*Ungathered Verse*, XVI). And only such poets, whose art "hath a Stomacke to concoct, divide, and turne all into nourishment,"[9] are thoroughly qualified to counsel the princes and patrons whose art is the ordering of society and the state. The structure of society severely limits the extension of friendship proper, on the pattern of the Tribe; that is a pity; but community of interest among good men may serve instead. And Jonson's poems record his constant care for that harmonious ideal.

9. *H&S*, VIII, 638.

G. A. E. PARFITT

Ethical Thought and Ben Jonson's Poetry†

I

The limited extent to which Jonson's poetry is known may be linked to the fact that the revival of interest in the metaphysical poets early in this century largely passed his work by, because the kind of density and compressed thought which characterize metaphysical poetry are usually absent from it. Previously, Jonson had been half-ignored because if he is not metaphysical he is not what we usually mean by Elizabethan either. Although he has his supporters there is little sign that critical comment on his poetry is based on the sort of comprehensive reading of it which we take for granted where Donne is concerned, or Pope or Wordsworth. One long-standing reason for this neglect has been a misunderstanding of his "classicism," a belief that he had little contact with anything English, linked to a persistent failure to define what is "classical" in his work at all closely. I now want to challenge this misunderstanding from the viewpoint of Jonson's ethical thought, and since "To Penshurst" is one of the few poems by Jonson which is both well-known and important it provides a good point at which to begin.

"Assurance" and "control" are the best general descriptive words for "To Penshurst." A complimentary poem to the Sidney family, it is written without a trace of sycophancy or servility, moves from one facet of its topic to another with calm conviction, and impresses us with a restrained certainty about exactly what values, what sort of civilization, are worthwhile. This certainty, as we should expect, is embodied in the style, as in the opening lines, with their distinction between real and apparent greatness:

> Thou art not, Penshurst, built to envious show,
> Of touch, or marble, nor canst boast a row
> Of polish'd pillars, or a roofe of gold:
> Thou hast no lantherns, whereof tales are told;
> Or stayre, or courts; but stand'st an ancient pile,
> And these grudg'd at, art reverenc'd the while.
> Thou joy'st in better markes, of soyle, of ayre,
> Of wood, of water: therein thou art faire.

The emphasis is two-fold, upon tradition (ancient pile) and upon the solid connection with Nature: both emphases involve ethical judgments—set against the glamour of "polish'd pillars, or a roofe

† From *SEL,* IX (1969), 123–134.

of gold" the attributes of age and of a connection with Nature are clearly, to Jonson, desirable. The position is not surprising but it takes certainty of belief to make it so clear, without discussion, right at the beginning of the poem, and it provides a strong departure point for the rest of "To Penshurst," in which Jonson develops his conviction that the harmoniously unified society which he evokes is morally admirable. The poem's assurance is such that Jonson can refer to Lady Robert Sidney as providing James I with entertainment which is "(great, I will not say, but) sodayne" (l. 82): Jonson feels so sure that he knows, and is communicating the worth of, the main moral values that he can emphasize the state of preparedness and ready hospitality at Penshurst without feeling impelled to exaggerate its lavishness. The distinction reflects that in the opening lines. The control of the whole poem is indicated by the way in which everything is finally brought to bear upon a distinction between men who "build" and those who "dwell," a distinction which, in context, is so much more than linguistic juggling.

I have already suggested that the poem grows from the ethical distinction made in the opening lines between types of greatness. Jonson extends this point, going on to make it clear that the valid fame of the house depends not on its natural setting as such, but on the existence of a harmonious "social" unit, of which the fusing of house in setting is both part and symbol. This harmony exists on several levels (in the selflessness of the fishes, the accessibility of the fruit, the local stone of the walls, the humaneness of the country people and also of the Sidneys) and depends upon the realization of several morally admirable qualities. Generosity and friendliness come easily to mind, but Jonson is also upholding a sense of responsibility and, at any rate implicitly, a sense of function and place. The fish function to serve Man (ll. 31–38 are less hyperbolic natural description than a formalized account of the relationship of creatures below Man in the Chain of Being to him) and the Sidneys, as the family of the great house, have the functions of providing hospitality and, more generally, of ensuring the peace and welfare of the neighborhood. But these various ethical views are in no sense imposed on the poem; there is no sense of nature being raped to yield moral lessons, for one of the poem's most remarkable features is the manner in which ethical views grow from, are proved "on the pulses" by, the controlled and vital embodiment of Jonson's imagined experience of Penshurst, an experience which seems to him to contain that ideal of the virtuous and satisfying life for which he is, in a sense, searching throughout his work, the ideal which underlies all his satire. We should also notice how secular the poem is, for although Christianity specifically enters towards its end, and although the *spirit* of Christian ethics is relevant throughout, the achievement which Jonson saw at Penshurst is essentially human and no attempt is made to suggest that it is only possible with God's grace and help—it is accessible to Man as Man and it is self-rewarding.

But "To Penshurst" can also be shown to demonstrate Jonson's awareness of his English environment, although a single point will have to be sufficient illustration. The poem was written about 1610 and among its themes, as we have seen, are the Sidneys' hospitality and the peaceful harmony of the whole social unit. A few years later James had to resort to a Royal Proclamation to make gentry return from London to their country homes. The proclamation probably did little good, and the forces which rendered it impotent overran Jonson's ideal also, but it emphasizes the seriousness with which James (and Elizabeth before him) treated the problems of hospitality, social responsibility, and, more loosely, local government. At the time of Jonson's poem, as throughout the sixteenth and seventeenth centuries, England was largely rural and local government still a meaningful term. Prosperity depended largely on agriculture and political stability on efficient administration at the level of Justices of the Peace. For both reasons the central government needed the gentry to be based on their country houses and viewed the centripetal force of London with concern. Although Justices of the Peace were not always efficient they were at this time indispensable. Crowley is characteristic in the way in which his statement of the gentry's responsibilities is given direct moral emphasis: "Thou shalt have delite in nothyng, Savinge in doyng thy duty: Which is, under God and thy Kyng, to rule them that thou doest dwel by."[1] Jonson's poem is not propaganda, nor is it an historical document, except in a minor sense, but part of its greatness lies in the imaginative weight given to a vision of life where responsibility is accepted and practiced by all for all, and as such is demonstrably rooted in his contemporary background.

II

"To Penshurst" has been used to point to the centrality of ethical attitudes in Jonson's verse, the assurance with which these are handled, and the connection between his verse and its background. We can now widen the scope of the discussion by looking at Jonson's ethical views with that bogey-word "classicism" in mind—a word which has been used of Jonson so much, and with so little useful definition, as to be of little use as a critical term. Examination of

1. *The Laste Trumpet*, E.E.T.S. ed., 1871, p. 92.

Jonson's ethics with Roman writers in mind has been mainly at the level of pointing out references in Latin writing which Jonson may have borrowed or which indicate views close to his own. The nature of the relationship between Jonson, Rome, and English ethical traditions has not been satisfactorily examined and his "classicism" is, in consequence, usually misunderstood. An attempt to sketch this relationship and to state what is unusual in Jonson's ethical position demands more detailed treatment than can be given here, but even a brief survey can suggest the main points.

The distinction between real and apparent greatness in "To Penshurst" is linked to what is, perhaps, Jonson's most prominent theme—the gap between seeming and being, which underlies most of his satire. His view of Man as individual is a development of this perception: he admires constancy, honesty, and self-sufficiency, while detesting hypocrisy, fickleness, and flattery. Extended to human relationships this attitude involves a refusal to admire birth or wealth as such, and admiration for generosity, humaneness, and a sense of function. This last point makes Jonson politically conservative, stressing hierarchy and arguing that the aristocracy should continue to rule, so long as merit matches birth, because this is their function, because they have the greatest potential for government, and because no other class has the abilities necessary for the good rule of the country as a whole. It is this set of ideas about government which produces the pressure of anxiety which makes "A Speach According to Horace" an important poem. To convey aspects of his ethical beliefs Jonson uses the concepts of the Golden Age and of the world's degeneration, while his view of the soul's superiority over the body is implied by his view of Man as individual. Finally, women in Jonson's poetry are viewed with a mixture of rough abuse and strong admiration.

This capsulated survey of Jonson's ethical views touches on all the main elements in his ethical thinking, and the first thing to notice in it is that most of the attitudes involved will be familiar enough to anyone who has read at all widely in medieval, Elizabethan, and Jacobean literature. The gap between seeming and being is a common theme in Jacobean drama; Chapman constantly emphasizes constancy and self-reliance; hypocrisy is a major target of all satire; the hatred of fickleness and distrust of wealth and its manifestations are both bound up with the themes of *ubi sunt* and *sic transiit* which have a continuous history in England from the Old English *Wanderer* and *Seafarer* onwards to Jonson's time and beyond; the refusal to admire wealth and titles in themselves involves Jonson in one of the greatest of sixteenth-century debates (we remember, for example, Marston's view that "birth doth ne'er enroll A man among monarchs, but a glorious soul");[2] the belief that the

2. *The Malcontent*, V. vi.

nobility are, nevertheless, better equipped to govern than any other class is the subject of another great debate; the ideas of the Golden Age, of the world's degeneration, of the soul's superiority over the body, and of the dual nature of women are all commonplaces of contemporary thought.

These strong similarities do not, as we shall see, make Jonson's views merely derivative, nor do they refute the connections which editors and scholars allege to exist between these views and Roman thought. It is one of the more striking naiveties of Jonson scholarship and criticism that his connections with Rome can be taken to exclude connections with England, for it requires no exceptional learning to see views which Jonson shares with Roman writers seeping into England from the twelfth century onwards. The notes to the poems in the Oxford edition of Jonson's works make it clear—although with an element of wishful thinking—that time and again his statements of moral attitudes are translations or close adaptations of statements by Roman writers, and, behind the particular links, there lies a more general resemblance of belief which demonstrates that Jonson was well aware of, and used, a number of Roman ethical attitudes. Verbally the links with Rome are far stronger than with other English writers, but this should not blind us to the fact that the attitudes which Jonson expresses in Roman terms remain ones already familiar in England: they do not in themselves isolate Jonson from his English environment at all. In fact, there are points in Jonson's ethic—in his view of the soul, his view of women, and his social outlook—for which Roman analogues are demonstrably incomplete and where English views have to be invoked in explaining the background to these points.

The point of this rapid and dogmatic statement of a complicated problem has been to suggest that Jonson cannot be termed "classical" because of what his ethical views were and thus to clear the way for a statement of what really is unusual about these views and an enquiry into the value, or otherwise, of this element of unusualness to his poetry.

If we compare Jonson's ethical position with those of other writers of his time three main things, I think, emerge: the actual ethical complex is unique, although none of its constituents is unusual; the consistency and coherence of the complex is unusual; and the centrality of ethical, as distinct from primarily religious, beliefs in the poetry is original. In a long and productive career Jonson's views changed remarkably little and, except for his views on woman, they all contribute to a coherent whole. His attitude to social organization depends upon an extension of the same principles which he sees as governing worthwhile personal relationships, and these in turn spring from the attributes which Jonson admires in individuals, while the concepts of the Golden Age and of degeneration, as well as his view of the soul, are used to support or illustrate aspects of these views. The resultant close-knit set of beliefs is, I think, unique: no other writer of the time has Jonson's complex of beliefs or holds ethical views with such firmness and constancy. Even Chapman, who at one time or another provides parallels for most of Jonson's views, changes his attitudes in the course in his career and reflects views which Jonson never held.

These distinctions lead to a more important one, the centrality of ethical beliefs in Jonson's poetry. It is frequently remarked that Jonson's religious verse lacks conviction and, although the point is often overstressed and misused, it is true that in general he has little feeling for transcendental aspects of Christianity—little sense of the great symbols of that faith, little interest in doctrine, little involvement with a personal God, and little concern with any aspect of supernatural power. Explanations are not necessary here, but it is important to note that this lack of transcendental religious feeling throws great weight upon the ethical beliefs themselves. Jonson's poetry is about Man as individual and social animal, about what Man should be and how he should behave. It is social and ethical poetry, and, since there is no strong feeling of supernatural control or of religious sanctions, the ethical views which Jonson holds must stand as valid and consistent in themselves, so that, as a result, the views become unusually prominent in their own right, lying at the heart of the poetry. How unusual this is can be briefly indicated. Except in "To Heaven" Jonson shows none of the specifically religious tension and involvement found in Donne or Herbert, and there is also a contrast between his satirical poetry and that of Skelton and Wyatt, where, although the attitudes are sometimes close to Jonson's, there is a strong religious framework. Nothing in his poetry and plays suggests any equivalent to the fascination with Heaven and Hell in Marlowe, or to that sense of the supernatural which informs so much Jacobean tragedy. Most Elizabethan and Jacobean writers show considerable interest in ethical matters, but, at the same time, they *feel* that the Christian God or some other supernatural agency overlooks, controls, and sanctions their ethical outlook, and their constant appeals to some such agency almost always carry more than conventional weight. What Jonson believed is not in question, but quite a lot of his unusualness is contained in his lack of interest in these aspects of religion and in the consequent weight placed on ethical views themselves.

By accident or deliberately Jonson's poetry shares this primarily ethical emphasis with Roman poets and philosophers and it is here that what we can usefully term "classicism" begins to emerge. There is, first of all, an undoubted similarity between Jonson and Roman writers in the prominence of ethical views in their work. Roman philosophy is mainly ethics, the only branch of the subject to which Rome made any really significant contributions, and the marked ethical emphasis in Seneca and Cicero is reflected not only in the philosopher/poet Lucretius, but also in Horace, Vergil, and Juvenal. The concern of Horace and Seneca, in particular, to find and apply standards for virtuous living represents an important facet of the greatness of Rome at her peak. But, and this is the second point, the relevant Roman poets (except Lucretius perhaps) are not ethical *thinkers*, in the philosophical sense, at all. Their views are largely derivative ones, expressed epigrammatically and used to sum up or comment upon the concrete experiences embodied in their vrse. Even in the formal philosophers there is little originality: Cicero and Seneca discuss conflicting views and select among them, but there is a reluctance to introduce any view which lacks Greek backing and an anxiety to find and hold to a system of principles which will guide their ordinary life. Seneca's letters are particularly good examples of the essentially practical nature of Roman ethics and the desire to refine ethical discussion to a set of commonplace, yet valid, *dicta*. The views which Horace holds are commonplaces, not because of vagueness or carelessness about ethical questions but because centuries of discussion and experience have led to their appearance as valid guidelines for human life. It is from this process of refinement that the compactness and assurance of Horace's ethical position come, and these are qualities which he shares with other Roman writers. Jonson . . . borrows Roman statements of ethical principles far more frequently and far more closely than any of his major contemporaries, and it is not surprising that his verse reflects the ethical certainty and centrality of his originals. Although Jonson's ethical statements almost always echo common English beliefs, the fact that they are so often translations or adaptations from Roman writers gives them a new distinctness and weight.

But we can, I think, take the matter one step further. Although Roman religious thought is a complex matter it is not unreasonable to claim that Roman civilization was not marked by real feeling for any religion which emphasized an afterlife, at the expense of the present, introduced a real connection between virtue and reward, or put forward a consistent and personal, yet still mysterious, deity. The Roman stress is upon earthly life and how to live it in the face of the fickleness of fate and the certainty of death. Far from reflecting the teaching of a deity and his prophets, Roman ethics is rather a defence against the arbitrariness, moral uncertainty, and general irrationality of the Roman pantheon. Even the oracles were consulted mainly about the earthly future and this emphasis upon earthly life is increased by the general belief that the only personal survival after death was the fame of a good name, a survival that would depend upon virtuous life and make it important to find the right ethical guidelines. This is something which goes far to explain Horace's and Seneca's concern with practical ethics: because of a lack of reasonable supernatural guidance, or because they were not concerned to seek such guidance, Roman poets and philosophers depend heavily upon the coherence and consistency of their ethical views *per se*. There is little sense of tablets handed down on Mount Sinai.

Jonson, of course, did not share this religious background. Many of his contemporaries felt that caprice was a feature of their lives, but this is seldom attributed to God. It is present because of Man's post-lapsarian weakness, or expresses an irrational force somehow independent of God, or is assimilated in references to pagan deities. Jonson alone shares with Roman writers their degree of emphasis upon earthly life, this lack of interest in the supernatural, and this belief that life must be organized upon self-coherent and self-sufficient ethical principles. So it is that, although Jonson's actual beliefs are within an English tradition, his emphasis upon them gives him a position of originality within that tradition and provides a significant link with Rome.

III

All this might be true, and yet Jonson's poetry might gain nothing valuable from it. There is, however, a consequence which I am tempted to see right at the point which Leavis stresses as one of Jonson's distinctive characteristics, his quality of "tough reasonableness." I should go beyond this to suggest a connection between the emphasis on practical ethics in Jonson and the linguistic feature of exclusion in his verse, a feature intimately bound up with the limitations in outlook which are the preconditions of Jonson's greatness.

"Tough reasonableness" is not always a feature of Jonson's work: occasionally one thinks more of "tough unreasonableness," but the ability to be both unsentimental and yet generously human marks his best poetry. We see it at its most generous and fullest imaginative embodiment in "To Penshurst" and "To Sir Robert Wroth," and again at full stretch in the less important but wonderfully human tribute to Shakespeare. But, in some ways, the achievement is most impressive in the epitaphs "On my first daughter" and "On my first Sonne" and in such poems about himself as the badly undervalued "Epistle Mendicant" and "My Picture Left in Scotland." To take a single example. "On my first Sonne" contains one of the most poignant endings I know in poetry: "For whose sake, hence-forth, all his vowes be such,/As what he loves may never like too much." Here the full charge of deep emotion which the poem contains (and I use that word in its fullest sense) and which has already put great pressure on the poet's self-control earlier, in "O, could I loose all father now," is given full expression. But what gives the ending this impact, and what has enabled Jonson to make something instead of merely indulging his strong and natural grief, is his ability to deploy a variety of technical devices to shape, control, and yet express, his grief. There is this sort of "toughness" in the pun on the boy's name in the first line, in the mercantile imagery (already a theological commonplace) in line three, in the mingled irony and word-play in the phrase "his best piece of poetry," and—above all perhaps—in the way in which traditional *consolatio* themes are tested and questioned by setting and rhythm, as well as in the use of Martial ("quidque ames, cupias non placuisse nimis") to give a framework of previous usage for the final statement of loss.

The connection which I would suggest between this quality and Jonson's emphasis upon practical ethics is not one which I find easy to clarify, let alone prove. But "tough reasonableness" indicates a strong secular element, a determination to give reason a full say, as well as the humanity to express sympathies in a balanced manner. Part of the strength of "On my first Sonne" comes from the way in which Jonson concentrates upon the earthly aspects of his son's death, for although the "lending" theme and the idea of death as an escape point outside earthly life, the poem is primarily focussed upon the human loss and questions of how this may best be coped with. Jonson examines *consolatio* themes with a telling mixture of desire to accept their consolation and uncertainty whether they can really be consoling: his *mind* is operating on conventional material and the inability merely to accept such material indicates some reservations of religious faith or, at least, an emphasis upon the human, individual, predicament—something which links Jonson with a common Renaissance stress, but which also leads back to the normal, humanist, emphasis of Jonson's poetry.

The further point at which this Jonsonian emphasis seems to be of real value in his poetry, is that it forms part of that limited created world which is Jonson's achievement as a poet. Here the point is a simple one, which I have argued elsewhere[3]: Jonson's achievement depends upon the restrictions of his world view. This world view is reached through the exclusion of important aspects of human experience, and depends upon the reduction of moral complexity to simplified clarity. A feature and tool of this simplification is a use of language in which association and paradox are reduced

3. In *Essays and Criticism* XVIII, No. 1.

to a minimum, in favor of precision and local meaning. All this points back to that firmness and assurance of ethical belief which lie at the heart of Jonson's poetry, for it is this firmness and assurance which enable Jonson to make impressive ethical distinctions, to erect a consistent standard of judgment, and to apply and embody the consequent view of life in his poetry. The kind of concentrated insight into aspects of humanity which is Jonson's enduring merit as a poet springs directly from the central position of ethical views in his verse.

L. A. BEAURLINE

The Selective Principle in Jonson's Shorter Poems†

I

Since art is a matter of choices, appreciation requires a knowledge of alternatives, and when we try to imagine the possible choices that lay before a poet, we can better understand his accomplishment. In other words, if appreciation is an act of imaginative sympathy, adequate criticism demands that we compare what a poet wrote with what he might have written. Such a comparison is important for a student of the shorter forms of poetry because the object that engages his attention is so small he may have trouble attuning himself to it. Whereas a play or a novel has the time to develop its own context, a short poem must depend most directly on the intuitions of the reader; a poet has much less immediate control over his reader's responses. Anyone who has read poetry from an anthology that conceals the dates and names of the writers understands what I mean. What might be very good William Morris would be bad William Wordsworth, and what is cliché in E. A. Robinson may be fresh language in Lord Tennyson. Therefore this desire to know the facts seems to be a perfectly legitimate motive: we want to know the proper context in which the poem lies. What are the author's special predilections, what was the conventional language of poetry of his time?

Ben Jonson's epigrams and songs are especially hard to bring before a modern reader because of their brevity. At the beginning of his "Epitaph on Elizabeth, L. H." he boasts of this quality— "Wouldst thou hear what man can say in little?"[1] The poems are

---

† From Criticism, a *Quarterly for Literature and the Arts*, Vol. VIII, No. 1, Winter, 1966, revised, March, 1972. Reprinted by permission of the author.

1. See Howard S. Babb, "The 'Epitaph on Elizabeth, L. H.,' and Ben Jonson's Style," *JEGP*, LXII (1963), 738–744.

often extremely simple and the circumstances of composition frequently unknown. Many of them as occasional poems fitted some particular moment and some particular relation that the speaker bears to the occasion, as Geoffrey Walton has observed.[2] But many of them can be brought within the range of our imaginative sympathy. Mr. Wesley Trimpi's *Ben Jonson's Poems: A Study of the Plain Style* (Stanford, 1962), goes a long way toward clarifying Jonson's predilection for a middle style, neither too high nor too low, a kind of epistolary style popular among learned writers on the continent, and transmitted to England by way of the Latin epistles of Justus Lipsius and Luis Vives. Mr. Trimpi also suggests that this style is appropriate to Jonson's poetic character of a "sincere" writer who emphasizes his personal involvement with his subject, who tells only the truth, in the most genuine language. Jonson aims for the normal word order of speech, flexibility in placing his caesura, and careful control of the connotations of words. But this does not tell us why we admire Jonson's greatest lyrics, nor why we find Jonson a master craftsman of some of the most fragile poems in the language. R. S. Walker, quite rightly, explained it in terms of Jonson's ideal of form or design for its own sake;[3] however I think it is more than a taste for design, and certainly Jonson believed that a poem has to "mean" as well as "be." The principles of selection, rejection, subduing and heightening, in order to affect meaning, to project thoughts and feelings—these bring us closer to the ineffable grace of Jonson's best verse. These principles can be shown to have prevailed in several aspects of his poetry: in choice of literary form, in adaptation from his sources, and in metrics.

As an example of form, we might look at the epigram "On my First Sonne," a frequently anthologized poem. We get an idea of the events that Jonson might have recounted from the story he told Drummond.

> When the King came in England, at that tyme the Pest was in London, he being in the Country at Sir Robert Cottons house with old Cambden, he saw in a vision his eldest sone (then a child and at London) appear unto him with the Marke of a bloodie crosse on his forehead as if it had been cutted with a suord, at which amazed he prayed unto God, and in the morning he came to Mr. Cambdens chamber to tell him, who persuaded him it was but an apprehension of his fantasie at which he sould not be disjected. In the mean tyme comes ther letters from his wife of the death of that Boy in the plague. he appeared to him

2. *Metaphysical to Augustan* (London, 1955), pp. 23–44.
3. "Ben Jonson's Lyric Poetry," *Criterion*, XIII (1933–34), 430–448. David Wykes' essay "Ben Jonson's 'Chast Book' —the *Epigrammes*," *Renaissance and Modern Studies*, XIII (1969), 76–87, is the best analysis of the design of the epigrams, especially of Jonson's use of people's names for striking effects.

he said of a Manlie shape and of that Grouth that he thinks he shall be at the resurrection.[4]

Almost none of that experience reappears in the poem: nothing of the vision, the cross on young Benjamin's forehead, nor Camden's friendly comfort. Apparently the poem was written after the boy was buried, and by that time Jonson was more concerned with his feelings as a mourning father than he was with the miraculous vision. Only one detail has any possible association with the poem: the mature shape in which his son appeared, "of that Grouth that he thinks he shall be at the resurrection." This curious detail may express in another way Jonson's high hopes for his son, his "too much hope" mentioned in the second line of the poem. But it is questionable, especially because theologians commonly remarked that the risen body would be in its perfect or mature state on judgment day. If the anecdote were made into a poem, it would probably have been more amazing than sad; Jonson committed himself to a funeral poem rather than a miraculous tale or dramatic lyric.

The poem that he finally wrote is remarkably subdued, conventional, and low-pressure; it contains many straightforward, prosy statements in plain words, and few images or bold touches. It implies more than it includes. It is extremely neat; yet it expresses powerful feelings. The very neatness of its design is a part of the discipline of the speaker's feelings.

An early seventeenth-century poet probably would not have thought about "disciplining" his feelings; he would speak of "curing" them, reducing an excess of feelings, which amounts to much the same thing. But again there was a choice: he could cure an excess of sorrow by the Galenic or Paracelsian method. Puttenham observed that the Galenists cured "with any medicament of a contrary temper"; the Paracelsians cured by "making one dolour to expell another."[5] To freely pour forth one's grief in formal lamentation "was a very necessary devise of the Poet and a fine, besides his poetrie to play also the Phisitian, and not onely by applying a medicine to the ordinary sickness of mankind, but by making the very greef it selfe (in part) cure of the disease."[6] Puttenham's remarks imply that the long elegy cures in the Paracelsian manner, but the funeral epigram cannot be expected to work in the same way. It is too brief and pithy. A truly Galenic cure would probably express joy at the death of a son, but Jonson does not do this either. It seems significant, however, that he tries to achieve the feeling opposite grief, and I think that much of the force of the poem

4. *Ben Jonson*, C. H. Herford and Percy Simpson, eds. (Oxford, 1925–52), I, 139–140. All subsequent quotations are from this edition, except that I have modernized u, v, j, i, and long s.
5. *The Arte of English Poesie*, Gladys Willcock and Alice Walker, eds. (Cambridge, 1936), p. 50. George Williamson called my attention to this suggestive remark.
6. Puttenham, p. 47.

comes from his struggles to achieve the proper feelings—the right kind of love. He grieves as a father, but knows that he should rejoice as a Christian.

> Farewell, thou child of my right hand, and joy;
>   My sinne was too much hope of thee, lov'd boy,
> Seven years tho 'wert lent to me, and I thee pay,
>   Exacted by thy fate, on the just day.
> O, could I loose all father, now. For why
>   Will man lament the state he should envie?
> To have so soone scap'd worlds, and fleshes rage,
>   And, if no other miserie, yet age?
> Rest in soft peace, and, ask'd, say here doth lye
>   BEN. JONSON his best piece of *poetrie.*
> For whose sake, hence-forth, all his vowes be such,
>   As what he loves may never like too much.

Like most epigrams, each detail in the poem leads to the brilliant climax, where the essence of his thought is pressed into a few words, here a little epitaph. The climax is a daring conceit, a strikingly appropriate understatement that reveals a depth of feeling seldom attributed to Jonson. After paraphrasing the formula *Requiescat in pace,* he begins the inscription with an equally conventional *hic jacet.* The neat trick is the implied pun on "maker"—to have a pun on a word that does not even appear in the poem. As the poet has traditionally been known as a maker, so the best piece of poetry that Jonson made was his son. No man was more proud of his verse than Ben Jonson; only Pope comes close to Jonson's habitual self-approbation. This is, therefore, Jonson's great effort to be humble, and he was least likely to be humble about his poetry. Then, for the sake of his dead son he takes an oath not to be too self-satisfied, too pleased with what he loves in the future. Jonson cogently restates a passage from Martial's Epigram VI. xxix, *Quidquid amas, cupias non placuisse nimis*; hence he means to have a distinction between *love* and *like* in the last line: "As what he loves may never like too much." Modern readers have difficulty at this point because the word *like* has changed in meaning since the seventeenth century. Most readers think that *like* is a weaker form of love, and they imagine that Jonson ends with a cynical turn of thought: he vows he'll not love as intensely in the future because he has lost his son. But such a reading destroys the movement of the poem. His sin was too much hope for his son—too much pride for young Benjamin, son of his right hand—not too much love. He had too much stock in the boy's success in this world, and possibly he was "making" the boy over in his own image.

The older meaning of *like, to please,* was common in Jonson's time, and his contemporaries would have understood as they did

Tamburlaine, who said, "I'll dispose them as it likes me best,"[7] or as Jonson said in the prologue to *The Devil is an Ass*, "If this play doe not like, the Divel is in't." Therefore I think the line means nearly the same as Martial's line: whatever he loves may never please him too much, may never be the object of self-congratulation. And as a Christian his love has been disciplined to God's will so that it should never be smug or selfish love. Such a simple remark rings with eloquence and high style, not the high style of elaborate ornament or rotund sentences, but the eloquence that resides in the speaker's ethos, his depth of conviction and integrity, when a poet and father is thoroughly honest with himself.[8]

By contrast the metaphor in the first quatrain does not seem so emphatic; it is a commonplace of borrowing and paying back, so it is enough to make the point. The occasion does not call for a desperate or hyperbolic or pretty metaphor. Anything but an ordinary illustrative comparison would intrude here. Its appropriateness comes from its place in the burial ceremony: "the Lord gave, and the Lord hath taken away." But at the moment in the poem when he has to make his point vigorously, he uses a fresh and vivid image, "here doth lye BEN. JONSON his best piece of *poetrie*."

This image is apt and striking at this particular point, for indirectly this is another expression of Jonson's pride. Just as he was too proud of his son, now he sees that he is too proud of his poetry—another worldly thing that he has been excessively pleased with. Therefore with his son he buries his highest aspirations to worldly fame. Another possibility concerns the muse of poetry, who like God confers the gift of expression, but who may take the gift away if it is misused. Whatever interpretation we choose, the image represents Jonson's chastened feelings.

The other striking passage in the poem has no metaphor: "O, could I loose all father, now." (Since *lose* and *loose* were spelling doublets, there is no new significance in the reading *lose* from the 1640 folio.) The statement is not entirely flat, of course, because *father* is not meant literally. He means that he wishes he could lose the feelings of a father—a direct exclamation, reduced to the fewest possible words.

The poem is indeed one of the "ripest of his studies," as Jonson said of all his Epigrams. All the words are simple and every word counts. The poem is difficult because it is condensed. Although the feelings are intense, they are expressed in plain language. The sub-

---

7. *Tamburlaine* Part II,IV.ii. 91; Irving Ribner's edition, *The Complete Plays of Christopher Marlowe* (New York, 1963).

8. The right kind of love is, of course, charity. W. David Kay, in "The Christian Wisdom of Ben Jonson's 'On My First Sonne'," *SEL*, XI (1971), 125–136, cites Augustine on the need to enjoy a person for his own sake, not using him; that is,

to love a person in God. But St. Bernard seems even more relevant, in *On the Love of God*, secs. 17 and 36–38, where he distinguishes between mercenary love and love of the soul for the sake of God. By the law of charity we subordinate our selfish gratifications and pride to the will of God, and thus we have no fear of the body's death.

dued tone is nicely appropriate to the restraint he is exercising over himself. In commemorating his best piece of poetry he wrote one of his best poems.

His choice of the elegy form probably depended upon its subject; he could have written a formal elegy that would have required the elevated style of formal public utterance, such as his ode on the death of Sir H. Morison; the pastoral elegy would have involved the elaborate artifice of Spenser's "Astrophel" or Milton's "Lycidas," neither of them writ in the language such as men do use. Instead he turned to the personal form of the epitaph. He still had considerable leeway. Scaliger had said that epitaphs usually have five parts: "Praise, demonstration of loss, lamentation, consolation, and exhortation."[9] Puttenham was not altogether clear about the epitaph, but he is worth consulting because Ben Jonson owned a copy of *The Arte* that survives in the British Museum. Puttenham, in one passage, restricts the content of an epitaph to "the report of the dead persons estate and degree, or of his other good or bad partes, to his commendation or reproch: an inscription such as a man may commodiously write or engrave upon a tombe in a few verses, pithie, quicke and sententious . . . if it exceede the measure of an Epigram, it is then . . . rather an Elegie then an Epitaph."[1] He does not mention lamentation as a part of an epitaph, but when he discusses the elegy, Puttenham makes lamentation the principal part. If a long epitaph is equivalent to an elegy and an elegy is a lamentation, then you would think that an epitaph contains an expression of grief too. Certainly the Greek Anthology and the epigrams of Martial offered models of epitaphs of that sort.

Jonson's practice suggests that he thought a short funeral poem could contain any one or combination of the ingredients of an elegy. In his epitaph on Salamon Pavy he limits himself to praise of the dead. In the epitaph on Elizabeth L. H., he praises and consoles. "On my First Sonne" is a kind of leave-taking and lament. There is not much about a seven year old boy that can be held up for public praise, only a father's hopes. Consolation is hard to find when you mourn a first son. Jonson tried to find consolation but his attempts to comfort himself merely dramatize his grief.

II

Jonson's ideal in poetry was fitness or propriety—appropriate thoughts in appropriate language, appropriate to the occasion and subject. His own standard allows us to differentiate between Jonson's kind of funeral poem and Donne's: Donne was much less

9. A full account of these conventions may be found in O. B. Hardison's *The Enduring Monument* (Chapel Hill, 1962), pp. 113–115, and in A. L. Bennett's "The Principal Rhetorical Conventions of the Renaissance Elegy," *SP*, LI (1954), 107–125.

1. Puttenham, p. 56.

concerned with propriety; it did not matter to him whether Elizabeth Drury deserved fulsome lament or whether her death could suitably be compared to the disorder and decay of the cosmos. He was eager to follow his thoughts wherever they went; Elizabeth Drury is chiefly an excuse for a display of brilliance. George Williamson's essay on the context of the Anniversaries has recently clarified Donne's side of the contrast,[2] but we need to see Jonson's side more clearly. Jonson's acid comment defines his notion of appropriateness: he said to Drummond "that Donnes Anniversarie was profane and full of Blasphemies[.] that he told Mr Donne, if it had been written of ye Virgin Marie it had been something" (I, 133). A passage in *Timber*, adapted from Quintilian, is more general in its attack on bold and hyperbolic writing:

> Indeed, the multitude commend Writers, as they doe Fencers, or Wrastlers: who if they come in robustiously, and put for it, with a deal of violence, are received for the *braver-fellowes*: when many times their owne rudeness is a cause of their disgrace; and a slight touch of their Adversary, gives all that boisterous force the foyle. But in these things, the unskilfull are naturally deceiv'd and judging wholly by the bulke, thinke rude things greater then polish'd; and scatter'd more numerous, then compos'd: Nor thinke this only to be true in the sordid multitude, but the neater sort of our *Gallants*: for all are the multitude: only they differ in cloaths, not in judgment or understanding. (VIII, 538)

"The slight touch" of a skillful fencer fascinates Jonson, and it suggests the kind of expertise that he aimed for. Such perfection had a surprising moral tinge also, for he praises the brief life of H. Morison as if it were a perfect poem. After asking what is the "measure of a good life, he replies, punningly, that it is "ample, full, and round,/In weight, in measure, number, sound."

> Life doth her great actions spell,
> By what was done and wrought
> In season, and so brought
> To light: her measures are, how well
> Each syllab'e answer'd, and was form'd, how faire;
> These make the lines of life, and that's her ayre.

Since Morison died young, he was like a day lily, the flower of light. "In small proportions, we just beauties see/And in short measures, life may perfect bee" (VIII, 244–245). Like the epigram on his first son, the best thing he can say about a short life is that it has the virtues of a good poem.

These bold writers, on the other hand, "utter all they can thinke, with a kind of violence, and *indisposition*; unexamin'd without relation, either to person, place, or any fitnesse else" (VIII, 586). Its

---

opposite, Jonson's ideal of propriety, lies not in copiousness or vociferation but in wisdom in "dividing," subtility in arguing, strength with which the author inspires his readers, sweetness with which he "strokes them," and most important of all, manliness of expression (VIII, 588). Like a good athlete, a poet has to exercise, and like a gymnast his performance is measured by the force and control of his movements.

Jonson objected to the breach of decorum in the Anniversaries because Elizabeth Drury did not deserve the fantastic praise Donne gave her. Puttenham made the same point in distinguishing further between an elegy and an epitaph: "the Poet in praising the maner of life or death of anie meane person, [does] it by some little dittie or Epigram or Epitaph in fewe verses & meane stile conformable to his subject"; only great princes or heroic personages deserve larger poems in the high style. And "in everie degree and sort of men vertue is commendable, but not egally: not onely because mens estates are unegall, but for that also vertue it selfe is not in every respect of egail value and estimation."[3]

It is possible to exaggerate the differences between Donne's manner and Jonson's, for we should remember that Jonson especially praised Donne for his talent in writing epigrams, and apparently respected Donne's literary judgment: he sent his epigrams to Donne for censure (see Epigram xcvi). He cast Donne in the role of "Criticus" in his lost preface to observations on Horace's *Art of Poetry*. Nevertheless there is a useful contrast between the characteristic work of the two poets. Donne is usually bold, copious, farfetched, witty and obscure. Jonson, in writing epigrams, aims for brevity, propriety, restraint, "manliness," and clarity.

III

The much admired "Drink to me only with thine eyes" illustrates Jonson's method of adapting a source, in a case where at first glance he seems extraordinarily unoriginal. It has long been recognized and frequently rediscovered that this perfect lyric was pieced together from sentences in five different Love Letters of Philostratus (numbers 33, 34, 2, 60, and 46). Although similar thoughts occur in other ancient writers, only Philostratus contains this combination of material. However Jonson's synthesis is not just an aggregation or a completed jigsaw puzzle, as the source hunters often imply, because, although no detail is original, the whole poem is strikingly different from its sources. It is instructive to read each of the relevant letters in its entirety and to read the nearby letters in a similar vein, to see what Jonson sheared off. Three letters address a girl (in one she is a wench at an inn), two address a pretty boy. They

3. Puttenham, pp. 44, 42.

abound with sensuous details: cheeks the color of wine, eyes more translucent than drinking cups, praise of the way the girl carries her glass in her delicate hand, and outlandish conceits such as "You seem to me to give men drink from your eyes as if they were fountains." He sent the boy a gift of roses, and the boy literally slept on them, so the speaker asks that the roses be returned, for they will truly "smell of you"! The whole group of letters is rather sordid and prosy, perhaps a cut above the average men's magazine today.

Jonson suppressed all these irrelevancies and put the emphasis on three little courtesies: silent and secret pledging, passing the cup, and sending or receiving a gift. In each case he has carefully excluded any implications that his beloved returns his affections. He worships from afar, and on the face of it she may be either indifferent or hostile. We might paraphrase the first request, to bring out implications not in Philostratus: "If you will not admit openly that you love, at least pledge with your eyes." I do not suppose that she gratifies his desires here, because he then is willing to settle for less, and at the place on the cup where she has touched her lips, he will place his, imagining that she has left a kiss for him. The support for these suggestions comes from the last two stanzas, where again he shows that he tried to make a compliment out of a rebuff. Apparently the girl did not accept his rosy wreath, the symbol of his love; she did not even touch it, much less sleep on it, but the determined lover chooses self-deception, imagining that the wreath smells not of itself but her; hence it seems to him a token of her affection returned. I believe that much of the delicacy of the poem resides in these subtleties, expressed in precise "short measures" to create a "just beauty," wholly unlike the crude sensuality of Philostratus.

A final example, from the third stanza of "Charis her Triumph," illustrates Jonson's powers of calculated art in the minutest details of meter. It is not probable that Jonson automatically fell into regular rhythms or that he lisped in numbers, for we have his testimony that, following Master Camden's advice, he wrote his poems first in prose and then shaped the meter, and early drafts of several poems survive in manuscript showing extensive metrical experimentation. (Camden's advice sounds significantly a reversal of Sidney's suggestion in *An Apology for Poetry* to find whether contemporary poems had any "sinews": one should translate them into prose, i.e. remove the ornaments, if a poem has no meaning, it is proof that "one verse did but beget another, with out ordering at the first what should be last; which becomes a confused masse of words, with a tingling sound of ryme, barely accompanied with reason."[4]) Mr.

4. *An Apology for Poetry*, in *Elizabethan Critical Essays*, ed. G. G. Smith (Ox-   ford, 1904), I, 196.

Trimpi noticed that the rhythm of "Charis her Triumph" is lilting and the feet are often trisyllabic, but I think the cause of the lilt lies in the deliberate alterations of tempo. The first, third, fifth, and following lines depend upon regularly spaced long vowels, separated by two short syllables. Hence these lines move in grand measure, like a stately dance,

> Hăve yoŭ sēēne bŭt ă brīght Lĭllĭe grōw

counterpointed by the iambic stress-time rhythm of the second and fourth lines:

> Befŏre rŭde hánds hăve tóuch'd ĭt.[5]

The feminine rhyme, used quite sparingly in his poems and always for deliberate effect in order to achieve a light touch, contributes to the quickness of the iambic lines. The result is a movement of slow line, fast line, slow, fast, slow, slow, slow, slow, slow, capped by very slow final line, where we expect the iambic rhythm to reassert itself. Instead, Jonson shaped it into a synthesis of quantity and stress:

> Ō sō whíte! Ō sō sóft! Ō sō swéet is shē.

He put the stresses on the short syllables at the beginning, and, at the last, finally brought length and stress together on the most important word of the poem.

As the metrical pattern synthesizes here, so does the thought; this line draws together the several aspects of beauty that were scattered in the previous lines. She is the epitome of all the beauties of the natural world, an archetype; beauties causes sleep in her. A *tour de force* such as this is a fusion of thought and technique that characterizes the highest art.

STEPHEN ORGEL

[Images of Heroic Virtue in Jonson's Poetry]†

Jonsonian drama presents no image of heroic virtue; but the poetry of the *Epigrammes*, *The Forrest*, and *The Underwood* celebrates numerous figures who have, like Hercules, made the exemplary

---

5. The contemporary musical setting, attributed to Robert Johnson, corresponds to my metrical analysis as far as the quantitative measure goes, except for the last line, where the anapestic feet are maintained:

♩ ♫ : O so whyte O so soft O so sweet

♩ ♪
is shee

Printed in *La Musique de Scène de la troupe de Shakespeare: the King's Men, sous le règne de Jacques I*[er], John P. Cutts, ed. (Paris, 1959), pp. 54–56.

† From *The Jonsonian Masque* (Cambridge, Mass., 1965).

choice and stand as models to mankind. It is, in fact, in this world and with this kind of heroic potential that the mature Jonsonian masque leaves us. The heroes of Jonson's poetry are—sometimes literally—simply masques unmasked. Lady Mary Wroth, a nymph in *The Masque of Blacknesse*, thus becomes a prototype of womanly virtue, capable of replacing the traditional sources of poetic inspiration:

> Madame, had all antiquitie beene lost,
> All historie seal'd up, and fables crost;
> That we had left us, nor by time, nor place,
> Least mention of a *Nymph*, a *Muse*, a *Grace*,
> But even their names were to be made a-new,
> Who could not but create them all, from you?[1]

Jonson then presents her, appropriately disguised, as several mythological figures:

> He, that but saw you wear the wheaten hat,
> Would call you more than CERES, if not that:
> And, drest in shepheards tyre, who would not say:
> You were the bright OENONE, FLORA, or *May*?
> If dancing, all would cry th'*Idalian* Queene,
> Were leading forth the *Graces* on the greene:
> And, armed to the chase, so bare her bow
> DIANA'alone, so hit, and hunted so.
> There's none so dull, that for your stile would aske,
> That saw you put on PALLAS plumed caske:
> Or, keeping your due state, that would not cry,
> There JUNO sate, and yet no Peacock by.
> So are you *Natures Index*, and restore,
> I'your selfe, all treasure lost of th'age before.

Here, as in the masque, the disguise is only an expression of the inner reality. It is what establishes the figure as a valid symbol, making of the heroine "Natures Index," in whom all the lost virtues are preserved. But at the same time, the disguise also serves to convey those virtues to a world of spectators, and thereby to recreate in the present the heroism of the past.

Similarly, to the Countess of Bedford—another nymph in the masques of *Blacknesse* and *Beautie* and a queen in *The Masque of Queenes*—Jonson not only gives all the social graces, but allows her to be untouched by the vicissitudes of sublunary life:

> a learned, and a manly soule
> I purpos'd her; that should, with even powers,
> The rock, the spindle, and the sheeres controule
> Of destinie, and spin her owne free houres.

---

1. Epigram CV [*Editor*].

Sir William Roe, returning from a journey, has the character of a classic hero:

> This is that good AENEAS, past through fire,
> Through seas, stormes, tempests: and imbarqu'd for hell,
> Came back untouch'd.

And Sir Lucius Cary and Sir Henry Morison, in the great ode written near the end of Jonson's career, become explicit heroic examples in a world that barely makes room for virtue:

> You liv'd to be the great surnames,
> And titles, by which all made claimes
> Unto the Vertue. Nothing perfect done,
> But as a CARY, or a MORISON.
> And such a force the faire example had,
> As they that saw
> The good, and durst not practise it, were glad
> That such a Law
> Was left yet to Man-kind.

Such figures fill the poems, safeguarding the classic truths in a society that has forgotten them. They embody the ideals of the masque in settings that suggest the plays.

There is one particularly striking instance where the masque itself is included in Jonson's poetic vision. In the epistle to Sir Robert Wroth, the hero's moral choice is seen in the traditional terms of the rejection of a court world for a pastoral idyll:

> How blest art thou, canst love the countrey, WROTH,
>   Whether by choice, or fate, or both;
> And, though so neere the citie, and the court,
>   Art tane with neithers vice, nor sport.   (lines 1–4)

Here, ironically, the masque, reduced to its most momentary and spectacular aspects, exemplifies the vices of society, and provides a center for Jonson's satiric comment:

> Nor throng'st (when masquing is) to have a sight
>   Of the short braverie of the night;
> To view the jewells, stuffes, the paines, the wit
>   There wasted, some not paid for yet!
> But canst, at home, in thy securer rest,
>   Live, with un-bought provision blest.   (lines 9–14)

The poem then modulates into the richness of a pastoral landscape, equally artificial, but also fruitful and lasting:

> Among'st the curled woods, and painted meades,
>   Through which a serpent river leades
> To some coole, courteous shade, which he calls his,
>   And makes sleepe softer then it is! . . .

The whil'st, the severall seasons thou has seene
    Of flowrie fields, of cop'ces greene,
The mowed meddowes, with the fleeced sheepe,
    And feasts, that either shearers keepe;
The ripened eares, yet humble in their height,
    And furrows laden with their weight;
The apple-harvest, that doth longer last;
    The hogs return'd home fat from mast;
The trees cut out in log; and those boughes made
    A fire now, that lent a shade!   (lines 17–46)

Here, within the pastoral world, the masque is summoned up again.
Now it is an expression of order and bounty, and it relates the
virtuous man to whatever is mythical and divine:

COMUS puts in, for new delights;
And fills thy open hall with mirth, and cheere,
    As if in SATURNES raigne it were;
APOLLO's harpe, and HERMES lyre resound,
    Nor are the *Muses* strangers found:
The rout of rurall folke come thronging in,
    (Their rudeness then is thought no sinne)
Thy noblest spouse affords them welcome grace;
    And the great *Heroes*, of her race,
Sit mixt with losse of state, or reverence.   (lines 48–57)

The hosts have, with the entrance of the gods, become a race of
heroes. Comus is not a villain in this setting, and the appearance of
"the rout of rurall folk"—like the cook's antimasque of sailors in
Neptunes Triumph—is here "thought no sinne." In fact, both appetite and rudeness, natural simplicity and good humor, belong to
this life. It is the city (on which the masque is "wasted," a mere
diversion) that denies and destroys what is human, and from which
nature is excluded:

Let this man sweat, and wrangle at the barre,
    For every price, in every jarre,
And change possessions, oftner with his breath,
    Then either money, warre, or death:
Let him, then hardest sires, more disinherit,
    And each where boast it as his merit,
To blow up orphanes, widdowes, and their states;
    And thinke his power doth equall *Fates*.
Let that goe heape a masse of wretched wealth,
    Purchas'd by rapine, worse then stealth,
And brooding o're it sit, with broadest eyes,
    Not doing good, scarce when he dyes.
Let thousands more goe flatter vice, and winne,
    By being organes to great sinne,
Get place, and honor, and be glad to keepe
    The secrets, that shall breake their sleepe:

And, so they ride in purple, eate in plate,
Though poyson, thinke it a great fate.

(lines 73–90)

This might be an anthology of evils from Jonsonian comedy and
represents the realities with which the hero is faced. But the hero,
in such poems as this, has a more evident and more important kind
of reality even than the world of Jonson's satire: he has the reality
of the masquer, the nobleman beneath the symbolic disguise, who
is capable of learning, choosing, and acting. It is such figures, steadfast in a world of vice, misrule, and decay, who provide the links
between the ideal vision of Jonsonian masque and the satiric vision
of Jonsonian drama.

RONALD BERMAN

Herrick's Secular Poetry[†]

The bed is ready, and the maze of Love
Lookes for the treaders; every where is wove
Wit and new misterie; read, and
Put in practise, to understand
And know each wile.
Each hieroglyphick of a kisse or smile;
And do it to the full; reach
High in your own conceipt, and some way teach
Nature and Art, one more
Play, then they ever knew before.[1]

In these lines from 'a Nuptiall Song' there are some concepts
central to Herrick's poetry. The 'hieroglyphick' character of the
verse is perhaps no less marked than that of Herbert, although a
different idea of form is dominant.[2] I think it may be helpful to
acknowledge the extended meaning of these lines, to find in them a

[†] From *English Studies*, LII (1971), 20–29.
1. This and succeeding quotations from *The Poems of Robert Herrick*, ed. L. C. Martin (London, 1965).
2. See Joseph Summers, 'The Poem as Hieroglyph'. *George Herbert: His Religion And Art* (Cambridge, Mass., 1954), pp. 123–4: 'A hieroglyph is "a figure, device, or sign having some hidden meaning; a secret or enigmatical symbol; an emblem". In the Renaissance, "hieroglyph", "symbol", "device", and "figure" were often used interchangeably. Because of special meanings which have become associated with the other words, "hieroglyph" seems more useful than the others today, and even in the seventeenth century it was often considered the most inclusive term. "Hieroglyphic", the older form of the noun, was derived from the Greek for "sacred carving", and the root usually retained something of its original religious connotation. Ralph Cudworth used it in its generally accepted meaning when he said in a sermon. "The Death of Christ . . . Hieroglyphically instructed us that we ought to take up our Cross likewise, and follow our crucified Lord and Saviour" '. I use the term in its extended sense, although Herrick, like Herbert, sometimes confines himself to a visual hieroglyph of which 'The *pillar of Fame*', the last poem of *Hesperides*, is an example.

general sense of the art of poetry and some particular reflections on its craft. For the poet, no less than the participants in the rite, finds in the scene before him a moralized form of experience. In effect the poem is an instruction to the imagination.

It is not simply that the bed is 'the maze of Love' and therefore offers to the newly married couple all the pleasures of discovery; it is one of those objects in Herrick's poetical world existing in metaphorical as well as literal circumstances. It suggests both a dance and a labyrinth and invokes the emotions connected with each. The latter is a figure particularly suitable for the writer who does not have available the novelistic form to express those complications of feeling and moments of discovery native to passion. The labyrinth, in short, might well be the most condensed psychological statement we could make about that passion, whether it is used in the poetry of Herrick and Donne or, eventually, in Proust's description of Swann in love. But there is an indirect function of Herrick's language which we ought to recognize. The bed as labyrinth or maze is a 'hieroglyphick' which takes the form of 'Wit' and 'conceipt' while it intimates the presence of 'misterie'. As such, it is an indication that Herrick's poetry, composed in a far more tightly structured intellectual world than ours, depends on the recognition that all things are related and exist in correspondence to each other. As Herrick suggests, 'every where' there are such signs. The business of the poet, no less than that of the lovers, is to 'read, and/Put in practise, to understand'. There are two contexts, of course, for this interpretation. The immediate context is the maze of love in which a rite of initiation into a highly specific mystery is about to proceed.[3] I am, with the permission of the reader, more concerned with extrapolating this: everywhere in nature there are such figures. Indeed, if there were no general sense of this then the immediate sense could have neither intellectual nor imagistic conviction. We 'read' this figure, as we do all of nature, as if it were part of a great and intelligible tapestry.

Probably one of our most current errors is to read Herrick's erotic poetry as if it were composed in the twentieth century. These lyrics to Anthea, Julia and Corinna are not simply erotic but contain meanings ranging from the innocent to the sensual. The kiss that is so often mentioned and the love that is so often implied in these poems are the subjects of a complex attitude. In its occasional con-

3. In explaining Milton's 'Rites/Mysterious of connubial Love' (*Paradise Lost*, Book IV, lines 742–3) Merrit Hughes states 'He calls it *mysterious* because St. Paul calls marriage "a great mystery" (Ephes. v. 32), and in *Colasterion* (C. E. IV. 263) he rebuts an objection to his description of marriage as "a mystery of joy"'. Hexameral literature was full of eulogies of marriage, a fair example of which is a speech of Joseph to Potiphar in Joseph Beaumont's *Psyche* I, 203–6:

Except the venerable Temples, what
  Place is more reverend than the
  Nuptial Bed?
Nay, heav'n has made a Temple too
  of that
For Chastitie's most secret rites . . .

In *John Milton Complete Poems and Major Prose* (New York, 1957), p. 295.

text the 'hieroglyphick of a kisse' stands for the feelings the lovers
have for each other, for the innumerable nuances of their relationship. It may also be a sign of something else: the dualistic character
of that relationship. To an age that pondered the meaning of 'Her
lips suck forth my soul' no act could remain *simply* sensual. If the
kiss is a 'hieroglyphick' it stands not only for the infinite variations
of human feeling but for a relationship that could only be theologi-
cally considered. The ethics of Augustine's *On Marriage and
Concupiscence* and *The City of God*, which I take to be those
accepted by Protestant humanism in Herrick's age, and practiced in
his profession, insist on the dual meaning of the sensate human
relationship. Reinhold Niebuhr writes of the parallelism between
Augustinian, Thomist and Lutheran thought on this subject:

> Whatever Augustine may say about the passions of flesh and
> however morbidly he may use sex as the primary symbol of such
> passions, his analyses always remain within terms of this general
> statement [Paul's epistle to the Romans]. He never regards sensu-
> ality as a natural fruit of man's animal nature. . . . Though St.
> Thomas defines original sin as concupiscence he still insists that
> concupiscence is a consequence of self-love: 'Every sinful act
> proceeds from inordinate desire of a mutable good. Now the fact
> that some one desires a temporal good inordinately is due to the
> fact that he loves himself inordinately'.
> The Lutheran interpretation does not differ materially from the
> Thomistic one, except that Luther eliminates the implicit Aristo-
> telian emphasis upon reason as master of the body. . . . Sensuality
> is, in effect, the inordinate love for all creaturely and mutable
> values which results from the primal love of self, rather than love
> of God.[4]

All this undeniably seems like a heavy if not intolerable burden to
lay upon a love lyric. But, when we see a Protestant minister writing
fairly complex poetry about sensuality, and when this poetry invites
us to make figural comparisons, we may suspect that the overtones
will range from the sensual to the sinful. The lovers in this and and
other poems of the *Hesperides* rejoice in their innocent sensuality,
but, as Milton was so well to depict, that state of sensual innocence
was long behind us. In all the *Hesperides* poems there is a highly
intellectual opposition or tension between the sensual life and the
Christian view of that life. I think it an error to conceive of Herrick's
eroticism as mediated by pagan *weltschmerz*; he is, however, very
much concerned with the play of values between eternal and earthly
love.

The 'hieroglyphick of a kisse' is, I suggest, a figure of love which

4. Reinhold Niebuhr, 'Sin as Sensuality', York, 1955), pp. 231–2.
The Nature and Destiny of Man (New

is beautiful, full of pleasure, as innocent as is humanly possible—yet it is fundamentally sensual and subject to the imperatives of fallen love. It is transitory where eternal love, by definition, is not; it is sensate where eternal love is contemplative; it is concupiscent where eternal love is selfless. It may symbolize the higher form of love, but never attains it.

Herrick could not have avoided the knowledge that love in general and the figure of the kiss in particular were the natural subjects of religious inquiry. He is aware, it would seem, of the dual meanings implied by the situation of the lovers: they experience the pleasurable nuances of emotion and sensation inherent in earthly love while that love is illuminated—and shadowed—by the light of eternity. As in much of the *Hesperides* the impulse to involve oneself in the sensate life, which is that life most real to us, is counterbalanced by the impulse to 'read' that life in all its connections to the created world. Neither the 'hieroglyphick of a kisse' nor the poem is entirely innocent. The passion signified by that kiss, however, is part of what Herrick calls the 'confusion' of love: his obvious pleasure in the erotic feelings and painterly attitudes of his lovers is qualified by the knowledge that they represent earthly love. If, like Titian's great picture of profane Love, they sum up all the beauty of the painterly imagination, then like that picture they intimate a hierarchy of values. Profane Love, we recall, is in itself incomplete—it is only half of a canvas.

Herrick was probably no less aware than Burton of the particular 'hieroglyphick' character of sensual love—he would have had to go no further than *Dr. Faustus* for its character. If Burton and his library of authorities[5] see in the kiss the unqualified signature of fallen sexuality, however, Herrick proposes a more subtle argument. The kiss is an acknowledgement of transcendence. It may in fact

---

5. The *Anatomy of Melancholy* has this moralistic summation: 'The soul and all is moved: with the shock of many kisses, saith Petronius, the lips ache, and breaths are mixt breathlessly, and in the stress of mutual embraces the soul is at its last gasp:

—Hotly cleaving each to each,
And by each other's eager lips
transpierced,
Your souls will stray: such lovers
may ye be.
(Petronius)

They breathe out their souls and spirits together with their kisses, saith Balthasar Castilio, change hearts and spirits, and mingle affections, as they do kisses, and it is rather a connexion of the mind than of the body'. One is tempted to remark that they did those things better in the seventeenth century. But it is of course not the psychology that is central to Burton's meaning, although that is, I think, acute and authentic: it is the immanence of the kiss which matters in this context. It is a visible 'sign' of fallen sensuality, if we are to follow Burton's argument to its conclusion: 'If, as Peter de Ledesmo holds, *every a kiss a man gives his wife after marriage be a mortal sin*, or that of Hierome, *whoever is hotly in love with his own wife is an adulterer*, or that of Thomas Secundus, *handling and kissing is a mortal sin*, or that of Durandus, *married folks should abstain from caresses during the entire time when the nuptial deed is interdicted*, what shall become of all such immodest kisses, and obscene actions, the forerunners of brutish lust?" From the edition of Floyd Dell and Paul Jordan-Smith (New York, 1951), p. 702.

be something more. He is writing not only of pleasure but of that primal state which in 'To Anthea' is described this way:

> Let's kisse afresh, as when we first begun.

I hope the reader will allow the double meaning I have extracted from this line. The idea of love in Herrick's poetry may, I think, be very like that in the poetry of Milton. If we are to follow the sense of Milton (*Paradise Lost*, Book IV, lines 736 ff.) we shall find that Herrick's celebration of love has analogues in the Christian *mythos*. The relationship of Adam and Eve before the Fall is both sensate and innocent, and it is towards this great Christian contradiction that Herrick's imagination is attracted.

The stanza is in its way a commentary on Herrick's general poetic method. He has warned us in the first verses of *Hesperides* that he will sing of '*Times trans-shifting*', and, no matter how slight his materials seem to be, that movement of time is part of the beat of his poetry. He has reminded us of the 'hieroglyphick' character of his imagery, so that we may see behind each object some larger correspondence and meaning. 'A Nuptiall Song' involves these ways of viewing the particular as if it were primarily a key to the universal.[6] The time marking the divisions of the poem is to be measured in hours:

> To bed, to bed, kind Turtles, now, and write
> This the short'st day, and this the longest night;
> But yet too short for you: 'tis we,
> Who count this night as long as three,
> Lying alone,
> Telling the Clock strike, Ten, Eleven, Twelve, One.

These are the hours from procession to consummation, a sequence unique, ritualistic, and finite. But they represent a larger system of time. They are signs of time universal and infinite. Some of Herrick's poetic statements give direct notice of the relationship:

> Strip her of Spring-time, tender-whimpring maids,
> Now *Autumne's* come, when all those flowrie aids
> Of her Delays must end.

In the most immediate sense human time and cosmic time are related. Yet, in another way they reflect multiple ironies. The end

---

6. See Douglas Bush, *English Literature in the Earlier Seventeenth Century* (Oxford, 1962), p. 118: 'In our day classical art on any level may be underestimated because its smooth surface is deceptive; we suspect lack of stress and depth if there is no huffing and puffing. *But Herrick's best poems have a vein of seriousness that is more than pagan,* and in this vein we find his emotional and artistic complexity and strength. Though the case for his religious consciousness in *Hesperides* can be overstated, he has the unified vision that was the common inheritance of his age, the vision that embraces God and the book of creatures in a divine whole' (italics added).

of innocence is emblematic of Autumn's occurrence—and a unique reminder of the cycle of recurrence. What on the human scene happens but once and irremediably happens on the cosmic scene time without number or end. The vulnerability of things human is implied as well as their participation in the vast analogies of the creation.

What Herrick called '*Times trans-shifting*' is more subtly pervasive. He has chosen to illuminate the relatedness of things human and cosmic by images that possess moving overtones of creation, ending, and resurrection. From the first image of the poem —'the spring of Day'—he intimates both temporality and recurrence. One is necessarily within another. The implication is supported by other groups of images: for example, the groom is like both the phoenix and the wedding torch, himself a 'hieroglyphick' of temporality within permanence. It is the *telos* of the torch to burn and die, but that fire signifies also something elemental hence imperishable. The bride's 'fire' will in one sense waste her husband 'to ashes', but, in another, will 'consume/His soule'. If the first meaning is carnal the second has a good deal to do with the ritual whereby matter is purified by fire. While that fire, then, is undeniably sexual—

>   Frie
> And consume, and grow again to die,
>   And live—

it indicates also what is for Herrick the central, animating principle of Nature: recurrence.

The circularity of this idea embraces all the *Hesperides* poems. Perhaps to call it an idea is to overstate; it can sometimes be simply an implication. The strategic use of images, metaphors, or even of rhythms allows Herrick to imply the fulness and recapitulation of experience. If his language describing the merely human dwells on the short and direct progress from life to death, the straight-line voyage of human destiny, it has also resources which depict another kind of life entirely. These concern the life of the seasons, the phenomena of changing but changeless Nature, the heavens, the flux and reflux of organic life, the birth, passing, and resurrection of beauty. He is a poet obsessed with the contrast between change and permanence. Needless to insist, this is not the kind of interest we usually ascribe to a minor poet. The material of his poetry is more ponderous than perhaps seems likely.

The persona of the aging poet came to Herrick from Ben Jonson. From his slightest lyrics to the fully modulated tones of 'To Charis' Jonson articulates a great distinction: that between the passage of human life and the permanence of that greater life in which it is located. This distinction became one of the great motifs of Herrick's own work. In 'To Perilla' he writes,

> Age cals me hence, and my gray haires bid come
> And haste away to mine eternal home.

In 'To his Mistresses' he writes, with a certain ambiguity,

> Old I am, and cannot do
> That, I was accustomed to.

And, in 'Corinna's *going a Maying*' he has given us the most famous statement of this theme:

> We shall grow old apace, and die
> Before we know our liberty.
> Our life is short; and our dayes run
> As fast away as do's the Sunne.

As critics have observed, Herrick often casts this theme in the terms of floral imagery and fertility ceremonies.[7] Perhaps one of our tasks ought to be that of connecting the floral images and the rituals of fertility to a larger and more inclusive body of ideas. That task ought certainly to include the matter of Herrick's reconciliation of individual existences with religious conceptions.

Herrick's supposedly pagan poetry shows certain correspondences to the language of orthodoxy. Even in 'Corinna's *going a Maying*' the 'hieroglyphick' quality of the verse indicates plainly that it concerns a Christian universe. It is not Catullus who is implied by these lines—

> And as a vapour, or a drop of raine
> Once lost, can ne'r be found againe—

but the 'Sic Vita' of Bishop King, the *Holy Dying* of Bishop Taylor, and the *Devotions* of Dr. Donne.[8] The human life which is the subject of these lines received its figural correspondence, as Jeremy Taylor writes, in the New Testament:

> *Homer* calls a man a *leaf*, the smallest, the weakest piece of a short-lived unsteady plant. *Pindar* calls him *the dream of a shadow*; Another, *the dream of the shadow of smoke*. But *S. James* spake by a more Excellent Spirit, saying, Our life is but a vapor; viz. drawn from the earth by a celestial influence.[9]

---

7. See Karl Wentersdorf, 'Herrick's Floral Imagery', *Studia Neophilologica*, XXXVI (1964), 69–81.
8. L. C. Martin notes that 'Herrick, however, is clearly indebted not only to Latin poetry but to the Bible (where the thought of "carpe diem" is introduced in order to be deprecated)'. Martin refers specifically to the lines I have quoted, and to the image of life as a vapor. In *The Poetical Works of Robert Herrick* (Oxford, 1956), pp. 514–15.
9. Jeremy Taylor, 'Preparatory to Death', *The Rule and Exercises of Holy Dying* (London, 1847), p. 3.

There are correspondences of this kind in other poems of *Hesperides* and *Noble Numbers*. 'To Daffadils' suggests a meaning for the vapor or rain drop involving a favorite Christian metaphor for decay:

> We die,
> As your hours doe, and drie
> Away
> Like to the Summers raine;
> Or as the pearles of Morning dew
> Ne'r to be found againe.

The tone is as important as the category of images; it is calm, resigned, above the temptations of self-pity. It acknowledges the limits of organic life. Both lyrical and eschatological, it brings to mind Robert Deming's observation that Herrick's poetic materials 'are not exclusively identified with pagan Rome, as any seventeenth-century Puritan would be quick to point out'.[1]

Like other metaphorical objects, the blossoms of which Herrick writes exist in a world of correspondences and oppositions. The former are implied by 'Divination by a Daffadill':

> When a Daffadill I see
> Hanging down his head t'wards me;
> Guesse I may, what I must be:
> First, I shall decline my head;
> Secondly, I shall be dead;
> Lastly, safely buryed.

In how many meditations and sermons have we seen this expressed? Sir Thomas Browne has put it best: 'Thus there are two books from whence I collect my divinity; besides that written one of God, another of his servant nature, that universal and public manuscript that lies expansed unto the eyes of all. . . . Surely the heathens knew better how to join and read these mystical letters than we Christians, who cast a more careless eye on these common hieroglyphics, and disdain to suck divinity from the flowers of nature'.[2] The power of this short but brilliant poem resides precisely in this 'hieroglyphick' quality. Stripped to its essentials, it moves on the energy of its verbs: 'Hanging down', 'I shall decline my head', 'I shall be dead', 'Lastly, safely buryed'. But this verbal simplicity and taut directness can only operate after the guiding conception has been laid down; after the poem has stated something not only witty but true. Surely the great thing about religious poetry is the fact that it never hesitates or is confused between a likeness and a

1. Robert Deming, 'Robert Herrick's Classical Ceremony', *ELH*, XXXIV (September 1967), 341. Deming's article is an important demonstration of the Christian content of *Hesperides*.

2. Sir Thomas Browne, *Religio Medici* (1682). Reprinted in *Seventeenth-Century Prose and Poetry*, eds. Alexander Witherspoon and Frank J. Warnke (New York, 1963), p. 336.

truth. The poem succeeds then, because it forces us to accept a metaphor as a fact.

Correspondence in the seventeenth-century sense of the term is no more important than its corollary, opposition. We must bear in mind that, in the poetry of Marvell and Herbert for example, the play of opposites is continually intimated. The tree that we perceive in its natural shape is a form of the cross; the garden is a form of Eden; other aspects of the landscape are as much a part of iconology as of geography. What does Protestant theology have to say about the play of opposition? Since so much of Herrick's poetry concerns organic nature I have chosen Paul Tillich's essay on 'Nature and Sacrament' as a guide. Tillich's main point is that natural objects have always held sacral meanings: the gold of medieval painting does not have an absolutely concrete existence of its own but 'is, so to speak, the transcendence of mere color and therefore the adequate expression for transcendence as such'.[3] The trees of the myth of Paradise 'are bearers of divine powers. . . . In the transcendent fulfilment, according to the Apocalypse, there will be the tree of life, by whose leaves the nations will be healed'.[4] It is Tillich's opinion that, intrinsic to Protestantism itself, is this mode of perceiving the relationship of natural life and religious meaning. At one extreme this mode declines into mere superstition, but we ignore it at the peril of ignoring the connection between matter and meaning.

Tillich's sense of 'the power and meaning of natural objects' is of the deepest interest for the study of a Protestant poet whose subject was nature:

> No realm of such objects is, in principle, excluded from a sacramental consideration. But, beyond this, power and meaning can be found in situations and configurations of nature. We refer to the old and also to the new belief that such complexes express something which can be 'read' out of them. . . . The power inherent in natural configurations is also visible in the rhythms of certain recurring events, like day and night, summer and winter, seedtime and harvest, and also in the rhythms of human life.[5]

As Tillich wisely observes, consciousness of these sacral relationships does not imply paganism, although it does imply syncretism. It is one of the modes by which Christian thought relates itself to what he calls 'the historical-realistic interpretation of nature'.

We should therefore be alive to the implications of opposition in these lines of 'To Blossoms':

> What, were yee borne to be
>   An houre or half's delight;
>   And so to bid goodnight?

3. Paul Tillich, *The Protestant Era* (Chicago, 1957), p. 105.

4. *Ibid.*

5. *Ibid.*, p. 106.

> 'Twas pitie Nature brought yee forth
> Meerly to shew your worth
> And lose you quite.
>
> But you are lovely Leaves, where we
> May read how soon things have
> Their end, though ne'r so brave;
> And after they have shown their pride,
> Like you a while: They glide
> Into the grave.

It would be quite superficial to see in these verses either pessimism or paganism, for they exist in relation to vast although unspoken qualities. It is altogether too easy to suspect of these lines that they reinforce for Herrick a sense of the insubstantiality of the universe. And it is altogether too easy to convince ourselves that they argue for going a Maying in a world that permits neither permanence nor transcendence. The whole point of Herrick's insight into mutability is that it is manifold and aware of great contradictions. The blossoms of this poem and other poems are part of a great analogy that is best revealed by Donne's meditation upon 'The Unfading Flower':

> Then was there truly a rose amongst thorns when through his crown of thorns you might see his title *Jesus Nazarenus*. For in that very name *Nazarenus* is involved the signification of a flower; the very word signifies a flower. Isaiah's flower in the crown of pride fades and is removed; this flower in the crown of thorns fades not nor could be removed; for, for all the importunity of the Jews, Pilate would not suffer that title to be removed or to be changed.[6]

It is one of the great faults of appreciations like that of Marchette Chute that they ascribe Herrick's use of religious imagery to a kind of aberration, rescued, of course, by the fact that he was a 'true poet'. Herrick's pointed use of correspondence and opposition is not absent-minded, nor does it reveal a signal failure to discriminate between classical and religious ideas. Nor is it, as Miss Chute even more vaguely suggests, a kind of blasphemy redeemed by the 'purity' of his intentions.[7] At the very simplest, 'To Blossoms', like Herrick's other poems on the transitoriness of life, uses the life of the flower

6. John Donne, Sermon XXXIII (1649). Reprinted in Witherspoon and Warnke, p. 111.

7. Marchette Chute, *Two Gentle Men* (New York, 1959), p. 253. See Erwin Panofsky's 'Iconography and Iconology: An Introduction to the Study of Renaissance Art', *Meaning in the Visual Arts* (Garden City, 1955), pp. 26–54. This is an essay of exceptional value on the subject of classical and Christian motifs. Panofsky points out that the coexistence of the two does not indicate a schizophrenic confusion between values but a way of 'moralization'. Classical motifs were absorbed into and became the vehicles of Christian allegory. See also Beryl Smalley, *The Study of the Bible in the Middle Ages* (Notre Dame, Indiana, 1964), pp. 8–9.

as an epitaph for our own. But these poems rarely exist at the simplest level. The crown of pride of which Donne writes is the subject of Isaiah 28: in that chapter we see that while 'glorious beauty is a fading flower' in the secular life, the 'crown of glory' and 'diadem of beauty' are floral metaphors for the life of religion. *The 'real' flower implies its opposite, the spiritual flower which never fades.*

Our understanding of the figural and typological habits of mind must allow for their natural presence in a religious poet of the seventeenth century. And our understanding of the 'configurations of nature' must allow us to see, as Paul Tillich states, the connection of natural objects to religious meanings and the connection of 'recurring events' to sacraments. Herrick's own statement that 'every where is wove/Wit and new mysterie' must be understood in the sense that 'the book of mysteries was also an encyclopaedia which contained all knowledge useful to man, both sacred and profane'.[8] For Herrick as for others brought up under the theology of the Fathers, the creation was that book of mysteries. Even those poems which seem most unreservedly pagan have their exegetical connections. 'The Hock Cart' begins with a magnificent quatrain about the Sons of Summer who 'rip up first, then reap our lands', and seems to release an earthly and secular joyfulness quite separate from religious meanings. Yet, if we recall Tillich, we will suspect that this harvest has sacral as well as natural meanings—and that these sacral meanings are specifically Christian. And if we study Isaiah, a book of the Bible evidently very much on Herrick's mind, we discover that the plowman is an exemplary figure of the first importance: 'For his God doth instruct him to discretion, and doth teach him' (Isaiah 28:23–6). It is through the plowman that the intentions of Nature are discovered. The harvest itself is a sign of the fulfilment of the covenant; the celebration confirms the possession of the land. The feast is a biblical motif—when Herrick writes of it 'this pleasure is like raine' he is true to Isaiah 44: 'For I will pour water upon him that is thirsty, and floods upon the dry ground: I will pour my spirit upon thy seed, and my blessing upon thine offspring'. The promise of 'spring againe' upon which the poem ends is indeed a religious statement linking the end of life with its resurrection. In Herrick's intellectual vocabulary the rose and daffodil are signs of human temporality. The rocky bottom of a stream has a moral quality; a kiss can be both sensual and an attempt to return to the time 'when we first begun'; the branch of a tree suggests a tabernacle; the whiteness of a sheet 'spotlesse pure, as it is sweet', has the symbolic power we find in the poetry of Vaughan. To summarize, in the *Hesperides*

8. Smalley, p. 26.

the transitoriness of beauty is connected to the perfected, static beauty of the divine world. One does not, in that age, observe beauty so much as see *through* it:

> Whatsover is rare and passionate carries the soul to the thought of eternity; and, by contemplation, gives it some glimpses of more absolute perfection than here 'tis capable of. . . . When I see the most enchanting beauties that earth can show me, I yet think, there is something far more glorious; methinks I see a kind of higher perfection.[9]

In this passage from Owen Feltham we see cogently expressed the belief that a natural object is not in itself complete, but is a key to the perception of sacral meaning. Herrick's obsession with human beauty and its passing is not pagan, and is of course not wholly secular, but an ardent and orthodox way of reaching the reality behind sensate appearances.

BRUCE KING

The Strategy of Carew's Wit†

Thomas Carew is often praised for his sophisticated gallantry, his urbane assurance, and for the way in which he seems to express the best values of a rich civilization.[1] However, if we try to put our finger on what is mature, firm, or civilized in Carew's poetry we find ourselves circling around his wit. This means that a study of Carew's wit is a study in what distinguishes him from other poets. Wit may serve a poet in several ways. There is, for example, the wit of a *double entendre* which allows the speaker to mention what is socially hidden. Donne's early poems offer obvious examples of this. There is also the wit of Dryden's satires which mocks its victims by comparing the lesser to the greater. And there is the wit of Hamlet's irony which, in its implications, reveals a personality caught between conflicting demands of conscience and society. Wit usually serves both a psychological and social purpose. It relieves psychic tensions while enabling the speaker to deal with matters that would otherwise be socially forbidden for discussion.[2] What is of literary interest is how the basic psychological functions of wit

9. Owen Feltham, 'Of the Worship of Admiration', *Resolves; Divine Moral and Political* (1628). In Witherspoon and Warnke, p. 320.
† From *Review of English Literature*, V (1964), 42–51.
1. F. R. Leavis, *Revaluation* (1936), p. 16.
2. See S. Freud, *Jokes and their Relation to the Unconscious*, transl. J. Strachey (1960), pp. 140–58. Since I am concerned with the social purpose of Carew's poetry, my essay ignores the sadistic element that Freud finds in aggressive wit.

are shaped into rhetorical strategies that attempt to deal with social realities. Even the light irony of Dryden's satires has a strategic purpose; it suggests that his victims are beneath contempt and that they are not worth taking seriously. It is in the shaping of a literary strategy that a poet reveals his personality and the values he holds in relation, or opposition, to society.

What is the basic attitude behind Carew's wit? What causes us to feel that we are dealing with a personality of superior intelligence and of a high complexity of values? This is easier to answer if we examine the social function of his wit. Carew's poems deal with courtship and the suasion of seduction. For many writers this would mean smallness of theme and pettiness of interest. However, Carew treats courtship as a battlefield upon which most problems of human relations are presented in microcosm. His poems attempt more intimate communication between people than manners allow. Carew's wit is often aggressive since it must not only break through social rhetoric, but it must offer him protection in his manœuvres. For this reason he twists conventional poetic rhetoric into a means of saying the unconventional. His urbanity is a pose which allows him to use social graces for self-protection, while it offers him a claim to disregard the limits which manners impose upon individuals.

The majority of Carew's poems in Grierson cleverly invert traditional poetic compliments to threaten, or to pretend to threaten, some woman.[3] 'To my inconstant Mistris', 'A deposition from Love', 'Ingratefull beauty threatned' and 'To a Lady that desired I would love her' are sophisticated poems of courtship, but they also threaten retaliation if the poet is injured by his mistress. I have, of course, singled out one theme from Carew's works, but it is a basic theme, and it is common to his best poems. Take, for example, 'Ingratefull beauty threatned', in which the wit functions to keep someone at disadvantage while protecting the speaker against injury. Behind the gallantry of the poem lies a struggle for dominance. Carew warns his mistress that she is merely an average woman whom he has picked from the crowd, and that the qualities attributed to her do not exist except in his verse. Having given her social prestige through his poetry, he can also 'uncreate' her if she causes him to doubt her fidelity. Notice that the concluding four lines of the poem, which are derived from Donne's 'Elegie XIX', use the imagery of mysticism for sexual advances. Donne inverts the conventions of such imagery

---

3. Four of the seven love lyrics which represent Carew in Grierson's *Metaphysical Lyrics and Poems* are aggressive or threatening. In the *Oxford Book of Seventeenth Century Verse*, seven out of nine love poems are aggressive. I include among these 'Good Counsell to a Young Maid', which is a warning against mistaking man's sexual desires for love. The proportion is somewhat less in Carew's total works; but I am concerned with the attitude behind Carew's best poems.

to expose, to say what he knows about woman's sexual organs and desires.[4]

> . . . all women thus array'd;
> Themselves are mystick books, which only wee
> (Whom their imputed grace will dignifie)
> Must see reveal'd. Then since that I may know;
> As liberally, as to a Midwife, shew
> Thy self: cast all, yea, this white lynnen hence,
> [Here] is no pennance, much less innocence.

Carew, however, appropriates the rhetoric to gain a position of mastery.[5]

> Let fooles thy mystique formes adore,
>   I'le know thee in thy mortall state:
> Wise Poets that wrap't Truth in tales,
>   Knew her themselves, through all her vailes.

The poetic strategy depends upon the power of a poet in a small courtly society where, like newspaper gossip, verses make and unmake reputations. Carew's claim is that his mistress is foolish to think that he will allow himself to be used for her social advancement, or that he will allow conventions of courtship to be used as a means to dominate over him. It does not matter whether this poem was written about a real woman since the problems with which it deals are basic. Like devices of modern warfare, Carew's poetry is perhaps more useful when theratening aggression than when employed. The literary value lies in the ease and sophistication with which the problem is handled.

Given this as the basic strategy of Carew's wit, many of his best poems are variations upon it. Some poems threaten; others, such as 'A deposition from Love', injure. The opening stanza of 'A deposition from Love' at first sounds similar to any petrarchan complaint about a pitiless mistress; however, it only appears petrarchan since key words ('fortresse', 'within', 'paradise', 'gate') are *double entendres*:

> I was foretold, your rebell sex,
>   Nor love, nor pitty knew;
> And with what scorne, you use to vex
>   Poore hearts, that humbly sue;
> Yet I believ'd, to crowne our paine,
>   Could we the fortresse win,
> The happy lover sure should gaine
>   A Paradise within:

4. Donne's 'Elegie XIX', lines 40–6. Also see Clay Hunt, *Donne's Poetry*, New Haven (1954), pp. 18–21.

5. All quotations of Carew are from *The Poems of Thomas Carew*, ed. R. Dunlap, Oxford (1949).

> I thought loves plagues, like Dragons sate,
>   Only to fright us at the gate.

The poem is not, as are some of Donne's early poems, merely a pyrotechnical display of hidden sexual meanings. We are told that the speaker 'did enter, and enjoy what happy lovers prove'. Now he is cast off by his mistress and his complaint is that having 'once possest' her his pain is greater than before. The strategy is very clever. Carew has taken the petrarchan convention of the lamenting lover and has used it as a form of revenge. The poem pretends to elicit sympathy for the rejected lover; however, the originality of the poem is the public disclosure that the poet has sexually enjoyed his mistress, and that she has now given herself to another man. The poem is neither a lover's lament, nor is it simply a poem of sexual frankness. In its description of sexual looseness, it is close to satire. Carew's genius is the way in which the satiric elements of the poem are carefully balanced and controlled by traditional Renaissance conventions, so that what is being said comes as a surprise and draws attention to itself. The second stanza with its bold 'But I did enter, and enjoy' is meant to shock; that it is understated and put casually only makes the effect greater:

> But I did enter, and enjoy,
>   What happy lovers prove;
> For I could kisse, and sport, and toy,
>   And tast those sweets of love;
> Which had they but a lasting state,
>   Of if in *Celia's* brest,
> The force of love might not abate,
>   *Jove* were too meane a guest.
> But now her breach of faith, far more
> Afflicts, then did her scorne before.

Even the beautiful final conceit of 'A deposition from Love' plays its part in reminding us of the disclosure:

> If the stout Foe will not resigne,
>   When I besiege a Towne,
> I lose, but what was never mine;
>   But he that is cast downe
> From enjoy'd beautie, feeles a woe,
> Onely deposed Kings can know.

It would be a mistake to see these poems as merely exercises in anti-petrarchanism. The inversion of Elizabethan amatory imagery was old-hat by the early seventeenth century, and it no longer had interest in itself except as a means within more complicated poetic strategies. Carew works within poetic conventions so that he may seem to speak with detachment and high self-control. The purpose is to avoid injury by keeping personal emotion at a distance. Carew uses poetic conventions to organize personal emotions for social warfare. Even the controlled stanzaic forms, the purity of diction, and the cold logic of the poems are means to deal with the social and personal realities of courtship while pretending that one does not care. A good part of what is best in Carew derives from this strategy of nonchalance. T. S. Eliot's famous phrase for it is 'a tough reasonableness beneath [a] slight lyric grace'. The genealogy of this strategy probably derives from Donne's early libertine poems with their exuberant delight in sexual frankness. However, the distance in sophistication and caution between, say, Donne's 'Indifferent' and Carew's poetry is great. Even Donne's later poems to Mary Herbert, such as 'The Blossom' and 'The Relic', only lightly play with the ironies of courtship and sexual aggression.[6] Donne's wit in this mode is mostly teasing. The serious use of embarrassing another as a poetic device is, in English poetry, primarily Carew's discovery. Nor is it a minor discovery; embarrassment and aggression may be a means to break through the rhetoric of social manners to establish contact with others. Fights sometimes make friends. What Carew attempts to achieve is a realistic relationship between man and woman.

'To a Lady that desired I would love her' bears out the usefulness of Carew's pose of worldliness in a sophisticated society. The poem is clearly an attempt to gain what chess players call equality. The situation is that the speaker has been offered the position of poet-courtier for a lady's affections. Carew realizes, however, that playful attitudes often camouflage a battle for dominance. The poem rejects the ploy of playful courtship, with its subservience to the lady's whims, and insists that the situation be seen in terms of mutual needs. The poet will write no laments and will not whine for love He knows that his mistress is mortal and that she has 'dishevell'd hayre'. If she wants compliments and the glamour that poetry can bring, she must realize that the poet's terms are equality and sexual fulfilment. Thus the subject of the poem is one of mastery, of jockeying for position. Even in the stanzas where the lady is complimented there is a threat not only of aggression ('Each pettie beautie can disdaine') but also of the rejection of the whole game.

The dialectic of Carew's poetry does not turn inward and attempt to track the movements of the mind, as Donne's images do, but rather it attempts to justify the poet's attitudes. Carew pretends to be reasonable, he ironically appeals to the reader to see the justness of his point of view. The fourth stanza of the poem cleverly argues that the images a poet creates are related to how he feels. The

6. See Hunt, pp. 44–50.

petrarchan subservient lover will create a 'puddle' of 'griefe' which will not reflect the lady's beauty:

> Griefe is a puddle, and reflects not cleare
> Your beauties rayes,
> Joyes are pure streames, your eyes appeare
> Sullen in sadder layes,
> In chearfull numbers they shine bright with prayse.

There is a threat of latent aggression in the next stanza with its grotesque perversion of petrarchan imagery. If satisfied with the lady's love, he will not mention 'Stormes in your brow, nets in your haire', 'betray' or 'torture'. The imagery not only parodies petrarchanism but becomes progressively more unflattering:

> Which shall not mention to express you fayre
> Wounds, flames, and darts,
> Stormes in your brow, nets in your haire,
> Suborning all your parts,
> Or to betray, or torture captive hearts.

'To a Lady that desired I would love her' is, however, a less aggressive poem than 'To my inconstant Mistris'; here Carew claims to play the part of a petrarchan lover not to win his mistress's affections but to use her in gaining another woman. The strategy is particularly complicated since it presumably courts the woman by belittling her. It is a naked display of superiority in gaining social, and therefore personal, dominance in the battle between the sexes. As in many of Carew's poems the main strategy involves a manœuvre to appropriate conventional poetic rhetoric for unconventional purposes. In this poem Donne's favourite analogy between sacred and profane love is transformed into a social weapon. In Donne's love poems religious imagery is used to express a state of mind similar to that of devotion, while in Donne's religious poems, amatory imagery suggests the direct sensuousness of spiritual experience. Carew however is not interested in investigating the various implications of this analogy. Instead he uses the images to injure. His demonstration of constancy ('strong faith') will achieve greater conquests ('The full reward, and glorious fate') with other women: 'A fayrer hand then thine, shall cure That heart, which thy false oathes did wound.' His mistress is mistaken if she thinks that because he has cried over her she has him in her power. His demonstration of love is a superior means to advertise himself to women of finer sensibilities ('a soule more pure Than thine').

There are of course many non-aggressive poems on standard themes among Carew's works. Carew, like Donne, often played at creating strikingly original compliments. 'Ask me no more where *Jove* bestowes' is perhaps the most beautiful song of its period. Few poets have ever created such purely lyrical lines where the logic of analogy is so completely compressed that the statements are untranslatable into prose paraphrase. The lyrical songs, however, are the minor side of Carew. Carew is too realistic, and perhaps too self-protective, to make many flights into irrational beauty. But the lyric poems do reveal an intense emotional warmth which Carew otherwise keeps under control and which would seem to explain his need to establish clear, secure personal relationships.

Carew's poetry deals with the side of reality that is often hidden from public discussion: sexual appetites, the desire to dominate over others, the need for warmth and security, and the need to protect oneself against harm. While these are usually thought of as psychological drives, we are often aware of their existence; our social values recognize a delicate system of checks and balances in the give and take between people. Manners are the common means to legislate over this potential battlefield. However, manners are too slipshod to rule over all areas of society where clashes between personalities occur. Individuals or social groups often manage to appropriate manners for their own use, and then injustice occurs. What was meant to be flexible becomes rigid; what was meant to give rights leads to serfdom. The great themes of literature often derive from this border area between social values and psychological needs. In the modern novel there is a constant search for some superior organization of personality which will enable us to respond to this personal side of reality. Lawrence's novels record, when he is not being self-willed and didactic, a constant oscillation between the assertion of the ego, with its desire to be independent, and the search for warmth and security, which results from the weakening of the ego and its fusion with others. While Lawrence was unable to solve this problem, he had a heightened awareness that both the constant assertion of personality and the annihilation of individuality lead to psychic sickness.

Nor is the concern with the proper relationship of individuals to others a peculiarly modern literary theme. The supposed immorality of Restoration comedy derives from its naked acceptance of the view that man is appetitive matter in motion seeking satisfactions. It proposes as morally superior the man who clearly understands human nature, and who manages to control it to his own advantage.[7] The heroes and heroines of Restoration comedy continually seek to discover what others are really like so that they may live on rational terms with them. This is the theme of *The Man of Mode* and the significance of the brilliant proviso scene in *The Way of the*

7. Recent studies that take this point of view include N. N. Holland, *The First Modern Comedies*, Cambridge, Mass. (1959); and D. Underwood, *Etherege and the Seventeenth-Century Comedy of Manners*, New Haven (1957).

World. The 'honesty' of Wycherley is that he refuses to play the game and insists upon a more rigorous moral code.

The attitude of Restoration comedy has its origins in the wit of Carew. Carew's achievement is to have created a social pose of urbane worldliness which opens communication between the sexes but which threatens retaliation if one is injured. It is a means of mastering reality so that one may live within society without being a dupe or a cad. Essentially this is a problem of love. Since courtship is a matter of personal relations, it provides us with a microcosm of the tensions between the individual and society. In love we desire union with another person, by which we may feel at once secure in our giving and taking of affections, and yet self-sufficient in the completeness of our personality in relation to the external world. There is, however, a masochistic perversion of this in which, through self-hate, the ego is totally extinguished. There is also an aggressive attitude in which the ego is never extinguished, but attempts to appropriate or possess others without returning affection.[8] Courtship creates both possibilities at once: the overly compliant person who sacrifices his identity to become part of the other's narcissistic universe. While Carew's poems may seem to injure others, they are actually attempts to correct the unequal relationship implicit within the petrarchan rhetoric of courtship. If Carew's poems do not speak, as some of Donne's do, of a fusion of personalities, they at least have the value of creating situations where the fullness of love is possible. It is a razor-sharp position from which slight deviations can result in a disagreeable toughness. However, there is in Carew's best poetry a rich awareness of the complexity of our relations with others.

I think that I can illustrate the many dimensions of Carew's awareness by using Sir John Suckling as a foil. I have no wish to devalue Suckling; in an age of excellent poets he is superior to most. However, Suckling has less insight into the complexities of life; he reduces a valuable part of existence to a few simple ideas. In 'Of thee (kind boy)' the themes are that man is merely appetite and that beauty is relative. Love is a pleasing folly ('Make me but mad enough') and a product of the fancy ('tis love in love that makes the sport'). Even Suckling's libertinism is grossly literal ('tis the appetite Makes eating a delight'), and lacks the intense philosophical scepticism that makes Rochester an important poet. Suckling's talent is in his technique. He is a master of the manipulation of syllabic rhythms, the use of tonal modulation within a poem, and the modification of rhyme patterns. However, he never comes to grips with the substance of reality. Carew's poems are less simple,

8. A useful discussion of this is N. O. Brown, *Life Against Death*, New York (1959), pp. 40–54.

and describe life's essential battles. In a sense each of Carew's poems has a double existence: there is the poetry of the brilliantly finished surface of the poem itself; and there is the poetry of Carew's attempt to impose civilized order upon the desperate chaos of man's inner realities.

HUGH RICHMOND

The Fate of Edmund Waller†

When Waller died in 1687, his tomb at Beaconsfield was dignified by an epitaph from the Historiographer Royal. It is in the usual fulsome, empty style which dissipates trust by overemphasis, but surprisingly its claim that Waller endeared English literature to the muses is approved by Waller's most distinguished literary contemporaries. In Dryden's preface to Walsh's *Dialogue Concerning Women* (1691), for example, we read, "Unless he had written none of us could write"; and in his preface to *The Second Part of Mr. Waller's Poems* (1690) Atterbury boldly declared, thinking primarily of Waller, "I question whether in Charles the Second's Reign *English* did not come to its full perfection; and whether it has not had its *Augustan Age.*"

Modern critics have, however, responded to this rather too liberal praise with equally immoderate censure. Mr. J. B. Emperor's study of "The Catullian Influence in English Lyric Poetry" (University of Missouri Studies, 1928) alludes to the poet as "the frigid and time-serving Waller, who rhymed insipidly under both Jameses, both Charleses, and the Protector." The same critic continues, "Perhaps none of the men considered in these studies had less of the truly poetic and lyric than he; in him the Augustan age definitely begins and begins indifferently. He is a thoroughly bad poet. His love verse is cold, artificial, and absurd." Such severity seems hardly more discriminating than the earlier elaborate praise, but it is nevertheless shared by the best modern authorities. "No poetical reputation of the seventeenth century has been so completely and irreparably eclipsed as that of Edmund Waller," writes Douglas Bush in his history of seventeenth-century literature. "Whereas Cowley and Cleveland can still give pleasure, Waller's name calls up scarcely more than two lyrics of attenuated cavalier grace, " 'On a Girdle', and 'Go Lovely Rose', and a dim memory of much complimental verse. . . . For us he remains a fluent trifler, the rhymer of a court gazette."

† From *South Atlantic Quarterly*, LX (1961), pp. 230–38.

The sharpness of the conflict between the views of the seventeenth century and of our own suggests that Waller would present an unusually interesting figure on which to focus a study of developing critical opinion. The motives which apparently govern his decline into disrepute are unexpected and revealing, both of Waller's age and of ours. Clearly the bitterness of J. B. Emperor, and also of Edmund Gosse, in his *Seventeenth Century Studies* (to whom Waller was "the easy turn coat" who wrote "smooth, emasculated lyrics"), stems ultimately not from critical analysis of the poet's works so much as from a transferred judgment on Waller's apparently regrettable life. There can be no doubt that Waller's career does tempt the censorious minded, and it is bizarre enough to demand close examination and review in the light of our experience since the time when Gosse and Emperor wrote. Only so can a dispassionate estimate of his work be accomplished.

Waller's life invites censure because of its unhappy central episode —his regrettable collapse of character under threat of execution in 1643. During the early stages of the clash between parliament and king, Waller had behaved with a wisdom and integrity which marked him out as a politician of exceptional promise. Stockdale, an early editor (1772), writes in his preface without much exaggeration that: "Waller at this time acquired a very great political reputation. He vindicated the rights of the people, but he likewise supported the dignity and authority of the crown; he had chosen that just and virtuous medium, to which it is so difficult to adhere in times of tumult, fanaticism and rebellion." He was welcomed by both parliament and the king as one of the commissioners sent to treat with Charles after Edgehill.

Nevertheless, seven months later Waller was under arrest for treason to parliament and was condemned to death soon after by a court martial. Pathetically, Waller's search for a peaceful compromise had involved him, accidentally, in a plot not merely to publicize the king's case, as Waller thought, but to further a revolt led by a royalist hothead, Sir Nicholas Crispe. Parliament refused, on discovering the plot, to disentangle these relationships, and Waller was condemned for intentions alien to his character and purpose. However, while some of his associates were hanged, Waller successfully deferred his death by desperate subterfuges—feigned madness, mass bribery, and informing on casual associates—until feeling against him declined and his sentence was reduced to fine and exile. After he spent a few penurious years abroad, Cromwell, to whom he was distantly related, allowed him to return.

This return, chiefly due to the threat of starvation if he remained abroad, is one source of censure, a rather superficial one under the circumstances. The earlier betrayals of confidence are the other

grounds on which he is chiefly attacked. In the modern world, conditioned by work like *Darkness at Noon* and *1984*, we may be less
harsh, if still critical of Waller's conduct under threat of unmerited
death. "Time-serving" scarcely serves to describe a man who surely
felt with Marvell that "the cause was too good to have been fought
for."

This brief account may serve to set a little more in perspective the
outraged censure of many of his critics who clearly share the views
of Plato and Milton—that good poetry can only be written by conventionally good men. There is, however, another obstacle to
Waller's return to popular esteem—ignorance. The latest edition of
his poems, a "pocket" one, first appeared in 1893; and in the last
twenty-five years *PMLA* lists only three slight references to Waller.
Since the turn of the century only Mr. F. W. Bateson's "A Word
for Waller" in his *English Poetry* (1950) makes a brief attempt at
examining Waller sympathetically. On the other hand, the standard
evaluation of him is stabilized because every history of English
literature stereotypes him as reference point for the dawn of
Augustanism. Bell's edition (1861) illustrates this interest-killing
appreciation by noting. "His principal merit is that of having been
the first who uniformly observed the obligations of a strict metrical
system." This editor's fullest praise is "There are very few of his
lines that do not read smoothly, and but one in which a syllabic
defect can be detected." Few histories improve on this approach—
with inevitable consequences on the interest of potential readers.

There is one more complex reason for Waller's lack of reputation—the historical myth of the "unified sensibility" which Mr.
Eliot fostered in his two essays "The Metaphysical Poets" and
"Andrew Marvell." Eliot seeks to demonstrate a deep and valuable
tension between thought and feeling in such poets as Donne which
later poets like Waller and Milton are held to lack. However, critics
like Mr. Leonard Unger, in his essay "Fusion and Experience" (in
The Man in the Name, 1956), have asked "Where in Donne's
poetry is there a 'felt thought,' or a 'thought feeling'?" and denied
that the concept of such fusions is relevant to any Stuart poetry,
Donne's included. Probably what we have in Donne is the blend of
intellectual ingenuity with strong verbal emphasis used in the context of various stock emotional situations—partings, betrayals,
attempted seduction. We value this verbal vigor and the intellectual
virtuosity which Donne uses to create the scene—but neither of
these resources has actually been forfeited by Waller as is usually
claimed. Each quality has merely been developed to suit the social
needs of a later, more urbane age. Waller's sense of conversational
flow is as sure as Donne's, but more discreet, and his intellectual
liveliness is at least equal to that of the author of "The Flea."

Perhaps the easiest illustration of Waller's capacity as a wit to transform a social situation by applying his quickness and felicity of mind to it is to relate two conspicuous examples from court life which Johnson notes in his life of Waller. The first occurred when Waller "upon sight of the Duchess of Newcastle's verses on the *Death of a Stag*, declared he would give all his own compositions to have written them; and being charged with the exorbitance of such adulation, answered that 'nothing was too much to be given that a lady might be saved from the disgrace of such a vile performance.' " Here we see the devastating cynicism and mocking slyness which Donne also exploits in a poem like "Woman's Constancy." Again, when Charles reproached him on the superiority of his *Panegyric* to Cromwell over his *Congratulation* to the King, Waller answered, "Poets, Sir, succeed better in fiction than in truth." Could Donne have found a more ingenious excuse? If these qualities of liveliness are transferred to his poetry, as I think they are, then surely Waller has a claim to our respect and is not wholly unworthy of the great predecessor to whom he is usually so unfavorably compared.

Let us examine some of these resources in his verse itself, avoiding thoe poems normally praised. For example, his poem about inconstancy, "Chloris! farewell," has never been noticed by either critics or editors:

> Chloris! farewell. I now must go;
> For if with thee I longer stay,
> Thy eyes prevail upon me so,
> I shall prove blind, and lose my way.
>
> Fame of thy beauty, and thy youth,
> Among the rest, me hither brought;
> Finding this fame fall short of truth,
> Made me stay longer than I thought.
>
> For I'm engaged by word and oath,
> A servant to another's will;
> Yet, for thy love, I'd forfeit both,
> Could I be sure to keep it still.
>
> But what assurance can I take,
> When thou, foreknowing this abuse,
> For some more worthy lover's sake,
> Mayst leave me with so just excuse?
>
> For thou mayst say, 'twas not thy fault
> That thou didst thus inconstant prove;
> Being by my example taught
> To break thy oath, to mend thy love.

The poem concludes with Waller's rueful departure. These stanzas illustrate fairly Waller's virtues as a poet. The style is bare and natural, the situation precisely visualized, and the outcome both ingenious and salutary. The most effective part of the poem is the poet's insight into social and psychological patterns. The shock which tragically overtakes Beatrice in Middleton's *Changeling* when she discovers that murder leads to self-victimization has in Waller's poem been transposed to the level of more normal relationships. The shock effect remains in the unexpected reversal of the predictable outcome, based on what can only be called moral insight.

Ingenuity thus here acquires both literary and social value in a way comparable but superior to Waller's epigram about the Duchess of Newcastle's poem. In Waller's verse we find then at very least the penetration of "metaphysical" wit and ingenuity into the finest texture of social relationships; and it is in this deft investigation of even conversational manners that the foundations of eighteenth-century sophistication were laid. It is not surprising that Waller's verse was so fashionable in that century, nor that, in less sophisticated modern society, he is disregarded.

Waller's resources are by no means so limited as modern critics pretend. In a stiffer, more Horatian style, Waller can be compared with Jonson or Herrick as we see in his poem "To a Lady in Retirement":

> Sees not my love how time resumes
> The glory which he lent these flowers?
> Though none should taste of their perfumes,
> Yet must they live but some few hours;
> Time what we forbear devours!
>
> Had Helen, or the Egyptian Queen,
> Been ne'er so thrifty of their graces,
> Those beauties must at length have been
> The spoil of age, which finds out faces
> In the most retired places.
>
> Should some malignant planet bring
> A barren drought, or ceaseless shower,
> Upon the autumn or the spring,
> And spare us neither fruit nor flower;
> Winter would not stay an hour.
>
> Could the resolve of love's neglect
> Preserve you from the violation
> Of coming years, then more respect
> Were due to so divine a fashion,
> Nor would I indulge my passion.

This is not the feeble writing which we are led to expect from Waller. The poem is firmly organized, and sophisticated. The subdued mockery of the couplet:

> The spoil of age, which finds out faces
> In the most retired places.

agreeably offsets the aureate allusions introduced discreetly into the text of the poem. It is not improper to note a hint in Waller's conclusion for the last lines of Marvell's first stanza of "To his Coy Mistress" since Waller's poems first appeared in 1645, some years before Marvell's best verse was probably written. That Marvell knew these poems and valued them is shown by the well-known and unmistakable debt owed by "The Bermudas" to Waller's "The Battle of the Summer Islands" (see Margoliouth's edition of Marvell).

In fact Waller's poem about "Dorothea" ("At Penshurst") also probably provided a popular model for that series of "promenade poems" praising ladies which includes "Appleton House," and of which this Waller poem is probably the first English example. It is no mean achievement to have set a precedent for Marvell's praise of the young Maria—and Cleveland's "Upon Phillis Walking in a Morning" as well. (Many lesser poets such as Hammond, Heath, and Hooke also conform to Waller's pattern.)

Waller is also by no means a trivial poet because he chooses to write lightly. The savage vehemence and aggressive ingenuity of Donne are by no means the only mood and method for effective comment on human nature. "Of Silvia" displays a lithe sinuosity of analysis coupled with an irony as inconspicuous as the poem's intention is razor-like:

> Our sighs are heard; just Heaven declares
> The sense it has of lover's cares;
> She that so far the rest outshined,
> Silvia the fair, while she was kind,
> As if her frowns impaired her brow,
> Seems only not unhandsome now.
> So when the sky makes us endure
> A storm, itself becomes obscure.
>
> Hence 'tis that I conceal my flame,
> Hiding from Flavia's self her name,
> Lest she, provoking Heaven, should prove
> How it rewards neglected love.
> Better a thousand such as I,
> Their grief untold should pine and die,
> Than her bright morning, overcast
> With sullen clouds, should be defaced.

Ostensibly this is the familiar lover's complaint, but the discriminations on which the progression of the poem depends are of unusually subtle character. The dogma of the moral nature of beauty, in the

Platonic style, is invoked with polished ease—that which is ungracious is shown to be not fair. How lightly the effective censure of fickleness is achieved can be seen in the phrase "seems not unhandsome now." The subjective and sentimental nature of the lover's sense of his lady's beauty is suavely stressed—but gallantly and moderately. "Not unhandsome" is a more original because a more poised mode of rejection than, say, one of Horace's blistering curses on Barine. However, the climactic irony lies in the mock gallantry of the second stanza. Lovers should not avow their loves, says Waller, because the regrettable lack of graciousness shown by a woman knowing of a lover's infatuation is bound to disgust him!

If this caustic yet urbane little poem is set against Donne's song, "Go and catch a falling star," which makes a somewhat comparable attack on female nature, it will be seen that Donne's poem is memorable for its stylistic virtuosity, while Waller's is distinguished for its poised evalution of social and moral tensions. Donne's poem is simply an assertion, though vivid and memorable; Waller's is an elegant algebraic demonstration. This is the quality which it shares with the first poem which we discussed; and it is that sharp sense of the significance of politely conversational exchanges which distinguishes all Waller's best verse.

This natural yet sensitive tone was certainly also his greatest social asset, restoring him to favor with the court even after his Cromwellian connection. And equally it was his political stock in trade, perfectly adapted to parliamentary eloquence. It was Waller's particular tragedy that in the middle of his life he found himself involved in events of a confusion and violence for which his unique talents were altogether unsuited. However, his contemporaries could distinguish these talents and admire them while admitting his public failures as a man.

We are less wise, and yet ironically even the one or two poems of Waller still conventionally admired, are good because of exactly those virtues which I have sought to display in his neglected verse and personality. Take this deservedly famous song:

> Go, lovely Rose!
> Tell her that wastes her time and me,
> That now she knows,
> When I resemble her to thee,
> How sweet and fair she seems to be.
>
> Tell her that's young,
> And shuns to have her graces spied,
> That hadst thou sprung
> In deserts, where no men abide,
> Thou must have uncommended died.
>
> Small is the worth
> Of beauty from the light retired;

Bid her come forth,
Suffer herself to be desired,
And not blush so to be admired.

Then die! that she
The common fate of all things rare
May read in thee;
How small a part of time they share
That are so wondrous sweet and fair!

It is ironic that Waller's best-known poem should so obviously lack that marked originality of intention which we noted in some of his other verse, for clearly this poem conforms in aim explicitly to Martial's famous admonition ("I felix rosa . . ."). However, this conventional frame allows us to see exactly where Waller's true originality lies. Compare the poem with Jonson's "To Celia" (in *Volpone*), Herrick's "Gather Ye Rosebuds," or Marvell's "To his Coy Mistress" and it will be seen that though all these pleas for love are impressive and picturesque, none is so economical and so devoid of the "poetic." The sentiment is expressed here with the minimum of effort—neither tone nor imagery is other than the actual situation permits. Perhaps for the first time in English the full force of poetic sensibility has focused on a social situation without distortion or heightening, and yet retained the magnetism of true art. The imagery is not exotic but drawn from immediate experience—the extraordinary tact of "Suffer herself to be desired" shows a sense of the pride of modesty which colors the poem as vividly as sensuous details. The swift conjunction of the second line, "Tell her that wastes her time and me," shows that mastery of reserved yet pointed expression which distinguishes Waller. But most of all the spoken flow of the whole shows something definitive in English. No poem can be read without false intonation more infallibly than this one. The control is not only metrically impeccable, it is socially speaking, masterly. Henry James could hardly seek more. Such a fascinating conversationalist as Waller here shows himself to be deserves to be more talked about himself.

EARL WASSERMAN

[The Topographical Dialectic of *Cooper's Hill*]†

***Although it is a historical fact that Denham's poem fathered a long line of loco-descriptive poems, the sins visited upon the offspring had their origin elsewhere than in their sire. One need

† From *The Subtler Language: Critical Readings of Neoclassic and Romantic Poems* (Baltimore, 1959), pp. 47–66.

only place *Cooper's Hill* in its own temporal setting, the troubled days of 1642, to sense that it is probably thematic throughout and that the primary function of its descriptive elements is to create a realizable and meaningful structure for the political concept being poetically formulated.[1] They are the linguistic terms whose implied syntactical relations make possible a self-containing embodiment of the concept; but the reference value of those terms is to be found in the events and ideas of England in 1642.

Denham himself succeeded in defining rather precisely for us the relation we are to find between the descriptive and thematic strands by postulating that the poem arises from a contest between his eye and his thoughts. Although he intends to describe the scene he surveys, his "Fancy" is more boundless than his eye (12); and yet the flight of his mental fancy is aided by his physical elevation at the top of Cooper's Hill—"By taking wing from thy auspicious height" (10)—as though his fancy were a bird winging through space. Eye and thought contract space with equal swiftness (13). He would continue his meditations if he could, but his "wandring eye" betrays his "fixt thoughts" (112), and it is all one whether he is raised in body or in thought (1642 version). Briefly, he moves from one scene to another by "untrac't ways, and aery paths" (11), for thought and vision contest with each other for possession of the scene until it becomes symbolic. The contest between eye and fancy is the struggle of each simultaneously to grasp the same subject matter through its own mode of perception, as thing and as meaning; and only the faculty psychology of his·day prevents Denham from identifying the two acts. Moreover, Denham insists in his opening lines that, in his conception, poetry is the act of transforming the physical world into values and meanings by way of metaphor, for if he can succeed in making poetry of his experiences at Cooper's Hill, the hill will become Parnassus for him (7–8). The object becomes a meaning through poetry; and poetic meaning derives only from the play of thought on things. Correspondingly, total poetic success must lie in the transformation of all the other topographical features in the poem into metaphoric relevance.

Even the opening lines of the poem require us to recognize that

1. That the poem is to be read in the context of its political circumstances has been recently proposed by Rufus Putney, "The View from Cooper's Hill," *University of Colorado Studies* (Studies in Language and Literature, no. 6, 1957), pp. 13–22.

The differences between the 1642 and 1668 versions are very numerous (a version published in 1655 is approximately that of 1668). See *The Poetical Works of Sir John Denham*, ed. Theodore H. Banks (New Haven, 1928). The existence of the two main versions makes the problem of analysis especially complex. On the one hand, if the poem is topical, the 1642 version is more closely related to the situation it deals with; on the other, it is the later version that has been known and that exerted its influence on Pope and others. I have tried to skirt the dilemma by making the later version my basic text and using the earlier version wherever it is especially helpful in clarifying the meaning of the poem.

the poet has taken a firm political position in addition to his physical one, and that from the political position he will survey a thematic scene. The analogue to the fact that Parnassus is wherever the poet succeeds in creating poetry is, we are told, the fact that the court is wherever the king may be: "as Courts make not Kings, but Kings the Court" (5). What is being denied is the inherent virtue of any particular place: Parnassus is not a place having the inherent power to inspire poetry in whoever may visit it, despite the ancient myth; the power lies in the poet, not outside him, and a Parnassus comes into being as a place wherever this power acts. In 1642, when the poem first appeared, men were seriously contemplating the thesis that the king owes his power to his election by the people. In mid-1642, moreover, Charles had removed from London to York and was enticing members of Parliament to join him. Parliament—the "high *Court* of Parliament"—insistently demanded his return to London in order that the parliamentary monarchy might function;[2] declared "the King's resolve to adjourn the next term of Parliament from Westminster to York, to be illegal"; and, after fining the members "now at Yorke attending on his Majestie," condemned them and those who had advised Charles to absent himself as "enemies to the peace of this Kingdome." The royal power, like the poetic power, Denham is saying, is not inherent in a place, but in a person. The source of government resides in the king alone, and wherever he governs, whether at Westminster or York, there is the place of Parliament, which is his own creation, just as Parnassus is the poet's.

Or consider the description of Windsor Hill that has so distressed some of the literalist critics: since the hill is the site of the monarch's palace.

> When Natures hand this ground did thus advance,
> 'Twas guided by a wiser power than Chance;
> Mark't out for such a use, as if 'twere meant
> T'invite the builder, and his choice prevent.
> Nor can we call it choice, when what we chuse,
> Folly, or blindness only could refuse.   (53–58)

As a naturalistic explanation, of course the lines seem unjustifiable exaggeration. But if poetry can make Cooper's Hill a Parnassus, and if Charles's presence localizes Parliament, poetry transforms Windsor Hill into meaning by identifying it with the King; the theme of the lines, therefore, is both the hill and Charles. In considering

2. See C. H. McIlwain, *The High Court of Parliament* (New Haven, 1934), chap. 3. The term "court" was regularly used for "Parliament" in the seventeenth century. James I, for example, defined Parliament as "nothing else but the head Court of the King and his vassals" (*Trew Law of Free Monarchies,* in *Political Works,* ed. C. H. McIlwain [Cambridge, Mass., 1918], p. 62).

Dryden's epistle we have already examined the complicated seventeenth-century debate over the sources of royal prerogative, and it is this subject that Denham is exploring with his metaphor. At a moment when a large number of the populace were insisting that the king is their own creation, to make or unmake, Denham is taking a position on the relation of divine anointment to popular appointment: the king is designated by "a wiser power than Chance," and popular election symbolized by the coronation, though real in itself, is predetermined by God. Denham's is the basic royalist conception of divine right: "the Coronation of the King is only a Declaration to the people that God hath given them a King; Outward Unctions, and Solemnities used at coronations, are but only Ceremonies, which confer no power to the King, For it was his from the Lord."[3] Only "Folly, or blindness"—indeed, only sin—could fail to choose (if we can "call it choice") as God has clearly designated.

So bold a stand by the poet on some of the most momentous issues of the day vividly suggests that the reader is consistently being called to look to the immediate affairs of state in the words that will follow. True, the reference to the place of Parliament appears casually as the subordinate part of a metaphor, and the poet's immediate subject at the opening is the nature of poetry, a subject that is extended into a discussion of the fancy. However, the subordinate but parallel relation of politics to poetry in those lines becomes a relationship of parallel coequality shortly thereafter: St. Paul's is secure while Waller sings of it in a poem on its restoration, and it is equally "Preserv'd from ruine by the best of Kings" (23–24). And now that the political theme has been raised to the surface and brought into a kind of identity with poetry, it takes over the further control of the poem.

The entire first half of the poem is now devoted to description and imaginative interpretation of three elevations that the poet views from his position on Cooper's Hill: St. Paul's Hill (14–38); the hill of Windsor Castle (39–110); and St. Anne's Hill with the ruins of Chertsey Abbey (111–56). It is almost explicit, however, that Denham is contemplating these not merely as discrete external objects but as coherently organized symbols generated by the friendly struggle between eye and mind. St. Paul's is significant to him not merely because the church-topped hill is a topographical feature to be painted with words but mainly because the "sacred pile," the cathedral church of the capital, had recently been "Preserv'd from ruine by the best of Kings" and now will stand secure despite "sword, or time, or fire"—or, he adds, "zeal more fierce

3. *Scutum Regale* (1660), p. 231.

than they" (21–24). By 1642 the fires of religious conflict had grown to white heat, and it is most unlikely that any poem of the moment touching on religious or civil affairs could fail to reflect the contemporary situation. Commons had, to mention only a few examples of its zeal, already meditated upon the Root and Branch Bill and the Bishops' Bill, which would have completely reconstituted the Church; the Puritan leader was already known as King Pym; and Charles, late in 1641, had felt the urgency to remind London of the recent "tumults and disorders" in the city and to pledge himself publicly to "maintaining and protecting the true Protestant religion, according as it hath been established in my two famous predecessors' times . . . and this I will do, if need be, to the hazard of my life and all that is dear to me."[4] Consequently, in focusing upon St. Paul's Cathedral, recently restored from decay by the efforts of Charles and of Archbishop Laud, the leader of the extreme Anglican group, Denham was calling attention to palpable evidence of the King's benevolent determination to preserve "the true Protestant religion" in the face of Puritan extremism and the impending civil wars. Charles had built against the ravages of sword, time, and fire, but the grestest threat against what he was preserving by his symbolic act was zeal, which threatened the entire Establishment.

On the other hand, Benedictine Chertsey Abbey, at the other edge of the poetic canvas, is now only a few crumbling walls, having been demolished by Henry VIII in "devotions name" (126). It is, therefore, the antithesis of St. Paul's and memorializes the vicious destruction of religion by the crown. By this sharp contrast of the restored cathedral and the ancient ruins, Denham is assuring that Charles, unlike Henry, is no religious hypocrite who crushes a religion after writing in its defense, but is sincere and unwavering in his Anglicanism and is determined to reform religion, not pull it down: "may no such storm/Fall on our times, where ruine must reform" (115–16), as Charles has reformed the ruins of St. Paul's to symbolize his reformation of the crumbling Anglican faith. The complex overtones of the contrasting symbols become evident when one recalls that the Puritans, now assuming Henry's former role, were demanding a complete leveling of church government and ritual and were accusing Charles and the Laudian party of Popery, the religion Henry had destroyed. There is gradually emerging, then, a kind of chiastic arrangement of thought that may well be an index to the structure and meaning of the poem. Charles has preserved the Church against popular destructive zeal while being accused of Popery; formerly it was the monarch, Henry, who had occupied the role now being played by the populace, and the result

4. *The Constitutional Documents of the Puritan Revolution*, ed. S. R. Gardiner   (Oxford, 1906), p. 201–202.

had been the ruined abbey that sharply contrasts with the newly refurbished St. Paul's. Moreover, this chiastic structure is further shaped by the facts that, like the current disorders among the populace, Henry's crime is also attributed to "Zeal" (153), a mere word with which civilization excuses its most barbarous acts, and that the zeal of both Henry and the present public is the product of their "luxury" (33, 124).

Between these topographical symbols of the benevolent and the tyrannical, sincere and hypocritical, altruistic and selfish management of religion, placed as though to allow the monarch to make his choice of either, stands the royal hill of Windsor. Wearing a "Crown of such Majestick towrs" (59), it is the natural correlative of the monarch.[5] But it is also more, for its very form is symbolic of the ideal king: Windsor hill is "an easie and unforc't ascent" (42), a "gentle height" (49). It is being implied, therefore, that the royal hill is Nature's manifestation of that harmony-through-opposition that the age continued to accept as the heart of the cosmic scheme.

The doctrine of *concordia discors* is at least as ancient as Pythagoras and Heraclitus, and had a remarkably vital history thereafter.[6] It is to be found in Plato, Empedocles, Cicero, Horace, Seneca, Plutarch, Ovid, Manilius, Quintilian, Nichomachus of Genasa, and Plotinus, among many others.[7] It recurs frequently among the Church fathers and spread widely in the Renaissance and thereafter. Very early the Pythagorean theory of the musical and celestial harmony of discords was assimilated into the doctrine; and even the Empedoclean thesis that friendship and hostility control the universe was almost regularly interpreted as identical with the

5. It is also likely that in comparing Windsor to Atlas (52) Denham had reference to the emblematic tradition reported by Alexander Ross (*Mystagogus Poeticus* [third ed., 1653], p. 37): "A King is the Atlas of his Commonwealth, both for strength and greatness."

6. The richest account of the concept is to be found in Leo Spitzer's "Classical and Christian Ideas of World Harmony," *Traditio*, 2 (1944), 409–64, 3 (1945), 307–64; a number of Mediaeval and Renaissance presentations of the theme have been collected by Rosamond Tuve, "A Mediaeval Commonplace in Spenser's Cosmology," *SP*, 30 (1933), 133–47; and there are helpful references in Maynard Mack's edition of Pope's *Essay on Man* (Twickenham ed., [1950], III, i).Professor Mack has been admirably perceptive in recognizing the importance of the idea for Pope. But there is great need of a comprehensive study of the idea in the sixteenth, seventeenth, and eighteenth

centuries, since it is one of the great controlling patterns of thought and of literature in this period. Perhaps the fullest application of the doctrine is to be found in the *De la Vicissitude ou Variété des Choses en l'Univers* (Paris, 1584) of Louis Le Roy, who expresses his central theme in this manner: "En telle manière est la terre, et toute autre chose en l'Univers, tempérée, et conservée par contraires et dissemblances. Ce n'est donc sans cause, que nature appète tant les contraires, faisant d'eux toute décense et beauté, non de semblables" (p. 10). Le Roy's treatise was translated by Robert Ashley as *Of the Interchangeable Course or Variety of Things in the Whole World* (1594), and part of it was twisted into English verse by John Norden in his *Vicissitudo Rerum* (1600).***

7. It is also the basic principle of the pseudo-Aristotelian *De Mundo* and the *De Mundo* of Apuleius.

doctrine of *concordia discors*.[8] For Heraclitus, as for others, the doctrine explained the design of the cosmos: "Existing things are brought into harmony by the clash of opposing currents. . . . All things come into being by conflict of opposites, and the sum of things flows like a stream."[9] One of the most charmingly blunt accounts of *concordia discors* appears in a couplet of the seventeenth-century John Norden: "Without a discord can no concord be,/Concord is when contrary things agree."[1] Since this was accepted as the cosmic principle, it was eventually sought everywhere in the microcosm—in the ways of man and society. Perhaps one of the most explicit transfers of the doctrine to the political order appears in a passage from Cicero preserved in St. Augustine's *City of God* (II, 21):

> As, among the different sounds which proceed from lyres, flutes, and the human voice, there must be maintained a certain harmony which a cultivated ear cannot endure to hear disturbed or jarring, but which may be elicited in full and absolute concord by the modulation even of voices very unlike one another; so, where reason is allowed to modulate the diverse elements of the state, there is obtained a perfect concord from the upper, lower, and middle classes as from various sounds; and what musicians call harmony in singing, is concord in matters of state, which is the strictest bond and best security of any republic, and which by no ingenuity can be retained where justice has become extinct.[2]

This it was that came to be the cosmic rationale for England's parliamentary monarchy and the model for the ideal attributes of the king of such a mixed state: the political harmony arising from

---

8. See, e.g., Pico della Mirandola's commentary on Benivieni's sonnet, in Thomas Stanley, *History of Philosophy* (1656), part 5, p. 101. For a compilation of early interpretations of the doctrine see Ralph Cudworth's *The True Intellectual System of the Universe* (1678), where it is a central principle in Cudworth's philosophy.

9. Diogenes Laertius, *Lives of Eminent Philosophers*, IX, 7–8 (trans. R. D. Hicks; Loeb Classical Library).

1. *The Labyrinth of Mans Life* (1614).

2. See also Juan de Solorzano Pereyra, *Emblemata regio-politica* (Madrid, 1651), emblem 48 ("Casura nisi Invicem Obstarent"), where the doctrine of *concordia discors* is very extensively applied to the structure and management of the state.

Edward Forset analyzed political *concordia discors* by way of analogy with the concord of contrarieties in the microcosm man: "For as in the bodie naturall, if the Wisdome of the Creator had not composed into a concord the contrarieties of the first Elements, it had (as still sticking in the confusion of the first Chaos) never attained the strength, beautie & order, which we now admire: So in the civill bodie, if prudent policie by advised tempering of the disparities of the people, should not conjoyne them to a well agreeing consent, how could any hope be conceived, but that the difference of poore and rich, vulgar & noble, ignorant and learned, fearfull and valiant, industrious and such as take their ease, must needs by their opposite qualities, not onely deface the dignitie, but also subvert the stabilitie of the state" (*A Comparative Discourse of the Bodie Natural and Politique* [1606], p. 38).

See also Jean Bodin, *The Six Bookes of a Commonweale*, trans. Richard Knolles (1606), where it is argued by analogy with cosmic concord and the "well tuned discord" of music that "of the very discord of the magistrates among themselves ariseth an agreeing welfare of all" (p. 498).

the conflict of monarch and populace is but an imitation of the cosmic harmony produced by the clash of the opposing elements. For example, one of Halifax' maxims of state directly draws on the analogy between the cosmic and political harmony-through-discord. Just as Ovid had said that all generation results from the discordant concord of fire and water (*Metamorphoses*, I, 430–33), so Halifax wrote that "*Power* and *Liberty* are like Heat and Moisture; where they are well mixt, every thing prospers; where they are single, they are destructive." And for this reason he gloried in

> . . . our blessed Constitution, in which Dominion and Liberty are so well reconciled: it giveth to the Prince the glorious Power of commanding Freemen, and to Subjects, the satisfaction of see-ing the Power so lodged, as that their Liberties are secure. . . . our Laws make a distinction between Vasselage and Obedience; between a devouring Prerogative, and a licentious ungovernable Freedom. . . . Our Government is in a just proportion, no un-natural swelling either of Power or Liberty.[3]

Even the Puritan Pym felt it not inconsistent with his political posi-tion to argue a variant of this same thesis.[4] And shortly after the Restoration, Davenant expected Charles II to imitate the ways of God by directing the warring factions into a political harmony:

> You keep with prudent arts of watchful care
> Divided Sects from a conjunctive War:
> And when unfriendly Zeal from Zeal dissents,
> Look on it like the War of Elements;
> And, God-like, an harmonious World create
> Out of the various discords of your State.[5]

Bishop Atterbury, then, was later merely repeating the common theme when he described England's political constitution as "nicely poiz'd between the Extremes of too much Liberty, and too much Power; the several Parts of it having a proper Check upon each other; By the means of which they are all restrain'd or soon re-duced, within their due Bounds." The very susceptibility of such a system to "Concussions within," he added, is ideal, for this "Dis-order . . . raises that Ferment which is necessary to bring all right again."[6]

In the ambience of this doctrine of *concordia discors* Denham's poem has its meaningful existence; and it quickly urges the reader to see that from this concept it will draw its poetic vitality. For Nature's design, expressed by the structure of Windsor Hill, now permeates the political world that the hill symbolizes; and the har-mony of tensions in Nature becomes both the symbol of the perfect

3. *Complete Works of George Savile*, ed. Walter Raleigh (Oxford, 1912), pp. 180, 62.
4. *The Speech or Declaration of John Pym* (1642).
5. *Works* (1673), p. 264.
6. *Sermons and Discourses* (fifth ed., 1740), I, 264–65.

balance of oppositions in the monarch and the proof of its necessity. Because the hill is an elevation and yet a gentle ascent, a perfect harmony of conflicting height and breadth, it corresponds to the fact that in its castle dwell Charles and his Queen, "Mars" and "Venus," who represent strength and beauty living in harmonious accord, not despite, but as a consequence of their antithetical attributes (39–40).[7]

Superficially considered, the reference to Charles and Henrietta Maria as Mars and Venus might well seem only deference to a panegyric convention: how better to praise the royal pair than to call the King martial and the Queen the goddess of beauty? But the perfect correspondence of this conjunction of opposites, Mars and Venus, to the already observable theme of *concordia discors* suggests that the mythological reference is integral to the poem, echoing as it does the union of the opposing dimensions of Windsor Hill and the chiastic relationship we have already noted between St. Paul's and Chertsey Abbey. How completely *concordia discors* as a mode of conception pervades the reference can be seen in the very structure of the parenthesis:

> . . . (where *Mars* with *Venus* dwells,
> Beauty with strength). . . .

The sense and the grammatical forms of the two clauses are the same, each occupies a hemistich, and both appear in the same couplet. Yet, they appear in opposite halves of different lines and differ in metrical length, although taken together they would constitute a complete heroic line. Moreover, although they are parallel, even almost redundant in meaning, the order of terms (Mars, Venus) is inverted in the second line (Beauty, strength), even to the extent of substituting for the monosyllable "Mars" the trochee "Beauty" and for the trochee "Venus" the monosyllable "strength." The passage, then, not only specifies a harmonious union of contraries; it is itself a verbal enactment of the theme, producing poetic harmony out of a complex system of similar opposites. For if *concordia discors* is the order of the universe, it must also be the source of harmony in man's arts.[8]

---

7. As John Norden had written ·in order to prove that even "The *Heavens* have their moving contrarie,/But equally disposed, uphold the rest":

> Milde *Venus* as a meane, is placed neere
> Unto fell Mars, to counterchecke his ire.

(*Vicissitudo Rerum*, stanza 89)

8. As would be expected, the idea of the harmony of discords was everywhere applied to theories of music; see, for example, Athanasius Kircher, *Musurgia* *Universalis* (Rome, 1650). For its application to theories of painting, especially with respect to chiaroscuro, see Frederick Hard, "EK's Reference to Painting," *ELH*, 7 (1940), 121; and H. V. S. Ogden, "Principles of Variety and Contrast in Seventeenth-Century Aesthetics," *JHI*, 10 (1949), 159. But it was understood that beauty in all its forms consists of the harmony of contraries; see, e.g., Pico della Mirandola, *Opera* (Basle, 1601), II, 634.

But the perfect fusion here of expression and concept is not merely the product of Denham's artistic contrivance. Rather, expression and concept are so contained in each other as to imply a single all-controlling mode of thought because this particular mythological reference is itself deeply rooted in the history of *concordia discors*. The myth of Mars and Venus had long been the traditional allegory for the theme because the offspring of their union was said to be the goddess Harmonia.[9] In his life of Pelopidas, for example, Plutarch saw in the myth the principle of civic order: the Thebans did well, he wrote, to make Harmony, the daughter of Mars and Venus, their tutelar deity, since where force and courage (Mars) are joined with gracefulness and winning behavior (Venus) a harmony ensues that combines all the elements of society in perfect consonance and order. In his treatise on Isis and Osiris he interpreted the birth of Harmonia from Venus and Mars as a symbolic expression of all the ancient dualisms, Heraclitean, Empedoclean, and Pythagorean: harmony is the balance of the creative and destructive powers. And similarly the unknown author of *De Vita et Poesi Homeri* found in the myth the whole Empedoclean doctrine of the cosmic order born of the clash of opposing elements.[1]

By reconciling perpendicular directions, then, the hill invites both "A pleasure, and a reverence from the sight" (46), corresponding to the harmonious beauty-strength of the royal pair. For the perfect marriage, even as Dr. Johnson was to define it in his remoteness from the tradition, is a "*concordia discors*, that suitable disagreement which is always necessary to intellectual harmony,"[2] although the intellectual factor is an especially Johnsonian addition. But even the individual elements of this ideal *concordia discors* at Windsor are independently a harmony of differences. The hill, being a "gentle height," not only symbolizes the union of Venus and Mars, but is also an "Embleme" of the King, in whose face one sees "meekness, heightned with Majestick Grace" (47–48) or (the earlier version added) "friend-like sweetnesse, and a King-like aw," gentle

<hr/>

9. Hyginus, VI, 148; Hesiod, *Theogony*, 937, 975; Lactantius on Statius' *Thebaid*, I, 288; Lactantius, *Divine Institutes*, I, xvii; Eustathius on Homer's *Iliad*, XXI, 416. See further, Erwin Panofsky, *Studies in Iconology* (New York, 1939), pp. 163–64. Alexander Ross (*Mystagogus Poeticus*) explained that Harmonia was born of Mars and Venus because "the two chief props of a kingdome are *Mars* and *Venus*, warre and propagation, and these two live in harmony and order." In his commentary on Benivieni's sonnet (trans. by Thomas Stanley in his *History of Philosophy*) Pico supported the claim

that beauty is "the union of contraries, a friendly enmity, a disagreeing concord" and "cannot subsist without contrariety" by the myth of Mars and Venus: "she curbs and moderates him, this temperament allaies the strife betwixt these contraries. And in Astrologie, *Venus* is plac'd next *Mars*, to check his destructive influence" (I, v).
1. In *Plutarchi Opera*, ed. Dübner (Paris, 1876), v, 127.
2. *Rambler* 167. Cp. Dryden, "To the Duchess on her Return from Scotland," 44: "Discord, that makes the harmony of hearts."

kindness and royal severity, mingled majesty and love.[3] That is, the King, even apart from his union with his Venus, is that harmony of power and liberty that makes England's parliamentary monarchy the true cosmic form of government. Shortly thereafter Denham again describes the perfect king in terms of the harmony of contraries, piety, or saintliness, now being substituted for the corresponding "friend-like sweetnesse" and martial prowess for "King-like aw." By virtue of his rank, the King is chief of the Knights of the Garter, whose patron is the soldier-martyr St. George; indeed, Charles does not need the emblem of the Garter, since, uniting contraries, he "is himself the Souldier and the Saint," and in choosing St. George as patron of the Order, Edward III (motivated by "love/Or victory" [83–84], corresponding to the Venus-Mars reference) had prophetically chosen a type of Charles, the perfect union of saintliness and military might (101–10). As soldier and saint, Charles belongs both to the world and to heaven, just as it has seemed uncertain whether St. Paul's is the earth reaching towards heaven ("a proud/ Aspiring mountain," [17–18]) or heaven descended to earth ("descending cloud"). As God's vicar, as soldier-saint, the King, like St. Paul's, is indifferently "a part of Earth, or sky" (16).[4] Through the same set of emblems Denham then extends the significance of Charles so that, as the concordance of clashing religion and war, he becomes a world monarch, the archetype of monarchy. The blue garter surrounding the insignia of the Order, he claims, symbolizes the sea surrounding England, recently again annexed as part of England's domain; but since these seas extend to "the Worlds extreamest ends," they bound not only England but also the "Endless" world (105–108). The extension is inevitable, not only because England is a microcosm of the world, but also because, *concordia discors* being the law of the entire cosmos, its perfect manifestation in Charles justifies his role as universal sovereign.

The hill of Windsor, then, which gave rise to these successive and complex modes of *concordia discors*, is certainly not merely a topographical feature, nor merely a convenient arbitrary metaphor; it is the symbol inherent in the concept because it is Nature's phys-

3. The miraculous paradox that the king joins the contraries, severity and kindness, or majesty and love, derives from the fact that he is viceroy to God, who unites His justice and mercy. Compare Jonson's praise of James I: "The contraries which time till now/Nor fate knew where to join, or how,/Are Majesty and Love" (*Love Freed from Ignorance and Folly*).

In the 1642 version the Queen is also described in paradoxically antithetical terms to reveal that she also is a perfect harmony: in her pregnancy—that is, in her perfection as woman—she is "proud," yet seems to make that pride her shame," and the poet, following the convention of comparing the lady's beauties with features of the landscape, compares her womb to the gentle height of Windsor Hill, just as he had compared the King's countenance to it.

4. The 1642 version comes closer to the traditional concept of man as a compound of heaven and earth: Charles has "That fortitude which made him [St. George] famous here,/That heavenly piety, which Saints him there."

ical expression of her divine formula for harmony and consequently expresses the fusion of popular freedom and sovereign authority essential for political order. "The whole world is kept in order by discord," wrote Owen Felltham; "and every part of it is but a more particular composed jar. . . . it makes greatly for the Maker's glory, that such an admirable harmony should be produced out of such an infinite discord. The world is both a perpetual war and a wedding."[5]

But if with this interpretation of Windsor Hill as symbolic of the politico-cosmic harmony arising from the proper tension of strength and beauty, war and religion, severity and kindness—or, inclusively, the King's combined regard for his own majesty and gentle concern for his people, and his saint-like determination to preserve the saving grace of religion even if he must do so with a soldier's arms—if with this we now return to the other two hills at the extreme edges of Denham's landscape, we find it has been an oversimplification to define them as symbolizing merely good and bad royal managements of religion.

For in viewing St. Paul's hill Denham has seen not only the re-built cathedral but also the tumultuous city of the populace at the base of the hill, a thick cloud of busyness (25–28). The zealous Londoners rush about, "Some to undo, and some to be undone" (32), toiling (according to the 1642 version) "to prevent imaginarie wants" and yet only feeding their "disease." This was the excessive acquisitiveness that caused the Londoners to protest Charles's tax levies and demand economic assistance; this the destructive zeal that led them to insist upon violent church reform. The earlier version, being directed more immediately to the political events, adds: "afraid to be secure" and "sicke of being well," "Some study plots, and some those plots t'undoe,/Others to make 'em, and undoe 'em too." In this extravagant and pointless commercial and religious energy of the citizenry, Denham was prophetic enough to foresee the civil wars: looking down upon this "thicker cloud/Of business" in the city, he is like those who

> . . . rais'd in body, or in thought
> Above the Earth, or the Ayres middle Vault,
> Behold how winds, and stormes, and Meteors grow,
> How clouds condense to raine, congeale to snow,
> And see the Thunder form'd, before it teare
> The ayre. . . . (1642)

This, too, is more than metaphoric, for, with precise knowledge of the prevailing meteorology, Denham is describing the disordered clash of the elements. Since the harmony of the physical world

5. Resolve 41.

results from the concordant opposition of the unlike four elements, the disorders formed in "middle air" result from opposition alone, without harmony. "Meteors" were known as the product of discordant strife among the elements; and in describing the "Thunder" (i.e. thunderbolt) as tearing the air, Denham was alluding to what was considered the most disruptive and destructive force in the war of the elements. The human correlative of this storm is the Londoners' running "with like hast, though several ways" (31). The crime of the citizenry, then, is not merely economic or religious or civil; it is a sin against the cosmic harmony. And therefore the gathering storm likened to the populace is, Denham insists, no mere metaphor; it is "to him who rightly things esteems,/No other in effect than what it seems" (29–30), for the clash in the heavens and the strife in the state are truly one.[6]

Just as the meteor metaphor represents discord without a controlling concord—chaotic energy alone—so the poet also attributes to the populace excesses resulting from the absence of any limiting opposition to its single energy; and in this sense the populace is quite unlike Charles, in whom each quality is balanced by its contending opposite. Even unopposed good, in terms of the dialectic of *concordia discors*, becomes evil through excess and thereby destroys itself, just as in the state too much power becomes tyranny, too much liberty chaos. Correspondingly, the populace is motivated by an unopposed greed, since the crown is symbolically represented in this tableau only by Charles's benevolent restoration of St. Paul's. The unchecked citizenry, therefore, only increases its desires by increasing its stores, and "feedes only the disease"; it causes itself to be "afraid to be secure," "sicke of being well," and "Blinded with light" (1642). It seeks its peace in tumult, its "heaven in hell." For when an appetite is not brought into concordant clash with a contrary force it paradoxically both grows to its own excess and in this act destroys itself by becoming its own opposite; and the appropriate metaphor for this endlessly circular and pointless mutability through excess is the rivers which grow until they are "lost in Seas" and then are reconveyed by secret veins, "there to be lost again" (35–36).

The populace therefore sins on both sides of *concordia discors*: as a forming storm it is a disconsonant strife; in another sense it is a single force that, through the absence of any contention to

6. Cp. Norden, *Vicissitudo Rerum:*
The Starres that wander, and that
  fix'd remaine,
Do cause in ayre great changes,
  Cold and *Heate,*
Windes, Thunder, Tempests, and
  great gusts of *Raine,*
And their *Aspects* and *Oppositions*

met,
Some strange presages of *Events*
  beget,
  Of *Warre,* of *Death,* of *Famine,*
    Drought, and *Pest,*
Yet nought befalles, but by
  supernall hest.

moderate it into a harmony, rushes to its two destructive extremes, excess and extinction. Consequently, not only is there chaotically undirected and therefore contradictory energy ("with like hast, though several ways, they run/Some to undo, and some to be undone," [31–32]); there is also an excessive energy that, by its excess, destroys itself (others study to make plots and "undoe 'em too" [1642]). Yet even worse than these disorders, the public has also mistaken irreconcilable and therefore mutually destructive extremes for a *concordia discors*, wishing to have both "luxury, and wealth" (33). But these only falsely seem to be like authority and liberty, which, by contending, moderate each other and preserve both. Instead, they are sheer contradictions, not reconcilable differences; they are "like war and peace" and therefore "Are each the others ruine, and increase" (33–34), just as excessive desire for security creates a fear which destroys the security and just as excessive quest for wealth results in an increase of desires, which then destroys the wealth.[7] As Ben Jonson expressed this dialectical extension of the doctrine of *concordia discors*,

> What though all concord's borne of contraries?
> So many follies will confusion prove,
> And like a sort of jarring instruments,
> All out of tune: because (indeed) we see
> There is not that analogie, twixt discords,
> As between things but merely opposite.[8]

The entire first tableau, therefore, consists of a symbol of the monarch's benevolent restoration and preservation of religion and, at the base of that symbol, a people zealously acquiring a chaotic and unbalanced power. Both a religious and an economic factor are involved, as indeed they were in the conflict between Charles and his people. Inversely, the ruin of Chertsey is attributed to Henry's tyrannical "rage," a chaos-making force like the modern Londoner's busyness, and to Henry's desire to feed his "Luxury," the analogue of which is the present overacquisitiveness of the Londoners. And just as the religious disorder in the shadow of St. Paul's has been attributed to the material appetite of the citizenry, not to a sincere religious impulse, so having assigned the destruction of Chertsey Abbey to Henry's desire for luxury, the poet adds that "this Act, to varnish o're the shame/Of sacriledge, must bear

---

7. Clearly, Denham is alluding to the popular proverb that described the endlessly circular mutability created by excess: "Warre bringeth ruine, ruine bringeth povertie, povertie procureth peace, and peace in time increaseth riches, riches causeth stateliness, stateliness increaseth envie, envie in the end procureth deadly mallice, mortall mallice proclaimeth open warre and battaile" (Thomas Fenne, *Fennes Frutes* [1590], quoted by Paul A. Jorgensen, "Views of War in Elizabethan England," *JHI*, 12 [1952], 478). For an extensive history of the proverb, see Swift, *A Tale of a Tub*, ed. Guthkelch and Smith, pp. 217–18 n.

8. *Cynthias Revels*, V, v, 9–14.

devotions name" (125–26). Both the scene at St. Paul's and that at Chertsey, then, represent the failure of a *concordia discors* between monarch and populace, between religion and wealth; but the relationships within the two scenes are inverted. For just as there is no possible harmony between Charles's gentle religious benevolence and the extravagant worldly energy of the populace, so there was no harmony between Henry's tyrannical acquisitiveness and the religious lethargy of his people, since

> Then did Religion in a lazy Cell,
> In empty, airy contemplations dwell;
> And like the block, unmoved lay. . . . (135–37)

Moreover, the present public sin against *concordia discors* in allowing unrestrained wealth to run to its two contradictory extremes, luxury and poverty, had previously been committed by Henry. Having "spent the Treasures of his Crown," he condemned public wealth as luxury and so destroyed public wealth to feed his own luxury (123–24). The consequence is that at every point Henry, like the present citizenry, rushed to extremes that deny each other. He wished his bold crime to be understood a "real, or at least a seeming good" (128). He did not fear to do ill, but feared "the Name" (129); and, not being restrained by the opposing force of conscience, he wished fame, which of course is directly contradicted by his infamous deeds (130). But the most precise similarity between Henry and the seventeenth-century populace results from his treatments of religion. Because it was Henry's character to fly to mutually destructive limits, he wrote an attack on Luther in defense of Catholicism and then abolished the Catholic church in England. Therefore, just as the excessiveness of the populace was defined by the fact that luxury and wealth are "each the others ruine, and increase" (34), so Henry's is defined by the fact that "he the Church at once protects, & spoils" (131).[9]

At St. Paul's, then, violent public greed, masquerading as religious zeal, is too powerful for reconciliation with the mere religious benevolence of the crown—the King appears as only saint, not soldier; at St. Anne's, violent royal greed, masquerading as religious

9. In the earlier version Henry's violation of *concordia discors* was somewhat more vividly expressed. According to a long tradition of statesmanship, princes should reconcile in themselves the rival pursuits of arms and letters, and the prince's union of sword and pen was a persistent theme in the emblem books (see R. J. Clements, "Pen and Sword in Renaissance Emblem Literature," *MLQ*, 5 [1944], 131–41; and "Princes and Literature," *MLQ*, 16 [1955], 114–23). In translating Henry's actions into this theme, Denham underscored the mere antagonism of these two pursuits in Henry and hence his failure to bring them into a necessary harmony:

> While for the church his learned pen disputes,
> His much more learned sword his pen confutes.

In the later version Denham sacrificed the irony of this violation of *concordia discors* for a pun on the word "stiles" (132).

solicitude, was too powerful for the religious lethargy of the people —Henry was the soldier, not the saint. But between the two stands Windsor, home of the Order of the Garter, in whose patron, St. George, is reconciled the rivalry of soldier and saint. In him, and consequently in Charles, power and religion are united in the harmony of oppositions. The three hills, therefore, are symbolic of three kinds of kingship—it is significant that the first is *"Crown'd with that sacred pile"* (15), that Windsor, like Cybele, wears *"A Crown of such Majestick towrs"* (59), and that St. Anne's was once with *"A Chappel crown'd* (114). And each of these kingships is defined in terms of the different relations of sovereign and populace, religion and activity. The central hill, Windsor, being the residence of Charles, is the perfect harmonious balance and interaction of the two powers, and there the natural and political ideals coincide. The other two hills, described in terms of the immediately pertinent religious and economic dissensions, illustrate the dangerous and unnatural imbalance of royal solicitude and popular zeal on the one hand, and of royal tyranny and public apathy on the other. The first may be read as the precarious imbalance of the moment—if Charles does not exercise greater force, or if the public does not moderate its zeal. The last is a historic warning to Charles not to crush the public and a reminder to the rebellious public of its past fate, but a fate that the benevolent Charles will not initiate. And the central tableau symbolizes the perfect *concordia discors* in the crown that requires only a corresponding but inverse perfection in the populace to form the ideal mixed monarchy.[1]

D. C. ALLEN

[Lovelace's *The Grasshopper*]†

This poem was written and sent by Lovelace to his fellow poet and royalist, Charles Cotton, sometime after the collapse of the great cause and the execution of King Charles. It is not unlikely that it was written by Lovelace in a moment of dejection after his own imprisonment and impoverishment. The story of the summer grasshopper that makes no provision for winter, that plays its violin while the ants are busy at harvest, obviously supplies the pre-text of

1. The remainder of Wasserman's article deals in some detail wtih "the image of the *concordia discors* of the total state," represented by the "Thames couplets" (ll. 189–192), and with Denham's account of the stag hunt. For a differing view of this episode, cf. Brendan O Hehir's extended discussion of the vari-ous drafts and printed texts of "Cooper's Hill" in *Expans'd Hieroglyphicks: A Study of Sir John Denham's Coopers Hill, with a Critical Edition of the Poem* (Berkeley, 1969), pp. 165–256 [*Editor*].
† From *Image and Meaning: Metaphoric Traditions in Renaissance Poetry* (Baltimore, 1960), pp. 80–92.

the poem. The cavaliers were grasshoppers, and when this poem was written they were learning the lesson of the insect. Any reader can find all of this in "The Grasse-Hopper," and it is not surprising that the poem has been usually described as a simple cavalier lyric, a powerful overflow of alcoholic feelings recollected in adversity. But the poem is richer than it seems on first reading, and an examination of the tradition, of the metaphoric history of the insect that is the subject, will suggest that the theme has emotional possibilities that have not been understood. [Quotes the entire poem.]

At first reading, the poem separates rather naturally into two parts. Stanzas I–V set a familiar measure by recalling in a submerged but personified fashion the literary ancestry of the insect that is the subject. We recognize the subtune at once; it is Anacreon, whose poem on the grasshopper had been earlier translated by Belleau and Cowley. But Lovelace's poem is no forthright rendering; it is a more complicated chorus of voices. With the sixth stanza the imaginative rhythm begins to alter, and not only is Horace heard, but there is also an immediate contrast between the past and the present, between the symbolic history of the grasshopper and the immediate history of the poet and his friends. The prudent morality of stanzas IV and V is rejected and, after a series of variations, replaced by a Horatian act of will. In this artistic voluntary there are both Christian and pagan tones. The remedy for the moment is provided by the doctrine of Horace, although the inner conviction of an infinite present, once satisfaction is procured, is totally Christian. This rough summation, however, must be annotated in terms of Lovelace's gift from his predecessors.

Almost at the beginning of the history of poetic transformations, Anacreon of Teos heard the grasshopper in the fields of summer and put him into song. He took delight in the insect because it could be as drunk as a happy king on dew, because it owned all that it saw about it and took tribute from the seasons. It is beloved of the Muses for its singing, he tells us, and blessed by Phoebus; and if this is not merit enough, the unsuffering song-lover is as ethereal as a god.

> Ἀπαθής δ', ἀναιμόσαρκος
> Σχεδὸν εἶ θεοῖς ὅμοιος[1]

This in substance is what Anacreon wrote, and the first twelve lines of Lovelace's poem[2] reproduce these themes against a now universal landscape. But in these stanzas there is obviously more than a

1. XXXIV.17–18. The Greeks do not distinguish clearly between the various singing insects, and it is not always clear what they mean when they use τέττιξ, καλαμαία, μάντις, and ἀκρίς. The translators have done little better, for Anacreon's poem is probably about the cicada.

2. I have used the text of C. H. Wilkinson (Oxford, 1930). The two last lines of the third stanza may be paraphrased as "days make men merry, yourself merry, and melancholy streams away" or "make melancholy streams (rivers) also merry."

pleasant rewarming of Anacreon's poem, and we do well to turn the hands of the poetic clock backward for a better understanding.

Hesiod had also known the "blue-winged" grasshopper that perched on green boughs, singing in the heat of the dog days when the beard grew on the oats;[3] the grasshopper that made sonorous odes in the luxuriant months when goats were fattest, wine best, women amorous, and men languid.[4] It is, however, Homer who creates a symbolic prejudice, when he compares the song of the grasshopper to the "lily-like voices" of the old Trojan aristocrats, who chattered on the wall as Queen Helen walked through the wide-way to the Skaian Gate.[5] From poems of this nature, the champions of Charles might imagine that the grasshopper, the βασιλεύς of Anacreon, had aristocratic pretensions; if they did not heed the whisper of these texts, there were those that flatly stated the case. "It is only recently," Thucydides writes of the Athenians, "that their rich old men left off . . . fastening their hair with a tie of golden grasshoppers."[6] The so-called Suidas states that the grasshopper was the insignia of the Athenian nobles because not only was the insect a musician, but like Erechtheus, founder of the city, it was also born of the earth.[7] So the insect that sings throughout the rich and prosperous seasons of the year, the insect of warmth and light, is given the colors of wisdom possessed among the Greeks by the noblemen of Athens.

If for the Greeks the grasshopper is a symbol of the gay months and their magic, if he is also the representative in nature of the ἄριστοι, he is most triumphantly the analogue of the poet-singer, whose verses he so delicately graced throughout antiquity.[8] For this reason Meleager is securely in the tradition when he invokes the grasshoppers as the "Muse of the cornlands (ἀρουραίη Μοῦσα), the song writer of the dryads, the challenger in voice and verse of the of the great Pan.[9] In one ancient myth, a singing grasshopper, by alighting on the peg from which the lyre string had broken, helped Eunomos of Locris win the prize at the Pythian games by supplying the wanting notes.[1] Another legend, probably invented by Plato, may be used to fortify this one.

Once, when Socrates and Phaedrus were talking, the old philosopher heard the grasshoppers singing and said that they had received gifts from the gods which, in turn, they imparted to men. When

3. "Shield of Achilles," *Opera,* ed. Flach (Leipzig, 1878), pp. 393–400.
4. *Theogony,* 581–86.
5. *Iliad* III.151–53.
6. *History* I.6.
7. *Historica* (Basel, 1564), col. 959.
8. It is everywhere part of rural decoration; see Theocritus XVI.94–96; Vergil *Eclogues* II.12–13; *Georgics* III.328;

"Culex" 151; *Copa* 27–28. The *Greek Anthology* is filled with poems to the grasshopper; see VII.189–94, 197–98, 201; IX.92.
9. *Greek Anthology,* VII, 195–96.
1. Strabo *Geography* VI.i, 9. Paulus Silentiarius (*G.A.,* VI, 54) puts this myth into elegant verse.

the exquisite Phaedrus inquired about the nature of these gifts, Socrates related the following story:

> A lover of the Muses should surely not be ignorant of this. It is said that once these grasshoppers were a race of men that lived before the Muses existed. When the Muses were born and song appeared, they were so moved by pleasure that as they sang, they forgot to eat and death caught them unawares. They live now in the grasshoppers, having that boon from their birth until their death. When they die, they inform the Muses in Heaven who worships them here below. Terpsichore, they tell of those who have honored her in the dance, and thus make them dearer to her; Erato, they tell of her lovers and to each sister they report according to her honorers. But to Calliope, the eldest, and to Urania, the second of the nine, they bear tidings of those who pass their lives in philosophic study and the observance of their special music; for these are the Muses, who having Heaven for their particular sphere and words both human and divine, speak most gladly.[2]

So with Plato, whose own musical voice was likened by Timon[3] to the "lily-songs" of the Hecademian grasshoppers, the insects become the apotheoses of human singers who have lost their lives through their love of art. "Dropt thee from Heav'n, where now th'art reard." The insect—Plato's myth and Anacreon's poem intermarry—is now a poet, and the evidence of its transformation, with a further qualification, is found in the writings of Flavius Philostratus.

Among the letters of the author of *Apollonius* and the *Imagines*, books popular with men of the Renaissance, is one commending the poet Celsus to a wealthy patron. This poet, Philostratus writes, has, "as do the good grasshoppers [οἱ χρηστοὶ τέττιγες], devoted his life to song; you will see to it that he is fed on more substantial food than dew."[4] At the touch of metaphor the poet is made a grasshopper; but in the *Apollonius*, Philostratus associates the grasshopper with the plight of men who have lost out. The philosopher Demetrius, exiled to Dicaearchia by the Roman despot, cries out in envy of the singing insects and says to Apollonius that they, at least, are never in danger of persecution and are above human calumny, for they have been set aloft by the Muses so that they "might be the blissful poets of that felicity which is theirs."[5] This comparison of Demetrius is close to the central tone of "The Grasse-Hopper."

By following the tradition through antiquity, we come on imaginative identifications that help us read this seventeenth-century poem. We know that the grasshopper was beloved of the Muses; that it

2. *Phaedrus* 259. I cannot find this legend in any text prior to Plato's; Photius mentions it as if it were common knowledge (*Bibliotheca* [*PG*, CIII, 1354]).

3. Diogenes Laertius *Lives* III.7.
4. *Opera*, ed. Kayser (Leipzig, 1870), p. 364.
5. *Ibid.*, p. 261.

had once been a human artist and continued to accompany and instruct human artists; that it was a king, an aristocrat, a badge of royalty, a poet; and that it was identified with men in political disfavor. This multiple suggestiveness may explain why Cowley translated Anacreon's poem and why Lovelace sought to remake it into something at once familiar yet novel. When we read the first three stanzas of Lovelace's poem, all that we have learned from the Greeks is born again. The grasshopper is drunk on dew, now a "Delicious teare"; he swings from the oaten beard on which Hesiod had placed him; but like the song-obsessed Platonic grasshoppers, he has been "reard" to Heaven. We see at once behind the literal front, for we know that the grasshopper is an aristocrat, a King. We have been reading a poem about a King and a cause that are dead on earth but living in Heaven. The poem has nothing to do with grasshoppers.

Choosing what in many respects was an optimistic symbol, Lovelace annotated it with melancholia. According to the bright Attic tradition, as represented by the poem of Meleager, the grasshopper's music was the anodyne of sorrow, and Lovelace remembers this in the latter lines of the third stanza. But the living grasshopper of the Greek solar months is made a poetic prelude to the inexperienced innocent, "poore verdant foole," who is in Heaven. In this interplay of life and death, tersely suggested by stanzas IV and V, we pass from what is light and warm into the cold darkness of inescapable defeat and death.

> But ah the Sickle! Golden Eares are Cropt;
>   *Ceres* and *Bacchus* bid good night;
> Sharpe frosty fingers all your Flowr's have topt,
>   And what sithes spar'd, Winds shave off quite.
>
> Poore verdant foole! and now green Ice! thy Joys
>   Large and as lasting, as thy Peirch of Grasse,
> Bid us lay in 'gainst Winter, Raine, and poize
>   Their flouds, with an o'erflowing glasse.

The quiet warning of the first stanza, which had been further muted by the bright Anacreontic quatrains, is now made into a torrent of trumpets. Behind the allegory of nature and the classical figments, the emotional current of the decade in which the poem was written comes plain. The grasshopper King, who symbolically loved the sun, has been harvested with the harvest. The flowers of his realm are topped by the "sithes" or, spared by these, shaved by the cruel winds. The merry men, faced by winter, look to the lesson of the summer singer. At this point, too, the poet makes his own self-identifications, for all that antiquity had attributed to the grasshopper—the sign of the aristocrat, the symbol of the poet singer, and the man in political ill favor—suit him. The emphasis is solemn enough and with it Lovelace remembers many things. He recalls, perhaps, the legend of the impotent Tithonus, but he expresses the tragedy of the summer-happy insect with that prudent variant of the Aesopica.[6] He leaves the myrtles and laurels of the Greek sea islands to inhabit for a while the north of cold and sunlessness.

In the gathering shadows of the world of death we hear for a moment an ancient funeral chant. The crops are harvested. Ceres and Bacchus have departed to a deeper sleep than that enjoyed by the sunlight grasshopper when its "Poppy workes." Winter has frozen even Fate. The North Wind strikes with "his frost-stretch'd Winges." December comes in tears far different from those that "Dropt thee from Heav'n." Sullenly, the "darke Hagge" hangs about "light Casements." Anacreon's season is over. Nature is now sternly present, thinly veiling with her realities the parallel actualities of the poet's life. We leave the dark external world to enter the poet's heart. In this black moment of cold, the Christian tone begins, for Lovelace remembers the once bright celebration of the wintered year.

> Dropping *December* shall come weeping in,
>   Bewayle th' usurping of his Raigne;
> But when in show'rs of old Greeke we beginne,
>   Shall crie, he hath his Crowne againe!

Pathos and hope, together with December memories of the Roman Saturnalia, are joined in this somberly happy stanza, but to increase its emotion we must remember the Christmas prince, who wore his crown during the festivities of the Christmas week as proudly as Charles had worn his.[7] But the royalty of Christmas, shared by all who kept the feast, had been despoiled, as the royalists were despoiled, by the new masters of the state. For a number of years John Evelyn recorded the dismal fall of the Christmas king. One of his entries reads: "Christmasday, no sermon any where, no church being permitted to be open, so observed it at home."[8]

Lovelace's solution, like Evelyn's, is based on privacy and withdrawal. The aristocratic poets may be the victims of a frosty fortune,

6. The fable of the industrious ant and the careless grasshopper was popularized in the Middle Ages by Alexander Neckham (*Novus Aesopus* XXIX). It also appears in various French redactions; see J. Bastin, *Recueil General des Isopets* (Paris, 1929), and Marie de France, *Poesies*, ed. De Roquefort (Paris, 1832), II, 123–25. Seneca suggests the legend in *Epistolae Morales* LXXXVII.19–20. The early Fathers think of the insect in the metaphoric manner of the poets (Ambrose, *Hexameron* [*PL*, XIV, 251–52]), or commend it for some Christian quality (Gregory, *Oratio* [*PG*, XXXVI,

59]; and Jerome, *Epistulae* XXII.18).
7. The career of such a prince, who had in his titles the distinction of "high Regent of the Hall" (probably Gloucester Hall, Lovelace's college) has come down to us in an eyewitness account; see G. Higgs, *An Account of the Christmas Prince, as it was exhibited in the University of Oxford in the year 1607* (London, 1816).
8. See the *Diary* (De Beer edition) for December 25 in 1652, 1654, 1655. The parliamentary order of December 19, 1644, abolished the observance of Christmas.

but they can "create/A Genuine Summer in each others breast," a summer that inwardly is more real than the winters of Nature and Fate. So when December comes lamenting the usurping of "his Raigne," the "his" means both the King of England and the King of Christmas. To emend this tragic state, Lovelace and Cotton can make bowers in each other's breasts where the two rejected kings may dwell with them. By this act of the imagination, Christian in its import (for "the Kingdom of Heaven is within you"), they will privately establish a reality greater than the facts allow. To the winter rains, which are December's tears as opposed to those that banished Ceres wept for the crops, the poets will offer a counter-blast, "show'rs of old Greeke," wine and perhaps, the Greek point of view. Both they and the mourning month can then say of the two dead kings, "he hath his Crowne againe."

It could be said that "The Grasse-Hopper," in spite of these more subtle undertones, is simply a cavalier drinking song, not unlike Cotton's "Chanson à Boire" or "Clepsydra." Alcohol had always been a cavalier cure, and Alexander Brome can advise his friends to seek refuge in wine, "in big-bellied bowls," "true philosophy lies in the bottle." Some of this drunken logic certainly seeps into Lovelace's poem; in fact, it is the ostensible mode. We must not forget that the poem, though it began in death, passed into warmth and light, that though we are now in the night and the cold, we shall emerge into an eternal beatitude that will cancel temporal despair. A consciousness of eternity is present in this poem even when the metaphors of death and despair are paraded in stanzas IV and V; it comes resolutely forward in "Our sacred harthes shall burne eternally/As Vestall Flames." Opposed to the North Wind, the savage symbol of death and evil, are the virginal fires of the ever burning hearth within the human heart. This is the kingdom of the heart—this "Aetna in Epitome"; but it is also something that cannot be lost because it is something "we will create." The general state has perished and Lovelace proposes to replace it with another state, one that is inner, private.

The kingdom of the heart that Lovelace would restore is not one of retreat and withdrawal, the resolution in isolation that charmed so many of his fellow sufferers;[9] it is rather a revision of his own cosmogony. The hovering emblem of the winged North Wind, against which Lovelace directs the symbolic fires of the "sacred harthes," makes firm this revision; for Lovelace must have seen in Aquilo, as Milton did, the bony face of death. The wind

9. On the cavaliers' praise of solitude as an escape from the evils of the Common-wealth, see H. G. Wright, "The Theme of Solitude and Retirement in Seven-teenth Century Literature," *Études Anglaises*, VII (1954), 22–35.

that the ancients called "horrisonus," "saevus," "ferus," "horrifer," and "crudelis" was a bitter symbol for this generation. Evil was North, from whence streamed the gonfalon of death, a banner that men said blew significantly "ab sinistro."[1] The vestal fires that blast with their heart heat the North and the cold, the "show'rs of old Greeke" that dry up tears and rain, are augmented in their symbolic services by the display of lights that whip the "darke Hagge" of Night from "the light Casements." Within themselves, the frozen poets will remake the lost summer of the grasshopper. It is more than a lost summer; it is a shore of light as Vaughan would have understood it. This will be done, Lovelace informs Cotton, by means of candles as potent as the planet Venus, the "cleare *Hesper*." They are candles in the way that the fire is a fire; in one sense they are wax, in another, they are an inward light. By them Night is stripped forever of her dark cloak, for they will "sticke there everlasting Day." The warmth and brightness of the grasshopper's year, realized literally and, consequently, finitely in the early part of the poem are thus made eternal. The poet puts down Gothic horror; the grasshopper is made immortal; antique fearlessness is restored.

With the last stanza, the king, who has until now been hidden from us by a series of artistic translucencies, is revealed in his clear title. He is more than king of the summer fields or of Britain, for in governing the world of his creative imagination, he is untempted by the world. The poet and his friend, who may also be the "himselfe" of the last line, have created a kingdom privately. This kingdom cannot go down because it is invincible to outward attack. With this last stanza, the Horatian music that we have heard steadily since the dreary center of stanza V seems to achieve symphonic fullness. We have the impression of the Horatian tone because we know it has to be here. Horace, who fought on the wrong side at Philippi, must have appeared to Lovelace and Cotton as a Roman cavalier who, when all was lost, found the good way. His metaphors repeat themselves once more. The tempest comes with the rain and the North Wind, but one forgets them before a heaped fire and a full cup. [Quotes Horace, *Epodes*, XIII. 1–8.] In Horace's poetic promises there is little eternity; this illusion is shunned. The fire on the Sabine hearth is as real as the wind and the rain. It is Lovelace who creates the illusion for which he lives. In another sense "himselfe" may not be Cotton at all, but the private world of the poet's heart, where all is warm and light and the grasshopper lives in a kingdom made eternal by his song.

---

1. For some associations, see St. Augustine, *In Iobam*, ed. Zycha (Vienna, 1895), p. 608 and his *Epistulae*, ed. Goldbacher (Vienna, 1904), p. 201; see also Eucherius, *Liber Formularum* (*PL*, L, 740–41).

T. S. ELIOT

A Note on Two Odes of Cowley†

The meaning of the term 'metaphysical poetry' is stretched to its utmost to include Cowley; and in considering Cowley as a metaphysical poet, our interest in that subject is stretched to its utmost too. It is quite right that specimens by Cowley should be included in a volume of selections from the metaphysical poets; but if we were making a selection from Cowley we might be justified in omitting all of those poems which show direct indebtedness to Donne. Cowley's relation to Donne, in *The Mistress* (e.g. *My Diet*), is that of an imitator; unlike Cleveland or Benlowes, he has no grain of originality, however perverse, to provide an interesting derivative. The poems included in Sir Herbert Grierson's anthology[1] exhibit Cowley at his mild best and most readable; and apart from these, he is perhaps best remembered by the few lines which provided Dryden with a magnificent parody in *MacFlecknoe*. But in Cowley's poetry there is another interest, which belongs rather to the history of thought and sensibility than to the pleasures of art.

Cowley is, I think, to be appreciated as an early Augustan as well as a late metaphysical. It has fallen to many small poets to be late followers of a distinguished school, and to be the authors of a few verses meriting a place in anthologies; and it has fallen to some to be interesting precursors. It cannot have fallen to many to occupy both positions, and in such a way as to provide the literary expression of a state of mind different from either. Cowley's moderate talent placed him in this unusual position; with a more original, or a more adaptable fancy, he might have been more completely assimilated to an earlier or a later generation. He is neither Caroline nor Restoration: his state of mind would appear rather to be that of the Exile. In our historical reading of poetry we are apt to skip from type to type; we are influenced, because of natural inertia, by the classifications of the history books. We can place ourselves in a position to accept Donne and his immediate followers; we can pass to the late seventeenth and the eighteenth centuries. Cowley is at a disadvantage compared with either those who preceded or those who followed him. I do not make pretensions for him by the standards of his greater precursors. But I think that there is a good case to be made out for him in a form in which he was preceded by Ben Jonson, and was followed by Dryden and by Collins and Gray, the so-called Pindaric ode.

† From *Seventeenth Century Studies Presented to Sir Herbert Grierson* (Oxford, 1938), pp. 235–242.

1. I.e., *Metaphysical Lyrics and Poems of the Seventeenth Century, Donne to Butler* (Oxford, 1921) [*Editor*].

Whether the Pindaric ode is in itself a form of verse unsuited to the English language is an idle speculation, because everything is impossible until some one has done it. We can only say that this is a form which no one has yet practised successfully in English. To have made something of it would have strained the powers of a Milton. No one with less mastery could succeed with it, and only poets of less mastery have attempted it. But of those who did attempt it, I claim that it was Cowley who practised it most successfully. To have practised an alien and unassimilated form of verse better than any one else may seem a negligible distinction; yet to assert that Cowley's odes are more interesting than those of Dryden, and much better than those of Gray and Collins, gives that distinction greater interest.

My familiarity with the Greek language has never been adequate to the appreciation of Pindar's odes in the original; and in translation they are very dull reading. I am therefore not in a position to affirm that those who profess to enjoy these odes are in reality mistaking their enjoyment of their own proficiency in Greek verse for enjoyment of poetry. But of English imitations, one may say that only a poet to whom sublimity came naturally, such as Milton, is qualified for such a task; and that to aim at sublimity and fail is one of the worst sins that a poet can commit. The odes of Dryden surprise and excite, and sustain a kind of interest to the end by the brilliance of *tours de force;* but content is sacrificed to magniloquence, and the music is harsh and metallic. The most admired odes of Gray, *The Bard* and *The Progress of Poesy,* have not even this virtue to recommend them; their laboured progress is very different from the powerful easy movement of Dryden. The wit of Dryden is replaced by romantic imprecision, and the language deteriorates, as for example in the use of the words 'ruin' and 'confusion' at the beginning of *The Bard.*

I do not pretend, however, that the odes of Cowley are *better* than those of Dryden, but only that in the ode we get Cowley at his best, and Dryden at his worst; and that it is more satisfactory to watch a small man making a good job than a great man wasting his talent. Cowley, in the best of his odes, such as the ode *To Mr. Hobbes,* the ode *Of Wit,* and the ode *Upon Dr. Harvey,* had something to say, was setting down something about his own age that was worth recording. There is no straining, as with Gray, after a false sublime; and a quality of wit, carried over from the earlier period, gives these odes an intellectual value absent from later productions in the same form. Cowley wrote, in these odes, of matters of intellectual importance.

While Cowley as a poet is derivative from the metaphysicals, as a mind he has very little in common with them. His use of the language is still Caroline: his mind is of the Restoration. He had considerable intellectual curiosity; but, in comparison with Donne, this curiosity is reduced and dissipated. Cowley knew Hobbes; he probably met men of science in Paris; and the science which he studied with the most attention was botany. He loved gardening. He was enthusiastic: he liked to formulate schemes for founding institutions and promoting scientific research. He belonged to a new world; a world which the metaphysicals could have made little of, a world which has lasted to our time; a world in which men lived in the expectation of perpetual, happy, and marvellous surprises of discovery and invention, surprises which were to have brought about a newer and happier world. The world of Cowley, indeed, is partly the world of Mr. H. G. Wells. When, therefore, he says in the ode *To Mr. Hobbes:*

> Long did the mighty Stagirite retain
> The universal intellectual reign. . . .
> But as in time each great imperial race
> Degenerates, and gives some new one place:
> So did this noble empire waste,
> Sunk by degrees from glories past,
> And in the schoolmen's hands it perisht quite at last. . . .

he is speaking, and speaking well, for the spirit of his time.

When, therefore, we admit that Cowley is inferior to his predecessors of the school of Donne, we cannot be contented to explain his inferiority simply by saying that he happened to be less of a poet. Nor is it sufficient to gibe, as did Johnson, at the apparent tepidity of Cowley's love affairs. The transference of attention from theology to science, or to sciences—the beginning of that slow disease which was to separate and then confuse thought and feeling —was a character of Cowley's time from which he could not escape. It is because he is so representative a man of his time—as a poet, the victim of his time—that he is interesting. We can say, I think, that belief is not a simple act of the mind, of such a kind that to 'believe' in the world of the schoolmen; and to 'believe' in the mechanistic universe, are as acts of believing identical. We might even suggest that 'believing' changes from age to age, although no age will possess the terms in which to define the difference between its believing and that of any previous age. In the age of Cowley the traditional form of belief was broken, and of this breach his ode *To Mr. Hobbes* is a monument. The romantic form of belief, belief in one's individual feelings, or in collective feeling, had not yet been evolved. There was, in Cowley's world, no object of belief capable of eliciting from him a response of the highest poetic intensity. There is therefore an *adequacy* in the ode to Hobbes, absent from *The Mistress*, which makes it satisfying.

Cowley's importance as a man who had some things to say about his own time, and who said them better than any one else, can be illustrated in a different way from his ode *Of Wit*. This ode is of course not Pindaric, and in form is much closer to Donne. In this ode Cowley gives an account of wit as it was just before Dryden. To appreciate the definition of Cowley we need to compare it with the attempts made later by Dryden and by Johnson; from which it should appear that wit meant something a little different to each of these three men. In the *Life of Cowley* Johnson observes:

> If, by a more noble and adequate conception, that be considered as wit, which is at once natural and new, that which, though not obvious, is, upon its first production, acknowledged to be just; if it be that which he that never found it, wonders how he missed it; to wit of this kind the metaphysical poets have seldom risen. Their thoughts are often new, but seldom natural; they are not obvious, but neither are they just; and the reader, far from wondering that he missed them, wonders more frequently by what perverseness of industry they were ever found.

It will be observed, I think, that for Johnson wit is still something serious, and not associated with 'humour'; but that wit for him appears to be less a spirit animating the whole of a serious composition, than the occasional dignifying and embellishment of it. In the loosest of Donne's compositions there is a kind of continuity in change, and we can perceive an effect of wit throughout the whole which is not merely the sum of the wit of the parts. In *The Vanity of Human Wishes* there is neatness and decorum, but these qualities do not constitute order. In that poem there are plenty of intellectual variations on a main theme; but the effect is on the whole monotonous. We do not find the exceptional power of creating a unity of feeling out of the most disparate elements.

With Dryden we find a larger conception of wit than Johnson's. He says:

> The composition of all poems is, or ought to be, of wit; and wit in the poet, or *Wit writing* (if you will give me leave to use a school distinction) is no other than the faculty of imagination in the writer, which, like a nimble spaniel, beats over and ranges through the field of memory, till it springs the quarry it hunted after; or, without metaphor, which searches over all the memory for the species or ideas of those things which it deigns to represent. . . . The first happiness of the poet's imagination is properly invention, or finding of the thought; the second is fancy, or the variation, deriving, or moulding, of that thought, as the judgement represents it proper to the subject; the third is elocution, or the art of clothing and adorning that thought, so found and varied, in apt, significant, and sounding words: the quickness of the imagination is seen in the invention, the fertility in the fancy, and the accuracy in the expression.

It would appear that wit has for Dryden a greater extension than for Johnson; but even Dryden's meaning is a contraction from what the word meant for Cowley. Even Cowley defines wit in contrast to what we should call cheapness; but it is probable that he is protecting wit against those who would mistake cheapness for wit, rather than against any who might identify wit and cheapness.

> Tell me, O tell, what kind of thing is Wit,
>   Thou who master art of it.
> For the first matter loves variety less;
> Less women love't, either in love or dress.
>   A thousand different shapes it bears,
>   Comely in thousand shapes appears.
> Yonder we saw it plain; and here 'tis now,
> Like spirits in a place, we know not how.
> .   .   .   .
>
> 'Tis not to force some lifeless verses meet
>   With their five gouty feet.
> All ev'ry where, like mans, must be the soul,
> And reason the inferior parts control. . . .
>
> Yet 'tis not to adorn, and gild each part;
>   That shows more cost, than art.
> Jewels at nose and lips but ill appear;
> Rather than all things wit, let none be there. . . .
>
> 'Tis not such lines as almost crack the stage
>   When Bajazet begins to rage. . . .
>
> In a true piece of Wit all things must be,
>   Yet all things there agree.
> As in the ark, join'd without force or strife,
> All creatures dwelt; all creatures that had life.
>   Or as the primitive forms of all
>   (If we compare great things with small)
> Which without discord or confusion lie,
> In that strange mirror of the deity.

This is not only good poetry, Cowley at his best, but it is better criticism of Donne than either Dryden or Johnson has made, while as a poem it was probably more congenial to either Dryden or Johnson than anything of Donne's.

M. Jean Loiseau, in his exhaustive work on Cowley, observes that the imagination of Cowley

> n'est pas inspirée par un enthousiasme visionnaire, mais elle est alimentée par ce que le XVIIe siècle appelait l'esprit, 'wit,' c'est-à-dire la faculté d'analyse qui découvre les rapports cachés des choses.

While I am ready to admit that Cowley himself never rises to a 'visionary enthusiasm' (by which I take M. Loiseau to mean a kind of hallucinatory intensity), I question whether Cowley, who may also have thought his own odes, as he thought Pindar's, more tumultuous than they are, means by wit a mere analytical faculty—even if it be conceded that a faculty for discovering the hidden relations of things is merely 'analytical'. Cowley seems to me to mean something much more profound, something which can only be observed at its best in poets of the first rank, though not in all of them.

To find out what a critic of a long-past age meant by a term, we have not only to examine carefully the literal contexts of that term in his statements, but also, as far as we can, the unspoken context. We have to try to discover, not only what that critic's mental furniture was, not only what authors he had read and admired, but the way in which he admired them. And we have to make the difficult and never wholly successful effort of erasing from our minds the ways in which they have been modified, in what they expect poetry to be, by everything that has been written *since* that critic wrote. And what we get, so far as we get it, will be something that we cannot adequately express in words. We cannot assume, in attempting to fix the earlier meaning of a word which has changed its meaning, that the words in which we define it will not have changed their meaning too. The *N.E.D.* mentions the word 'wit' as having acquired the 'reference to the utterance of brilliant or sparkling things in an amusing way'. Of course the term 'amuse' has changed its meaning too; and what right have we to assume that that constellation of references to contexts, which is what we *mean* by 'amuse', existed for a person of our level of education and sensibility in the middle of the seventeenth century? We must conclude that we cannot arrive at a full understanding of what either Cowley or Dryden or Johnson meant by wit. We can only be fairly confident that they did not mean quite the same thing, though there is of course a relation between their various meanings, and a relation of them all to our own; and that, to the extent of the general changes taking place—for we need not assume that every word changes its meaning at a uniform rate—they did not understand each other, just as we fail to understand them.

I am therefore driven back to a kind of personal confession instead of a definition of wit. It seems to me, however, the best that I can contribute, to a volume designed to honour a scholar[2] who has done more than any other in our time towards removing the obstacles between ourselves and the poetry of the seventeenth cen-

2. I.e., Sir Herbert Grierson [*Editor*].

tury. My frequentation—unscholarly, I admit, and perhaps capricious and haphazard—of the poetry of that century has led me to feel that the word 'wit' represents far more for me than anything that I could enclose within a definition. It has come to represent for me the essence of that strange period of poetry which ends with the Martyrdom and the Exile, and is as much a part of that period's religious intensity as of its levity. The age of Donne, and of Herbert, Crashaw, and Vaughan seems to me the most 'civilized' age of English poetry; in consequence the age of Gray, Collins, and Johnson even, and *a fortiori* the nineteenth century, decadent. 'Wit' stands for a kind of balance and proportion of intellectual and emotional values, in which the poetry of the nineteenth century is lamentably deficient. Yet what I mean by wit is related to other meanings of the word, and even to that which connotes mirth— though there especially, perhaps, to what is most alien to our age, a holy mirth. But I am quite aware that when I employ the terms 'civilized' and 'decadent' I am employing them in a private and arbitrary sense—until some one else employs them in the same way.

Selected Bibliography

The definitive survey of the literature of this period is that by Douglas Bush, *English Literature in the Earlier Seventeenth Century 1600–1660*, 2nd ed., rev. (New York, 1962), which includes extensive bibliographies for a wide range of topics and for individual authors.

The best historical account of the period is that by Godfrey Davies, *The Early Stuarts 1603–1660* (Oxford, 1937). An invaluable socioeconomic study is *The Crisis of the Aristocracy 1558–1641* (Oxford, 1967), by Lawrence Stone. Among the many other works that discuss the history, thought, and cultural milieu of the period, the following may be particularly helpful: G. P. V. Akrigg, *Jacobean Pageant* (Cambridge, Mass., 1962); R. F. Jones, *Ancients and Moderns*, 2nd ed. (St. Louis, 1961); L. C. Knights, *Drama and Society in the Age of Jonson* (London, 1937); three studies by D. Mathew, *The Age of Charles I* (London, 1951), *The Jacobean Age* (London, 1938), and *Social Structure in Caroline England* (Oxford, 1948); and Basil Willey, *The Seventeenth Century Background* (London, 1950). Oliver Dick's edition of *Aubrey's Brief Lives* (London, 1950) is recommended.

The most authoritative modern editions of the poems of each author represented in this Critical Edition are noted individually, by author, in the Textual Notes.

The following bibliography is not intended to be absolutely comprehensive; it includes those books and articles which, in the editor's judgment, will be especially helpful to readers of this edition. Books concerned primarily with Jonson's dramatic art are not included, although the student of Jonson's nondramatic verse will profit from, for example, the discussions of his rhetorical practice in Jonas Barish, *Ben Jonson and the Language of Prose Comedy*, and A. H. Sackton, *Rhetoric as a Dramatic Language in Ben Jonson*. Again, only those studies that bear directly on the early poetry of Henry Vaughan are included. Finally, articles reprinted in this edition are not included in these lists, which (with some exceptions) do not take account of books or articles published before 1945.

LITERARY CRITICISM AND POETIC PRACTICE: GENERAL

Atkins, J. W. H. *English Literary Criticism: The Renascence.* London, 1947.

Bush, Douglas. *Mythology and the Renaissance Tradition in English Poetry.* New York, 1963. Chapter XI.

Finney, Gretchen. *Musical Backgrounds for English Literature, 1580–1650.* New Brunswick, N.J., 1962.

Hall, V. *Renaissance Literary Criticism: A Study of Its Social Content.* New York, 1945.

Hardison, O. B. *The Enduring Monument: A Study of the Idea of Praise in Renaissance Literary Theory and Practice.* Chapel Hill, N.C., 1962.

Hollander, J. *Untuning of the Sky: Ideas of Music in English Poetry 1500–1700.* New York, 1961.

Keast, W. R., ed. *Seventeenth Century English Poetry: Modern Essays in Criticism.* New York, 1971.

Leavis, F. R. *Revaluation: Tradition and Development in English Poetry.* London, 1962. Chapter I.

McEuen, Kathryn. *Classical Influences upon the Tribe of Ben.* Cedar Rapids, Iowa, 1939.

Maddison, Carol. *Apollo and the Nine: A History of the Ode.* Baltimore, 1960.

Miles, Josephine. *The Continuity of Poetic Language: The Primary Language of Poetry in the 1640's.* Berkeley, 1948.

Miner, E. *The Cavalier Mode from Jonson to Cotton.* Princeton, 1971.
Nevo, Ruth. *The Dial of Virtue: A Study of Poems on Affairs of State in the Seventeenth Century.* Princeton, 1963.
Nicolson, Marjorie. *The Breaking of the Circle: Studies in the Effect of the New Science upon Seventeenth Century Poetry.* Evanston, Ill., 1950.
Palmer, D. J. "The Verse Epistle." *Metaphysical Poetry,* Stratford-Upon-Avon Studies, 11, ed. M. Bradbury and D. Palmer. New York, 1970.
Piper, W. B. *The Heroic Couplet.* Cleveland, 1969.
Richmond, H. *The School of Love: The Evolution of the Stuart Love Lyric.* Princeton, 1964.
Rostvig, Maren-Sofie. *The Happy Man: A Study in the Metamorphosis of a Classical Ideal.* 2 vols. Oslo, 1954–1958.
Saunders, J. W. "The Social Situation of Seventeenth Century Poetry." *Metaphysical Poetry,* Stratford-Upon-Avon Studies, 11, ed. M. Bradbury and D. Palmer. New York, 1970.
Sharp, R. L. *From Donne to Dryden: The Revolt against Metaphysical Poetry.* Chapel Hill, N.C., 1940.
Skelton, R., ed. *The Cavalier Poets.* New York, 1970. Introduction.
Summers, J. *The Heirs of Donne and Jonson.* New York, 1970.
Tuve, Rosemond. *Elizabethan and Metaphysical Imagery.* Chicago, 1947.
Ustick, W. L. and H. Hudson. "Wit, 'Mixt Wit,' and the Bee in Amber." *HLB,* VIII (1935), 103–131.
Wallerstein, Ruth. *Studies in Seventeenth-Century Poetic.* Madison, Wis., 1950.
Walton, G. *Metaphysical to Augustan: Studies in Tone and Sensibility in the Seventeenth Century.* London, 1955.
Wedgwood, C. V. *Poetry and Politics under the Stuarts.* Cambridge, 1960.
Williamson, G. *The Proper Wit of Poetry.* Chicago, 1961.
———. *Seventeenth Century Contexts.* Chicago, 1969.

BEN JONSON

GENERAL STUDIES
Bamborough, J. B. *Ben Jonson.* London, 1959.
Castelain, M. *Ben Jonson: L'Homme et l'oeuvre.* Paris, 1909.
Chute, Marchette. *Ben Jonson of Westminster.* New York, 1953.
Dunn, Esther. *Ben Jonson's Art.* Northampton, Mass., 1925.
Evans, Willa. *Ben Jonson and Elizabethan Music.* Lancaster, Pa., 1929.
Johnston, G. B. *Ben Jonson: Poet.* New York, 1945.
Nichols, J. G. *The Poetry of Ben Jonson.* London, 1969.
Palmer, J. *Ben Jonson.* London, 1934.
Swinburne, A. C. *A Study of Ben Jonson.* London, 1889.
Trimpi, W. *Ben Jonson's Poems: A Study of the Plain Style.* Stanford, Calif., 1962.
Wheeler, C. F. *Classical Mythology in the Plays, Masques, and Poems of Ben Jonson.* Princeton, 1938.
Whipple, T. K. *Martial and the English Epigram from Wyatt to Ben Jonson.* Berkeley, 1925.

CRITICAL POSITIONS
Bredvold, L. I. "The Rise of English Classicism: Study in Methodology." *CL,* II (1950), 253–268.
Calder, D. G. "The Meaning of 'Imitation' in Jonson's *Discoveries.*" *Neuphilologische Mitteilungen,* LXX (1969), 435–440.
Clark, D. L. "The Requirements of a Poet: A Note on the Sources of Ben Jonson's *Timber,* Paragraph 130." *MP,* XVI (1918–1919), 412–429.
Fieler, F. B. "The Impact of Bacon and the New Science upon Ben Jonson's Critical Thought in *Timber.*" *Renaissance Papers 1958–60.* Durham, N.C., 1961, 84–92.
Redwine, J. D., Jr., ed. *Ben Jonson's Literary Criticism.* Lincoln, Neb., 1970.
Schelling, F. E. "Ben Jonson and the Classical School." *PMLA,* XIII (1898), 221 ff.

Walker, R. S. "Ben Jonson's *Discoveries.*" *Essays and Studies of the English Association,* N.S. V (1952), 32–42.

———. "Literary Criticism in Jonson's Conversations with Drummond." *English,* VIII (1951), 222–230.

NONDRAMATIC VERSE

Babb, H. S. "The 'Epitaph on Elizabeth, L. H.' and Ben Jonson's Style." *JEGP,* LXII (1963), 738–744.

Ben Jonson: Quadricentennial Essays. Studies in the Literary Imagination, 6 (1973). [Includes essays on Jonson's nondramatic verse by Ian Donaldson, William Kerrigan, Edward Partridge, Richard S. Peterson.]

Blanshard, R. A. "Carew and Jonson." *SP,* LII (1955), 195–212.

Brown, A. D. P. "Drink to Me, Celia." *MLR,* LIV (1959), 554–557.

Cope, J. I. "Jonson's Reading of Spenser: The Genesis of a Poem." *English Miscellany,* X (1959), 61–66.

Cubeta, P. " 'A Celebration of Charis': An Evaluation of Jonsonian Poetic Strategy." *ELH,* XXV (1958), 163–180.

———. "A Jonsonian Ideal: 'To Penshurst.' " *PQ,* XLII (1963), 14–24.

———. "Ben Jonson's Religious Lyrics." *JEGP,* LXII (1963), 96–110.

Davis, T. "Ben Jonson's Ode to Himself: An Early Version." *PQ,* LI (1972), 410–421.

Everett, Barbara. "Ben Jonson's 'A Vision of Beauty.' " *CritQ,* I (1959), 238–244.

Hart, J. "Ben Jonson's Good Society." *Modern Age,* VII (1963), 61–68.

Hibbard, G. R. "The Country House Poem of the Seventeenth Century." *JWCI,* XIX (1956), 159 ff.

Kay, W. D. "The Christian Wisdom of Ben Jonson's 'On My First Sonne.' " *SEL,* XI (1971), 125–136.

Levine, J. A. "The Status of the Verse Epistle before Pope." *SP,* LIX (1962), 658–684.

Marotti, A. "All About Jonson's Poetry." *ELH,* XXXIX (1972), 208–237.

Miller, P. "The Decline of the English Epithalamion." *TSLL,* XII (1970), 405–416.

Parfitt, G. A. E. "Compromise Classicism: Language and Rhythm in Ben Jonson's Poetry." *SEL,* XI (1971), 109–124.

———. "The Poetry of Ben Jonson." *EIC,* XVIII (1968), 18–31.

Rackin, Phyllis. "Poetry without Paradox: Jonson's 'Hymne' to Cynthia." *Criticism,* IV (1962), 186–196.

Spanos, W. V. "The Real Toad in the Jonsonian Garden: Resonance in the Nondramatic Poetry." *JEGP,* LXVIII (1969), 1–23.

Sternfeld, F. W. "Song in Jonson's Comedy: A Gloss on *Volpone.*" *Studies in the English Renaissance Drama.* 1960, 310–321.

Talbert, E. W. "New Light on Ben Jonson's Workmanship." *SP,* XL (1943), 154–185.

Van Deusen, M. "Criticism and Ben Jonson's 'To Celia.' " *EIC,* VII (1957), 95–103.

Walker, R. S. "Ben Jonson's Lyric Poetry." *Criterion,* XII (1933–1934), 430–448.

Wallerstein, Ruth. "The Development of the Rhetoric and Metre of the Heroic Couplet, Especially in 1625–1645." *PMLA,* L (1935), 166–209.

Williamson, G. "The Rhetorical Pattern of Neo-Classical Wit." *Seventeenth Century Contexts* [noted under Literary Criticism and Poetic Practice], pp. 240–271.

Wilson, Edmund. "Morose Ben Jonson." *The Triple Thinkers,* rev. ed. New York, 1948, pp. 213–232.

Wilson, G. E. "Jonson's Use of the Bible and the Great Chain of Being in "To Penshurst,' " *SEL,* VIII (1968), 77–89.

Winters, Yvor. *Forms of Discovery: Critical and Historical Essays on the Forms of the Short Poem in English.* Denver, Col., 1967. [Includes essays on Jonson's nondramatic verse, notably "To Heaven."]

Wykes, D. "Ben Jonson's 'Chast Booke': The *Epigrammes.*" *Renaissance and Modern Studies* [Nottingham], XIII (1969), 76–87.

ROBERT HERRICK

Brooks, C. "Corinna's Going A-Maying." *The Well-Wrought Urn.* New York, 1947, pp. 54–64.

Capwell, R. L. "Herrick and the Aesthetic Principle of Variety and Contrast." *SAQ*, LXXI (1972), 488–495.

Delattre, F. *Robert Herrick.* Paris, 1912.

Deming, R. H. "Herrick's Funereal Poems." *SEL*, IX (1969), 153–167.

———. "Robert Herrick's Classical Ceremony." *ELH*, XXXIV (1967), 327–348.

DeNeef, A. L. "Herrick's 'Corinna' and the Ceremonial Mode." *SAQ*, LXX (1971), 530–545.

Gilbert, A. H. "Robert Herrick on Death." *MLQ*, V (1944), 61–68.

Godshalk, W. L. "Art and Nature: Herrick and History." *EIC*, XVII (1967), 121–124.

Hinman, R. B. "The Apotheosis of Faust: Poetry and New Philosophy in the Seventeenth Century." *Metaphysical Poetry*, Stratford-Upon-Avon Studies, 11, ed. M. Bradbury and D. Palmer. New York, 1970.

Jenkins, P. "Rethinking What Moderation Means to Robert Herrick." *ELH*, XXXIX (1972), 49–65.

Kimmey, J. L. "Order and Form in Herrick's *Hesperides*." *JEGP*, LXX (1971), 255–268.

———. "Robert Herrick's Persona." *SP*, LXVII (1970), 221–236.

———. "Robert Herrick's Satirical Epigrams." *ES*, LI (1970), 312–323.

Moorman, F. W. *Robert Herrick.* London, 1910.

Musgrove, S. *The Universe of Robert Herrick.* Auckland, N.Z., 1951.

Reed, M. L. "Herrick among the Maypoles: Dean Prior and the *Hesperides*." *SEL*, V (1965), 133–150.

Regenos, G. W. "The Influence of Horace on Robert Herrick." *PQ*, XXVI (1947), 268–282.

Rollin, R. B. *Robert Herrick.* New York, 1966.

Ross, R. J. "Herrick's Julia in Silks," *EIC*, XV (1965), 171–180.

Spitzer, L. "Herrick's 'Delight in Disorder.' " *MLN*, LXXVI (1961), 209–214.

Starkman, Miriam. "*Noble Numbers* and the Poetry of Devotion." *Reason and the Imagination: Studies in the History of Ideas 1600–1800*, ed. J. Mazzeo. New York, 1962, pp. 1–27.

Staudt, V. P. "Horace and Herrick on *Carpe Diem*." *Classical Bulletin*, XXXIII (1957), 55–56.

Swinburne, A. C. "Robert Herrick." *Studies in Prose and Poetry.* London, 1894.

Wentersdorf, K. "Herrick's Floral Imagery." *SN*, XXXVI (1964), 69–81.

Whitaker, T. R. "Herrick and the Fruits of the Garden." *ELH*, XXII (1955), 16–33.

Woodward, D. H. "Herrick's Oberon Poems." *JEGP*, LXIV (1965), 270–284.

THOMAS CAREW

Blanshard, R. A. "Carew and Jonson" [noted under Ben Jonson, Nondramatic Verse].

———. "Thomas Carew and the Cavalier Poets." *Transactions of the Wisconsin Academy of Sciences, Arts, and Letters*, XLIII (1954), 97–105.

———. "Thomas Carew's Master Figures." *Boston University Studies in English*, III (1957), 214–227.

Martz, L. *The Wit of Love: Donne, Carew, Crashaw, Marvell.* Notre Dame, Ind., 1969.

Parfitt, G. A. E. "The Poetry of Thomas Carew." *Renaissance and Modern Studies* [Nottingham], XII (1969), 56–67.

Praz, Mario. "Literary Resurrections." *ES*, XLII (1961), 357–362.

Richmond, H. *The School of Love* [noted under Literary Criticism and Poetic Practice].

Selig, E. I. *The Flourishing Wreath.* New Haven, 1957.

EDMUND WALLER

Allison, A. W. *Towards an Augustan Poetic: Edmund Waller's "Reform" of English Poetry.* Lexington, Ky., 1962.

Bateson, F. W. "A Word for Waller." *English Poetry: A Critical Introduction.* New York, 1966.

Chernaik, W. L. *The Poetry of Limitation: A Study of Edmund Waller.* New Haven, 1968.

Korshin, P. J. "The Evolution of Neoclassic Poetics: Cleveland, Denham, and Waller as Poetic Theorists." *Eighteenth-Century Studies,* II (1968), 102–137.

Nevo, Ruth. *The Dial of Virtue* [noted under Literary Criticism and Poetic Practice].

Wallerstein, Ruth. "The Development of the Rhetoric and Metre of the Heroic Couplet" [noted under Ben Jonson, Nondramatic verse].

Wikelund, P. R. "Edmund Waller's Fitt of Versifying: Deductions from a Holograph Fragment, Folger MS. X.d.309." *PQ,* XLIX (1970), 68–91.

Williamson, G. "The Rhetorical Pattern of Neo-Classical Wit." *Seventeenth Century Contexts* [noted under Literary Criticism and Poetic Practice], pp. 240–271.

SIR JOHN SUCKLING

Beaurline, L. A. "An Editorial Experiment: Suckling's *A Sessions of the Poets.*" *SB,* XVI (1963), 43–60.

———. "New Poems by Sir John Suckling." *SP,* LIX (1962), 651–657.

———. "The Canon of Sir John Suckling's Poems." *SP,* LVII (1960), 105–126.

———. " 'Why So Pale and Wan': An Essay in Critical Method." *TSLL,* IV (1962), 553–563.

Berry, H., ed. *Sir John Suckling's Poems and Letters from Manuscript.* London, Ont., 1960.

Gray, P. H. "Suckling's 'A Sessions of the Poets' as a Ballad." *SP,* XXXVI (1939), 60–69.

Henderson, F. O. "Traditions of *Précieux* and *Libertin* in Suckling's Poetry." *ELH,* IV (1937), 274–298.

SIR JOHN DENHAM

Dobrée, B. "Sir John Denham," in *As Their Friends Saw Them.* London, 1933.

Korshin, P. J. "The Evolution of Neoclassic Poetics: Cleveland, Denham, and Waller as Poetic Theorists" [noted under Edmund Waller].

Nevo, Ruth. *The Dial of Virtue* [noted under Literary Criticism and Poetic Practice].

O Hehir, B. *Expans'd Hieroglyphicks: A Study of Sir John Denham's Coopers Hill, with a Critical Edition of the Poem.* Berkeley, 1969.

———. *Harmony from Discord: A Life of Sir John Denham.* Berkeley, 1968.

Wallerstein, Ruth. "The Development of the Rhetoric and Metre of the Heroic Couplet" [noted under Ben Jonson, Nondramatic Verse].

Williamson, G. "The Rhetorical Pattern of Neo-Classical Wit," in *Seventeenth Century Contexts* [noted under Literary Criticism and Poetic Practice], pp. 240–271.

RICHARD LOVELACE

Evans, Willa. "Lovelace's Concept of Prison Life in *The Vintage to the Dungeon.*" *PQ,* XXVI (1947), 62–68.

———. "Richard Lovelace's 'Mock-Song.' " *PQ,* XXIV (1945), 317–328.

Hartman, C. H. *The Cavalier Spirit and Its Influence on the Life and Work of Richard Lovelace.* London, 1925.

Holland, N. H. "Literary Value: A Psychoanalytic Approach." *Literature and Psychology*, XIV (1964), 43–55.

Jones, G. F. "Lov'd I Not Honour More: The Durability of a Literary Motif." *CL*, XI (1959), 131–143.

King, B. *"The Grasse-hopper* and Allegory." *Ariel*, I (1970), 71–82.

———. "Green Ice and a Breast of Proof." *CE*, XXVI (1965), 511–515.

Richmond, H. "A Note on Professor Holland's Psychoanalytic Approach." *Literature and Psychology*, XIV (1964), 125–127.

Scoular, Kitty. *Natural Magic.* Oxford, 1965.

Wadsworth, R. L. "On 'The Snayle' by Richard Lovelace." *MLR*, LXV (1970), 750–760.

Weidhorn, M. *Richard Lovelace.* New York, 1970.

ABRAHAM COWLEY

Elledge, Scott. "Cowley's Ode 'Of Wit' and Longinus on the Sublime: A Study of One Definition of the Word *Wit.*" *MLQ*, IX (1948), 185–198.

Ghosh, J. C. "Abraham Cowley (1618–1667)." *Sewanee Review*, LXI (1953), 433–447.

Goldstein, H. D. *"Anglorum Pindarus:* Model and Milieu." *CL*, XVII (1965), 299–310.

———. *"Discordia Concors,* Decorum, and Cowley." *ES*, XLIX (1968), 481–489.

Hinman, R. B. *Abraham Cowley's World of Order.* Cambridge, Mass., 1960.

Korshin, P. J. "The Theoretical Bases of Cowley's Later Poetry." *SP*, LXVI (1969), 756–776.

Nethercot, A. H. *Abraham Cowley, The Muse's Hannibal,* rev. ed. Oxford, 1967.

Nevo, Ruth. *The Dial of Virtue* [noted under Literary Criticism and Poetic Practice].

Taaffe, J. *Abraham Cowley.* New York, 1972.

Williamson, G. *The Donne Tradition.* Cambridge, Mass., 1930.

HENRY VAUGHAN

Blunden, E. *On the Poems of Henry Vaughan: Characteristics and Intimations.* New York, 1969.

Hutchinson, F. E. *Henry Vaughan, a Life and Interpretation.* Oxford, 1947.

Marilla, E. L. "The Secular and Religious Poetry of Henry Vaughan." *MLQ*, IX (1948), 394–411.

Simmonds, J. D. *Masques of God: Form and Theme in the Poetry of Henry Vaughan.* Pittsburgh, 1972.

———. "Vaughan's Love Poetry." *Essays in Honor of Esmond Linworth Marilla,* ed. T. A. Kirby and W. J. Olive. Baton Rouge, 1970, 27–42.

MINOR FIGURES

Blunden, E. "Thomas Randolph." *Votive Tablets* (London, 1931), 47–52.

Bradbrook, Muriel. "Marvell and the Poetry of Rural Solitude." *RES*, XVII (1941), 37–46. [Fane]

Brooks, C. "The New Criticism and Scholarship," *Twentieth-Century English,* ed. W. S. Knickerbocker. New York, 1946, 371–383. [Corbett]

Crofts, J. E. V. "A Life of Bishop Corbet." *Essays and Studies of the English Association,* X (1924), 61–96.

Moore Smith, G. C. "Thomas Randolph." *Proceedings of the British Academy,* XIII (1927), 79–121.

Praz, Mario. "Stanley, Sherburne and Ayres as Translators and Imitators of Italian, Spanish and French Poets." *MLR*, X (1925), 280–294, 419–431.

Wedgwood, C. V. "The Poems of Montrose." *Essays and Studies of the English Association,* N.S. XIII (1960), 49–64.

Wilson, E. M. and E. R. Vincent. "Thomas Stanley's Translations and Borrowings from Spanish and Italian Poets." *Revue de Littérature Comparée,* XXXII (1958), 548–556.

Withington, Eleanor. "The 'Fugitive Poetry' of Mildmay Fane." *HLB,* IX (1955), 61–78.

———. "Mildmay Fane's Political Satire." *HLB,* XI (1957), 40–64.